ONE PALESTINE, COMPLETE

AN OWL BOOK

Henry Holt and Company · New York

ONE PALESTINE, COMPLETE

*Jews and Arabs Under
the British Mandate*

TOM SEGEV

TRANSLATED BY HAIM WATZMAN

Henry Holt and Company, LLC
Publishers since 1866
115 West 18th Street
New York, New York 10011

Henry Holt ® is a registered trademark
of Henry Holt and Company, LLC.

Originally published in Israel as *Yamei Kalaniot* by Keter Publishers, Jerusalem, in 1999.

Library of Congress Cataloging-in-Publication Data
Segev, Tom, 1945–
    [Yeme ha-kalaniyot. English]
    One Palestine, complete : Jews and Arabs under the British Mandate / Tom Segev.
        p.   cm.
    Includes bibliographical references (p.) and index.
    ISBN 0-8050-6587-3
    1. Jews—Palestine—History—1917–1948. 2. Palestine—History—1917–1948.
3. Great Britain—Foreign relations—Palestine. 4. Palestine—Foreign relations—
Great Britain. I. Title.
DS126.S38513 2000
956.94'004924—dc21   00-039536

Henry Holt books are available for special promotions and premiums.
For details contact: Director, Special Markets.

First published in the United States in 2000
by Metropolitan Books/Henry Holt and Company

First Owl Books Edition 2001

DESIGNED BY FRITZ METSCH
MAPS BY JEFFREY L. WARD

*Frontispiece photograph by Underwood & Underwood,
Frank and Frances Carpenter Collection,
courtesy of the Library of Congress*

Printed in the United States of America

1   3   5   7   9   10   8   6   4   2

CONTENTS

———•—•———

PART III: RESOLUTION (1939–48)

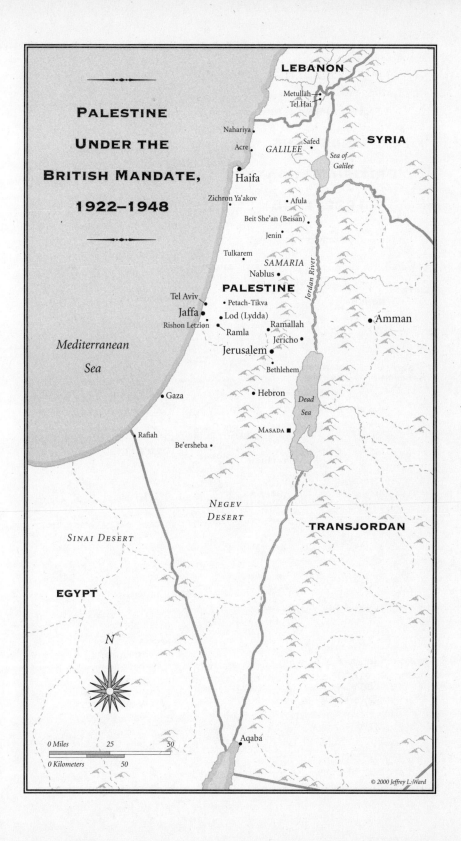

PALESTINE
UNDER THE
BRITISH MANDATE,
1922–1948

LEBANON

Metullah
Tel Hai

Nahariya

Acre   *GALILEE*   Safed   SYRIA

Haifa   Sea of Galilee

Zichron Ya'akov   Afula

Beit She'an (Beisan)

Jenin

Tulkarem

SAMARIA   Jordan River

Nablus

PALESTINE

Tel Aviv   Petach-Tikva

Jaffa   Lod (Lydda)

Rishon Letzion   Ramallah   Amman

Ramla   Jericho

Jerusalem

Bethlehem

Mediterranean
Sea

Gaza   Hebron   *Dead Sea*

Rafiah   MASADA ■

Be'ersheba

NEGEV DESERT

SINAI DESERT   **TRANSJORDAN**

EGYPT

N

Aqaba

0 Miles   25   50

0 Kilometers   50

© 2000 Jeffrey L. Ward

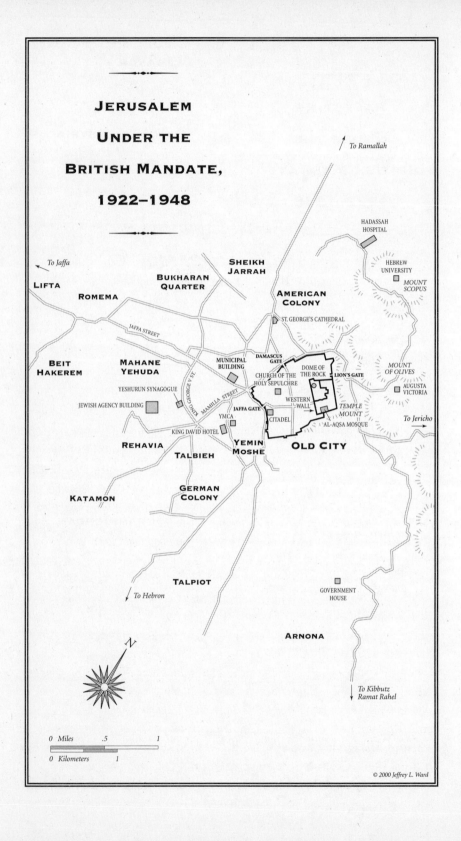

JERUSALEM
UNDER THE
BRITISH MANDATE,
1922–1948

To Ramallah

HADASSAH
HOSPITAL

To Jaffa

LIFTA

ROMEMA

BUKHARAN
QUARTER

SHEIKH
JARRAH

AMERICAN
COLONY

HEBREW
UNIVERSITY

MOUNT
SCOPUS

ST. GEORGE'S CATHEDRAL

JAFFA STREET

BEIT
HAKEREM

MAHANE
YEHUDA

MUNICIPAL
BUILDING

DAMASCUS
GATE

CHURCH OF THE
HOLY SEPULCHRE

DOME OF
THE ROCK

LION'S GATE

MOUNT
OF OLIVES

YESHURUN SYNAGOGUE

JEWISH AGENCY BUILDING

WESTERN
WALL

AUGUSTA
VICTORIA

JAFFA GATE

TEMPLE
MOUNT

To Jericho

YMCA

CITADEL

AL-AQSA MOSQUE

KING DAVID HOTEL

REHAVIA

YEMIN
MOSHE

OLD CITY

TALBIEH

GERMAN
COLONY

KATAMON

TALPIOT

To Hebron

GOVERNMENT
HOUSE

N

ARNONA

To Kibbutz
Ramat Rahel

0   Miles   .5   1

0   Kilometers   1

© 2000 Jeffrey L. Ward

Introduction:
Until We Meet Again

On the southern slopes of Mount Zion, alongside the ruins of biblical Jerusalem, lies a small Protestant cemetery. The path to it wends through pines and cypresses, olive and lemon trees, oleander bushes in pink and white, leading to a black iron gate around which curls an elegant grapevine. Perhaps a thousand graves are scattered over the terraced hill; ancient stones peer out from among red anemones. Not far away, on the top of the mountain, is a site Jews revere as the grave of King David as well as a room in which Catholics say the Last Supper was held; in a nearby basement chamber, they believe, eternal sleep fell over Mary, mother of Jesus. The Muslims have also sanctified several tombs on the mountain.

Bishop Samuel Gobat consecrated the cemetery in the 1840s to serve a small community of men and women who loved Jerusalem. Few had been born in the city; the great majority came as foreigners, from almost everywhere between America and New Zealand. Engraved on their headstones are epitaphs in English and German, Hebrew, Arabic, and ancient Greek; one headstone is in Polish.[1]

When the first of the dead were interred here, Palestine was a rather remote region of the Ottoman Empire with no central government of its own and few accepted norms. Life proceeded slowly, at a pace set by the stride of the camel and the reins of tradition. Outsiders began to flock to the country toward the end of the century, and it then seemed to awake from its Levantine stupor. Muslims, Jews, or Christians, a powerful religious and emotional force drew them to the land of Israel. Some stayed only a short time, while others settled permanently. Together they created a magical brew of prophecy and illusion, entrepreneurship, pioneerism, and adventurism—a multicultural revolution that lasted almost a hundred years. The line separating fantasy and deed was often blurred—there were charlatans and eccentrics of all nationalities—but for the most part this period was marked by drive and daring, the audacity to do things for the first time. For a while the new arrivals were intoxicated by a collective delusion that everything was possible.

An American brought the first automobile—that was in 1908. He traveled the length and breadth of the country and created a sensation. A Dutch journalist arrived in the Galilee, dreaming of teaching its inhabitants Esperanto. A Jewish educator from Romania opened a nursery school in Rishon LeTzion, a tiny experimental Zionist settlement, and was among the editors of the first Hebrew children's newspaper. Someone began making ice cream—that was Simcha Whitman, who also built the first kiosk in Tel Aviv. A man named Abba Cohen established a fire department, and a Berlin-born entrepreneur built the first beehives. A Ukrainian conductor founded a local opera company, and an Antwerp businessman set up a diamond-polishing shop. A Russian agronomist who had studied in Zurich planted eucalyptus trees, and an industrialist from Vilna launched Barzelit, the first nail factory. A Russian physician, Dr. Aryeh Leo Boehm, set up the Pasteur Institute, and a man named Smiatitzki, who came from Poland, translated *Alice in Wonderland* into Hebrew.[2] George Antonius, a prominent Palestinian Arab, dreamed of an Arab university and in the meantime sought funds to support the publication of an Arab dictionary of technological terms.[3] Antonius had come to Jerusalem from Alexandria, Egypt. Others of the country's Arabs had come from Turkey and Morocco, from Persia and Afghanistan, and from half a dozen other countries; there were also former black slaves who had escaped from their masters, or who had been freed.[4]

Tens of thousands of people, most of them Jews, came from Eastern and Central Europe. Among them were courageous rebels searching for a new identity, under the influence of Zionist ideology. Others had fled persecution or poverty; most came unwillingly, as refugees. A. D. Gordon, a white-bearded farmer-preacher, a kind of local Tolstoy, proclaimed a gospel of manual labor and return to nature in the Galilee. He had come from the Ukraine and was one of the fathers of labor Zionism, the political movement that led the Jews to independence. A young woman, fanatic and mad, galloped over the Galilee mountains dressed in Arab garb; her name was Manya Wilbushewitz. She came from Russia, where, in great spiritual turmoil, she had pledged her soul to the Communist revolution. In Palestine she was among the founders of a communal farm, an early incarnation of the kibbutz, and one of the first members of HaShomer, a forerunner of the Israel Defense Forces.[5] Some Jewish immigrants embarked on new lives in the first Zionist agricultural villages; others decided to build themselves a new city on the Mediterranean shore. It was called Tel Aviv.

The Christians, for their part, brought with them the imperial aspirations of their native lands; they were drawn largely to Jerusalem. "And so Palestine, and particularly Jerusalem, became a veritable Tower of Babel," remarked Chaim Weizmann, who led the Zionist movement.[6] Indeed, the Christians all tried to mold the city in their spirit and in their image, as if it were an international sandbox. The Russians covered their church with onion domes, like the Kremlin in Moscow; the Italians built a hospital and next to it erected the tower of the Palazzo Vecchio in Florence. On Mount Zion, the Germans built a church inspired by the cathedral in Aachen, Charles the Great's capital. The German Colony in the southern part of the city looked like a Black Forest town—a few dozen small stone houses with red-shingled roofs, inhabited by a community that was largely made up of members of the Templar sect. "Odd people are safe in Palestine," wrote Estelle Blyth, the daughter of the man who built the Anglican cathedral in Jerusalem, a structure inspired by Oxford's New College.[7] A lawyer from Chicago settled not far from there. He and the members of his sect established the American Colony, and dreamed of spreading love, compassion, and peace throughout the world.[8]

The founding fathers of the American Colony are also buried in Bishop Gobat's little cemetery. Not far from them lies the son of a German banker who financed the first rail link between Jaffa and Jerusalem. The grave of a Polish doctor is nearby. He opened the first children's hospital, on the Street of the Prophets. On that same street, Conrad Schick, buried next to the doctor, constructed houses that made his reputation as the greatest builder of modern Jerusalem. In his native Switzerland Schick had built cuckoo clocks. On a higher terrace lies an Englishman, William Matthew Flinders Petrie, considered by some the father of modern archaeology. He did much work in Egypt and excavated in Palestine as well. In his old age he settled in Jerusalem, dying at nearly ninety. Before his burial, his widow had his head severed from his body. The head was placed in a jar and covered with formaldehyde, and after being packed in a wooden crate was sent to London for a pathological examination meant to discover the secret of the late man's genius.*

In the Protestant cemetery lie the many foreigners who fell for Palestine, among them soldiers who fought in the strife-torn decades of the Mandate period. Enemies and comrades-in-arms are buried side by side. Adolf Flohl, a German pilot during World War I, had come to join in the defense of his country's ally, the Ottoman Turks. He was shot down and killed in mid-November 1917, less than four weeks before the British victors marched into Jerusalem and took control of Palestine. Not far from Flohl lies Sergeant N. E. T. Knight, an English policeman. He was killed in April 1948, less than four weeks before the British left Palestine. Together they frame an era of promise and terror.

The Great War that shoved Europe into the twentieth century changed the status of Palestine as well. For more than seven hundred years the land had been under Muslim rule. In 1917, as part of the British push into the Middle East, it passed into Christian hands; indeed, many of the conquering British soldiers compared themselves to the Crusaders. However, even as the British took control of Palestine the tide was going out on their empire; when they left the country thirty years later Britain had just lost India, the jewel in the crown. Palestine was little more than an epilogue to a story that was coming to an end. In the history of empire, then, Palestine was an episode devoid of glory.[10]

It was an odd story from the start. Altogether, the British seemed to have lost their bearings in this adventure. They derived no economic benefit from their rule over Palestine. On the contrary, its financial cost led them from time to time to consider leaving the country. Occupying Palestine brought them no strategic benefit either, despite their assumptions that it did. Many top army officers maintained that Palestine contributed nothing to the imperial interest, and there were those who warned that rule over the country was liable to weaken the British. There were early

---

*Israeli writer Meron Benvenisti relates that when the crate reached London there was no one to identify it and that it was lost in the huge basement of the British Museum. "Flinders Petrie's head," Benvenisti wrote, "thus lies in the most fitting location—among the treasures of the past that he excavated and studied." This legend is so captivating, so quintessentially Jerusalem in its bizarre eccentricity, that one hesitates to touch it, lest it be revealed as mere fantasy. Forty years later the genius's head was rediscovered.[9]

signs that they were getting themselves into a political problem that had no solution. These were reason enough not to take over the country. But the Holy Land elicited a special response; its status was not determined by geopolitical advantage alone. "Palestine for most of us was an emotion rather than a reality," one official in the British administration commented.[11]

At first, the British were received as an army of liberation. Both Arabs and Jews wished for independence and assumed they would win it under British sponsorship. Confusion, ambiguity, and disappointment were present at the very beginning. Before setting out to war in Palestine, the British had gotten themselves tangled up in an evasive and amateurish correspondence with the Arabs, who believed that in exchange for supporting the British against the Turks, they would receive Palestine. Just before the conquest of the country, however, His Majesty's Government announced, in the famous words of the Balfour Declaration, that it "views with favour" the aspiration of the Zionist Jews to establish a "national home" for the Jewish people in Palestine. For all practical purposes, the British had promised the Zionists that they would establish a Jewish state in Palestine. The Promised Land had, by the stroke of a pen, become twice-promised. Although the British took possession of "one Palestine, complete," as noted in the receipt signed by the high commissioner, Palestine was riven, even before His Majesty's Government settled in.

The British kept their promise to the Zionists. They opened up the country to mass Jewish immigration; by 1948, the Jewish population had increased by more than tenfold. The Jews were permitted to purchase land, develop agriculture, and establish industries and banks. The British allowed them to set up hundreds of new settlements, including several towns. They created a school system and an army; they had a political leadership and elected institutions; and with the help of all these they in the end defeated the Arabs, all under British sponsorship, all in the wake of that promise of 1917. Contrary to the widely held belief of Britain's pro-Arabism, British actions considerably favored the Zionist enterprise.

In standing by the Zionist movement, the British believed they were winning the support of a strong and influential ally. This was an echo of the notion that the Jews turned the wheels of history, a uniquely modern blend of classical antisemitic preconceptions and romantic veneration of the Holy Land and its people. In fact, the Jewish people were helpless; they had nothing to offer, no influence other than this myth of clandestine power.

The British pretended, and perhaps some of them even believed, that the establishment of a national home for the Jews could be carried out without hurting the Arabs. But, of course, that was impossible. The truth is that two competing national movements consolidated their identity in Palestine and advanced steadily toward confrontation. "To be a Palestine nationalist hardly left any room for compromise with Jewish nationalism and its backer, the Western powers," wrote historian Isa Khalaf.[12] From the start there were, then, only two possibilities: that the Arabs defeat the Zionists or that the Zionists defeat the Arabs. War between the two was inevitable.

And Britain was caught in the middle. High Commissioner Arthur Wauchope compared himself to a circus performer trying to ride two horses at the same time. Of these two horses, he said, one cannot go fast and the other would not go slow.[13] For a time the British clutched at the hope of creating a single local identity in Palestine, common to both Jews and Arabs, and in this context they even spoke of the "people of Palestine." These were empty words. The British were fooling the Arabs, fooling the Jews, and fooling themselves, Chaim Weizmann once commented. He was right.[14] It is a fascinating story, but not always a laudable one. As with national revolutions elsewhere, both peoples in Palestine tended to put nationalism above democracy and human rights. The leader of the Arab national movement even made common cause with Adolf Hitler.

Twenty years after the British conquest, the Arabs rose up to throw them out. By 1939, the Arab rebellion had brought the British to the verge of a decision to go home. It would have been better for them had they left then, but it took them nearly ten more years to act. In the meantime, World War II broke out, and after the war British forces were hit by Jewish terrorism as well. Thousands of them paid for the adventure with their lives.

Indeed, most of those interred in the back plots of Bishop Gobat's cemetery were killed in the outbreaks of violence that were regular features of the thirty years of British rule. Lewis Andrews is buried there; he was murdered by Arab terrorists. Not far from him lies Thomas Wilkin; he was killed by Jewish terrorists. Andrews, a forty-one-year-old Australian, was assistant to the district commissioner of the Galilee. In September 1937 he came to Sunday evensong at the Anglican church in Nazareth. Four pistol-wielding Arabs ambushed him near the church. They fired nine shots and killed him on the spot; the policeman who accompanied him was also hit and later died of the wounds he received.

Andrews was a friend of the Zionists. Judge Anwar Nusseibeh described him as an Arab hater. The circumstances of Andrews's death, on the way to church, elicited from Nusseibeh this comment: "He met his creator at a time when he was in the process of seeking him."[15] Thomas James Wilkin was a member of the Criminal Investigation Department (CID) of the Palestine police; he was killed in 1944 for his part in the arrest and death of "Yair," the leader of an underground Jewish terrorist organization. Wilkin did not hate all the Jews, however. Among those in his funeral procession was Shoshana Borochov, the daughter of one of the founders of Jewish socialism in Russia. She and Wilkin were lovers.[16]

Looking out from Bishop Gobat's cemetery on Mount Zion over the Hill of Evil Counsel, one sees Government House, the British administrative headquarters. To the west, one can see in the mountainous vista other stone structures the British left as memorials to their generation in Palestine. They radiate authority and majesty. The first of these that catches the eye is the Scottish church, with its rectangular bell tower; at the beginning of the summer it used to be surrounded by a sea of wildflowers. Farther west lies Talbieh, a neighborhood of luxurious mansions inhabited largely by affluent Arabs, many of them Christian—they did well during the British period. One resident, an attorney named Abcarius Bey, built a large house for a Jewish woman he loved, Leah Tennenbaum. She was thirty years younger than he was, and when she left him he rented the Villa Leah to Haile Selassie, the exiled emperor of Ethiopia.[17]

Then one's gaze catches a broad avenue the British built to give the city a look befitting one of the empire's capitals. They named it after their king, George V. At the end of the avenue stands a luxury hotel bearing the name of King David. It opened in 1930 and was considered one of the wonders of the East, an object of pilgrimage for aficionados of the good life from all over the world. "It is magnificent!" exulted Edwin Samuel in a letter to his mother, wife of the first high commissioner. One tourist from America thought it was the renovated Temple of Solomon. Jerusalem mayor Ragheb al-Nashashibi had his hair cut there.[18]

The hotel was famous for its kitchen and service staff. The waiters were towering black Sudanese athletes in tight-fitting red jackets who circulated among the guests, offering them whiskey and coffee from golden trays. The King David turned into a center and symbol of British power, and one of its wings held British administration offices. On July 22, 1946, Jewish terrorists managed to sneak several milk cans filled with explosives into the hotel's basement. Ninety-one people were killed; most of them were buried on Mount Zion. Some of the tombstones proclaim that the dead gave their lives for Palestine. Others say simply, "Until we meet again."

Across from the King David, a huge stone phallus rises among the neighboring roofs. This is the YMCA tower, a fertility symbol. It, too, was erected in the 1930s and was considered one of the architectural marvels of its time, designed by the same firm that drew up the plans for the Empire State Building in New York.[19] Mandatory administration officials and high society sipped lemonade on its terrace. The men sported pith helmets and the women shaded their faces with white silk parasols. They carefully observed the rules of good English society. In the afternoon they had tea, and they dressed for dinner. From time to time they could be seen at evening lectures or concerts; sometimes they attended the dances held in their honor by Miss Annie Landau, an ultra-Orthodox Jewish school principal, or they might pay a visit to the house of Katy Antonius, wife of George Antonius and a legendary Arab hostess.

The British preserved a rigid class consciousness: soldiers and NCOs spent their time in pubs and brothels; the officers went on fox and jackal hunts. The British hunting club in Ramle offered its members the opportunity to purchase red coats and buttons emblazoned with the club name, Ramle Vale Jackal Hounds. (None of the club's members forgot to mention the jacket in their memoirs.)[20] The road paved by the authorities between Latrun and Ramallah was meant mostly to serve British officials off on weekend picnics. [21] And they played tennis. People played soccer in Palestine even before the Mandate, but the British brought tennis; it was part of their colonial culture and mentality.[22] Ronald Storrs, governor of Jerusalem, documented the following scene in his diary: Colonial Secretary Lord Milner came to visit Palestine. He drank tea with the governor of Hebron and his guests and afterward they went to play tennis. Two Arab criminals were brought specially from the prison to run around the court and collect the balls; their legs were in irons throughout the game. Milner seemed to endure it with fortitude, Storrs wrote.[23]

The colonial method of government, wrote District Commissioner of the Galilee Edward Keith-Roach, was "totalitarianism tempered with benevolence."[24] Many of the British brought with them imperialistic arrogance and a powerful sense of cultural superiority. There were those who saw their dominion as a destiny and a mission. Herbert Samuel, the first high commissioner, proposed that his government conquer Palestine in order to "civilize" it.[25] When he eulogized one of his men who had died, Samuel honored him with the warmest praise he knew: "as head of the civil service staff he bore the brunt of the work of building up almost from the foundations the structure of a modern state."[26]

There were those in the British administration who identified with the Jews and those who identified with the Arabs. There were those who found both repugnant. "I dislike them all equally," wrote General Sir Walter Norris "Squib" Congreve. "Arabs and Jews and Christians, in Syria and Palestine, they are all alike, a beastly people. The whole lot of them is not worth a single Englishman!" This was a common sentiment. Police officer Raymond Cafferata put it more politely: "I am not anti-Semitic nor anti-Arab, I'm merely pro-British." So felt many, perhaps most, of those who served in Palestine.[27]

Their regime was a kaleidoscope of perceptions and positions and conflicting interests constantly tumbling over one another and rearranging themselves. Officials, diplomats, and politicians, military men and journalists contended and competed in a never-ending torrent of words, intrigues, alliances, and betrayals. The Prime Minister's Office, the Foreign Office, the Colonial Office, the Treasury, the India Office, the War Office, and the different branches of the military were only some of the agencies that sought a role in governing Palestine. The local administration also had a bureaucracy that was full of opposing forces and contradictions, a checkerboard of branches and departments and subdepartments and bureaus full of people. They wrote memoranda and reports and letters, a total of hundreds and thousands of sheets of paper. Almost every paper they wrote begat at least one more piece of paper—and generally more than one—that said the reverse.

The British had found an underdeveloped country when they arrived, and they left behind much progress, especially among the Jews. But they also left behind much backwardness, especially among the Arabs. Shortly before leaving the country one senior official estimated that the British had never in fact had a policy for Palestine, "nothing but fluctuations of policy, hesitations . . . no policy at all." [28] He was right. Commissions of inquiry came one after the other, studied the Arab-Jewish situation, and left. The British government generally adopted their recommendations, then changed its mind and sent more commissions. "If all the books of statistics prepared for the nineteen commissions that have had a shot at the problem were placed on top of one another they would reach as high as the King David Hotel," wrote Henry Gurney, the last of the Mandatory government's chief secretaries.[29] Like most of his colleagues, he departed

Palestine disappointed, cynical, disgruntled, and sad. The last high commissioner claimed that the British left "with dignity," but that was incorrect. Gurney wrote that they departed with a clear conscience, and that, at least, was true of many of them.[30] "England is an odd country," David Ben-Gurion concluded.[31] Still, as the British were about to leave, he went to London to convince them to stay, just for a little while longer.

PART I

ILLUSION

(1 9 1 7 – 2 7)

———•◦•———

Jane Lancaster was an odd person, an Englishwoman, Christian, not married. She lived in a Jewish neighborhood in southern Jerusalem. No one knew why she had come to Palestine, but there was one thing that they did know— Miss Lancaster loved the land of the Bible. Once a year she would set out for the Judean hills to plant narcissus bulbs and cyclamen and anemones.

———•◦•———

Khalil al-Sakakini
Receives a Visitor

1.

In the early-morning hours of Wednesday, November 28, 1917, someone knocked on Khalil al-Sakakini's front door and brought him great misfortune, indeed almost got him hanged. Sakakini, a Christian Arab, was an educator and writer, well known in Jerusalem. He lived to the west of the Old City, just outside the walls.

He'd had trouble falling asleep that night. He'd tossed from side to side, then got up, lit a lamp, set up his nargileh, and sat down to write a letter. "Even the worst—it's not so bad," he wrote. By the time he'd finished, three o'clock was approaching. Sakakini went back to bed, but a few minutes later he heard the boom of mortars very close by—it seemed as if they were firing on his street. He got up again, as did his wife, Sultana; they climbed to the upper floor and listened. The noise came from the west, from the area of Mea She'arim, the Jewish neighborhood, but Sakakini and his wife saw nothing. It was now around 4:30 A.M. They had just gone back to bed, thinking they might still manage an hour or two of sleep, when the artillery barrage began. The shells were falling closer than before and crashing like thunder. "We were afraid the whole house was going to collapse on top of us," Sakakini wrote in his diary.[1] The British army was advancing swiftly; Prime Minister David Lloyd George wanted Jerusalem before Christmas.[2]

At dawn Sakakini went to draw himself a bath; at that moment he heard a knock at the door. He went down to open it and found himself facing Alter Levine, a Jewish insurance agent and an acquaintance. Levine asked Sakakini's permission to hide in his home. The Turkish police were after him, he explained. In recent nights he had been running from house to house and now he had nowhere else to turn.

Levine's troubles had begun in April, when America entered the war on the side of the Allies. Levine, a U.S. citizen, thus became, along with his country, an enemy of Turkey. The departure of the American consul from Jerusalem signaled the end of Levine's protection; he was slated for deportation. The count of Ballobar, the consul of Spain, which had remained neutral in the war, had advised Levine to leave the city. Levine moved to Petach Tikva, a Jewish town near Tel Aviv, while his family went to Rehovot, a Jewish settlement south of Petach Tivka. In September, Levine learned from Count Ballobar that the Turkish authorities suspected him of being a spy.[3]*

Levine was indeed a man of mystery. He traveled frequently and maintained contacts with diplomats at a large number of embassies. The American consul, Otis Glazebrook, had been one of his friends, and Levine had very probably briefed him from time to time on the situation in Jerusalem. However, Levine's personal papers contain no hint of espionage.

Levine returned to Jerusalem as soon as he could. At one point he was arrested. The reason is unclear—at the time many people were arrested for no specific reason. Perhaps it was simply his U.S. citizenship; other American citizens were being deported from Jerusalem.[5] Perhaps a book of poems he had published had led to suspicions that he was fomenting pro-Zionist, anti-Turkish sentiments.[6] Whatever the reason, Levine had apparently managed to bribe someone and was released. But he continued to be a wanted man. "From that time on my father became elusive and hid with various acquaintances," his daughter Shulamit later wrote, "because he was afraid of spending too much time in any one place lest they discover his hideout."[7] Levine's wife and three daughters also went

---

*Years later, Aziz Bek, a Turkish intelligence officer, wrote in his memoirs that contrary to the accepted view—that the British capture of Palestine had been best aided by the famous Jewish spies of the Nili network in Zichron Ya'akov—one particular Jew living in Jerusalem had been even more helpful. Aziz Bek identified this master spy by name: Alter Levi. According to Aziz, Levi (that is, Levine) traveled freely among the cities of the Levant and set up a chain of brothels in which intelligence information was obtained from clients through extortion.[4]

into hiding. "In the afternoon we left where we had been in the morning, and come the morning we left where we had been at night," Shulamit Levine wrote.

The Turkish police found the family anyway. The girl watched the police rough up her mother. In prison they whipped Gittel Levine in order to extract her husband's whereabouts. Consul Ballobar confirmed afterward that the woman had been tortured severely and that it had affected her nerves. In fact, she lost her mind.[8] Levine, in the meantime, had knocked at the door of Khalil al-Sakakini, "a teacher, Christian and friend," as Levine would later describe him.[9]

Sakakini was alarmed: "God save me from bringing a spy into the house," he thought, but his conscience would not permit him to send Levine away. He did not know what to do. He had never faced such a momentous decision.[10]

2.

Three years earlier, in 1914, a few days after Turkey had linked its fate with that of Imperial Germany and entered the World War, a small crowd staged a demonstration under the window of the Spanish consul's home in Jerusalem. The count of Ballobar, Antonio de la Cierva Lewita, came out to his balcony to greet the crowd, and afterward made a note that the city's residents were demonstrating their loyalty to the sultan. At a prayer assembly conducted at the Al-Aqsa Mosque it was announced that Turkey's cause was a jihad—a holy war. The Jewish community was also quick to declare its allegiance. Many of its members donned tarbushes, albeit unwillingly, and ostensibly became patriots, related Meir Dizengoff, the mayor of Tel Aviv. When they heard that British Secretary of State for War Lord Kitchener had drowned at sea in June 1916, the Jews of Tel Aviv decked out the streets and organized parades to celebrate. The Christian residents of Jerusalem, the Spanish consul wrote in his diary, were profoundly frightened.[11]

At the outbreak of war, Khalil al-Sakakini was planning a big celebration in honor of his son Sari's first birthday, but the party was canceled. "Because of the current situation we have decided to make do with kissing him a thousand times," Sakakini wrote. Like many people, he believed the war would be short. God willing, he thought, it would be possible to have a big party for Sari on his next birthday.[12] In the meantime, Sakakini did all he could to avoid joining the Turkish army. Most Jews were afraid of enlisting, too.

Many of the immigrants to Palestine had not renounced their previous citizenships; among them were thousands of Jews, most of them Russian subjects. With Russia allied to France and Great Britain, the Jews of Palestine were faced with a cruel choice. They could leave the country or wait until they were expelled; alternatively, they could accept Ottoman citizenship and enlist. The threat of deportation prompted a Zionist initiative in favor of accepting Ottoman citizenship despite conscription; its purpose was to prevent a decline in the number of Jews in the country. Proponents of the initiative included two seminal figures in the cause of political Zionism: Jerusalem linguist Eliezer Ben-Yehuda, later to become known as the father of the Hebrew revival, and David Ben-Gurion, a low-ranking politician then in his twenties.

As he went around trying to persuade Jews to take on Ottoman citizenship, Ben-Gurion sported a tarbush and dressed like a Turkish government official; when he spoke about the Ottoman Empire he called it "our country." He believed the Turks would win the war and hoped that after the hostilities they would help establish Jewish autonomy in Palestine in exchange for their subjects' loyalty. For this reason he proposed setting up a Jewish battalion within the Turkish army, in opposition to a vocal group of Zionists who, convinced that Britain would win the war, preferred to throw their lot in with the Allies. This group advocated establishing a Jewish force as part of the British effort. "Maybe we were wrong, maybe we weren't," Ben-Gurion would later write.[13]*

Although the Ottoman authorities had restricted Jewish immigration to Palestine and the purchase of land on which to settle immigrants, by 1914 the Zionist movement had a number of achievements to its credit. In the decade that preceded the war, tens of thousands of Jews had settled in Palestine; the Turks had allowed them to establish agricultural villages, as well as an independent Hebrew school system.[14] But largely pro-Western, of Allied citizenship, and a threat to Islamic hegemony, the Zionists found themselves increasingly persecuted during the course of the war.

Many of the Jews living in Palestine did not support Zionism; indeed, much of the pre-Zionist Jewish population—that is, those who lived in Palestine before the 1880s—were ultra-Orthodox. They were deeply hostile to the notion of secular Jewish autonomy in the Holy Land, which, according to religious doctrine, would be redeemed only through divine

---

*Despite his loyalty to the regime, Ben-Gurion would soon be expelled from Palestine because of his political activity. He would go to the United States.

intervention in the messianic age. To the traditional Jewish population of Palestine, the Zionist ideal of secular redemption was sacrilegious. "A deep abyss separates the two parts of the Yishuv,"* Ben-Gurion wrote, calling for war against "the rabbis who are betraying their people." In addition to their abhorrence of Zionism's secular ideals, they feared that Zionist activity would cause the authorities to act against all the Jews, and saw the increasing power of the Zionists as competition for the leadership of the community.[16] Knowing of this split, Jamal Pasha, the sultan's governor in Palestine, was always careful to claim that he was opposed only to Zionism, not to all the Jews. Consul Ballobar recorded in his diary a piece of gossip that had reached his ears—that Jamal Pasha had in fact married a Jewish woman. He received later confirmation of the rumor from Jamal himself. People in the streets of Jerusalem's Old City said his wife was a whore.[17]

Jamal also carefully monitored Arab aspirations for independence. In his journal, Ballobar described with trepidation the first executions of members of the Arab national movement. The Turkish practice was to exhibit the bodies of hanging victims at the city gates, and Ballobar could see them from his consulate window. At least once he identified among the hanged men a personal acquaintance—the mufti of Gaza. Jamal once joked that he would hang Ballobar as well. The consul was not amused.[18]

By the time the war reached its end Ballobar, a pivotal figure in Ottoman Jerusalem, simultaneously represented a dozen countries, many of which had fought each other, including the Russian, Austro-Hungarian, and German empires, France, the British Empire, and the United States. It is doubtful whether the annals of diplomacy could produce another man who became the envoy of so many countries.[19] When the war began, the count was still in his twenties. His mother was Jewish; his father had met her while serving as military attaché at his country's embassy in Vienna. A short, thin man with a pointed nose and large mustache, the consul dressed carefully, always wearing pressed suits and a fancy Panama hat. He was remembered as an "attractive and amiable young man."[20] A pilgrim

---

*The term has its roots in ancient sources of the Hebrew language, and one of its meanings, according to Eliezer Ben-Yehuda's dictionary, is "a small number of Jews living in non-Jewish villages." *Yishuv*, which literally means "settlement," is also the opposite of "wasteland" and of "destruction." The word was used, consciously or not, to indicate that the Jews were living in a wilderness devoid of human beings, that is, Arabs. One Zionist leader objected to the use of the Hebrew word *moshava* to designate Jewish agricultural towns. *Moshava* literally meant "colony," and thus bore imperialistic connotations. The issue was hotly debated.[15]

from his country whom he met in Jerusalem became the love of his life. Ballobar was famous for the sumptuous meals he served at his home in west Jerusalem, opposite the Ethiopian church and next door to Eliezer Ben-Yehuda. Jamal Pasha was a frequent visitor. The two men would sip champagne, then smoke fine cigars and sit on the verandah for a game of poker that would last until after midnight. Indeed, they saw much of each other, often going horseback riding together in the Judean wilderness.

Ballobar's interest in Palestine was primarily guarding the monasteries and the churches, but he was sympathetic to Jewish concerns as well.[21] His diary paints local politics as a colorful kaleidoscope of intrigue, deception, and duplicitous schemes, of pashas and patriarchs, captains and chargés d'affaires, merchants and mercenaries. Their voracious appetite for fine food and flattery at an endless round of dinners and receptions was matched only by the verve with which they cheated, exploited, bribed, and spied on one another, trading gossip and innuendo while wallowing in the decay and corruption of a crumbling empire.

The young count bore his yoke of responsibility with a good deal of winning self-irony. He was a sensible man and a good observer and writer who learned much from what he saw. He described the wretched-looking Turkish soldiers setting out to capture the Suez Canal, their uniforms ragged, their discipline loose. He observed the frequent victory parades they mounted before their departure; at one of these, Ballobar noticed a soldier pushing his drinking water in a baby carriage most likely stolen from a Jewish courtyard. He recorded a scene he witnessed at the southern exit from the city, on the road to Bethlehem: a group of women and children were at forced labor, digging trenches. The Turkish soldier overseeing them was knitting. With such an army, the count thought, the Turks could not win. "We'll meet on the other side of the canal—or we'll meet in heaven," Jamal Pasha had once said to Ballobar. The diplomat considered the second possibility more likely, but was careful not to make the Turk party to his assessment.

In January 1917 Ballobar noticed five military trucks loaded with Turkish soldiers parked by his house. They remained there all day, plagued by an irritating drizzle. The consul noted that the soldiers did not eat the entire time. A bit before five in the evening they were each given a tiny roll and a can of thin lentil soup. Ballobar watched the hungry young men with pity. Off to the desert to save the empire, they didn't stand a chance.[22] If the enemy didn't get them, then surely hunger would. Some soldiers robbed the city's flour mills and some slaughtered their own camels for the meat. One Jerusalem boy recalled a Turkish soldier rushing at him on his way to school, grabbing his half pita.[23]

Many Turkish soldiers fled the army. Bertha Spafford Vester, whose parents founded the American Colony, saw a group of conscripts arriving in the city. Their commanders had put them in chains.[24]

3.

Sometime after the unsuccessful Turkish attack on the Suez Canal in the spring of 1917, the British army launched its campaign to conquer the city of Gaza. They tried twice and were repelled both times. The battle for the city cost thousands of soldiers' lives on both sides, and Gaza's inhabitants suffered greatly.[25] Many were forced to leave by the Turks, who feared the population would get in the way of the troops. "A terrible panic has fallen not only over the residents of Gaza but over the entire country," wrote Moshe Smilansky, a farmer and leading Zionist thinker and writer. "What is the purpose of this expulsion? Will the whole country be expelled before the British come?" The roads were filled with refugees, Smilansky wrote, all of them ravaged by hunger, fear, and disaster.

One Gazan woman provided an account of the Turkish evacuation. Soldiers went from house to house, whips in hand, lashing out left and right and forcing residents onto the street without any of their belongings. According to Smilansky, 40,000 people were expelled from Gaza, including a few Jewish families. Arab historian Aref al-Aref, later governor of the city, estimated the number at 28,000; about 10,000 had left the city ahead of the fighting.

The well-off Gazans settled in Hebron, Ramle, and Lydda; the poor ones scattered among Palestinian villages or lived in orchards and fields. According to Smilansky, the Ottoman authorities had plans to settle some of the Arab refugees in Jewish villages. "We were very anxious about having these particular guests," Smilansky wrote, "because of the crowding, the filth, the general disturbance. But we took some comfort—better the Arabs should be sent to us than we should have to go to the Arabs."[26] The plan was never implemented, but a few weeks later—as the fighting came closer—many residents of Jaffa and Tel Aviv were also forced to leave their homes; some of the Jewish exiles did take refuge among the Arabs.

At that time there were 50,000 people living in Jaffa, among them some 10,000 Jews; about 2,000 Jews also lived in nearby Tel Aviv.[27] The authorities claimed that the evacuation of Jaffa was necessary to protect the civilian population. The soldiers wouldn't be able to fight for the city while hearing the screams of women and children, Jamal Pasha explained to Consul Ballobar.[28] A few young Jews were allowed to remain in the city and guard the houses; the rest were forced to go.[29]

The evacuation took two weeks. Orderly at first, it quickly turned to chaos. A local reporter described a confused crowd of people, horses, and mules, and piles and piles of belongings. Men, women, and children lay sprawled on their bundles for days, waiting under the open sky for their turn to leave. Wagon after wagon set out, tens and hundreds—wagons loaded with pianos, rugs, heavy furniture, Torah scrolls, wheat, and other foodstuffs. They left a trail of dung behind them. Smilansky observed a baby carriage hitched to a donkey, with two children driving it.[30] "Tel Aviv is a wasteland," he wrote. "A deathly silence pervades the streets. It is as if the place has been blighted by a plague." A local journalist made out some graffiti scrawled on a wall in a child's hand: "Goodbye Tel Aviv."[31]

The expulsion from Jaffa and Tel Aviv brought an end to the Jewish community's willingness to support the Turkish interest. "We will never forgive Jamal Pasha this crime!" wrote Mordechai Ben-Hillel Hacohen, a businessman and public figure who was one of the founders of Tel Aviv. He had a personal reason to be angry; his son David was serving in the Turkish army. Hacohen had taken pride in his son's officer rank, but on being driven from his home he felt that his son had risked his life in the service of a rotten empire; all were now praying for its collapse.

Ben-Hillel (Marcus Hillelovitch) Hacohen had come to Jaffa from Mogilev in White Russia. At the first Zionist Congress in 1897 he had been the first delegate to give a speech in Hebrew. A founding father of the Zionist establishment in Palestine, he saw one of his daughters married to the son of influential writer and philosopher Ahad Ha'am and another to Dr. Arthur Ruppin, a major figure in the Zionist settlement enterprise. When he first learned of the order to evacuate Jaffa, Hacohen toyed with the idea of resisting. If Jamal came to realize that the Jews were not prepared to go like "lambs to the slaughter," he wrote, the pasha might be deterred from carrying out the expulsion. But that was only a passing thought, an expression of helpless anger, "because in the end," he concluded, "what can a herd do, and how can sheep range themselves against the wolves of the desert?" The choice before Hacohen was one that Zionist society in Palestine would confront repeatedly: between compliance and resistance, restraint and combat; between Jewish patriotism, which could endanger the population, and communal responsibility, which often called for compromise, even to the point of impotence.

But Hacohen's own weakness infuriated him, and he vented his rage by accusing the Arab population of primitivism and disloyalty. Many of the Arabs had succeeded in remaining in Jaffa despite the evacuation order, and many others were able to return to their homes soon afterward. "We are Europeans, loyal, accustomed to obey orders and to follow them precisely on time," Hacohen wrote partly with arrogance, partly in self-pity. As he faced the inevitable and left his home at 11 Herzl Street in Tel Aviv, Hacohen gave a last look at his two oleander bushes, one by the fountain, the second by the verandah. In a few days their beautiful flowers would release their scent, he realized, but who would be there to smell them? He choked on his tears and swore he would return. "Our entire existence has collapsed," he wrote.[32]

Most of the Jewish exiles settled at first in Petach Tikva, to the east. As the fighting threatened to spread, they were forced to move again, northward to the Galilee. Writer and teacher Yosef Chaim Brenner was on this journey; he recorded the sight of a woman sitting on the ground next to a dead baby. Many of the exiles were housed in harsh conditions; within a few weeks typhus was raging among them. "One disaster after another," Moshe Smilansky wrote.[33]

Conditions were similar throughout Palestine. In some Jewish villages laborers ate only once every two days. A few soup kitchens were set up here and there, but these barely sufficed. Many people died of cholera. Consul Ballobar doggedly documented the spread of the disease—he himself stopped brushing his teeth out of fear that his water was contaminated. Moshe Smilansky recorded his impressions of a visit to the ultra-Orthodox neighborhood of Mea She'arim, where he had been deeply shaken. "My God!" he wrote. "I never imagined that such wretched poverty really exists and that there really are such dark and filthy corners. . . . [O]ld men and women bloated with hunger. Children with an expression of horror, the devastation of hunger written on their faces. And they cry as well, a miserable, ceaseless whimper in their throats—the whimper of hunger. And all of them are almost naked, covered with tattered rags and crawling with all sorts of vermin. . . . On their faces and hands and all over their bodies, slime, filth, disease, and sores. . . . That people can live like this without losing their minds!" One source noted that many people killed themselves by jumping off roofs or throwing themselves into wells, just so they didn't have to watch their children die.

Smilansky found equally horrific conditions among the Arabs. In some villages, as many as a third of the residents had died of hunger and disease.

"On all the roads," Smilansky wrote, "under every fence and in every stream and well there are dead bodies. If a man gets sick, he might be left in his field or on the road for days until he dies, and no one comes to his aid." Bertha Spafford Vester reported that Arab women had appeared in the yard of the American Colony offering to sell their babies for food. Boris Schatz, a local artist and founder of the Bezalel School of Art, recorded the story of a Jewish woman who, having heard the dog in her Arab neighbor's yard barking incessantly for several days, went to see what was going on. "When she opened the door to the house," Schatz wrote, "she saw three children lying dead on the ground and the mother embracing her eldest daughter as they sat on a pile of rags in a corner of the house. She approached them and was aghast to see that they, too, were dead. Rushing out of the house, she left the door open as she went to call some other neighbors. Returning to the house, they found that the dog had already eaten one of the children." Izzat Darwazza, a leader of the Arab national movement in Palestine, wrote that there were women who ate the flesh of their babies.[34] Estimates are that by 1917, the prewar population of 700,000 Arabs and 85,000 Jews had shrunk by 100,000, including 30,000 Jews. Some were killed or died of hunger; others fled, were exiled, or were deported from the country.* Of those who remained, many longed for the British to arrive.

4.

The British troops set out from Egypt in the spring of 1917, advancing from south to north, via the Sinai desert. Their progress depended on the construction of railroad tracks, an enterprise that employed 56,000 laborers and 35,000 camels. Pipes also had to be laid to supply water. The force was commanded by General Sir Edmund Allenby, a tall man with an impressive aquiline nose who exuded strength, authority, and charisma. He set his command tent at the front, earning the admiration of his soldiers. The scion of a family that claimed Oliver Cromwell among its ancestors, he was a professional soldier, fifty-six years old, a great believer in feint, surprise, and the power of the horse. Before being dispatched to Palestine he had fought in South Africa and France.

Allenby was an avid reader of the Bible and took an interest in the history, geography, and flora and fauna of the country he was about to con-

---

*Most of the Arab population was Muslim and lived predominantly in villages or nomadically in the desert. Most of the Christian Arabs lived in the cities, as did most of the Jews; more than half the Jews lived in Jerusalem.[35]

quer. In letters to his wife he told her about the birds and the trees and, like an anthropologist on a field trip, he reported on the people, who all looked like biblical characters, he wrote. His biographer wrote that "birds, beasts, and flowers interested him more than his soldiers." At the end of October 1917, Allenby's forces took Be'ersheba and, on the third try, Gaza.[36]

The battle gave birth to one of the classic tales in the history of counter-intelligence. At its center was a British colonel, Richard Meinertzhagen, whose mission was to convince the Turks that the British intended to attack Gaza a third time, when in fact they planned to attack Be'ersheba first. Meinertzhagen recorded the plan in his diary:

I have been busy lately compiling a dummy Staff Officer's notebook containing all sorts of nonsense about our plans and difficulties. Today I took it out to the country north-west of Be'ersheba with a view to passing it on to the enemy without exciting suspicion. . . . I found a Turkish patrol who at once gave chase. I galloped away for a mile or so and then they pulled up, so I stopped, dismounted, and had a shot at them. . . . They at once resumed the chase, blazing away harmlessly all the time. Now was my chance, and in my effort to mount I loosened my haversack, field-glasses, water-bottle, dropped my rifle, previously stained with some fresh blood from my horse, and in fact did everything to make them believe I was hit and that my flight was disorderly. They had now approached close enough and I made off, dropping the haversack which contained the notebook and various maps, my lunch, etc. I saw one of them pick up the haversack and the rifle, so now I went like the wind for home and soon gave them the slip. . . . If only they act on the contents of the notebook, we shall do great things.

According to Meinertzhagen, the ruse worked—the attack on Be'ersheba surprised the Turks. The story spread: one of the top officers in the German army thought it necessary to defend the reputation of Germany's allies and deny it.

Meinertzhagen invented another method of hitting at the enemy. At sunset British planes would circle over concentrations of Turkish forces and drop opium cigarettes on them. Allenby forbade this, but according to Meinertzhagen, the scheme continued without Allenby's knowledge. The result: "On 6 November a high percentage of the Turkish army at

Sheria and Gaza were drowsy and fuddled. Some of the prisoners taken were scarcely coherent and quite incapable of resistance."[37]

The British soldiers were tormented mostly by the heat of the desert. "We have now completed the second stage of our long journey," one soldier wrote from the desert. "I must say that I'm not feeling particularly cheerful just now. Am writing in a beastly tent the temperature being 106 in the shade so if you notice a few grease spots on the paper you will know what it is. Before sitting down to write I had to chase a small snake out of the tent, a dear little thing about 18 inches long, some other beastly animal has just taken a flying leap over my legs. I think it was a lizard. It was about 10 inches long, but moved so quickly I hadn't time to get a good look at it. This is a glorious place you get all sorts of animals crawling all over you and the flies are lovely. I'm one mass of bites and blisters already."[38]

Allenby's force was composed of 75,000 infantrymen, 17,000 cavalrymen, and 475 artillery pieces. More than half of this force participated in the battle of Be'ersheba; six tanks took part in the attack on Gaza, and the city was almost leveled.[39] The force continued northward; two weeks later, in mid-November, it reached Jaffa and Tel Aviv.

The first British soldiers who entered Tel Aviv were most impressed by the opportunity to obtain fresh bread and a bath. "Europe! Europe!" they cried happily. Mordechai Ben-Hillel Hacohen, who quickly returned home, took this as a compliment. The British had not expected to find, in the wilds of Asia, a well-ordered city with pretty houses and clean, straight streets, he wrote proudly in his diary.

Some of the soldiers looted. They broke into Tel Aviv homes whose tenants had not yet returned, destroying furniture, mutilating books, pulling down doors and window frames to burn for heat. One of the city's veteran residents recalled that her mother had managed at the last minute to save a piano soldiers had stolen. She also heard about "all kinds of undesirable incidents that happened to little girls." Hacohen and community leaders from Jaffa went to complain to the commanders of the force. The commanders "suggested" they forget about the complaints; otherwise the looting soldiers would be court-martialed and sentenced to death. Hacohen and his associates thought it best to back down—there was no choice but to accept the soldiers' rowdiness with love, Hacohen wrote. He comforted himself with the idea that maybe they thought Tel Aviv was a German neighborhood and were engaged in short-term vengeance. The British, he believed, would eventually bring law and order, justice and discipline. "We have been saved, we have been redeemed!" he wrote.

Many of the soldiers fighting in Palestine were Australian. "They are all charming, and their faces are handsome," Hacohen noted. "They have good faces like big children," he added. "The Australians were generous and freehanded," one of the city's girls later wrote. "Once, when I was jumping rope in front of the house, an Australian soldier joined in and jumped with me. Both of us laughed. He took the rope and wrapped it around his hand and I tried to jump high with him. At the end he gave me a big bar of chocolate." The soldiers brought an orchestra with them, and Tel Aviv sent them Moshe Hopenko, one of the city's first violin teachers.[40]

Moshe Smilansky met his first Australian while wandering through an orange grove. The soldier was a shepherd by profession. "He had left his herd of sheep to volunteer for the army that went to conquer Palestine," Smilansky wrote. "As a schoolboy he studied the Bible and knew that the land of the Bible had been taken from the people of the Bible and that it was under the yoke of Turkish rule. . . . And when the world war broke out and the Australian people were called to volunteer and the ladies of Australia collected money for the war in Palestine, he too put his hand to the sword and his mother and his sister gave him their blessing and said: Go restore the homeland to the one nation left without a homeland." Smilansky recorded the young man's name and so ensured his place in history: Sid Sheerson.[41] The war was not yet over, however. German planes bombed Jaffa, Petach Tikva changed hands several times, and in late November Allenby turned to his next objective: Jerusalem.

The British marched to the city along two major routes: one from the south, parallel to the Hebron road, and the second from the west, along the Jaffa road. The Turks fought back. On several occasions they succeeded in halting the British advance and even in repelling it. The Turks controlled fortified mountain redoubts, like Kastel and Nebi Samuel; the British attacked from below. Here and there the forces engaged in hand-to-hand combat, with bayonets and swords. "Galloping horses are hard to handle one-handed while you have a sword in the other," wrote a British cavalry commander. "Hindered by the clutter of rifle butt and other equipment, troopers found it nearly impossible to get at a low dodging Turk. One missed and missed again until the odd Turk wasn't quite quick enough. . . . I have been asked how one felt on that day. In all honesty, I think it was the only occasion I was not frightened—probably one was too occupied and the final excitement was pretty intense. Altogether like champagne on an empty stomach."[42]

The British were well organized. Unlike the Turks, they were not hungry. They received all their provisions, including bread, from Egypt. The supplies came part of the way by train; on the last section of the tracks, which stopped at Be'ersheba, the British used mules to pull the cars. Then from Be'ersheba supplies were sent northward by mule, after which they were loaded on trucks, and then finally onto camels. Many of the camels could not manage the muddy, soggy journey through the mountainous approach to Jerusalem, and several died. The soldiers shot other camels to end their suffering and rolled the carcasses down into the wadis. "They were quickly seized upon by watchful natives . . . and no doubt afforded excellent dinners to numerous Palestinian families," one of the officers later reported. Battle memoirs of the time also describe the suffering of the horses scrabbling to climb the Judean mountains; many were hit by Turkish shells. Finally, Allenby ordered a thousand donkeys to be brought from Egypt. The heavy cannons transported from Egypt had to be left behind.

But the common enemy of the Turks and the British was now the winter. At the end of long weeks of combat that had begun in the heat of the desert, many British soldiers were still wearing summer uniforms, including shorts. The British force included Egyptians, Indians, New Zealanders, and Australians—all of whom were plagued by the cold. One general compared the Judean hills to the Himalayas.[43]

Life in Jerusalem went on almost as usual, even as the city was about to fall. Next to the famine-ridden lanes of Mea She'arim, Smilansky wrote, "sit people with full bellies in clean homes . . . and they are not driven mad by what they see."[44] Count Ballobar attended a masked ball held at the home of the Mani family, one of Jerusalem's elite Sephardic dynasties. He dressed as a Turkish woman and everyone thought he was the governor's daughter. It was great fun.[45] An advertisement published a few days later in *HaHerut*, the last newspaper still being published in Jerusalem, promised the Jewish residents "a sidesplittingly funny Purim play" and an appearance by a comedian. At the end of March, as Gaza suffered its first assaults, the Fig cinema screened a Sherlock Holmes film. His tricks and maneuvers would provide "uplifting enjoyment," the ad claimed. Only a few days later the newspaper was shut down; the lead type was confiscated by the authorities and melted down to make ammunition.[46]

In April, following the evacuation of Jaffa and Tel Aviv, Jamal Pasha summoned the consuls remaining in Jerusalem to an urgent meeting at his headquarters on the Mount of Olives. The meeting took place in a castle inspired by a Hohenzollern palace in Germany and was named after Empress Augusta Victoria. Jamal intended to notify the foreign consuls that in preparation for battle he had decided to evacuate Jerusalem as he had done in Gaza and Jaffa. But Count Ballobar made a prediction in his diary: Turkey's German allies would force the Ottomans to preserve the integrity of Jerusalem and abandon it without a fight.[47] He was right: Berlin understood that the city was of no military value and it was better to give it up than have the Germans bear responsibility for destroying holy places. By November, after the fall of Be'ersheba, Gaza, and Jaffa, Jerusalem's residents could hear the thunder of the approaching cannons and knew they were on the verge of a new era. "Jerusalem is about to fall, tomorrow or the next day," wrote Khalil al-Sakakini on November 17. He was off by only three weeks; in the meantime, Alter Levine appeared at his door.[48]

5.

Sakakini was afraid to take the Jewish fugitive into his home. He knew that if he was caught, the Turks would charge him with treason. But if he sent Levine away, Sakakini told himself, he would be a traitor to his cultural heritage. He believed Levine was not seeking his personal protection, but rather the refuge offered by traditional Arab hospitality. "He asked for sanctuary in the culture of my people, which preceded Islam and will remain after it," Sakakini wrote. "I have to say that he has granted me a huge honor with his request of sanctuary in my house, because it allows me to represent the spirit of our history and the spirit of our culture. . . . I hope my people will rejoice in a foreigner having requested sanctuary among them and through me, and I have received him in their name, after his own people denied him and his family shut their doors to him."[49] Levine promised that no one knew of his arrival. Sakakini let him in.

In the days that followed the two had many long conversations and got to know each other well. Both were extremely complex men, full of contradictions and with many doubts and questions about their cultures and their identities. Levine, who had been born in Russia, was then about thirty-five years old, the father of three daughters. Sakakini, a native of Jerusalem, was thirty-nine and had one son. Levine's father, Morris, who had managed estates in the Minsk area, had come to Palestine with his family at the beginning of the 1890s, but shortly thereafter had left for the United States to raise money for a yeshiva and a hospital in Jerusalem. Most of Jerusalem's Jews then lived off donations collected overseas by emissaries like Morris Levine. A few years later he obtained American citizenship. His son Alter had studied in yeshiva but later left the Orthodox world in which he had grown up. As an adult, he considered himself a traditional Jew, but since he was a Zionist, ultra-Orthodox Jews saw him as a traitor.[50]

Khalil al-Sakakini's father had been a carpenter and, like Morris Levine, had taken an active part in his community. Sakakini himself had studied at the Greek Orthodox church school and then at the Anglican school founded by Bishop Blyth.[51] Later, he quarreled with the Greek Orthodox patriarch and his followers over corruption in the church and its Arab national character, which Sakakini supported. "I cannot be under the leadership of this corrupt, base priest, nor be numbered among this hateful denomination," he explained, and he left the church. "I am not Orthodox! I am not Orthodox!" he wrote emphatically. Like Alter Levine, his inclination was to define his identity according to a liberal nationalism while adhering to his religious roots; in his will he instructed his son to live in the spirit of the Sermon on the Mount.[52]

Levine was a modern businessman, conscious of the spirit of the new century in which he had come of age. He began work as an agent of the Singer sewing-machine company, whose product was a revolutionary innovation in Palestine, and went on to import typewriters. Next he represented several foreign insurance companies, specializing in life insurance, itself a novelty. He did well in business and was soon known as Palestine's "King of Insurance," with agents and subagents in many Middle Eastern cities. When he came to hide in Sakakini's house, Levine was a rich man who owned land and houses around the country, and he was a moneylender as well. Before deciding to hide, he was careful to transfer power of attorney for all his interests to his father-in-law.[53]

Sakakini was a pioneer in his field as well, in the spirit of the new century. In the school he founded, he instituted a revolutionary method of education. The language of instruction was Arabic, not the usual Turkish, and the pupils did not learn by rote; instead they were expected to understand the material. There was no homework, no tests, no report cards. Sakakini preached the "liberation of the pupil"—he said he hated nothing more than a school run on violence. The teachers were not supposed to punish children or humiliate them, as was common practice, but rather to help develop their personalities. Relations between teachers and pupils were supposed to be open. He encouraged the pupils' social activities, including the publication of a school newspaper, as well as sports, all quite exceptional at the time. Both Sakakini and Levine had an almost mystic faith in the power of physical activity to purify the soul. The school also had a dormitory and a kindergarten, further innovations.[54]

Sakakini had joined one of the Masonic lodges in Jerusalem, and Levine was also one of the "brothers." The two had much in common. They would talk each evening, late into the night, men of books and action given to soul-searching. As church bells rang in the background, the muezzins' cadences floated in the air, and distant cannons thundered, they exchanged ideas and visions of Palestine. Levine hoped to see a million Jews living between the Mediterranean and the Euphrates, the biblically promised borders. At the same time, he conceded that the dream of reviving the Jewish nation in Palestine was dead: the country could not absorb all the Jews of the world—at most, it could take two or three hundred thousand. He advocated Jewish-Arab coexistence. "The Land is our sister," he wrote in a poem, "a single crescent has made the two of us into nomads in the night."[55] For his part, Sakakini said he hated Zionism because it tried to build itself on the ruins of others; in conquering Palestine, Sakakini felt as if Zionism were trampling the heart of the Arab nation.[56] He too, however, could soften his approach, and assert that the world was heading toward unity. The day would come, he'd say, when there would be only one nation on earth.[57] In less sober moments, though, the two were extremely conscious of cultural and political contention, almost national enmity.

Sakakini tried to distinguish between Jews and Zionists; to Levine this meant little. While he had cast aside most religious observance, Levine preserved various Jewish practices, as did most secular Zionists. He would eat only kosher food, which meant he could not partake of the Sakakinis' cooking. His host noted that Levine ate only bread with olives and drank only tea, and this offended him: "May God forgive you, man," he wrote. "Why shouldn't you eat our food? If you consider our food impure, then we too are impure because we eat impurity. Why, then, did you ask for sanctuary among us?" He recorded the incident as if Levine stood for all Jews and Sakakini represented all Christians: "How many crimes have you committed against us and how numerous are your victims!" he wrote.[58]

But Sakakini's annoyance was more than just cultural conflict; he had good reason to be exasperated with his guest. Levine had no intention of remaining hungry—a day or two after arriving at the Sakakini residence, he had spotted a Jewish passerby from the window and asked him to make contact with his mother-in-law. The man did so, and Levine's mother-in-law began to bring him kosher meals. Two or three days later she also brought the Turkish police.

At three in the morning on December 3, a large police force surrounded the house; Sakakini heard the policemen coming up the steps, and he heard them cocking their guns. He had no doubt they had come to arrest Levine. "I jumped out of bed and went to our friend's bed," Sakakini wrote. "I knocked on the door, perhaps I would manage to get him out. But he did not wake up. In the meantime the soldiers were standing at the inner door of the house and there was nothing for me to do but surrender." He opened the door and they broke in; Levine's mother-in-law was with them. They arrested Levine and took Sakakini with them as well.[59]

6.

Five more days remained of Turkish rule. "Fear overcame us all," wrote Aliza Gidoni, a Jerusalem resident who had been a girl at the time. She remembered oxcarts carrying the dead and wounded, both Turks and the German soldiers who had fought on their behalf. "The screams and groans of the soldiers were appalling, their blood dripped on the road." The wounded were taken to improvised hospitals in Jerusalem and elsewhere, and Gidoni asked herself whether any would survive.* Antonio de Ballobar was moved by the dreadful sadness on the faces of the wounded. There was an exceptional amount of commotion in the city, Judge Gad Frumkin later recalled. "The road from the train station and Bethlehem was full of vehicles and mules and infantrymen, disorganized and undisciplined, heading eastward by way of the post office to Jericho. It was obvious that this was not an orderly retreat but a hasty flight." In one neighborhood, Frumkin saw a Turkish soldier sprawled helplessly on the ground, begging for bread and water. He clearly had not eaten for several days. In other parts of the city, Ottoman soldiers were reportedly willing to hand over their weapons in exchange for food. Many abandoned their arms so as not to be weighted down as they ran; some fled barefoot.[61]

Khalil al-Sakakini described the view from the window of his prison cell. "The war was at its height," he later noted, "shells falling all around, total pandemonium, soldiers running about, and fear ruling all." The last of the foreign diplomats finished burning their documents and left the city.[62]

---

*Fighting for his life in one of those hospitals lay a German soldier named Rudolf Hoess, later commandant of Auschwitz.[60]

At Augusta Victoria castle, Sister Theodora asked commander in chief General Erich von Falkenhayn what she and the few remaining nuns should do if a mob broke into the building after the soldiers left. In previous months von Falkenhayn had opposed those of his countrymen who wanted to evacuate Jerusalem without a battle, but his opinion was overruled. Now he did not really know what to tell the good sister; he probably suggested that she pray. He ordered a large oil portrait of the kaiser to be removed from the church vestibule; the portrait, at least, would be protected from the mob.[63]

Throughout the chaos, Count Ballobar had continued to dine with commanders of the German army, enjoying until the end his daily custom of sharing a glass of cognac with one of them. Ballobar also continued to record faithfully all he heard and saw, but during the last week of Turkish rule, even he conceded in his diary, "I don't understand anything!" His connections were still of some use, though. As a macabre farewell gift, the Turks planned to blow up Jerusalem's flour mills. When he learned of this, Count Ballobar borrowed a carriage and rushed to army headquarters on the Mount of Olives, where he succeeded in persuading the soldiers to spare the mills.

Then the chaos in the city finally reached the Spanish consulate and produced the following operatic scene. Ballobar had agreed to grant asylum to two leaders of the Jewish community: Jacob Thon, a Zionist representative in Palestine, and Siegfried Hoofien, the movement's banker. Both were designated for deportation, together with a number of other Jewish public figures. Once he learned of the two men's whereabouts, the Turkish police chief appeared at the Spanish consulate and demanded that the count hand them over. The consul, however, had sent them to hide behind a curtain. As the police chief entered, Ballobar promised to hand the two men over the next day. The two Zionist leaders, quaking behind the curtain, were convinced that the consul intended to give them up.[64] But Ballobar was fairly certain that twenty-four hours later the Turks would have left the city, and he proved correct: Izzat Bey, the city governor, hammered the last telegraph machine to smithereens. He left a writ of surrender, meant for the British, in the hands of Jerusalem's mayor, then stole a carriage from the American Colony in order to depart from the city, as befitted him, in honor.

On December 8 a violent rainstorm raged over the Judean mountains; a heavy fog reduced visibility to zero. The British forces had to halt. That same day they had already marched through Bethlehem, where they were received as liberating heroes; some of the forces had already reached Ein Kerem, John the Baptist's village, just southwest of Jerusalem. Toward evening the storm began to subside.

Count Ballobar went out to the roof of his house to take in the view. The sky was sprinkled with stars. A sudden stillness had fallen over the city. Just a single cannon firing at regular intervals disturbed the night, and a few dogs barked. Ballobar heard a car in the distance and tried to guess who its passengers were. He meditated a moment on the vicissitudes of time and went to sleep. There was shooting that night, but he slept soundly.[65]

2

❖

"A Contract with Jewry"

1.

The British entered Palestine to defeat the Turks; they stayed there to keep it from the French; then they gave it to the Zionists because they loved "the Jews" even as they loathed them, at once admired and despised them, and above all feared them. They were not guided by strategic considerations, and there was no orderly decision-making process. The same factors were at work when they issued the Balfour Declaration, their proclamation of support for Zionist aspirations in Palestine. The declaration was the product of neither military nor diplomatic interests but of prejudice, faith, and sleight of hand. The men who sired it were Christian and Zionist and, in many cases, antisemitic. They believed the Jews controlled the world.

The first British proposal to conquer Palestine and eventually establish a Jewish state there appeared before the cabinet in the form of a memorandum in January 1915, less than three months after Turkey entered the war. Its author was the postmaster general, Herbert Samuel, a Jew. In his characteristically cautious way, Samuel was a Zionist; he seems to have seen Zionism as a bridge between his Judaism and his liberal values. He was thirty-four years old when the World War broke out.[1]

Samuel was aware of the difficulties. "The attempt to realise the aspiration of a Jewish State one century too soon might throw back its actual realisation for many centuries more," he wrote in his memorandum. The time is not yet ripe, he explained. Jewish minority rule should not be imposed on an Arab majority—a Jewish majority should be created first. Palestine was, in any case, too small to absorb all the world's Jews, and so could not provide a solution to the Jewish problem in Europe; but there was room there for three or four million Jews, he concluded.

The proposal to seize Palestine accorded with the way people in London were thinking at the time. When they spoke about the dissolution of the Ottoman Empire, there was a tendency to think of it as a large cake: this country would get one slice, that country another; the territory the Ottomans were about to lose was considered booty to be shared out among the victors.[2] "We have arrived at a supreme moment in the world's history. The map of the world is to be remade," wrote one of the Zionist periodicals in England.[3] There were also thoughts about an exchange of territory; if France conceded on Palestine, as one proposal suggested, it would receive some colony in Africa in exchange.[4]

But Samuel's memorandum was a document unlike most foreign-policy papers placed on the cabinet table—it was all myth and prophecy, an "almost lyrical outburst," said Foreign Secretary Edward Grey.[5] "Let us not presume to say that there is no genius among the countrymen of Isaiah, or no heroism among the descendants of the Maccabees," Samuel wrote, quoting historian Thomas Macaulay. He promised that if only it were given a body in which to reside, the Jewish soul would return and enrich the world. In a private conversation, Samuel also spoke of the need to rebuild the Jewish Temple.

The annexation of Palestine and settling it with Jews, Samuel wrote to his colleagues, would allow Britain once again to fulfill its historic calling of bringing civilization to primitive lands. He outlined the situation in Ottoman Palestine: the despotism, the corruption, the backwardness, the filth. For hundreds of years the country had given the world no benefit. The Jews would bring progress and enlightenment; under British rule, the land would be "redeemed." Palestine would raise the prestige of the great empire, and its conquest "would add lustre even to the British crown." The British public needed Palestine, and would be disappointed were the war to end without any real gain. The German colonies in Africa were not sufficient, nor was it wise to take them. "Widespread and deep-rooted in the Protestant world is a sympathy with the idea of restoring the Hebrew people to the land which was to be their inheritance, an intense interest in the fulfillment of the prophecies which have foretold it," he wrote. "The redemption also of the Christian Holy Places ... would add to the appeal" of the policy, he maintained, and make access to them easier.

Samuel went on to say that the link between the Jews and the land of Israel was as ancient as the world. The Jews had been longing to return for eighteen hundred years. If Britain were to annex Palestine with the intention of one day establishing a Jewish state, millions of Jews scattered around the world, including the two million in the United States, would show lasting gratitude for all generations. The goodwill of "a whole race," Samuel wrote, "may not be without its value." He noted that while living in Palestine, the Jews had produced many great men—statesmen, prophets, judges, and soldiers. The Jewish brain is a "physiological product not to be despised."

Only briefly, and apparently without any real concern, did Samuel mention the possibility that one of the European powers might take control of Palestine and endanger Britain's hold on the Suez Canal. He was thinking of France, which had its own territorial ambitions in the Middle East.

Foreign Secretary Grey ridiculed the memorandum. Apparently, he wrote, there really is something to the maxim that Disraeli so liked: "race is everything."* The prospect that all the world's Jews might gather in a single country gave him the shivers: "What an attractive community!" he sneered. But when he actually spoke with Samuel, Grey claimed "a strong sentimental attraction" to the idea of giving the Jews Palestine. Still, he thought Britain should not assume any more colonial responsibilities; he feared Britain would get badly entangled in Palestine.[6]

After speaking with the foreign secretary and other officials, Samuel decided to redraft his memorandum. He struck out the first version's overly sentimental statements and added that even those Jews who did not support Zionism were favorable toward his proposal. He also reduced the suggested number of Jews who should settle in Palestine, from "three or four million" to "three million." In the amended version he no longer spoke of the "annexation" of Palestine to the British Empire, but rather of a British "protectorate." These were cosmetic changes, however; the gist of the proposal remained the same.

A few months later, an interministerial committee was established in London to discuss the future of the Ottoman territories. The committee members weighed largely strategic issues. Palestine's importance was

---

*The British generally used the word *race* to mean "nation." This is important with regard to those who spoke of Jews disparagingly: it is not always correct to consider their comments as racist. There were those who spoke of "race" even when they did not mean to express antisemitism.

weighed in the context of securing Britain's access to India, but Britain did not need to control the country for this purpose; indeed, the committee did not recommend its conquest. In any case, there would have been no strategic reason to give Palestine to the Jews. It could also be given to the Arabs.

At the beginning of the war, Britain had acted on the assumption that the best way to strike at Germany was by direct confrontation, in Western Europe. The possibility of outflanking it from the east, via the Ottoman Empire, was not yet part of the battle plan. The action Samuel proposed therefore ran against his colleagues' strategic thinking. It did, however, appeal to their sense of historical justice, to their inclination to perform an act of biblical compassion for the Jews, to their vague but deep-seated belief in the great power of world Jewry, and apparently also to their hope that they might be rid of them.[7]

It was those feelings that had prompted Britain's earlier engagement with "the Jewish Question," chiefly its offer in 1903 of a tract of land for an autonomous Jewish settlement under Zionist auspices in British East Africa. At the time, the Zionist movement in London had obtained the services of an attorney to facilitate its contacts with the Foreign Office; his name was David Lloyd George. *The Jewish Chronicle* attributed to Lloyd George an ardent belief in the Zionist cause, and Samuel consulted him when he wrote his memorandum.[8] Indeed, Lloyd George did believe in the return to Zion.

2.

Lloyd George was one of those Englishmen who had grown up on the Bible. "I was taught in school far more about the history of the Jews than about the history of my own land," he once recalled. "I could tell you all the Kings of Israel. But I doubt whether I could have named half a dozen of the Kings of England and no more of the Kings of Wales." He told David Ben-Gurion that he had known the names of the rivers, valleys, and mountains of Palestine before he knew even a single geographical name in his own country. In his memoirs, he referred to Palestine by its ancient name, "Canaan."[9] The return to Zion was thus anchored deeply in his Christian faith. Indeed, there was a long English tradition of Christian Zionism, and Herbert Samuel made a calculated appeal to that tradition in his memorandum. Edward Grey called it an updated version of *Tancred*.*

---

*As early as the beginning of the seventeenth century, books and public discussion in England had taken up the idea of returning the Jews to the land of their fathers, in the spirit of the biblical prophets.

The comparison was germane. Tancred, the hero of Benjamin Disraeli's eponymous 1847 novel, is a young British noble who goes to the Holy Land and inspires the East to fight a war of liberation. "Palmerston will never rest until he gets Jerusalem," one character says during a conversation on the state of the world. Thirty years prior to the novel's publication, Foreign Secretary Palmerston had instructed the ambassador in Turkey to pressure the government there to allow Jews to return to Palestine. The London *Times* devoted a sympathetic editorial to the idea.[10]

Lloyd George would later write that Palestine had not even been under discussion at the beginning of the war and that it was put on the agenda only at the end. In fact, as early as 1915 he himself had proposed conquering Palestine. At the time, he supported his proposal with one of the less pertinent arguments in Samuel's memorandum, that Palestine would add luster to the British Crown.[11] Lord Horatio Herbert Kitchener, the secretary of state for war, was infuriated by the proposal and by Lloyd George's rationale, saying, "Palestine would be of no value to us whatever." His loss of temper might have had more to do with his famed intolerance of anyone challenging anything he said.[12] Either way, the following year Kitchener drowned at sea and his strategic approach—limiting the war to the western front in Europe—drowned with him. Six months later, in December 1916, Lloyd George was elected prime minister and British policy changed: the Germans would now also face Allied attacks on their southern and eastern fronts via the Ottoman Empire.

In line with the new battle plan, the British troops in Egypt were poised to enter Ottoman territory, but the army's first two attempts to conquer Gaza failed. Lloyd George decided to send the troops a more effective commander. He first thought of General Jan Smuts from South Africa, but Smuts preferred to serve in the imperial war cabinet. Allenby was his second choice.[13]

According to Edward Grey, Lloyd George had no interest in the Jews, neither in their past nor their future. What he really wanted was to keep the holy places in Palestine from getting into French hands. That wasn't the whole story, though. Lloyd George did indeed despise the French and had no intention of allowing them to control Palestine. But in his own way he despised the Jews as well—or, to put it another way, he feared them.[14]

By the time Lloyd George wrote his memoirs, toward the end of the 1930s, the common wisdom in Britain was that the country had erred in supporting the Zionists; Lloyd George wanted to convince the public that he had been right to do so. Writing six years after the Nazis came to power, he could simply have pointed to the persecution of the Jews in Europe as reason to have supported the Zionists and argue that British actions in Palestine had been a way of providing some sort of justice for the Jewish people. Instead, he explained his support for the Zionist movement as an alliance with a hugely influential political power whose goodwill was worth paying for. The war had made such an alliance inevitable; the Zionists, he claimed, had in effect forced his government to support them. It was a distinctly antisemitic claim.

"The Jewish race," Lloyd George explained in his memoirs, had worldwide influence and capability, and the Jews had every intention of determining the outcome of the World War—acting, he said, in accordance with their financial instincts. They could influence the United States to intensify its involvement in the war, and as the real movers behind the Russian Revolution, they also controlled Russia's attitude toward Germany. The British feared that Russia would sign a separate peace with Germany, which would have enabled the Germans to direct all their forces to the western front. The Jews offered themselves, of course, to the highest bidder, and had the British not been expeditious in gaining their favor, the Germans would have bought them. Lloyd George believed that the friendship of the Jewish people would benefit Britain while Jewish hostility would harm it. The British had thus had no real choice—they had had to "make a contract with Jewry."[15]

Lloyd George's view was widespread. "I do not think that it is easy to exaggerate the international power of the Jews," Lord Robert Cecil, who was undersecretary at the Foreign Office during the final years of World War I, once said. Similar assessments came from no small number of British diplomats around the world. The ambassador in Turkey reported that an international conspiracy of Jews, Freemasons, and Zionists was the real power behind Attatürk's Young Turk revolution. "The influence of the Jews is very great," noted the British ambassador in Washington. "They are well-organised and especially in the press, in finance, and in politics their influence is considerable." According to the ambassador, "most people" said that American Jewish sympathies were generally with the Germans.[16]

"Away behind all the governments and the armies there was a big subterranean movement going on, engineered by very dangerous people," John Buchan wrote in his classic spy novel *Thirty-nine Steps*. The director of information for the British government during Lloyd George's administration, Buchan was talking about the Jews. They pulled the strings of war in accordance with their interests, he had one of his characters say: "Things that happened in the Balkan War, how one state suddenly came out on top, why alliances were made and broken, why certain men disappeared. . . . The aim of the whole conspiracy was to get Russia and Germany at loggerheads. . . . The Jew was behind it and the Jew hated Russia worse than hell. . . . The Jew is everywhere . . . with an eye like a rattlesnake. He is the man who is ruling the world just now and he has his knife in the empire of the Tsar."[17] Chaim Weizmann did his best to encourage that impression.

3.

Weizmann settled in England in 1904, at the age of thirty, soon after Herzl's death. Born in Russia, he had spent several years in Switzerland. A chemist, he was already a prominent figure in the Zionist movement, having acquired a reputation as a powerful public speaker.

While a key activist, Weizmann held no office in the Zionist movement, but nonetheless he immediately took charge of the situation in England. Within a few weeks he managed to secure a meeting with Lord Eustace Percy, then undersecretary of state for foreign affairs. A few days after the meeting, Weizmann sent Percy a draft summary of their discussion. The Foreign Office raised an eyebrow; Percy had not been aware that Weizmann had been conducting an official "interview," but he took Weizmann seriously and requested a few corrections to the wording of the document, as if it were indeed the summary of a meeting between the representatives of two nations.[18]

Chaim Weizmann's remarkable ability to gain access to British policy makers and leave a strong impression on them was the Zionist movement's chief asset in that period: he saw them all, more or less whenever he wanted. When he arrived in England, his English was less than fluent; his conversation with Percy had been in French, and he still thought in Yiddish. In a somewhat pathetic attempt to assimilate into British society, he took an English name, Charles. A lecturer in chemistry at the University of Manchester, he lived under constant financial pressure. In many ways, Weizmann was a typical Jewish immigrant from an Eastern European shtetl who had come to seek his fortune in the great world beyond.

If he trembled like a leaf in the corridors of imperial power, Weizmann made sure the great and the mighty did not notice. He was blessed with audacity and discernment, courage, craftiness, and great personal charisma. He had, wrote Jerusalem governor Ronald Storrs, "almost feminine charm." In time, he learned how to dress, how to express himself, and even how to think like the British, becoming a sworn Anglophile. More than anything else, people believed him because he believed in himself. Storrs said, "Did he not explain Einstein's Relativity to my sister and myself at luncheon until for a moment I dreamed that even I understood?"[19] Sometimes he appeared as a beggar pleading for charity: he made an art of emotional blackmail, and almost everywhere he found good Christians who wanted to help. At other times he behaved like a statesman among statesmen, looking them directly in the eye, speaking in the name of the Jewish people. On occasion, he could summon a threatening tone. But it was all bluff: the Jewish people had not sent him, and he had no power.

By the beginning of the war, Weizmann had gotten to know quite a few people in the political system, including Winston Churchill. For much of his access, he had C. P. Scott, editor of the *Manchester Guardian,* to thank. It was Scott who had managed his most important introduction—to Arthur James Balfour, a former Liberal prime minister and foreign secretary in David Lloyd George's cabinet.

Balfour was no stranger to "the Jewish Question." He had been prime minister in 1903 at the time of the East Africa, or "Uganda," proposal, often called the "first Balfour Declaration."[20] The Zionist Congress rejected the offer, having firmly fixed its sights on Palestine, but when Weizmann and Balfour first met in 1906, they spoke of it again, in an exchange that yielded one of Zionism's most famous anecdotes. Had Moses been offered Uganda in exchange for Palestine, Weizmann said, he surely would have broken the tablets. After all, would Balfour agree to exchange London for Paris? "But Dr. Weizmann," Balfour responded, "we have London." True, Weizmann replied, "but we had Jerusalem when London was a marsh." Surprised, Balfour asked Weizmann whether there were many Jews who thought like him and was told that there were millions. "It is curious," Balfour said. "The Jews I meet are different." Weizmann's response: "Mr. Balfour, you meet the wrong kind of Jews."[21]

The two continued to see each other from time to time. Once Balfour told Weizmann about a conversation he had had with Cosima Wagner, the composer's widow, and remarked that he shared some of her antisemitic ideas. This was no secret. In 1905, Balfour had been among the sponsors of the law to restrict immigration to Britain, a largely anti-Jewish measure, which had led to his vilification as an antisemite.[22] But Weizmann, a master of self-restraint, knew how to respond temperately in such fraught conversational moments. The Zionists also subscribed to "cultural antisemitism," Weizmann reassured him; and they also believed that those German Jews who identified themselves as "Germans of the Mosaic faith" were "an undesirable, demoralizing phenomenon." Still, he said, Wagner's antisemitic worldview failed to take into account that the Jews had contributed significantly to Germany's greatness, as they had to the greatness of France and England. He told Balfour about what was happening in Palestine—about the struggle to make Hebrew the official language of its Jewish community, about his dream of founding a university, about Boris Schatz's art school, Bezalel. Balfour, Weizmann wrote, was moved to tears.

One night in 1916 Weizmann dined as a guest of Balfour's, who was now foreign secretary. It was already after midnight when Weizmann left. Balfour walked with him for a few minutes, as far as the Duke of York's column. Once they reached the column, Balfour persuaded Weizmann to walk back with him, and at the house the two retraced their steps to the column. They walked back and forth this way for two hours, Weizmann doing most of the talking. He laid out his much-repeated argument—that Zionist and British interests were identical. The Zionist movement spoke, Weizmann said, with the vocabulary of modern statesmanship, but was fueled by a deep religious consciousness. Balfour, himself a modern statesman, also considered Zionism as an inherent part of his Christian faith. It was a beautiful night; the moon was out.[23] Soon after, Balfour declared in a cabinet meeting, "I am a Zionist."[24]

Weizmann was aware of his image as "king of the Jews"; every so often he would send out letters that looked as if they had come from a center of world power: "American friends must strain every nerve to influence our Russian friends favour of vigorous support British and Entente policy and counteract all adverse forces there," he once cabled a Zionist activist in Washington. "We are doing from here the same. Wire steps you are taking."[25] In a telegram to American Supreme Court Justice Louis Brandeis, Weizmann wrote, "We must do our utmost to prevent Germans obtaining footing South Russia." He said he had received information that the Germans intended to purchase merchandise and fuel in southern Russia and warned that this was liable to damage the effectiveness of "our embargo" and endanger the "Allied and Palestinian cause." He added, "We think that Jews of South Russia who control trade could effectively couteract German and Bolshevik manoeuvres in alliance with Ukraine," noting that "We have telegraphed our friends Petrograd Rostov Kiev Odessa and beg you to do the same appealing to them on behalf of Allied and Palestinian cause. . . . Every influence must be used now. . . . Jews have now splendid opportunity show their gratitude England and America." This was no doubt meant for the eyes of the British censor. Like one conspirator to another, or perhaps with a wink to the censor, Weizmann warned the American jurist to keep the matter strictly confidential. At the same time he wrote to his acquaintances in Russia and urged them to act swiftly, making a point to wire Petrograd in English. British intelligence showed an interest in Weizmann's activities, and he was glad to report to one of the senior officials in the Foreign Office.[26*]

In 1917, Weizmann had reason to conjure up the myth of Jewish power and influence, and he rose to the occasion admirably. In May of the previous year, Great Britain and France had agreed on a secret convention with the assent of Russia on the dismemberment of the Ottoman Empire. Named for its two chief authors, Sir Mark Sykes and Georges Picot of France, the Sykes-Picot Agreement would give Syria and Lebanon to France and divide Palestine into zones of British and Anglo-French control. Weizmann learned of it from C. P. Scott and was deeply disturbed, as the division of Palestine would threaten the chances of establishing a Jewish state there. As one of the Zionist leaders warned, the French were liable to impose their language in Palestine at the expense of Hebrew. Weizmann went to the Foreign Office to protest; according to one description he arrived "in a fine rage." By 1917, the Foreign Office was already having second thoughts about the agreement—the Arabs had been scandalized by it, Russia had defected from the war, and Italy wanted to share in the spoils; the Zionist protest further strengthened their inclination to break it. Weizmann's influence could only reinforce Sykes's predilection for seeing the Jews everywhere and behind every decisive event. Lloyd George himself thought that it would be best to take Weizmann's opposition into consideration.[28]

Weizmann's principal achievement was to create among British leaders an identity between the Zionist movement and "world Jewry"—Lloyd George referred to "the Jewish race," "world Jewry," and "the Zionists" as if

---

*Like many of his colleagues, Balfour took note of the involvement of Jews in Russia's Communist revolution. In conversation with Justice Louis Brandeis, Balfour mentioned a piece of news he had heard a few days earlier, from a "well-informed person," that Lenin's mother was Jewish.[27]

these were synonyms. He also succeeded in persuading them that British and Zionist interests were the same. Yet none of it was true. No real national interest dictated support for Zionism. Moreover, the movement that was supposed to be a center of world influence in fact occupied four small, dark rooms in Picadilly Circus in London; its entire archives were kept in a single box in a small hotel room, under the bed of Nachum Sokolow, a leader of the World Zionist Organization.[29] Most Jews did not support Zionism; the movement was highly fragmented, with activists working independently in different European capitals. Weizmann had absolutely no way of affecting the outcome of the war. But Britain's belief in the mystical power of "the Jews" overrode reality, and it was on the basis of such spurious considerations that Britain took two momentous decisions: the establishment of a Jewish legion and the Balfour Declaration.

The participation of Jews in the war in Palestine in separate battalions was, from their point of view, meant to promote recognition of their national identity and guarantee them a share in the spoils of the war. The assumption among Jews was that the soldiers would be participating in the battle for their own country. However, the War and Foreign Offices in Britain considered the legion a needless bother and resented its imposition by the Prime Minister's Office. The establishment of the legion involved considerable operational and legal difficulties, and the secretary of state for war couldn't see the need for it. But as one of Lloyd George's aides explained, the prime minister was concerned that the influential Jews of the world were agitating for the war to end; "they" needed peace in order to resume "their" commerce, the aide noted. It was hoped that the establishment of a Jewish unit to take part in the conquest of Palestine would encourage the Jews to support the continuation of the war.

From a military point of view the Jewish Legion was of no significance—Jerusalem was conquered before its soldiers even reached Palestine. The legion did, however, give the Zionist movement a certain amount of military experience and a myth of defense and heroism. And more than anything else, its creation illustrated the threatening image of the Jews and the significance of biblical romanticism for Lloyd George and Balfour.[30]

4.

Many years afterward, Lloyd George described the Balfour Declaration as a prize awarded by a generous and benevolent ruler to his court Jew. Weizmann had developed a method of producing acetone from maize, and acetone was needed for the production of artillery shells. According to Lloyd George, he wished to reward Weizmann for his diligence, but Weizmann responded that he wanted only support for his people. The result was a letter from Foreign Secretary Balfour expressing the British government's backing for the Zionist cause. Weizmann hated the story. "I almost wish it had been as simple as that," he wrote, "and that I had never known the heartbreaks, the drudgery and the uncertainties which preceded the declaration." But the story is not entirely specious.

Beginning in 1915, Weizmann worked on his project in one of the admiralty's laboratories near London and then later in the service of the Ministry of Munitions. This was a distressing experience: Weizmann was dissatisfied with his job title and his salary, and once he succeeded in perfecting the process there was the question of the patent's ownership. There were all kinds of bureaucratic delays in establishing Weizmann's claim; officials created problems, which Weizmann tackled the way he knew best—by calling on his connections. Again and again, he enlisted C. P. Scott, who helped wherever he could. Scott spoke on Weizmann's behalf to party colleagues, the first lord of the admiralty, and the minister of munitions. Early in the war, the first lord of the admiralty happened to be Arthur James Balfour; the minister of munitions was David Lloyd George.

Weizmann comes out of this chapter of his life looking like an unrelenting gadfly. While he was sending C. P. Scott to intervene on his behalf with the empire's ministers, these men, responsible for more than four hundred million subjects, had in excess of eight million soldiers at the front.[31] It is doubtful whether Weizmann would have gotten to Lloyd George and Balfour without Scott's help, and to Scott's good fortune, his protégé did not let him down; Weizmann's research was of some importance to the war effort, and so Scott could continue to represent Weizmann to Lloyd George and to Balfour after 1916, when the two men became, respectively, prime minister and foreign secretary.[32]

During the course of the war Weizmann spoke with Lloyd George at least seven times; once, they dined together at the home of Lady Astor. Now that he had made a significant contribution to the empire, Weizmann felt justified in asking for the government's formal support of Zionism. He had spent years priming Britain's leaders on the Zionist cause, so when he asked for a letter of support, he did not have to begin at the beginning. "It would appear that in view of the sympathy towards the Zionist movement which has already been expressed by the Prime Minister, Mr. Balfour . . . and other statesmen, we are committed to support it," stated one of the Foreign Office officials with whom Weizmann was in contact.[33]

Balfour, however, was careful not to get carried away. When he said, "I am a Zionist," he did not envisage Britain remaining in Palestine long enough to advance the cause of Jewish independence, and in any case he did not think that Britain should bear the burden alone. He on no account wanted to annex Palestine to the empire. But he devoted considerable time to the subject and was apparently delighted to do so. Palestine gave him a spiritual break from the horrors of the war. He described it as a great ideal: returning the Jews to their homeland was a historic project, and he wanted his name linked to it. He was also enthralled by the experiment and challenge: "Are we never to have adventures?" he asked his colleagues imperiously in the House of Lords. A world without grand exploits was, for him, a world without imagination. George Antonius, a prominent Jerusalem Christian Arab, thought Balfour saw Palestine as a kind of "historico-intellectual exercise and diversion," which, in a rather snobbish way, he did.[34] Always in the background was his evaluation of Jewish power. "Zionism, be it right or wrong, good or bad," Balfour wrote, is "of far profounder import than the desires and prejudices of the 700,000 Arabs who now inhabit that ancient land."[35]

The British government had still not defined its objectives in the Middle East; its intention was to "muddle through" and satisfy everyone.[36] So it groped its way, intuitively, not only between the conflicting interests of the Zionists and the Arabs but also between piles of position papers and the egos of its officials. In the War Office and the Foreign Office, in the residence of the British high commissioner in Cairo, and in the India Office people were drafting their own foreign policies. Some objected to Weizmann's request for a declaration of support.

The most comprehensive memorandum against the declaration bore the same title as Herbert Samuel's memo of nearly three years earlier: "The Future of Palestine." Its author was Lord George Nathaniel Curzon, a member of the war cabinet. It has been said that he opposed the declaration out of envy of Lord Balfour. Whatever the reason, his memorandum was well argued. Curzon conceded that some sort of European administration would probably be established in Palestine to defend the holy sites and to ensure equal rights to all the country's citizens, including the Jews, but not to them alone. He did not reject out of hand the possibility that this administration would open the country to Jewish immigration and allow Jews to purchase land. "If this is Zionism, there is no reason why we should not all be Zionists," Curzon wrote. But the draft declaration promised more, and for that reason he opposed it. Curzon was warning his colleagues that they were about to get into trouble, and he was right. The difficulties he laid out weighed on the British administration in Palestine to its last day.

The declaration did not refer to a Jewish "state" but a "national home." The phrase was a Zionist invention, promulgated in the first Zionist Congress and intended to camouflage Zionism's true intention so as to mitigate opposition. Curzon argued that a "national home" was a vague entity. Some understood it to mean a state independent in all respects; others were talking of a "spiritual center" for the Jews. Curzon felt the British government was assuming an obligation whose substance was not clear, and that was asking for trouble.

Second, the country was small, poor, and frayed by the war. There was no possibility that a large portion of the world's twelve million Jews could be settled there. The entire settlement operation would require a huge financial investment. Moreover, the country was not empty; it was inhabited by Arabs. They would not agree to be dispossessed of their land or to be the Jews' hewers of wood and bearers of water. Jerusalem could not in any case serve as the capital of this national home—too many religions had a deep emotional attachment to it.

In addition, British representatives in Cairo had invested great efforts in organizing an Arab rebellion against the Ottoman Empire, with Thomas Edward Lawrence, better known as Lawrence of Arabia, spearheading the push. In return for support against the Turks, the British had promised the Arabs independence. Sir Henry MacMahon, the high commissioner in Egypt, had said as much in a letter to the sharif of Mecca, in October 1915. Later, the question would arise about whether Palestine was included in that promise. Apparently it was, but the letter's wording was vague, perhaps deliberately so, either to mislead the Arabs or out of carelessness. The matter of Britain's promises to the Arabs continued to vex the government—during the 1920s it came up for discussion in Parliament at least twenty times. The Arabs claimed that the British had broken their word. MacMahon claimed that he had not intended to give the Arabs Palestine.[37]

About six weeks before the Balfour Declaration was issued, Brigadier General Gilbert Clayton, Allenby's chief political officer, warned that a pro-Zionist proclamation would anger the Arabs and recommended that the statement not be issued.[38] The government did not take the advice of its man in the field; indeed, over the next thirty years it would frequently ignore the professional evaluations from military men in Palestine.*

Minister of Munitions Edwin Montagu, Herbert Samuel's cousin and later secretary of state for India, considered Zionism a threat and raised yet another objection. His view is important since it reflects an eternal source of conflict in Jewish public discourse. Montagu rejected the idea that the Jews are a nation and argued that the demand to recognize them as a separate nation put at risk their struggle to become citizens with equal rights in the countries in which they lived. Every country that recognized Palestine as a Jewish "national home" would want to get rid of its Jews.†

Montagu thought that Christian Zionism in Britain did in fact reflect an aspiration to expel English Jews to Palestine, where they would live in one large Jewish ghetto. In a letter to Prime Minister Lloyd George, he wrote that if Palestine were declared the national home of the Jewish people, every antisemitic organization and newspaper would ask by what right a Jewish minister served in the British government. "The country for which I have worked ever since I left the University—England—the country for which my family have fought," Montagu wrote, "tells me that my national home, if I desire to go there . . . is Palestine."[41] Montagu was right: Great Britain was about to declare that the Zionist movement represented the entire Jewish people.

While the cabinet deliberated, some of Weizmann's colleagues in the movement accused him of working like a dictator—he wasn't consulting them and wasn't keeping them informed; some also hated his wife, Vera. His biographer Jehuda Reinharz described many of the moves made by the "Chief," as he was called, as the improvisations of a man following his intuition. Weizmann was hurt by the criticism—or perhaps only made out that he was, as he did on occasion. Either way, in September 1917 he complained that the atmosphere around him was laden with lack of confidence, jeal-

---

*At least some British supporters of Zionism, including those who despised Jews, backed the Zionists because they hated the Arabs even more. The Arabs of Palestine had, after all, fought for Turkish rule, Lloyd George wrote in his war memoirs. In fact he knew no more about Arabs than he knew about Jews. His Arab policy, to the extent that it was a policy, suffered from misunderstanding, internal contradiction, and ignorance; part of the latter was his dismissal of emergent Arab nationalism.[39]

†Theodor Herzl had also thought of this eventuality but, unlike Montagu, considered it positive. "The antisemites will become our most loyal friends, the antisemitic nations will become our allies," he noted in his diary.[40]

ousy, and a kind of stridency preventing him from doing any productive work. Lamenting the vicious air of intrigue, he wrote to his friend C. P. Scott that his colleagues had begun importing "Soviet tactics" into the Zionist movement.[42] He urgently needed a concrete achievement to win out over his opponents. As part of this struggle within the movement, he redoubled his efforts to enhance the impression of Jewish influence.

Meanwhile, Nachum Sokolow had spent some months traveling from one world capital to another, collecting declarations of support for Zionism, kinds of preliminary Balfour Declarations. Everywhere, he was received as the emissary of a great power. He went to Paris and Rome and enjoyed an audience with the pope. Chaim Weizmann used Sokolow's journey as reason to inform the British Foreign Office that the German government was also considering a declaration of support for the Zionists' aspirations, which was true.[43]

At this point in October Edwin Montagu succeeded in convincing his colleagues that the declaration should not be promulgated without first consulting the president of the United States, Woodrow Wilson. As he suspected, the White House recommended against putting out the declaration, almost knocking the entire matter off the agenda. But Weizmann lobbied his friend Brandeis, who in turn spoke with someone on Wilson's staff, and the White House reversed its position. The marginal significance President Wilson assigned to the matter is evidenced by a note sent to one of his aides, to the effect that he had just found in his pocket the declaration the Zionist movement was requesting from Britain; he had no objections. The change in the president's position was little more than the product of good public relations work by the Zionists in Washington, but in London it raised eyebrows. Lloyd George could hardly construe it as anything other than confirmation of his conviction that the Jews controlled the White House.

Simultaneously, Herbert Samuel was promising that the conquest of Palestine would also bring Britain the gratitude of the world's Jews.[44] His opinion was echoed retrospectively in a report issued by the Royal Institute of International Affairs at Chatham House some years later. The report confirmed that the Balfour Declaration had been anchored in deep sentiment toward the Holy Land, but the war cabinet could hardly have made such a decision for the sole reason of doing right by the Jews. Based on a speech given in Parliament by David Lloyd George after the war, the institute determined that London had been inundated with reports from all over the world, asserting that the sympathy of the Jews was vital to winning the war. The Balfour Declaration, the institute resolved, had indeed been a means to victory. The fact was that other countries had also competed for Jewish support, the report noted.[45]

The final draft of the declaration did not give the Zionists everything they wanted; the British government stopped short of designating Palestine a Jewish state. The wording incorporated the various objections raised during the debate and reflected all-around caution. Thus it did not say that Palestine would become the national home of the Jews, but that the national home would be established in Palestine—in other words, only in part of it. The Arabs were not mentioned explicitly—there was no sense of Palestine as an Arab land—they were described as "non-Jewish communities," and the establishment of the Jewish national home was conditional on nothing being done to prejudice Arabs' civil and religious rights. In order to ease Montagu's mind and those of other anti-Zionist Jews, the national home was also predicated on the rights and status of Jews in other countries not being compromised. The Zionists managed to get in one amendment, almost at the last minute: the British had referred to "the Jewish race" but made no fuss about changing that to "the Jewish people."[46] *

In the early afternoon of October 31, 1917, Weizmann sat waiting outside the room where the war cabinet met until Mark Sykes emerged, calling, "Dr. Weizmann, it's a boy!" Weizmann would later write that this was not the boy he had prayed for; time after time the Zionist movement would make do with less than it hoped to achieve. But that evening the Weizmanns had good reason to celebrate. They had friends over for dinner, and all of them performed a Hasidic dance.[48]

The publication of Lord Balfour's letter was delayed so as not to endanger Allenby's campaign; he was then on his way to Be'ersheba, and London intended to issue the declaration only after he entered the city. But by the time word of Be'ersheba's fall arrived there was no room in that week's edition of the *Jewish Chronicle,* which came out on Fridays. For the *Chronicle*'s sake, everyone agreed to put off publication for a week, and the declaration, dated November 2, was finally made public on Novem-

---

*A writer "must formulate and observe certain literary principles if he wishes to be completely understood," wrote Robert Graves in a handbook for writers. He noted, however: "Granted, he may not always wish to be so understood: a good deal of play is made in English with deliberate looseness of phrase." He cited the Balfour Declaration as a classic example.[47]

ber 9. The timing couldn't have been worse—the news was completely overshadowed by Lenin's victory.[49]

Here was one nation promising another nation the land of a third nation, wrote Arthur Koestler, who, dismissing the declaration as an impossible notion, an unnatural graft, called it a "white Negro."[50] But the Zionist movement knew how to give the event biblical majesty: "Since Cyrus the Great there was never, in all the records of the past, a manifestation inspired by a higher sense of political wisdom, far-sighted statesmanship, and national justice towards the Jewish people than this memorable declaration," Weizmann wrote to Balfour.[51] Throughout the world there were assemblies of thanksgiving. In Palestine, people heard the news by word of mouth. Nachum Gutman, an artist and writer, related this story: an Australian officer, a music lover, entered Tel Aviv with his soldiers and heard the sound of a violin floating from the window of one of the houses. He halted, listened to the melody, and then went up to the house to thank the musician. In passing, he also mentioned the Balfour Declaration, and word spread quickly from house to house. There were those who doubted the Australian's news, but the violinist claimed that people who love music do not lie.[52]

5.

On Sunday, December 9, 1917, the sun came out in Jerusalem. Antonio de Ballobar noted in his diary that it was a day of "astounding beauty"—the first Sunday of a new life, the consul wrote.[53] In the dawn light, Mayor Hussein Salim al-Husseini went to search out the city's new rulers. A scion of one of the most powerful Arab families in Jerusalem, he had inherited his office from his father. He spoke English well. On his horse, he set out to submit to the British the writ of surrender deposited with him by the Turkish governor; he took along several people, including the police chief.

The first stop they made was at the American Colony to share the news. The neighborhood's residents sang "Hallelujah," and the mayor, who had graduated from the colony's school, joined in. Then, Bertha Spafford Vester related, "Mother warned him not to go into town without a white flag." So they took a sheet, tied it to a broom handle, and bid the mayor godspeed. One of the colony's residents, the Swedish photographer Hol Lars Larsson, joined the entourage. As for the rest of the mayor's journey, there are countless versions.[54] Over the years, the story took on legendary dimensions, but thanks to Larsson's pictures it is clear that at least some of the events really happened. Actually, the nebulousness of the account has only added to its charm. What it comes down to is this: Jerusalem surrendered no fewer than seven times.

As the mayor was knocking on the gate of the American Colony, an officer of the British army, which was already bivouacked at the northern limits of the city, hankered after eggs for breakfast. He sent his unit's cook and another private to search for a chicken coop in one of the nearby villages. The cook and his comrade set out and quickly got lost. They walked and walked and suddenly found themselves facing a party of civilians bearing a white flag. They were the first British soldiers to encounter the mayor. He presented himself and announced ceremoniously that the city of Jerusalem welcomed His Majesty's army and wished to surrender. The two soldiers had a hard time understanding what it was that the man wanted. They were on another mission—their major was still waiting for his English breakfast. So the two groups parted ways, and Husseini proceeded westward, in the direction of Antonio de Ballobar's house.

Ballobar woke up that morning to the sound of a crowd at his door. When he peeked from his window he made out a few dozen hysterical women. Over the last few days, their husbands had been arrested by the Turks and taken in an unknown direction. The women pleaded with the consul to intervene. One of them was Sultana al-Sakakini and another was Gittel Levine. In the days since their husbands had been arrested, the two had gone to the gates of the military prison to bring them clothes, food, and money. But the soldiers had taken their money and sent them away.[55] That morning, however, the consul was no longer in a position to involve himself in everything, as he had been during the Turkish regime, and he knew it. Unfortunately, at this juncture his influence was too small to be of use, he told the weeping women.

Only a few hours previously, Khalil al-Sakakini and Alter Levine had been taken from their cells. Turkish soldiers led them through the Old City to the Lion's Gate and from there by foot to Jericho. It was an agonizing journey, which ended in a Damascus jail. They were bound with a single rope. "I was tied by both hands to my fellow sufferer Alter Levine," Sakakini later wrote, "and the knots were so tight I was afraid the blood would burst out of my hands. When I asked them to loosen the knots a bit, they said: 'We don't care if you die.'" All around, masses of retreating soldiers were fleeing; a British airplane circled in the sky.[56]

Ballobar knew nothing of the two men's fate. After their wives left, a black servant from the Fast, a German luxury hotel, came to report that the mayor was on his way to the British. The consul set out for the hotel, where he found the residents of the German Colony, mostly members of the Templar sect. As enemy nationals, they were afraid of the British. From the hotel, Ballobar went out for a stroll through the city. He walked down Jaffa Street and witnessed the looting: everywhere people were taking whatever they could lay their hands on, from furniture to telegraph wires, from houseplants to the wheel hoops of broken wagons. Pediatrician Helena Kagan saw people robbing not only houses and offices and abandoned property but also the Italian hospital for contagious diseases, taking the blankets and sheets. At about a quarter to nine, the first of the British soldiers reached the Zion Gate, on the south side of the Old City.[57]

The news swept through Jerusalem. Attorney Gad Frumkin went anxiously into the street; an Arab neighbor, Mahmud al-Husseini, told him there was nothing to be afraid of—the English had arrived and his cousin, the mayor, was on his way to them.[58] Menashe Elyashar, from one of the most respected Jewish families in the city, set out to return home; the Turks had put a machine gun in his yard and the Elyashar family had moved in with relatives. Now he was going back to investigate the situation. On his way he ran into the mayor, a frequent guest in his house. Husseini invited Elyashar to join his entourage. "Witness a historical event you'll never forget," he said. They proceeded in the direction of Upper Lifta, where the Jerusalem neighborhood of Romema would later be built.

Suddenly they heard a cry. "Halt!" Two British sergeants leaped out from behind a half-ruined stone wall with their weapons at the ready. The mayor put up his hands, once again waving the white sheet. He turned to the two sergeants and notified them ceremoniously that the city of Jerusalem welcomed His Majesty's army and that he wished hereby to submit to them the Turkish governor's writ of surrender. Sergeants Sedgewick and Hurcombe, both in short pants, were scouts from a unit that had not yet entered the city. Neither agreed to accept the surrender, but they did consent to having their pictures taken with the mayor and his party and asked for cigarettes. They promised to report to their superiors. The mayor waited at Lifta.

The next Englishmen he saw were two artillery officers, Beck and Barry. The mayor tried to surrender for a third time, but the two officers also declined the historic role, promising to report back to their unit, and the mayor continued to wait. A while later Lieutenant Colonel Bailey appeared, and again the mayor announced that the city of Jerusalem welcomed His Majesty's army. The lieutenant colonel radioed to one Major General Shea; in the meantime, Brigadier C. F. Watson showed up. The mayor tried to surrender for the fifth time. Watson consented to accept the writ of surrender and asked where he could get a cup of tea. The entire company headed back to Jaffa Street, to Dr. Moshe Wallach's Sha'arei Zedek Hospital.

Wallach had emigrated from Germany. He was one of those people who did things in Palestine that no one else had done before. Together with *Schwester* Selma, chief nurse Selma Meir, he based his hospital practice on a unique blend of the latest medical innovations and Jewish religious law. At Sha'arei Zedek, Wallach received the mayor and the English general in keeping with Jewish tradition—he came out to greet them bearing bread and salt. Consul Ballobar dropped in soon thereafter. Everybody drank tea and ate biscuits while the British officers asked all about their enemies—when General von Falkenhayn had left the city, how many German soldiers were fighting with the Turks, what was the state of the Turkish army. Ballobar, eminently cautious in keeping with his neutral status, and a bit haughtily, as also befit him, said he had no military intelligence; his concern was entirely for Jerusalem's civilians. He emphasized to Watson the need to expedite provisions to the hungry population and asked that a police force be organized immediately. He also demanded that the residents of the German Colony be protected. Watson hurried on his way, and the consul continued his tour.

Crowds began to flood the streets. Ballobar had never in his life seen such spontaneous popular enthusiasm. Both Jews and Arabs joined in. Every British soldier who came down the street was greeted as a hero. Admiring civilians surrounded him, touched his uniform, patted him on the head, blessed him in every language of the Orient. The crowd's wonder knew no bounds, Ballobar wrote. After hiding for months out of fear of conscription or expulsion, people poured into the streets. They had long been waiting for this army of liberation. Ballobar identified with them but reminded himself not to show his feelings—he was supposed to be neutral. Even when summing up the day's events in his diary, he warned himself not to be foolish, but it was so hard to hold back: "Goodbye, hateful Turks!" he wrote.[59]

Mayor al-Husseini had still to surrender one more time that day. His sixth attempt, in the afternoon, was delivered to Major General Shea on the steps of David's Tower in the Old City. Shea appeared in the name of

General Allenby, who was sitting in his command tent near Jaffa. Allenby received the news of Jerusalem's conquest together with Major T. E. Lawrence of Arabia and invited him to join the official entry into the city, two days hence.

Allenby's entrance occasioned Mayor al-Husseini's seventh and final surrender. This one, a full ceremony, was planned out in careful detail. Allenby reined in his horse at the Jaffa Gate and entered the Holy City on foot. The elders of all the city's communities and faiths awaited him, dressed in picturesque robes and intricately decorated hats. Allenby brought with him representatives of France, Italy, and the United States. He read a declaration drafted with great care in London; it was then translated into Arabic, Hebrew, French, Italian, Greek, and Russian. Its central point was a promise to preserve the city's holy sites. Among the guests presented to him was Consul Ballobar, who was thanked for his efforts during the war. "Allenby was extremely gracious," the consul observed, noticing also that there was a moving-picture camera. If only Jamal Pasha could see it, he thought to himself.[60]

Shooting was still going on here and there in the city. A few Turkish soldiers had holed up on the Mount of Olives; hand-to-hand, bayonet-to-bayonet combat was necessary to defeat them. The British later established a military cemetery on the mountain's slopes. In the battle for Jerusalem, the British had deployed 26,000 troops, including 8,000 cavalry. Of these, 1,667 men were killed; 5,000 horses also died. Since setting out from Be'ersheba, the British had suffered about 18,000 casualties, the Turks 25,000. Many thousands of Turkish soldiers had been taken prisoner.[61]

A day or two later another little war took place in Jerusalem, this time between Major General Shea and Brigadier Watson. When Shea learned of Hol Larsson's photographs memorializing al-Husseini's surrender to Watson, he immediately ordered that the negatives be destroyed. The surrender of Jerusalem was to be remembered as his story. Larsson tried to get around the order; Shea made threats, and the photographer was forced to obey, saving only the pictures of the two sergeants. The British also took care to preserve the surrender flag—the historic sheet was sent to the Imperial War Museum in London.[62]

Jerusalem being Jerusalem, the conquest was decked in the trappings of myth. The Jews saw it as a Hanukkah miracle; on the evening of the conquest they lit the holiday's first candle. Avraham Yitzhak Hacohen Kook, the Yishuv's leading rabbi, who was then in London, later composed a special prayer of thanks. Across the city people quoted a prophecy the Arabs used to tell to glorify the Ottoman Empire: the Turks would leave Palestine only when a prophet of God brought the water of the Nile to Palestine. The British had laid pipes that supplied their army with water in the desert, and so Allenby was called *Allah an-nabi,* a prophet of God.

The British army newspaper published the following tale in its Hebrew edition: an old man, Rabbi Shmuel Schmilkis, had left his house every Sabbath eve waving a red handkerchief to greet the Messiah. As the years went by it became harder for him to walk, but he performed the task week after week. Three days before Allenby arrived, Rabbi Schmilkis returned to his maker. "He lived in his faith in the coming of the Messiah," the newspaper wrote, "and he died in his faith in the coming of the Messiah, and who knows . . . perhaps in his last moments, he was privileged to hear the sounds of the redeemer. . . . [W]ho knows?"[63] Only two bearers of the cross had succeeded in liberating the Holy City, Major Vivian Gilbert wrote: the crusader Godfrey of Bouillon and Edmund Allenby.[64]

James Pollock, a British soldier, would have given anything to take part in the battle for Jerusalem. When he arrived in the city a few months later, he had a religious experience that changed his life. He sat alone on the Mount of Olives, gazing on the city before him, and his heart went out to Jesus of Nazareth, who had suffered so for him and for all mankind. He so much wanted to do something for him, Pollock wrote to his parents, and then it was as if a voice from heaven called out: the greatest and most difficult of wars still rages—go to battle. During the coming months the British army had still to complete the conquest of the northern part of the country. "I felt then that he really understood that the fighting we were going through was worthwhile. I almost felt him standing beside me and a great peace entered my soul and I thanked God," Pollock wrote. It was, he said, a widespread feeling—one minister had told him that the demand for copies of the New Testament among the soldiers was greater than the supply. "Jerusalem has made us all feel that Christ can be our Pal."[65]

In London, the bells of Westminster Cathedral pealed for the first time in three years. News of the conquest was delivered to Parliament, and King George V sent Allenby a personal telegraph of congratulations.

Allenby himself was not one to express his feelings; the letter he sent his wife after his arrival in Jerusalem was devoid of all emotion. Even when he and Lady Allenby had lost their beloved only son, Michael, who was killed on the French front six months previously, Allenby's response was remarkably restrained. Had he been doomed not to know Michael at all, his sorrow would have been deeper than the sorrow of mourning over the temporary separation that had been imposed upon them, Allenby wrote to his wife, thanking her for twenty-one years of perfect happiness. On Christmas, he placed in his letter a scarlet anemone.[66]

3

◦•◦

Self-Service

1.

A few days after the conquest of Jaffa, one of the city's wealthiest Jews reported to the British military governor. He was Yosef Eliahu Shlush, a contractor and dealer in building materials, a founder of Tel Aviv. During the Turkish expulsion from the city, the Shlush family had taken refuge in a small Arab village, Kafr Jamal, in Samaria, where they had been warmly received. At some point after their arrival, Shlush's mother died and he asked to purchase a burial plot for her. The village elders told him he was free to bury his mother there, but they would not sell him the plot. In his memoirs, Shlush recounted an exchange reminiscent of the bargaining between Abraham and Efron the Hittite over the purchase of the Cave of Makhpela, Abraham's burial site in Hebron. Abraham was able to persuade the Hittite to sell him the cave for four hundred shekels of silver; Shlush bought his mother's grave for forty Turkish mejidi.

Now Shlush wanted a permit to transfer his mother's body to the Jewish cemetery in Jaffa. The war was still in progress; Allenby and his soldiers were preparing to conquer the northern part of the country on their way to Damascus. Restoring normal civilian life was not easy, and Shlush's request came as a test of the military government's ability to keep municipal services operating.

The army passed with flying colors. Shlush was sent to the Ministry of

Health to receive instructions from the government doctor, and the next day he was permitted to travel to Kafr Jamal with two physicians, one civilian and one military. He took two caskets, one of wood and the other of zinc. Also accompanying the group were a metalworker and ten laborers. All of them lodged in the village. When they opened the grave, they found that the body was well preserved despite having been interred for ten months. The laborers transferred the body to the zinc casket, which was then placed in the wooden casket. The metalworker sealed the coffin, the doctors filled out the necessary forms, and the body was reburied in Jaffa, all in accordance with Ottoman law. The legal and administrative systems remained unchanged, as prescribed by the laws of war.[1]

Antonio de Ballobar's impression was that the British were ruling the entire country from a simple camp—all told, just a few big tents equipped with electricity and a telephone. Allenby invited him for lunch and explained the structure of his administration. It followed the well-established British colonial model: alongside the supreme commander, Allenby, there was a chief political officer and a financial adviser. Reporting to Allenby was also a chief of staff and under him a chief administrative officer. The latter ran the various departments: general administration, finance, trade, health, legal, police, and public works; the British also appointed district governors and assistant district governors. At first the army preserved the existing Ottoman district boundaries and also left the municipal governments in place. The central British administrative headquarters remained in Egypt; later, the first general headquarters in Palestine was set up in Bir Salim, near Ramle, southeast of Jaffa.[2] Allenby and two of his top officers rode around the country in Rolls-Royces; brigadiers had Vauxhalls, colonels Sunbeams, and the rest of the administration officers shared a fleet of fourteen Ford Boxcars.

Allenby offered his guest large quantities of sausages; for dessert there were various undefined puddings. There were no waiters—the men got up and took their food themselves from a large table at one end of the tent. Amazed, and with some disapproval, Count Ballobar noted that the British called this practice "self-service."[3]

In the meantime, the Zionist movement's men in London were spinning fantasies of a provisional administration headed by a Jewish president, whose authority would resemble that of a high commissioner in a British colony. They prepared a working paper on the proposal, and though the paper was written in English, its authors gave their Jewish president the title *nasi,* a Hebrew word with biblical and Talmudic resonance. They envisioned an executive council under the *nasi* to run the treasury; the departments of communications, public works, immigration and land settlement, trade and industry, and justice; and an office of home affairs, which would oversee the police force—a Jewish police force.

The paper went into a fair amount of detail, and it completely ignored the qualifications so carefully inserted into the Balfour Declaration with regard to Palestine's non-Jewish communities. The Jewish president would govern all of Palestine; the British army was expected to tell the local residents that the country would henceforth be the national home of the Jews. In order to implement the plan, the Zionists proposed that a special delegation, headed by Chaim Weizmann, set out for Palestine to work together with the army.[4]

2.

With Christmas approaching, Consul Ballobar briefed the new military governor, Ronald Storrs, on the situation in Jerusalem. On the eve of the war the city had had between 80,000 and 85,000 inhabitants; at the end of 1917, there were only 50,000 to 55,000. About 27,000 were Jews, half the prewar population. The looting had stopped, the bakeries had opened, but people were still dying of hunger. In the past, food had been brought in from the region east of the Jordan River, but the Turks were in control there and had cut off the supply route. Masses of refugees had begun flowing into the city, and this had made the situation worse. There were epidemics of malaria, trachoma, and other diseases; the hospitals were packed; there was a severe shortage of medicines and medical equipment. "Everywhere was more or less chaos," Edwin Samuel wrote to his father, "in the Pentateuchal sense of the word—the sea hadn't separated from the sky and the land was not."[5]

Three thousand homeless Jewish children roamed the streets; there were thousands of Arab orphans as well. Local boys sold British soldiers forbidden alcoholic drinks; local girls worked as prostitutes. Venereal disease soon spread through the city. "The heart aches when one looks at it all," Chaim Weizmann wrote to his wife. The winter was extremely cold, and everywhere there was a shortage of fuel and wood for heating. Only collectors showed any interest in Turkish paper money, and the Egyptian banknotes that the British had declared legal tender had not yet won the public's confidence.* Schools and banks were closed, and there was no mail. The British quickly declared a state of emergency.

Upon arriving in the city, Ronald Storrs ran into an acquaintance in the lobby of the Fast Hotel, from whom he heard that "the only tolerable places in Jerusalem were bath and bed." The truth was, of course, that across the entire breadth of the empire there was no more enticing position than governor of Jerusalem; Storrs had accepted the appointment with a "wild exhilaration" and brought to the city a "deep enthusiasm." Jerusalem is "a great adventure," he wrote to Herbert Samuel; he liked to pen letters in red or green.[7] Within a short time he managed to overcome some of the city's most immediate problems.[8]

Consul Ballobar made Storrs party to titillating scraps of gossip on the top men in the old Turkish administration and allowed Storrs to read his diary. The two discovered a common nostalgia for the oysters at Shepheard's Hotel in Cairo. Both were by nature susceptible to the charms of Jerusalem politics, so small and petty, contained within two or three city streets, yet so international, lusty, unbridled, and stimulating. Storrs was a very political man, keenly interested in the city's people, their beliefs, their mores. He discovered dozens of sects in Jerusalem—Jewish, Muslim, and Christian—all attired in elaborate robes and ornate miters, all chanting an endless, mysterious litany of covenants and betrayals, piety and corruption. Insatiably curious and sociable, Storrs lived and breathed local politics and played it as if it were a private game of chess. Indeed, he founded a Jerusalem chess club; he was wise enough to allow Mordechai Ben-Hillel Hacohen to beat him in their first game.[9]

A graduate of Pembroke College, Cambridge, Storrs was a bright and witty man, haughty, crafty, and cynical, and a snob. He was a master of flattery and intrigue, with an eye for the ironic and the grotesque. He was an avid reader, always ready with an apt reference from classical literature, and fluent in several languages, including Arabic. He knew some Hebrew, too. He listened to classical music and was interested in architecture. Distant, even patronizing, Storrs tended to examine people as if they were rare insects, all the while considering whether they warranted the attention of being speared with a pin and added to his collection. Egocentric to the point of absurdity, he identified himself with Jerusalem as if he were

*The Egyptian lira, or pound, containing 100 piastres, or *grush*, was close in value to the British pound sterling. In 1921 the British pound became legal tender in Palestine as well. The local pound was instituted only in 1927, and it too was close in value to the British pound.[6]

the city's emperor and it was the center of the world. As governor he arranged an interview with the American president Warren Harding, visited the king of Italy, and was received twice by the pope. In one story, the holy father, wearing golden shoes that immediately caught Storrs's scornful eye, asked with concern about the prostitutes in Jerusalem. Storrs explained the problem at length and probably with considerable relish. His Majesty's Government was doing its best to purify the Holy City, he said.* But what was to be done? he asked the pontiff. Even a holy city had its needs and couldn't be cleaned up entirely.

At the beginning of his tenure, Storrs had almost unlimited authority and ruled as an enlightened despot without any public scrutiny—there were no courts and no newspapers. He would later describe his first months as "a state of innocence."[11] Like Herod, who had ruled nineteen hundred years before him, Storrs imposed his aesthetic tastes on Jerusalem. He tended to think of the city in spiritual, romantic, and extremely conservative terms; the Old City was to be protected, surrounded by a belt of green, as if it were a rare museum piece.[12] To preserve the look of the city, he forbade the use of a whole range of construction materials, limiting people to building with local limestone.

Storrs never forgave the Turks for allowing Jerusalem's merchants to set up stalls along the Old City wall. It was hard getting rid of these, but he made sure to demolish the fancy Ottoman clock tower built on the wall. The Pro-Jerusalem Society, which he founded, funded the renovation of the walls and of the Dome of the Rock and installed street lighting. The society was his pride and joy; from time to time Storrs would travel overseas to raise money for it. Among other things, the society brought in and trained craftsmen—rug weavers, glassblowers, ceramicists—to give the Old City a kind of colorful folkloristic charm. The society further ordered street signs from Armenian ceramicists.[13]

Storrs took an active role in naming the streets, using his imagination and great historical presumption. There was Salah A-Din Street and Tancred Way, Suleiman the Great Street, St. Francis Street, and Allenby Square. Street

---

*In a memorandum composed after this conversation, Storrs wrote that the pope had agreed, "with something approaching a smile." Storrs omitted these words from the book he later wrote. At the end of the war, there were by one estimate five hundred prostitutes working in the city, many of them Jewish. Storrs restricted prostitution to specific areas, such as the Nahalat Shiva and Mea She'arim neighborhoods, as was done in other cities. Outside those areas where prostitution was explicitly permitted, Ottoman law, still in force, forbade women even to wink at a strange man in public. Some time later prostitution was prohibited entirely, throughout the country.[10]

naming was a sensitive subject, with international implications, and Storrs felt that the world was watching him. When the time came to name the music school Storrs established, the political ramifications were apparent. The honorary treasurer was Consul Ballobar, and Storrs himself was president. He kept careful records of the diplomatic aspects of the project. The Jews, it seems, wanted to call it the Anglo-Jewish School and objected to Storrs's proposal that a Muslim representative sit on the board. President Storrs decreed that the school would simply be called the Jerusalem School and that there would indeed be a Muslim on the board. Similarly, he took a close interest in other cultural developments, establishing a Russian nuns' choir, which he conducted himself, performing selections from Wagner's *Die Meistersinger.* He also organized a local boys' soccer team. Harry Luke, deputy governor, described him as a "cultural Robin Hood."[14]

Most of the officials in the military administration serving with Storrs had fought in the war and either did not want to return home or had nothing to go back to. The war had molded them and become their home; they had no other. The routine of ordinary civilian life repelled them. Douglas Duff, a member of the military police and afterward chief of the Jerusalem police force, wrote that many were simply unable to sit on their hands after their experiences on the front. He described these soldiers as a "Legion of the Lost," and he was one of them. During the war he had served as a sailor, after which he had considered joining a monastery, but he could not handle monastic life and instead enlisted in the Royal Irish Constabulary. In Ireland he had learned about civil war: "There is nothing more beastly," he wrote.[15] But this was the only professional experience he had, and he did not intend to waste it. "Generations of Duffs have served in practically every army and navy around the world," he noted. His father, an admiral, had encouraged him to follow in their footsteps, so he came to Palestine.

When Ronald Storrs surveyed the backgrounds of the members of his staff, he found a wealth of military experience, but a strange assortment of administrative knowledge. There was "a cashier from a bank in Rangoon, an actor-manager, two assistants from Thos. Cook, a picture-dealer, an army coach, a clown, a land valuer, a bo'sun from the Niger, a Glasgow distiller, an organist, an Alexandria cotton-broker, an architect, a junior service London postal official, a taxi driver from Egypt, two schoolmasters, and a missionary."* None of them had been trained to run a country.

---

*This is a much-quoted passage. Storrs was certainly the type who could have made the whole thing up, but a document preserved among his papers shows that he actually took some pains to ascertain the professions of the men who worked with him.[16]

The commanders of the military government in Palestine, however, included several men who had years of experience gained in the colonial service, mostly in Egypt. The chief administrative officer, Arthur Wigram Money, came to Palestine after having served in the empire's colonies for thirty years, more than twenty of them in the Middle East. Storrs himself, thirty-nine years old, had worked in Cairo; his deputy, Harry Luke, thirty-six, had served in Sierra Leone, Barbados, and Cyprus.

Edward Keith-Roach, who would eventually succeed Storrs, also brought colonial experience with him. At seventeen he had begun working as a bank clerk in London. The bank posted him to one of its branches in Bombay. Three years later he returned to England, married, had a son, and worked as an accountant in Manchester. When the war broke out, he volunteered for the army, participated in its aborted attack at Gallipoli, and was afterward made governor of a remote area of the Sudan, where nothing much happened and Keith-Roach got bored. Once, he sentenced a murderer to death but had to wait for several months for permission to carry out the sentence. In the meantime he became friendly with the prisoner; nevertheless, when the necessary permission arrived, Keith-Roach personally hanged him. He read the Bible, felt lonely, and missed his wife and children, whom he did not see for four years. When he heard that Palestine had been conquered, he asked for a transfer. He was thirty-five years old at the time, looking for a career and advancement.[17]

At the start of World War I, twenty-one-year-old James (Shamus) H. H. Pollock was a student at the University of Leeds. He enlisted in the London regiment of the Royal Irish Rifles, was wounded, and was transferred to Egypt; at the time he had the rank of captain. His first job in Palestine was a temporary stint with the military administration, issuing exit visas. Pollock hadn't decided whether to remain in Palestine or to return to the family business in Ireland. In the end, he "received a district" and chose to stay: he foresaw a good career in the colonial service, rapid promotion, and a fine salary. In letters to his father Pollock wrote about a soldier's difficulty adjusting to a world at peace. He wondered what the politicians at home had in store for Palestine. He found their policies "absolutely incomprehensible" and could not figure out where they were leading the world.[18]

The men of the military government were at times torn between conflicting interests and contradictory orders, including sudden instructions from the people in London—civilians—who did not understand conditions in the field. The army detested civilians: "The soldier makes a country in six months, the civilian ruins it in two years," they would say, quoting one of their generals.[19] Most stayed in their jobs for only a short time, and the large turnover made it difficult to set up a well-run, efficient administration. The soldiers frequently found it hard to get along with one another and never managed to agree on a clear division of authority.

3.

The Zionists' proposal to send a Jewish delegation to Palestine was accepted by the British government; the appointment of a Jewish *nasi* was not. The British agreed to the delegation only as an advisory body to liaise between the Jewish community and British representatives. The Zionists were disappointed. This dynamic characterized Zionist-British relations—the Zionists never got all they wanted and always felt they weren't getting what they'd been promised. At times the Zionists only made a show of feeling this way, since in general they received a great many of their demands: army units, support for a national homeland, and now this delegation. The Zionist Commission, as it was called, was headed by Chaim Weizmann and remained in Palestine for three and a half years. It was supposed to be a kind of embassy, Weizmann said, but it soon began functioning essentially as the first Zionist government. The commission often worked in cooperation with the British military administration, but by the nature of things the two bodies were frequently locked in a power struggle.

The establishment of the Zionist Commission came in stages similar to the formation of the Jewish Legion and the drafting of the Balfour Declaration. Once again, the willingness of the government in London to work with the Zionists ran into opposition from the army and from those who warned that the commission was liable to foment unrest among the Arabs. The government's vacillation almost left Chaim Weizmann with a new top hat and nowhere to wear it.

He related the story with some charm. In anticipation of the commission's journey, Weizmann had been granted an audience with King George V—another gesture of British commitment, goodwill, and respect for the Zionist leader. Weizmann purchased a top hat specially for the interview. By previous arrangement, he reported first to the Foreign Office, where he found a flustered Sir Mark Sykes replete with apologies. Sykes had just received cables from Cairo, in which British officials reported that the Arabs were beginning to ask unpleasant questions. Sykes thought it best to cancel the audience.

Weizmann insisted on seeing the king, as promised. He later described the argument as "heated and sometimes painful," but he considered sticking to the meeting a matter of principle and protocol. As on so many occasions, Weizmann threatened scandal—the only weapon in his arsenal. Without an interview, the commission would not depart for Palestine. Sir Mark did his best. The argument went on for a long time, the two men standing in a corridor at the Foreign Office. At some point they noticed Lord Balfour on the stairs and agreed to refer the matter to him. Sykes suggested that Weizmann present the dispute to the foreign secretary; Weizmann, shrewd as ever, suggested that Sykes present the argument, and so he did. Half an hour went by. Weizmann waited for the verdict, top hat in his hand, in the company of Major William Ormsby-Gore. A Conservative member of Parliament and later colonial secretary, Ormsby-Gore had helped draft the Balfour Declaration and was now assigned to accompany the commission and serve as liaison officer to the military authorities in Palestine.

Balfour decided that the interview should take place, but in the meantime the appointed hour had passed. Balfour called Buckingham Palace and apologized for having made His Majesty wait. The tardiness, he said, was his fault for having gotten to the office late. The king was not angry; another audience was granted. Balfour was always late, he told Weizmann.

The establishment of the commission, long before the British government had decided to remain in Palestine, long before it received the League of Nations' Mandate to rule the country, and despite the objections of army men in the field, was once again a reflection of the presumed power of Zionism and Chaim Weizmann's influence in London.

Weizmann took a pretty odd crew with him. The commission's initial six members represented British Jewry, Zionists and non-Zionists, as well as the Jews of France and Italy. In time, representatives from the United States, Russia, and Holland were added. In Palestine they were joined by Ze'ev Jabotinsky, who served as something vaguely between official spokesman and liaison officer.[20] Jabotinsky, one of the men behind the establishment of the Jewish Legion, was a well-known Zionist journalist from Russia, a writer, translator, and orator. While still in Russia he had organized a kind of militia to defend the Jews of Odessa. In 1903 Jabotinsky went to Kishinev to cover the aftermath of the infamous pogrom, and among the people he met there was the Hebrew poet Chaim Nachman

Bialik. He would later translate into Russian Bialik's great Hebrew poem on the pogrom, "City of Slaughter."*

As head of the commission Weizmann ensured that his men, the British Zionists, would maintain control. One of these, Montague David Eder, would eventually run the delegation single-handedly. Eder, a boyish adventurer, had successively fallen under the spell of three of the twentieth century's most prominent ideological movements: socialism, psychoanalysis, and Zionism. In his colorful history, he had once been captured by a tribe of cannibals; Sigmund Freud referred to him as a man who had "a great capacity for love." Not many remember his name, but he ought to go down in history as the Zionists' first prime minister.

4.

David Eder had a scar on his forehead. He had acquired it during the famous Trafalgar Square riots of November 1887—popularly known as Bloody Sunday—in which unemployed laborers clashed with the Metropolitan police. Eder was then a medical student at the University of London. The son of a successful Jewish diamond merchant, he belonged to several of the first socialist organizations founded in England, including the Fabian Society. Eder, a rather opinionated man, once received an angry letter from prominent Fabian George Bernard Shaw: "I cannot explain my political position to you," Shaw wrote. "There is something inherent in your germ-plasm which makes you congenitally incapable of understanding anything that I say. I have explained in writing over and over and over and over and over and over and over and over and over and over and over and over and over and over and over and over and over and over and over with the most laborious lucidity."

While at the university, Eder lived in bachelor's quarters together with his cousin, the well-known writer Israel Zangwill. A Zionist, Zangwill had hosted Theodor Herzl in London; like Herzl, he too assigned little exclusive importance to Palestine—any available, secure, and fertile territory would serve for the settlement of the Jews, he believed. To that end, he founded the Jewish Territorial Organization, or JTO. Sometime later, his

---

*Jabotinsky did not meet Chaim Weizmann in Kishinev. This is worthy of note because Weizmann liked to claim that when he heard of the pogrom he rushed to Kishinev and organized a group of Jews, armed with pistols, "to defend the women and girls." Jehuda Reinharz, his biographer, discovered that the story was baseless. Weizmann lied to history, or perhaps fantasized this act of heroism.[21]

cousin Montague completed his studies. Zangwill sent him to Brazil to assess the potential for Jewish settlement.

Eder was no stranger to South America. He had already been to Colombia to visit an uncle who owned rubber and coffee plantations, and to Bolivia, as the head of a medical delegation. His travels took him to remote parts of the Andes, where he found himself in the midst of a civil war and was accused of espionage; at one point he fell ill and could not travel farther and almost died. The natives took good care of him, nourishing him with what they said was a baby's head but which turned out to be the head of a young monkey. Eder discovered that his hosts really did eat human flesh, although they did not kill people for this purpose. During his illness Eder fantasized about what a good meal he would make if he died.

A passion for psychoanalysis took Eder to Vienna and Sigmund Freud. After their meeting Freud wrote that he identified in Eder something he could see in himself. "We were both Jews and knew of each other that we carried in us that miraculous thing in common which—inaccessible to any analysis so far—makes the Jew." When Eder tried to disseminate psychoanalysis in Britain, he ran into great hostility, but he managed to practice the discipline through working with children in poor London neighborhoods and setting up the first clinic to treat battle fatigue. Most of his patients came from the Dardanelles front, the site of great defeats, where the members of the Jewish Legion also fought.

Eder supported the legion, along with his boyhood friend and brother-in-law, Joseph Cowen. It was Cowen, a Zionist, who brought Eder and Chaim Weizmann together, although Eder did not yet subscribe to Zionism; he defined himself as a Jew and atheist and instructed that his body be burned when he died, something forbidden in religious law. Moreover, Zionism clashed with his socialist ideals of a world in which people would overcome differences of religion, nationality, and race. As a cynic and humanist, he summed up his life experience as follows: "We are born mad, acquire morality, and become stupid and unhappy." Weizmann would eventually win him over to Zionism and describe him as his best friend.

Eder joined the Zionist Commission as a medical officer and representative of the JTO, but it was another friend, D. H. Lawrence, who identified the adventuristic element in his personality that drew him to Palestine: "One must go somewhere, I suppose, it is abominable to keep still in nothingness," Lawrence wrote. But he refused to understand Zionism: "Why do you go with the Jews? They will only be a mill-stone round your neck. Best cease to be a Jew and let Jewry disappear—much best."

Still, to be with Eder, Lawrence later wrote, he was prepared to follow him even to Palestine.[22]

5.

Twenty minutes after the Zionist Commission left the train station in Paris on their way from London to Rome, the Germans bombed Paris from the air. "This is my military service," Weizmann wrote to his wife, Vera, who was staying with her sister in France, "service for the good of [our] native land." Invoking Joshua's words to the children of Israel as they entered Canaan, he urged her, "Be strong and of good courage."[23]

Weizmann convened the commission's first meetings while its members were still in transit, at the Excelsior Hotel in Rome and on the deck of the SS *Canberra*, which was taking them to Egypt.[24] Official minutes were recorded from the beginning: indeed, during the course of its work, the commission produced an enormous quantity of paper, including tens of thousands of letters received and sent, each one numbered and filed, as if its members had been born administrators. In fact, they were groping in the dark at first: none of them had been trained for the challenges before them. The abundance of documents left behind reflects the wide variety of concerns the commission dealt with, a unique blend of charity, welfare, personal problems, and statesmanship.

As soon as the commission opened its office on Jerusalem's Jaffa Street, a great deal of the members' initial energies went into handling the countless requests with which the Jews, especially those in the city, deluged them. Many of these were submitted in writing—thousands of little notes, in many languages, some in high literary, quasi-biblical style and ancient Hebrew calligraphy. The supplicants asked for money to buy bread, medicine, and clothes for the winter, to pay rent and finance lessons for their children. "A woman in desperate straits am I, a widow, and my son is still dependent on his mother," Rachel Bitshekov wrote. "I apply to you in the name of all that is merciful and compassionate . . . for I have nowhere to turn in my troubles . . . and if God forbid you turn away from me I and my orphan son will face starvation."

A penniless woman named Kimche managed to persuade Consul Ballobar to intervene on her behalf—her husband had abandoned her. The commission was swamped with requests to locate relatives who had left the city during the war; it searched for them everywhere between Sydney and Mexico City. "If you could see the kind of petitions and requests that are coming to us, you would be amazed," Chaim Weizmann wrote to his wife. "From long-term loans to granting a divorce, and from building a synagogue to getting a thief released from prison." He was impatient. "Tiresome people!" he concluded. Palestine was a community with a thousand tragedies, and its only hope was organized begging. "There is no other city in the world, where almost eighty percent of the inhabitants receive support of various kinds and in this support they see no dishonor, baseness and diminishment of the soul," wrote Mordechai Ben-Hillel Hacohen.[25]

Most of the Jews in Jerusalem had always lived off the donations they received from Jewish communities in Europe; this was the *chalukkah* (distribution) system. The Jews were meant to represent their European communities in Jerusalem and engage in Torah study and prayer in their names. Most of them had no independent income and since the war had lived without any income at all. The Zionist Commission functioned as a direct successor of the *chalukkah* system, providing a daily bread ration to more than 1,000 elderly Jews, 7,000 students, 800 invalids, and 1,500 orphans. It granted a monthly stipend to 448 families and 1,684 widows, and supported religious elementary schools and yeshivas. About 65 percent of the commission's funds, approximately 10,000 Egyptian pounds, or $40,000 a month, was expended in Jerusalem; most of this money was given in direct support to the needy.[26]

Before the commission had set out, Chaim Weizmann had asked the Zionist movement's representatives in the United States to raise a million dollars for its activities. During the three and a half years in which it functioned, the commission had at its disposal more than a million pounds sterling, equivalent at that time to roughly $4 million, a little less than 40 percent of all the Jewish public funds that reached Palestine during that period.[27] Hadassah, the women's Zionist organization, helped by sending a medical delegation to Palestine; the Joint Distribution Committee opened soup kitchens and aided orphanages and old-age homes.

The commission quickly understood that the state of dependency of the Yishuv, the Jewish settlement in Palestine, was not healthy. Its members had not pictured their work as charity. They had known that dealing with the Jews who lived off *chalukkah* would not be easy, but they had expected that the major portion òf foreign support would help the indigent help themselves. Members of the Zionist movement living in Palestine submitted plans to create jobs in the cities and aid farmers,[28] and the commission initiated all sorts of quasi-productive projects: print shops, textile shops, vegetable gardens organized by Jerusalem's women. It tried to encourage industry and investment, gave credit to agricultural settlements, and funded the establishment of several kibbutzim. It also helped raise the salaries of teachers. The commission considered programs for populating the country, assisted the first Jews who began to arrive from overseas, and arranged for the purchase of land and the founding of settlements. The charitable institutions that received commission money were enjoined to make proper use of it and show evidence of efficiency. The commission also tried to define support to individuals as loans.

But despite all this the commission was largely considered a wasteful and debilitating philanthropic body. The daily newspaper *Ha'aretz* accused the commission of having "committed a grievous sin" by fostering humiliating listlessness and rot and encouraging people to beg instead of work. Edwin Samuel, who was attached to the commission as a liaison officer to the army, reported to his father in Parliament that the support system was having a bad influence in Jerusalem. Weizmann knew that the system was breeding "complete moral corruption" and that 90 percent of its recipients would remain idle. He was "ashamed and frightened," he wrote. Mordechai Ben-Hillel Hacohen thought the residents of Jerusalem were taking advantage of the commission's lack of experience.[29]

Before long a board of inquiry from the U.S. Zionists demanded that the commission be managed on a more rational and solid economic foundation. David Eder was hurt by the criticism; the situation was horrible and people needed help, he claimed. Weizmann tried to mollify him. "To bring order into that hell—it's a job that is going to take a long time and require the strength of a giant and the patience of an angel!" he wrote to his wife.

Weizmann, however, had political motives in continuing to foster Jerusalem's dependency. The willingness of its ultra-Orthodox residents to accept money from the Zionist Commission was tantamount to recognizing its authority. The ultra-Orthodox community had long scorned the Zionist movement; the personal dependency of many in the community worked to strengthen the Zionist position. Weizmann even tried to impose a condition on the ultra-Orthodox yeshivas—financial support in return for conducting studies in Hebrew rather than in Yiddish—though with little success. He also tried to intervene in local politics, but he failed in this effort—nothing had prepared him for that kind of tangle.[30]

Weizmann detested Jerusalem. For him the city symbolized the very opposite of the Zionist dream: the old Jew. "I have been here in Jerusalem nearly a week trying to make some order out of this mess," he wrote to his wife. "There's nothing more *humiliant* than 'our' Jerusalem. Anything that could be done to desecrate and defile the sacred has been done. It's impossible to imagine so much falsehood, blasphemy, greed, so many lies." He hated the city in a very concrete way, too: "It's such an accursed city, there's nothing there, no creature comforts," he wrote. He complained that Jerusalem had all the disadvantages of a big city without any of the advantages. It "hasn't a single clean and comfortable apartment," only filth, ugliness, and beggars. When Weizmann tried to convince a top official in the military administration that the "quality" of the Jews in the country was higher than the "quality of the natives," he was hard put to argue that this included the ultra-Orthodox Jews in Jerusalem.[31]

The conflict between the ultra-Orthodox and the Zionists had already emerged as a central political issue. According to rabbinic stricture, God had enjoined the Jews not to "break the wall," meaning not to take the land of Israel by force of arms, and not to "rebel against the nations" who ruled over the Jews. The Jews were to wait for rather than "push toward the end"—the messianic age in which the land would be restored to the Jews. Mordechai Ben-Hillel Hacohen believed that the ultra-Orthodox needed "reeducation" that would take many years.[32]*

To strengthen Zionism's position with the ultra-Orthodox, Weizmann determined to purchase the Western Wall from the Waqf, the Muslim religious trust. "The minarets and the bell-towers and domes rising to the sky are crying out that Jerusalem is not a Jewish city," Weizmann wrote to his wife. He found them "oppressive, threatening!"[34] Ownership of this most holy Jewish site would also improve the Zionists' standing vis-à-vis the Moslems and Christians in Jerusalem, Weizmann believed. Thus the Western Wall was transmuted from a place of prayer into a national symbol.

Several attempts had been made to purchase the wall and the houses facing it in the previous century. Mordechai Ben-Hillel Hacohen had kept track of these efforts and felt that the Jews had missed their chance because they had not handled the negotiations wisely. Instead of settling the transaction with the Ottoman government, they had let too many

*Some members of the ultra-Orthodox community complained to the British authorities that the Zionists were discriminating against them. "Just imagine," Weizmann told his wife, "some of the representatives of Orthodoxy denounced us to the government as a dangerous lot, we intended to overthrow the King, etc. The informants were pronounced to be crazy, but even so this is characteristic of the Jerusalem bunch." David Eder did inform on the ultra-Orthodox. They could not be trusted to be loyal, he told the military governor of Jaffa: "Yiddish means the tendency of those who speak it to draw their cultural inspiration from Germany."[33]

middlemen have a hand in the project, as if it were an ordinary real estate deal, until the opportunity slipped through their fingers. The commission had discussed the idea of purchasing the wall while still on the SS *Canberra,* and they continued to discuss it in Palestine. Money should be no object, they felt. Whatever sum was required had to be found.

Weizmann worked as he knew best, through lobbying and diplomacy. He spoke with Allenby; he wrote to his liaison officer, William Ormsby-Gore; he wrote to Balfour. Describing the Western Wall as "part of one of the original walls of the Temple," he claimed that the buildings around it were neglected and decrepit and that the entire place was "from the hygienic point of view a source of constant humiliation to the Jews of the world." The houses, he wrote, belong "to some doubtful . . . religious community," and the open space in front of the wall was "the haunt of Arab loafers and vagrants, whose presence and conduct do not tend to the peace of mind of the Jewish devotees." In fact, the impression that the Western Wall made on Jews from overseas "is painful beyond description." The place must be purified, he insisted.

The military authorities had agreed to the transfer of the wall to Jewish hands, Weizmann wrote, but were afraid of the Muslim reaction. Ronald Storrs confirmed this and even tried to help the Zionists. Weizmann linked the transfer of the wall to the Jews with the anticipated renewal of the national life of "Jewry." He promised to compensate the Muslims generously, and to Balfour he promised political benefit: "I only wish to state that the satisfactory settling of this point would mean an enormous access of prestige to us. It would make the Jewish World fully realise what the British regime in Palestine means; it would help to rally all the Jews, especially the great masses of orthodox Jewry in Russia, Galicia, and Romania as well as England, Germany, and America round the platform which we have created, namely a Jewish Palestine under British auspices." Balfour, infinitely cautious, responded that the matter should be approached "gradually" and that in any case it should be done through direct contact with the Muslim leadership. "Government intervention in the matter would tend to intensify rather than to diminish the difficulties in your way," he said.

The Western Wall remained under Muslim ownership; it is doubtful whether there was ever a real chance of it being sold to the Zionists. The episode followed the well-established dynamic between the Jews and Arabs: the Jews believed that they could buy the Arabs' consent to Zionist rule with money but managed to bribe only a few collaborators here and there.[35] To

Mordechai Ben-Hillel Hacohen, this most recent effort to buy the wall was simply one more missed opportunity. But he and Weizmann respected each other; on occasion the two would meet in Hacohen's home in Jaffa, Weizmann reclining on the couch, and talk in Yiddish about the Zionists' dreams and concerns and diplomatic contacts.[36] Hacohen threw himself into another passion of Weizmann's—building a Hebrew university.

According to Weizmann, a Jewish state without a university would be like Monaco without a casino. He also compared the university to the Third Temple, and the speakers at the cornerstone-laying ceremony used similar analogies. Like the Temple, the university was meant to be a spiritual-national center, but unlike the Temple, it was supposed to foster secular nationalism. For this reason, some rabbis threatened to boycott the ceremony.[37]

6.

At least three people, two of them rabbis from Jerusalem, had dreamed of establishing a university in Jerusalem even before the idea was proposed at the first Zionist Congress in 1897. After the congress, however, the idea became an inseparable part of the Zionist dream. The university's main role would be to promote Jewish nationalism in Palestine. Weizmann, being a practical man, knew that the university, like the state itself, would have to develop gradually. A plot had already been acquired on Mount Scopus. Weizmann intended to build the university institute by institute, as contributions came in. In the meantime, he concentrated on laying the cornerstones as a way of "raising the flag." The ceremony in which they were laid demonstrated what the Zionist movement was best at: public relations. Symbolically, the cornerstones of the Hebrew University stood for the cornerstones of the Jewish state.

The British army commanders in Palestine opposed the ceremony at first. Allenby claimed that Weizmann had chosen the worst possible moment, since the war was not yet over: the Turks were liable to renew their attack on Jerusalem at any moment, and parts of the country still remained under their control. In Europe, too, the war was far from decided: the Germans were close to the gates of Paris. Weizmann responded by reassuring Allenby that "we" would win the war. He overcame the army's objections in his usual way—by going over its head to Balfour.

Organizing the ceremony had not been easy. Ben-Hillel Hacohen, who had undertaken the project, thought of having twelve stones laid, representing the twelve tribes of Israel. He hoped that the number would be enough to fittingly honor all the organizations and professions and important people who had demanded the right to lay a stone of their own. But then Weizmann wanted to lay a stone "in the name of Zionism," and so a thirteenth was added to the original twelve. Hacohen also had to deal with the question of payment for the stones; naively, he had assumed the stonemasons would consider it a patriotic duty to donate their work and materials. Instead, they presented him with a bill that dumbfounded him. "When I told them what I thought of their attitude," he wrote in his diary, "they looked at me as if I were strange and were even insulted."

Close to six thousand guests gathered on Mount Scopus in the late afternoon of July 24, 1918. A large tent was erected and decked with flowers. General Allenby brought Weizmann in his Rolls-Royce, and Balfour cabled greetings. The mufti and the Anglican bishop, together with the city's rabbis, laid a foundation stone "in the name of Jerusalem." Consul Ballobar, who considered the bishop antisemitic, teased him for having attended and wrote in his diary that the mufti hadn't managed to hide his true feelings about the whole thing—his face was as yellow as a rotten melon. In Ballobar's opinion, the ceremony was an unnecessary and harmful political spectacle—he was not fond of Weizmann.

Allenby had refused to allow the soldiers of the Jewish Legion to participate, but Weizmann laid a stone "in the name of the Hebrew army." The rest of the stones represented Baron Rothschild, Y. L. Goldberg—a Jewish millionaire from Russia who had contributed money to buy the plot—the city of Jaffa, the agricultural settlements, the university's educational committee, future teachers, academics, writers, artists, workers, and the next generation. Several dozen children were roped into the ceremony. They were given candy and told that the university building was a "holy house."

Weizmann's evening was not yet over. He was very tired, but masses of people, many more than the number of invited guests, went from the ceremony to another celebration at the Amdursky Hotel to wait for him. Weizmann arrived only toward midnight—he had been having dinner with Mordechai Ben-Hillel Hacohen. By the time he reached the hotel, the people had lost their patience and some were drunk. The crush was intolerable, the crowd demanded a speech, and Weizmann got angry. Hacohen managed to appease him the next day by presenting him with the trowel that had been used to lay the cornerstones.

Weizmann would later describe the ceremony with poetic nostalgia: "The declining sun flooded the hills of Judea and Moab with golden light, and it seemed to me, too, that the transfigured heights were watching, wondering, dimly aware perhaps that this was the beginning of the return of their own people after many days. Below us lay Jerusalem, gleaming like a jewel." The assembly stood for a long moment around the stones, but even after "Hatikva" and "God Save the King" had been sung they still would not go. "We stood silent, with bowed heads, round the little row of stones, while the twilight deepened into night," Weizmann wrote. From far off there were explosions, echoes of the war for Palestine that was not yet over.[38]

7.

Allenby needed some time to redeploy for the continuation of his campaign; meanwhile, he had to transfer part of his forces to Europe. The Turks and Germans made one last effort to retake Jerusalem in early 1918 and were repelled. Allenby's soldiers crossed the Jordan but were pushed back from Amman. Several months went by before the British were able to launch their attack on the north; the major battle took place at Megiddo, the biblical Armageddon—Allenby would later add the name to his title. Megiddo was the last cavalry victory in history, and both native-born Jews and Arabs served in the campaign.

Leaders of the Jewish community were torn over whether to enlist in the British forces. Mordechai Ben-Hillel Hacohen and the Jews in Jaffa received an offer from the army proposing that enlisted men enter the Jewish Legion, whose members had come from Britain and the United States. The army also promised that when the conquest of Palestine was completed, the enlisted men could transfer into the police force, since the country was to be handed over to the Jews.

Hacohen and his colleagues were leery of the idea. The war itself scared them. They were anxious about the fate of Jewish residents in the north—the Galilee was still in Turkish hands. Hacohen was also worried about prisoners who had been taken to Damascus, among them Meir Dizengoff, the Tel Aviv council chairman. And who knew whether the soldiers would be allowed to remain in Palestine? If the war required it, they could be transferred to another front. "We should not spur our young men to enter any army and we must not have any force of ours go beyond the borders of Palestine," Hacohen wrote. Young people were urgently needed for the Zionist "rebirth." He was also afraid of conflict between the Jewish soldiers serving in the British and Turkish armies, which would mean a war of brother against brother. A few hundred weak, hungry, nervous young men had nothing to contribute to the British war effort, he felt, and he saw no national value in the service of a small number of Palestinian Jews in such a large army.

But soon the small community found itself caught up in a turbulent debate, one of those fundamental controversies that would ignite Hebrew public discourse many times in the future. Ze'ev Jabotinsky, who had helped found the Jewish Legion in England and was now in Palestine, began encouraging people to enlist in Allenby's army. Mordechai Ben-Hillel Haco-hen had him over to his house, where Jabotinsky demanded that he support enlistment. They had a cup of tea and a friendly conversation; Hacohen and his colleagues in the community did not want to make Jabotinsky angry.

At one point the conversation took a fairly abstract turn, touching on Judaism and militarism. Jabotinsky argued that all human beings are militarists; Hacohen said that Jabotinsky was asking young people to make an unjustified sacrifice, a concept foreign to the spirit of Judaism. In his diary, an astonished Hacohen wrote: "How much heart, how much energy and talent, has this alien militarism taken from Jabotinsky. How much courage and strength—what courage! what strength!—has he devoted to this strange cult."[39] Previously, Jabotinsky had told Hacohen he was close to despair and considering suicide. Hacohen was taken aback until Jabotinsky explained that he didn't really mean to kill himself; perhaps it would be best for him just to stop dealing with the Jewish Legion's affairs and devote himself to writing and making money. Hacohen didn't dare say so, but he thought that an excellent idea.[40]

Those community leaders who supported service in the legion believed it would bring young people together around the national idea and prepare them to become a nucleus of the future national army. "We want to spill our blood in this country," said writer Moshe Smilansky, "because without blood the stones of our future building may dissolve into sand." A report composed by the Zionist Commission stated, "Practically the whole of Jewish young manhood of military age came forward to join the Jewish Legion." This was not accurate: only a few hundred men enlisted, and they engaged in actual combat for two or three hours at most. Their enemies were mainly malaria and the Spanish flu, which was already raging in Europe. Hundreds fell ill, and dozens died.[41]*

---

*By the time he had completed his conquest of Palestine, Allenby had deployed more than 350,000 troops, among them more than 100,000 Egyptians and tens of thousands of Indians—one soldier for every two of the country's inhabitants. They took with them some 160,000 horses and camels and captured about 90,000 Turkish and German prisoners. They left more than 12,000 British graves behind them.[42]

A few days after Allenby's soldiers entered Nazareth, Antonio de Ballobar set out for a tour of the north. The land of Jesus of Nazareth has been
cleared of the heathen conquerors, the consul wrote in his diary. The
October skies were cloudless and Ballobar was in high spirits, but the trip
took him through a battered and troubled landscape and along the way
he encountered macabre sights that he would never forget. He described
rusting iron wrecks, tin cans, empty bottles, ammunition crates, pieces of
wagon, fragments of a plane, rifles that soldiers had thrown away mid-
flight, abandoned artillery, and the unbearable stink of dead horses and
camels. The consul and his companions stopped their car to collect war
souvenirs and photograph the sites. North of Nablus they saw a convoy of
burned automobiles; then suddenly they made out the remains of soldiers, in various stages of decomposition. They saw piles and piles of bodies, some charred and some skeletons—wild animals had fed on the meat.
Planes still circled in the air. It was like a film, Ballobar wrote.

He spent the night in liberated Haifa and fell in love with the view from
Mount Carmel and the pine trees. At the Carmel Hotel the consul ran
into Ronald Storrs and heard that the British had reached Damascus.[43]
Among the other guests at the hotel was Meir Dizengoff, who had just
been freed from prison. Ballobar began working to bring back the other
captives, most of them residents of Jerusalem, including Khalil al-
Sakakini and Alter Levine.

8.

Nine months had gone by since Sakakini's arrest on the last day of Turkish rule in Jerusalem, when he had been dragged out of the city bound to
Alter Levine with a single rope. At first they were led for four days on foot,
via Jericho to Amman. From there they were taken by train to the Damascus prison, where they slept on the same mattress. In their interrogation,
the two gave a coordinated story, according to which neither of them
knew the other and Levine had not been hiding in Sakakini's house—
only by coincidence were they arrested in the same place. They were not
brought to trial, although the Turkish authorities continued to detain
them.

Both men wrote diaries in jail; both were racked with longing for their
families. "Return my family to me and then sentence me to permanent
exile," Sakakini wrote.[44] "My heart resounds like the ocean on a stormy
night," wrote Levine, "like the beating of an eagle's wings I hear the echo

of the voice of my beloved daughters, dearer to me than life." They were very lonely together. Sakakini wrote on New Year's Eve: "I could not help it, I wept bitter tears . . . the last night of 1917 in Damascus prison, far from my loved ones . . . fate! Fate!" On the eve of Passover, Levine noted, "A holy night of the Seder, in impure imprisonment, like a juniper tree in the desert, among two hundred impure souls."

Levine described Sakakini as a friend, but Sakakini wrote, "I do not understand him and he does not understand me." He felt Levine believed that the Jews were a chosen people, better than all others, but wondered whether Levine didn't attribute a similar arrogance to him.[45] But in fact Levine was enamored of Sakakini's world: he identified a continuous thread from the biblical Hebrew past to the Arab culture of Palestine. He venerated the sun and the desert, adorning his poems with camels and crescent moons; he asked that a palm tree be planted on his grave. In many of his poems he fantasized about Arab love legends in terms that are sensual and violent. He also wove many Arabic terms into his writing, learned from his Arabic teacher, Khalil al-Sakakini. In one letter he wrote: "I am a foreigner in the world of Aryan culture; my place is in the East and my paths lead to the sun." He was attracted to a stereotype—the "Arab," in his imagination, was a noble savage, romantic, erotic, and cruel.*

Once Levine had himself photographed dressed as an Arab sheikh, in robe and headdress. The photograph is preserved among his papers, pasted next to another picture in which he is in the same pose but dressed in a tailored suit and expensive tie. One is labeled "East" and the other "West." His attempts to bridge the two cultures produced, among other things, a long ballad telling the story of Snow White as a desert legend: "In the name of Allah and Mohammed! / From the heavens is known to me Snow White, who is called Taljia," Levine wrote, his narrator being an Arab prince, a sheikh of the mountains.[46] Levine also marveled at the

---

*Levine's papers contain hundreds of unpublished poems. Many of them glorify the majesty of Jerusalem—the stones and the light, the charm and the Shekhina, God's divine presence. He developed an almost erotic love for the city, and his poems, following a medieval and even biblical tradition, read like poems of longing for a beloved woman: "You are all radiance softness and silk . . . a neck, a curl, the feet of a doe, your breast, your hand, all your body / your voice, your look they have banished and my passion they have vanquished." He assumed a pen name: Asaf Halevy the Jerusalemite. However, Levine is not considered a great poet. Critics who sought to praise him seem to have had trouble finding the right words. The poet Rachel wrote that the simplicity of Levine's juvenile expression touched the heart, but she seems to have felt more comfortable praising the design of his poetry collection, which, she noted, was printed on fine paper.

Arabs' religious piety. He described the devotions of the Muslim prisoners, the clanking of their leg irons blending with the ululation of their prayers: "Anyone who has not seen this drama has never seen anything reverent," he wrote in his diary. Sakakini, for his part, decided that all prisons should be abolished. Countries should deal with the sources of criminality rather than focusing on the criminals themselves.

Handwritten notations preserved among Levine's papers reflect a great admiration for American culture, something else he shared with Sakakini; both of them envisioned the United States as a symbol of national independence and personal freedom. Levine also identified the American dream with the Zionist vision. He wished to see the Jews of New York invest their capital and energies in Palestine so that the Jewish state would be born as part of a worldwide process of Americanization. New York was, in Levine's eyes, second only to Jerusalem. "It is an awesome and sublime sight," he wrote once of the Manhattan skyline, "the glorious endeavor of mortal man, the work of a human artist, perfection . . . exaltation, the eternal aspiration of man for the heavens, a song of ascent . . . freedom casting its glow on stranger and inhabitant and calling the peoples and races to be blessed in the new emerging nation, the American nation." Wall Street appears in his notes as "Western Wall Street."[47]

Like Levine, Sakakini had spent some time in the United States. While he had still been a young man, a few years before the war, Sakakini had gone there to seek his fortune, and he might well have stayed had things gone well. He meditated on this, writing, "Anywhere I am I will see myself as a patriot and will act to advance the society I live in, be it American or English society, Ottoman or African, Christian or Muslim or pagan; I will act only in the service of science, and science has no homeland. If patriotism means to be a man with a healthy body, strong, energetic, enlightened, of good character, gracious and well-mannered—I am a patriot. But if it means preferring one religion to another, or aggression by a man against his brother because he is not of his country or religion—I am not a patriot."

In the United States Sakakini attended lectures at Columbia and took part in editing an Arabic periodical. To make a living, he gave private lessons in Arabic, hawked goods in an open-air market, and worked in a factory. He found it hard to be away from Jerusalem. "I would like to fly to Jerusalem like a bird," he wrote then in his diary, "and to throw my worry and sorrow at the feet of Sultana. I wrote to her and said: 'Give me one more year, and if I do not succeed—judge me as you wish.' "[48] He did not manage to hold out; in less than a year he came home.

In prison, he returned to thoughts about America. "If I live," he wrote, "I will impose on myself exile from Jerusalem to America and there I will put my son into the best of its schools. There he will learn their mores and be educated in their culture. . . . Nothing could make me happier than to see my son in gym clothes, his arms and shins bare, his head uncovered, the wind ruffling the gold of his hair, skipping down the stairs of Columbia University in New York on his way to the athletic field, where he will be one of the participants in those games that train the body and which require quickness, elegance, energy, daring, discipline, and alertness."

The two men thought a great deal about their children. Sakakini wanted his Sari to be a teacher, and if not that, a doctor: "I don't want him to marry, but if he marries, let him marry someone who will elevate him and not humiliate him." Levine wanted his daughters, Rivka, Shlomit, and Rachel, to flower "modest and hidden from the eye of man." Both insisted that their children play the piano.

Sakakini tried to help Levine. "From the time we left Jerusalem I have not ceased to have compassion for him, as one brother has compassion for another, and I calm his spirits and attribute the misfortunes that have fallen on both of us to fate and bad luck."[49] But Levine blamed himself for Sakakini's situation. "He is the miserable victim of circumstances that I am guilty of creating," he wrote to his beloved wife, Gittel, and instructed her to maintain contact with Sultana al-Sakakini.

While Sakakini held on to what he described as his "philosophy of happiness"—"Laughter proves a generous soul, sorrow and pain are a grievous sin"—Levine had it out with his Maker: "My God, my God, is this how you mistreat the Hebrew sons of the land? Is this how you have thrown them into the abyss, into depths, without light and without liberty?" Levine admired Heine; Sakakini, Nietzsche for his "philosophy of power." They identified with Cervantes and with Oscar Wilde, writers who had spent time in jail.

Both men wanted to go home and used their connections to do so. Levine wrote to various leaders of the Zionist movement with whom he was acquainted. He sent letters to Istanbul and Basel, Amsterdam and Washington. A relative in New York, a journalist named Samuel Harkabi, published an emotional article, in Yiddish, in which he demanded that Levine be released; the Jewish Distribution Committee asked the new American consul in Jerusalem to intervene.[50] Somehow, Levine managed to obtain a bit of money.

Sakakini's connections were not the world-girdling ones of insurance agent Levine, but he found support among young intellectuals from Palestine and was in fact released before Levine, in January 1918. While he was waiting for a way to return to Jerusalem, he rented a room in Damascus and made a living teaching English. He gathered around him a small group of educators and journalists, who would sit at a café each morning and dream about the future of the Arab national movement. "I am not a politician," Sakakini now wrote, "but I am first of all an Arab." One day the group was joined by a young man from Jerusalem named Musa Alami, a former pupil of Sakakini's. The two lived together for a few months. Alami, who was then twenty-one, would later become a prominent leader of the Arab national movement in Palestine. Sakakini wrote an anthem for the movement, "Saving the Homeland," which was, he said, the Arab "Marseillaise."

Sakakini visited Alter Levine regularly in jail and from time to time borrowed money from him. Levine was finally released at the end of April 1918, largely, it seems, due to the efforts of Consul Ballobar.[51] He was allowed to remain in Syria and spent his initial weeks in Damascus in the company of Sakakini and his friends. Sakakini wondered why Levine continued to be friendly with him and found no answer; apparently the two found it difficult to part. In August, Sakakini left Damascus to join the forces of the Arab revolt, led by Prince Faisal. "We were some three hundred or more on camelback, and I was in the vanguard, riding a noble horse, like a celebrated commander," Sakakini wrote. The troops sang the anthem he wrote for his people and the desert echoed it back to them.[52] Within two or three months he was at home, in Jerusalem. Levine stayed a while longer in Syria, working for a German insurance company. In letters he managed to smuggle to Jerusalem in all sorts of indirect ways he wrote over and over again that he did not lack money. But he did not stay for long, either; within a few months the word was out in Jerusalem: the king of insurance was back.[53]

9.

Before taking up his new post as assistant district governor of Ramallah, Captain James (Shamus) Huey Hamill Pollock completed his temporary work at the offices of the military administration, where he issued exit permits. There was great demand for travel to Egypt for the purpose of importing food and other merchandise needed in Jerusalem, but the trains were always full of soldiers. Ramallah was not far from Jerusalem, so Pollock rented an enchanting stone house in the city, surrounded by pine trees and complete with towers and pediments and roofs with shingles laid at capricious angles. It stood next to Count Ballobar's house, on the street that had always been called Consuls' Street until it was renamed the Street of the Prophets by Ronald Storrs. Architect Conrad Schick had named the house Tabor, after the mountain in the Galilee. James Pollock and his wife, Margaret, had the name printed on their stationery, as if the house were their family estate. They described it frequently in their letters and furnished the rooms lovingly.

"Shamus gave me for my birthday a most wonderful hand worked curtain, a really marvelous piece of work," Margaret Pollock reported to her mother. "Our walls are white so it looks splendid on them. The colours in it are red black white green and blue, not over bright, just blended to a nicety. I have covered the sofa in a dull blue and made brilliant coloured silk cushions. This looks very well. The floor is black and white marble, the walls are white and wood work white, so the dull blue and the bright cushions give a beautiful tone to the room. Our rugs are really old ones and beautiful in color. Then we have lovely brass work and a splendid old brass candelabra." She sent her mother a drawing of the candelabra. That same evening she had her first dinner party, and recounted for her mother the entire seven-course menu.

The British officials loved to have each other for dinner parties. Often, they had invitations printed up for a "do," as they liked to call these events, and had them hand-delivered by servants. Preserved among James Pollock's papers is a stiff cardboard card announcing:

THE MILITARY GOVERNOR

AT HOME

MONDAY FEBRUARY 23

4–6.30

The British community was a small, tight group of strangers who fostered a strong social tradition. Everybody knew everybody else, and they all gossiped about one another; everybody suffered from mosquitoes and boredom. They liked to pretend they were scattered among distant estates separated by a ride of many hours or in an imaginary international metropolis, not stuck in a backward little city. The colonial service did well by them: they often lived far better in Jerusalem than they ever could have lived at home.

Helen Bentwich, the wife of a British official, recalled how they had "found" a nine-room house in the German Colony and had gone to the custodian of enemy property to choose some furniture, also left behind by the Germans.* The movers who brought the furniture to the Bentwich house were prisoners. Officers, she related, were permitted to put prisoners to work in their homes or gardens without pay. An Arab policeman would bring them from the jail; those sentenced to death came dressed in red. But then an order was issued requiring the prisoners to wear irons on their waists and legs. Bentwich could not endure the sight and stopped using prisoners.

One day the Bentwiches invited the chief administrator and his wife for a meal. Unfortunately, their cook had just been arrested. Bentwich was "panic-stricken," but the police generously released the prisoner, on condition that, after the meal, he be immediately brought back to the prison.[55]

Margaret Pollock also had a cook who was central to her life. "I feel lonely and quite unable to compete with the cook," she wrote. She wrote a great deal about the cook to her mother, much of it complaints. The cook did not know her work, but at one point she learned to make "nice griddle scones" like in England and was the only cook in Jerusalem who knew how. This brought Mrs. Pollock great success with the guests she invited for afternoon tea. Sometime later she boasted that her cook was considered the best in town.

But the servants continued to irk her. In addition to the cook there were a valet, a housemaid, and a nurse for the Pollocks' baby son, Patrick. They don't know how to work, she complained. They claim they work too hard. They are very expensive. Mrs. Pollock also fussed about rising prices. Living at home would not cost less, she moaned. A fundamental assumption of hers had been that life in a distant country would be not only more comfortable but also more economical. Her husband now needed a costly evening suit. "I don't know how the poor people live here," she remarked. She couldn't have known, for she had no contact with poor people.[56]

Once a week, Margaret Pollock went to visit the wife of Colonel E. L. Popham, the assistant administrator to the military governor; the two did

---

*The British deported most of the German residents—Ballobar accompanied them to the train station—and years passed before they were allowed to return. The first British officers and officials to arrive in Palestine expropriated German homes and property. Edward Keith-Roach, who was responsible for abandoned property, demanded detailed lists of what had been taken, but many of his countrymen were inclined to disregard his request.[54]

voice exercises together. Once Mrs. Popham invited her to pay a courtesy visit to a cardinal who had come to visit the city. Margaret Pollock set her eyes on his "lovely red silk cape." She asked to have it as an opera cloak, she wrote.[57]

When the Pollocks had settled into their new house, Captain James wrote with satisfaction to his mother that it was in truth "very similar to any English home." In the afternoons they would go out riding. From time to time they ran into a pleasant fellow, their neighbor the Spanish consul, and once James Pollock wrote to his father that he might soon meet the famous Lawrence of Arabia.[58]

Lawrence sometimes materialized in Jerusalem. The small community would sit up and take notice, and then he would disappear as suddenly as he had appeared. Storrs described the following scene: He was sitting in his house early in January 1919. A snowstorm was raging outside, and suddenly his butler entered and announced that a barefoot Bedouin was at the door and wanted to come in. It was Lawrence. He remained until evening, and when he left he took with him a volume of Virgil.[59]

Pollock began to study Arabic; he had his picture taken, like Lawrence, wearing an Arab headdress. James and Margaret Pollock now sent letters home almost every day. "Life is beginning to whirl," Margaret wrote to her mother.[60]

4

———•◦•———

Ego Versus Ego

1.

When Weizmann first arrived in Palestine as the head of the Zionist Commission, he lodged in Allenby's camp near Ramle. One morning, as Allenby was driving by, he saw Weizmann standing near his tent. He told his driver to stop and invited Weizmann to accompany him to Jerusalem. Weizmann badly wanted to accept, but "something within" deterred him. Perhaps, he suggested, Allenby would not feel right being seen with the Zionist leader as he entered Jerusalem. Allenby got out of his car, stood next to Weizmann, considered the matter for a moment, and then smiled. He held out his hand and said, "You are quite right—and I think we are going to be great friends."[1]

"I can't say that he has a deep appreciation or understanding of the moral and political significance of the movement," Weizmann wrote to his wife, Vera, "but he definitely showed a willingness to understand and help." In the weeks that followed the meeting near Allenby's camp, Weizmann wrote to his wife that Allenby expressed "warm sympathy and keen appreciation." Even if the general was dubious about the possibility of establishing a Zionist state in the country, Weizmann's assessment was that "Allenby is with us and for us." At nights, Allenby told Weizmann, he read the Bible.[2]*

---

*Allenby seems to have been taken by Weizmann's personal charm. Weizmann had earlier made a fine impression on Lady Allenby and believed that the general treated him well in part under the influence of a "very nice" letter he had received from Lady Allenby.[3]

Soon after his conquest, Allenby made official visits to Jerusalem and Tel Aviv, and everywhere was received with massive enthusiasm. The people of Tel Aviv named a street after him, a main thoroughfare leading from the Zionist Commission headquarters to the sea; it had previously been New Society Road.[4] The Zionist Commission viewed Allenby's visits as gestures of recognition of Zionism.

The general frequently stressed that his job was to hold Palestine temporarily until the establishment of a civilian administration; in the meantime he promised to govern with "benevolent neutrality." As a soldier, Allenby's inclination was to see Zionism principally as a nuisance, a common view in the military administration. A few of its officers had sympathy for Zionism; others supported the Arabs. Overall, the army did not reject Zionism as an idea, or on moral or political grounds, but felt that Britain's support for the movement was liable to complicate matters in Palestine, and warned the government in London.[5] As a rule, however, the army considered the government's policy on a Jewish national home an order to be carried out.

The military regime lasted for two and a half years, during which time the country came back to life. The health department successfully fought cholera and typhus epidemics; starvation ended as supply lines were reinstituted, with most of the food coming from Egypt. The administration provided seed, seedlings, and instruction for both Arab and Jewish farmers. The water supply, especially to Jerusalem, was significantly improved. The city, previously dependent on rainwater collected and stored in cisterns, was given running water, pumped from Solomon's Pools, south of Bethlehem. The Zionist Commission considered this the military administration's most important achievement. Cleanliness in the streets was also improved, and the city government was reorganized. Jerusalem's mayor, Feisal al-Husseini, died a few months after the British conquest; Ronald Storrs appointed the departed mayor's brother, Musa Kazim al-Husseini, as his successor.

Schools and banks were opened, and the court system was rehabilitated. The judges, both Arabs and Jews, received higher salaries, and this reduced corruption. Tax collection was refined. The Egyptian pound gained the population's confidence. Roads destroyed during the war were repaired, and new roads were paved, providing employment for thousands who had been out of work. Here and there private cars traveled the roads. New railway lines were laid, and soon passenger service began running between the country's cities. Consul Ballobar traveled from Lydda to

Kantara on the night train; his car contained a bed and a place to eat, and the consul was very impressed. New telegraph lines were erected, and a few private telephones were installed. The mail service was made more efficient; for the first time, one could send a letter and trust that it would reach its destination.[6]

All these changes were fairly straightforward, requiring nothing more than authority, organization, and money. But when Mordechai Ben-Hillel Hacohen went to W. F. Stirling, the governor of Jaffa, and demanded that all administration announcements be published in Hebrew as well as in English and in Arabic, the governor found himself in a difficult spot. He did not know Hebrew, but he knew this was a manifestly political demand.

From the start, the Zionists viewed the British administration's attitude toward the Hebrew language as indicative of its attitude toward Zionism; the resurrection of a national language was at the heart of the Zionist dream. Countless applications to the authorities on this matter tried to make the point that the national-home policy was meaningless if the Hebrew language was not given parity with Arabic. Stirling and Ronald Storrs found the request amusing. Most Jewish settlers did not know Hebrew, Stirling noted. "They had to sit down and learn their supposedly native tongue," he related. To Storrs, the Jews were fighting a pointless symbolic battle, characteristic of "samovar Zionism," as he called the ideology of Weizmann and others who came from Russia.[7]

Zionist leaders protested that Hebrew letters were not used on license plates. Stirling recalled that at one settlement the Jews removed the signs from the local post office because they had Arabic lettering in addition to English and Hebrew. He considered the act "foolish" and it angered him. "I gave [them] three days to replace the notices and told them that if they failed to put them back in that time they would have to go all the way to the head office in Jerusalem to collect their mail. The notices were put up at once." The episode contributed to his impression that individually Jews were intelligent and industrious, but collectively they were abysmally foolish.

There was probably nothing the military administration disliked more than local politics. Unlike Ronald Storrs, most of the British were not interested, did not understand, and did their best to avoid the whole tangle. They had come to fight, conquer, and rule, not to engage in politics, Stirling told a representative of the Zionist movement.[8] But the military administration quickly discovered that in Palestine politics were the main thing. The Zionist Commission turned almost every event and decision into a political issue. When the military authorities planned a new sewage system in several Jewish neighborhoods in Jerusalem, David Eder agreed to help fund it, but on one condition—that the work be given to a Jewish contractor. A member of the Zionist Commission asserted that the Jews should purchase Jerusalem's water sources, even at a loss.[9] The commission took a manifestly tribal attitude, in which the commercial interests of individual Jews were considered part of the national interest. So the Zionist Commission had no qualms about intervening in the future of Jerusalem's Fast Hotel, as if it were a project of national importance.

Two bulging files of documents tell the story. In 1918, some Jewish investors had expressed an interest in leasing the hotel building from its owners, the Armenian Patriarchate. The Zionist Commission tried to help; a luxury hotel would, they thought, bring prestige to the Zionist movement. The major investor, a Jewish businessman from Cairo named Barsky, demanded that the hotel be handed over with its furnishings and equipment, but these were under the control of the custodian of enemy properties, as the hotel proprietors, the Fast brothers, were German members of the Templar sect. In a deal negotiated through the good offices of Consul Ballobar, the brothers had already agreed to sell Barsky what he wanted, but the custodian held up the transaction. Without the furnishings and equipment, Barsky would not proceed with the deal.

The Zionist Commission devoted considerable energy to resolving the dispute. The documents speak of "victory" and "defeat." Then, when all obstacles had been overcome, Barsky added a new condition: he would complete the deal only if the commission arranged a loan on extremely good terms. The commission put pressure on the Anglo-Palestine Bank, a Zionist establishment, which suggested that the commission bear a part of the costs of the loan. Now the commission made its own conditions: first, the hotel's kitchen would have to be kosher. Barsky refused. The bank proposed a compromise: there would be two kitchens, kosher and nonkosher, and two dining rooms with equal levels of service and prices. Second, the commission demanded that the menu be printed in Hebrew; it finally agreed to Hebrew and English. The lengthy correspondence between the Zionist Commission and the bank continued, however, since Barsky insisted that the interest rate on his loan be no higher than 6 percent. Throughout all this, everybody agreed that a luxury hotel in Jerusalem was an extremely important political asset for the Jews.*

With equal nationalist fervor, the commission pursued a variety of projects, including the transfer of the Tiberias hot springs into Jewish hands, efforts to obtain a franchise to operate telephones and manufacture electricity, and a program to exploit the resources of the Dead Sea. In fact, the Zionist Commission functioned as a government in almost every respect, with a staff of one hundred employees. In keeping with the policy dictated by London, the army reluctantly recognized the commission as representative of the entire Jewish community, as if the Zionist movement were the exclusive agent of Jewish nationalism. Thus, the commission was empowered to collect taxes from the Jewish agricultural settlements—an important political achievement.[11]

The commission was also allowed to take control of the Jewish secular schools, which had until then used German as their language of instruction; now the students would be taught in Hebrew. When Jerusalem ophthalmologist Arieh Feigenbaum refused to pay his taxes because there was no Hebrew on the receipts, Ronald Storrs announced that this would be rectified. The train company eventually acceded to demands to print Hebrew on its tickets and schedules, and the military government finally agreed to add Hebrew to all its government proclamations; English would be printed in the center, Arabic on the right, and Hebrew on the left. Stirling, the governor of Jaffa, was willing to employ a Hebrew secretary sent to him by David Eder. This was Ehud Ben-Yehuda, son of the great lexicographer. He brought along a Hebrew typewriter.[12]

2.

Wyndham Deedes, Allenby's intelligence officer—who became the number-two man in the administration—was a devout Christian and Zionist. The more he could assist in the return of the Jews to the Holy Land, the quicker he would hasten the second coming of the Lord, he once said to one of his colleagues. He believed there was an unwritten compact between

*Storrs's contribution to the story was a proposal to change the hotel's name to The Allenby; he wrote to the general to ask his permission. Of course, he noted, the hotel could be called The Continental, or The Bristol, or The Savoy, but these names were "of unsavoury, unsuitable association." Unfortunately, the name "The Jerusalem Hotel" was already taken, by an "obscure inn" belonging to a Jew named Kaminetz. To call it the Zion Hotel would, of course, be to take sides politically. So Allenby agreed and the hotel earned his name. In the same letter, Storrs reported "a marked and pleasant improvement in our relations with the Zionists."[10]

the British Empire and world Jewry, and he saw the establishment of the national home as part of a common effort to bring about world peace. His colleague Norman Bentwich called him "a modern saint."[13] Bentwich himself was a British jurist, a Zionist and a Jew, who became attorney general, filling one of the most powerful posts in the administration.

The Zionists had another ally in Edwin Samuel, liaison officer to the Zionist Commission and also the Jewish affairs expert on Allenby's staff. He was particularly enthusiastic about serving in Jerusalem—even were he offered ten thousand pounds or more he would not agree to another posting, he wrote to his father.[14] The letters he sent home show that he in fact served as a kind of double agent. Alongside his work for Allenby he sent detailed reports to his father in London, which, in turn, affected policy. "I know you are very interested in the PI [Political Intelligence] side of here— that is why I came," he wrote. Herbert Samuel made good use of the information he received from his son; during that period he was of considerable assistance to Weizmann in planning the Zionist movement's tactics.

Allenby's chief political officer and chief administration officer, Brigadier General Sir Gilbert Falkingham Clayton, had opposed the Balfour Declaration and was against handing Palestine over to the Zionists immediately. That would be unjust, he argued: 90 percent of the country's inhabitants were not Jews, and the Zionists still had no administrative experience. Clayton did not, however, oppose the gradual installation of the Zionists as the country's rulers, and he did support giving Hebrew official status. Formal but not hostile, he once paid a visit to Tel Aviv. The gymnasts of the Maccabee sports organization put on a display, and the music school presented a short concert. He ate at Dizengoff's house. Mordechai Ben-Hillel Hacohen noted that the visit was quite obviously political—Clayton's department in the military administration would not have organized such a visit without a reason. Weizmann developed a correct working relationship with him, and others, among them Jabotinsky, also stated that Clayton took a sympathetic position. Ronald Storrs claimed that he and Clayton shared a common view; Storrs was a Zionist.[15]

Storrs himself was often at odds with the Zionist Commission, but he considered the return of the Jews to their land an act of salvation and historic justice. He even described Zionism as a divine enterprise; in his memoirs he used the Hebrew word *Shekhina*. For generations the Jews had contributed their genius to the world, and every country had done them immeasurable injustice, he believed. Now human civilization had recognized its moral and political debt to the Jews, and he, Storrs, had been chosen to discharge the debt. This version of events appealed to Storrs's megalomania.[16]

Storrs displayed a profound and sincere interest in Hebrew culture, conversing with Ahad Ha'am and Chaim Nachman Bialik, the leading Hebrew poet. At the same time, he saw Palestine as a kind of loyal Jewish Ulster, perhaps as part of a regional federation, and thus strove for cooperation between the Zionists and Arabs. The symbol of his Pro-Jerusalem Society, founded to spur building in the city, combined the Arab crescent and the Star of David with the Christian cross. His presumption that he could find common ground between Zionist and Arab demands reflected his tendency to see himself as having taken possession of a large stage whose actors he could direct as he saw fit.

Toward the first anniversary of the Balfour Declaration, the Zionist Commission organized a parade. Governor Storrs approved, on the condition that no flags be displayed and that the parade disperse some distance from the Old City's Jaffa Gate. He honored the parade with his presence and made a speech. But a group of high school students violated the governor's prohibition and marched toward Jaffa Gate carrying a banner. Two young vagrants dressed in rags, one Muslim and the other Christian, snatched the banner, broke the stick to which it was attached, and beat a teacher who was part of the group. The two were arrested on the spot and taken to the police station. Later in the day, David Eder lodged a complaint with the governor. Storrs called Major Bentwich at the court, and as a result the two "ragamuffins" were sentenced to four months in prison. The sentence was harsh, and they appealed.

In Storrs's evaluation the incident had not been premeditated, but it was undeniable that there was very strong anti-Zionist sentiment in the city. The next day the governor heard a fuss outside his office and found himself facing Mayor Musa Kazim al-Husseini at the head of a procession. The delegation had come to protest Britain's intention to give Palestine to the Jews. Storrs accepted their petition and then, in consultation with Bentwich, suggested to David Yellin, a Jewish community leader, that he arrange a reconciliation ceremony between Jews and Arabs. Yellin demanded that the head of the al-Husseini clan come to him, and Husseini refused. They compromised on meeting in Storrs's office, shook hands, and Yellin agreed to withdraw the Zionists' complaint against the two youths. The court then reduced their sentence to six days, the amount of time that had passed since their arrest, and the two were released.

In accordance with the arrangement reached by Storrs and Yellin, the two Arab youths apologized to the teacher and promised to pay for the broken stick. However, they had no money. "Both the boys being absolutely penniless there appears to be every chance of the bill for the banner having to be settled by myself," Storrs wrote. There was a mocking tone in his words, a haughtiness that would cost him in the future. But the historical significance of this minor incident was not lost on him. It contained many of the elements of Palestine's nascent conflict: the national, social, and symbolic tensions, the force of honor, the insignificance of the courts system, the illusion that the authoritative bearing of a British official was enough to reconcile the natives. Last but not least, it demonstrated that the British paid the bills.[17]

"I am not for either, but for both," Storrs wrote. "Two hours of Arab grievances drive me into the Synagogue, while after an intense course of Zionist propaganda I am prepared to embrace Islam."[18]*

Some British officers explicitly and adamantly opposed their government's Zionist policy. Lieutenant General Sir Walter Congreve, who commanded troops in Egypt and Palestine, believed in the idea of the Jewish national home, with all its limitations, and had even expressed "cordial sympathy" for Zionism.[20] Chaim Weizmann described him as a friendly gentleman who knew little about Zionism; he felt sure he could train the general. However, Congreve feared that support for Zionism would lead to a conflagration throughout the Arab world, and he tended to blame the Jews for this development. Had the Jews acted wisely, quietly, and slowly, he later wrote, everything might have worked out; but the Jew is "aggressive, contentious, and unbridled." He expressed the hope that the Balfour Declaration would be revoked. "We might as well declare that England belongs to Italy because it was once occupied by Romans," he wrote, claiming that many of the military administration's officers shared his opinion.[21] They were convinced that the Zionists wanted to flood the country with Jews, especially with lower-class Jews from Russia, Poland, and Romania, so as to create a Jewish majority in Palestine. When they got strong enough, Congreve argued, the Jews would crush the Arabs, expel them from their land, and get rid of the British as well.[22]

British officials frequently said "Jews" when they were in fact referring

---

*Weizmann once complained that Storrs was present at an occasion in which an anti-Zionist speech was made, and that he did not protest. The "speech" turned out to have been made in a school during a student production called *Sheikh Hamlik*. It was, Storrs said, an "infinitely tedious" version of *Hamlet*.[19]

to the Zionists, but some of the men in the military government were unequivocally antisemitic. Intelligence officer Wyndham Deedes showed Chaim Weizmann reading material he had found among army men in Egypt, *The Protocols of the Elders of Zion,* and faith in the world Jewish conspiracy permeated the evaluations the officers wrote.[23] According to Congreve, "Weizmann and the other Zionists accuse us all out here of being anti-Zionists, and I do not doubt that in our hearts we are." He explained that those who lived with the Jews in Palestine had a hard time distinguishing Zionist theory from the people who were putting it into practice, and that the people were not nice. One should keep in mind the link between the Jews and the Bolsheviks, he continued, and centuries of British hostility to the Jews—it was only natural that they not be pro-Jewish. The third chief administrative officer in Palestine, General Arthur Wigram Money, made quite a few antisemitic remarks in his diary.[24] They made their way into his telegrams as well.[25*]

Still, most British officials did not use antisemitic expressions. Either way, Congreve asserted, their personal views had no effect on policy. Each official, he maintained, acted in accordance with the government's Zionist agenda; they were not anti-Zionist, but were strictly fair in their treatment of all beliefs and all interests. It was precisely for this reason that the Zionists did not like them, he felt. They wanted preferred treatment.[27]

For the time being, the Zionists held back with certain controversial demands. The Ottoman prohibition on the sale of land was still in force, and the commission did not ask for it to be rescinded immediately. At this point the Zionist movement did not have the money to buy a lot of land, and the prohibition prevented speculators from driving up prices.[28] The Zionist movement also did not demand at this point that the country be opened to any Jew who wanted to come, although thousands deported by the Turks were allowed to return. So long as the Zionists were not prepared for mass absorption, restricting entry to the country served their interests. That made relations with the British easier.

Once again, the Zionists did not get everything they wanted. They were not allowed to print banknotes, and the commission was denied exclusive

---

*Horace Samuel, a Jewish jurist, warned that the derogatory expressions used by British officers and officials when speaking of Jews were meaningless: "Damned Jews and bloody Jews—in my view all this is much ado about nothing, the words in question being practically hyphenated in the ordinary vocabulary of a certain type of military officer." They used rude terms to refer to the Arabs as well. "We scarcely regarded these people as human," police officer Douglas Duff wrote.[26]

rights over the entry of money into the country, an arrangement that would have allowed them to block the flow of *chalukkah* money to the ultra-Orthodox. Weizmann wanted to purchase the Augusta Victoria castle from the army to serve as the Hebrew University library but was rebuffed. His request for a rail line from Jaffa to Jerusalem was turned down, as were a long series of other requests he submitted to the authorities.[29] More than once, Weizmann protested the military administration's decisions, but when all was said and done, the commission granted that its relations with the military administration had been "of the friendliest description." The administration officials had displayed a "spirit of fairness" and "sympathetic understanding" and had done all they could to be of assistance, the commission wrote.[30] In turn, the commission had provided the army with intelligence reports and situation evaluations, and had even absorbed the expenses involved.[31] This cooperation dwarfs almost to insignificance any claim that the military administration acted in opposition to Zionist concerns; the mutual intelligence work was directed against Arab national interests.

The major source of conflict between the commission and the military administration stemmed from neither political differences nor some officers' antisemitism and opposition to Zionism. Rather, it was a matter of ego versus ego. "The existence of the Zionist Commission in its present form is a standing insult to the British administration," General Congreve wrote, noting that the commission had a bureaucracy whose structure precisely paralleled the structure of the military administration.[32] "They went about dressed in khaki and wearing Sam Browne belts . . . [and] raised many questions," Edward Keith-Roach observed. In his words, "they were often more enthusiastic than tactful or prudent." The commission's policy was, he complained, "aggressive." Maybe all the Zionists did was talk to the officers as equals, as Weizmann spoke with the politicians in London. But the British officers were not used to natives who looked them in the eye. Keith-Roach found among his soldiers a tendency to prefer the Arabs to the "hordes of Jews from Eastern Europe." James Pollock wrote to his father: "The Jews are the most intolerant and arrogant people in the world."[33]*

---

*David Eder, however, was universally admired. "One of the strange things about him," said Wyndham Deedes, "was that he was so English and at the same time so Jewish. And in his relations with the administration it was the Englishman arguing on behalf of the Jews who confronted them; with this difference, that his Jewishness gave an inflexibility and a force to his arguments which no Englishman alone could bring." In this, Eder was like Chaim Weizmann, although Weizmann insisted that none of the other members of the commission knew how to understand both the English and the Jews. This characteristic, he believed, only he possessed.[34]

The Zionist Commission paid great attention to the statements of the administration officers. James Pollock wrote to his father: "Another amusing and at the same time fairly serious incident occurred. The Zionists have decided that I am anti-Jewish and are I believe trying to have me quickly removed."[35] Pollock explained that they wanted to get rid of him merely because he treated Jews and Arabs equally. "All I ask is—why not?"[36] The answer was that the Zionist Commission was not interested in fairness, as Congreve had noted—whoever was not for Zionism was against it. Pollock was not mistaken: from time to time the Zionist movement did have hostile officers transferred out of the country.

"Colonel Gabriel should not be allowed to return to Palestine," Weizmann ruled at a Zionist Commission meeting. Edmund Vivian Gabriel was responsible for the military administration's budget, and the Zionists considered him an enemy. He supported the interests of the Catholic Church and the Arabs, Weizmann charged. Weizmann sent Herbert Samuel to speak with Winston Churchill about the matter and spoke to Balfour himself.[37] Gabriel did not return. Foreign Secretary Lord Curzon was angry. "This is allowing the Jews to have things too much their own way. . . . It is intolerable that Dr. Weizmann should be allowed to criticize the 'type of men' employed by H.M. Govt.," he wrote.[38]

Weizmann indeed acted imperiously, as if it were the Zionist Commission, rather than the British Empire, that employed Gabriel. He not only succeeded in ousting the men he didn't like but also in arranging appointments for those he did, among them Richard Meinertzhagen, at once a great antisemite and a great Zionist. "I am imbued with anti-semitic feelings," Meinertzhagen wrote in his diary. "It was indeed an accursed day that allowed Jews and not Christians to introduce to the world the principles of Zionism and that allowed Jewish brains and Jewish money to carry them out, almost unhelped by Christians save a handful of enthusiasts in England." Meinertzhagen liked Weizmann to such a degree that he had a hard time reconciling his admiration with his disdain for Jews. When Gilbert Clayton left his position as chief political officer, Weizmann was instrumental in having Meinertzhagen appointed to replace him.[39]

Louis John Bols, Palestine's fifth chief administrative officer, described the Zionist Commission as an administration within the administration— the Jews obey their own people, not mine, he wrote.[40] Bols was disappointed. In December 1919, a month after arriving in the country, he sounded like a child who had received a new toy, all enthusiasm and great aspirations to succeed. He believed that Zionism had a chance, he wrote to Allenby. Weizmann's activity was helping reduce tensions. During Bols's first weeks in Palestine he was certain that there was nothing to prevent the settlement of large numbers of Jews in the country, despite Arab propaganda, provided it was done quietly without ostentation. He wanted Herbert Samuel to come to assist him. He needed the help of a "big financial fellow."

If Bols could get a loan of £10 or £20 million for the development of the country, it would be possible to increase the number of inhabitants from 900,000 to 2.5 million. There was enough room in the country, he wrote; a million people could be settled in the Jordan Valley itself. "I feel I can develop the country—and make it pay," he wrote. He could promise Allenby that within ten years Palestine would be a land flowing with milk and honey free of anti-Zionist agitations.[41]

Five months later Bols demanded that the Zionist Commission be dismantled. He had not become an enemy of Zionism; he was simply an English general, no smarter than any other man, who was sick and tired of receiving orders from those subservient to him. He was motivated not by politics but by indignity. In his written demand, he quoted several letters he had received from the commission. They were hardly submissive. In fact, they were insolent.

In one, the Zionist Commission protested that the police force had enlisted Jewish men without the commission vetting the candidates. "Only by this method can the Zionist Commission exercise an indirect control and be in some way responsible for the efficiency of the Jewish Gendarmes," wrote the commission's secretary, as if it were understood that the commission was responsible for every Jew in Palestine, including those serving in the police force. The British authorities agreed not to accept Jewish candidates without the recommendation of the commission, but Bols sensed that the Zionists were trying to impose their own people on the police force.[42]

The police were an important Zionist objective. Few policemen in the country were Jewish, most were Arabs, and the force was routinely brutal and corrupt. The Jerusalem police in particular were considered "the rottenest in Palestine," General Money observed. But it was not easy to find Jews willing to serve as policemen. As an incentive, the commission supplemented their salaries. Bols objected to this as a kind of bribery. "You must agree that in principle it is wrong that King George's servants should be paid by an outside body," he told Eder. "Yes," Eder responded, "on condition that King George's servants are properly paid by King George." The force remained, until the very end, the British administration's weakest link, partly because of the low salaries paid to the policemen.[43]

Bols also complained of threats against Jewish parents who dared send their children to British-run schools. He quoted articles to that effect from the Hebrew press. The newspaper *Do'ar Ha-Yom* called for a boycott of all Jews who sent their children to foreign schools and described such people as traitors to their nation; it threatened to print their names. The newspaper's editor, Itamar Ben-Avi, son of linguist Eliezer Ben-Yehuda, attacked a whole range of public figures for not Hebraicizing their names. Among these were poets Chaim Nachman Bialik and Shaul Tchernikovsky, and Zionist leaders Menachem Ussishkin and Meir Dizengoff. Bols attributed these articles to the Zionist Commission, which he referred to as a tyrannical and Bolshevik organization.[44]

3.

In the meantime, a national awakening was taking place in Palestine, an inevitable consequence of relief from oppression. No sooner had the Turks left than the small Jewish community began sprouting scores of organizations and councils and associations and societies, cultural and sports and consumer clubs, trade unions, ethnic committees, and political parties. All of them held conventions, all organized elections; all competed to demonstrate greater Zionist patriotism. One measure of national loyalty was the degree of suspicion and hostility displayed toward the British administration. To be resentful and protest against injustice was to be patriotic.[45]

Toward the end of the summer of 1919, a group of Jerusalem high school students set out for a trip to Mount Hermon. The teacher was a well-known educator, Chaim Arieh Zuta. When the students reached the mountain, they wrote their names on a sheet of paper and put it in a bottle, which they buried. Then they planted the national flag on the spot and returned to Metulla, a farming village in the valley below the mountain. Arabs who saw the flag called the police, who took down the flag and removed the bottle. Newspapers in Damascus interpreted the incident as evidence that the Jews intended to occupy the entire country. Zuta explained afterward that the flag had been planted merely as a sign that Jews had been there, but he later changed his story, probably in accordance with instructions he received from the Zionist Commission. The flag, he claimed, had been meant only to mark the students' location and had no political significance. Just a rag, a secretary of Metulla said, a sign that the hikers had arrived safely.

A few days after the event the authorities prohibited the display of national flags; this followed a previous decree against playing national anthems other than "God Save the King." The decree had produced an extended correspondence between David Eder and Colonel Popham, Storrs's assistant, which included a debate over the meaning of the Zionist anthem "Hatikva," translated into English for the purpose of proving that the words were not anti-Arab.[46]

The Yishuv demanded that the Zionist Commission defend national honor in the matter of the flag. The commission was not enthusiastic: "To me and a majority of the Zionist Commission, such things seem entirely gratuitous," Mordechai Ben-Hillel Hacohen commented. Some commissioners viewed the fight for the national symbol as a manifestation of extreme chauvinism, but the commission was afraid of losing its influence over the public, so it took up the issue of the flag, with no success.[47]

The commission received countless complaints from irate Jewish settlers, but two subjects predominated: the Hebrew language and the Jewish Legion. "The rights of the Hebrew language are a symbol of the rights of the Hebrew nation in our land," some prominent Jerusalem Zionists wrote to the commission. The major agitator in this regard was Ze'ev Jabotinsky.[48] Within days of the British conquest the Provisional Assembly—a group of activists who assumed leadership of the Jewish public and represented it to the British regime—decided that the right to vote and be elected was conditional on knowledge of the Hebrew language.[49]

One of the first demands received by the Zionist Commission was a list of books that Zionists in Jaffa wanted translated into Hebrew, including Turgenev's *Fathers and Sons,* Swift's *Gulliver's Travels,* and Edmondo De Amicis's *The Heart.*[50]* At one public meeting Chaim Weizmann wanted to speak in German or Yiddish in order to express himself with greater precision. He switched to one of these languages whenever he wanted to create an atmosphere of comradeship, Moshe Shertok later recalled. Local

---

*Jabotinsky composed a hundred-word Hebrew-English lexicon for the use of British soldiers. "Whatever you think of Zionism," he wrote in the preface, "there is one thing which every civilized man, Gentile or Jew, should support: it is the revival of Hebrew as a spoken language." The first word that Jabotinsky wished to teach the British soldiers was *shalom.*[51]

participants discussed his request, rejected it, and forced him to speak in Hebrew. David Ben-Gurion regularly attacked the commission members for their foreignness. People walk around the country and don't even know its language, he griped. Most of the commission did not know Hebrew; the members typically conducted their meetings in English. But there were exceptions. Menachem Ussishkin, a leading fighter for the status of Hebrew, came from Russia and did not know English, and not all of the commissioners knew Yiddish. When Ussishkin joined the meetings, everyone used the only language they all shared—German.[52]*

The Jewish Legion gave rise to similarly heated passion. Commanding Officer John Henry Patterson, an engineer from Ireland, was world famous as a lion hunter. In his best-selling book on his exploits along the Tsavo River in East Africa, he described a problem that arose in his camp. Each night, he related, a lion would enter the camp and eat one of the Swahili laborers employed in the construction of a bridge. Patterson killed one lion after another, for a total of eight. He too had grown up on the Bible. "When, as a boy," he later wrote, "I eagerly devoured the records of the glorious deeds of Jewish military captains such as Joshua, Joab, Gideon and Judas Maccabaeus I little dreamt that one day I myself would in a small way be a captain of a host of the Children of Israel." He thought that Judah Maccabee would feel at home in his camp. "He would have heard the Hebrew tongue spoken on all sides and seen a little host of the Sons of Judah drilling to the same words of command that he himself used to those gallant soldiers who so nobly fought . . . under his banner."[54]

Patterson had hoped to receive a larger force. He complained that he was denied adequate supplies, that his men were excluded from the conquest of the Galilee, and that they did not receive proper treatment in the hospitals. Jabotinsky detailed Patterson's grievances in a series of letters to Weizmann, Eder, and Allenby. He cultivated the thesis that Allenby wanted to conceal the role of the Jews in the conquest of Palestine. That was not true. Allenby praised the Jewish Legion, and his words were quoted throughout the country.[55]

After the conquest of Palestine, many of the legion's soldiers wanted to

---

*Theodor Herzl did not know Hebrew and did not believe that it could serve as a language of daily intercourse. "Who of us knows Hebrew well enough to ask for a train ticket in that language?" he wrote in *The Jewish State*. He believed that the Jewish state would have a Swiss type of linguistic federalism—"Everyone will hold to his language, which will be the dear homeland of his thoughts."[53] German was generally the language spoken at the Zionist Congresses.

go home; some wanted to stay in the country. Weizmann hoped to expand the battalions and integrate them into the remaining British forces. A number of legion soldiers were stationed in Haifa but were removed when Arab leaders in the city complained after a series of incidents between Jewish conscripts and young Arabs.[56] The legion was transferred to the Rafiah area near Gaza and assigned to guard a prison camp. Jabotinsky considered this exile. Soon thereafter the British decided to transfer some of the legion's men to Egypt, and a mutiny broke out.

When David Eder learned of the legion's rebellion, he rushed south to mediate between the soldiers and their commanders. He tried to persuade the rebels and spoke to army commanders in Cairo as well. "I was inwardly quaking if outwardly calm," he later wrote. He succeeded in resolving the problem: the soldiers agreed to go to Egypt, and the British agreed to bring them back a few days later. Eder returned to Tel Aviv. Those forty-eight hours of diplomacy were the hardest in all his years of work in the country, he noted.[57]

Jabotinsky proposed protesting about the legion's treatment to King George and demanded that Eder join him.[58] Eder refused. The rebels had not been motivated by patriotic loyalty to Palestine, he said. The soldiers had mutinied because one battalion had not received salt and another was angry that a soldier had been punished severely for neglecting his mule. David Ben-Gurion claimed that Eder had said "horrible and hair-raising things" and threatened to sue. Eder rebuffed him coldly.*

Eder also refused to promise that discharged legion soldiers would receive employment in Palestine. Without such a commitment, the military authorities refused to allow them to remain. Ben-Gurion demanded that Eder issue false commitments. Eder, who had been raised to respect the law, could not believe his ears. Ben-Gurion had grown up on the assumption that the government—any government—was hostile to the Jews and there was thus no reason not to mislead it. This was a confrontation between cultures, but also between Israel and "the Exile," as it was called—leaders in Palestine had their own ideas how to run matters and saw the commission as a foreign body. This conflict would deepen over time.

---

*Shabtai Teveth, Ben-Gurion's biographer, wrote: "If this incident strengthened Eder's opinion that Ben-Gurion was nothing but a small-time factional hack who liked to flex his muscles, an impetuous young man who liked to show off and get publicity through sensational lawsuits, an ambitious person who got pushed into actions that bordered on the irresponsible—it would be hard to blame him. Such an impression had begun to find a way into the hearts of others."[59]

Some years later, David Ben-Gurion asked Chaim Weizmann why he had accepted the promise of a national home in Palestine rather than holding out for a state. Weizmann responded that he did not demand a state because he would not have gotten one. "That is a tactical question," he said.[60] Whereas Ben-Gurion was a young politician with no responsibilities, Weizmann saw himself as a statesman shaping the future of his people. He believed in cautious, gradual action, in a doctrine of stages.

An old fox in Jewish politics, Weizmann tended to view public life in Palestine as a provincial dance of midgets. He rejected the local leadership's demand to participate in the Zionist Commission's decisions. His approach was arrogant, almost colonial: Weizmann came from London and claimed to represent the entire Jewish people. The process of nation-building was meant to happen according to set priorities and the pace set by the "nation," the "nation" being the provider of funds for the rehabilitation of Palestine. Or rather, the Zionist movement, that is, Chaim Weizmann himself. "We demand discipline of you!" Weizmann once said to local Zionists.

Reporting to his people in London on relations with the authorities, Weizmann accused the Jews in Palestine of tactlessness. He considered some of the demands it made of the administration parochial and unnecessarily provocative. He believed that the Palestinian Jewish community "takes itself much too seriously."

Between Mohammed and
Mr. Cohen

1.

On January 23, 1919, Khalil al-Sakakini celebrated his birthday. "On this day, forty-one years ago," he wrote, "I was born and named Khalil, after my older brother, who died in childhood. My earliest boyhood memory is that we lived in our house in the Old City. My hair was red, the color of Sari and Sultana's hair today, and it was flowing, so that they sometimes braided it as they braid girls' hair. I was fat, so much so that because of my low stature I looked like a rolling ball."[1]

Like Alter Levine, Sakakini agonized over his identity. "I am not a Christian nor a Buddhist," he wrote, "neither a Muslim nor a Jew. Just as I am not Arab or English, nor French nor German nor Turkish. I am just one member of the human race." He had calling cards printed that read "Khalil al-Sakakini—human being, God willing."

Sometimes, however, Sakakini was inclined to define himself first and foremost as an Arab, and believed it was his duty to work for the rebirth of this "miserable nation." Their interest, he wrote, "is to be a single people, to be educated in a single culture and to a single way and to hope a single hope"; he added that this was not an impossible mission for a true patriot. "We have a place, we have a language, we have a culture," he explained. "Independence! Independence!" he wrote in his diary. He was among the founding fathers of Arab national consciousness in Palestine, one of the first activists in the joint Muslim-Christian literary clubs that served as the nucleus of the Arab national movement.

After his return from Damascus, Sakakini made a living teaching Arabic. One evening, on his way back from giving a lesson, he ran into a young man he knew, Amin al-Husseini. They spoke of the general situation in Palestine. "I hate politics," Husseini said, "but I have no choice to be involved in it now." Sakakini replied, "If politics means working for the country's freedom, we must all be politicians."

At the time of this meeting, Amin al-Husseini was in his twenties. Before the war he had been a student in Cairo, in training to inherit his father's position as mufti of Jerusalem. A pilgrimage to Mecca with his mother gave him the right to add the title "Haj" to his name. When war broke out he enlisted in the Turkish army, returning to Jerusalem in 1917; he had been discharged for medical reasons. Apparently he made a quick recovery, for as soon as the British reached the city he helped to enlist two thousand or more volunteers into their service. Here was a pious Muslim in the service of a Christian army—against a Muslim enemy. Khalil al-Sakakini, a Christian, sneered at such people and condemned their hypocrisy: "Yesterday they fawned over the Ottoman government, serenaded it with hymns of praise and gratitude—and today they fawn over the English government," he wrote in his diary.[2]

Just like the Jewish Legion, the Arab Legion was intended to foster nationalism. The Arabs also wanted to serve only in Palestine and demanded a national flag of their own. They fought in the Arabian deserts, shoulder to shoulder with the soldiers of the Jewish Legion; a single army, a single front, a single enemy, and a similar aspiration—independence in Palestine.[3]

When the British arrived, the Arabs too experienced a release of suppressed political activity. Arab politics was largely urban in nature and had the character of a family rivalry. "Every Muslim family in Jerusalem has a tradition distilled into its blood, handed down from father to son," Sakakini wrote. "The family interest comes before any other interest and the family's influence comes before any other influence. If you assign someone to vote for a representative in a house of delegates, or a city council, or a board of education, or a national association, he will vote for the elder of his family, whether or not that person is fit for the job. Ask him who the most loyal patriot is, the one with the most superior qualities, with the broadest knowledge or with the best opinions and he will cite his father, or brother, or cousin."[4]

In 1920, some forty Arab national associations with approximately three thousand Muslim and Christian members were active in Palestine.[5] From time to time people would meet at Sakakini's house; Haj Amin al-Husseini also came. In his diary, Sakakini recorded his own pronouncements made at these meetings: "These are the most important times in the chronicle of this country. . . . It is incumbent upon us to cultivate the nationalist sentiment, perhaps it will live again, after its days nearly reached their end. . . . We must invigorate the nation's youth, breathe hope into it. . . . We must make ourselves heard everywhere—in the homes and on the streets, in all the clubs and congresses. The national question must become part of every conversation. . . . We must capture the world's attention. In short, we must show signs of life." Actually, he had been determined to keep away from public affairs, he wrote, but circumstances prevented him from isolating himself. "I have almost become the leader of the national movement," he noted.[6]

Signs of an incipient Arab national consciousness in Palestine had been apparent in the previous century, in the early confrontations between Zionist settlers and Arab farmers. The Jews had purchased land to establish agricultural settlements, and in many cases Arab tenant farmers resided on the property. The new settlers evicted the tenants, sometimes forcibly, with the aid of the Ottoman authorities. There were incidents of violence, some of them deadly.[7] As early as the 1880s, the conflict was a struggle between two peoples, an inevitable part of daily life in Palestine.

Ahad Ha'am addressed the issue in his pamphlet "Truth from Palestine," published in 1891. The Jewish settlers, he wrote, "treat the Arabs with hostility and cruelty, trespass unjustly, beat them shamelessly for no sufficient reason, and even take pride in doing so." He offered a psychological explanation for the phenomenon: "The Jews were slaves in the land of their Exile, and suddenly they found themselves with unlimited freedom, wild freedom that only exists in a land like Turkey. This sudden change has produced in their hearts an inclination toward repressive tyranny, as always happens when a slave rules." Ahad Ha'am warned: "We are used to thinking of the Arabs as primitive men of the desert, as a donkey-like nation that neither sees nor understands what is going on around it. But this is a great error. The Arab, like all sons of Shem, has a sharp and crafty mind. . . . Should the time come when the life of our people in Palestine imposes to a smaller or greater extent on the natives, they will not easily step aside."[8]

Once, an Arab notable in Jerusalem had implored Theodor Herzl, "The world is big enough, there are other, uninhabited lands in which millions of poor Jews could be settled. . . . In the name of God, leave Palestine alone!" That was in 1899. Two years later several leaders of the Arab community sent a petition to their Turkish rulers demanding that the entry of Jews into Palestine be restricted and that they be prohibited from purchasing land.[9] These two issues became the core of the Arab struggle against Zionism. In 1905, Najib Azuri, a harbinger of Arab nationalism, published a book in Paris announcing the Arab national awakening, which was coming just at the time that the Jews were attempting to reestablish the ancient Israelite kingdom. The two movements were destined to wage war until one defeated the other, Azuri prophesied, and the fate of the entire world depended on the outcome of this struggle.[10]

Arab national activists closely followed developments in the Zionist movement. One of them, Mohammed Izzat Darwazza, later recalled reading a translation of Herzl's *The Jewish State* in an Arabic newspaper. Some Arabs expressed the opinion that their nation should learn how to run their affairs from the Zionists, including how to promote education and raise money. Sakakini once saw a welcoming ceremony in Jerusalem honoring Baron Rothschild. "The Arab nation needs a man like Rothschild, who will put up money for its revival," he wrote in his diary.[11]

But when he styled himself as a leader of the Arab national movement, Sakakini was exaggerating. The Arabs in Palestine had no organized national movement comparable to the Zionists', nor did they have a recognized leader. At the time, the most prominent spokesman for Arab nationalism was Musa Kazim al-Husseini, the mayor of Jerusalem. Still, the nationalist sentiment was widespread and agitation was on the rise. Cafés in Jerusalem were full of people talking national politics; in every village locals were gathering around the teacher to hear him read the newspapers.[12]

In May 1919, at the Zohar cinema in Jaffa, the local chapter of the Muslim-Christian Association held a public assembly. Printed invitations had been sent out, stating that important national issues would be discussed. The meeting began at ten in the morning on a Sunday and lasted for over two hours. More than five hundred residents of Jaffa and nearby villages attended. The keynote speaker, who also served as chairman, was a Christian, while the three other speakers were Muslims, among them a blind sheikh from Ramle. All spoke in the same vein: the residents of Palestine had experienced cruel repression during the Turkish period and now their hour of freedom had arrived. The speakers praised the British government, noting as well that the Arab nation had a great future, just as it had a great past—Arabs had, after all, brought enlightenment to Europe. Therefore, they too deserved national independence. Muslims and Christians were united in one religion, the religion of the homeland, which granted equal rights to all.

The assembly promised equality for the country's Jewish inhabitants, but would not agree to additional Jewish immigration. "We do not at all oppose the Jews," one speaker said. "We only oppose Zionism. That is not the same thing. Zionism has no roots at all in Moses' law. It is an invention of Herzl's." He noted happily that many Jews also opposed Zionism, and these, he said, would not be denied entry. Another speaker remarked that the Arabs should show their hospitality to the Jews, so long as the Jews did not espouse separatist aspirations.

The backdrop on the stage was composed of four cloth screens—red, green, black, and white. Each screen bore a caption explaining the color's significance. Red symbolized blood: "In the name of Arabia we will live and in the name of Arabia we will die," the caption read. Green symbolized liberty: "Arabia will not be divided," it said. The white screen was an homage to Prince Faisal, the leader of the Arab revolt, and the black one represented the Zionist migration.

At the meeting's conclusion, a resolution was agreed: Palestine is part of Syria; it will be given autonomy in the framework of Greater Syria under the rule of Prince Faisal; there will be no national home for the Jews. Someone proposed that everyone sign a declaration to that effect, and there was an uproar. People were unwilling to sign their names; they had not been told in advance. There was shouting and shoving, and here and there people traded blows. One angry young man jumped on the stage and yelled at the crowd, "You have no national consciousness! You are a herd! You don't understand what this day is for our nation! At this moment its fate is being sealed for generations to come! We will not allow ourselves to be led like lambs to the slaughter!" Tempers finally ebbed, but then the military governor appeared and ordered the meeting dispersed.[13]

Also from Jaffa came a report on a play performed at the Arab Club— five acts on the tyranny of fallen Ottoman governor Jamal Pasha. In the last scene he finds himself face-to-face with the dead Arab underground fighters he ordered hanged. They are wrapped in sheets, and each one is inscribed "the Arab awakening." At the end the entire cast sang the anthem adopted by Prince Faisal's men, perhaps the one Sakakini wrote in Damascus. The audience joined in, and the actors waved the Arab national flag.[14]

The Arabs made three basic demands: independence, no Jewish immigration, and a prohibition against Jewish land purchases. The demands were reworded from time to time at national congresses but remained unchanged in principle. Countless petitions inspired by these conditions were sent to the British administration; many protested the authorities' support for Zionism and discrimination against the Arabs.[15] They repeatedly cited the right to national self-determination and the democratic principles the world had adopted after the war. Like the Jews, who based their demand for a national home in Palestine on historical justice, the Arabs also appealed to history. Arab rule in Spain had lasted for more than seven hundred years, one petition noted. The Arabs had considered Spain their home and had left their imprint on its culture. Would anyone dare suggest they should now be allowed to return there?[16]

No less than the Zionist movement, the Arab nationalist movement was divided by different factions and approaches. Their attitude to the British administration was determined largely by their own internal politics. "Why do people hate General Storrs?" Sakakini wrote. "I believe the reason is that the Husseini family are the only people he knows. He listens only to their opinion." Among themselves, the Arabs debated a long list of tactical questions; they argued over attitudes toward the Jews, the use of violence, and even the aspiration for independence. Once, at Sakakini's house, his guests discussed whether the Arabs were ready for independence. "Is there among our people anyone who is fit to be a director-general, chief of the treasury, an educational superintendent, a postmaster, a police chief?" Sakakini had his doubts.[17]

Sakakini recalled a discussion he had held with Benyamin Ivri (Berstein), a Zionist activist from Russia, who had been involved in buying land for the Hebrew University on Mount Scopus. Ivri had brought Sakakini to the Fast Hotel for Arabic lessons, and the two men also talked about Zionism. Sakakini said that the country belonged to the Arabs; Ivri argued that the Arabs had neglected it. On the contrary, Sakakini said, they had spread their culture and language throughout Palestine. He could not deny that once, in the distant past, the Jews had had a right to the country, but it had expired, he said. The Arabs' right, he insisted, "is a living one." Ivri responded that the Jews' eternal yearning for the land entitled them to return to it. Sakakini had no objections to Jewish independence, but he would not consent to the Jews "killing an entire nation in order to live." The Jews did not want to expel the Arabs, Ivri countered; they wanted to live together with them. "The land is spacious and its soil is fertile," he claimed.

Sakakini was not persuaded. "You are a star that has gone out," he told Ivri. "Don't expect the entire universe, every sun and every moon, to revolve around you." He was convinced that Jewish settlement in Palestine endangered the entire Arab world. "If you want to kill a nation—conquer its land and tear out its tongue. That is exactly what the Zionists want to do to the Arab nation," he said.[18] "The Jews need you," Ivri told Sakakini, wanting to win his sympathy.

The Zionist movement tried to prove that Jews and Arabs could live together. "They want to mix with you. They need your blood," Ivri said to Sakakini. "Undoubtedly in the future they will accept your customs and speak your language. And if many Jews come to Palestine, it will be a country with more than one language. Like Switzerland."* Ivri shared with the influential writer Ahad Ha'am the minority view that Palestine would serve mainly as a spiritual center for the Jews and that a Jewish state would not be established there. For this reason he could tell Sakakini that the Arabs had nothing to fear: Palestine could not take in all the Jews; in any event, no more than 200,000 to 300,000 would come.† But in general, the Zionist movement felt otherwise: it was striving to create a Jewish majority in Palestine and establish a state based on European culture.

To allay tensions in the present the Zionists tended to idealize the two peoples' common past. "The relations that have so far prevailed between the Jews and the Arabs in Palestine have been good and satisfactory," stated a document presented to the Zionist Commission. "We were like a single family," wrote Ya'akov Yehoshua, a longtime Sephardic resident of Jerusalem, on the relations between his community and the Arabs.

However, Sephardic public figures accused Zionist activists, almost all of whom were Europeans, of not making them party to policy decisions. Governor Ronald Storrs thought that the Sephardic Jews would be better

---

*An article published by teacher Yitzhak Epstein in 1907 provoked a debate over the right of the Jews to establish their home in Palestine and over the proper attitude to the Arabs. Both subjects have been a source of conflict within the Zionist movement from its beginnings to the present.[19]

†Theodor Herzl had tried to convey a similar message to Yussuf Dia al-Khaladi, a mayor of Jerusalem and member of the Ottoman parliament. Herzl claimed that the Jews would help increase property values in Palestine. Nachum Sokolow spoke to the same effect in an interview with an Egyptian newspaper. The benefits of Jewish immigration to the Arabs was a central Zionist argument.[20]

at dealing with the Arabs because of their cultural affinities. Arab leaders were also inclined to claim that until the Zionists came they had enjoyed excellent relations with the Jews. Musa Alami liked to say that he had a Jewish "brother"—a boy who had been born close to his parents' home, whom his mother had wet-nursed. Yehoshua told of Arab women who wet-nursed Jewish children and of Jewish *mohelim*—ritual circumcisers— who circumcised Arab children.[21] Both sides had their own reasons for embellishing this supposed former golden age of Jewish-Arab relations.*

The Zionist movement closely followed the development of Arab nationalism, and the Zionist archives in Jerusalem preserve reports from dozens, perhaps hundreds, of Arab informers located in every city and in many villages. The Hebrew press frequently printed translations of Arab articles condemning Zionism. David Ben-Gurion knew of Najib Azuri's book and said it contained "seeds of hatred."

2.

While on his way to Palestine with the Zionist Commission soon after the British conquest, Weizmann had stopped off in Cairo to meet with a number of Arab leaders. He tried to convince them they had nothing to fear from Zionism, and as a gesture of good faith he sent the University of Cairo a donation of one hundred pounds. Weizmann claimed that there was no national conflict between Arabs and Jews; at the most there were economic disparities that would not be hard to bridge. At the same time, he denied the existence of an Arab nation in Palestine. "The poor ignorant fellah does not worry about politics," he wrote to his colleagues in London, "but when he is told repeatedly by people in whom he has confidence that his livelihood is in danger of being taken away from him by us, he becomes our mortal enemy." He tended to dismiss the Arab position, seeing it as propaganda that the Jews had to live with, just as they had to live with the mosquitoes. "The Arab is primitive and believes what he is told," Weizmann stated.[23] As for Zionist ambitions for an independent state, Weizmann instructed members of the Zionist Commission to evade

*The assumption that relations between Sephardic Jews and Arabs had been better than those between Ashkenazim and Arabs developed over the years into a full-fledged political and cultural position.[22] It had been true, however, only so long as Zionist activity in Palestine was not on the upswing. In fact, some of the first people to devote themselves to improving Jewish-Arab relations were born in Eastern and Central Europe. Ashkenazim were also prominent among academic Orientalists, and one of them, Yosef Yoel Rivlin, translated the Koran into Hebrew during World War I. He also translated *The Thousand and One Nights*.

the question. The Zionists did aspire to an independent Jewish Palestine, but the less they spoke of it the better, he told them.[24]

Speaking with senior Arabs and British officials, Weizmann scrupulously followed his own instructions. "We don't desire to turn out Mohammed in order to put in Mr. Cohen as a large landowner," he wrote to General Money. The statement is worth a second reading for the patronizing attitude beneath the conciliatory tone, and for the perceptions it reveals. The Arab was merely "Mohammed," but the Jew was "Mr. Cohen." Weizmann left no room for doubt as to his feelings: "There is a fundamental difference in quality between Jew and native," he stated.[25] He believed that it was neither possible nor worthwhile to negotiate with the Arabs of Palestine. He himself was not prepared to do so, he explained to the military administration, because the Palestinian Arabs were "a demoralised race." In a letter to Balfour he suggested keeping a careful eye on the treacherous Arabs, lest they stab the army in the back.[26] To his wife he wrote, "I feel that I do not have to concern myself with the Arabs anymore." He said he had done all that was necessary to explain his position to them, and they could take it or leave it.[27] They appreciated only force, but could probably be won over with bribes, Weizmann believed, intending to buy the goodwill of Prince Faisal, as well.

The British had urged a meeting between the two heads of Jewish and Arab nationalism: Weizmann and Prince Faisal, son of Hussein, ruler of Mecca, and leader of the Arab revolt against the Turks. In June 1918, Weizmann prepared to travel to Aqaba, across the Red Sea, near where Faisal was camped in the desert. "I propose to tell him," Weizmann wrote, "that if he wants to build up a strong and prosperous Arab kingdom, it is we Jews who will be able to help him, and we only. We can give him the necessary assistance in money and organising power. We shall be his neighbours and we do not represent any danger to him, as we are not and never will be a great power." He described the Jews as natural intermediaries between Great Britain and Arabia.[28]

The British had encouraged the Arab rebellion against the Turks, provided military and financial assistance, and had promised independence. Prince Faisal was extremely popular throughout the Arab world, including Palestine. The Arabs "put his name into every song," Sakakini noted.[29] He represented their national aspiration to unity, and he considered Palestine, or "southern Syria," as part of his kingdom.

Sir Mark Sykes made certain to prepare Faisal for his meeting with Weizmann. "I know that the Arabs despise, condemn, and hate the Jews," he wrote to the prince, but warned that it would be best to learn from those who had persecuted the Jews—the Spanish and tzarist Russian empires were no more, he noted. "Believe me," Sykes wrote, "I speak the truth when I say that this race, despised and weak, is universal, is all-powerful and cannot be put down." Jews could be found, he said, "in the councils of every state, in every bank, in every business, in every enterprise." He promised that the Jews were not plotting to expel the Arabs from Palestine and suggested the prince see them as Prime Minister Lloyd George did, as a powerful ally.[30]

Weizmann's journey to Aqaba took several days. "In the heat of June it was no pleasure jaunt," he later wrote. First he went by train to Suez. There he boarded a ship that took him across the Red Sea. "It was a small, grimy, and neglected vessel," he recounted. The crew was Greek. The heat was intolerable, the food bad, the bathrooms unusable. "We devised what substitutes we could," Weizmann wrote. Major William Ormsby-Gore, liaison officer to the Zionist Commission, was also in the party, but came down with dysentery and could not go on.

At Aqaba, Weizmann set off for Faisal's camp with a car, an escort, and an Arab guide. The car broke down after three hours. The group continued on camel and walked part of the way. "There was no trace of any vegetation, no shade, no water, no village wherein to rest," Weizmann recalled. "Only the Mountains of Sinai on the horizon, bounding a wilderness of burning rock and sand." They finally reached a British air force camp, where they received a new car and driver. This car could not withstand the rigors of the journey either, so again they continued on foot. Before long they were met by camel riders sent by the prince, carrying water and fruit. By the time the travelers reached the camp in Wadi Wahadia, evening had fallen.

Weizmann later wrote of the beauty of the moonlit night. As he often had before, he conjured up a biblical fantasy: "I may have been a little light-headed from the sudden change in climate," he wrote, "but as I stood there I suddenly had the feeling that three thousand years had vanished, had become as nothing. Here I was, on the identical ground, on the identical errand, of my ancestors in the dawn of my people's history, when they came to negotiate with the ruler of the country for a right of way that they might return to their home. . . . Dream or vision or hallucination, I was suddenly recalled from it to present day realities by the gruff voice of a British sentry: 'Sorry, sir, I'm afraid you're out of bounds.'"

The next day, Weizmann was received, as was customary, with great ceremony. The prince's men whirled around him in a *fantasia,* an Arab dance. Lawrence of Arabia was there, Weizmann noted. He seemed to be preparing a sortie, apparently to sabotage part of the vast Hejaz railway line. Weizmann saw Lawrence hand out gold sovereigns to his men; he assumed these had been in the heavy chests he had seen on his boat.[31] He also witnessed the arrival of a German airplane trailing a white flag. The passenger, a Turkish emissary, had come to persuade Faisal to join the Turkish side in exchange for piles of gold.

The conversation between Faisal and Weizmann lasted about an hour. A British colonel called Joyce served as interpreter—Weizmann knew no Arabic, while Faisal was not fluent in English; here and there they spoke French. The two men exchanged many pleasantries and greetings. Weizmann said that the Jews wished to develop Palestine for the benefit of all its residents, under British protection. He offered financial and political support. He would soon be traveling to America, he said, where the Zionists had a great deal of influence. Faisal asked many questions, and Weizmann received the impression that the prince knew something about the Zionist movement. He expressed a desire to cooperate with the Jews but was careful to make no commitment. Faisal could not say anything about the future of Palestine, he said, being cautious and prudent. Toward the end of the conversation Faisal suggested that he and his guest have their photograph taken together as a souvenir.

"He is a leader!" Weizmann wrote to his wife, adding that the prince was "handsome as a picture." This was the first real Arab ruler he had met. Palestine did not interest the prince, Weizmann told his wife; he wanted to control Damascus and northern Syria. "He is contemptuous of the Palestinian Arabs, whom he doesn't even regard as Arabs," he continued, praising the prince as "quite intelligent" and a "very honest man."

The British were also satisfied. They were convinced the meeting had created "excellent personal relations" between the two men. To Weizmann the conversation had "laid the foundations of a life-long friendship."[32] But no historic agreement had been reached. At most, the trip was a public relations success.

Nonetheless, the journey seemed to inspire Weizmann to send Balfour one of his audacious letters, the kind that helped create his reputation as a statesman with worldwide influence and place Palestine in a global context, between Washington and Delhi. Weizmann explained that Zionism was closely linked to Britain's power in the East. There should be no weak link along the London-Cairo-Jerusalem-India axis. He proclaimed his support of Faisal. So long as the Arab national movement developed and succeeded under his leadership, Weizmann stated, there would be minimal tension between the Arabs and Zionism. "The Arab question in Palestine" would remain a purely local issue, he asserted, adding that none of the experts thought it should be taken too seriously. Then he gave Balfour a few pieces of advice on how to streamline the decision-making process in His Majesty's Government. With effusive, almost obsequious politeness, he tipped Balfour off to some discord between the army's headquarters in Cairo and in Palestine—they were acting at cross-purposes and General Clayton could not work properly under the circumstances. While he was at it, Weizmann also requested that Major Ormsby-Gore, a great friend of Zionism, be appointed the new political officer.[33]

Almost offhandedly, Weizmann threw in mention of "our friends in America," reminding Balfour of the Jews' international reach. The reference was to Supreme Court Justice Louis Brandeis and to Professor Felix Frankfurter, who would later succeed Brandeis on the high court. Weizmann was planning to send an emissary to Washington to update President Wilson and "the friends," but only with Balfour's approval, of course, he added courteously.

In the fall of 1918, Weizmann was again in London. Prime Minister David Lloyd George invited him to lunch. On the designated day, November 11, an armistice was declared and World War I came, for all intents and purposes, to an end. Despite the momentous news, the Prime Minister's Office notified Weizmann that the invitation remained in force. At close to 1:30 P.M. Weizmann arrived in Green Park; cheering crowds had gathered around the iron gate leading to Downing Street. A policeman prevented him from proceeding. Weizmann spoke of his invitation to dine with the prime minister. The policeman remarked dryly that he had heard the same thing from any number of people who wanted to pass. When Weizmann was finally allowed to enter, he found the prime minister "moved to the depths of his soul, near to tears, reading the Psalms."[34]

3.

While Weizmann was downplaying Arab-Jewish tensions to his diplomatic contacts around the world, the Jewish community in Palestine was less sanguine about future relations with the Arabs. A discussion held by members of the Provisional Assembly, a body that represented the Jewish community in Palestine, revealed their concerns. Indeed, the minutes of the discussion are worth reading, because they show that everything that would ever be said about the subject had already been said back then. Chaim Margalit Kalvarisky, a Polish-born agronomist who had been living in the Galilee since the 1890s, opened the discussion. As part of his management of the Jewish Colonization Association, which purchased land and encouraged Jewish settlement in Palestine, he had frequent contacts with Arab leaders, including Prince Faisal. It was his belief that the Arabs could simply be paid off. At the same time, he maintained that the Zionist movement could conduct a "dialogue" with the Arabs, and throughout his life he argued that Zionism had missed a chance for peace.

Kalvarisky began his statement with a story, about the first time he had dispossessed Arabs of the land on which they were living. Typical of many such Zionist accounts, Kalvarisky's story was full of self-pity.

> The question of the Arabs first appeared to me in all its seriousness immediately after the first purchase of land I made here. I had to dispossess the Arab residents of their land for the purpose of settling our brothers. The doleful dirge of the Bedouin men and women who gathered outside the sheikh's tent that evening, before they left the village of Shamsin, next to Yama, which is Yavniel, did not stop ringing in my ears for a long time thereafter. I sat in the tent and concluded my negotiation with Sheikh Fadul Madalika. The Bedouin men and women gathered around the fire, prepared coffee for me and for the rest of the guests. And at the same time they sang songs of mourning for their bad fortune, which forced them to leave the cradle of their birth. Those songs cut through my heart and I realized how tied the Bedouin is to his land.

He had been dispossessing Arabs for twenty-five years, Kalvarisky said. It was not easy work, especially for a man like him, who did not see the Arabs as a flock of sheep but rather as human beings with hearts and souls. He had to turn them off the land because the Jewish public demanded it of him, Kalvarisky said, but he always tried to ensure that the people did not leave empty-handed and that the land-speculating effendis with whom he did business did not rob the simple folk of their money.

This prologue led to his central argument: the Zionists should strive to reach an agreement with the Arabs, something the movement had neglected to do. The Zionist movement could not continue to deny the existence of a problem and maintain that the Arabs were "just a bunch of ignoramuses and bootlickers willing to sell everything for a mess of pottage." Ultimately, Kalvarisky seems to have envisaged a form of Jewish autonomy in the framework of an Arab kingdom, probably under Faisal. He proposed a political agreement, having already conducted talks with Arab leaders, among them Prince Faisal. "We don't have to concede anything of our fundamental program," he promised. "Palestine should be a national home for us, the Hebrew language should be recognized as the national language, together with the Arab language. Total freedom will be given to Jewish immigration and Jewish settlement and the management of immigration and settlement will be given over to the Jews themselves."

Kalvarisky complained of the plethora of Zionist declarations, which served to alarm the Arabs. The Arabs believed that the Jews wished to expel them from the country, he warned, and he told of his efforts to persuade them that this was not the case. Arabs everywhere received him warmly, he claimed, adding, "I must confess to you that I found many intelligent young people among them. The Jerusalem Arabs have nothing to be ashamed of when they compare their young people to the Jews." All that was required of the Jews, he argued, was "to behave like a progressive cultured nation, and not to make any distinction between one religion and another." He suggested that they learn Arabic, noting that he had established, in Tiberias, a school in which Jewish and Arab children studied together in Hebrew, Arabic, and English.[35] As long as the Jews don't do to the Arabs what they don't want done to themselves by the gentiles in the Diaspora, and so long as they did not build their homes "on the ruin of others," there was a chance for détente, Kalvarisky concluded.

A discussion ensued. Efraim Gissin, a farmer from Petach Tikva and a volunteer in the Jewish Legion, said, "Let's not fool ourselves. We know the Arabs. . . . 'Friendship' with the Arab 'people' is impossible!" Yosef Sprinzak of the nonsocialist Labor party HaPoel HaTzair scoffed, "Maybe we should wear a tarbush or an Arab headdress? No, that we will not do! It's ridiculous to demand that our Jews learn Arabic when most of us still don't know Hebrew." David Remez, also a member of the labor movement, said it was necessary to create the best possible relations with the Arabs but also "to keep contact as near as possible to the minimum," articulating what would come to be called the policy of separation. "Remez is right," said a man named Blumenfeld. "We have to minimize our contacts. We need to bring about a situation in which only Jews

...in in Palestine and we manage all aspects of life." A speaker named Shochat thought the whole discussion was superfluous: "Have we solved all our other problems yet?"

On a different occasion, David Ben-Gurion said, "Everybody sees the problem in relations between the Jews and the Arabs. But not everybody sees that there's no solution to it. There is no solution! . . . The conflict between the interests of the Jews and the interests of the Arabs in Palestine cannot be resolved by sophisms. I don't know of any Arabs who would agree to Palestine being ours—even if we learn Arabic . . . and I have no need to learn the Arabic language. Woe to us if we have to conduct our lives in Arabic. On the other hand, I don't see why 'Mustafa' should learn Hebrew. . . . There's a national question here. We want the country to be ours. The Arabs want the country to be theirs." Both peoples, Ben-Gurion concluded, should wait for decisions made by the great powers at the Versailles peace conference.[36]

4.

The peace conference that convened at Versailles in January 1919 was the pinnacle of Weizmann's diplomatic achievements. He managed to ensure that the British would remain in Palestine. The conference met to determine, among other things, the fate of the former Ottoman Empire. Weizmann, at the head of the Zionist delegation, pleaded for the international ratification of the Balfour Declaration. As a result, the League of Nations agreed to grant a mandate to the British, empowering them to govern Palestine, that included an explicit responsibility to help the Jews establish a national home in the country. The mandate was Weizmann's own personal achievement.

Prime Minister Lloyd George and Foreign Secretary Balfour continued to view Weizmann as a leader possessed of some mysterious, world-encompassing power to pull the strings of history. Britain, together with the rest of Europe, had endured one of the most dramatic periods in its history. Close to a million British soldiers had been killed in the war and two million wounded; the Spanish influenza epidemic had cut a swath through Europe; millions were out of work. Britain was in a state of shell shock, forced to confront a new world, new values, and new ways of life that were causing much agony. With all this, doors stayed open to Weizmann: the prime minister and all the other officials made time to see and hear him whenever he asked for their attention.

To prepare the case he would put before the peace conference, Weizmann had convened an advisory panel, headed by Herbert Samuel, which held discussions about opening the country to Jewish immigration and the purchase of land for settlements. Weizmann was very clear about the Zionist movement's aim: Palestine would be a Jewish state. Perhaps it would take ten years or twenty, twenty-five or thirty, but it would happen. He compared the struggle for Palestine to a fencing match. Several army officers and government officials were present at the meetings, and one complained that it was hardly proper to provide advice to a man who was essentially a foreign agent. Samuel promised that no one would know of the discussions' content.[37] His assumption was that British and Zionist interests were one and the same. These meetings and others like them enabled Weizmann to evaluate, with a large measure of precision, what he could expect to achieve at the peace conference.

The document the Zionist delegation finally submitted to the conference in Versailles was a compromise, particularly with regard to the movement's ultimate goal. The Jewish community in Palestine had grappled with the wording. The original formulation of the "Claim of the Jewish People" asserted, "Palestine should become [the Jewish people's] national home." Ze'ev Jabotinsky had altered the text by hand to read, "Palestine should once again become a Jewish commonwealth." The final claim submitted to the peace conference attempted to satisfy all camps by postponing the demand for a "commonwealth" but not omitting it. "Palestine shall be placed under such political, administrative, and economic conditions as will secure the establishment there of the Jewish National Home and ultimately render possible the creation of an autonomous Commonwealth."[38] In Versailles, when Weizmann was asked to say what he meant by the term "national home," he replied that the country should be Jewish in the same way that France is French and England English. That, he said, was "the most triumphant moment of my life."[39]

By the time the final wording of the Mandate was agreed on, in July 1922, the Zionists had experienced a series of disappointments. The major setback was that they had to concede a large portion of the land of Israel as they defined it. The Zionist dream map submitted to the conference had included southern Lebanon, the Golan Heights, and a large area east of the Jordan River. In the end, the area designated by the British for the Jewish national home was half the size of the land on the map.[40]

The discrepancy between the Zionists' demands and what they actually received continued as a source of resentment. But, as in the past, the Zionists could comfort themselves with having achieved the most important thing. The fight had not been easy. Weizmann, a self-taught diplomat, had to overcome countless obstacles, including the impatience of the Jewish community in Palestine and attempts made by non-Zionist Jews to keep the peace conference from adopting the Zionist program.[41] Hardest of all had been the fight against Zionism's opponents in London. For a while there was a possibility that the United States, rather than Britain, would assume control of Palestine. The episode was ultimately of negligible historical importance, but it does fire the imagination.

The mandatory system was designed to give colonialism a cleaner, more modern look. The Allied powers refrained from dividing up the conqueror's spoils as in the past; rather they invited themselves to serve as "trustees" for backward peoples, with the ostensible purpose of preparing them for independence. This new form of colonialism was said to incorporate international law, as well as the principles of democracy and justice, and respect the wishes of the inhabitants of each country. Awarded by the League of Nations, mandates could, theoretically, be revoked by it.[42] In reality though, the postwar system was merely a reworking of colonial rule.

The conventional wisdom in London was that the empire should not be expanded. *Round Table*, a journal published by a circle with major influence over British foreign policy, urged the United States to assume part of the responsibility for the new world order, and in this context suggested that it accept the Mandate for Palestine. The author believed that the United States' "vast Jewish population preeminently fits her to protect Palestine." Lord Balfour and other ministers had once voiced a similar notion, and the idea was current among several members of the military administration as well. Ronald Storrs told Consul Ballobar that he thought the plan a good one, but Ballobar believed that the English would not leave Palestine even if they were shot in the feet.[43]* Lloyd George discussed the proposal with President Wilson's chief aide, Colonel Edward M. House, who was not enthusiastic. The United States did not know how to run colonies, he said. Colonialism required a special skill that the

---

*Ballobar himself was about to return home. As one of his last activities, he ate supper with General Allenby; the general bored him, he wrote. Before he left, the Jews of Jerusalem held several farewell parties in his honor, and they presented him with an honorary scroll that described him as a savior.[44]

United States lacked. The Philippines, he noted, had not been a success story.[45]

Some Americans conceded one argument in favor of governing Palestine. If the Jews were to receive their own state, maybe they would in exchange halt the Bolshevik revolution, which was threatening to spread to other countries. In his diary, Colonel House summed up a conversation with Balfour on the subject. "[Balfour] is inclined to believe that nearly all Bolshevism and disorder of that sort is directly traceable to Jews. I suggested putting them, or the best of them, in Palestine, and holding them responsible for the orderly behaviour of Jews throughout the world. Balfour thought the plan had possibilities," House wrote. House later discussed the idea with Wilson himself.[46]

The Zionists opposed U.S. control of the country on the grounds that American democracy ran counter to the plan for a national home. "Democracy in America," explained a publication issued by the Zionist Organization in London,

> too commonly means majority rule without regard to diversities of types or stages of civilisation or differences of quality. Democracy in that sense has been called the melting pot in which that quantitatively lesser is assimilated into the quantitatively greater. This doubtless is natural in America, and works on the whole very well. But if the American idea were applied as an American administration might apply it to Palestine, what would happen? The numerical majority in Palestine today is Arab, not Jewish. Qualitatively, it is a simple fact that the Jews are now predominant in Palestine, and given proper conditions they will be predominant quantitatively also in a generation or two. But if the crude arithmetical conception of democracy were to be applied now or at some early stage in the future to Palestinian conditions, the majority that would rule would be the Arab majority, and the task of establishing and developing a great Jewish Palestine would be infinitely more difficult.[47]

The problem at the heart of the Zionist claim was rarely articulated so clearly: the Zionist dream ran counter to the principles of democracy. The Zionists sometimes argued that they were speaking in the name of fifteen million Jews against half a million Arabs. The fact that these Jews had not yet "returned home" did not diminish their right to determine the fate of their country.[48]

Balfour saw another way around the issue. After all, the problem was only temporary. The Jews would soon be a majority in the country. Furthermore, Balfour judged, the Arabs would not in any case establish a democratic government. According to Weizmann, "Only those who had some notion of the structure of Arab life understood how farcical was the proposal to vest political power in the hands of the small Arab upper class in the name of democracy." But when it was suggested that the country's Arab inhabitants be asked what they thought, Balfour objected. He knew what they would say, and the right to express their opinion would create difficulties for the establishment of the Jewish national home.[49]

The suggestion to consult the Palestinian Arabs had come from Howard Bliss, son of the founders of the American University in Beirut and an old acquaintance of President Wilson's. Bliss hoped that the country would be handed over to the United States, and he traveled to the Paris Peace Conference ill with tuberculosis and close to death to meet with Wilson. His last request, he told the president, was that the Arabs in Palestine be asked what they wanted. Prince Faisal, also in Paris, was concerned about the extent of French influence in the region. Determined to keep France out of Palestine, he too suggested sending a commission to find out how the country's Arabs felt.

Thus was born the King-Crane Commission. Henry Churchill King, the president of Oberlin College in Ohio, was a church and missionary activist and a leader of the Young Men's Christian Association. Charles Crane was an industrialist and businessman from Chicago, one of President Wilson's supporters. The commission traveled throughout Palestine and heard from Arabs everywhere that they wanted American rule. Even the Bedouin in the desert, Crane later wrote, said they wanted the Americans to come and do for them what they had done for the Filipinos. The Zionists treated the King-Crane Commission with all due seriousness, submitting to it large amounts of material meant to prove that only the British could rule Palestine. They even purchased the signatures of several dozen Arabs in support of the Zionist position.[50]

Speaking to Ronald Storrs, Khalil al-Sakakini said, "I will not conceal from you that nearly the entire public wishes the Mandate to be given to the U.S., because they have seen that England promised to give the Jews Palestine as a national home. They have also seen how the English act in the country—they encourage the Zionist movement." He further explained that the Palestinian Arabs did not want England because that would mean France would get Syria, and they did not want the region divided between the two. "We want the country to be under the sponsorship of a single power, and so we will preserve our unity. . . . The country that saves us from Zionism and from partition—that country we will prefer above all others."

But Sakakini was quite sure that the Arabs would not in any case be allowed to choose the regime they wished. There was no chance that Palestine would receive independence, because the powers had decided it was unable to govern itself. He did not believe that American rule was a real possibility: America was too far away and had no interests in the country. When it came down to it, there were only the British.[51]

The King-Crane Commission concluded that a majority of the country's inhabitants wanted American rule and made its recommendations accordingly. Its report was completed in time to bring joy to Howard Bliss a few days before he died, but Wilson never saw it. He had already fallen ill and would soon cease functioning as president. The report was filed away and first published several years later, as a great scoop, by an American newspaper.[52]

5.

Shortly after his meeting with Weizmann near Aqaba, Prince Faisal went to Paris to represent Arab interests. Felix Frankfurter, among the leaders of the American Jewish community, arranged an interview for him with President Wilson. Sometime later, Faisal met again with Weizmann, and together they signed a document that contained Faisal's consent to the creation of a Jewish majority in Palestine, provided he received a large and independent Arab kingdom.

Major J. N. Camp, deputy to Palestine's chief political officer, contended that the agreement was not worth the paper it was written on nor the effort expended on getting the two men to sign. If, however, the document were to become public, it would turn into a noose around Faisal's neck. The Arabs would consider him a traitor. "No greater mistake could be made than to regard Faisal as a representative of Palestinian Arabs," Camp wrote. "He is in favour of them so long as he embodies Arab nationalism and represents their views, but would no longer have any power over them if they thought he had made any sort of agreement with Zionists and means to abide by it." Camp's evaluation depended in part on conversations with Sakakini in which Sakakini had voiced three nationalist "no"s: no to Zionism, no to the division of Faisal's Arabian empire, no to Jewish immigration.[53]

Upon returning home, Faisal entered Damascus and in March 1920 crowned himself king of Greater Syria, which, in theory, included Palestine. Weizmann considered the gesture a plot hatched by British military officers in Palestine who opposed the Jewish national home.[54] Once the French took control of Syria, they ejected Faisal; the English allowed him to stay in Palestine for a short while, along with his dozen assistants, twenty-five wives and concubines, 175 bodyguards, two automobiles, twenty-five horses, and four tons of baggage. The exiled king lived in Haifa in the home of Frances Newton, an Englishwoman, receiving delegations of admirers and granting interviews to the press.[55] After a while, he moved on to Europe and eventually became king of Iraq.

The agreement between Weizmann and Faisal has been cited many times as proof that it was possible for Zionism and moderate Arabs to accommodate each other.[56] Mordechai Ben-Hillel Hacohen, however, never trusted Jewish-Arab agreements. "The Arab—his promise is no promise, his agreement is no agreement," he wrote in his diary when Weizmann told him about his planned trip to Aqaba. He sincerely hoped that the Zionist enterprise would not be dependent on the consent of the Arabs.[57] In the three years that followed Weizmann's meeting with Faisal, the confrontation in Palestine turned bloody in the Galilee, in Jerusalem, and in Jaffa, and the Jews suffered heavy losses. Those experiences—traumatic and formative—would shape relations between Jews and Arabs in the decades that followed, sending a clear signal: the conflict with the Arabs would be decided not by words but by force.

6.

On Monday morning, March 1, 1920, several hundred Arabs gathered at the gate of Tel Hai, an isolated Jewish farm in the upper Galilee. The area was then in limbo—the Turks had been defeated, and Britain and France had agreed that the upper Galilee would be included in the French sphere of influence. The arrangement was temporary, since no one really knew who would control the area in the end. Bands of armed men roamed around—soldiers, freedom fighters, adventurers, thugs, highway robbers. It was hard to know who was who. The Arabs who collected outside the Tel Hai courtyard had been in pursuit of some French soldiers and believed them to be hiding with the Jews. The Arabs demanded to search the yard.

Slightly more than one hundred Jews lived in the upper Galilee then, most of them young men, a minority women, all laborers, herders, and farmers. They had first settled in Metulla, near Mount Hermon, then spread among three nearby sites, one of them Tel Hai. The settlers saw themselves as pioneers and emissaries of the Jewish people; in their view, their presence on the land was a national mission, a step toward realizing a dream. They stayed put as long as they could, despite tensions with their Arab neighbors. Some had been born in Palestine, some came from Eastern Europe, and some had arrived from America with the Jewish Legion. They were armed.

Their inclination was to steer clear of local trouble, but that was impossible. From time to time they had given shelter to Arabs, or allowed French soldiers to stay on their land. When tension in the area had increased, Jewish leaders were divided on whether to send defense forces to the Galilee or to instruct the settlers to leave. This was one of those fundamental doubts that periodically tormented the Jewish community. Ze'ev Jabotinsky, one of the more militant voices, judged that there was no way to defend the settlers of the upper Galilee. He demanded that they be told so and moved south. Since the World War, martyrdom had been severely devalued, he wrote.

David Ben-Gurion opposed Jabotinsky: if the Jews fled the upper Galilee they would soon be forced to leave all of Palestine. The dispute quickly developed into an argument over politics and fundamental, existential values—who was a patriot and "for" the Galilee, who was a defeatist and "against" it.[58] In the end, a Zionist delegation, which included David Eder, went up to the Galilee. By the time the delegation arrived, it was too late.

Exactly what happened at Tel Hai on the morning of March 1, 1920, has never quite been understood. There were no French soldiers hiding in the farm that day, and the Jews at Tel Hai put up no resistance to being searched by the Arabs. One of the settlers fired a shot into the air, a signal to call in reinforcements from Kfar Giladi, two kilometers away. Hearing the shots, some ten men set out to assist the settlers at Tel Hai. They were led by Yosef Trumpeldor.

Famous throughout Palestine and admired as a hero, Trumpeldor was a dentist by training. He had served as an officer in the Russian army and had lost his left arm in the Russo-Japanese War.[59] His handicap made a new profession necessary, and he began to study law at the University of St. Petersburg. At the same time, he gathered around him a group of young Zionists, and in 1912 they came to Palestine. At first Trumpeldor joined a farm on the shores of the Sea of Galilee; later he worked as a laborer at Kibbutz Deganya. During the World War he left Palestine to fight with the Allies and was instrumental in setting up the Jewish Legion.

Upon being discharged, Trumpeldor returned home to St. Petersburg, or Petrograd as it had become known in his absence. He organized Jews to defend themselves and began to engage in Jewish politics in the framework of Hehalutz—the Pioneer—a socialist-Zionist party he founded. Several dozen of the party's members planned to settle in Palestine, and Trumpeldor went in advance to prepare for their arrival. He was visiting Metulla at the time of the attack on Tel Hai, and was due to return to Russia soon.

When he reached Tel Hai, Trumpeldor took command. He may have opened fire, and he may have done so too soon. Perhaps it had not been necessary to fire any shots at all. One of the first reports from Tel Hai speaks of "misunderstanding on both sides."[60] Whatever the case, at some point everyone was shooting at everyone else. Trumpeldor was wounded, first in his hand and then in his stomach. Only toward evening did a doctor arrive, and then an attempt was made to evacuate Trumpeldor to Kfar Giladi. He died on the way. Five other Jews were also killed. All were buried in Kfar Giladi in two common graves: four men in one, two women in the other. Five Arabs were also killed in the fighting. The settlers at Tel Hai and Kfar Giladi left.

During the days that followed, Trumpeldor's last words were quoted—in several different versions: "No matter, it is worth dying for the country"; "It is worth dying for the land of Israel"; "It is good to die for our country." A year later one of the newspapers wrote, "A year has passed, and the marvel of a national myth is blooming on the graves of Kfar Giladi." On the wall in the nursery school at Kibbutz Hulda a sign was hung, woven of green branches, that read, "It is good to die for our country." Beneath the words was Trumpeldor's picture. The message of Tel Hai, the newspaper wrote, was the importance of holding on to the soil of the homeland, through the power of thousands of young men and women.[61] Thus Tel Hai became a legend; like many national legends, its potency far outstripped the strength of its heroes.*

---

*As the first anniversary of the Tel Hai incident approached, the weekly *HaPoel HaTzair* published a different interpretation of Trumpeldor's last words: "It is better to die for the homeland than to die for a foreign land, but it is better to live for the homeland."[62]

The Zionist movement needed its heroes and martyrs, and it needed them at that moment, just as the dream of Jewish independence was on its way to being realized. Had the events at Tel Hai not happened, the Zionists would have needed to invent them. Settlement, especially in agricultural areas, was a fundamental element of the national identity, like the Hebrew language. An attack on a settlement was thus an attack on the very foundation of the Zionist collective. As a slogan, "It is good to die for our country" elevated the nation and the land over the lives of individuals.

Tel Hai also came to symbolize the principle that no settlement should be abandoned. The fact that two settlements were evacuated after the attack was generally not mentioned. The defeat was turned into a victory.[63] Trumpeldor, a hero in life, a modern Judah Maccabee, was a fitting mythic figure. No less important, he had belonged to the labor movement, which would soon take control of Jewish public life and monopolize the formulation of its value and symbols. The writer Yosef Chaim Brenner eulogized the Yishuv's first mythological hero in biblical terms: "Yosef Trumpeldor—the beloved and the handsome, the bold and the chosen, the symbol of pure heroism, slain upon thy high places. His blood was spilt by the sons of evil. . . . Is it good to die for our country? It is good! Happy be he who dies knowing this—and at Tel Hai he lays his head to rest."[64] Sometime later, a huge stone statue was placed at the site, a lion.

Labor leader Berl Katznelson wrote a eulogy for the dead fighters that came to embody the Yishuv's national consciousness: "May the nation of Israel remember the pure souls of its faithful and brave sons and daughters, people of labor and peace, who followed the plow and gave their lives for the honor of Israel and the love of Israel. May the people of Israel remember and be blessed in its seed and mourn the radiance of the lost ones and the delight of heroism and the sanctification of desire and the devotion that fell in the heavy battle. May the mourning be not stilled or comforted or pass until the day Israel returns to redeem its despoiled land."*

The myth of Tel Hai not only provided the Jewish community in Palestine with a tale of heroism, it also served to divert attention from the failure of the leadership to help the settlers in the upper Galilee. In a letter to

---

* Modeled on the ritual memorial prayer, Katznelson's eulogy was manifestly secular: it contains no mention of God. It was later revised as a national-religious prayer. The references to the labor movement were removed and "May the people of Israel remember" was replaced by "May God remember."[65]

Weizmann, Eder warned that the incident should not be presented as proof of enmity between Jews and Arabs. The Zionists should be very careful not to harm the Arabs, who were also seeking martyrs, he warned.[66] A *Ha'aretz* correspondent in Damascus described a mass memorial service in honor of seven Arab nationalists who had been executed by the Turkish regime. All the speakers claimed the dead commanded the living to fight the Zionist movement to the death. "There is no death more beautiful than death for the sake of the homeland," one of them declared.[67]

— • • —

Nebi Musa, 1920

1.

In the early morning hours of Sunday, April 4, 1920, Khalil al-Sakakini walked over to Jerusalem's municipal building, outside the Old City's Jaffa Gate. It was his custom to do this each year, to watch the Nebi Musa procession. Passover, the Greek Orthodox Easter, and the traditional Muslim procession to a shrine associated with Moses—or Nebi Musa to Arabs—all happened to fall that year during the same week of the "cruelest month." The outbreak of violence that marred the celebrations, driven by the mixture of "memory and desire" evoked by T. S. Eliot, was in essence the opening shot in the war over the land of Israel.[1]

"The Nebi Musa festival in Jerusalem is political, not religious," Sakakini wrote. At this time of year, Christians from all the countries of the world would flock to Jerusalem, he explained, and so Muslims had to mass in Jerusalem as well, to prevent the Christians from overwhelming the city. They came from all over the country as well as from neighboring countries, tribe after tribe, caravan after caravan, with their flags and weapons, as if they were going to war, Sakakini wrote. The Turkish authorities used to position a cannon next to the Lion's Gate in the Old City and escort the procession with large contingents of soldiers and police. The religious aspect of the holiday was designed only to draw the masses, otherwise they would not come. Food was handed out for the same reason, he wrote.

Sakakini liked to watch the celebrants, and he liked the poems they chanted. He believed that poetry was good for fostering national identity and proposed that every village establish a "Council of Poets," which would compose new works and teach the village's young people the traditional dances. "We will teach them to use weapons and to dance with the sword and other things to ensure their hearts will reawaken; the era of chivalry will renew itself and the nation will be fired in a new forge," he wrote.*

When he arrived at the city square, sixty or seventy thousand people had already congregated there. Some were from Hebron and some from Nablus. They carried banners and waved flags. The VIPs stood on the balcony of Jerusalem's Arab Club, but not all of them were able to deliver their speeches because of the commotion and noise. One man angrily tore up the text of his speech.

The time was now about 10:30. In the Old City, Arab toughs had been brawling in the streets for more than an hour. Gangs surged through the walkways of the Jewish Quarter, attacking whomever they passed; one small boy was injured on the head. They broke into Jewish stores and looted. The Jews hid.[2]

Meanwhile, the speeches from the balcony of the Arab Club continued. Someone waved a picture of Faisal, who had just crowned himself king of Greater Syria. The crowd shouted "Independence! Independence!" and the speakers condemned Zionism; one was a young boy of thirteen. The mayor, Musa Kazim al-Husseini, spoke from the balcony of the municipal building; Aref al-Aref, the editor of the newspaper *Suriya al-Janubia* ("Southern Syria"), delivered his speech on horseback. The crowd roared, "Palestine is our land, the Jews are our dogs!" In Arabic, that rhymes.

No one knew what exactly set off the riots. In testimony given to a British court of inquiry, people said that a Jew had pushed an Arab carrying a flag, or that he'd spat on the flag, or that he'd tried to grab it. In another version, the violence began when an Arab pointed at a Jew who was passing by and said, "Here's a Zionist, son of a dog." Many testified that Arabs had attacked an elderly Jewish man at the entrance to the Amdursky Hotel, beating him on the head with sticks. The man had col-

---

*The Nebi Musa celebrations led Sakakini to meditate on the difference between Arab and Jewish holidays. The Jews cry a lot because most of their holidays are in memory of catastrophes that have befallen them, he posited, whereas the Muslims celebrate with great enthusiasm, with poetry, flags, and colorful parades. Sakakini drew a lesson from this: "A nation whose holidays are only occasions for crying has no future."

lapsed, his head covered with blood. Someone had tried to rescue him but was stabbed. People said they had heard gunfire. "The furor almost turned into madness," Sakakini wrote. Everyone was shouting, "The religion of Mohammed was founded by the sword," and waving sticks and daggers. Sakakini managed to get out of the crowd unhurt. "I went to the municipal garden, my soul disgusted and depressed by the madness of mankind," he wrote.[3]

2.

During the preceding year, relations between Arabs and Jews in the city had worsened considerably. A confrontation had taken place between Mayor Husseini and Menachem Ussishkin, who had been appointed head of the Zionist Commission when Chaim Weizmann returned to London. David Eder, who had always managed the commission's affairs in Weizmann's absence, did not like his new boss. The two had little in common: Eder was very British, Ussishkin very Russian. Eder was often quiet, Ussishkin loquacious. Eder was temperate, almost inconspicuous, while Ussishkin was bombastic, insistent on getting the respect he thought was his due. Eder believed that the success of Zionism depended on working with restraint and avoiding flagrant spectacles so as not to aggravate the Arab population. Ussishkin believed in large demonstrations of national pride. Inevitably, his introductory meeting with the mayor was hostile from the start, and it quickly deteriorated into explicit talk of war.

The two men needed an interpreter—Ussishkin spoke Hebrew, Husseini Arabic. Ussishkin needled him: How is it, he asked, that the streets of Jerusalem are full of potholes and thick with such awful dust? The mayor explained that the city engineers were unable to pave the streets with asphalt because the streets were not flat. Furthermore, asphalt is dangerous, he said, and people and animals could slip on it. Ussishkin would not let up. Certainly it must be possible to level the roadbed, he said. The mayor explained that there was no money.

Then Husseini asked how things were going at the Paris Peace Conference. Ussishkin said there was still no treaty but everything was pretty much settled: Syria would be put under French protection, and Palestine would remain with the British. "The Arabs will not consent to that," Husseini responded. Ussishkin interrupted him. "Look, I said everything is settled," he repeated, and mentioned that Prince Faisal had agreed to the Jewish national home in Palestine. As far as Husseini was concerned, the Arabs in Palestine had not authorized Faisal to make concessions in their name. He had nothing against the Jews, he said. Those who already lived in the country were welcome, but the Arabs opposed the immigration of more Jews. He tried to explain to Ussishkin that style was important. The Zionists did not understand Arab culture, he said, and they spoke to the Arabs in a contemptuous and patronizing way.

For example, the mayor went on, there was supposed to be a ceremony to commemorate the first anniversary of the British conquest and suddenly the Jews demanded that the invitations be printed in Hebrew. Ussishkin argued that Hebrew was the language of the majority of Jerusalem's residents, but Husseini was unimpressed. First, most of the Jews understood Arabic, he noted. Second, most of them did not understand Hebrew. Third, the demand to print the invitations in Hebrew was meant solely to force the municipality to give in to Zionist demands. The municipality would not give in.

Ussishkin did not deny that Jews had injured Arabs. These things could be resolved, he said, but on no account would the Jews concede their national demands. There was no room for compromise. We do not want war, he went on. In fact, we are doing everything to prevent war. Yet the Jews are not afraid of war, he said, if it is necessary. As his excellency knew, Ussishkin told the mayor, the Jews were currently equipped with everything needed for war. A war would hurt both sides, but the Arabs would suffer more, he concluded.

There was little left to say. Ussishkin reminded the mayor that the Jews had wandered the wilderness for forty years before reaching the Promised Land. Musa Kazim al-Husseini smiled. It had taken forty years because the Jews had not listened to Musa, he said, and suggested that they listen to Musa now, lest it take them another forty years to get where they wanted to go. Reporting back to the commission, Ussishkin summed up the meeting: Husseini was an enemy of the Jewish people.[4]

Throughout 1919, the leaders of the Jewish community warned the authorities of Arab plots against Jews. In Jaffa the Jews reported the activities of an Arab terrorist group called the Black Hand. Its members planned attacks on Jews in order to deter other Jews from settling in Palestine, the Zionist Commission claimed. And before the Nebi Musa festival that year the commission had warned the British authorities that the procession was liable to deteriorate into violence. In the end it passed without incident.[5] Then in the winter of 1920 the Arab leadership organized demonstrations calling for independence, condemning Zionism, and opposing the British. The authorities permitted the demonstrations, and thousands attended. The demonstrations were generally peaceful, although here and there some demonstrators and Jewish pedestrians exchanged blows.

As the day of the 1920 Nebi Musa celebration approached, the Zionist Commission again warned the authorities to expect disturbances. General Louis Bols, the chief administrative officer, promised that his forces were prepared for all eventualities. The Jewish residents of Jerusalem sent a representative to Governor Storrs to talk about the procession; he assured the man that everything would be done to prevent the celebration from degenerating into riots.[6]

Still the Jews were wary. "The pogrom is now liable to break out any day," Ze'ev Jabotinsky had written to Chaim Weizmann. Weizmann was on his way to Palestine from Egypt. When he arrived in Jerusalem he went to see General Allenby at the Augusta Victoria castle, where he found another guest, Herbert Samuel, who had come to assess the situation in Palestine on behalf of the British government. General Bols was there as well. Weizmann warned of the tension in the city. A pogrom is in the air, he said. Bols and Allenby reassured him that the army was in control of the situation, and wished him a good Passover. Weizmann went to Haifa to celebrate the Seder with his mother, who had recently settled in Palestine. His son Benjy, soon to be bar mitzvahed, was with him. After the Seder, they returned to Jerusalem.

An incident at the Church of the Holy Sepulchre gave a hint of what was to come. Richard Adamson, a soldier, found himself in a bizarre situation. He had been sent to keep order in the church, which is built over the supposed site of Jesus' grave. A large crowd of Christians had gathered for the traditional ceremony of the holy fire. Each year, fire would appear in a small cell close to the sepulchre; the fire supposedly came from heaven, an annual miracle. It is "a brilliant mystery," Ronald Storrs wrote, "half political, half pagan, marred sometimes by drunkenness, savagery, and murder." While Richard Adamson was keeping watch, the church door burst open and a throng of Arabs poured in. Adamson saw one man about to deal a death blow to the patriarch, but before he could do anything, the holy fire suddenly appeared. The thug retreated in panic and the patriarch's life was saved.[7]

The next day, a Sunday, Storrs went to St. George's Cathedral for Sunday worship, accompanied by his father and mother. At the end of the service, someone informed him of disturbances near the Jaffa Gate. "It was as though he had thrust a sword into my heart," Storrs later wrote. He rushed to the British headquarters, located in the Austrian hospice, near the Nablus Gate. General Bols had already summoned his staff for an emergency meeting. Without warning, Chaim Weizmann stormed into the room. He had just heard news of unrest in the city and demanded concerted action to restore order.[8] Weizmann was extremely upset and angry; he had, after all, given the British advance warning of the riots. Storrs reminded him that the Zionist Commission had warned him of riots the year before as well, yet everything had gone peacefully.

In truth, Storrs had blundered. A few days earlier, he had issued warnings to Arab community leaders, but had done nothing else. He would later argue that his critics did not understand the difficult circumstances: the Old City streets are steep, narrow, and winding, with many stairways—impassable to cars and horses, he explained. A whole family could be murdered out of sight or sound of police stationed not a hundred yards away. And then there was the city's psychology, Storrs claimed. In Jerusalem, the sudden clatter on the stones of an empty petrol tin could cause a panic. Finally, the police available to him were inexperienced and not properly trained. They weren't English, and many were Indian. Storrs had a total of 188 men, including just eight officers.[9]

Storrs could have learned from the experience of the Turks, who usually deployed thousands of soldiers to keep order during the Nebi Musa procession. The peaceful celebrations of the previous year should not have misled him. As a political man, he should have realized that the events of the previous weeks, including the incident at Tel Hai, the crowning of Faisal, and especially the heightened passions of nationalism, were liable to cause trouble, just as the Jewish representatives had warned and the assessments available to him had confirmed.[10] He failed not only in preventing the riots, but also in suppressing them: three days went by before they were stopped.

Several hundred Jews had spent the previous month organizing themselves for self-defense. Many of them belonged to the Maccabee sports club, and some had served in the Jewish Legion. Their training consisted largely of calisthenics and hand-to-hand combat with sticks. Khalil al-Sakakini saw them some hours after the Nebi Musa riots broke out, marching in formation, four abreast, carrying truncheons and singing. Sakakini mocked them, saying they reminded him of the words of a poet: "When the field has emptied, the coward sets out alone to war."[11]

In command was Ze'ev Jabotinsky, who had been discharged from the British army sometime earlier as an "indiscreet political speaker" and a "firebrand." Jabotinsky had given too many speeches and had inundated top officers with imperious letters, accusing them of hostility to the Zionist movement.[12] After his discharge, he and his wife, Johanna, and son, Eri, settled in Jerusalem, where Jabotinsky translated poetry and published articles in the daily newspaper *Ha'aretz*.

Jabotinsky had frequent guests. He lived in the center of town, not far from Feingold House, which served as Chaim Weizmann's residence in Jerusalem, and close to the offices of the Zionist Commission and the central post office. His house was a popular meeting place for commanders of the Jewish Legion, staff and members of the Zionist Commission, and the people of the Hadassah medical mission. Some of the guests took up residence on the ground floor, which housed a kind of studio apartment. Jabotinsky hosted writers and journalists, among them Ahad Ha'am and Itamar Ben-Avi, the son of the lexicographer Eliezer Ben-Yehuda. Ben-Avi, an advocate of the new secular Hebrew identity, thought the language should be written in the Latin alphabet; Jabotinsky agreed. Another guest was Pinhas Rutenberg, who had helped set up the Jewish Legion and been a minister in the Russian revolutionary government. Ronald Storrs compared Rutenberg to the Egyptian sphinx—his head was hard as granite, he wrote—and believed that in a time of crisis both Jews and Arabs would be willing to obey him. Rutenberg was involved in the initiative to organize Jewish self-defense in Jerusalem.

Jabotinsky made a point of training his volunteers in the open. He considered acting freely and visibly a matter of principle, defending his views against members of the labor movement, who wanted to set up an underground defense organization. Training and inspections were held in a schoolyard; on at least one occasion Jabotinsky took his people out for a parade through the city. Headquarters were in two rooms in the offices of the Zionist Commission, which donated the space. The commission kept the authorities informed about the enterprise and asked that the defenders be equipped with weapons. The British rejected the request.[13]

When the riots broke out, Jabotinsky and Rutenberg went to look for Storrs but couldn't find him; apparently the governor was still in church. Toward noon they met in the street. Storrs was a frequent guest of Jabotinsky's and also a friend of the family, especially fond of Eri. "No more gallant officer, no more charming and cultivated companion could have been imagined than Vladimir Jabotinsky," Storrs wrote in his memoirs, using Jabotinsky's Russian name. He also quoted an English translation of a poem by Chaim Nachman Bialik, "Take Me Under Your Wing," that Jabotinsky had prepared for him. But Storrs also believed that Jabotinsky was liable to bring Palestine to war.[14]*

Jabotinsky suggested deploying his self-defense group; Storrs demanded to know where he kept the group's weapons and ordered Jabotinsky and Rutenberg to hand over the pistols they were carrying. Actually, Storrs said, he should jail them for bearing arms. Then he asked the two men to come to his office later that afternoon to discuss the possibility of establishing an unarmed Jewish guard unit. One of Storrs's aides favored the idea; Storrs himself opposed it.

Then he changed his mind and instructed Jabotinsky to report to police headquarters in the Russian Compound together with two hundred of his men in order to be sworn in as deputies. The volunteers made their way to the compound, and Colonel Popham, Storrs's aide, began to administer the oath. Suddenly an order was received to desist. There was no need for the defense group, Popham was told, and the men were all sent home. The authorities had also invited Arab volunteers to join the security forces; these too were sent home.[16]

Rachel Yanait, a labor leader and educator, heard about the riots from her neighbors. That day David Ben-Gurion had come to visit her and her husband, Yitzhak Ben-Zvi. The three had talked politics until noon. Those weeks were the climax of a fairly stormy political campaign: the Jews in Palestine were electing representatives for the first national assembly. When they learned of the disturbances, Ben-Gurion and Ben-Zvi quickly headed toward the center of Jerusalem. The Arab landlord locked all the doors and closed the shutters. Yanait then decided to see what was happening in the Old City. She reasoned that if she dressed elegantly, she would not be arrested. From an old suitcase she took a dress she had worn only overseas and a small hat that had been her mother's back in the Ukraine. Then she set out, but not before shoving a pistol into her pocket.

She was allowed to enter the Old City and for some hours wandered around without any clear destination. The alleys of the marketplace were empty; from time to time she heard the sound of a mob. She got lost; a Russian nun passed by and Yanait asked her the way to the Jaffa Gate. The frightened nun did not answer and hurried on her way. Near the Holy Sepulchre she caught a brief glimpse of two soldiers carrying a wounded man on a stretcher. She thought she identified the two soldiers as Ben-

---

*In the manuscript of his book Storrs described Jabotinsky as a "brilliant and fascinating" man; in the printed version he changed the adjectives to "versatile and violent."[15]

Gurion and Ben-Zvi, but it must have been an illusion. Ben-Gurion in fact spent most of the day at the Zionist Commission's office outside the Old City. Yanait went on, saw Storrs from a distance, and then ran into Nachman Syrkin, a socialist Zionist thinker and Russian-born American in Palestine on a visit. They walked together to the Jewish Quarter and suddenly found themselves in a cloud of feathers. Arabs were ripping open the quilts and pillows of their victims; to Yanait and Syrkin this was a well-known sign of a pogrom.[17]

At the end of the first day the British imposed a night curfew; given the weakness of the police and the army, the curfew should probably have been enforced day and night. As Monday dawned, the disturbances began again and grew worse. Several dozen rioters had been arrested the night before but were allowed to attend morning prayer and then released. Arab toughs continued to attack passing Jews and break into Jewish homes, especially those in buildings where most of the residents were Arabs.

Rabbi Zorach Epstein related that vandals broke into his house and made off with everything. They took the mattresses, the blankets, the pillows, the quilts, the silver candlesticks, and his wife's jewelry. Then they raided the Toras Chaim Yeshiva, tearing up Torah scrolls, throwing them on the floor, and setting fire to the building. Two pedestrians were stabbed to death. The Old City was sealed off; even Jews who sought to flee were not allowed to leave. That afternoon martial law was declared. Private Richard Adamson later remembered that he and his comrades had frisked Arab women in particular. It turned out that most of the illicit weapons had been concealed on their bodies.[18]

The looting and burglary continued. A few homes were set on fire, and some tombstones were shattered. In the evening, the soldiers were evacuated from the Old City. A court of inquiry later termed this "an error of judgment." The Jews living in the Old City had not been trained to protect themselves and had no weapons; Jabotinsky's volunteers had concentrated their efforts outside the Old City.[19] That decision also turned out to be a mistake.

On Tuesday morning vandals burst into the courtyard of Hannah Yafeh, not far from the Gate of Forgiveness, leading to the Temple Mount in the Muslim Quarter. Three Jewish homes adjoined the courtyard; since the beginning of the riots their occupants had been virtually under siege. When the attackers broke down the doors, the residents fled to the upper story. The rioters smashed furniture and took valuables before ascending to the upper floor, where they began beating the Jews. Moshe Lifschitz was hit over the head with an iron rod and was critically injured. His children were beaten as well. Then the attackers took turns raping Lifschitz's two sisters, one twenty-five years old and married, the other fifteen.

In the meantime, two of Jabotinsky's men, both carrying hidden pistols, had put on white coats and entered the Old City in a Hadassah ambulance. One, Nehemia Rubitzov, had served in the Jewish Legion, having enlisted in the United States. Originally from the Ukraine, he had immigrated to America, sold newspapers, worked as a tailor, been active in the Jewish tailor's union, and studied at the University of Chicago. Years later, Ben-Gurion claimed that he had personally enlisted Rubitzov in the legion. When Rubitzov first applied to the legion he was turned down because of a minor leg problem. He tried his luck at another enlistment office, changing his name to Rabin for the purpose, and was accepted.

Upon entering the Old City, he and his comrade, Zvi Nadav, tried to organize the residents to protect themselves, and instructed them to prepare rocks and place boiling water on their roofs to throw at the rioters. Then they helped get some of the Jews out of the Old City. One of them, Rosa Cohen, was Mordechai Ben-Hillel Hacohen's niece. She had arrived from Russia only three months previously. Red Rosa, as she was known, was a Bolshevik who had managed a military explosives factory in Russia. No Zionist, her intention had been to settle in the United States, but she had attached herself to a group of young immigrants who had come to Palestine on the *Ruslan*.* She and Nehemia Rabin would fall in love, marry, and within two years have a son, Yitzhak.[21]

Outside the Old City, several members of Jabotinsky's self-defense force got caught up in a gunfight with some gypsies who were camped between the Jewish neighborhood of Mea She'arim and the Arab quarter of Sheikh Jarrah. Khalil al-Sakakini was a witness: "I hate the Jew when he assaults an Arab and I hate the Arab when he assaults a Jew and I hate all humanity when it is a humanity of hatred and hostility," he wrote. At some point, the Muslim-Christian Association demanded that Storrs resign and the Jews be disarmed.[22]

The British army sent several men to search Jews for weapons. One of the places they looked was in Chaim Weizmann's apartment, where they

---

*The *Ruslan* renewed the link between Palestine and Russia, which had been severed during the war, and symbolized hope for the reinforcement of the Jewish community. It was a kind of Jewish *Mayflower*—several of the ship's passengers went on to become famous, among them the poet Rachel and the historian Joseph Klausner.[20]

found nothing. At Jabotinsky's house, however, they found three rifles, two pistols, and 250 rounds of ammunition. Altogether, nineteen men were arrested and imprisoned, but not Jabotinsky. Indignant, he went to Kishla, the prison at the Jaffa Gate, accompanied by attorney Mordechai Eliash, and demanded that he be arrested. The police obliged, but a military judge released him because he had not been at home when the rifles were found. A few hours later, he was arrested again.

Storrs came to the jail to see for himself that Jabotinsky was being properly treated. He personally led his friend to a more comfortable cell; he tried to be polite, Jabotinsky later wrote, "like the owner of a palace ushering a guest into his anteroom." Storrs ordered that his prisoner receive a bed with a mattress and a washbasin. Jabotinsky's food was brought to him from the adjacent Amdursky Hotel; he was served wine as well.

Afterward, Storrs went to Jabotinsky's apartment and, with the help of Johanna, his wife, packed two suitcases with clothing and other items, including paper and a fountain pen. When he brought all this to the jail, the governor opened the suitcases for a security check before they were given to Jabotinsky, all according to the rules. Jabotinsky later wrote, "You have to live with the English for seven straight years, as I did, in order to become familiar with this muddle and this chaos from which, like a swamp plant, little by little, without rules and without any predetermined pace, their order develops, sometimes belatedly." In this incident, though, the muddle of Jabotinsky's arrest, release, rearrest, and preferential treatment exemplifies the conflicts, the contradictions, the hesitations, and the helplessness that characterized British rule from the very beginning.

Jabotinsky was brought to trial a few days later, accused of possessing weapons and disturbing the peace. The chief witness for the prosecution was Ronald Storrs. The hearing was confused and rather comical: Storrs claimed he "did not remember" Jabotinsky telling him about the self-defense organization.[23]

After the riot, Storrs went to pay an official condolence call to the chairman of the Zionist Commission, Menachem Ussishkin. "I have come to express to his honor my regrets for the tragedy that has befallen us," he began. "What tragedy?" Ussishkin asked. "I mean the unfortunate events that have occurred here in recent days," Storrs said. "His excellency means the pogrom," Ussishkin suggested. Storrs replied emotionally that there had been no pogrom. He knew very well what a pogrom was—an attack on Jews under the sponsorship of the authorities.

Characteristically, Ussishkin did not let up. "You, Colonel, are an expert on matters of management and I am an expert on the rules of pogroms." There was no difference, he asserted, between the riot in Jerusalem and the Kishinev pogrom. He was not saying this, Ussishkin said, to Governor Storrs but to Storrs the English gentleman. What depressed him was not the death of a few Jews—in Russia more had died. He was despondent because of the betrayal. History would remember that the pogrom had occurred during the tenure of Ronald Storrs. How would the colonel feel if his sister had been raped, or his daughter-in-law? His regrets were useless and his explanations were of no help. He, Ussishkin, could not accept them, just as the world did not accept the Jewish explanations about the crucifixion of Jesus.

Storrs asked whether he should resign. Ussishkin said it was too late. Had he been a decent man, he would have resigned when the riots broke out. Storrs made no response. He hoped that the next time they would meet under happier circumstances, he said, and went on his way.[24]*

Jabotinsky had meanwhile been convicted, among other things, of possessing the pistol he had handed over to Storrs on the first day of the riots. Sentenced to fifteen years' imprisonment, he was sent by train to a jail in Egypt; his guards put him in a first-class carriage. The day after arriving they returned him to Palestine, to the prison in the fortress of Acre. No one knows why he was sent to Egypt or why he was brought back; on his return trip he again traveled first-class. His trial and sentence created an uproar. The London papers, including the *Times,* protested, and there were questions in Parliament. General "Squib" Congreve, commander of the British forces in Palestine and Egypt, did not wait for the *Times* editorial. Even before it appeared he wrote to Field Marshal Henry Wilson, complaining about the sentences given to the Jews convicted of possessing weapons. "They [are] much too severe compared with those passed . . . for worse offenses and I shall have to greatly reduce them. Jabotinsky to one year instead of fifteen and the other nineteen to six months instead of three years."[16]

The final tally was 5 Jews dead, 216 wounded, 18 critically; 4 Arabs had been killed and 23 wounded, 1 critically; 7 soldiers had been wounded, all apparently beaten by the Arab mob. One of the Arab dead was a small

---

*By the time he wrote his memoirs, Storrs had managed to recover his sardonic tone. His audiences with "Czar Menachem" were among the most difficult parts of his job. "When he was announced for an interview I braced myself to take my punishment like a man," he wrote.[25]

girl. She had been shot before the eyes of Edward Keith-Roach. He had left the Church of the Holy Sepulchre after services and walked into sudden shooting. The girl fell from the window of her house—a stray bullet had hit her in the temple.[27]

3.

More than two hundred people were put on trial in the aftermath of Nebi Musa, among them thirty-nine Jews. One of the rapists who had assaulted the Lifschitz sisters was sentenced to fifteen years in prison. Haj Amin al-Husseini and Aref al-Aref were each given ten years for incitement to riot, but they were no longer in the city—the two of them had fled.[28]* Mayor Husseini was removed from his post and replaced by Ragheb al-Nashashibi, a member of a powerful Jerusalem family involved in a long and bitter feud with the Husseinis.

"There had been no clashes like these for a hundred years," Moshe Smilansky wrote in *Ha'aretz,* asserting that the conflict was one between two nations. The same newspaper ran an article by the historian Joseph Klausner containing the warning "If the Arabs imagine that they can provoke us to war and that because we are few they will easily win, they are making a huge error. Our campaign will include all 13 million Jews in all the countries of the world. And everyone knows how many statesmen, how many opinion makers, how many people of great wisdom and great wealth and great influence we have in Europe and America."

Not only did Klausner's statement exploit yet again the image of the world-dominating Jews, but it was also among the first expressions of the reversal that would eventually take place in Zionism's purpose. Instead of seeing the Jewish state as a means of saving the world's Jews, the Zionists were now demanding that the world's Jews defend the Jews of Palestine.[31]

The Zionists blamed the riots on the British: "This regime has declared open war on the Jews of Palestine," wrote one labor movement leader.[32]†

---

*Aref al-Aref, before his departure, seems to have come to the conclusion that attacks on Jews harmed the Arab cause. "Let us work in the way our opponents are working: in order, discipline and courage," he said, according to an intelligence report by the Zionist Commission.[29] Al-Aref and Husseini both now tended to speak of the Arabs of Palestine as a separate entity, no longer as the inhabitants of "southern Syria." They would soon mean Jerusalem, not Damascus, when they spoke of "the capital." The Nebi Musa riots were thus not merely an expression of Palestinian Arab nationalism but also one of its catalysts.[30]

†The charge was published in one of the labor movement's periodicals. Berl Katznelson, the editor, was told to apologize. Katznelson refused. This led to a debate over freedom of expression and criticism in the Hebrew press.

General Allenby had to defend his men against an even more serious accusation: his political officer, Richard Meinertzhagen, claimed that several of the military administration's officers had initiated the riots to prove there was no chance of carrying out the Jewish national home policy. Allenby's chief of staff, Colonel Bertie Harry Waters-Taylor, had given Haj Amin al-Husseini explicit instructions on how to "show the world" that Palestine's Arabs would not stand for Jewish rule, Meinertzhagen maintained. The officers involved were antisemites and anti-Zionists, under the sway of Arabic romanticism, he charged. Meinertzhagen also called the riot a pogrom. Ten years previously he had visited Odessa, where he had stumbled into an anti-Jewish pogrom, and he had never gotten over the shock of it. He registered his accusations directly with Foreign Secretary Curzon. Allenby threatened to resign; Meinertzhagen was ordered out of Palestine.[33]

Meinertzhagen had his own reason for blaming the riots on his colleagues. Only four days before Nebi Musa, he had written to the Foreign Office that all was quiet. "I do not anticipate any immediate trouble in Palestine," he predicted.[34] Thus he attributed the events to a plot hatched by British officers. In his diary, Meinertzhagen sounds like something of a lunatic and is therefore a doubtful source for such a serious charge. But his accusations did represent a general feeling.*

The Zionist Commission tried to support the conspiracy theory with a line of circumstantial evidence. They noted that the Arab milkmen who had come to Mea She'arim that Sunday morning had demanded to be paid on the spot, which was unusual. They would no longer be coming to the neighborhood, they explained. Christian storekeepers had marked their establishments in advance with the sign of the cross, so they would not be looted by mistake.[36] An earlier commission report had accused Ronald Storrs of deliberately fanning the flames of Jewish-Arab tension, according to the time-honored British method of divide and rule. Storrs supported the Arabs because he was afraid that the Jews would take over the country and get rid of him, the report claimed, adding that one of Storrs's Arab aides had sabotaged Weizmann's attempt to purchase the Western Wall.[37]

The court of inquiry appointed to investigate the riots reached a more logical conclusion. Governor Storrs, it found, had failed because of over-

---

*Insurance agent Alter Levine gathered signatures of his acquaintances, all American citizens like himself, on a letter to the American Consul Otis Glazebrook to protest that the British had prevented the Jews from defending themselves.[35]

confidence; he had believed that the police force could preserve order during the Nebi Musa procession just as it had done in previous demonstrations. "Overconfidence" was an understatement; "arrogance" might have been a more accurate choice. More than anything else, Storrs was guilty of criminal negligence.[38] The Nebi Musa riots revealed an administration lacking central coordination and a uniform policy: different men acted according to contradictory orders, divergent worldviews, and unreliable intuitions. "The trouble about Storrs is that he had neither the confidence of the Arabs, the Jews, or the British officials here," David Eder wrote.[39]

The conclusions reached by the court of inquiry came as no surprise to anyone who had been in Jerusalem at the time of the riots: the security forces had not been prepared and the main victims were the Jews. Beyond this assessment, the court, made up of two generals, a colonel, and a legal counsel, put together a historical survey of Palestine, beginning with Jewish sovereignty in ancient Israel, which had lasted for a mere three hundred years, they noted. The Balfour Declaration "is undoubtedly the starting point of the whole trouble"; there could be no doubt that the Zionists' intention was to establish a Jewish state. In their assessment, Chaim Weizmann, a moderate, had lost control of the Zionist movement, which was now in the sway of extreme elements. They portrayed the movement as nationalist and dictatorial, with a clear plan to expel the Arabs from Palestine. Thus they reached the conclusion that Arab fears were not unfounded.

Bolshevism flowed in Zionism's inner heart, the court stated. Many of the Jews coming to settle in Palestine brought Bolshevik views with them. The court mentioned one such person by name: Lieutenant Jabotinsky, identifying him with the Poalei Zion Party, which the court called "a definite Bolshevist institution." The association of the fiercely antisocialist Jabotinsky with a Marxist party was not the only nonsense in the report. The court proudly asserted that 152 witnesses had been heard speaking eight languages: "English, French, Arabic, Hebrew, Yiddish, Jargon, Russian, and Hindustani." The court did not know that "Jargon" was a dismissive Hebrew term for Yiddish. The historical survey took up more than half the report. It is not an intelligent document, and it was never published. By July 1920, when it was signed, the military administration had been dismantled and replaced by a civil administration. This was another one of Chaim Weizmann's notable achievements.[40]

4.

Immediately after Passover, Weizmann set out for San Remo in Italy, where the British and the French were holding final discussions over the Mandate in Palestine. He made a stop to see Allenby in Cairo; while speaking of the events in Jerusalem, he burst into tears. "I'm tired, worn out, crushed, and sick of the whole world," he wrote to his wife, telling her how much care he had taken during the riots to ensure the safety of little Benjy. "It was just as though we were in a mouse-trap, cut off from the whole world, not knowing whether we would wake up alive after nightmarish nights." He needed her, he wrote to his wife, he wanted to pour out his heart to her. "The whole of the outside world is so awful," he wrote. No, perhaps it was not true to say that the English had organized the pogrom, but they had undoubtedly played a passive role in it. With the exception of Wyndham Deedes and Richard Meinertzhagen, they were all wolves and jackals, he wrote.

Yes, he had checked the prices of the carpets she had asked him to buy in the Jerusalem bazaar, but that was before the days of terror. He had managed to buy only a rug for the stairway. He had not bought the large carpet she had asked for. "One doesn't care and one doesn't think," he wrote to her.[41]

But in San Remo he did what he knew how to do. The French representatives had expressed many reservations about the inclusion of the language of the Balfour Declaration in the Mandate Declaration. Only after the exertion of Zionist pressure on the British, who in turn persuaded the French, did the conference conclusively decide to incorporate the commitment to establish a Jewish national home in the terms of Britain's mandate to govern. Furthermore, the nature of the government in Palestine had yet to be determined. The shock of the Nebi Musa riots, and Weizmann's presence as a firsthand witness, led to the conclusion that a civil administration would be more effective and less inflammatory than the military forces. The British acted on the basis of the same considerations that led them to issue the Balfour Declaration: they wanted to prevent the country being given to the French and they submitted to Zionist pressure.[42]

David Eder was in San Remo as well. He had been in London for the Passover holiday and on his way back to Jerusalem made an overnight stop at the Hotel Royale. In the afternoon he had tea with Weizmann, Nachum Sokolow, and Herbert Samuel in the hotel lobby. Prime Minister Lloyd George suddenly appeared. Samuel rose to greet him, and Lloyd

George asked Samuel to come with him. Twenty minutes later Samuel returned and informed the Zionists that the prime minister had authorized him to tell them, confidentially, that he, Samuel, had been offered the post of high commissioner in Palestine's civil administration. "Well, my darling," Weizmann wrote to his wife, "our trials have come to an end."[43]

5.

Upon returning to London, Weizmann worked to obtain Jabotinsky's release from prison. One of the people he petitioned was Colonial Secretary Winston Churchill. Weizmann assumed that when Samuel arrived in Palestine a few weeks hence, Jabotinsky would be freed. But a storm was raging among the Zionists in Palestine. Jabotinsky had become a symbol of injustice, and his ongoing imprisonment fed anti-British sentiment. In a protest in Tel Aviv, people took down the street sign bearing Allenby's name and replaced it with Jabotinsky's name instead. In a bold, rare gesture, Rabbi Avraham Yitzhak Hacohen Kook, soon to be appointed chief rabbi of Palestine, violated the sanctity of the seventh day of Passover and while still in synagogue signed the petition protesting the arrest of Jabotinsky and his associates. Hundreds of other worshipers did the same.[44]*

Jabotinsky spent his time in jail translating poems by Omar Khayyám and a few of Arthur Conan-Doyle's Sherlock Holmes tales. But he was far from calm. He felt abandoned. "He is in a pathological condition and I really have some fears for the state of his mind. He is tremendously excited and working himself up to ever greater excitement," David Eder wrote to Weizmann, in his capacity as psychiatrist. He also reported a plot that had reached his ears—an attack on the Acre prison to free Jabotinsky by force. Weizmann was furious. A jailbreak might well mark the beginning of a Jabotinsky dictatorship, he wrote. "From the heights of Sinai he will summon the Jews to the struggle against Perfidious Albion, against Samuel, against the Zionist Organization, which sold out the Jews, etc., etc. . . . All this loud, adventurous, pseudo-heroic cheap demagogy is repulsive and unworthy. Behind it no doubt there hides petty, raw ambition."[46]

---

*In his memoirs, Storrs accused Rabbi Kook of hypocrisy, saying that he wore his "cruciform Order of the British Empire" hidden in the folds of his robes.[45]

He had never been so angry with the Zionist leadership. When he wrote to Ben-Gurion and Berl Katznelson he did so in Russian, because only in that language could he berate them in a way that expressed his rage. "The hysterical state" into which part of the Jewish population had apparently worked itself, he wrote, "the spirit of bitterness and vindictiveness," the "pressures," the "enormous exaggerations," the "constant shouting of 'wolf,'" the "cheap heroism" and "false martyrdom"—all these brought him to sympathize with the British administration more than ever before. Above all he was enraged because the politicians in Palestine were trying to interfere with the work of the Zionist leadership in London.[47]

The internecine wrangling could not dim Weizmann's achievement. A chapter had come to an end. Now the building of the land would begin, Weizmann wrote to his wife. In San Remo, Lloyd George had parted from him with the words *You have got your start. It all depends on you.* "Hotels are always optimistic," Weizmann wrote at the time, thanking Vera for her support. He had in the meantime sent their Benjy to Paris, and given the carpet to a colonel who promised to get it over the border without paying customs. He would bring her the amber necklace and the halvah himself.[48] Ronald Storrs, who would now be leaving Jerusalem, quickly sent a letter of congratulations to Herbert Samuel. A "great adventure" awaits you, Storrs wrote in red ink. In truth Storrs thought the appointment of a pro-Zionist, Jewish high commissioner "mad."[49]

—•—

A Steady Gaze and a Firm Jaw

1.

With the army about to transfer power to the civilian administration, Generals Waters-Taylor and Bols held a farewell reception for Arab community leaders; Khalil al-Sakakini served as their spokesman. He told the two generals that they were admirable as individuals, but they were leaving the Arabs with open wounds. One of the things he was referring to was the appointment of Herbert Samuel as high commissioner. He requested a favor of the two British officers: "Please convey to Europe that we do not trust Europe, we do not respect Europe, and we do not love Europe."[1]

Since returning from Damascus, Sakakini had established excellent ties with the top figures in the military administration. Some of them studied Arabic with him. The director of the education department consulted him on the Arab educational system and appointed him and his wife, Sultana, to the board of education. Within a short time he became head of a teachers college. Sakakini put the same energy into his new work that he devoted to politics, and believed that the two fields complemented each other. "We need schools that will instill in students the spirit of freedom, pride, independence, courage, sincerity, and other such principles that can serve to raise nations from the depths of degeneration and enable them to shake off the semblance of servitude they have worn for generations," he told the director of the education department. He founded a library for his students and required them to take daily cold showers, as he himself did.[2]

At some point in 1919 he moved to the western side of the city, not far from the Ratisbonne Monastery. Some of the city's better-off Jews had begun to build their homes in the area, and the place would soon turn into a fashionable neighborhood called Rehavia. There was an old wind-mill, and the Sakakini family rented it to live in. From time to time Sakakini would run into Alter Levine, who tried to be friendly. Levine arranged and cosigned a loan for Sakakini at the Anglo-Palestine Bank and bought young Sari al-Sakakini candy and pajamas. Sakakini recorded all this in his diary.[3] He and Levine responded to the news of Samuel's appointment quite differently: Levine published a poem in *Ha'aretz*, signed with his pen name, Asaf Halevy the Jerusalemite. It was a hymn to a new age. "The dawn enraptures and casts its light / We said it would come . . . We rebelled against the mist / Because our hearts yearned / For the sun."[4] Sakakini, on the other hand, prepared to resign from the teachers college.

The resignation was an act of protest and was not well received. Ronald Storrs summoned Sakakini and issued a warning. He had heard that Sakakini was among those Arab public figures who were encouraging Arab officials in the British administration to quit their jobs—an error, in Storrs's view. The administration would simply hire Englishmen or Jews in their place and would not take them back. Storrs tried to dissuade Sakakini from leaving his job. In England, he claimed, no one asked what anyone else's faith was. He, Storrs, had never known whether his school chums were Catholics or Protestants or heathens. The British government considered Samuel an Englishman and had appointed him on the basis of his qualifications.

Storrs was aware that the Arabs viewed Samuel first and foremost as a Jew, he told Sakakini. Had a Christian been appointed the Jews would claim that the high commissioner was acting against them because he was an antisemite. The government had preferred to appoint a Jew precisely to avert such a possibility; Samuel would be able to carry out British policy without anyone claiming that he hated Jews. In fact, many Jews were aware of the government's intention and opposed the appointment. Some Jews had told Samuel, Storrs averred, that during the first few weeks of his tenure he would need British policemen to protect him from the Arabs, but afterward he would need Arab policemen to protect him from the Jews. Sakakini was not persuaded. He made sure everyone knew why he had resigned—he would not work under a Jewish high commissioner. From exile, Aref al-Aref warned that the appointment would lead to bloodshed.[5]

In response to Samuel's impending appointment, Captain James Pollock considered going home. "No really self-respecting Britisher can stay here," he wrote to his father. "Britain may be about to commit the greatest injustice that has ever been done by any nation in modern times." He felt as if he were standing on the edge of a volcano, he wrote. Later he calmed down somewhat, but he still expected disaster. "All faith in British honesty and justice has gone from the Arab of the Near East," he wrote. The country would be handed over to the Jews, despite the wishes of the Arabs. The Jews would come from southeastern Europe—rich, educated Jews would not leave England and New York. Britain needed God's mercy, Pollock wrote. Allenby also opposed Samuel's appointment. The choice was extremely dangerous, he warned Foreign Secretary Curzon.[6]

Field Marshal Sir Henry Wilson, the highest-ranking British soldier in the Middle East, reiterated that the British had no business being in Palestine and the sooner they left, the better. For years Wilson had been warning the government that the empire could not afford the luxury of spreading itself too thin. Great Britain should withdraw from all lands that were not its own, he maintained, and concentrate its strength in England, Ireland, Egypt, and India. "The problem of Palestine is exactly the same . . . as the problem of Ireland," Wilson wrote, "namely, two peoples living in a small country hating each other like hell." Only a powerful authority could enforce its will on both parties: "[E]ither we govern other people or they will govern us," he maintained. Britain had to control Ireland because it could not afford to lose it; Britain could not control Palestine because it did not have the force to do so.

Over and over again Wilson castigated the civilians—he called them the "frocks"—for not understanding that spreading Britain's forces over such a large empire would bring about its decline. Again and again he demanded that Palestine, or "Jewland," as he called it, be abandoned: "The best thing we can do is to clear out of Jewland as soon as we can and let the Jews run that country as quickly as they can." Wilson, whose military career had taken him from one end of the empire to the other, saw no strategic value in Palestine.[7] General Congreve felt the same way. "It is a beastly country and most unpopular with the soldiers," Congreve wrote to Wilson. This was hardly surprising to him, since the government expected the army to impose peace between the Jews and the Arabs, as a result of which it had to fight both of them.[8] It was in this climate that Samuel packed his bags.

2.

He landed at Jaffa in July 1920, wearing a white uniform and a steel-spiked pith helmet, also white. A purple sash crossed his chest, displaying the medal his king had bestowed on him when he set out. His stiff collar was embroidered with gold, as were his large cuffs; he wore a slender ceremonial sword against his left thigh. Samuel looked like an operatic character—elegant, handsome, younger than his fifty years, very colonial. A special boat had been sent to bring him from Italy; now a fighter plane circled above it, and a cannon fired a seventeen-gun salute to honor his arrival. An incident occurred immediately: Meir Dizengoff, chairman of the Tel Aviv municipal council, made a welcoming speech in Hebrew, even though it had been agreed in advance that he would speak in English, as the Arab mayor of Jaffa did. "It was wrong of him to have done so," Samuel commented. He was surrounded by exceptional security precautions; the Zionist Commission had warned that the Arabs were plotting to blow up his train on its way to Jerusalem.[9]

Once Lloyd George's government had thrown its weight behind Jewish aspirations in Palestine, it could not have appointed a more suitable man to the post of high commissioner. Herbert Samuel had not been chosen for the job because of—or despite—his Jewishness, nor for his abilities and experience. Samuel was sent to Palestine because he was a Zionist.

The scion of a wealthy Liverpool banking family, Samuel had been raised in a home where Jewish dietary laws and the Sabbath were observed. The family was active in the Jewish community and in politics; another son was a member of Parliament. Samuel studied at Oxford and went into politics himself, joining Lloyd George's Liberal Party. He served as postmaster general, and as home secretary he instituted daylight saving time in Britain, proposed the law allowing women to stand for Parliament, and was involved in suppressing the riots in Ireland. Bernard Shaw thought he would become prime minister.[10]

From the time of his 1915 proposal calling for the establishment of a Jewish state in Palestine, Samuel had been involved in every stage of the Zionists' success: the Jewish Legion, the Balfour Declaration, the Versailles peace conference, the Mandate. He had intervened countless times on problems Weizmann had laid before him, and Balfour frequently asked him to persuade the Zionists to moderate their demands. Samuel's letters to his son reflect both a commitment to political Zionism and a profound spiritual and cultural attachment to the movement. He compared events in Palestine to a mummy rising up from its sarcophagus, shedding its shroud, and returning to life. He and his wife took Hebrew lessons.[11]

But Samuel was plagued by doubts before he accepted the post. Perhaps it was not wise to have a Jewish commissioner govern Palestine— his appointment was liable to make things more difficult for both the Zionists and the British.[12] He raised the issue with the prime minister as well; Lloyd George thought the difficulties were not insurmountable. Encouraged, Samuel's optimistic, liberal, and rationalist nature quickly reasserted itself. He was imbued with a deep historical consciousness and thought a great deal about the future. He believed that with prudence and restraint it would be possible to establish a Jewish state in Palestine without war. For the time being, there would be no Jewish state, he wrote to his niece, only limited immigration and settlement, accomplished cautiously. Five years down the road the British could perhaps increase the rate of immigration and add to it gradually. Fifty years from now there might be a Jewish majority and Jewish rule for all practical purposes, and possibly a generation later a Jewish state might be plausible. The opportunity to realize all this, he continued, infused him with "a fine enthusiasm." In a letter to his wife he wrote of "the joy of creation." His elderly mother also advised him to accept the appointment. He had lost his seat in Parliament a year and a half previously and was without gainful employment.[13]

Chaim Weizmann treated the new high commissioner as if he were on his staff. Before Samuel arrived in Palestine, Weizmann ruled that he was "weak, frightened and trembling," altogether too cautious. "He will need a big shaking up before he understands the real situation," Weizmann wrote. But the Jewish public received Samuel as if he were the Messiah, the redeemer of Israel. They sent him parchment scrolls inscribed with praise and poetry written in ancient Hebrew calligraphy; they wove his picture into tapestries, just as they did with the image of Theodor Herzl.[14] He was a Jew, a Zionist, and an Englishman—thrice worthy of adulation. The Zionists identified themselves and their political vision with European culture. They had always sought to tie their fate to one of the great colonial powers in Europe.

3.

The Zionist movement arose in Europe, drew its inspiration from Europe, and was part of Europe's history. Its nationalism, romanticism, liberalism, and socialism were all products of Europe. The movement's founding fathers had from the outset charged it with a cultural mission. The Jewish state in Palestine, Theodor Herzl wrote, would be Europe's bulwark against Asia: "We can be the vanguard of culture against barbarianism."[15] Writer Max Nordau believed the Jews would not lose their European culture in Palestine and adopt Asia's inferior culture, just as the British had not become Indians in America, Hottentots in Africa, or Papuans in Australia. "We will endeavor to do in the Near East what the English did in India," he said at an early Zionist Congress. "It is our intention to come to Palestine as the representatives of culture and to take the moral borders of Europe to the Euphrates River."[16] The Jews in Palestine defined their European self-image in contrast to the Arabs and to the Jews from Arab countries, such as the Yemenite Jews, who had settled in Jerusalem.

"We are here in Palestine the more cultured part, and there is not in Palestine any other part that can compete with us culturally," Mordechai Ben-Hillel Hacohen wrote. "The great majority of the country's residents are fellahs and Bedouin, all of them wild, whom world culture has still not reached." Hacohen foresaw little change. "It will be a long while before they learn to live lives in which there is no robbery, thievery, and larceny; lives in which they feel shame and embarrassment at walking around half-naked and barefoot; lives of possessions and property and established boundaries; lives in which there is a need for level sidewalks and paved roads, organized schools and charitable institutions, courts without bribery, and so on." Many writers, journalists, and politicians shared Hacohen's view, often describing the Arabs as "savages" or "semi-savages," the opposite of the "cultivated" Jews. Hacohen also had a penchant for comparisons between the Arabs and the Sephardim—both were Levantine, not to be imitated and to be kept at arm's length.[17]

Aharon Avraham Kabak, a teacher and author, wrote about the differences between children whose parents had come from Russia and Galicia, who were "a storehouse of mental energy and intellectual talents," and children whose parents had come from Yemen. Of the latter he said, "The Yemenite child, after so many generations of idleness, penury, abjectness, and servility under the fierce Yemenite sun, brings with him, together with Oriental sharp-wittedness and wiliness, a tendency for delusion, negligence, slowness of movement, with bodily lethargy and weakness of the nerves." Educator Shmuel Yavnieli said of the Yemenite Jews, "They are people who need education. They cannot, in a cultural sense, take any action. This action, so necessary for our rebirth, can only be taken by young Ashkenazi people."[18]

According to Ze'ev Jabotinsky, "We Jews have nothing in common with what is called the 'Orient,' thank God. To the extent that our uneducated masses have ancient spiritual traditions and laws that recall the Orient, they must be weaned away from them, and this is in fact what we are doing in every decent school, and what life itself is doing with great success. We are going to Palestine, first for our national convenience," he wrote, and second, "to sweep out thoroughly all traces of the 'Oriental soul.' As for the Arabs in Palestine, what they do is their business; but if we can do them a favor, it is to help them liberate themselves from the 'Orient.'"[19]

Here and there Jews made attempts to acculturate into the Orient. People put on Arab headdresses, made Turkish coffee in Arab coffeepots, and learned Arabic. Some Hebrew writers and artists tried to create a blend of ancient Hebrew culture and contemporary Arab culture. The upright, independent Hebrew farmer who appeared in the new Hebrew literature, art, and folklore, was inspired by an Arab ideal: the son of the sheikh.[20] But such borrowings were in no way an abandonment of Western values and convention. Alter Levine, one of the first of this school, held his own cultural world in great esteem. A series of letters sent to his wife and daughters, who were in Vienna for rest and relaxation, reads like a book of etiquette for nineteenth-century European society women. Levine wrote to his wife, Gittel, in Yiddish. She did not have a good command of Hebrew; to his chagrin, she could not read his poetry. In one letter he enjoined her to have herself photographed in a fur coat. The coat should be worn open and have a drooping collar and a flower on the lapel. She should put on pearls and a hat—a pretty hat, he demanded. He wanted his Gittel to wear a silk glove on one hand and leave the other hand bare. Likewise, he insisted that she wear silk stockings and small, dainty shoes. The picture was supposed to be a winter portrait, and Levine intended to have it copied in oils.

He wrote to his daughters in Hebrew but inserted key words in German. He wanted them to learn languages (French, German, and English), take dancing and piano lessons, and listen to a great deal of music, especially Beethoven and Meyerbeer. They should read, he instructed, and send him book reports. He also urged embroidery and tennis. From Jerusalem, he told them what to eat—lots of goose fat—and advised them on personal hygiene: "A woman's beauty and delicacy are reflected in her attention to her delicate hands and the way she cleans her nails." He ordered them to use Odol, a popular mouthwash in Vienna at the time, and to have massages.

He wrote to them about undergarments and bid them not to wear girdles. They were girls from Jerusalem, he reminded them, and they should beware of a permissive "counterfeit culture." The real Europe, prewar Europe, Levine explained to his daughters, was rational, all harmony and cleanliness, diligence and beauty, order and tolerance. This was the culture he wished to instill in them. Like Mordechai Ben-Hillel Hacohen, he identified Europe with Zionism. Arab culture was the opposite, "primitive," and lacking "harmony."[21]*

Khalil al-Sakakini was also steeped in European culture. Like Levine, Sakakini read widely, from William Shakespeare to Friedrich Nietzsche. He too tried to mold his children, down to the very last bourgeois detail. "How happy I will be when I get up from supper and enter the living room and Sari sits at the piano to play and sing, or plays the flute or violin," he wrote. He hired a Jewish piano teacher; Sultana al-Sakakini also liked Beethoven.[23] While Levine shared his cultural affinities with the Jewish community in Palestine, Sakakini's admiration of European culture was exceptional among the Arabs. In fact, Sakakini felt uncomfortable about this inclination of his: "I do not want to shed my Orientalism," he wrote. "I cannot be other than a son of the East."[24]†

In the Zionists' adoration of Europe, England held a special place. The HaPoel HaTzair publishing house produced a 1921 booklet containing an admiring collective portrait of the English. The author was identified only as "P." Because of "their courage and immense will, the English will triumph and succeed wherever they turn," he wrote. "In their competence

---

* As Levine was writing his letters, *Ha'aretz* published an advertisement for a Jerusalem department store, depicting ideal customers: a man and a woman, she in high heels and a hat and he in a tailored suit and homburg. A little black boy carries their packages.[22]

† Sakakini's case was particularly complex: his maternal grandmother was a Greek native of Istanbul. At one stage Sakakini gave himself over to his Greek heritage, learning how to curse in modern Greek and falling in love with Greek music. His admiration of ancient Greek philosophy was boundless, leading him to call himself "Socrates." Mordechai Ben-Hillel Hacohen wrote about people like Sakakini, Christian Arabs who had "gotten a whiff of the culture of Europe." They adopted the "well-pressed appearance" of European culture, but "their souls are still full of the filth of savagery," Hacohen wrote. "Their souls are impure," he added.[25]

at establishing colonies, they are superior to almost all the nations of Europe." P went on to say: "It is puzzling that most English boys like to put themselves at risk. You will always find dozens of volunteers willing to participate in a dangerous hunt, to climb up a tall tree, to swim across a surging river, and so on." This is how they built an empire: "With these characteristics the English succeeded in enforcing their rule over far lands, subjecting many peoples, and all treat them with deep respect, even in places where they are not loved because of their iron hand."[26] The Hebrew reader could rest assured: the Zionist movement had chosen the best governmental subcontractor in the world.

Mordechai Ben-Hillel Hacohen considered the English cultural allies. "England will come to establish a government in Palestine and will link us with Europe," he wrote in his diary. To Chaim Weizmann the Turkish regime was "of inferior culture," while the British applied "honest European methods."[27] Some years later, David Ben-Gurion amplified this view: "We have come here as Europeans. Although our origin is in the East and we are returning to the East, we bring with us European civilization and we would not want to sever our connections and those of the country with the civilization of Europe. We see in Great Britain the chief standard-bearer of this civilization in the world and Palestine should serve as the bridge between East and West. We do not see a better representative of western civilization than England."[28]

Cultural identification affected political outlook, and vice versa. "We stand with Europe," *Ha'aretz* asserted six months before Samuel's arrival. "Here in the East one thing is needed more than any other: European order and European government. This condition is more important than all the other conditions—even national rights." The newspaper praised the British and the French for having educated the nations living in their colonies to live lives of "law and order." Ze'ev Jabotinsky wrote similar things.[29]

As Europeans, the Jews in Palestine felt stinging indignity when the British described them as "natives." They resented the authorities' tendency to consider the two populations in Palestine as equal—Jewish natives and Arab natives. Senior Zionist official Frederick Kisch felt that the treatment of both peoples recalled the attitude of the British to the colored populations in their colonies, and he quoted officials who had compared events in Palestine with the situations in Sierra Leone or Fiji. Relating to Jews and Arabs in the same way brought the Jew down to the level of the Arab, Kisch insisted. He demanded that the British be enlightened as to the difference between the European Jew and the Arab, who treated his wife as if she were a beast of burden—he rides a donkey, and she walks on foot, heavily loaded with baggage.[30]*

There were some in the British administration who viewed Zionism as a cultural movement with a European mission. "They are eager to visit in our homes," Hacohen wrote, "we being the only Europeans in the country."[32] Others, however, felt no such affinity. "On the whole the British administrator—especially in the lower ranks—prefers the native to the Jew, not out of any reason of unfairness or anti-Semitism, but simply because the native is a much simpler proposition than the Jew in Palestine," Chaim Weizmann wrote. Humphrey Bowman, director of the education department, felt that English officials found it easier to relate to Arabs than to Jews; the connection was based on a common inclination to freedom, daring, and adventurousness. Not that the average English official was antisemitic, Bowman wrote. On the contrary, nearly all of them counted Jews among their friends. According to Bowman, they were impressed by "spiritual Zionism," the revival of the language, the establishment of the university. They did not like political Zionism, though, because it threatened the status of the Arabs. William Ormsby-Gore wrote, "One can't help noticing the ineradicable tendency of the Englishman who has lived in India or the Sudan to favour quite unconsciously the Moslem against the Christian and Jew." One Zionist activist remarked in his memoirs that the English were in the habit of saying "our little friends" when speaking of the Arabs.[33]

The place of Zionists in the social firmament was an emotional and cultural issue, and since it touched on the new identity the Jews wished to create in Palestine, it had political ramifications as well. Given the Zionists' claim that their return to the land of their fathers was a natural right, not something granted to them as a gift, they should have been pleased to be called "natives"; their foreignness weakened their claim. "I am no stranger in this country, even if I was born and bred in the far north," Weizmann said at a meeting with Arabs in Jerusalem. During the final stage of drafting of the Mandate document, Weizmann wrote to Samuel and demanded that it not refer to the Jews as a "native population." The natives were the Arabs.[34]

---

*Sometime later Kisch wrote to Lord Rothschild about the two groups of "natives": "The Jewish population contains many persons at least as intelligent as the average British official, while masses of the Arabs are entirely illiterate and little removed in intelligence from the donkeys these gentle people habitually accelerate with the aid of rusty nails."[31]

4.

Before Samuel took over from the military government, the chief administrative officer asked that he sign one of the most quoted documents in Zionist history: "Received from Major General Sir Louis J. Bols, K.C.B.—One Palestine, complete." Samuel signed.[35]*

He remained in Palestine for five years, a glorious era, according to Judge Gad Frumkin: "A period of spiritual elation, of national maturation, of enhanced Jewish self-respect, of the sanctification of the name of Israel in the eyes of the gentiles and especially in the eyes of the Arabs." Frumkin was hyperbolizing, but in essence he was right. Samuel led the country in its first steps into the twentieth century. When he went home he left behind a fairly efficient administration, a generally stable economy, a measure of law and order, and relative tranquillity. The principal effect of his achievements, however, was to advance the Zionist interest. The Arabs considered him an enemy and claimed he left the country worse off than when he arrived.[37]

Samuel's black mustache, always well trimmed, exuded a kind of military vigor and frigid aloofness. "He had a rather wooden face with a searching, almost furtive expression," wrote District Commissioner Edward Keith-Roach. It was easier to squeeze a tear out of Cromwell's statue than to sway Samuel from his position, they said of him in Parliament. Frederick Kisch, who married Samuel's niece, described his routine audience with the high commissioner as a cold shower. Margery Bentwich, the sister of Attorney General Norman Bentwich, had Samuel for tea and considered him pompous. "H. S. is stiffish and must always be feeling very uncomfortable as he never seems able to forget and shed his office—at any rate in company. He seems more the official than the man."[38] Even his letters to his son exude a kind of stern, almost formal, correctness.

He lodged in the north wing of the Augusta Victoria castle on the Mount of Olives. "Government House," as it was now known, had a hundred rooms, was pleasant in the summer, and proved hard to heat in the winter. At first Samuel devoted a fair amount of time to organizing the household.

---

*Many years later this odd "receipt" was offered for sale at an auction in New York. Newspaper reporters contacted Samuel, then in his nineties. The elderly lord was angry. The receipt wasn't a historical document, he wrote in his memoirs, it was a joke. Its value as a curiosity might be a couple of shillings or perhaps a dollar in the United States, no more. The piece of paper in fact sold for $5,000. Samuel remarked dryly, "The price realized was astonishing but there is often a difference between price and value."[36]

His wife had remained in England to pack and arrange for the rental of their house. She and their two small children joined him six months after his own arrival, by which time he had already seen to furniture and books, a soup tureen, silverware, and curtains. The reception hall would be furnished at government expense, but they could not be extravagant, he cautioned his wife—the lifestyle in Palestine was simpler than in England.[39]

The house had come equipped with a French chef, who soon departed for home because his wife was ill. General Allenby loaned the Samuels his own chef from Cairo as a temporary expedient. The gardener at Government House prepared a list of seeds he wished brought from England. Local women, Russians, took care of the bedding, but it would be well to bring a pair of personal servants from England, Samuel advised his wife. A house had been prepared for them on the grounds. Samuel's wife had shipped one crate after another; the first contained a Torah scroll. She had not sent his top hats, however. "I am anxious to discourage the use of high hats in this country," Samuel had written. Beatrice Samuel pondered what duties she should fulfill, as the country had never had a first lady. She decided that her job was to be nice.[40]

The high commissioner also tried to be pleasant to everyone. He toured the Zionist agricultural settlements and thought that the residents were happy people. On the Sabbath following the Ninth of Av fast he descended the Mount of Olives on foot to pray at the Hurva Synagogue in the Old City, bringing his top officials with him. Crowds gathered to see and cheer him. At the synagogue he had the honor of chanting the week's reading: Isaiah, chapter 40, which promises the redemption of Zion. Samuel remarked with satisfaction that his atrocious pronunciation made it impossible to determine whether he spoke Hebrew with an Ashkenazic or a Sephardic accent, so no one would be insulted. It was the most moving ceremony of his life, he wrote.*

He ordered the immediate release of Ze'ev Jabotinsky and also pardoned two senior Arab figures who had been arrested in the Nebi Musa riots. During a visit to the new principality of Transjordan—also under British control—he was asked by local Arabs to rescind the convictions of Aref al-Aref and Haj Amin al-Husseini and allow them to return to Jerusalem; he

---

*Samuel was not observant, however. He sometimes worked on the Sabbath, and while he fasted on Yom Kippur, he explained to his wife that he did so only because the country's inhabitants believed that he fasted and he did not want to deceive them. In principle, he rejected the fast, he said.[41]

acceded immediately. He made frequent visits to Arab villages and regularly conferred with the leaders of the Christian communities. He was pleased and astounded by the country's tranquillity; his term as Britain's postmaster general had been turmoil in comparison, he wrote.[42]

Soon after his arrival he found himself facing two surprises. Despite the impatience displayed by the Zionists, the movement, hobbled by an acute financial crisis, was not yet ready to carry out its program.[43] One manifestation of this was the low immigration rate. Samuel offered the movement 16,500 immigration permits, but the Zionists were willing to make do with 1,000. In a letter to branches of the Zionist Organization around the world, the leadership instructed its officials to warn people not to liquidate their businesses in the hope of soon setting out for Palestine. The time had not yet arrived for that, the Zionist Organization in London announced; for the moment, patience and discipline were called for. Samuel was disappointed, and Weizmann thought it necessary to apologize to him. He explained that American Jewry was at fault, for not taking care of the movement's financial needs, but the money would come, he promised. In the end, 8,000 Jews immigrated that year while just over 1,000 Jews left the country.[44]

Samuel's second surprise was the discovery that not everyone considered Palestine a strategic asset worth funding. The British treasury informed him soon after his arrival that it would not finance this adventure: local taxes, tariffs, and other income would have to cover all the administration's outlays and development expenses. The treasury even sent him a bill for the railroad tracks the army had laid during the conquest of the country; the railroad was now being used by civilians and the treasury saw no reason why Palestine should receive it as a gift. Samuel might have been better off suggesting that the army dismantle the tracks and take them back to London, but instead he tried to argue with the treasury and failed. The track running from Rafiah to Haifa cost the Palestine administration a million pounds sterling. In a letter to his son, Samuel wrote that the only troubles he had in Palestine were in London. "There is a very strong current running in favour of economy and the prevailing question is 'Why should we be spending all this money in Palestine?'"[45]

In this atmosphere Samuel found it difficult to obtain a development loan for the country or to persuade his government to fund the construction of a port in Haifa Bay: the price was too high. "It has been repeatedly pointed out," the War Office maintained, "that Palestine is of no military value from an imperial point of view. It should be regarded as an entirely separate administration and the troops in the country should be . . . at the disposal of the civil power." Colonial Secretary Churchill himself warned the government that in the 1922–23 fiscal year the garrison in Palestine, 8,000 men, would cost British taxpayers more than £3.3 million.[46]

Churchill inherited responsibility for Palestine once the Mandate was implemented. During and after the war he had expressed doubts about Britain taking upon itself the realization of the Zionist program; he supported having the United States do it. At one point he had proposed that Britain simply give up Palestine. Churchill was concerned with not only the financial cost but also the political cost: the confrontation between the Jews and the Arabs would only cause problems for Britain.

He had been one of the first public figures to meet with Chaim Weizmann, soon after the latter's arrival in Britain. Even though Churchill was not caught up in the same fervor that produced the Zionism of David Lloyd George and Balfour, he shared their sense that the Jews were highly influential and therefore their goodwill was worth acquiring. He believed that the "international Jew" had brought down Imperial Russia; the revolution was a "sinister conspiracy" the Jews had hatched against Western culture. He called the Bolsheviks "a bacillus," an expression frequently applied to Jews in antisemitic publications. The Zionists, he theorized, would "provide the antidote to this sinister conspiracy and bestow stability instead of chaos on the Western world."*

In the spring of 1921 Churchill took Lawrence of Arabia with him to Jerusalem. During his stay in the city he painted its vistas in oil; Samuel politely called the paintings "effective." And then, "One Sunday afternoon," as Churchill remarked contemptuously, he crowned Prince Abdullah king of Transjordan. This allowed the British to say that they had fulfilled all their obligations to the various parties.† Musa Kazim al-Husseini, the former mayor of Jerusalem, demanded that Churchill revoke the Balfour Declaration, close the country to Jewish immigration,

---

*As the Colonial Office accepted responsibility for Palestine, British newspapers were writing a great deal about *The Protocols of the Elders of Zion*. The *Times* of London wondered whether it might not be a forgery, but left the question unanswered.[47]

†The Versailles peace conference had decided to carve a state, Transjordan, out of Ottoman territory—and include a large area of eastern Palestine—to give to the sharif of Mecca's family in an effort to satisfy its territorial claims. Prince Abdullah, brother of Faisal and son of the sharif, had agreed to the arrangement in exchange for £5,000. Thus the Arabs received independence, the French received Syria, and the Jews received Palestine.[48] But no one in Palestine was happy: the Arabs felt the country had been torn away from Syria; the Zionists were bitter because Transjordan had been torn away from Palestine, and the northern bor-

and undo the partition between Palestine and Syria. Churchill responded with a firmness that bordered on disrespect. Even if he could revoke the Balfour Declaration he would not do so, because the national home policy is "manifestly right" and would benefit all the inhabitants of Palestine, he asserted. He promised the Arabs that the policy would not be fully implemented immediately: their generation and also their children and their children's children will have passed from the earth before the Jewish national home is realized, he reassured them; and in the meantime British rule would continue. Of course, Churchill's comments also implied that the Arabs would not see independence in Palestine in their lifetimes.

As for the Zionists, Churchill gave them to understand that the pace of developing their community depended only on their ability to raise the necessary funds; the Zionist movement leadership in Palestine was pleased. When Churchill went to visit the Jewish settlements, he was received, justifiably, as a great friend. On the night before his visit to Tel Aviv employees of the municipal council cut down several trees and stuck them in the sand next to Meir Dizengoff's house to make an impression on the guest. The crowd that gathered at the house to greet Churchill was so tightly packed that one of the trees was knocked down and the deception was revealed. "Mr. Dizengoff, without roots it won't work," Churchill commented. *Ha'aretz* editor Moshe Glickson, who had arrived only a year and a half previously on the *Ruslan,* declared that Churchill had displayed "moral fortitude."[51]

A few days before Churchill went home, the mufti of Jerusalem died. The Muslim establishment needed a new religious leader, and Samuel agreed to the appointment of Haj Amin al-Husseini. Twenty-six years old and an up-and-coming figure, Husseini was ambitious and forceful. Bernard Wasserstein, Samuel's biographer, always sympathetic and often admiring, described the appointment of Husseini, however, as "a profound error of personal and political judgment"; many share this opinion, citing Husseini's militant strain of Arab nationalism. But, in fact, the appointment was entirely reasonable.

Husseini came from the right family: his grandfather, father, and elder brother had all served as mufti. He was not able to get himself elected in

---

der differed significantly from the Zionists' map.[49] Arabs and Jews would thus claim for many years afterward that a national injustice had been perpetrated on them. But had France lost Syria it probably would have withdrawn its consent to leaving Palestine with the British, and then the national home might never have been established.[50]

the first round of voting, but displayed an ability to organize broad public support for himself. Husseini's late brother had done much to help the authorities, in return for which the British decided to grant his widow and five children a "political pension," almost ten times higher than the pension they were entitled to by law. It would be difficult to exaggerate the value of the services the previous mufti had rendered to the government, an internal memo noted. The Husseini family had already lost the post of mayor; the new mayor was a member of the rival Nashashibi family, and that was another good reason to leave the post of mufti with the Husseini clan. In this matter, Samuel acted in accordance with the advice of Ronald Storrs, who was more experienced than he, intimately acquainted with Jerusalem politics, and knew Husseini well.

In early April 1921 Storrs took Husseini to meet the high commissioner and Samuel was favorably impressed. Husseini said he believed in Britain's good intentions toward the Arabs and undertook to use his family's influence to maintain the peace in Jerusalem.[52] He kept his word. The Nebi Musa celebration went by that year without incident. Jerusalem remained peaceful several months later as well, when other parts of the country were in turmoil. In fact, Jerusalem remained tranquil for years.

Husseini would later lead the Arab struggle to evict the British from Palestine, something Samuel could not have predicted, just as he could not have conceived that the Jews would also one day act to expel the British.[53]

Some months after his arrival, the high commissioner established an advisory council of twenty members. Half were British officials, and the rest consisted of public figures—four Muslims, three Christians, and three Jews. The forum met once a month at Government House and discussed education and transportation, the water supply, health, and other issues that, while important, were not explicitly political. Samuel tried to evince open-mindedness and a cooperative sympathetic spirit. In a letter to Lord Curzon, the foreign secretary, he wrote that he had no wish to impose British will autocratically, to govern a country "flowing with licensed milk and registered honey." The advisory council members had no real power; they listened and expressed opinions. The atmosphere was friendly, and votes were unnecessary, since they always reached a consensus, Samuel wrote many years later, as if he still believed in the optimism he had conveyed upon his arrival.

The advisory council had no impact on legislation, though, and over the years fairly extensive laws were enacted. In 1922 a kind of constitution was instituted, a document issued by the king in the Privy Council. The public was granted the right to express its opinions of proposed legislation drafted by the high commissioner's legal counsel, but the actual legislative process was not democratic and not liberal. The document prescribed the death penalty as well as collective punishment.[54]

5.

The high commissioner represented the king of Great Britain. When Samuel wore his official uniform and summoned to the Mount of Olives carefully selected notables in order to make government proclamations, he seemed to speak with the collected might of the British Empire itself. The high commissioner had the authority to pass laws; there was no elected parliament to check his power. The judicial system was formally independent, however, and from time to time the judges made rulings that contradicted the government's position; but fundamentally the courts considered themselves part of the regime, not an independent estate whose job it was to restrain it. The "fourth estate" was free to criticize the regime only to the extent that the high commissioner allowed. He was, on the face of it, an omnipotent ruler.

In reality, this was an illusion. The high commissioner had trouble doing anything at all without approval from the Colonial Office in London. Ostensibly, there was also international oversight: Britain ruled Palestine by virtue of a League of Nations Mandate, and a league commission was charged with ensuring that the administration acted according to the Mandate document. In this sense, Palestine was not a regular crown colony and did not belong to the empire; its inhabitants were citizens of Palestine.*

The League of Nations Mandates Commission had no teeth, however. Real influence was concentrated in London. The colonial secretary had the authority to confirm or void laws initiated by the high commissioner, the expenditures he proposed, and the appointments he wished to make. Besides the Colonial Office, other government ministries had interests and opinions that also constrained the high commissioner. But colonial

---

*The country did not have its own flag only because Samuel's efforts to come up with a design that would represent all the country's inhabitants were for nought. He realized that the flag's symbol could not be a Star of David, a cross, or a crescent, and a combination of all three was not acceptable either. Perhaps, he thought, it would be best to choose one of the country's native animals; then he thought of a torch within a circle—the torch would symbolize enlightenment, the circle eternity. In the end, the administration simply used the British Union Jack.[55]

secretaries did not hold the post for long. By the end of Britain's thirty years in Palestine, the colonial secretary had been replaced no less than seventeen times. During the same period there were seven high commissioners. This left most power in the hands of the Colonial Office's senior officials; possibly one in a thousand documents actually reached the colonial secretary's own desk, Edward Keith-Roach wrote.[56]

The correspondence between the high commissioners in Jerusalem and the Colonial Office in London, a huge quantity of paper, reflected an ongoing battle of wills between the man in the field and one "Sir Humphrey" or another, the archetypical omnipotent bureaucrat who acted on the assumption that he knew what should be done better than the high commissioner did. As often as not helpless, the high commissioner could only grit his teeth and make excuses for his superiors, trying at least to conceal how short his reach was. Indeed the high commissioner often acted as if his job were to lobby London, rather than to represent a regime with great power.*

Samuel took advantage of Churchill's 1921 visit to Palestine to get him to make several decisions on matters that Samuel had not been able to resolve in his contacts with the Colonial Office. He had been trying for some time to persuade the office to commence the construction of the Haifa port. Everything favored the project, but the bureaucrats were blocking it. He was also trying to expand the train network, a good source of government revenue. All he had requested was a meager allocation of 200 Egyptian pounds to conduct a preliminary survey. The high commissioner sent a memorandum, number 675, but the officials turned him down. He had to send many more dispatches before they approved the expense.

For months, Samuel added, he had been trying to obtain authorization for the repair of the western leg of the Jerusalem-Jaffa road, between Jaffa and Ramle. Experts had proposed filling in the potholes with stones; in Jerusalem there was a quarry that could supply the material. The office had turned this down as well. Samuel shared his frustration with Churchill. There was heavy traffic on the road. The potholes were causing damage to automobiles, whose owners had paid high license duties. The scandal had already been reported in the local press. Even worse, tourists

---

*"Official correspondence became a fetish before which every head must bow," complained Humphrey Bowman, director of the education department. The files multiplied and swelled, the exchange of cables, memoranda, and reports became the major preoccupation of the administration, and the connection with the situation in the field grew more and more tenuous.[57]

from all over the world had no choice but to use this road.[58] Samuel's distressed memorandum on the Jerusalem-Jaffa road—the Jaffa-Ramle leg—was addressed to the colonial secretary, a man concerned with a worldwide empire that held sway over hundreds of millions of people. The high commissioner's position in this system sounds, from his letters, like that of a most junior village chief.

Yet he headed a government of departments, quasi ministries, each one responsible for a defined area: finance, justice, education, immigration, health, agriculture and fishing, antiquities, commerce and industry, public works, trains, mail and telegraph, customs, surveys, statistics. To coordinate the system the high commissioner was aided by a secretariat; the chief secretary, the number-two man in the British administration, more than once served as Samuel's temporary replacement. Their fundamental assumption was that the administration existed to develop the country and provide services. Much of the responsibility for daily life devolved to local officials, or district commissioners. While their titles, job descriptions, and range of powers changed from time to time and place to place, one thing remained constant: these men were the most senior representatives with whom most of the population came in contact; they were the face of the civil administration. Among their duties were tax collection, security, and the trial and sentencing of criminals.

The position was an excellent one for a man in the first stages of a colonial career. "For a junior colonial administrator there is nothing to compare with one's first independent territorial command. I was lucky to get Ramallah," Edwin Samuel later wrote.[59] Of course, his name did not hurt him, although his father was no longer high commissioner at the time. Ramallah was then no more than a large village of about three thousand inhabitants; Samuel's jurisdiction included the surrounding villages. Typically, the local chief, the *mukhtar,* served as liaison between commissioner and village. Some mukhtars were chosen for the job with the consent of the villagers; others were imposed by the government. Some, as members of the village's principal family, inherited their position; others had to compete with rivals to get the job. In the larger villages there might be several mukhtars. They recorded births and deaths, and sometimes also functioned as judges. They were in charge of internal security and tax collection, keeping a few percent for themselves.[60]

Before taking up his position in Ramallah, Edwin Samuel went to consult an old acquaintance, Mayor Ragheb al-Nashashibi of Jerusalem. "What should I do if a Mukhtar refuses to come and see me when summoned?"

Samuel asked. "The Turks would have flogged him," Nashashibi noted. "You won't, but he isn't sure enough of that to run the risk. . . . So he'll come as soon as you call."

They came, and Edwin Samuel frequently went to them as well. He spent most of his time as district commissioner visiting the villages under his jurisdiction, two or three a day. He drove in his own car, flying the government flag, or rode on horseback. He generally gave advance notice of his arrival; the mukhtars received him ceremoniously, slaughtering a sheep. On occasion he lodged in the villages. The mukhtars presented their requests—this one wanted a classroom, that one a new road, here they needed seeds, there a doctor. Sometimes they complained of robbers and asked Samuel to intervene in local conflicts or conduct reconciliation ceremonies. They would eat, drink, talk about this and that, and then get around to the main purpose of the visit: tax collection.

Edwin Samuel did not like being in the position of taking the villagers' money. He saw wretched farmers, at times burdened with heavy debts. Like James Pollock, who had also served in Ramallah, he occasionally listed a village's arrears as "lost debts" that could not be recouped. The tax, a kind of tithe that had been imposed by the Turks as well, was supposed to reflect the harvest, but in fact the amount was set in a process of bargaining between the commissioner and the mukhtar.

More than once Samuel resorted to threats, delivered in broken Arabic. In English, he would speak to the villagers in quasi-biblical language: "If you pay now what I ask, oh my children, I shall be as dew upon your fields, as honey on your lips. But if you do not, then I shall come as a wolf in your sheep-fold by night and you shall be consumed as by fire on your threshing floor." Then, when he saw their eyes fairly popping out of their heads, he said, he would tell them to scurry home and bring something on account. A tax collector, sitting at his side, would keep the record. Samuel was assisted by a force of fourteen policemen; their principal task was to defend the tax collectors when they traveled on the roads with money in hand.

He tried to impose various modern farming methods such as iron plows, but came to the conclusion that it was better to leave the village in its backwardness; it had a certain romantic charm and confirmed his self-image as a man of progress. "I was someone from the twentieth century back in the eleventh century with all the powers of feudal baron," he wrote. "The peasants might be miserably poor and illiterate, but they were *mine*. I protected them against tyranny from my own liege lord and expected them to pay me homage accordingly."[61]

In the cities, district commissioners supervised the work of the municipalities. Since all municipal matters required approval from the civil
administration, supervision included everything from writing the budget
to preventing people from pasting notices on walls, from the control of
epidemics to zoning plans. The municipalities were glad of the administration's intervention in such matters because the government also took
responsibility for urgent needs, funding the water system in Jerusalem, a
hospital in Tel Aviv, and so on. Like a village mukhtar, a city mayor served
as a kind of liaison between the populace and the authorities; real power
rested with the district commissioners.[62]* Indeed, the authorities tended
to treat the mayors as high-level mukhtars. During the first years of the
Mandate, mayors were appointed, not elected. "The result is that the
people have far less share in the government than in Turkish times," Herbert Samuel maintained.[64]†

The administration grew from year to year. Herbert Samuel worked
with twenty departments, the last high commissioner with more than
forty. Parallel to the dramatic increase in the population, the number of
civil servants rose also. Samuel began his term with fewer than 2,500
employees; toward the end of the Mandate there were more than
30,000.[65] The administration was the largest employer in the country, and
salaries consumed 75 percent of its budget.[66] "The Holy Land with its
large administration and its small area is like a baby wearing his father's
clothes," critics wrote. Arab locals complained about contradictions,
duplication, and lack of clarity: "We see a Tower of Babylon in Palestine,"
they stated. Every commissioner in Palestine "rules as he likes." Furthermore, they added, the government is amateurish, and in fact the director
of customs and duties "is an actor by profession."[67]

As the years went by, one was less and less likely to find an actor collecting duties, or the organist or the Glasgow distiller that Ronald Storrs had
identified among the first members of his staff. As in other parts of the
empire, British bureaucrats in Palestine increasingly belonged to the
colonial administration ranks trained in London according to fairly strin-
gent political and professional standards.

*In Jaffa, W. F. Stirling complained that his job required running up large official
expenses—time and again he had to host all kinds of important people, some of them local
and some guests of the government. But no one compensated him, he said.[63]

†Elections to local councils were delayed, mainly to make legal arrangements allowing the
country's Jews to participate. Most of the Jews held foreign citizenship, and Turkish law, still
in force, permitted only local citizens to vote. The first municipal elections were held in 1926.

6.

The administration officials were supposed to be "English gentlemen"—demobilized officers or university graduates. If a man had gone to private school, was an active sportsman, and looked good, he could probably get a job in the colonial service. Instructions regarding the candidates' physical appearance almost created a kind of pedigree breed. The criteria referred not only to a man's style of dress and his manner of speech but also to his physique, the color of his hair and eyes, the shape of his mouth, and the state of his fingernails. "Weakness of various kinds may lurk in a flabby lip or in averted eyes," one of the service's veteran members enjoined his colleagues, "just as single-mindedness and purpose are commonly reflected in a steady gaze and a firm set of mouth and jaw."

Young men frequently followed their fathers into the colonial service and in going overseas continued a family tradition. Their enlistment, however, was often the result of their inability to find suitable employment at home and of the expansion of the colonial administration. There was considerable demand for colonial jobs, and at a certain point demand surpassed the supply. Service was always temporary, a few years in Malta, a few in Tanganyika, a few more in Sierra Leone, then a few in Jerusalem.

Manly, chivalrous, imbued with a sense of moral mission, colonial officials were supposed to carry the principles of British administration overseas—proper, fair, apolitical management.[68] But their image of themselves reflected a fiction: they were hardly neutral, and they did not come from the elite of British officialdom. The salaries of government officials in the colonies were lower than those of parallel rank in England, and consequently the colonies did not attract the most talented young people.

The British themselves filled no more than 10 percent of the jobs; a majority of employees were locals. In the early 1920s there was a notably high proportion of Jews and Christian Arabs, far beyond their presence in the population. The Muslim Arabs were severely underrepresented. Over the years their share grew, while the percentage of Jews in government service declined until it was below their presence in the population, although they filled a disproportionate number of senior positions. The segment of Christian Arabs remained relatively high. The fact that the British took pains to record the national and religious identities of the officials and to produce statistics belies their claim to have set up a professional, apolitical administration. British Jews in the bureaucracy were counted as Jews.[69]

The Palestinian Jews in senior positions were prominent principally during Samuel's tenure. Together with the British Zionists, they held the key positions in his administration, complained Lieutenant Colonel Percy Bramley, the director of public security in Palestine. In fact, Bramley wrote, Samuel's was a "Zionist-controlled government." The high commissioner, the chief secretary, and the attorney general were good people, wrote Colonel Stirling, who governed in Jaffa, but the fact that the British had chosen these particular people for these positions "blackened the good name of England in the Middle East and led to the downfall of our reputation for fair play."[70]

The British believed their main job was to ensure that everyone live together peacefully. More often they found themselves caught in the breach between Jews and Arabs. Harry Luke, Storrs's assistant, blamed the Balfour Declaration for having created an impossible situation. The declaration led, inevitably, to partition—not a new thing, Luke commented, in the land of King Solomon.[71] The British were supposed to bring culture to Palestine, but in contrast to France's cultural imperialism, they did not seek to impose their values or their identity on the colonies. They tended to keep their distance from the population, at most displaying folkloristic wonderment at the native heritage and some interest in preserving it.[72]

This reluctance was not just a political consideration; it also reflected a romantic tendency to relate to Palestine as the land of the Bible and treat it as a huge wax museum. Architect Charles Robert Ashbee, an adviser to Storrs, made tremendous efforts to save Hebron's glassblowing craft from extinction. His ideal Palestine was backward, to be sure, but so harmonious and heartwarming. To him, the Arab villagers personified beauty and dignity. The Jews who had come to the country had brought with them the squalid ugliness and disharmony of the cities of southeastern Europe and America. Ashbee couldn't imagine a worse combination.[73]*

In keeping with their stance, the authorities refused to prohibit child marriage, an accepted practice among Arabs and Jews from Arab countries. A Jewish women's organization launched a campaign to halt it, but the administration tried to evade the issue. Member of Parliament

---

*Thomas Hodgkin, Samuel's personal secretary, later attributed "something splendidly eternal" to the Arab villagers, and predicted that this quality would be preserved even when all the empires, officials, soldiers, and policemen went home: "Shepherds will go on playing pipes when all the brass bands are scrapped and wearing Palestinian clothes when all the tail-coats have been destroyed by moths."[74]

Eleanor Rathbone intervened to little effect. In the early 1930s Rathbone was still protesting the Palestine administration's tolerance of the marriage of thirteen-year-old girls; the age of consent was raised to fifteen only in the mid-1930s.[75] Some of the leading figures in British government, among them David Lloyd George, lent their names to an organization that defended Arab child marriages, warning Rathbone that protests against the practice were part of the Zionist movement's plot to take over the country. After robbing the Arabs of freedom and opportunities for economic development, the Zionists now wished to impose their moral norms on Palestine. The British administration also resisted granting women the right to vote. "Seeing that strong objections are entertained not only by Moslems but also by certain Jews to the participation of women in public affairs, you will, I am sure, agree that it would be impracticable to lay down a general rule in Palestine," an official of the Colonial Office wrote to Rathbone.[76]

The British were swept away by the charms of the colorful human mosaic they found in Palestine. Luke enumerated the servants in his home: they had brought the nanny from England; Vladimir, the butler, was a "white" Russian refugee from the Soviet Union who had been a counterrevolutionary officer. There were also red Russians in Jerusalem, loyal to the revolutionary regime. Luke had brought his valet, a Turk called Halil Ali, from his previous posting in Cyprus. Ahmed, the cook, was a black Berber from Egypt, the kitchen boy was an Armenian who had one day turned out to be a girl in disguise, and the housemaid came from the Russian convent on the Mount of Olives. When Edwin Samuel described his household, he mentioned, along with the nanny and the houseboy, "our two Yemenites."[77]

At times the British wrote of the Palestinian population with arrogant, derisive irony. Edward Keith-Roach described the Arabs as "a naturally indolent people." He wrote, "Arabs are a pleasant people to live among, and their long loose garments cover a multitude of sins." Keith-Roach related how the mayor of Jerusalem had demanded that he dedicate the new public toilet the municipality had built not far from Zion Square. According to Keith-Roach, he had to "induce" the municipality to build the structure, which would continue to function for many years to come. He claimed also to have "induced" the mayor to do without the opening ceremony: "For once, a public building was opened without speeches," Keith-Roach wrote with an air of victory, his wit a sign of progress and wisdom, so different from the backward population whose leaders were ignorant, corrupt, power-hungry, honor-seeking and, especially, less intelligent than he.[78]

In his memoirs Humphrey Bowman ridiculed the errors he saw on the English signs Arabs put up in buses and other public places. In fact, as director of the department of education he bore responsibility for these mistakes, but to his way of thinking his job did not include ensuring that the Arabs were fluent in English.[79] A similar sense of superiority guided the first British judges to arrive in Palestine.

7.

One sunny morning seven men went out onto the roof of the courthouse in Jerusalem to have their picture taken. Six of them were judges of the appeals court; one was apparently the bailiff. The courthouse was located in the Russian Compound, in a nineteenth-century structure built as a tzarist hospice for pilgrims. The photograph shows a domed roof tiled with stone; in the background is another picturesque dome and, at a distance, some cypress trees. The six judges sit on a stone railing, the bailiff behind them wearing boots, jodhpurs, and a military jacket with large pockets and metal buttons; a leather belt cuts diagonally across his chest. In his hand is a ceremonial staff, under his nose a large mustache, and on his head a tarbush. Ramrod straight, punctilious, not young, he looks as if the Turks had forgotten to take him with them when they fled the city.

The judges at his feet radiate an avuncular, almost genial air. All are in black robes with white starched collars. Two are Muslims, one a Christian Arab, and one, Gad Frumkin, is Jewish. The three Arab judges in the picture also wear tarbushes, while Frumkin's head is bare. In the center sits Chief Justice Sir Thomas Haycraft, together with the other British judge. Both are wearing white wigs, a professional tradition and status symbol they brought from home. They do not appear to feel ridiculous; rather, they convey superiority. The wigs on their heads separate them from the local judges—only British justices were entitled to wear a pile of horsehair.

The British judicial system was considered far superior to the Ottoman system it had replaced. Nevertheless, the authorities saw no reason to grant the local population all the advantages of British justice. For years they ruled that "the customs and habits, mode of life, mode of thought and character of the English people are very different from those of the inhabitants of Palestine." Hence it would be a "grave injustice" to impose British

common law, with which the people are not acquainted, on Palestine.*
Thus, unlike courts in Britain, there were no juries in Palestine; the
assumption was that juries would be too political and corrupt. During the
Turkish era, one lawyer wrote, the position of judge was analogous to that
of "a waiter in a hotel, where it was officially forbidden by the management
for waiters to accept tips."[80] Bribes were common currency, people's way of
influencing decisions that determined their fate. Years went by before the
population began to trust that the British administration was indeed honest and fair. The reduction of corruption in the judicial system was one of
the main British achievements. The judges also believed that the natives
had to be educated to respect the independence of the courts.[81]

In principle, the court system did enjoy a great deal of independence
from the government. But when the judges had to address political matters
they often tended to adjust their rulings to the needs of the administration,
and their individual political positions also influenced their decisions. Still,
the courts maintained a fiction that the great national conflict, so dominant
outside the courtroom walls, was dwarfed among the robes, as if it were just
one matter of contention among countless others that could be resolved
disinterestedly. The system thrived because everyone involved preferred to
subscribe to the fiction of the courts' impartiality and accept the courts'
conventions. The population of the court was spectacularly contentious
and diverse; at the same time there was a familial air, as if everyone knew
everyone else—judges, attorneys, plaintiffs and defendants, rapists, thieves
and murderers, con men and terrorists, prostitutes, clerks and bailiffs,
reporters, onlookers, Jews from all corners of the world, Arab citizens,
Christians of all sects, and British bureaucrats. In their various languages
and particular brands of humor, the people of the court enacted their conflicts and compromises, loyalties and betrayals, all laced with politics.

The judges lived their own fiction. The chief justice of the Supreme
Court in Jerusalem carried himself as if he were the lord chief justice of England. Edward Keith-Roach wrote that those who entered the judicial
departments in the colonies were the ones who had failed at the English or
Irish bar. Still, the courts in Palestine were considered one of the more effective judicial systems in the empire, alongside those of Ceylon and Cyprus.[82]

---

*Within less than ten years other British judges ruled that the six hundred thousand Jews
and a million and a half Arabs living in Palestine were sufficiently imbued with Western culture and ideas to enjoy the benefits of the common law. In the meantime, the judges had
been replaced; they were now less conservative and less arrogant. In time they also permitted the local judges to wear wigs.

8.

Herbert Samuel was proud of the achievements of his five-year administration: the construction of nearly a thousand kilometers of roads, progress in the fight against malaria, two hundred new classrooms, punctual and effective rail and postal systems. Measures had been taken to protect antiquities. Samuel cited other achievements, but what seemed to please him most was the budget surplus he left behind of about a quarter of a million pounds. Except for the cost of maintaining the army, the British taxpayer had not been required to finance Palestine, and even the army had reduced its expenses by 80 percent, Samuel declared.[83]

From time to time the Mandatory administration took loans to cover a deficit, but so long as there was relative tranquillity, the government managed its finances prudently and conservatively. In the period preceding World War II it spent only 10 to 12 percent of its budget for health and education; the same was true in other colonies as well. In Britain itself, nearly 50 percent of the budget went for welfare services.*

Both the Arabs and the Jews frequently claimed that the budget was not distributed equitably. The Zionist movement argued that the Jewish population provided a greater proportion of the Mandate's revenues than the services it received, meaning that the Jews were financing Arab welfare. Chaim Weizmann complained to Samuel that the Jews were funding part of the Arab educational system.[85] The Arabs, for their part, remonstrated that the government's tariff policy favored Jewish industry and harmed Arab interests, and that high taxes were required to fund a bloated administration that principally provided for the needs of the expanding Jewish population. Most of the new roads were paved to serve the Jews, they argued.[86]

The British not only allowed the Zionist movement to bring capital and to purchase land, they also granted the Jews important economic concessions, including the franchise to produce electricity and the franchise to exploit the resources of the Dead Sea. Tariffs were intended to bring money into the public purse, but they essentially aided Jewish industry while putting pressure on the Arab population, especially the

---

*Other government expenses were administration (29%), internal security, including courts (29%), and services such as road construction and communications (30%). Government revenues came almost entirely from local taxation, largely of agricultural produce, and tariffs; an income tax was instituted only in 1941. Grants received by the Palestinian administration from London did not amount to more than 10 percent of its budget and were needed mostly for security requirements.[84]

villages. Moreover, Jewish workers in government service demanded and received higher salaries than Arab workers. But the large gap between the strength of the two economies, Jewish and Arab, was not for the most part a reflection of British economic policy, but rather of the momentum of Zionist entrepreneurship.[87] The government encouraged economic separation between Jews and Arabs.[88] To the Zionists, an independent economy was part of the aspiration for political independence.

Herbert Samuel believed the tensions between Jews and Arabs could be neutralized through the benefits of effective health and education systems. He tended to view the conflict in social and economic terms, which was an illusion. The conflict between the Jews and Arabs in Palestine was not principally economic but national. The prisoner of his conception, Samuel repeated it again and again, as if that would make it real. His reports to his king reflected his indefatigable optimism.*

Soon after his arrival Samuel had set out on horseback to visit Malha, an Arab village on the outskirts of Jerusalem. He was hosted in the home of the most important family in the village. Among those who greeted him there was one of the leading provocateurs during the Nebi Musa riots, who had been released from prison on Samuel's order. Samuel was glad to see the man. He wrote to his wife that "all that agitation is as dead as if it had taken place a hundred years ago." With amazement, he told her that the bloodshed had been "forgotten."[91] Everything is quiet, Samuel wrote to Chaim Weizmann as well, in one of his optimistic reports: "you could hear a pin drop." Less than a year later the country was burning.

---

*Direct contact with Buckingham Palace was a flattering innovation in Samuel's life. He requested and received instruction in how to address the king. "In old days when letters were written by hand, it would have been sufficient for the commencement to be merely 'Sir Herbert Samuel presents his humble duty to Your Majesty' and then no ending to the letter. But with a type written communication, an autograph signature is necessary to establish its genuineness. So to be correct your letter, which finished 'I am Sir Your Majesty's loyal subject and Obedient Servant' should have begun with 'Sir': Otherwise it would have been sufficient to have signed Herbert Samuel at the end, having begun Sir Herbert Samuel presents his humble duty to Your Majesty."[89] From time to time Samuel sent the king stamps from Palestine. He also tried to use his connections to arrange a knighthood for Weizmann, but failed.[90]

Jaffa, 1921

1.

Beyond the orange groves, southeast of Jaffa, in an Arab neighborhood called Abu Kabir, stood the Red House, named for the color of its upper floor. A high wall surrounded the courtyard; within was a well and a barn. In the spring of 1921 the Yatzker family was renting the place; no other Jews lived nearby. Yehuda Yatzker was fifty-five and had come, some six months earlier, from Russia, where he had been in the livestock feed business. In Palestine he became a dairy farmer and kept several cows. The house itself was fairly spacious: in typical Arab style, the front steps led into a large central space from which other rooms branched off. The Yatzkers rented some of these rooms to boarders, all of them Jews. "The house attracted people who were searching for seclusion, quiet, and a cheap place to live," Yatzker's daughter, Rivka Yatzker-Schatz, later wrote.

One of the tenants was a chemist-inventor who wanted to produce cheap blocks for building, and there was a poet or two waiting for inspiration and a publisher. Also living in the house was Josef Chaim Brenner, an author, editor, translator, and journalist, a man of some fame and many admirers. His room contained a simple table and a crate to sit on; he slept on a folding cot.[1] At the time, he was editing the letters of Yosef Trumpeldor, recently killed at Tel Hai.

This was not a good time in his life. Almost forty, he had just separated from his wife; she had taken their son, Uri, and gone to Berlin. Brenner had been born in the Ukraine. He studied in a yeshiva, then abandoned religious orthodoxy, and began writing articles and stories in Hebrew. He served for a while in the Russian army until the Russo-Japanese War broke out, in 1904. Unlike Trumpeldor, Brenner deserted rather than fight in the war and escaped to London, where he put out an influential Hebrew literary journal, *HaMeorer*. In 1909 he settled in Jerusalem. For a short time he worked as a laborer and then joined the staff of the socialist-Zionist weekly *HaPoel HaTzair*. During World War I he taught at the Hebrew Gymnasium high school in Jaffa. When the Turks expelled the city's residents he went to the north with his students, and after various wanderings settled in Tel Aviv and again earned his living as a teacher and editor. He published his first stories in the periodicals he edited.

Brenner radiated an air of boyishness; he was dreamy, romantic, melancholy, and very Russian; when he came to Palestine he grew a thick beard, which added to his charisma. "We all clung to him with love," wrote one of his followers. Hailed as a prophet of Hebrew secularism, he was a gaunt man with jutting cheekbones, which gave his face a distinctly Slavic look, but his admirers saw in him a Hebrew masculinity, charged with an almost erotic passion for the land. One night after a lecture, some of Brenner's disciples accompanied him on his way back home. "Suddenly Brenner fell down onto the plowed field," wrote a follower, "took a handful of earth, kissed it and, weeping, cried out: Land of Israel, will you be ours?"[2]

Brenner's writing was vehement and combative, sometimes rancorous and hostile. Philosophically, he sought to detach himself from Jewish life in the "Exile," as the Diaspora was then called. In his stories Diaspora Jews were contemptible, degenerate, shifty, and filthy. His depiction was almost antisemitic, and he frequently found himself at the center of fierce controversies. His critics accused him of self-hatred. In truth, though, the new Hebrew culture never replaced his Jewish identity. Moreover, Brenner belonged to a Jewish literary environment that mostly flourished, in Hebrew and in Yiddish, more powerfully outside Palestine than in it. The great Hebrew literary figures such as Bialik, Ahad Ha'am, and Tchernikovsky had not yet settled in Palestine, and S. Y. Agnon had just left for a long stay in Europe. In fact, once he had moved to Palestine, Brenner found he actually preferred living among the Jews of the Exile to having Arabs for neighbors.[3]

In an article he wrote for *Kuntress,* one of the publications of the labor movement, Brenner described an incident with his Arab neighbors. He had come home; the neighbors were sitting on their doorstep, and Brenner greeted them. They did not respond, and he felt hurt. "The lack of response was deliberate, malevolent," he wrote. He thought he saw an expression of triumph on the face of the Arabs, as if to say, "We managed to restrain ourselves from returning the Jew's greeting." Brenner, in his anger, wondered whether the Arabs in Palestine really were the descendants of the ancient Hebrews, as some people said—they hardly deserved such a lineage, he thought.* Either way, he had to walk past them, whether they wanted him to or not, Brenner wrote, but he would prefer to deal with a neighbor in Kovno, Lithuania.

As he continued on his way home, a "colossal Arab" leaped out at him. To his surprise the giant turned out to be a boy of about thirteen. Brenner tried to strike up a conversation but understood only a few words, and he agonized at not having learned Arabic. He imagined the boy was telling him about his tribulations and felt a paternal responsibility for the boy's future: "Indeed, it is for me to bring light to your eyes, to bring you into the human fellowship," he wrote. Previously Brenner had written of the Arabs, "We are arch-enemies." He understood that the Arab-Jewish conflict was one of two national movements. "Living in tiny Palestine," he wrote, are "no fewer than six or seven hundred thousand Arabs who are, despite all their degeneracy and savagery, masters of the land, in practice and in feeling, and we have come to insert ourselves and live among them, because necessity forces us to do so. There is already hatred between us— there must be and will be." Everything belongs to them, Brenner noted as he gazed at the citrus groves around him.[5] A Muslim graveyard lay across the street from the Red House. He related to the Arabs with alienation and arrogance, anxiety and hostility.

The week of Passover went by quietly. But on Saturday, April 30, 1921, the residents of the Red House were concerned that there would be clashes between Jews and Arabs in the city the next day, May Day, when the socialist Jews held a parade. Brenner suggested that they guard the house at night—Zvi Schatz, Rivka Yatzker's husband, had a rifle. As it turned out, the night passed without incident. The following morning Rivka and her husband set out for Tel Aviv on a donkey, taking their little

---

*While in exile in the United States, David-Ben Gurion and Yitzhak Ben-Zvi wrote a book on Palestine in Yiddish that promulgated the idea that the Arab fellahs were nothing less than the descendants of the ancient Jews. This was meant to prove that the Jews had continued to engage in agriculture in the land of Israel even after they lost their independence.[4]

girl Devorah and Rivka's mother with them. Yehuda Yatzker and his son Avramchik escorted them and then returned. The three boarders, Brenner among them, remained at home.

Rivka and Zvi Schatz wanted to see the May Day parade in Tel Aviv. They found a large crowd at the workers' club waving red flags and a picture of Karl Marx. Suddenly they heard gunshots. Rivka Schatz sent Zvi to find out what was happening, but he returned with only vague information.[6] Maybe a police officer had fired for some reason, perhaps it was Toufiq Bey al-Said, one of Jaffa's most senior police commanders. Schatz made no further inquiries, as he was frantically trying to obtain a vehicle to evacuate the people from the Red House: Jaffa was raging with a kind of violence unknown in the country since the World War.

2.

The first shots had apparently been fired to disperse a procession marching from Jaffa to Tel Aviv without a permit. The parade had been organized by the Jewish Communist Party, officially called the Socialist Workers Party, though its opponents used an acronym of the party's Hebrew name to nickname it "Mops," which means "pug dog" in German. The previous night the party had sent boys out to distribute leaflets in Arabic and Yiddish emblazoned with slogans calling on the workers to topple the British regime and establish the Soviet Union of Palestine. That morning, police officer Said had appeared at the party's headquarters in Jaffa, warning the sixty people present not to participate in the demonstration. But they managed to slip away and headed for Tel Aviv via Menashia, a border neighborhood populated by both Jews and Arabs.

Meanwhile in Tel Aviv, a large May Day parade had been organized by Achdut HaAvoda, the major Jewish labor party at the time, and sanctioned by the authorities. Tensions ran high between the rival parties. At some point the communists and Achdut HaAvoda people ran into one another, and a fistfight ensued. The police chased the "Mopsies" members back in the direction of Jaffa, where the Communist parade clashed with Arabs, who were equally unsympathetic to a Soviet Union of Palestine.

A commission of inquiry later appointed to investigate the riots found that the fight between the communists and Achdut HaAvoda was the spark that lit the fire. The American consulate in Jerusalem concluded, in contrast, that violence between Jews and Arabs was bound to erupt in any case.[7] Whatever the reason, dozens of witnesses—Jewish, Arab, and

British—all told the same story: Arab men broke into Jewish buildings and murdered the occupants; women came afterward and looted. Bearing clubs, knives, swords, and in some cases pistols, Arabs attacked Jewish pedestrians and destroyed Jewish homes and stores. They beat and killed Jews, children included, in their homes; in some cases they split the victims' skulls open.

In testimony reminiscent of the Nebi Musa riots of the previous year, many witnesses recounted how the mob had torn apart quilts and pillows and scattered the down in the alleys, just as Russian thugs did during pogroms. The commission of inquiry later described the riots as "an orgy of pillage." Many witnesses identified their neighbors among the attackers and murderers; in some places Arabs had come to the defense of Jews and gave them refuge in their houses. A number of witnesses said that there had been Arab policemen among the rioters.[8] About 45,000 people lived in Jaffa at the time, roughly half of them Muslims, a third Jews, and the rest Christians.

3.

At about noon two British officers were walking through the alleys of the marketplace in Jaffa's Muslim Ajami neighborhood. They were on vacation and had come to visit the city along with their wives. After making their purchases they suddenly found themselves surrounded by an angry crowd; people ran around them hysterically, brandishing wooden boards and iron rods. Reginald Samuel Foster was not sure what he was seeing—there was a man taking knives from people and sharpening them on a stone; the knives were very long, he later testified. He had a feeling that something horrible was about to happen. Foster and his companions slipped into the nearby French hospital to protect the women, he explained. He went up to the building's roof, where he heard gunshots. His friend, Sergeant Major Euclid Brooks Wager, had remained on the ground floor; his wife had fainted from the excitement. Wager then went up to the roof himself but did not see much and soon came back down to check on his wife. Foster in the meantime saw a crowd trying to break down the gate of a nearby building.

The crowd's target was an immigrants' hostel, run by the Zionist Commission; about a hundred people were staying there that day. Most had arrived just weeks or days before. Sometimes the young men and women living at the hostel would walk down to the beach with their arms around each other, and the locals said they were polluting Arab morality. How could it be that Britain, a country committed to Christian morals, was allowing such people to take over the country? This argument would be repeated in the years that followed.[9]* The hostel, both a Zionist stronghold and a den of iniquity, was thus an obvious symbolic target. On the other hand, perhaps the house had no symbolic value but was simply an unprotected site full of defenseless people in the heart of a neighborhood of Arabs run amok.

When the attack came most of the hostel residents were in the dining room, where they had just finished lunch. At close to 1:00 P.M. they heard shouting from the street, according to twenty-five-year-old Rachel Rudenberg, a new immigrant from the Ukraine, in her testimony six weeks later. Some of the immigrants went out to the yard, locked the gate, and leaned against it with their backs to keep the mob from storming the hostel. Rocks began landing in the yard; suddenly there was an explosion. Then they heard the sound of gunfire. A few minutes later another bomb went off. Most of the residents fled to the second floor of the building; Rudenberg and a few others hid in the reading room. The gate in the yard was rammed open, and the mob poured in. Through the window of the reading room Rudenberg saw a policeman. She told the others that everything would be all right, the police had arrived. But the shooting did not stop. At first she thought the police were firing in the air to disperse the crowd, but she soon realized that the policemen were aiming at the building. Rudenberg and her companions retreated into a back room and blocked the door with chairs and tables. Someone banged on the door and tried to break in, and the hinges began to give.

Out in the yard the mob was running wild. One immigrant was killed by a policeman's bullet, fired at short range. Others were beaten with sticks and stabbed. Inside the building the rioters continued to batter the door, trying to break it down. Nineteen-year-old Shoshana Sandak, who had arrived from Lithuania five months previously, recounted the scene: the door began to splinter; the bookcase pushed up against it inched forward. Five women fled through another door into the courtyard, with a policeman on their heels, firing his pistol.[11] Three managed to escape.

Devorah Meler, the house mother, was trapped in a corner with one of the girls, who hid behind her. A policeman wanted to get at the girl. Meler

---

*The governor of Jaffa later recalled complaints he had received from Arab community leaders to the effect that young Jews were engaging in "mixed bathing in the nude."[10]

shielded her, and the policeman struck Meler on the head. She tried to placate him with her gold necklace, but the policeman was not satisfied. Meler motioned that she had nothing more to give him. He gestured that she did have something he wanted and began to unbutton his trousers. As she tried to escape, he shot at the floor to frighten her and began to lift up her skirt. Meler tried to flee again and he shot at the floor a second time. Finally, she managed to shake free and run; the policeman fired his pistol in her direction but missed.[12]

Some of the immigrants escaped into the street. Reginald Samuel Foster, still on the roof of the French hospital, heard a woman scream and made out several men chasing a girl of about fourteen. The girl fell. Foster saw a man beat her head with an iron rod. Sergeant Major Wager, still going up and down from the roof to care for his wife, saw a man running; others ran after him and grabbed his clothes, bringing him to the ground. As he lay on the road the crowd beat him with an iron rod, jumped on his body, and then jabbed at him with the rod. A few minutes later Wager saw another man fall; he was beaten to death with wooden boards.

Wager later reported all this to the commission of inquiry. He was asked whether he had considered going out to the street to see whether he could do something. His answer summed up the British dilemma in Palestine: "When we found it was a question between the Jews and the Arabs we did not think it was for us to interfere. . . . Which were we to stop?"[13]

4.

Herbert Samuel tried his best to bring a halt to the riots. He was stunned, as was his wife. One administration official recalled the high commissioner consulting with his staff, while Lady Samuel paced back and forth in the long corridor at Augusta Victoria, muttering over and over, "They are killing our people, they are killing our people." Samuel sent his two most senior officials, Wyndham Deedes and Norman Bentwich, both ardent Zionists, to Jaffa. At the same time, he called for reinforcements from Egypt; Allenby sent two destroyers to Jaffa and another to Haifa. The administration declared a state of emergency. The press was subjected to censorship, and in the days that followed, newspapers appeared with blank spots.[14]

Samuel met with Arab representatives and tried to calm them. Former Jerusalem mayor Musa Kazim al-Husseini demanded that he suspend

Jewish immigration. As two or three small boats holding some three hundred immigrants were even then approaching Palestinian shores, Samuel asked Allenby for permission to redirect them to Port Said or Alexandria. Allenby refused. Samuel permitted the commissioner of Ramle to announce the suspension of immigration, and the boats, which were not allowed to land, were forced to return to Istanbul.[15] At the same time, Samuel notified Haj Amin al-Husseini that he had made his final decision to appoint him mufti of Jerusalem.

Weizmann, Ussishkin, Jabotinsky, and Ben-Gurion all happened to be out of the country. Thus David Eder, Yitzhak Ben-Zvi, and Arthur Ruppin took the helm of the Jewish community, and Nachum Sokolow, who was visiting Palestine, joined them. The minutes of their meetings reveal a sense of terror, indignation, and helplessness. They pondered the future of the Jews in Palestine but were most concerned with immediate questions, such as how to explain the riots to the high commissioner. The Zionist movement had always taken the position that Arabs and Jews could live together peaceably in Palestine. But now, Ben-Zvi argued, "if the entire Arab world is against us, we must say so." One of his colleagues disagreed. Any statement confirming that the Jewish presence in Palestine inevitably led to violence would only serve Arab propaganda, he said. The Zionists should continue to argue that the clashes were the result of deliberate agitation and did not express the Arabs' true national sentiments.[16]*

Sokolow demanded that Samuel revoke the suspension of immigration. He was simply rewarding terror, Sokolow said. He suggested halting immigration quietly, without an announcement; the Zionist movement would cooperate, he promised. Such surreptitious action would not have helped, of course. To assuage the Arabs, a public announcement was precisely what was needed. Samuel showed Sokolow the draft of his statement and, Jew to Jew, Zionist to Zionist, the two began to bargain over the wording and then continued to argue about the riots. Samuel warned that Palestine was liable to become another Ireland. Sokolow said there was no reason to worry—a small gang of Arab nationalists had stirred things up, but there was no basis for saying that the entire Arab world opposed Zionism. "You are wrong," Samuel corrected him. "This is a war of the Arab nation against the Hebrew nation." Members of the Zionist Com-

---

*A few days later Eder presented this position before the British commission of inquiry: "I do not think there is a genuine Arab national movement," he said.[17]

mission described the events as a pogrom. "I was in Kishinev during the pogroms," Rabbi Y. L. Fishman told his colleagues.[18] Kishinev was cited the way Samuel cited Ireland, as one trauma to trump another, claim versus claim.*

5.

All this time Zvi Schatz had been running around pleading with different members of the recently established Tel Aviv defense committee, trying to persuade them to send a vehicle to evacuate the residents of the Red House. His daughter Devorah Yatzker-Schatz later related that until he mentioned Brenner, no one paid any attention. By the time a car was found, it was close to five in the afternoon. Leaving his wife and daughter in Tel Aviv, Schatz drove to Jaffa, accompanied by an Arab policeman. Meanwhile, three Jewish beekeepers had appeared at the Red House, the Lerer brothers from the agricultural settlement Nes Tziona, who had come to inspect the hives they had left in a nearby citrus grove. So there were now nine people to be evacuated, but only three places in the car. The three Lerers went: Zvi Schatz remained behind in the Red House. The Lerers later said that Brenner had insisted they go.[20]

By late afternoon the news from Jaffa had reached the Sarafand military camp, about twelve miles away. The Jewish Legion, which no longer existed but had not yet been officially disbanded, was billeted at the camp, and several soldiers set out in the direction of the riots. Wyndham Deedes, who was kept apprised of the situation, agreed that the men be given rifles. In addition Pinhas Rutenberg, Jabotinsky's partner in the Jerusalem self-defense efforts, had arrived in Tel Aviv and was helping the Jews organize.[21] The next morning armed Jews went into the streets of Jaffa to take revenge. Arab accounts of the Jewish violence are very similar to the Jewish testimonies about the Arab riots. The Jews looted homes and stores. They broke into Arab houses, beating and killing the occupants; in one house, a woman and child were murdered. A hunchbacked Arab and his children were killed in an orange grove; their bodies were disfigured. A Jewish policeman took part.[22]

---

*The comparison between the events in Jaffa and the Kishinev pogrom later appeared in the *Haganah History Book,* an official history of the Jewish community's self-defense campaign. But Zionist leader Chaim Arlosoroff wrote to his mother, "It is definitely not, in my opinion, a pogrom." One participant in the discussion used another word to describe what had happened in Jaffa: Holocaust.[19]

Still no one returned to evacuate the people left in the Red House. At around eleven on Monday morning, the six remaining occupants apparently decided to make their own way to Tel Aviv. They locked the door and set out but managed to get only a short distance. By the Muslim graveyard near the house, they ran into the funeral of an Arab boy killed the day before, the son of policeman Mahmoud Zeit. Had they stayed at home, they might have lived. Confronted by the crowd of mourners, the six men had no chance. Brenner and Schatz were shot; the others were murdered with sticks and hatchets. The bodies were discovered in the evening by a search party that included labor leader Berl Katznelson. By the time the police consented to move the bodies, one of them had disappeared; it was never found. The murderers had mutilated the victims: Brenner was found lying on his stomach, naked from the waist down. An eyewitness said that in his hand he held a bloodstained piece of paper with a few lines of writing on it.[23]

The bodies were finally taken for identification to the foyer of the Hebrew Gymnasium high school and were then buried in a common grave. The road leading to the cemetery was named after Yosef Trumpeldor. "What a harmonious end!" wrote Rabbi Benjamin, one of Brenner's friends. "What a beautiful death!" Brenner had been in no hurry to flee, he said, and had not been afraid of dying. S. Y. Agnon wrote that Brenner "sanctified his life in his death and sanctified his death in his life."

Brenner himself might have said the same about Trumpeldor. In fact, the two men became part of a single myth. They were particularly well suited to being mythologized. Like Trumpeldor, Brenner had been an object of worship while still alive, almost a patriotic symbol, and like Trumpeldor he was shot by Arabs. Thus the shots that killed him, people said, had been meant to kill Zionism. The headstone over the communal burial site reads: "A fraternal grave for holy and pure souls . . . in their blood the people of Israel will live and in their sanctity be sanctified."* In addition, the national myth created around Brenner's death

---

*The spirit behind Trumpeldor's purported final words—"It is good to die for one's country"—had taken root in the developing national culture of mourning. Moshe Gissin of Petach Tikva, whose son was among the casualties of the riots, eulogized his child with the words, "I am gratified that I was a living witness to such a historical event in the life of Petach Tikvah."[24]

Jerusalem, December 9, 1917: Mayor Salim al-Husseini surrenders to the British for the second time. (Central Zionist Archive)

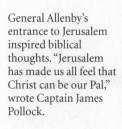

General Allenby's entrance to Jerusalem inspired biblical thoughts. "Jerusalem has made us all feel that Christ can be our Pal," wrote Captain James Pollock.

Count Antonio de Ballobar, Spanish
counsel, Jerusalem 1918 (*Kol Ha'ir*)

Jerusalem governor Ronald Storrs, posing
for posterity (*Orientations*, Storrs, 1939)

Lod, 1918: Chaim Weizmann (second from right) and the Zionist Commission—"a standing insult to the British administration," according to General Congreve (State Archive)

Alter Levine as a European . . .

. . . and as a man of the Middle East
(The National Library)

Khalil al-Sakakini
with his
daughters (Hala
and Dumia
al-Sakakini)

Herbert Samuel, Jerusalem, 1923
(State Archive)

Samuel (right) and Storrs, 1921. "It's so quiet
you could hear a pin drop," wrote Samuel.
(Central Zionist Archive)

"The government agreed to
add Hebrew to all its
proclamations: English
would be printed in the
center, Arabic on the right,
and Hebrew on the left . . ."

High Commissioner Herbert Charles Onslow Plumer, Jerusalem, 1925 (Central Zionist Archive)

"A loathsome country . . ." High Commissioner John Chancellor, 1928. (Central Zionist Archive)

"One sunny morning seven men went out onto the roof of the courthouse in Jerusalem to have their picture taken . . ." The judges, 1925. (Central Zionist Archive)

The Western Wall, 1928 (State Archive)

"I'm not anti-Semitic and I'm not anti-Arab. I'm simply pro-British." Raymond Cafferata, Hebron, 1929. (Veronica Robertson)

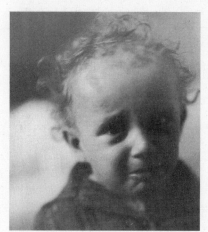

Thirteen-month-old Shlomo Slonim survived the massacre in Hebron. Both his parents were killed. (Central Zionist Archive)

Chaim Shalom Halevi, né Yeffim Gordin, 1929 (Central Zionist Archive)

A lost generation: only three out of every ten Arab children learned to read and write. (State Archive)

British soldiers in search of Arab nationalists in Samaria. "Who would have believed that Palestine has such heroes?" wrote Khalil al-Sakakini. (Central Zionist Archive)

served to expiate a sense of guilt: Brenner, like Trumpeldor, could have been saved.[25]*

The tension in Jaffa continued for a few more days, spreading to the nearby settlements of Petach Tikva, Hadera, Rehovot, and Kfar Saba. Samuel ordered that the Arab rioters be bombed from the air. A total of 47 Jews and 48 Arabs were killed in the disturbances, and the wounded numbered 146 Jews and 73 Arabs.[27] Palestine was at war, as Samuel told Sokolow, and war required a new kind of thinking.

6.

A few days after the events in Jaffa, the Tel Aviv municipal council discussed the future employment of a worker whom the minutes identify only as Mohammed. Someone had vandalized the council's generators, and there was a suspicion that the culprit was Mohammed. One of the council members proposed firing Mohammed, but the others preferred to defer the decision for a week or two. In the meantime, they decided, Mohammed would continue to receive his salary, although he was suspended from work. Ten days later the council discussed the issue again. They would have been happy for Mohammed to go back to his home in Jaffa and remain there but were concerned that this would make a "bad impression on the public." They decided to give him a different job, away from the generators.[28]

Between the council's first and second discussions, Tel Aviv had ceased to be part of Jaffa; the high commissioner had granted the town independent status. Tel Aviv had begun lobbying for municipal independence prior to the May riots; the events in Jaffa only served to spur the British to grant the town autonomous status, just as the Nebi Musa riots in Jerusalem a year earlier had influenced the decision to include the Balfour Declaration in the language of the Mandate.[29] In fact, Tel Aviv's autonomy was the most important Zionist achievement since Britain was given the Mandate. It was a cornerstone of Jewish autonomy in Palestine. Splitting Tel Aviv from Jaffa also formalized the principle that had moved the Jews to leave Jaffa in the first place: separation between Jews and Arabs.

---

*Nahum Kramer (later Shadmi) had experienced a pogrom in his native Russia. Newly arrived in Haifa, he was shocked by the news of Brenner's murder. Would pogroms continue to pursue him here? He went to the immigrants' hostel in Haifa, where self-defense was being organized. A woman who answered only to the name of Rosa handed him a pistol; she was "Red Rosa" Rabin. Suddenly a British police officer entered and Kramer was alarmed. But to his astonishment the policeman turned out to be "one of us"—a Jew. He had come to advise the defenders.[26]

Tel Aviv had been founded by Jews who were tired of living among Arabs. The formation of the town had not been a political act; nor was it necessary for security reasons. The founders of Tel Aviv simply wanted a European quality of life. "After my wedding in 1888," wrote Rachel Danin, a Jewish resident, "my father rented us an apartment in Jaffa, close to the road leading to the port, next to the Arab marketplace. The place was squalid; our apartment was full of smoke from the Arab houses, especially their bathhouses. The Arab houses were extremely close to ours and the close quarters were excruciating, especially when our son, Moshe, was born. The filth, the cursing, the nasty habits of the Arab children created a bad atmosphere in which to bring up a child. . . .

"We adults also felt isolated in this foreign environment; there was no cultural life and the Jews were scattered in different places in the town. The harshness of our life gave my husband Ezra the idea of creating a neighborhood some distance away from the Arabs—different, modern, where the houses wouldn't be on top of one another or attached like barracks. . . . He imagined a neighborhood where every resident would have a garden with flowers and chickens—a garden city."

Ezra Danin's new home in Tel Aviv had five bright and airy rooms. "The large, spacious bathrooms were not at all common," he wrote. "You can't imagine how happy the children were to see a faucet when they were used to waiting for Abu Halil or Abu Hassan to bring water in skins that stank; sometimes we would wait the whole day for Abu Halil to do us the favor of bringing our precious water. But in Tel Aviv the children could run to the faucet whenever they wanted, turn it on and, wonder of wonders, water came out . . . without Abu Halil."[30]

After the May Day disturbances, thousands of Jewish residents fled Jaffa for Tel Aviv, where they were housed in tent camps on the beach. Caution was necessary. Tel Aviv was still dependent on Jaffa; most of its residents worked there, and food and other services were supplied by the Arab city. One Arab fruit and vegetable vendor was given a note confirming that he had helped save Jews during the riots and the residents of Tel Aviv were thus obliged "to treat him with friendliness." Whoever harmed him would be severely punished. The home of another Arab had been damaged by his neighbors because he had given shelter to Jews; the people of Tel Aviv were called on to contribute to a special fund established for him, "so he does not think there is no support for a person who does good to a Jew in this or any other way." Dizengoff tried to maintain working relations with the Arab leadership in Jaffa. At a festive gathering held at Tel Aviv's Segal restaurant a year after the May riots, Dizengoff welcomed his colleague the mayor of Jaffa in a thoroughly Zionist way. "Both Jaffa and Tel Aviv will soon be beautiful European cities," he promised.[31]

These were faint gestures of goodwill, however. *Kuntress,* which Brenner had helped edit, reacted to the events in Jaffa with an article entitled "Entrenchment." Its message was clear: We wanted peace, and you, nefarious brother, have rejected our outstretched hand. We have no choice but to be here. We have burned all our bridges—Palestine is our last stand. So we will not be forced out. Quite the contrary: we will work even harder to build our homeland. And we will not forget what you have done to us. The article's language seems to have been influenced by the Haggadah, which the Jews would have read on the first night of Passover, just a few days before the riots: "And the more they afflicted them," the article read, "the more the children of Israel multiplied and grew." *Kuntress* referred to the Palestinian Jewish community as "the children of Israel" and as "us"—first person plural—as opposed to "the Arab"—third person singular. On May 1 the age of innocence had ended, *Kuntress* declared. Henceforth, the Jews could trust only in themselves, in the spirit of Brenner: "To the extent that we still have the breath of life in us, we will rejoice at the opportunity to spill our blood and the blood of others for a Jewish homeland."[32]

Only a few months earlier, news of the dreadful pogroms in the Ukraine had reached Palestine. According to various estimates, between 75,000 and 200,000 Jews had been murdered. The Zionist newspapers expressed deep emotional identification with the tragedy, describing the victims as "sheep led to the slaughter." The rabbinate called for a day of mourning and the suspension of all work; a collection was taken up. Then Yisrael Belkind, an educator who had led one of the first groups of immigrants in the early 1880s, initiated an operation to bring some 150 orphans from the Ukraine to Palestine. In 1903 he had established an agricultural school for children whose parents had been killed in the Kishinev pogrom. As in the case of the Kishinev children, Belkind's current plan gave rise to many arguments. Local leaders wanted to know who would pay for the children's care and what kind of education they would receive.

Compared to the dimensions of the catastrophe, reaching out to the orphans was essentially a symbolic gesture. But as Ahad Ha'am had written about the rescue of the Kishinev children, "It is such a beautiful idea!" Moreover, it was the original Zionist idea: the Jewish state in Palestine was to be a refuge for persecuted Jews from other lands. Max Nordau, a founding Zionist, proposed bringing to Palestine, within a few months, 600,000 immigrants, regardless of the country's economic absorption capacity.[33]

However, the clashes in Jerusalem and Jaffa made the local Jewish population acutely aware of its dependence on the Jewish communities of the world. *Ha'aretz* made an emotional appeal: "Do not leave us alone at the front. Do not slight the blood of the pioneers you sent ahead of the nation! Come to us in your masses, come to us in your multitudes to strengthen the Hebrew position, to bring us more working hands, more hands for defense!" This was the voice of a Jewish community in distress. Zionist representatives called on the Jews of the world to donate money to Palestine. Zionist thinking had entered a new stage. No longer a means of saving the Jewish people, Palestine turned into a national objective in its own right: "All our hope is in immigration, all our strength is nothing without the uninterrupted flow of people and resources to the country," *Ha'aretz* wrote. Jewish politicians in Palestine, among them David Ben-Gurion and Berl Katznelson, continued at the same time to fulminate against the Diaspora and to accuse Chaim Weizmann of all sorts of blunders.[34]

There is no evidence that the Jaffa riots were premeditated. Arab leaders and spokesmen, first and foremost Musa Kazim al-Husseini, condemned them. Haj Amin al-Husseini shifted his position as a result of the violence; he had been a vocal advocate of terror against Zionism, and though the appointment he received from the British did not soften his view, he turned to mostly legitimate political means to further the Arab cause and worked to prevent repetition of the rioting.[35] The Arabs put together a petition that they submitted to the League of Nations, in which they expressed their grievances; the essence of their demands—independence and democracy—remained unchanged through the end of the Mandate. The petition noted that the Arabs of Palestine included hundreds of young people, graduates of universities, among them architects and engineers, doctors and lawyers and teachers, and that many Arabs held senior positions in the governmental services of other countries. There was then sufficient Arab talent and experience to establish a stable, representative parliamentary government in Palestine, in accordance with the universal principles of self-determination accepted by the international community after the World War, they wrote.[36]

Khalil al-Sakakini was in Cairo as the riots were taking place, serving as the principal of a school. During the day he spent much time sitting in coffeehouses, smoking and meditating on the transformation the Arab world was undergoing, from a traditional society to a modern one, and thinking about the meaning of Levantinism. "The European city has made contact with the Oriental man before it has reached the Oriental woman. So the man is left between two elements—the European city outside and the Oriental woman inside. It would seem that the influence of the woman is stronger than the influence of the city," he wrote.[37]

7.

Herbert Samuel moved quickly to appoint a commission to investigate the events in Jaffa. A more astute body than the Nebi Musa court of inquiry, the commission was headed by Sir Thomas Haycraft, the chief justice of the Supreme Court in Palestine, and included among its members Harry Luke, aide to Ronald Storrs. The investigation focused on similar questions: Were the riots premeditated? Would it be fair to consider the riots an antisemitic pogrom? Had the authorities done everything in their power to halt the disturbances? The commission ruled that the rioting had broken out spontaneously, and that its perpetrators were not Jew haters but opponents of Zionism. In addition, the commission deemed that actions taken by the authorities had been satisfactory, although it confirmed, in understated language, that policemen had participated in the riots and the pillage. The corruption and weakness of the police, it argued, reflected the policemen's low pay. Most of them were Arabs; few Jews were willing to serve under the conditions the force offered.

Unlike the Nebi Musa court of inquiry, the Haycraft Commission did not go back to the dawn of history. It placed the blame squarely on the Arabs but evinced a great deal of understanding for their motives. Zionism scares them, it said, and the Zionists were not doing enough to mitigate the Arabs' apprehensions. In the process, the commission made an anthropological observation: Arabs are more obedient, but have a predilection for violent outbursts; Jews are less obedient, but also less prone to violence.

The commission's report angered the Jews in England. The *Jewish Chronicle* published a fitting Zionist response: "Imagine the wild animals in a zoological garden springing out of their cages and killing a number of spectators, and a commission appointed to enquire into the causes of the disaster reporting first and foremost that the animals were discontented with and hostile to the visitors who had come to see them! As if it were not the first business of the keepers to keep; to know the habits and disposition of the animals, and to be sure that the cages were secure!"

Spokesmen for the Jewish community in Palestine were also enraged. A few days before the report was published, on November 2, 1921, the anniversary of the Balfour Declaration, Arab thugs again went on a rampage through the Jewish Quarter in Jerusalem's Old City; five Jews and three Arabs died.[38] The Arabs were killed by explosives thrown by the Jews.

Jewish leaders demanded that Jerusalem commissioner Ronald Storrs be dismissed. "Leave!" *Ha'aretz* trumpeted, repeating this demand daily over a period of weeks. Storrs's way of governing, the newspaper insisted, was amateurish and romantic. "Can one look on spilling of Jewish blood as entertainment, as the Romans did?" the newspaper asked.[39] The anger was justified, though not because Storrs had incited the Arabs against the Jews, but rather because he had arrogantly believed his personal prestige was sufficient to hold them back. He had given the Arab leaders several warnings to control their community, and when disturbances broke out nevertheless, he behaved as if the violence were a personal slight. He found the angry criticism of his management by the Jewish leadership even more insulting. David Ben-Gurion described Storrs as "one of the top bloodstained officials of iniquity," and maintained that his presence in the country was a danger to the Jewish community. The Arabs were murdering the Jews because that was their nature, Ben-Gurion explained, but pogroms—that is, the murder of Jews under state sponsorship—were not a necessary part of reality. The fact was that the Turks had known how to keep the Arabs down.[40]

Storrs took cover behind a wall of patronizing sarcasm. "I am still unable to understand how I did not emerge from [the Zionist criticism] an anti-Semite for life," he wrote. And, he added in a sentence he later chose not to include in his memoirs, "Never was a Goy more mercilessly pogrommed."[41] He continued to treat Palestine as a colonial pet—fun to bring up, but not worth getting in trouble over with the neighbors.

Some villages whose residents had participated in the riots were heavily fined. A few of the rioters were brought to trial; one man was sentenced to fifteen years in prison, and a boy was given a public lashing. When three Jews, including a policeman, were convicted of participating in the murder of Arabs, the Jewish community raised a hue and cry: "There are judges in England," wrote historian Joseph Klausner, "who are concerned with nothing but justice and truth; but in Palestine, the land of the prophets, the prophets of truth and justice, where is truth, where is justice?" The consequences of the court's decisions, Klausner wrote, would be serious: "The foundations of the world crumble the moment justice is brought to its knees." The Supreme Court later acquitted the Jewish defendants on the grounds that they had acted in self-defense, but the crisis of confidence between the Jews and the authorities continued. Some months after the riot, three Arab men were tried for the murder of Brenner, but they were acquitted because of reasonable doubt.[42]

Police officer Toufiq Bey al-Said resigned from the Jaffa police force. One day, he was walking down the street when a man addressed him from behind. When Said turned around, the man shot him. The bullet pierced his skull and Said died on the spot. An Arab newspaper claimed he had been murdered as revenge for his part in the attack on the Jaffa immigrant hostel. A Hebrew newspaper responded that the accusation was vicious slander—Jews do not engage in acts of revenge. That was not precisely true, since HaShomer, the Jewish self-defense organization that operated in the Galilee before World War I, did avenge attacks on its members.

A man named David Bar was charged with Said's murder but acquitted.[43] The real perpetrator was never apprehended. He was Yerahmiel "Luka" Lukacher, a legendary figure from the Galilee. Apparently, he had been sent by HaShomer veterans to avenge Brenner's death. Lukacher came from Russia; his acquaintances remembered him as a handsome man, full of personal charm, a pioneer and adventurer, a romantic bandit and Communist spy. David Ben-Gurion once hinted that Lukacher was planning to murder him over ideological differences. Some time after Said's death, Lukacher returned to the Soviet Union and disappeared.[44]

8.

In early June 1921 Samuel gave a speech at Government House on the occasion of the king's birthday and stressed Britain's commitment to the second part of the Balfour Declaration—the provision stating that the establishment of a Jewish national home would not hurt the Arabs. Immigration would be allowed only to the extent that it did not burden the country's economy, he said. Samuel's speech conformed strictly to the declared policy of his government, but those who heard him received the impression that he was trying to appease the Arabs at the expense of the Jews. David Eder was outraged. "The word 'traitor' crossed my lips," he wrote to his colleagues.[45]

Eder had always been among the moderates who believed it was important to make approaches to the Arabs: he had rejected the tendency toward separation, including the severing of Tel Aviv from Jaffa, and had not ruled out the possibility that the Jewish state might be part of a regional federation with Arab countries. But after the events in Jaffa Eder was moderate no longer. Terrorism exacted a heavy price; not least it impaired people's ability and willingness to consider problems rationally. Eder responded to the Jaffa riots with a proposal to cancel the Mandate. Better to let the Jews handle the Arabs on their own, he said, estimating that in Palestine there were 10,000 Jews able to bear arms, at least 3,000 of whom had already served in the army. In his testimony to the commission of inquiry, Eder said that the Arabs in Palestine had been taught by their leaders to respect nothing but force. So long as they believed the Jews were armed with justice but not with guns, he maintained, they would continue to regard the Jews as legitimate targets for murder and pillage.[46]

As he returned from Samuel's speech, still furious, Eder determined to cable Weizmann and demand that he immediately begin working to oust Samuel. Once he had calmed down, Eder called Samuel, and a conversation between the two persuaded Eder that ousting the high commissioner would cause more problems than it would solve. Eder opted for a boycott of official ceremonies in which the high commissioner participated.[47] The lines were drawn between these two English Jews, both of them Zionists. Samuel had been concerned that the Arabs would consider him a Zionist agent. Now he found that the Jews thought he was an Arab agent. "Until yesterday he was like God; now he is castigated as a traitor," Arthur Ruppin wrote in his diary.

Ruppin, a dry, Prussian-born jurist and economist, and a founder of Tel Aviv, identified with Samuel. The best thing would probably have been to put down the Arabs by force, he wrote, but being a liberal, "European, and a rather pure man," Samuel was not capable of doing this. "In that sense I feel a spiritual identification with him," Ruppin stated, deciding that if the Zionist program required the use of force, he would resign his position in the movement. He estimated that Samuel would probably leave. "The job is too burdensome for a Jewish man," he wrote. Samuel's presence in Palestine also made matters difficult for the Jewish community. "He is a Zionist," Ruppin noted, "and so we cannot complain about him." But when Samuel threatened to resign over the Jews' stinging criticisms, the Zionists retreated somewhat; they did not want him to leave, even though they resented him bitterly.[48]

Yitzhak Ben-Zvi and other National Council members sent Samuel extremely emotional letters, expressing a sense of tribal indignity. As a Jew, Samuel was expected to be "one of us" above all else. But in fact he represented the British Empire and was responsible for the Arab population as well, and did not intend to deny that responsibility. So the Zionists felt betrayed, or at least acted as if they did.[49] It was hard to know when they truly felt victimized and when they were feigning bitterness as a tactical move.

Chaim Weizmann, cautious, astute, and now a man of abundant experience, perfected this tactic as a diplomatic art. His expressions of pessimism were deliberate, carefully governed and measured.[50] To his colleagues, Weizmann denounced Samuel as a coward: "There he is, trembling and imploring everybody to 'make peace' with the Arabs, as if we were quarreling with them," Weizmann said. He was particularly angered by a decision Samuel had recently made to hand over hundreds of thousands of dunams—a measurement equal to four acres—of government land in the Beit She'an Valley to a Bedouin tribe.[51] One of Weizmann's aides had returned from Palestine with "a great deal to say about our nonentity of a hero," he wrote to Ahad Ha'am.[52] The aide, Frederick Kisch, claimed that Samuel was being too fair; "he established a sort of 'fifty-fifty' attitude as between Jews and Arabs," instead of favoring his own people. His inclination, Kisch maintained, was to mold Palestine into a colonial territory with a single population of natives, Jews and Arabs.[53] But Weizmann's letters to Samuel following the riots expressed not anger but great appreciation, almost commiseration, and a near-abject willingness to help. "It is essential that we appreciate his very difficult position, supporting him with all our power," he wrote to David Eder. "To embarrass him would play into our enemies' hands at home and abroad. We are on trial. We must show patience and forbearance."[54]

Weizmann's "enemies at home" were not the Arabs but David Ben-Gurion and Ze'ev Jabotinsky, whom he considered too hotheaded and reckless. Ben-Gurion railed against the "Jewish Commissioner," criticizing his cowardice and his frailty.[55] Jabotinsky continued to send the Colonial Office anti-British rants, which led one of Winston Churchill's aides to inform his minister that Mr. Jabotinsky was "a little crazy."[56] Denunciations of British "betrayal" were seen as proof of patriotic loyalty. Weizmann, always navigating between the extremes, demanded that the

Zionists display more understanding for Samuel.[57] He had obviously considered the possibility of forcing Samuel's dismissal, but had decided it would be best to leave him in office. "Respect him but suspect him," Weizmann stated, quoting a Hebrew proverb.[58]

In fact, Herbert Samuel had not betrayed Zionism; his emotional and political commitment to the national-home policy was undiminished. His royal birthday speech has often been described as an expression of a "major public shift" in his political vision. According to one theory, the events in Jaffa had pushed him to change his position. His British-Jewish background was also cited: he could handle Arab nationalism, but his definition of himself as a British Jew did not allow for Jewish nationalism.[59] None of this was true. Samuel was and remained a Zionist.

To the end of his life, Samuel believed that Zionism would achieve its goal gradually. His son Edwin, who had arrived in Palestine before him, expressed this view succinctly. Zionism should work slowly, he wrote his father as early as 1917: "Nothing can be lost by waiting and colonising slowly and introducing development carefully while a lot can be destroyed by rushing." This was the position Samuel articulated to Lloyd George on the eve of his departure for Palestine, and it echoed Chaim Weizmann's own belief.

No less committed to Zionism than Weizmann, Samuel was, however, aware of the ever-deepening fear that governed relations between the Jews and the Arabs; he knew that on both sides there were those who were deliberately fanning that fear. As a consequence, he felt the Zionists should exercise restraint and abstain from symbolic gestures liable to anger the Arabs. He came to regard the Arabs as a minority in need of protection. As a Jew and a liberal Englishman he would be ashamed, he wrote, if it turned out that the establishment of a Jewish state involved injustice toward the Arabs. "Nothing could be worse than if it were to appear that the one thing the Jewish people had learnt from the centuries of their own oppression was to oppress others," he wrote. But when he defended the rights of the country's Arabs, he was referring only to their economic, religious, and cultural welfare; he did not view them as a separate nation. He believed wholeheartedly that a Zionist Palestine coincided with the interests of England.[60] And since that was his government's position as well, there was, for him, no issue of conflicting loyalties.

The Jaffa riots brought home to Samuel that his job was going to be harder than he thought; he had been misled by the calm that greeted his arrival. The riots made him aware that he was dealing with a war between two nations. But Samuel was by no means too "pure," as Ruppin had written. His objection to suppressing the Arabs harshly grew out of a cold calculation: such suppression would only increase the violence, which first and foremost would harm the Zionist interest, he explained to Nachum Sokolow.[61]

Samuel warned that the British public would not consent to advancing the Zionist program on the bayonets of the British army. The tension between Jews and Arabs in Palestine was likely to raise hostile questions in Parliament, and the foundations of Britain's Zionist policy were not stable enough to withstand such assaults, he asserted. Some of the British newspapers were evincing growing sympathy for the Arabs; there were rumblings that the British presence in Palestine threatened to cost too much money.[62] Field Marshal Wilson continued to oppose Britain's role. Winston, he said of Churchill, appears to think he can govern Palestine with hot air, airplanes, and Jews. Wilson himself doubted that anyone would agree to be governed with hot air and airplanes; he also detested the tendency of the politicians to avoid taking responsibility by granting self-government to small nations not trained to rule themselves. Inevitably those nations would fall into the hands of extremists. Altogether, he simply could not understand what the British were doing in Palestine, he wrote.[63]

At one point, Weizmann succeeded in getting his hands on a document from General Congreve's London headquarters stating that, as in Ireland, the army could not avoid taking a position in favor of one side or another, and it was clear enough that in Palestine its sympathy was with the Arabs. The British government would never countenance a policy that made Palestine for the Jews what England was for Englishmen, the document said. Weizmann sent copies to Balfour and Prime Minister Lloyd George. "The Colonial Office is rather upset about the circular having got into my hands," he wrote. "I have told them that I am going to press this point until the Government makes up its mind whether it is going to remove such officials (or tear up the Mandate)."[64]

Churchill and Samuel both acknowledged to Weizmann that most British officials could not be counted sympathetic to Zionism. "The policy of the Balfour Declaration is an unjust policy," one of them, Charles Robert Ashbee, stated, quoting George Adam Smith's *Historical Geography of the Holy Land:* "Palestine is emphatically a land of tribes. The idea that it can ever belong to one nation, even though this were the Jews, is contrary to both nature and the Scripture."[65] Cooperation between the

Zionists and the British seemed about to collapse. But in fact the relationship was growing ever stronger. On Tuesday, July 22, 1921, Weizmann arrived at Balfour's home to discuss the situation. At Weizmann's request, Balfour had invited Prime Minister Lloyd George and Colonial Secretary Churchill.[66] Also present were the cabinet secretary and another official from the Colonial Office. It is doubtful whether anywhere in the empire there were many other national leaders able to arrange such a high-level meeting. Weizmann led the discussion; Lloyd George and Balfour went out of their way to please him. Churchill put forward some arguments but ultimately behaved cooperatively, almost obediently. The encounter was extraordinary from every point of view.

Weizmann first reported on a dispute with leaders of the American Jewish community that he had won. Lloyd George complimented him. Balfour then suggested that he give the prime minister an overview of the state of the Zionist movement. Weizmann complained about the situation in Palestine, saying the tension made it difficult for him to run the movement. He complained about Samuel's royal birthday speech, arguing that it contradicted the Balfour Declaration; without immigration the Jews would never be able to establish a majority in Palestine. Churchill disagreed with Weizmann's interpretation; Lloyd George and Balfour conceded that the speech had been unfortunate. The Balfour Declaration had always meant the eventual creation of a Jewish state, they said.

This statement promised more than the British government had ever said before; Churchill was surprised. He maintained that nine out of every ten British officials in Palestine were opposed to the Balfour Declaration, and that many Jews rejected it as well. He contended that a representative government should be established in Palestine; Weizmann was opposed, since the Jews were a minority. Lloyd George also disagreed with Churchill: "You mustn't give representative government to Palestine." Churchill proposed that the matter be brought before the cabinet.

Weizmann further argued that suspending immigration encouraged Arab violence. The threat to the Jews was so severe, he said, that rifles were now being smuggled into Palestine—without his authorization, of course, he added cautiously. Churchill responded: "We won't mind, but don't speak of it." As if he could not believe his ears, Weizmann asked whether he had understood the secretary correctly. Did the prime minister of Great Britain sanction Zionists smuggling rifles into Palestine? Apparently, he did. Weizmann would soon thereafter budget money for the purchase of weapons.[67] Everyone present agreed that the suspension of immigration was a temporary measure; when Churchill asked how many immigrants the Zionists wished to bring to Palestine, Weizmann had no answer. Churchill commented that the country should not be flooded with immigrants without means. They all agreed on this as well. Within a few months immigration resumed.

The men continued to talk, Weizmann rejecting as utter nonsense Samuel's report that Palestine was an imposition on British taxpayers. Lloyd George and Balfour concurred; Churchill did not. Weizmann then dismissed as "absurd" the charge that the Jews were stealing the Arabs' livelihood. Lloyd George broke out laughing. He asked how much money the Zionists had invested in Palestine and was "much struck" by the answer he received, Weizmann later recorded. Churchill brought up Musa Kazim al-Husseini: he was coming to London at the head of an Arab delegation and Churchill heartily wished the Zionists would reach some sort of accommodation with the Arabs. Weizmann said he could not come to terms with the Arabs unless he was sure of the government's position. "Frankly speaking," Lloyd George said, "you want to know whether we are going to keep our pledges." "Yes," Weizmann said. Balfour nodded positively. "You will have to do a lot of propaganda," Lloyd George advised, adding that Samuel was "very weak and has funked the position."

The prime minister got up to leave; at some opportunity, Balfour should probably repeat one of his pro-Zionist speeches, he suggested. When he reached the door he suddenly said, "Bribe the Arabs." Weizmann cautiously said that would be immoral but added, with the British dryness he had, with much effort, acquired over the years, that bribery was no longer so effective because British policy had driven up the Arabs' price. Two years ago he could have easily bought his way into becoming an Arab national leader.

Balfour walked the prime minister to his car. On his return Balfour told Weizmann that he had Lloyd George's support and high regard. Was there anything else he could do? Balfour asked. Weizmann demanded that responsibility for the defense of Palestine be taken from Congreve, whom he described as an enemy. Churchill consented.[68] Weizmann proposed for the government's consideration a series of actions to reinforce the Jewish community in Palestine: removing administration officials opposed to a Jewish police force, punishing Arab villages when their residents caused damage to Jewish settlements, strengthening the settlements, granting the Jews economic franchises, and increasing Jewish involvement in the selection of immigrants.

Field Marshal Wilson wrote, with much justification, that only one thing could explain this wholesale kowtowing to Weizmann: "The 'Frocks' seem to think, and I wholly disagree with them, that by handing over Jewland to the Jews they will make friends of those other Jews who govern finance in Chicago, Washington, London, Paris, Berlin, Moscow, etc."[69]

9.

The Zionist movement in Palestine had prior to the riots set up new administrative institutions. The Zionist Commission, always a temporary body, was transformed into the permanent Zionist Executive, a kind of cabinet, which would head the new Jewish Agency, officially responsible for cooperation with the administration but acting as an unofficial Jewish government. David Eder left the commission's helm to return home; in his place came Frederick Kisch, a British Jew and a great patriot.

Had Kisch been sent to Palestine as part of the colonial apparatus, he might have served his country better. A former British officer, a colonel, he had been born in India; his father, from a family whose origins were in Prague, had been the director of the Bengal mail. Kisch had served in the Royal Corps of Engineers, was wounded in Flanders, and had been transferred to one of the intelligence headquarters in London, where he dealt with various diplomatic matters. One day in June 1917, his commander summoned him to meet Chaim Weizmann. Kisch had been put in charge of organizing a diplomatic mission for Weizmann.

In his search for a replacement for Eder, Weizmann naturally turned to the British establishment. He consulted Lieutenant General Sir George Macdonogh of intelligence, and Macdonogh, "a loyal friend of the Zionist movement," according to Weizmann, sent him to Kisch. The young colonel had wanted to remain in the army, but he had not been promoted and was filled with a sense of frustration and failure. From Weizmann's point of view Kisch was an ideal choice; his father was a Zionist and he himself was a demobilized officer with diplomatic and political experience, including an assignment to the British delegation at the Versailles peace talks. He was meticulous, precise, and coolheaded, the very traits that Weizmann admired in the English. Moreover, he saw himself as a British officer, which would make his contacts with the administration much easier. Kisch dressed like an Englishman, spoke like one, and thought like one; he invited other Englishmen to tea and played cricket with them. When he arrived in Jerusalem, he knew no Hebrew.

Weizmann warned him that the Jews might not accept him because he was too much of an Englishman, while the British might come to regard him as an Englishman "gone native." Weizmann was right. Kisch generally received the authorities' understanding, but not always their agreement. He usually obtained the Jewish leaders' agreement, but not always their understanding.[70] He was up against the same tangle of conflicting expectations and loyalties that made things so difficult for the Jewish officials serving in Samuel's administration and for Samuel himself. "It is not that these people are bad Jews," Kisch said, "it is that each is too much of a Jew." He wrote that Samuel had forbidden dogs to be brought into his house, out of respect for his Muslim guests, and had also prohibited his waiters from wearing tarbushes, so as not to anger his Jewish guests. One of the administration's men protested this caution in his own way: he bought a dog and called him Tarboosh.[71]

Like Chaim Weizmann, Kisch believed the British could and should do more than they had done to move the Zionist cause forward; he too was never satisfied and always felt unjustly treated. But despite his frustrations, he shared Weizmann's belief that, ultimately, British colonialism needed Zionism as much as Zionism needed the British administration.

The Zionists would have needed the British even if Palestine had been empty of Arabs, Kisch wrote, because the Zionists did not understand the fundamentals of governing a country. It might well take them another fifty years to gain enough experience to run an independent state. "We have to learn from [the British] not only the technical methods of public administration but standards of public administration, as to which so few of our people have any experience or understanding," he explained. He had no doubt about the importance of the British presence. As he put it, "The Mandate, all the Mandate, and nothing but the Mandate."[72] However, in London, two officials in the Colonial Office, one senior and one junior, were taking stock: what, really, had Britain gotten out of the Balfour Declaration?

10.

The fifth anniversary of the declaration had just passed when Sir John E. Shuckburgh, assistant undersecretary for the colonies and head of the Middle East Division, was concluding a routine morning meeting in his office. Shuckburgh asked one of the participants, Sydney Moody, to stay behind for a private chat. A graduate of Eton and Kings College, Cambridge, Shuckburgh had served in India; Moody, twelve years his junior, had studied at Oxford and spent several years as district commissioner of Safed. He had been sent back to London to study and would later return to Palestine to work for the British administration in Jerusalem. Discussing Palestine, the two men were close to despair, Moody remembered. They talked about the illusions, the constraints, the doubts, the disappointments, and the trap. The notes Moody made of their conversation reflect a sense of helplessness, confusion, shame, and anxiety. In the twenty-five years that followed, no one better expressed the frustrations of Palestine.

He saw no purpose to the Mandate and no way out, Shuckburgh said. His office had tried to bring about a settlement between the Arabs and the Jews, but seemed to have failed. The Arabs were embittered, the Jews were dissatisfied, constantly accusing British administration officials of taking an anti-Jewish line. "We are unfortunate in our clients," Shuckburgh said with a touch of self-righteousness, almost self-pity.

He felt that Britain was operating in the dark, with no idea what it was doing or where it was going. There were only two options: to implement the Zionist policy by force or to abandon it. Protracted equivocation was not possible, Shuckburgh said. Britain could not hop from one compromise to another, the first embarrassing and the next degrading. This two-faced policy was not appropriate for the British government, and it disgraced him personally. The matter was particularly complicated now because Palestine was no longer considered a strategic asset. The House of Lords had concluded that the region was not a source of power but of weakness.[73] Shuckburgh had heard these things in army circles as well.

Soon afterward, Shuckburgh sat on a panel of military experts convened to examine the strategic value of Palestine. There was no clear agreement. Some participants thought in terms of the previous war: if the Turks were to return to Palestine they would endanger Britain's position in Egypt; Palestine was needed to defend the Suez Canal. Shuckburgh contributed the "imperial interest," as he liked to say: "To lose Palestine is to lose Arabia." The air force maintained that holding Palestine facilitated contact between Egypt, Iraq, and India—and kept the enemy away from Egypt. The first lord of the admiralty complained about Palestine's ports; Cyprus was a better base for protecting the Suez Canal, in his view. To the general staff, Palestine was not necessary to defend the canal; the forces stationed in Egypt were sufficient. In fact, the need to defend Palestine was liable to place a burden on the army in Egypt. The chief of the general staff ridiculed the thesis that Palestine was important as a link between

Egypt and India: "If we are to hold and garrison increasingly broad areas of the earth's surface in order to confine foreign aerodromes to a safe distance from our own territories, we shall presently, as the range of action of aircraft increases, have to hold most of the world." The occupation of Palestine had greater moral than strategic value, he said. The secretary of state for war summed up the discussion: while, in present circumstances, Palestine was not of real strategic value, it was desirable to keep it. Who knows, maybe one day oil would be discovered there. It was unfortunate, Shuckburgh said, that one could not depend on military experts—they were always in dispute and kept changing their positions every six months.[74]

During that same period calls were made in the press and in Parliament for the unilateral evacuation of Palestine: there was no way out of the Arab-Jewish predicament, and the whole thing was too expensive. Against this background a book was published in 1923, written by *Times* correspondent Philip Graves, presenting a well-argued political and military case for continued rule of Palestine. Graves's fundamental assumption was that if Britain left Palestine, the country would descend into anarchy and war and before long another power would invade. Turkey, France, or Italy—any one of these would endanger Britain's hold on Egypt. Graves mentioned the Suez Canal and the air route between Egypt and India. He furthermore argued that rule of the Holy Land, guarding the Western world's holiest sites, enhanced Britain's honor and prestige, and was therefore worth the price. But even a person willing to forgo Palestine's sentimental value, he added, should remember that tearing up the Balfour Declaration would mean losing the support of America's Jews. This prospect should not be taken lightly, especially given the great influence the Irish already enjoyed in the United States, Graves maintained. Breaking a promise made to the Jews would push many of them into the arms of communism.[75]

Shuckburgh had once spoken with David Eder about Arab-Jewish relations. "Why don't you bang our heads together and make us agree?" suggested Eder.[76] Shuckburgh had liked the idea. Recalling his private chat with Shuckburgh, Moody remembered his boss making a similar suggestion. They should summon the Arabs and Jews, he said, and tell them something like, "Look here, we have made certain promises to both of you. We promised the Jews a National Home in Palestine. We promised the Arabs national independence. Now you must agree together. We will give you independence provided you agree on a basis of settlement about the National Home. Now you must get round a table and come to some mutual arrangement. We give you six months to make up your minds. If you have not reached a settlement in that time we will simply resume our liberty of action and regard our promises to Arabs and Jews in Palestine as non-existent and simply govern the country as we think best quite unembarrassed by preconceived policy." No independence and no national home. Of course, Shuckburgh added cautiously, it should be made clear that even if they reached an agreement the British would not get up the next day and leave. First they would ensure that the agreement worked.

Shuckburgh seems to have been thinking of Jewish autonomy in the framework of an Arab state. If the Arabs would only consider the matter, he tried to convince himself, they would reach the conclusion that his proposal would bring them closer to achieving independence; the Jews, for their part, would agree out of fear of losing Britain's support and having to face the Arabs alone. He became quite enamored of the idea: he would no longer have to live with the feeling that his country was breaking its promises; British rule would enable a compromise between the two sides; Palestine would be a placid crown colony. He asked Moody what he thought. Yes, Moody agreed, the compromise Shuckburgh was proposing would finally release them from the anguish of contradictory promises.

Moody had a great many thoughts and doubts that he did not share with the assistant undersecretary; in his records of their conversation he placed those thoughts in brackets. Palestine was an underdeveloped, underpopulated country, and only the Jews could develop it for the good of all its citizens, because only they had the necessary money, enthusiasm, and manpower. No, they apparently did not intend to develop the country for the good of the Arabs as well, but Moody thought of the Jewish colleague in his office who was always telling him why the British should help the Jews—a Jewish Palestine would be stuck like a bone in the windpipe of an Arab empire. Moody thought that good. He opposed Arab unity.

Palestine required patience, Moody told his superior. A solution would turn up: one just had to hold on. Whoever digs in the longest wins. The British taxpayer would in the meantime continue to finance the army's expenses, but these were progressively declining. He supported Shuckburgh's proposal of Jewish autonomy in an Arab state, but with great hesitation. His conscience plagued him: yes, the Jews would receive a measure of self-rule, but he knew they were clinging to the Balfour Declaration and would see Shuckburgh's initiative as a betrayal.

Moody recalled the scene. He had sat in a leather armchair; Shuckburgh faced him, his back to the fireplace. Moody noted that his trousers were baggy at the knees. He asked his boss whether he thought Britain had gotten its money's worth when it gave the Zionists the Balfour Declaration. Sir John responded like a gentleman in distress. He was inclined to think that the Balfour Declaration had not been worth it. Nevertheless a bargain had been struck, and even if Britain was disappointed, that did not affect the binding nature of the bargain.

9

—·•·—

Culture Wars

1.

Jerusalem was aflutter at the beginning of 1923—Albert Einstein was in town, the most famous man in the entire world, *Ha'aretz* wrote.[1] The visit was part of a public relations campaign to help promote the establishment of the Hebrew University; Einstein had already accompanied Weizmann to the United States on a fund-raising tour. Getting the celebrated physicist and Nobel laureate to lend his name and his time to the project was a considerable achievement for Weizmann personally and a political coup as well, since the Hebrew University was a Zionist initiative. Kisch wrote that Einstein's cooperation was a blow to the enemies of Zionism.[2]

From the moment he arrived in Jerusalem, Einstein was dragged from one reception to another, from fete to fete, from ceremony to ceremony. He lodged at Government House as a guest of the high commissioner, but he was a hostage of the Zionist movement. At every stop he was forced to listen to long speeches in Hebrew, which he did not understand. The Zionists wanted to show him everything, and would have done anything to gain his favor. They also tried to persuade him to settle in Jerusalem and took him to admire Hehalutz Street in Beit Hakerem, a new garden neighborhood.* "The heart says yes," Einstein wrote in his travel diary, "but reason says no."

*Richard Kaufmann, who planned Beit Hakerem, also planned the Rehavia and Talpiot neighborhoods; they were inspired by the garden suburbs of Europe. Talpiot was meant to

Einstein gave a lecture on the theory of relativity in one of the rooms of the only building then available to the university, on Mount Scopus. The organizers had distributed too many tickets, and the room was unbearably crowded. Herbert Samuel and Ronald Storrs were there, as were the foreign consuls with their wives. Helen Bentwich, the wife of the attorney general, wrote that none of those present had come with any hope of understanding Einstein's theory, but everyone wanted to be able to say they had seen the great man. Sixty-seven-year-old Ahad Ha'am had to stand.

Einstein knew no English, so he spoke in French. This was in everyone's best interest, he suggested to his audience, since they could all say they would have been able to understand relativity had the lecturer's French not been so poor. Given his own mental deficiencies, Einstein said, there was no hope he would ever learn Hebrew. "The poor professor was miserable during his Hebrew introduction which he read most laboriously from a text in Latin characters," Colonel Kisch wrote, adding, "This performance made him look very ridiculous but possibly may have some good propaganda value, although I doubt it." *Ha'aretz* reported that despite the lecturer's efforts to explain himself with the help of diagrams and despite the attentiveness of his audience, there must have been very few who were able to grasp the "wondrous theory." The concept that nature has not only three dimensions but also a fourth one, time, "is hard to take in," *Ha'aretz* lamented, as if this were the only difficulty. The newspaper also noted that no Arabs had been present. "Those people are apparently still far from the world of science," *Ha'aretz* remarked.[4]

Einstein enjoyed himself immensely. He was touched by all the receptions given in his honor. The only thing that put him off was the sight of Jews praying at the Western Wall; to him, they were people stuck in the past, oblivious to the present. In a synagogue in Jerusalem's Bukharan neighborhood, he saw "filthy Jews," he wrote.[5] He marveled at Kibbutz

---

be "the Grunewald of Jerusalem," Grunewald being a well-known suburb of Berlin. When Kaufmann submitted his Talpiot plans to the authorities for approval, Charles Robert Ashbee, adviser to Storrs and secretary of the Pro-Jerusalem Society, saw that they included a large building that had not been identified. He asked about the building's purpose and was told, "That is the home of our parliament." Ashbee mocked Kaufmann's fantasy as an expression of nationalist megalomania. But there was something naive and captivating in Kaufmann's hope that the Jewish parliament would be established in, of all places, his garden neighborhood on the edge of Jerusalem, and also something bold, a daring to do what had never been done before. Either way, Ashbee demanded that the dream be expunged. The plan was amended and the future home of the Jewish parliament was marked as an art gallery.[3]

Degania—a "communist colony," he observed. Their communism will not last long, he predicted, but in the meantime they were raising a new generation. One evening he went to the home of Norman Bentwich to play the violin in a Mozart quintet. The attorney general's sister Margery also played violin; another sister, Thelma Yellin, was a well-known cellist.[6] The gathering was the kind of event that gave Storrs the feeling Jerusalem was worthy of his talents; he played the piano.

The original purpose of a Jewish university had been to set up an institution to take in students excluded from other universities, especially in Eastern Europe, because of anti-Jewish discrimination. Just as Weizmann had, early on, been willing to consider establishing a Jewish state outside Palestine, he had not ruled out the possibility of establishing the university, at least in its first stage, in England or Switzerland. Nor had he insisted that the language of instruction be Hebrew.[7] Within the Zionist movement, there were those who opposed the project, among them Max Nordau and Arthur Ruppin. They argued that the plan was too ambitious and too expensive. Others were afraid that the existence of such an institution might lead to the expulsion of Jewish students from universities in Europe. A similar concern had motivated Jewish opponents to the Balfour Declaration; the conflict was one between Jews and Zionists.[8]

The idea also had its critics among the Jews in Palestine. Along with the ultra-Orthodox, who opposed the university as being too secular, a number of labor movement figures spoke out against it. Yosef Chaim Brenner had dismissed the idea derisively: "Do those laboring on the rectification of our people really have no concerns other than the university?"[9] In the yearly meetings of the Zionist Congress, members of the socialist Poalei Zion Party consistently argued that "concrete needs" in Palestine should take precedence; establishing a university was like "building roofs before putting up houses." Berl Katznelson, an inspirational labor leader, attacked scholars who, he said, were only interested in publishing "papers" to win international fame instead of providing for the country's needs. Still, he was willing to give the university a chance, but only if it could prove its usefulness for building the country. Science, he wrote, "was created for the nation." Fields of knowledge that do not directly serve society and the nation might be important in their own right, but not to us, Katznelson stated.

Other leaders of the labor movement expressed a similar strain of anti-intellectualism: "What will the hundreds of doctors do who graduate each year from the university?" wondered one opponent of the university.

A. D. Gordon, an influential thinker who preached the importance of Jews returning to work on the land, feared that the country would be flooded with physicians, engineers, agronomists, and teachers, who would simply educate another generation of academics. "And who will be our farmers and our workers?" he asked. "Once again people of another nation?" At one Zionist Congress a Poalei Zion member complained that the party had come "with the weighty question of how to create the Jewish worker of the land, the Jewish farmer, and the Congress's answer was: 'Hail the Hebrew University!'" He noted, "The enthusiasm for the diploma was stronger at the Congress than was the fragrance of the earth." These Zionist leaders were also making a cultural and emotional protest against everything they associated with Jerusalem and its residents—*chalukkah* money, dependency, and the weakness they so detested and scorned. Even after the university was established, this political and ideological debate persisted: one labor movement member later warned the university's students that they had better not think their status was higher than the workers'.[10]

Since the university's thirteen cornerstones had been laid in 1918, not much had happened. Weizmann tried to raise money but made only slow progress.[11] In Jerusalem, there was a feeling that the project had reached a dead end. Eliezer Ben-Yehuda, Ahad Ha'am, Joseph Klausner, Menachem Ussishkin, David Yellin, and others did not blame Weizmann for the failure; they understood the difficulty of raising sufficient funding. By 1922, however, they too had come to see establishing the university as an important plank in building the national home and felt that any further delay was liable to harm their ultimate goal. A long memo on the subject leaves no room for doubt: the Hebrew University had become above all a national enterprise, all the more urgent in the wake of the Nebi Musa and Jaffa riots. "The events of the last two years have caused our political and spiritual standing to be profoundly shaken and our honor has paled in all eyes," they wrote. "The respect that other nations evinced toward us is turning into an attitude of disparagement, among both our enemies and friends. Everyone is laughing at our expense, everyone is contemptuous of us for being unable to accomplish even a part of what we say we've done." Contempt constitutes a real danger to the Jews, the memorandum stated; government officials who had supported Zionism as long as it was winning had withdrawn their support, and this would only lead to more Arab violence.

In the meantime, "foreign elements" had initiated the establishment of an English university—in fact, this was Ronald Storrs's idea—and were already making preparations for its opening. And Arab leaders had begun to speak of the possibility of an Arab university.[12] Young Jews were leaving the country to study overseas and becoming "Christianized in spirit" as a result, according to the memorandum. Most professors overseas were either total antisemites or partial antisemites. "And since they are truly great, each in his field, our young people cannot but respect them and so they drink the evil waters and swallow, together with true wisdom, mistaken and flawed ideas about their people and their heritage, and it is difficult for them to free themselves of this afterward, because of their respect for the foreign scholars." Even worse, members of the Yishuv who could not afford studies overseas might enroll in Arab universities, and clearly what they would learn there would not be desirable for Jewish life in Palestine. The Hebrew language was endangered as well. An entire generation had fought for the status of Hebrew. Their victory was "one of the strongest foundations of the demand for our rights to a national home in the land of our fathers." This victory would be for nothing if schoolchildren did not know that a Hebrew university awaited them, the memo argued.

Ussishkin, Ben-Yehuda, and their colleagues understood that it was not easy to establish a Hebrew college, so they proposed making do in the meantime with an institute for the humanities—by which they apparently meant a Jewish studies department. Everyone agreed that only in the land of the Bible was it possible to achieve a full understanding of the Torah and the prophets. A humanities institute, with superior scholars and a good library, would attract students from overseas and would thus also be an important source of income for the city of Jerusalem. Other cities in the country would develop commerce and industry, but Jerusalem's only hope of becoming a "great and wealthy city" lay in "the enrichment of the spirit, the industry of wisdom and the sciences."[13]

The dream of the university thus switched directions. No longer intended as an educational haven for Jews in distress, its major role would be to promote Hebrew nationalism in Palestine. Weizmann, arguing for the inclusion of the sciences, promised that scientific research would develop new methods of agriculture and in this way the university would promote the national home.[14] Although this added dimension would please the labor movement, humanities scholars raised objections. "Useful sciences are not national," wrote Simon Bernfeld, a well-known rabbi who had translated the Bible into German. It makes no difference whether a chemist or biologist works in Jerusalem, Berlin, or Paris, he argued. Nor would applied sciences cause the Jews of the world to view

Jerusalem as their spiritual center. They would pay attention to Jerusalem only as a "Historical Hebrew Center," he wrote. Jewish studies would "maintain what earlier generations have preserved and prepare the enrichment of Judaism in the generations to come." The Jewish heritage "is the established base of our people and the backbone of our historical existence," Bernfeld concluded.

The Institute of Jewish Studies opened in December 1924 and, like the British conquest of Palestine, it was seen as a "Hanukkah miracle." The institute developed as a secular research school. Its faculty, all European-born, represented a variety of scholarly and political approaches, but they were united in their goal of strengthening the foundations of Zionist ideology. The university was also meant to do its part to reinforce the European character of the national home. Its founders' intention was to attract "our brothers in the lands of the West, in Europe and in America."[15]

The first professor hired was Andor Fodor of Hungary; he taught in the Institute of Chemistry. The university's development remained a subject of contention. Now the question was whether research or teaching would best serve the institution and the Jews of Palestine. Weizmann believed the wiser course was to concentrate on research. It would be easier—and cheaper—to bring to Jerusalem top-flight scholars who would enhance the university's prestige rather than to operate a teaching program on a high level. Locating good scholars who knew Hebrew and would agree to leave their countries would pose enough of a challenge. Thus the first students, unable to graduate with a degree, had the status of auditors; they were not required to pay tuition.[16]

Most of the funding for the university was raised in America. David Yellin, a Jerusalem scholar and educator, had tried to tap into the generosity of a Chicago businessman, Julius Rosenwald, who supported the promotion of education for black Americans. Yellin brought with him a verse from the Book of Amos, "Are ye not as children of the Ethiopians to me, O children of Israel?" On the wall in Rosenwald's office he found a large map marked with schools throughout the United States that had received support from him. Rosenwald had spent more than $2 million on the education of "niggers," Yellin wrote to his wife. How wonderful it would be if he would donate just a fraction of that to Jewish education in Palestine. "It is hard for us to accept the idea that one of ours gives his money to backwards people," Yellin wrote, but he was quick to correct himself: "Do we have the right to be resentful when we see a Jew acting righteously towards the least educated of human beings?" It was all a matter of business, he concluded. Rosenwald's emporium, Sears, Roebuck & Co., made huge amounts of money each year from its business with blacks, and he was thus obligated to give them something back.[17]

Sufficient money was raised to plan for a permanent campus. Patrick Geddes, a biologist and sociologist and one of the pioneers of urban planning, was invited to design the new campus. The central structure in his design was to bear the largest dome in the world. He related to the building, which was to overlook a breathtaking desert vista from the top of Mount Scopus, as if it were a house of God. His plan was never realized, rejected as too grandiose by some and too expensive by others, and there were those who said it was inappropriate to give such a project to a non-Jewish architect.[18]

2.

In the early 1920s the Jews lived with the sense that they were making history, that they were creating a new nation, a new society. Local Jewish leaders had always assumed that the Jewish community would be organized in the same kind of para-parliamentary system that had governed the Zionist movement in Europe, which included general elections. Now, the Yishuv inaugurated an elected body, the Elected Assembly, which appointed the National Council, the community's official governing body. Recognized by the British administration, the National Council was empowered to oversee local civil matters.

The community split into dozens of parties. The largest political block was composed of the parties of the labor movement, but these never achieved an absolute majority in the Elected Assembly.[19] Some of the movements active in Jewish communities overseas also organized as political parties in Palestine. Indeed, the strength of the various parties derived to a large extent from their links to their mother parties abroad. All were engaged in a power struggle over the division of Zionist resources.

The labor movement drew its organizational strength mainly from the Jewish Labor Federation of Palestine, better known as the Histadrut, established in 1920. The federation's rhetoric spoke of "workers" and "the proletariat," but the Histadrut strove to enroll all wage earners, including middle-class employees like teachers and office clerks. The Histadrut's power derived from its success in improving working conditions, and even more from its ability to supply its members with work and services, including health care. To that end, the Histadrut had set up a large construction company, Solel Boneh, as well as various other industrial enterprises and a bank. It established settlements, mostly kibbutzim; the Haganah, a military organization; and youth movements engaged in educational, cultural, and sporting activities.

The parties of the left viewed themselves ideologically as part of the socialist world, but very few of them advocated class warfare aimed at transferring power to the proletariat. Most took positions in line with Western European social democracy. The Histadrut considered its objectives synonymous with those of the Zionist movement and evolved over the years from a labor union into a far-reaching national organization— largely under the leadership of David Ben-Gurion—with the primary goal of advancing Jewish autonomy toward independence. When the labor movement ran into contradictions between its socialist and national identities, it always, in every case, came down on the side of Zionism.[20]

A sense of common purpose prevented real conflict between the parties of the left and the civil block—the umbrella name given to the various parties in the center and the right—which tended to believe in letting free-market forces operate unhindered and wished to minimize the use of public capital. But civil-block members, too, were first and foremost Zionists. On occasion, the level of rancor between left and right suggested imminent civil war, but in retrospect, such a rift was clearly never a possibility so long as the factions within the Jewish community were united against the Arab threat and joined in the fight to create a Jewish state.[21]

For the same reason, the common national goal guaranteed the democratic character of public life, in a tradition already set by the Zionist Congresses and under the influence of the British system of government. The Elected Assembly might have been a rowdy forum, with shouting and whistling, but in general conduct it never exceeded the norms of parliamentary discussion; the rules of the game were consensual, more or less. Despite the impression created by the different parties, and perhaps despite their members' inner convictions, the left and right were not enacting a confrontation between Bolsheviks and Fascists. Their combat took place in a Zionist center with fairly broad margins.[22]

The essential stability of that center was made apparent in 1923, when Ze'ev Jabotinsky withdrew from the Zionist establishment to organize his opposition Revisionist movement. Jabotinsky, an Anglophile and a liberal, broke with Chaim Weizmann, also an Anglophile and a liberal, over his cautious and moderate approach to the British. But their dispute was about tactics, not principles. Jabotinsky wanted to see faster, more radical progress. Among other things, he demanded that immigration be increased and a Jewish army established.* Jabotinsky's creation of an aggressive opposition forced the labor movement to take more "activist" patriotic positions against the English and the Arabs—and against the ultra-Orthodox as well. Jacob Israel de Haan, a Zionist who went over to the Orthodox camp, paid with his life.

De Haan was one of those eccentrics, adventurers, and fanatics drawn to Palestine as if to an open frontier, where all norms of behavior were suspended, where everything seemed possible. Jerusalem, especially, stirred up primal passions. An attorney and journalist, de Haan came from Holland; in Jerusalem he consorted with Arab boys and wrote homoerotic poems.

At first he was a respected Zionist intellectual: Chaim Weizmann wrote him a letter of recommendation, and Ze'ev Jabotinsky introduced a lecture by de Haan on the care of abandoned children. He wrote for a large Dutch newspaper and taught law; he knew everyone and everyone knew him. When he was drawn to the charismatic ultra-Orthodox anti-Zionist leader Rabbi Yosef Chaim Sonnenfeld and began to espouse the religious cause, the Zionists denounced him. David Ben-Gurion accused him of treason, and *Ha'aretz* called him antisemitic scum. De Haan denied statements attributed to him: it was not true, he said, that he had told Lord Northcliffe, the British media magnate, that the Balfour Declaration should be rescinded; he had said only that it should be amended to recognize the rights of the ultra-Orthodox community.[24]

No one believed him. Students boycotted his classes at the new school of law. *Ha'aretz* implied that he was crazy. "What we have before us is a psychological riddle," wrote Rabbi Benjamin, a writer and no small eccentric himself. "Is this man really of sound mental health? Are we not dealing with a pathological delusion? Has something not gone wrong in his brain?" Colonel Kisch, who described de Haan as a "Jewish Jesuit," wrote that the man suffered from a "persecution mania."[25]

---

*"Jabotinsky, the passionate Zionist," Weizmann wrote, "was rather ugly, but immensely attractive, well-spoken, warm-hearted, generous, always ready to help a comrade in distress. All of these qualities were, however, overlaid by a certain touch of the rather theatrically chivalresque . . . a certain irrelevant knightliness, which was not at all Jewish."[23] Few knew Jabotinsky better: in London Jabotinsky had lived in an apartment together with Vera and Chaim Weizmann.

Mania or not, de Haan did have enemies. He received death threats and had premonitions of his own murder: "As a tender bird flies / Fly my song / Until the pistol shoots my heart," he wrote. A roundish man, with a golden pince-nez on his nose and a bowler hat on his head, he was killed one evening as he left the Sha'arei Zedek Synagogue on Jerusalem's Jaffa Street. Three bullets hit him; one pierced his heart. The date was June 30, 1924; he was forty-three. The murderer was a twenty-one-year-old immigrant from Odessa, Avraham Silberg, later Tehomi. He was active in the Haganah, together with Yitzhak Ben-Zvi, who had been involved in the decision to do away with de Haan.[26]

The authorities kept a careful watch on Ben-Zvi, who was considered a possible Bolshevist. While the British did not seem to think he would lend his hand to political murder, Ben-Zvi was warned to restrain himself. Ben-Zvi and his comrades hated de Haan to the same extent that they loved Yosef Trumpeldor; the two figures were symbol and countersymbol. One was an officer, a Russian war hero, a Zionist patriot, a socialist, a virile man and loving friend; the other, a flabby, balding Diaspora Jew, an eccentric with a taste for boys. Ultra-Orthodox mythology adopted de Haan as a martyr. "He died desperately alone and perplexed in the extreme," wrote Ronald Storrs.[27]

De Haan was a victim of the extreme clash between secular Zionism and ultra-Orthodoxy, the enemy of Zionism. A similar such battle had raged over the issue of women's suffrage.

3.

In the home of Baron Edmond de Rothschild in Rishon LeTzion a special meeting convened in the spring of 1921 in honor of Dame Millicent Fawcett from London. The meeting involved "an entirely unexpected experience," Fawcett later wrote, referring to an effort by the settlement's women to explain to her the importance of granting the vote to all women; Fawcett, then seventy-four, had for fifty years fought for the right of women to participate in parliamentary elections. Now, in the postwar years, she was seeing the first fruits of her struggle.

In advance of her visit, Chaim Weizmann had sent a letter to David Eder. The kind of impression foreign guests received in Palestine depended on whom they met, Weizmann cautioned. "It is therefore very important that Fawcett should not be captured by our enemies, Jewish or non-Jewish."[28] Apparently Weizmann had mistaken Fawcett's identity; he thought she was the sister of Lady Astor, the first woman to be elected to

Parliament, also a well-known suffragette. But Fawcett had many admirers in her own right and was therefore still deemed worthy of lavish attention: the Zionist movement made great efforts to foster its liberal image. An offshoot of European liberalism, its disposition from the start was to recognize the equality of women, and beginning with the third Zionist Congress in 1899, women had the right to vote.[29] In this, the Zionist movement was ahead of several European countries, Britain included.*

When Dame Millicent went home she wrote a book about her journey to Palestine. She did not endorse Zionism's political goal of Jewish independence but was impressed by the movement's achievements and marveled that, of the seven members of Rishon LeTzion's local council, four were women.† In contrast, she was shocked by the condition of Arab women: in one village she was the guest of a sixteen-year-old girl who had given birth four times, each baby dying soon after it was born.[31]

The political vitality that animated the Jewish community in the wake of the expulsion of the Turks had also led to a proliferation of women's organizations. At first, these groups concentrated on efforts to rehabilitate the destroyed society. They established orphanages, soup kitchens, and sewing workshops for girls and ran evening classes, all in coordination with the Zionist Commission and the military authorities. "Our leader Herzl, who led us toward political independence," said Sarah Azariahu, one of the first activists of the women's movement, "taught us to be faithful to the spirit of democracy." The organized struggle for the status of women in Palestine was from the start considered part of the national struggle. "The women's right is the right of Zionism," stated historian Joseph Klausner.[32]

The debate over women's suffrage sometimes used terms taken from ethics and philosophy; at other times it sounded like a rehash of the argument between Adam and Eve. In one settlement, the women protested the first section of the local elections charter, which granted the vote to "every

---

*The first battle over the right of Jewish women in Palestine to participate in elections took place in the settlement of Zichron Ya'akov in 1903. The women fought to take part in elections for a committee to represent the small Jewish community to the Turkish authorities, but they failed. Sarah Thon, the wife of Zionist leader Ya'akov Thon, wrote a watershed article in 1910 in which she demanded that women be given the vote. The principle was eventually accepted by all the Zionist parties. A notice published in 1919 by the Zionist Commission's press office based the movement's egalitarianism on the writings of John Stuart Mill.[30]

†However, not every Jewish settlement was as egalitarian as Rishon LeTzion. Elsewhere, the struggle for women's votes continued for some time, particularly with regard to elections to national Zionist institutions.

person (male)." This implied that women were not part of the human race, the settlement's women maintained. A women's assembly in Haifa was cut short when a few men took over the stage and began to berate the audience about the harmful role of women in life and in history; as proof they cited the evil deeds of Cleopatra. The women in the hall drowned out the men with catcalls and whistles, and the gathering dispersed. Itamar Ben-Avi published a kind of historical apology. Men had oppressed women for five thousand years, he noted. "We have not done to a dog what we have done to her, and when we praised her as a daughter of the gods it was a lie. We lied, we lied, we lied," he wrote. "At most," he added, "we praised her as a mother and housekeeper."[33]

Writing in a women's magazine, Hannah Thon, Ya'akov Thon's second wife and an activist in her own right, decried a woman's lot as "slave to her husband" and called for her sex's liberation, which included freedom from housework. But on the whole, the women's organizations took care to limit their struggle to the political arena. The same monthly warned against a tendency by liberated women to "cast off the yoke" and sever their marriage ties. This danger should be resisted; a woman should restrain her "individual selfishness" for the good of the family. Some women did fight for the right to enter professions from which they were barred—Rosa Ginossar, daughter of Mordechai Ben-Hillel Hacohen and daughter-in-law of Ahad Ha'am, overcame many obstacles to become Palestine's first female attorney—but women's organizations were not for the most part concerned with achieving equal personal and sexual freedom for women. They accepted their roles as mothers, wives, and housekeepers who saw to their husbands' needs, and to the cleaning, cooking, mending, and child rearing. The limited nature of women's demands explains why the male establishment supported their right to vote: it did not threaten the traditional division of labor within the family. To avoid any misunderstanding, the Women's Association declared that its object was not to imitate some new world fashion and that it was not acting out of boredom but out of a desire "to participate in the building of the land," in other words, as part of Zionist patriotism.[34] This made it possible for all the Zionist parties to support the women's struggle.*

---

*Berl Katznelson suggested that women train themselves in preparation for their immigration to Palestine. Upon arrival, they should already know something of work in the kitchen and in the home. This is difficult work, demanding "talent and taste and great understanding, and it does not always bring intellectual rewards," Katznelson wrote, adding that women should also familiarize themselves with "family life and the prospects of newborn children."[35]

Most Zionist politicians, almost all of whom were men, were far more concerned with imposing Zionism on the ultra-Orthodox than with freedom for women. David Ben-Gurion took the position that women were not allowed to participate in general elections in many countries, and he saw no reason why Palestine had to be the first. On the other hand, the ultra-Orthodox were opposed to giving women the right to vote, and Zionists should never surrender to them. Otherwise, he said, "there will be nothing in our lives that they won't want to bury beneath esoteric laws of one sort or another."[36] The Zionists assumed that ultra-Orthodox women would not participate in the national vote; giving suffrage to their own women would thus nearly double the movement's relative strength.

At the same time, however, the Zionists wanted to ensure the broadest possible turnout for the elections—including the ultra-Orthodox—as a demonstration of national strength and unity to the Arabs and English. Mizrahi, the major religious Zionist party, suggested a number of compromises. One repeated suggestion was to differentiate between women's right to vote and their right to serve in office. The halacha, Jewish religious law, did not forbid women to vote, Mizrahi argued, but for men to serve together with women would be a violation of the rules of modesty. At one point Mizrahi suggested that the issue be put to public referendum, but then there was an argument over whether women would be able to vote in the referendum.[37]

For political reasons, then, women were asked to give up their right to vote, or at least to suspend it for a while. The national interest came first, and holding the elections to the assembly, which had been put off time after time, was paramount. "There is no choice, we must give in this time," Joseph Klausner wrote, "lest they say that the Yishuv's institutions do not represent it in its entirety." Was national unity worth breaching over a question that Europe itself had not yet resolved, asked *Do'ar Ha-Yom*, calling emotionally on women: "Act heroically—concede this time."[38]

The parties scrambled for a compromise. The labor movement, champion of the principle of equality, agreed at one point to an arrangement whereby women would participate in the elections, but ultra-Orthodox men in Jerusalem would vote at separate polling stations, and the vote of each ultra-Orthodox man would be counted twice, as if his wife had also voted. The assumption was, naturally, that she would vote as her husband did.[39]

None of these compromises took effect, however, and in 1920 women did gain the right to vote for the Elected Assembly—and the right to hold office. They established their own party, and five representatives of the women's slate were elected to the first assembly, fourteen women altogether (4.5 percent of the total number of delegates). On the other hand, they were unsuccessful on other issues, such as establishing civil courts for marriage and family affairs—under Ottoman and Mandatory law, marriage and divorce remained under the sole jurisdiction of the religious courts. In January 1926 the Elected Assembly passed a formal resolution recognizing the equal rights of women "in all branches of civil, political, and economic life." Only one settlement, Petach Tikva, stood fast against allowing women to participate in its local elections; as late as 1930 women organized a protest rally under the slogan "It's a disaster to be a woman in Palestine."[40] Ten more years passed before the women of Petach Tikva were allowed to vote.

Sometime after Jewish women had gained the vote for internal Zionist institutions, the British authorities initiated legislation to deprive all Palestine's women of this right in local elections. In England, MP Eleanor Rathbone protested. The government responded that women had in fact never received the right to vote in Palestine except in community institutions. In certain cases, the Colonial Office conceded, such as Tel Aviv, the high commissioner had issued special instructions granting women this right. The new legislation would state that only men were allowed to participate in elections, but Rathbone could rest assured that the high commissioner would be empowered to permit women's participation where he saw fit, and would most likely do so. "Seeing that strong objections are entertained not only by Moslems but also by certain Jews to the participation of women in public affairs," a colonial official explained, "you will, I am sure, agree that it would be impracticable to lay down a general rule in Palestine."[41]

At a suffrage meeting in Jerusalem, Millicent Fawcett called on Jewish women to fight for the rights of their Arab counterparts. Aware of the sensitivity of the issue, she later wrote, she took care to read these parts of her speech from written copy. "The Holy Land will not truly have fulfilled its destiny until Jew, Mohammedan and Christian are strong enough to set aside their strife and antagonism and unite to make Palestine a strong nation," she wrote. "Palestinian nationality" was still the government's hope, and Lady Samuel, who attended the lecture, liked what she heard.[42]* Fawcett's call had little resonance, of course. Jewish women could not and did not want to "unite" with Arabs; they had enough to fight for without trying to change Arab society.†

During her visit, Fawcett was impressed by two women in particular: Annie Landau and Frances Newton. Landau was an ultra-Orthodox woman of about fifty-five, headmistress of the Evelina de Rothschild School for Girls. She was born in England and had studied in Germany; her school was funded by a Jewish charitable organization in England. Her students received, in addition to religious studies, a general education and vocational training in secretarial and other skills.

The school occupied a building that had once served as the residence of an Ethiopian princess; the street that led to it was full of potholes. On her visit to the building, Fawcett asked why the street was not repaired, and Landau said that the municipality had no money. The British made it very difficult to get things done, she said, because they insisted on functioning according to the rigid rules of orderly administration. Under the Turks, things had been different. Someone had once left a dead camel in front of the school's door. Day by day, the stench had grown stronger, and despite Landau's protests, the municipality would not haul away the carcass. So she had written a letter to the governor telling him that if the camel was not taken away within twenty-four hours she would, at her own expense, have it dumped at his own front door. The camel had been removed immediately. Those were the days, Landau said, but methods like that didn't work with the British. Fawcett loved the story.

Landau was no Zionist. "She was more British than the English," Ronald Storrs wrote, "flying the Union Jack continually," and "more Jewish than the Zionists—no answer from her telephone on the Sabbath, even by the servants." She instituted two languages of instruction in her school: Hebrew and English. The school's culture was religious, in an

---

*Gerda Arlosoroff, the wife of labor leader Chaim Arlosoroff, attached great hopes to the encounter between Arab housemaids and Jewish women. Working in Jewish homes would "broaden the horizons" of the Arab maids. They would develop an appreciation of European women's fashions and would demand that their husbands buy them similar clothes. The transition to European ways of life would pave the way for more understanding between "one woman and another," Arlosoroff wrote.[43]

†At the beginning of 1919 two Arab women's associations organized in Jerusalem, one Christian, one Muslim. Their declared goal was to improve women's education. They began their activity with a telegram to the Duchess of York, the wife of King George V. In Lebanon in 1920, women demanded the right to vote. The Arab national movement frequently supported the women's organizations in their petitions to the authorities.[44]

ultra-Orthodox spirit, but it also meant to instill in the girls civic loyalty to Great Britain. The students elected a parliament and established a government. On the occasion of Fawcett's visit they reenacted a coalition crisis and conducted a debate on appropriate modes of punishment.[45*]

Frances Newton hosted Fawcett in her home on Mount Carmel. The daughter of an English missionary, Newton had lived in Palestine for twenty-five years, together with a woman Fawcett referred to as her hostess's secretary. People described Newton as a "masculine" woman who smoked a pipe.[47] When she first came to Palestine she established a hospital in Jaffa using contributions raised in English church circles. She later became a kind of poor man's lawyer, Fawcett wrote. The lower floor of her home was, at all hours of the day, full of people needing "physical, moral, or political" assistance. All of them were Arabs; Newton was fluent in their language. She helped people who had run into problems with the authorities, and she organized reconciliations between feuding tribes, the traditional Arab *sulha*. She devoted herself to the Arab national struggle and operated a kind of communications center out of her home.[†]

Weizmann once considered setting up a meeting in London with Newton and an Arab delegation from Palestine. Colonel Kisch had hosted her for dinner in an attempt to explain the justice of the Zionist cause. Henrietta Szold, the leader of the Hadassah women's Zionist organization in the United States, was also present. The dinner was a total failure—"Miss Szold overdid it," Kisch maintained after he had accompanied Newton home, "and her long speeches were somewhat tedious." Apparently Szold and Newton did try to work together, in a Jewish-Arab women's movement, but not much came of it. Kisch received reports that guests to Newton's home were shown *The Protocols of the Elders of Zion*.[49]

Kisch himself was increasingly busy with preparations for the opening of the Hebrew University. The ceremony was to be the greatest symbolic production ever mounted by the forces of Zionist public relations. Thousands of guests from many countries had been invited.[50] The guest of honor was a fragile old man of seventy-seven named Arthur James Balfour.

---

*Once every two weeks Landau would organize a dance party, inviting members of the administration, young British officers, and teachers from other schools. The event was a focus of Jerusalem social life. "Most wonderful parties," Deputy Governor of Jerusalem Edward Keith-Roach glowingly observed.[46]

†In her efforts to explain Arab opposition, Newton often mentioned that the Zionists were instituting equal rights for women in Palestine, which gave rise to great anxiety among Arab men, who saw it as a threat to their status.[48]

4.

By the time the Hebrew University opened formally, on April 1, 1925, two institutes had been established, one for chemistry and the other for Jewish studies. There was also a department of microbiology, a library, and a faculty consisting of seven professors and another thirty or so instructors. Judah Leib Magnes, the university's chancellor, was a Reform rabbi born in Oakland, California; his German-speaking parents had gone to the United States from Poland. Magnes had studied in Berlin and Heidelberg before he settled in New York.

A prominent opponent of America's entry into World War I, Magnes was a leader of the New York Jewish community noted for his attempts to build bridges between the city's rich Jews, who were of German origin, and the poor immigrants from Eastern Europe. He also served as liaison between the police and the leaders of the Jewish mafia. His ability and inclination to move among cultures and find common ground led him to try to bring Jews and Arabs together in Palestine. He came to Jerusalem with his family in 1922, intending to return home after a short visit, but leaders of the American Jewish community persuaded him to accept the new university's chancellorship. He proved able to stand his ground with Zionist movement leaders and even faced down Albert Einstein in a disagreement over the running of the university. As a result, Einstein stopped working on the institution's behalf.[51]

As the grand ceremony approached, Magnes felt uneasy. When referring to the "opening," he put it in quotation marks, as if the event were a lie, *ein Jüdischer Bluff,* as he said to Felix Warburg, another leader of the New York Jewish community. In correspondence, Colonel Kisch also referred to the "opening" with quotation marks.[52] In fact, there was very little to open. Magnes was unhappy that the university was serving the Zionist movement's political propaganda. The Palestinian Arabs declared a general strike on the day of the ceremony, flying black flags over their homes. "Could not the University have been inaugurated without stirring up the Moslem world against us?" Magnes wrote to Ahad Ha'am. He also objected to Balfour's participation, which required surrounding the campus with "100 extra British gendarmerie," he complained; the university would look like a stronghold of British imperialism.

But to Weizmann this was precisely the point. No man symbolized better than Balfour the obligation of the British empire to aid the establishment of a Jewish state. Weizmann had worked on the visit for more than a year. Balfour's trip was termed a "private visit," but in Jerusalem he stayed in the high commissioner's residence. General Allenby also came to Jerusalem to participate in the ceremony. The fight over tickets to the amphitheater, specially constructed for the purpose, led to insults that were never forgotten.[53]

As at the cornerstone-laying ceremony, the speakers at the inauguration compared the Hebrew University to the Holy Temple. Chaim Nachman Bialik called the opening of the university a "holiday to our Lord and our people," saying "the holy fire" would burn within its buildings. The university, he later said, is "our sanctuary," the sanctuary of the Zionist religion.* As for Balfour, "with his hands raised to the skies and his white hair floating in the wind, he looked like a prophet," Colonel Kisch wrote. Samuel gave "the most Jewish speech" Kisch had ever heard him make. At the end, he recited the *shehechiyanu,* the thanksgiving blessing in Hebrew. Ronald Storrs, ever a snob, said a few words in Latin and asked the forgiveness of the ultra-Orthodox in the audience. Magnes answered for them: no matter, he said, we long ago forgave Titus. Kisch estimated that twelve thousand people attended.[55]

Balfour was taken to visit farms and kibbutzim and was enthusiastically received everywhere. He was obliged to hear and make speeches wherever he went. In Tel Aviv he dedicated a street named after him; Kisch managed at the last minute to prevent Balfour from being forced to climb up the local water tower to take in the view of the city. As a departing present he was given a scroll of the books of Ezra and Nehemiah; his hosts sensed that he was moved to the depths of his soul. A few hours before the night of the Passover Seder he set out by train to visit Damascus, where he was almost killed.

Out of concern for his security, Balfour disembarked a station early, and was transferred to an automobile. The train continued on its course. An angry crowd awaited him at the Damascus station, but Balfour had in the meantime arrived by car at the Victoria Hotel. When the protestors realized they had been tricked, they streamed toward the city. There were perhaps six thousand of them. Mounted police tried to disperse the mob.

A correspondent for the London *Times* was positioned on one of the roofs facing the hotel. The mob, he wrote, surged forward again and again, "with ever growing fury." There was a pile of cobblestones for

---

*Chaim Weizmann's brother Hilik once attended a dinner where Frances Newton was also a guest. When she asked him whether the Jews intended to rebuild the Temple, he reportedly told her that there was no need—they had the university.[54]

repairing the road, and people began throwing them at the hotel. The police opened fire, and hand-to-hand combat ensued between policemen and rioters. Some of the crowd tried to topple the policemen from their horses and steal their weapons. The correspondent described the confrontation as a "monster outbreak." One demonstrator was killed. Some hours after Balfour's arrival, at around 2:00 P.M., the army moved in and chased the mob into the alleyways. At 3:00 the French high commissioner arrived, entering the hotel and leaving at once. Two airplanes had appeared above the hotel, dropping smoke bombs. A few minutes later Balfour was taken from the hotel and driven by car in the direction of Beirut, which he reached at about eight in the evening, immediately boarding the *Sphinx* and sailing for Alexandria. For a while his life had been in serious danger, the *Times* reported.

Questions were asked in Parliament. Yes, the possibility that Balfour's visit might cause trouble had been taken into account, the colonial secretary said. A few days before Balfour's departure for Damascus word had been received that there might be an attempt on his life. The information was duly transmitted to the French authorities, who had promised to take all necessary steps. Balfour himself expressed his regrets over the incident; all he had wanted was a "pleasure trip" to Damascus. Had he known what would happen he would not have gone.[56]

Balfour's visit to Palestine had also been a mark of recognition of Herbert Samuel's work on behalf of the national home; he was soon to end his term. He wanted very much to settle in Haifa, but his replacement, Lord Herbert Charles Onslow Plumer, objected. Samuel acceded unwillingly. Before leaving, he made one last effort to correct an embarrassing error that had crept into the history books. He had not permitted prostitution in Jerusalem, he wrote firmly—precisely the opposite. His administration had made a great effort to eradicate it.[57]

5.

Alter Levine, a.k.a. Asaf Halevy the Jerusalemite, continued in the meantime to strive to bring ever greater glory to his city of enchantment. He had his book of poems reprinted and sent it to many people. Acceptance as a poet was dearer to him than money. Writers sent him flattering letters, among them the prominent poet and editor Avraham Shlonsky. It seems Levine's fellow writers were not too enthusiastic about publishing his poems; but surely Levine, "friend and writer," would agree to place an advertisement—"a large advertisement," Shlonsky emphasized—in their various literary digests to help cover the costs of publication. The idea was that the king of insurance would place a few advertisements and the editors would print a few of his poems.[58]

British rule was good for Levine; his business flourished. To him, Zionism was synonymous with economic entrepreneurship, and he apparently believed with all sincerity that the Zionist capital flowing into the country had improved the quality of life for the entire population, just as the movement's spokesmen always claimed. Like many other industrialists and businessmen, he tended to identify his own private business interests with the national ideal, as if he were selling insurance policies not to make a profit but for the future of his people. In an interview with a British newspaper he exuded optimism; his life and work in Palestine were a great adventure. His interviewers were impressed with his "engaging" personality—so the prophet Ezekiel would have looked, they wrote, if he had tried to sell you an insurance policy.[59] Before long he had purchased a Cadillac and hired a chauffeur to drive him around Jerusalem. On the wall in Levine's office, in a silver frame, was a telegram from the queen of England thanking him for his kind wishes: he had sent the king a message wishing him a speedy recovery in the name of the city's Jews.[60] The list of people who took interest-bearing loans from him is a veritable Who's Who of Jerusalem, and it includes many Arab names.

From time to time Levine participated in the meetings of a small Jewish-Arab group that tried to preserve some level of cooperation between the two communities. Judge Gad Frumkin was a member; Khalil al-Sakakini was present on the Arab side. "It was a group of friends that engaged in mutual assistance and in disseminating knowledge of the country," Frumkin wrote. They spoke of establishing a formal club and organized language classes—Arabic for the Jews, Hebrew for the Arabs, and English for both. According to Frumkin, "all these were artificial and brought no real results."[61] The meetings might have been among the activities funded by the Zionist Organization in an attempt to neutralize extreme Arab nationalism.[62] Al-Sakakini could not have known this; perhaps Levine did not know it either.

Both men were square-jawed, not tall, but with full, solid physiques. In one photograph Levine looks like a scheming Mephisto; in others his eyes are full of soft, boyish romanticism. "He had velvet eyes caught in a flame," wrote Uri Keisari, a journalist for the *Do'ar HaYom* daily. "He would walk casually, flexibly, ready at any moment to pounce. . . . His small, square, black beard gave him the appearance of an Assyrian figure who had been reincarnated in modern times. . . . There was a whiff of the Orient about him, with his dreaminess and craftiness, his fiery imagination and his petty account keeping." When he spoke, Levine would lean a bit forward and bow his head slightly; he was a man of "proud subservience, of restrained arrogance," Keisari wrote. Another writer, Dov Kimche, described him as a "dandy" and marveled especially at the monocle that hung from the front of his white suits. Sakakini was much the same. "I love to dress well and cultivate my youth and beauty," he wrote.[63]

Keisari first met Levine in the corridors of the Anglo-Palestinian Bank. "I am Alter Levine, King of Life and Death," he introduced himself. Keisari laughed, captivated by Levine's flamboyance and pathos. The insurance agent drew a sheaf of notebooks and forms out of his briefcase and explained that there was nothing worse than death and that one should protect oneself from it. "I laughed in his face," Keisari recalled, "and asked him what cologne he had sprinkled on his hair. Levine was taken aback for a minute, but immediately smiled and said: 'The perfume is among the treasures of the Orient. I love perfume, poetry, and colors.'" They spoke no more of life insurance on that occasion.

A while later the two men ran into each other again in a dentist's waiting room. "I wanted to speak to him about poetry and feeling," Keisari wrote, "but Levine was quick to ask: 'So, when are you going to get some life insurance?' I told him 'Be quiet, Alter Levine, and let Asaf Halevy speak.' Levine just smiled. When he left, someone in the waiting room said, 'That's Alter Levine . . . he'll skin you alive. He'd sell his soul for a halfpenny.'"

On the strength of his prosperity, Levine had built himself a house in Romema, a new neighborhood to the north of Jaffa Street. He was one of the neighborhood's founders, all of whom were wealthy businessmen. The houses were built with Levantine grandeur, like the homes of the rich Arabs in Talbieh, Katamon, and Baka. They were impressive in their architectural diversity, at once European and Mediterranean, stone and iron, with colored glass windows and many columns, especially at the entrances; some had vases of geraniums placed on their capitals. There were lots of outer staircases and small columns shaped like pawns from a chessboard.[64] David Ben-Gurion was furious—the construction company that built Romema proclaimed its adherence to Zionism but did not employ Jewish workers, he complained.[65] The Levine house stood just a few minutes' walk from the site where Mayor al-Husseini had handed his writ of surrender to General Allenby on the day Levine and Sakakini were taken to Damascus. A memorial had been built on the spot. Levine had planted a date palm in his garden.

Levine and Uri Keisari met for a third time in Paris. Levine was indulging his passion for grand hotels; his papers include stationery from the Excelsiors, the Savoys, and the Regencys in every city between Beirut and London. Keisari was impressed by the uniform worn by the doorman at Levine's hotel and by Levine's bulging suitcases. He wondered what was in them and Levine showed him. "I saw elegantly tailored suits and expensive silk pajamas, but also hundreds of books. New books that had just appeared yesterday and old obscure books the insurance agent from Jerusalem had sniffed out at the bookstalls on the banks of the Seine."

Then Levine dug out of a special crate paintings he had just purchased from famous artists. Keisari wondered at the extravagance, and suddenly Levine seemed to take off a mask, as he said: "Colors . . . colors . . . I would give everything I have for colors." He was in fact one of the best-known art collectors in Palestine and sponsored local artists. "I am a bridge between West and East," he explained to Keisari.

Levine initiated the next meeting between the two men. He called Keisari and asked whether he would like to come to Damascus. They agreed to meet at Levine's office in Jerusalem, where Keisari found himself in a dark room with black furniture and green walls and curtains. "Levine sat at his desk like the prince in a fairy-tale," Keisari wrote, but when he spoke, he demanded that his guest purchase an insurance policy. "Be quiet, Alter Levine," Keisari again told him, as before, "and let Asaf Halevy speak." Levine responded, his lips compressed: "If Levine did not speak, Asaf Halevy could not sing."[66]

Among Levine's papers is a letter he received from the great Hebrew writer Shmuel Yosef Agnon. Levine had asked Agnon to put in a good word for him with the editors of a literary anthology and had taken the opportunity to offer Agnon an insurance policy. In response, Agnon had supplied the address of an editor in Tel Aviv and expressed no desire for insurance. "I have just returned from a journey and I am traveling once again," he wrote in tiny, flyspeck letters, responding, perhaps, to the two souls of his correspondent—Alter Levine, insurance salesman, and Asaf Halevy, poet of Jerusalem.[67]

————•─••─————

Yefim Gordin Comes
to Palestine

1.

In June 1926 Yefim Gordin, a young man of eighteen, landed at the port of Haifa. A recent graduate of the Hebrew Gymnasium in Vilna, he had been encouraged by his teachers to continue his studies in Switzerland or Italy, but Gordin wanted to live in Palestine. He was a Zionist. "This postcard is the last one I write as a European; today, in a few hours, I will become an Asian," he wrote to his parents from the port of Constantsa in Romania. "I have absolutely no regrets for that nice, cultured label European. May God grant that all be for the best and that we soon meet face to face on Mt. Zion and in Jerusalem."[1]

In the years that followed, Gordin wrote home almost every day; his letters were at least four pages long, written in a tiny, crowded hand to save on paper and postage. Mail left Palestine for Vilna twice a week. Gordin wrote in Hebrew; his letters and handwriting demonstrate considerable fluency. He told his parents everything, shared with them his nationalist dreams and personal troubles, from the conflict with the Arabs to the first holes in his socks. In his first three years in Palestine nothing preoccupied him more than the effort to obtain immigration permits for his parents and his sister, Hannah. To do so, he had to prove that he could support them. Officially, all he needed was a certificate from the British authorities, but he soon discovered that much depended on connections and patronage.

Most of Europe's 10 million Jews remained in Europe; a majority of Jews in Arab lands also stayed where they were. Close to 2.5 million Jews left Europe prior to World War I; most went to the United States. In the 1920s three-quarters of a million Jews emigrated; more than half went to the United States. Even at the height of Jewish immigration, only 4 out of every 1,000 of the world's Jews came to Palestine.[2] These were the limits of the Zionist adventure. All told, during the 1920s about 100,000 Jews, mostly from Eastern Europe, immigrated to Palestine, doubling the size of the Jewish community.[3] They came in two waves—the third and fourth *aliyas*.*

Zionist mythology depicts the people of the third aliya as agricultural laborers and those of the fourth aliya as bourgeois city dwellers.[5] In fact, only a small minority of those who came at the beginning of the 1920s actually engaged in agriculture, and some farm workers came during the second half of the decade, as part of the fourth aliya. The qualitative distinction between the two waves of immigration is thus artificial. Most of those who settled in the country during the 1920s came in search of a better life and chose Palestine only after the United States shut its doors to mass immigration in 1924. One out of every four newcomers did not remain in the country. Eight out of every ten settled in the cities; the central story of those years is the story of Tel Aviv. The Jewish city on the Mediterranean was poised between Moscow and Warsaw on one side and Paris and New York on the other, between a memory of the past and a dream of the future. Tel Aviv's residents were immigrants with sky-high expectations and were, for this reason, vulnerable to abysmal despair.[6]

2.

Populating the country with Jews was one of the Balfour Declaration's implicit obligations. The incorporation of the declaration into the Mandate the British had received from the League of Nations turned Jewish immigration from a unilateral and nonbinding promise to a legal, international obligation. Although the Zionists spoke about "millions" of immigrants, their immediate goal was to create a Jewish majority, both to strengthen the Jewish community and to create the impression that the

---

*Aliya, literally "going up," is the Hebrew term for immigration to Palestine and, later, Israel, and is also used to identify a particular wave of immigration. The first aliya began in the 1880s; the second aliya preceded World War I. The immigrants in both waves came mostly from Yemen and Russia.[4]

national home was grounded in democratic values and justice. The Arab majority argued that the national-home policy contradicted the principle of democracy and Arabs' own right to self-determination. There was no chance the Arabs would change their minds about the national-home policy, so the Zionists set about changing the country's demographic mix instead.

The Zionist movement had begun by demanding free immigration, but Herbert Samuel warned that the principle was dangerous, as it would most probably mean opening up immigration for Arabs as well. As an alternative, Samuel implemented a quota system, with the number of immigration permits to be set in bilateral negotiations between the Zionist movement and the British government, in the framework of the latter's commitment to the establishment of a national home. In this manner, Jewish immigration could be given preference.[7] And that is what happened. Year after year, Arab protests were heard and duly noted, but British policy insisted that the Arabs had no standing in the negotiations on immigration. Once again, the Zionists did not receive everything they wanted, but they received a great deal.

Each permit was ostensibly issued by the British administration; in practice, though, the British ceded authority to the Zionist movement to decide where the immigrants would come from, and in each country its representatives chose the candidates.[8] Thus most Jews who wanted to settle in Palestine turned not to the nearest British consulate but to the office of the local Zionist Organization. This process ensured that newcomers would indeed be Jewish and allowed for a selection process that became one of the movement's principal sources of power. It was also up to the movement to decide which relatives the immigrant would be allowed to bring and which route they would take to reach Palestine. Then there was the question of whether the immigrants should pay customs on their belongings. The Zionists demanded an exemption for personal items, including books and scientific instruments, as well as on raw materials and machinery.[9]

Although the Zionists had argued for free immigration, there was nothing that scared them more than uncontrolled and unplanned population growth. "If we were to grant entry permits to workers in excess of demand, we would not be enriching the country but leading it into an economic crisis," explained the movement's leaders in an internal memorandum. "That way we might well put the new immigrants in danger of starvation and place an intolerable burden on the Zionist Organization," they added. They warned their representatives to dissuade even people with capital from coming to Palestine in large numbers: "Our agents must make absolutely clear what kind of conditions currently prevail in Palestine," they wrote, explaining that disappointment would probably lead people who lost their money to leave the country.[10]

Chaim Weizmann wrote to Samuel that Jewish victory in Palestine did not depend on a million Jews coming there. He believed that the critical number was 100,000. "If we succeed in bringing in 100,000 productive working Jews, the way to the Jewish commonwealth will be paved and we may see it in our lifetime," he wrote.[11] His position was shrewd, producing an implicit agreement between the Zionist movement and the British government to link immigration to the country's capacity to absorb new arrivals, that is, the ability to provide them with work.

Once every six months the Zionist Executive and the British set the quota of immigrants and determined their desired professional training—so many agricultural workers, so many construction workers. Job creation for immigrants was largely dependent on the Zionists' ability to raise money, especially in the United States. The movement promised to guarantee every immigrant upkeep during his or her first year in the country. This policy was also in the movement's interest, Herbert Samuel explained: by assuming such responsibility, the movement would more easily be able to reject those candidates unable to support themselves.*

Immigrants with money—"capitalists"—were not included in the quotas and were allowed to come without restrictions. Early British regulations required them to prove they could bring at least £500. The sum fluctuated, and from time to time the Zionist leadership demanded that the amount be reduced. The authorities were not inclined to agree. "Everything appears to depend on the continuous influx of new immigrants bringing capital with them," asserted Sir John Shuckburgh of the Colonial Office.[13]

Throughout the 1920s and '30s there were debates over whether the rate of immigration should match the "absorptive capacity" of the Jewish economy alone or whether the condition of the Arab population should also be taken into account. Occasionally, the Zionists demanded an

---

*On one occasion, when Samuel reduced the number of immigrants because of a rise in unemployment, he told Weizmann that had he not done so the Zionist Executive would have had to do it, becoming the target of criticism currently aimed at the administration. "I hope you will appreciate my friendly service," Samuel wrote.[12]

increase in the quota, even if there was no guarantee of employment, arguing that immigration spurred the economy and therefore created work. At other times, the Zionist Executive complained that the British were reacting to Arab opposition rather than setting the quotas on purely economic grounds. The Yishuv's representatives would draft public protests, and the Hebrew newspapers would attack British immigration policy. On occasion Chaim Weizmann had to use all his connections in London to resolve the differences.[14] But on the whole, the Zionists worked in tandem with the government and with its consent, both on the basic principle of immigration policy and the details of its execution. The British tended to trust the Zionist Executive.

Samuel put several Jewish officials in charge of the administration's immigration department, one of them being Albert M. Hyamson. Like the high commissioner, Hyamson was a Zionist and sometimes the object of considerable hostility. However, he too did not consider his Jewish origins a reason to give preference to Zionist interests over those of his government. Hyamson habitually worked until late at night, personally examining immigrant applications and often making the final decision.

At one stage Edwin Samuel served as Hyamson's deputy; the senior Samuel was no longer in Palestine at the time.[15]

3.

Requests for immigration permits poured in from Iran to Argentina and every country in between. "Masses and masses are coming to our offices to demand visas," wrote Zionist representatives in Lithuania. Awarding the visa was largely a political affair: the movement had agreed that the permits would be allocated to each region and each political party according to its relative strength in the Zionist Congress. The various parties were constantly jockeying for power, and their members in Palestine were actively involved. Everyone concerned well understood that immigration would determine political power in Palestine. "The Exile is building us," David Ben-Gurion said.[16] The British did not intervene, except to rule out Communists.*

---

*Herbert Samuel feared a "deluge" of immigrants, including those of an "unsuitable type," thinking particularly of Communists. To weed them out, Samuel suggested that the Zionist offices in different countries serve as "sieves." He was in favor of preparing "blacklists" of people not allowed to come and did not rule out the deportation of undesirables. Weizmann promised that Zionist Organization representatives were carefully checking the political backgrounds of applicants to prevent the entry of Bolsheviks.[17]

The Zionist Executive demanded that visas be given only to those "elements who will not be a burden to us, those elements who will build the country," assuming that Jewish immigration should serve Palestine's needs, not the other way around. The principal and decisive goal was Palestine and its future. "We are obligated to be cruel," wrote one labor movement ideologue, referring to pogroms in the Ukraine and the many Jews in need of asylum. "We must restrain ourselves and declare that though the killings continue, we must save the Yishuv and its future, because the fate of all our people depends on it." This was also Ze'ev Jabotinsky's position.[18]*

The most desirable candidates for immigration were young unmarried men, "brave and idealistic," who would commit to work for two years in the agricultural settlements. "There is a great need for you here," wrote immigrant Chaim Bratschneider to his friends, stressing that "only the continuous mass immigration of young people who know how to wield a hoe and hold a rifle can save the Yishuv from obliteration." The Zionists assumed that the individual should "contribute" to the advancement of society. As one woman wrote to her friends, "Don't send people who have no profession. In Jaffa there are many pioneers without work. And every week new ships bring more of them."[20] Women were also considered an "element" whose arrival should be restricted.[21] An effort was made to prevent the arrival of people with infectious disease, the mentally ill, criminals, prostitutes, and drunks. The Zionist Commission complained about penniless, unhealthy types turning up on Palestine's shores. "Sometimes utter invalids manage to get permits as people fit for all work," the immigration department griped. There were hundreds of such cases, the department said. Its top officials sent the movement's overseas representatives a list of names of sick people. Under no circumstances should these people have been granted visas, the department ruled, demanding that the doctors responsible be fired.[22]†

*The socialist periodical *Kuntress* went so far as to describe the persecution of Ukrainian Jewry as a danger to Jewish existence in Palestine. The fear was that not enough potential immigrants would remain.[19]

†The Zionist Organization even paid for sick immigrants to return to their country of origin. Mr. Neifeld of Warsaw, one of the files said, had tuberculosis. "We will have to put out larger sums for him than we would for his trip back." Nevertheless, that was an exceptional case. "We are not permitted to expend even small sums to get people out of the country. The money at our disposal is designated solely for people remaining in Palestine who need our help," one of the Zionist Commission leaders wrote.[23]

Aware of the responsibility given them by the British, the Zionist immigration officials instructed their representatives to observe the rules and file truthful reports. Time and again newcomers were discovered with other people's permits, pretending they were relatives and lying about their professions. A man might receive a visa as an agricultural laborer and turn out to be a tailor. Such people would be sent back, the department warned. There were quite a few cases of this sort, and the Zionist Executive worried that the British might revoke the privilege of choosing the immigrants.

Most immigrants came at their own expense and at their own risk. The Zionist movement's commitment to ensure the newcomer's livelihood for a year was meant to satisfy the authorities, not the immigrant. "Receipt of a recommendation," the movement informed its representatives, does not give anyone the right "to make demands of the Zionist Organization." Subsidizing immigrants would attract undesirable "human material," it explained.[24]*

To a British officer in the border guard, the new arrivals looked like a ragtag but happy group. Douglas V. Duff described them with amazement. They stepped ashore after long weeks of horrible crowding on the decks of barely serviceable vessels; the conditions were worse than on old-time slave ships, Duff wrote, without bathrooms or showers. The immigrants had brought all their food along in bags, generally dry bread and smoked fish. To reach the shore they had to transfer into lighters; Arab sailors would toss them off the ship's deck as if they were packages. The stench of the travelers was evident at long range. "I often vomited as we put the medical officer aboard," Duff wrote. Piles of garbage and excrement were scattered all over the ship.

Amazingly, he saw no misery among the passengers, only exultation. A strange light shone in their eyes. When the immigrants made out the cliffs of Mount Carmel and the blue mountains of the Galilee, they would break out in song. Duff, a little carried away, wrote that they sang "ancient Hebrew melodies."

There was always a great commotion in the port, necessitating harsh, even heartless treatment, Duff wrote. Hundreds of people would come to

---

*The distinction between different types of "human material" has accompanied the Zionist movement from its origin. Theodor Herzl himself used the term in his book *The Jewish State*. It was a common phrase, showing up in, among other places, an early article written by Berl Katznelson.[25]

receive the immigrants, hysterically breaking through the barbed-wire fence, wanting to hear news of relatives left behind in Europe. According to Duff, the Arab policemen would get nervous and use their sticks and camel-hide whips to hold back the crowd. When they failed to maintain order, they would drag the culprits to the bathhouse together with the immigrants. On the way, they had to pass through the shipyards, where Arab workers would jeer at the strange procession of people in their ragged European clothes, smelly, exhausted, staggering under their bundles, and all the time singing those ancient Hebrew melodies. "Few of us fully appreciated what was happening in front of our eyes, nor grasped the historical significance of what we saw," Duff wrote.

After walking a few hundred meters, the arrivals would reach the bathhouse, where they had to drop their belongings to be searched. Then they had to strip naked, men in one room, women in another, to be checked for contraband firearms and explosives. Next they were taken to the disinfection facilities, not far away. Many also slept at the port, for a night or two, in tents, without sheets or mosquito netting; anopheles mosquitoes swarmed everywhere. The conditions were frightful. Duff did not want to describe them; "they may be easily imagined," he wrote.[26] The drama of the newcomers was one of fantastic journeys across continents, reversals of fortune, and newly minted identities. Such was the story of Yefim Gordin.

4.

Upon arriving in Haifa, after having been disinfected and receiving shots against smallpox and typhus, Gordin went first to the post office to send a telegram to his parents. Then he went to the Reali School, the focus of Jewish communal life in the city, to find the address of his Uncle David. His bundles remained in quarantine in the meantime; he was allowed to take with him only two small packages.

Haifa was then on the verge of the most dramatic transformation in its history. The small fishing town was turning quickly into a city, a center of government, and a magnet for Arab migrants from the surrounding villages and for Jews from Europe.*

*In the 1920s the number of Arab inhabitants of Haifa grew from about 18,000 to 24,000. The number of Jews nearly tripled, from 6,000 to 16,000 (this figure included a few thousand non-Arab foreigners). The proportionate size of the Jewish population also rose: at the beginning of the 1920s one out of every four people in the city was Jewish, whereas one-third of the population was Jewish in the early 1930s.[27]

In the 1920s the city's Jews began to settle in separate neighborhoods. The Hadar HaCarmel neighborhood was built around the Technion, the technical college, which had developed parallel to the Hebrew University in Jerusalem and was also considered a foundation stone of Zionist culture. Hadar HaCarmel had also been planned by Richard Kaufmann and was meant to be a quiet residential area of one- and two-story homes surrounded by gardens. Like Tel Aviv and the garden neighborhoods of Jerusalem, Hadar HaCarmel enabled Jews to live apart from the clamor of the Arab city.

Some time after Tel Aviv gained its municipal independence from Jaffa, Hadar HaCarmel also received autonomy to manage its residents' affairs. The neighborhood committee collected taxes, supplied water, and paved sidewalks. There was a kindergarten and a school.[28] Preferring to keep commerce at a distance, the residents opposed opening stores in the neighborhood. When Yefim Gordin came to join his aunt and uncle, there were three thousand people living in Hadar HaCarmel.

Uncle David and Aunt Rachel welcomed him warmly. David Ettinger was a fairly well off businessman; he had settled in Palestine in 1918, starting a company that unloaded oil from ships. They had five or six rooms, Gordin reported to his parents, and a view of Haifa Bay. There were beautiful furniture, carpets, and a maid—she came in the morning and left in the evening. Gordin slept on the couch in the living room. Like many immigrants, he quickly came down with a fever and spent three days in bed.

Gordin's first impressions: Aunt Rachel hates every minute in Palestine. She calls it a cursed land, in Yiddish. She can't forgive herself for leaving Germany and compares everything to Berlin. Even though she lives very well in Palestine, Gordin told his parents, she is perpetually angry and upset and always threatens to go back to Germany. Uncle David, on the other hand, tends to go too far the other way and tries to prove that everything is fine. They have lots of fights, including arguments about Uncle David being late for lunch.

Gordin's assessment was that the general situation in Palestine wasn't awful, but then neither was it all that great. "There are good things and bad things," he wrote. He was concerned by the high prices. When he recovered from his fever, he went to collect the bundles he had left at the quarantine station. The wagon driver took ten piastres, Gordin reported with some alarm. In the days that followed he searched out acquaintances to give them letters he had brought from Vilna. He noticed a lot of construction, and soft-drink stands everywhere. Soda is called *gazoz*, he wrote to his little sister.[29]

Gordin began to think about looking for work. In the city, of course: "Working in the villages is stupid, because they only have farm work and it's very hard labor," he explained to his parents.[30] How nice it would be to get a job at the customs house, he thought, but although he knew a little English, that plan didn't work out. Instead he decided to visit his Uncle Ya'akov and Aunt Anita in Jerusalem.

He went by bus, via the Jezreel Valley. A "pioneer" who had come six years earlier traveled with him, as did an old man who looked like an Arab because he wore Oriental clothes and a tarbush. It turned out that he was a Caucasian Jew who had lived in Palestine for thirty-five years and traded in cotton wool. He had just returned from a business trip to Beirut. Ten minutes out of Haifa Gordin saw the Nesher cement factory, the biggest plant in the country, like an entire city. The bus passed Nahalal, a cooperative farming village, also planned by Richard Kaufmann, and nearby Ein Harod, a kibbutz that had just celebrated its fifth birthday. The small buildings were pretty, and the fields nicely plowed, Gordin wrote. He saw Beit Alfa, a four-year-old kibbutz, from a distance. A few months previously the settlers there had uncovered an ancient synagogue with a stunning mosaic floor. "The valley has been conquered. To be more precise, it is still being conquered, because there is more to redeem and that is a duty and the order of the day and we must not miss this opportunity," he noted.

"Here and there you run into Arab villages—they live like real pigs," he wrote. Their fields were full of rocks. In one field he noticed stones that had been arranged in some specific order. It was a Muslim cemetery. His fellow travelers explained that the Arabs were not very concerned with their dead and did even less for the living: "If you saw how and what they eat and where they sleep, you'd feel real revulsion at touching them," Gordin explained. Yes, Jewish laborers demand higher pay than Arab ones, he meditated, but there was good reason to be proud of that, since a Jewish worker couldn't make do with half a loaf of bread but needed a newspaper as well and soap and toothpaste. It was not enough just to rinse yourself in water. "It looks to me as if the Arabs don't even know that," he added.

The bus stopped in Jenin, an exclusively Arab city. The only Jew there was a doctor; Jewish doctors also lived in other Arab cities. "Our neighbors are still underdeveloped," wrote Gordin.[31] On the way to Jerusalem

Gordin also noticed a few monasteries. They "really pollute the country. . . . There is a monastery at every place that has some Biblical tradition attached to it. Be grateful that Tel Aviv wasn't mentioned in the Holy Scriptures—thanks to that we have one city in Palestine without a monastery." The old man traveling in the bus pointed out where Joseph's brothers had thrown him into the pit. "He insisted on showing me as if he'd been a witness to the act."

Uncle Ya'akov and Aunt Anita Ettinger received him pleasantly. They lived in a one-bedroom apartment on Bezalel Street. Uncle Ya'akov had a shop for making blueprints. They put Gordin on the couch in their front room and tried to convince him to remain in Jerusalem. They knew a professor, Klein, and Klein had promised to speak with Professor Magnes from the university. Maybe the university would give him a five-pound monthly living stipend. The idea appealed to Gordin. He liked Jerusalem—spiritual life there is more interesting, he wrote. There were lectures and a library; Haifa did not have a decent library.

He had a distant relative who was an influential lawyer, Mordechai Eliash. Gordin went to introduce himself, hoping that Eliash would give him a letter of recommendation for an office job at the Hadassah medical center. Eliash did not want to lift a finger to help, Gordin wrote, but sometime later the attorney promised to speak to Magnes on the matter of the stipend.

In the meantime, Gordin managed to find office work with a Mr. Halliday, the director of Ronald Storrs's Pro-Jerusalem Society. Gordin's hours were seven in the morning to two in the afternoon; he was promised five pounds for the first month. He really wanted to work in the Hebrew National Library, but its director, Hugo Bergmann, was in Europe and no new employees were being accepted in his absence. At the Pro-Jerusalem Society Gordin spent most of his time typing. The first question asked of every immigrant was, Do you know how to type, and with how many fingers? he related. He would advise anyone planning to settle in Palestine to learn how to type.

In the afternoons he went to the Jewish Studies Institute and sat in on lectures. Uncle Ya'akov and Aunt Anita were about to move into a new apartment with another room, a European toilet, and running water. Gordin would be able to have his own corner, almost a whole room, he wrote. But then Uncle David wanted him to come back to Haifa, offering him an office job. In any case, Gordin had not managed to get command of the formal language Mr. Halliday expected him to use. He did not know what to do or whose advice to ask; he keenly felt the lack of his parents. His new socks already had holes in the toes, he wrote; he was now wearing the new pants he had brought from Vilna.[32]

Two months after arriving in Palestine, Gordin was back in Haifa, working for his Uncle David from morning until afternoon. The work was very easy, also mostly typing. Uncle David promised him between five and six pounds each month, but Gordin would have liked more. During the morning he would go to a restaurant and drink a glass of milk for one piastre. At noontime he would go home with his uncle for lunch. They ate vegetarian meals on weekdays; meat was only for the Sabbath. Uncle David was as strict with his nephew as he was with all his employees, calling him Gordin in the office. Aunt Rachel continued to complain about the living conditions. He had brought her, from Jerusalem, two boxes of pudding powder, very good, made in Palestine, but his aunt used only what she received from Germany.[33]

All sorts of plans popped into his head. There was a nice, well-ordered hotel run by the daughter of Rabbi Hildesheimer, but she didn't really know the business and it had gone bankrupt. Uncle David knew the creditors; were he to buy the hotel, for six or seven hundred pounds, Yefim's father and mother could come from Vilna and manage it. But Uncle David opposed having the Gordins immigrate unless they could bring enough money to live on for at least six months.

For the time being, Gordin moved to the Vilna Hotel. His room had a bed, a fairly large table, two chairs, and a bay window that could be used as a closet. After much haggling, the rent was set at 160 piastres a month, including tea in the morning and evening. Gordin was troubled by flies and mosquitoes in his room, but as a temporary arrangement it wasn't bad. The rooms for rent on Mount Carmel were unfurnished and went for two and a half pounds. He would have liked a roommate to share the rent and the boredom. Sometimes he went for a walk on Mount Carmel. He began to study the Talmud with five other young men, decided to look for a bicycle, and began to put out a kind of typewritten newsletter, called *BeArtzeinu*, "In Our Land."

On the newsletter's masthead he put a three-part slogan: "It is good to live in our land, it is good to suffer in our land, it is good to work in our land."[34] In the first issue he described the view from Mount Carmel. "Far far off where the sea ends lies Europe; Poland is there—so many memories are tied to it," he wrote. It was not easy for him to become an "Asian." His loneliness troubled him, and he missed home. "The tears roll down my cheeks one after another," he wrote to his parents. He wanted to know about everything over there, from the state of Aunt Rivka's health to the latest gossip from the gymnasium. His parents sent him a pillow with someone who came from Vilna; Gordin went to Tel Aviv to fetch it; his Uncle Chaim lived there on HaYarkon Street, not far from Menachem Ussishkin's house, near the Casino.

5.

The Casino was not a gambling establishment but a coffeehouse. Its flamboyant name was appropriate in Tel Aviv, itself a fantasy built on sand that fueled the imaginations of visionaries and charlatans from all over the world. The money to build the Casino had come from investors in America; the architect, Yehuda Maggidowitz, had come from the Ukraine on the *Ruslan*. Those who saw the Casino were reminded of the dachas rich families in Odessa built on the beach, although it looked more like a huge circus tent. The official name, Galei Aviv, was inscribed on two wheel-shaped signs, and these gave the building's facade the look of a huge fan or a fantastic windmill. There were awnings and bunting, decorative balconies, and elegant Chinese lanterns. "Around the terrace we have installed fountains and lighting effects," stated one advertisement, "which by day spurt jets of water to raise the spirits and at night dazzle with electric fire."

Mayor Meir Dizengoff and municipal officials treated the Casino like a public structure of national importance. They diverted Allenby Street from its planned route so that it would end precisely at the building's entrance. A dance band played the fox-trot and the Charleston. "The British commanders ate lunch there," one of the barmen later recalled. "They met the Jewish girls at the Casino, treated them to drinks, and sometimes it ended in marriage. The place was cheery with a good atmosphere."[35]

Tel Aviv was built according to every whim of the imagination, in a great celebration of kitsch, wastefulness, crazy stylistic juxtaposition, and the spirit of the roaring twenties. From the sands of Tel Aviv emerged one residence that looked like a Chinese pagoda but that was inspired by a coffee shop in America; another house resembled a castle from *Grimms' Fairy Tales,* with sharp metal spires like Pierrot hats. Round balconies rested on pseudoclassical columns decorated with metallic reliefs of the menorah from the Holy Temple; window frames suggested the harems of Arab *khalifs;* entranceways were surrounded by plaster lions and eagles.

Facades of buildings sported colorful ceramic tiles produced by the Beza-lel School of Art in Jerusalem using a technique and style imported from Vienna, depicting prophets and biblical tribes, camel caravans, and palms, lots of palms. In Bialik's house ceramic palms adorned an impressive fireplace he had constructed in the living room, apparently in expectation of Russian winters. One home owner had himself memorialized in clay on the facade of his house; the sculpture bore a caption: Samuel Wilson, American contractor. Alter Levine was excited by this brash blend of East and West: "It was not avenues you planted and gardens, not houses that you built on a hill," he wrote in a poem to the people of Tel Aviv. "You opened sanctuaries to the sun. Sanctuaries with golden gates, a joyous city facing the waves! You raised a lookout and a tower, at the portals of eastern Eden, for every home in Israel."[36]

This was the decade of the building contractors. In 1920 Tel Aviv had some 2,000 residents; by 1924 there were 20,000; that number doubled to 40,000 the following year. In 1925 investment in construction reached 1.5 million Palestinian pounds, more than 70 percent of the total investments in Palestine. A record was broken that year—some 35,000 immigrants arrived. Never had so many Jews come in a single year. For the first time, immigrants to Palestine outnumbered Jewish immigrants to any other country, including the United States. Almost half of them came from Poland, largely because of a new economic policy enacted by Polish finance minister Ladislav Grabski that hit hardest at the middle class, including many Jews.* Many of the "Grabski immigrants," as they were called, came as "capitalists" and settled in Tel Aviv.[38] Few other cities in the world grew so rapidly.

That same year Tel Aviv's municipal government asked Patrick Geddes, the urban planner who had drawn the design for the Hebrew University, to devise a master plan for the city. The construction craze had made its mark, and the built-up areas would remain as they were, but Geddes laid out a grid for the land still empty—broad north-south avenues running parallel to the sea and perpendicular east-west streets to ensure the flow of sea air. Tel Aviv would be a green city, with many public squares and parks. Geddes liked the life in Tel Aviv: it was, he said, a real live Jewish city "free from the constraints which are so tragic everywhere in Jerusalem."[39]

---

*At least eight out of every ten immigrants were Ashkenazim, more or less reflecting the demography of the Jewish people at the time. The Polish immigrants, however, represented twice Polish Jewry's proportional share in the world Jewish population.[37]

Tel Aviv was "small, quiet, and bright," one of its elder citizens wrote. The city had three colors, he said: the blue of the skies, the yellow sand, and the white houses, scattered like building blocks. "Oh, how good those times were!" recalled Mordechai Ben-Hillel Hacohen. The Herzliya Gymnasium high school was a building any European city would be proud of, as were Tel Aviv's broad, straight roads, so different from the dark, twisting alleys of Jaffa. There was no Arab influence, no shadow of the Jewish ghetto—the city was entirely Hebrew and European. The traditional Purim parade, with Mayor Dizengoff at its head mounted on a white horse, evinced a naive, winning, almost juvenile intimacy.[40] "Herzl, were he to go down Tel Aviv's Allenby Street," declared Dov Kimche, "would bear himself even more erect, and perhaps a tear might fall from his eyelashes."

Herzl, a man of the world, might well have thought of Tel Aviv what Weizmann did: too provincial for his tastes. "People are on top of each other," Weizmann complained. "They're always together and a word spoken in one house immediately gets round to all the others; everyone talks too much and they're all too self-conscious. Every Jew there is his own 'trend' an 'organization' and this is at once sad and very funny."[41] A traveler from France called it "a city with no history, devoid of legend, whose face is to the future. . . . When I looked for a past more than twenty years old, I found nothing but sand." Nahum Gutman, an artist who extolled the city in his work, also noted its transient nature: "Tel Aviv, I can write your name from right to left and from left to right, just as we used to write the names of those we liked when we were children—with one finger on the wet sand of the beach. The sea's waves erased them, washed them out."[42]

In 1923, *Ha'aretz* moved its offices from Jerusalem to Tel Aviv, both a recognition of the city's commercial and political status and a cultural statement: Tel Aviv was the capital of the new secular Hebrew culture. When Chaim Nachman Bialik settled in Tel Aviv in 1924, he was received as a national hero; the city chained off an area around the house it gave to Ahad Ha'am, to prevent the wagon and automobile traffic from disturbing the great man's siesta.[43] There was Hebrew theater, and important works of world literature were translated into Hebrew, but for a long time the people of Tel Aviv tended to think, speak, love, and hate in Russian, Polish, German, and Yiddish. Aunt Rachel, Yefim Gordin wrote to his parents, spoke to her husband in German, Russian, and Yiddish, and to her children in German. Her husband talked to them in Hebrew, which is what the children spoke among themselves.[44]

Many of the new immigrants, perhaps most, lived in their new country as they had in the Exile. The bulk of the community had been in the country for less than five years. In the early 1920s the median age of the country's Jewish population was close to twenty-two. Six out of ten people were not married; there were three single men to each single woman. Four out of ten couples did not have children.[45] A factory that produced cotton socks built in that period proudly bore the name Lodzia. The Polishness that is considered part of the Israeli cultural kaleidoscope derives largely from the immigrants of the twenties. The mythological figure of the "Jewish mother"—overprotective, overdemanding, and overdressed, always suffering from a vague sense of reproach, always a sanctimonious victim, making those around her feel guilty—was deemed a Polish import. Yefim Gordin told his parents about life with Aunt Anita: all day she bemoaned her bad luck. She had no maid, and when she cooked lunch she would never fail to remark that she had cooked just for him; had he not come, she would have been spared the work, she said over and over again. She did not wash the dishes properly, and when he offered to wipe them she was insulted.[46]

Gordin, a serious young man, was not impressed with Tel Aviv. "A person who comes from Warsaw, from Europe," he wrote home, "cannot be dazzled by a four-story building, a decent floor tile, a sidewalk, an electric street light."[47] He couldn't live in the city. "You can't at all imagine the frivolousness and the impulsivity, the hedonism and empty-headedness that pervade Tel Aviv," he wrote to his parents. "Jerusalem seems to me in comparison so serious, dignified, and deliberate, and I like that."[48]

The two cities represented vastly different cultural and political worlds. Jerusalem was very religious, political, intolerant, even fanatical, five thousand years old, and built on rock. Tel Aviv had no history, was built on sand, and exuded up-to-the-minute, secular frivolity—neither past nor future but rather life itself was the agenda. "We will not ask where to and where from—the world is wine," the poet Avraham Shlonsky wrote.[49] Yefim Gordin decided to live in Jerusalem.

6.

Gordin settled in the city toward the beginning of the university's 1927–28 academic year. His excellent high school grades from Vilna got him accepted easily, and there was still no charge for tuition. Uncle Ya'akov gave him a room in his apartment for three pounds a month, all inclusive, but Gordin did not feel comfortable in his house. With his cousin, he rented a single room in Achva, a neighborhood in the city's northwest. The roads were planted with acacia trees, and the air was clean and good. There was also a kind of municipal park, but because of the water shortage it wasn't much of a park. Whoever wants greenery should go to Hadar HaCarmel or Safed, our Switzerland, Gordin wrote.[50] But the street was paved with asphalt, unlike most of Jerusalem's streets, which were not properly paved. On rainy days they turned into pools of mud and mire.

His room had all the conveniences. The water came out of a tap—Gordin called it a "spring"—and not from a well. The apartment had a "good European toilet" and a washroom with a bathtub and shower. He and his cousin paid a pound and a half a month each, a very reasonable price. Finding the room hadn't been easy; they had searched for an entire month. They bought themselves a small table and two simple chairs, all for forty piastres. Unfortunately, they had only one bed and a hammock, so they traded: one month Gordin slept in the bed and his cousin in the hammock, and the next month they switched. But he was very pleased with the arrangement. Mr. Ben-Zakkai, the landlord, was a Jewish Agency official and a translator. He and Gordin had a mutual acquaintance in Vilna. Mr. and Mrs. Ben-Zakkai were nice, intelligent people, Gordin reported. They had no small children; only a twenty-year-old relative lived in the apartment. It was always quiet.[51]

Gordin ate breakfast and supper at home, tea or coffee with canned milk, bread, butter, olives, oranges, dates, jellies, halvah, and cheese—"not all at once, of course," he reassured his mother. Apparently she demanded that he tell her everything, and he, a young man who had just left home, obeyed her like a good boy, always precise with the details, always devoid of humor. He ate two eggs in the morning and two in the evening; a dozen cost fifteen piastres, or three shillings. He ate lunch at a vegetarian restaurant, which was very nice and clean. The menu changed every day; a meal cost three piastres, he wrote.[52] On Friday nights he ate a Sabbath meal at the workers' kitchen run by HaPoel HaMizrahi, the religious Zionist labor movement: gefilte fish, bouillon with rice, meat with a puree of beans, and compote. He ate Saturday lunch there, too: gefilte fish, cholent and bean puree, and meat with little noodles and raisins, finishing off with compote. They served good wine for making kiddush. The two meals cost ten piastres.[53]

His mother sent him packages, and Gordin would confirm that everything had arrived: the poems of Yehuda HaLevy, a jar of goose fat, a sausage, a box of butter cookies, plum jam, candy. Aunt Bracha sent some canned pears, in a small round box, Gordin was careful to note.[54] His mother also sent a kerosene stove, as well as a kettle and a jar of cherries and a prayer book. Sometimes his parents sent him a little money, and sometimes he sent them a little. Both sides protested. His was the life of an immigrant: mostly eating what he had eaten in Poland, washing himself with soap sent from home, and reading books he received from Vilna. Sometimes he would ask for specific books and instruct his parents where to find them, and when he began studying at the university he sent summaries of the lectures—seeking to foster cultural harmony between Jerusalem and the Jerusalem of Lithuania, as the Jews called their Vilna. He also sent his parents a *lulav* and *etrog*—fruit and foliage used in Sukkot holiday ritual.[55]

Against this background, the declaration Gordin made to his parents a year after his arrival seems somewhat pathetic: "I can be proud that during the year I have been in Palestine I have thrown off the defilement of the Diaspora, have purified myself as much as possible. . . . I defy the Diaspora and the Exile. . . . I wanted a homeland, to be a man like all men, to be an equal among equals, to be bold among the bold, proud of being a Hebrew, of being an Israeli. That was my desire and that's what I've achieved. The minute my feet walked on this land of our fathers I severed all my ties with Europe and America."[56] He renounced his Polish citizenship and obtained a Palestinian citizenship. "While it cost me half a pound," he wrote, "the money is worth it to stop being registered as the citizen of a country that is not mine and not my children's."[57] He had changed, he told his parents: he felt younger and had thrown off the psychology of exile.[58] He changed his name, too, calling himself Chaim Shalom. "I am a Hebrew and my name is Hebrew," he declared, "because from the land of the Hebrews I hail."[59]

But Gordin remained deeply attached to his family in the Exile. He wore the clothes of the Exile as well: a Panama hat and gray and white three-piece suits. He once reported to his mother that he had taken his garments in for mending and cleaning, and he also told her exactly how much that had cost: nightshirt, 1.5 piastres; underpants, 1 piastre; towel, 1 piastre; pants, 5 piastres; three handkerchiefs, 1 piastre; two pairs of socks, 1 piastre. He asked his father to instruct him about how to use that stuff, half-powder, half-lotion, that removed facial hair—the kind used by religious Jews who, in keeping with a Halachic injunction, would not take a razor to their skin. When he finally began shaving with a razor, he reported this also.[60]

Gordin's daily routine, indeed, his entire world, revolved around the mail. If there was no letter from home, he was devastated. He tried to find a job, preferably in an office. If he earned sixteen pounds a month, he would be able to bring over his parents and his sister. In the meantime, he took temporary work in the offices of AMZIC.

7.

AMZIC, the American Zionist Commonwealth, was a company head-quartered in New York that purchased land in Palestine and established Jewish settlements. The company was a commercial, profit-seeking ven-ture, but AMZIC's goals included mobilizing American Zionists to take part in the development of Palestine. Gordin's tenure in Jerusalem coin-cided with AMZIC's largest-ever project: establishing the city of Afula, slated to be the municipal center of the Jezreel Valley.

Al-Fula was a small Arab village that made its first appearance on the map Napoleon used in his Palestinian campaign. Later, the village found itself at the junction of the Damascus-Haifa-Nablus railway lines. At the beginning of the century, the Jewish National Fund—the major Zionist development organization—purchased land surrounding al-Fula from Elias Sursuq, an Arab businessman who lived in Lebanon. The sale required the eviction of several Arab tenant farmers, and from that time on al-Fula became an Arab national symbol, evidence of the Zionists' intention to dispossess the Arabs.

Hebrew Afula was intended to fulfill the urban dream of the Polish Jews. AMZIC sold lots using intensive and innovative advertising that depicted a modern city, planned more carefully than Tel Aviv. Once again Richard Kaufmann was hired. He conceived Afula as the ultimate garden city. The project was so popular that the land sold for twice as much as in Tel Aviv. More Arab farmers were evicted; some agreed to take compensa-tion and move elsewhere.

A report composed by Lieutenant Colonel Percy Bramley, a former director of public security in Palestine, states that only a quarter of the one hundred Arab families who had lived in the area left of their own free will. They received between five and twenty pounds each, accord-ing to the size of their families. Bramley explained that the compensation did not ensure the family's economic future; in many cases the farmer was destitute because he used the money to buy a new horse or a new wife.

The British administration offered the al-Fula farmers other plots but, according to Bramley, some of this land also belonged to the Sursuq family and was also up for sale. A number of the farmers were assigned to villages that did not want them, so they refused to leave their land. The Supreme Muslim Council in Jerusalem had proposed an alternative policy: helping the farmers purchase Sursuq properties at the same price the Zionists were paying for them. The Supreme Muslim Council retained the services of a lawyer, but by the time he prepared his proposal, the Afula sale had gone through. An American reporter who followed the story described the joy of the nearby Jewish settlers—all night they sang and danced and drank.

The next day some of the Jews set out for their newly acquired land. The British police were present to defend them, as required by law. Some of the al-Fula farmers threw stones. One of the Jews opened fire, and an Arab was killed. *Ha'aretz* regretted the incident. Colonel Kisch of the Zionist Executive was concerned that the event would increase the difficulty of purchasing land in the future. "No one should have been carrying firearms," he wrote. Two Jews were arrested, charged with murder, convicted, and sentenced to jail terms. They were, however, acquitted on appeal; their trial provoked great public interest.[61]

Afula staked out a prominent place in the pantheon of Zionist illusions. Polish and American Jews bought lots in the "city center" and even "close to the opera house," investing some half a million dollars, but twenty years later Afula was still a backwater with no more than two thousand residents, many of them working in agriculture. The plan had been too grandiose, a symbol of great ambitions, like the Casino in Tel Aviv. Richard Kaufmann could say in his own defense that he had never intended an opera house for Afula—his plan spoke only of "theaters."[62]

Gordin soon lost his job at AMZIC. In the meantime, he continued to chase down all-important connections and recommendations; everything depended on them. Perhaps some acquaintances of his parents living in Palestine could help; in Vilna he'd heard that one of them, Goldberg, ran "a big firm." Gordin looked for him all over the city and, in the end, found the man in the Bukharan quarter. It turned out that Goldberg ran a corner grocery store. Still, Gordin suggested, maybe Goldberg could give him a recommendation to someone? Goldberg just laughed.[63]

8.

On Rosh Hashanah Uncle Ya'akov took Gordin to services at the Yeshu-run Synagogue. The place was aristocratic, Gordin told his parents—many of the worshipers spoke to each other in English. He saw some of the city's biggest names: Judges Gad Frumkin and Mordechai Levanon, Attorney General Norman Bentwich, Professor Magnes from the univer-sity, and Dr. Mordechai Eliash, the attorney. There were so many people who could fix all of Gordin's problems if only they would write just a little recommendation, but how could he approach them? Eliash greeted him with a nod. When Gordin heard that Keren Hayesod, a Zionist fund-raising organization, was looking for office workers, he asked Eliash to intervene on his behalf. Eliash refused, but allowed Gordin to give his name as a ref-erence. This proved insufficient. Gordin tried to reach Leib Jaffe, a top official at Keren Hayesod, but Jaffe was out of the country. Gordin's par-ents, however, knew his wife, so he went to visit her.[64]

Mrs. Jaffe received him graciously. What was new in Vilna? she wanted to know, and she asked after various people. Of course he could mention her name, she said. She offered Gordin coffee, but he was in a hurry to get to the Keren Hayesod office. He was almost too late: actually the list of candidates was closed; but when he mentioned Mrs. Jaffe, his application was accepted. A week later he wrote to his parents: "The joy of my life!" He had received a letter from Keren Hayesod. Mr. Jaffe would see Gordin on his return.

He went back to Mrs. Jaffe and asked again that she speak to her hus-band on his behalf. "A nice woman," he told his parents. She invited him for lunch and gave him a note to her husband stating that Gordin was a cousin of Rachel Broide's. Aunt Anita said Mrs. Jaffe must have fallen in love with him. When Leib Jaffe returned from his travels he received Gordin graciously. After all, he was a cousin. Unfortunately, however, he had no position to offer him. Gordin was in shock. "What can I do? Even a recommendation is no help!" He had hung all his hopes on this job.[65]

Uncle Ya'akov offered him work in his blueprint shop at a salary of twelve pounds a month, which was enough to bring at least Gordin's mother over. The trouble was that Uncle Ya'akov refused to let him con-tinue his university studies.[66] Gordin tried, unsuccessfully, to find work in the Jerusalem municipality; he took on some schoolchildren who needed private lessons in Hebrew and English. Finally, he managed to speak to one of the members of the Yeshurun congregation, Reuven Katznelson, who worked in the statistics department at the Hadassah Medical Center.

Katznelson arranged a half-time job. "He said nothing about the salary and I didn't ask. You don't ask about something like that," Gordin wrote.[67]

The job was a beginning, a basis for hope. Gordin thought of first bringing his mother and sister, supposing they might be granted visas on the strength of his Hadassah salary and the income from his private students. Mordechai Eliash opposed the idea and refused to write in support of the application. Gordin submitted his request anyway; a professor at the university had agreed to sign the required form.

Gordin described the procedure: the Mandatory government's immigration department was open to the public in the afternoon. Applicants were given numbers to mark their place in line; Gordin had number 25. By a quarter to four the staff had only gotten to number 13. "VIPs" kept pushing ahead of the line, as did good-looking girls. Finally, he managed to get in before his turn. The interview was protracted and laborious, the application forms thick, lengthy, and very detailed. Then came a nerve-racking waiting period. Jerusalem was a small town where everybody knew everybody else, and Gordin happened to be familiar with the official who processed the requests. Every so often he was informed of his application's status. Gordin reported every rumor and every development to his parents.

While all this was going on, he negotiated changing the family name with his parents. He wanted them to be party to the decision. His father proposed "Gordin Ish Levi," meaning "Gordin the Levite," but Yefim objected. "That's just the same thing all over again," he complained, "neither here nor there." He wanted to sever himself from the Exile. No, not to sever himself from his past, he reassured his parents, just from the past of the Exile. He tried to meet his father halfway: Ish Levi, or Ish Halevi, or Levi, or Halevi, which was best because there were too many Levis and, anyway, it sounded better. The family finally settled on Halevi.[68]

The newly named Halevi lost one of his students and this reduced his income. He worried that this development might hurt his immigration application.[69] And then his request was rejected. He was in shock and appealed. The appeal was rejected as well. "There is a horrible feeling in the heart and the throat," he wrote.[70] Several months later he submitted a new request. Eliash had now agreed to support the application. In April 1929 Halevi received a raise at Hadassah, but he was still earning only twelve pounds. Everything now depended on Albert Hyamson, the British head of immigration. He was known in Vilna as a Jewish anti-semite and as first-class scum, Halevi commented.[71]

9.

At the university, Halevi delved into Jewish studies and humanities. His teacher, Joseph Klausner, professor of Hebrew literature, instructed him to compile a bibliography on Ya'akov Shmuel Bik, a playwright and translator from the early 1800s who had lived in Galicia. Halevi asked his sister to inquire whether the principal of the Vilna Gymnasium might be able to help.[72]

Klausner, an animated and hot-tempered encyclopedist from Russia, was a controversial man. An expert on the Second Temple period, he had wanted to teach history. But the university would not allow that. Klausner was too famous, too popular, too involved in the politics of the new Hebrew culture. His colleagues, especially those who came from Germany, considered him a charlatan. A book Klausner wrote in 1922 about Jesus of Nazareth created a sensation. It described Jesus as a radical nationalist Jew and maintained that even though the Jews could not recognize him as the son of God, he was nonetheless a "man of great morals and a master allegorist." The time would come when Jesus' "ethical book," the New Testament, would be accepted as "one of the most beautiful pearls of Jewish literature of all time," Klausner wrote. His newspaper articles exuded extremist, belligerent patriotism, which also made him insufferable to the professors from Germany who were committed to a restrained conservative liberalism.[73]

But Klausner represented an unusual blend of openness to world culture and Hebrew nationalism. Chaim Shalom Halevi looked up to his professor and shared a great secret with his parents: he was lending his support to Klausner's effort to turn the Institute of Jewish Studies, as it was called, into a general institute of the humanities. This was, he said, a fight against "the dark forces of orthodoxy."[74] In his letters the plan sounds like a conspiracy to overthrow the government; in fact, the struggle was between religious and secular Hebrew Zionist culture. Occasionally, Klausner would invite his students to his house in Talpiot: at the end of the academic year he bid them farewell in tears.[75]

Halevi's day began early. At five-thirty he recited the morning prayers. He now ate breakfast in a restaurant, generally a glass of milk with cake. At seven he was already in his office at Hadassah. At eleven he took a break, during which he drank a glass of yogurt and ate another piece of cake. At two o'clock he ate lunch at the vegetarian restaurant, and then he went to the university on Mount Scopus. He returned home at seven-thirty, ate supper, usually read a little, and went to sleep.[76] Sometimes he went to the theater. Klausner said that a cultured and educated person should also go to the opera. Halevi saw *The Dybbuk, The Golem, Jacob's Dream,* and *The Eternal Jew,* which shocked and impressed him: "Actress Hannah Rubina cries and wails," he wrote to his parents. "I cried with her."[77]

He would also take walks with his fellow students. He went to Tel Aviv to see the Purim parade but did not really enjoy it, and he attended Ahad Ha'am's funeral. Once or twice he went to a party. The students would sit around long tables, tell satirical jokes, and poke fun at their teachers and themselves, and they would dance, too. At the end of the evening the men would walk the women home.[78] Most of the time, Halevi was still very much alone.[79]

One night, upon returning from Mount Scopus, he wrote, "A moon twice as large as the one in Poland lights up the night like day and you can read small print without straining. I walk and have visions and dream dreams and think deeply and you are always the subject of my thoughts, my ideas, my notions."[80] He complained of attacks of depression. "Like a swarm of locusts it comes suddenly, settles on my soul and eats away at all that is good there." In his loneliness, he would sometimes wander the dark alleys of Jerusalem, gazing at the stars and agonizing over the insignificance of man in the vastness of space. What is the value of my thoughts and aspirations, he wondered. He began to keep a journal, and when he leafed back through it he found to his horror that almost no page was without some reference to death.[81] He tormented himself with doubts, sensing that his parents blamed him for not doing enough to obtain their immigration permits; his father perhaps was angry at him for having considered getting a permit only for his mother. "I fought a difficult and horrible inner battle deciding to postpone the request until I could ask for you both together," he wrote them.

Almost three years after Halevi's arrival the permits for his parents and sister were finally granted. "Now I can tell you," he wrote, "that Uncle Ya'akov once threw out a comment saying I didn't really want you to come"; at that moment he had felt "both a burning fire and a chill" and had choked back his tears. After a night of dejection and sleeplessness he had gotten up, "turned into stone," and redoubled his efforts to bring his family over. But perhaps they didn't really want to come, Halevi now wondered. Perhaps they were coming only because of him. Had he gone to Australia or Cuba, would they have followed him there as well, he asked himself?[82] Their permits had arrived, so why didn't they sell their house once and for all? Why were they postponing their departure?

The family had, in fact, begun to pack. Halevi instructed them on what to bring and what to leave behind: no pots and pans, but bring pillows and bed linens. Bring clothes, although only short underwear. He had very firm ideas: "I am definitely in favor of bringing the rocking chair. Shipping it will not cost much and there is a good chance it will arrive in one piece. Here the chair will be useful and pleasant and buying a new one would cost a lot. But I'm against dragging the bookcase." He urged his parents to pack the velvet things separately, because they could get damaged by the fumigation. "Everyone who comes to Palestine seems to be born again," he wrote. "It's all in your hands now."[83]

—•◦•—

11

A New Man

1.

Some of the immigrants who arrived in Palestine in the 1920s became farmers, but they barely amounted to 20 percent of the 100,000 or so newcomers—in other words, no more than 20,000 people.[1] Most chose to live in established farming towns. Only a few hundred organized the communes and settled in kibbutzim, where everything, including property and the education of children, was cooperative.

The kibbutz was an original social creation, yet always a marginal phenomenon. By the end of the 1920s no more than 4,000 people, children included, lived on some thirty kibbutzim, and they amounted to a mere 2.5 percent of Palestine's Jewish population.[2] The most important service the kibbutzim provided to the Jewish national struggle was military, not economic or social. They were guardians of Zionist land, and their patterns of settlement would to a great extent determine the country's borders. The kibbutzim also had a powerful effect on the Zionist self-image.

The cooperative way of life was a blend of necessity and idealism. Conditions were harsh. Kibbutz members lived in tents or huts; a long time went by before they built stone houses. Generally, they knew Hebrew. They planted trees, cleared fields of stones, and paved roads. Equality between the sexes was one of the fundamental values of kibbutz society, but when it came to the practical routine of daily life, the matter provoked constant controversy; the women usually found themselves cooking, cleaning, and sewing.[3]

Partly soldier-pioneers in the service of an idea, partly mystical cult devotees, and forever prisoners of the European culture they had left behind, kibbutz members read voraciously and spent a great deal of time pondering what one of them described as "cosmic and moral questions."[4] Representing different branches of the labor movement, they were emotional and ideological enthusiasts of factionalism, and often sounded as if they were engaged in a war between light and darkness. Indeed, their diaries and memoirs, the letters they sent back to parents in Europe reveal the early years of the kibbutz as a hyperintense adolescent fantasy come true. One such diary was kept by a member of Commune B, which later founded Kibbutz Mishmar HaEmek.

The commune was a beautiful camp of sparkling white tents, with three or four beds to a tent. Men and women generally slept separately. A few boards around the central tent pole functioned as a table, with the beds used as chairs. In early 1922, the commune, which was affiliated with the Hashomer HaTzair youth movement, was working on paving a road to connect Neve Sha'anan, a new Jewish neighborhood on Mount Carmel, to the lower part of the Haifa. The diary's author is identified by his nickname, "Takhi," as if he had no past or personality beyond his role as one of the commune's many components. The name was short for Takhamoni, he wrote. Commune members admonished one another to take their work seriously, by which they meant not reading Nietzsche and Freud on the job. But some were indifferent to their comrades' criticism; the main thing, they believed, was to live their communal life "in the most profound way possible."

Making communal life richer and more profound was, apparently, one of the goals of the shared clothing pool. "For the present," Takhi explained, "the commune has not made this mandatory. Whoever wants to can put his clothes into the common pool. Most comrades were enthusiastic and right away a procession of suitcase-bearers formed in the yard, marching toward the storage area next to the kitchen. Other members oppose the clothing pool. In the debate they argued that it's too early for that, we haven't yet created the necessary conditions—meaning, intensive, communal life that is broad and deep. When that develops, the clothing pool will just come into being naturally."

A few days after this entry, Takhi wrote: "Congratulations! We put up a hut without a floor and installed a shower. This is how it looks: there's a barrel on the ground and another one close to the ceiling; the two are connected with a pipe. A hand pump is fixed in the lower one and if you want to take a shower, you have to pump for at least half an hour to force the water up to the second barrel. H. organized a kind of central heating device, which is a little unreliable. It burns almond or nut shells, but generally there isn't enough fuel . . . and not enough water."

Takhi described numerous commune discussions. "The talk yesterday was nice, deep. We spoke—actually only one of us spoke and the rest kept quiet—on Eros in society, on the individual and freedom of the individual." The meeting took place at midnight. "The mess tent was half in darkness, somewhere in the corner a little lamp flickered. On the floor, against the walls, people sat huddled together, and from one of the corners, as if from the depths, arose the voice of Y.B. like a spirit, full of mystery. Disembodied words broke through the dim space, the speaker kept his head bowed. 'I called for a talk (long silence) . . . because I . . . that is, we, every individual (long silence) . . . the society, one family (long silence) . . .' All the comrades sat with their heads bowed, their faces concealed. I rested my chin on my knees and listened." Takhi soon fell asleep, but the next day he heard there had never been a talk as beautiful and profound as this one.

The comrades liked to talk about how they visualized the commune. "In his last talk, H. described the commune like this," Takhi wrote. "A moving train. A camel strides slowly on the roof of the train, and on the camel is a donkey and on the donkey a white rooster, with his wings extended." Takhi could not quite figure out the meaning of this allegory, but he wrote, "It is really important that every person have his own vision of the commune."

The members were so far from home, so uncertain, so full of expectations for the commune and for their own personal lives, yet so lonely within the group. "Sometimes you are lying on your bed, thinking about the commune, about its life and the people, and suddenly you hear the sound of weeping," Takhi wrote. "You get up and step outside to help your comrade in his distress. But next to the tent where you hear the crying several girls have gathered and they gesture to you, 'don't come near!' They're watching and helping. There are already quite a few experts in hysteria."

But he also described ecstasy and elation. The commune's first organized dance party developed into something almost cultic: "We all wrapped ourselves in white sheets, lit by the moonlight, and danced a magical dance. Actually, it wasn't a dance, but mystical and fantastical motion. H., who had started the party, was wonderful. Wrapped in a white sheet, his hands stretched high, he swayed to the rhythm of the harmonica. He looked like some mythical figure from the six days of creation. We experienced huge cultural enjoyment." In the days that followed, the members spent much time analyzing what had happened, telling one another that on the night of the dance, "the commune's soul melded into a single unity." It had been a kind of initiation, a coming-of-age ritual. In the meantime, the girls from Warsaw were growing close to the boys from Galicia. "Not for nothing does Eros have such an important place in our talks," Takhi wrote in his diary. "The individual bares his soul before the fellowship," he added, "and the entire commune sits together in the dimness of the dining room and listens with an open heart to the person's uncertainties." Other communes and kibbutzim recorded similar experiences. "Soul touched soul," wrote one member of Kibbutz Ginnosar, explaining that much of the emotional agony was a reaction to the gulf between people's expectations and the difficulties they encountered.[5]

After six months, the Neve Sha'anan road was finished and the commune moved to Nahalal, a collective farm, to work at swamp drainage. The hammer and chisel were replaced by the pick and shovel—"entirely unromantic tools," wrote Takhi, but he was aware of the importance of the work, as swamps spread malaria. The comrades spoke a great deal about their jobs now; Takhi was bored. "Isn't it enough that we work all day, why do we have to talk about it all night?" he wondered. Unfortunately, he wrote, some people were more concerned with the business of work and livelihood than with the commune's social-spiritual life. Before long, all the members came down with malaria. They swallowed quinine pills and ate cocoa and powdered sugar to get ride of the taste. At night they played practical jokes on one another—painting the faces of sleeping comrades, frightening the donkey—and munched on herring and halvah and raisins in the kitchen.

Takhi recorded several crises that shook the group in the summer of 1922, expressions of internal tensions, both personal and ideological. Some members had gone to the children's hut, where the commune's first four babies, Ariela, Uriel, Eitan, and Amira, slept, and rearranged its spartan look to resemble a European Jewish family home. Takhi described the scene: "Two beds, made, with slippers placed beneath them; on the husband's bed was a pipe and various accessories typical of a petit-bourgeois family." The tableau was a protest against the way the couples with children were beginning to isolate themselves, not "sharing the life of the greater family—the commune." The incident caused much agitation. One girl cried.

In the discussions that ensued, one member suggested that the whole commune live in a single hut, so that the connection between people would become a "great, uniting spiritual unification." Others spoke of a split among the comrades; some had stopped believing in the commune and were in despair, Takhi wrote. "They're always angry and in conversations among themselves, they try to prove that our group is just a collection of lazy intellectuals, trapped in illusions, that there's no tolerance for simple, healthy people, laborers with a straightforward attitude toward work. They say that the intellectuals are driving the simple people crazy."

At the end of September it happened: "Leaving! Today ten comrades left the commune all at once. Ten of the angry ones, the simple ones, the unintelligent, as they proudly call themselves. They left the commune and went to Haifa. How is this going to affect our lives? Some say that the ones who left didn't really belong in the commune. They were just an obstacle, not fit for intense, broad, deep communal life." Two weeks later Takhi noted that the commune was getting on with its life and overcoming the hurdles. "The weak will go and the strong will remain," he asserted.

December brought winter. Work slowed down, and the members read a lot of books. *Jean Cristophe* by Romain Rolland was the most popular, but Otto Weininger's *Sex and Character* also drew much attention. They now had a small library in one of the huts. Draining the swamps came to an end; instead the comrades collected stones for building or road paving— they didn't exactly know the purpose. The food was bad and usually burned. The stove was kept outside, next to the mess hut, and fueled with twigs and branches. The mess hut was covered with a tarpaulin, but rain leaked through and turned the ground into a puddle of mud. The tents tore, and the rain came in.

Takhi, always optimistic, tried to turn the winter into a romantic experience. "At night, when the wind wails and brings down the tents and you're left with your bed outdoors, exposed to the rain and wind, there's nothing better than to go to the bakery, where they're making bread from the flour that gets delivered from Haifa during the night. Homeless and tentless, felled by the wind, everyone comes to the warm bakery to enjoy a pita and a glass of black coffee without sugar. We stay all night. In the morning we put the tents back up."

But people continued to leave. "They're going one by one. Some of us think it's a kind of natural selection, but in the meantime there's a vacuum.

Sometimes people talk about it among themselves. And inside, in the heart, doubt gnaws. Can we persevere? Can we go on?" March 1924: "There's no work, but there is hunger and malaria." And there was music. One comrade could play the violin and another played the flute. "Music has begun to take a prominent place in our lives," Takhi noted and, a year and a half later, in May 1925, he wrote in his diary, "Believe it or not, we have received a piano as a gift from Prague. It stands in its place of honor in the library. We'll have to remove the tenant." The group also received two mules, Tzipora and Devorah: the commune purchased them with a loan. After swamp clearing and stone gathering, the commune was sent to work on another road on Mount Carmel. Then, in May 1924, it partici-pated in a new fantasy sweeping Palestine: tobacco.

The story began when the British imposed a tariff on imported ciga-rettes. Almost at once people began to invest in tobacco cultivation; some initial success attracted more investors. The new enterprise provided work for Commune B, but ultimately tobacco growing was a failure. Peo-ple who knew nothing about growing, drying, processing, and marketing tobacco entered the field with great enthusiasm and the obsessiveness of habitual gamblers. They took a bad fall: the first year's harvest produced twice the demand, and the quality was mediocre at best, certainly not good enough for export. A millionaire from Berlin, Lubliner, had promised to buy a large part of the harvest, but when the time came, he was nowhere to be found. Thousands of people were left without work.[6]

With the approach of the commune's second anniversary, its members had no clear sense of their future. The five young children in the group presented all kinds of new problems. At nursing time someone had to beat on gasoline cans to scare away the mice, because they frightened the mothers; on feminist grounds the women refused to wash the babies' dia-pers. There was an ongoing debate over whether the children should be cared for by their parents or in a communal children's house.

At Kibbutz Degania the arrival of children led to a thorough reexami-nation of the kibbutz ideal and much reflection on human nature. "When we saw our first children in the playpen, hitting one another, or grabbing toys just for themselves, we were overcome with anxiety," wrote one member. "What did it mean that even an education in communal life couldn't uproot those egotistical tendencies? The utopia of our initial social conception was slowly, slowly destroyed."[7]

On the occasion of a conference at Kibbutz Beit Alfa, Takhi wrote in his diary, "The mothers left their young ones and went. The only one who remained was H., since Amnon's birth was only weeks ago. The mothers ruled that since H. recently gave birth, she'll have enough milk for all the children." Perhaps their decision was a bit harsh, Takhi noted, but more than likely they knew best since they were mothers. The comrades continued to be tormented by doubts about their future, but they put down roots nonetheless, establishing a tiny kitchen garden. Homegrown radishes began to appear on their tables.[8] They also had a dovecote.

2.

They were *halutzim,* or pioneers. The Hebrew word appears in the Bible, where it is used in a military sense, meaning "vanguard," the troops who move in advance of the camp and at its head. Ben-Gurion described the *halutzim* as "the army of Zionist fulfillment."[9]*

The pioneer was part of a movement, expected to "enlist" in the collective effort. The movement itself served a noble moral goal. Just as the conquering soldiers of Joshua had crossed the Jordan "armed (*halutzim*) before God," so the *halutzim* of the Zionist movement came to fight for a national and social ideal. One of the labor movement's posters stated, "Whoever is among you of all his people, the Lord his God be with him, and let him go up!" This verse of the Bible is King Cyrus of Persia's call for the construction of the Temple in Jerusalem. The poem Chaim Nachman Bialik described pioneering as both a religious and erotic experience. The pioneers, he wrote, were willing "to empty all the strength of their youth into the bowels of this blasted ground to bring it to life." They knew how to raise simple labor to the level of "supreme holiness, to the level of religion," he said. Berl Katznelson wrote, "Everywhere the Jewish laborer goes, the divine presence goes with him."[11] Theirs was a religion of labor.

The pioneer concept had consolidated gradually, principally after World War I; over the years its significance was greatly pondered and debated. Were the *halutzim* the harbingers of the pioneering idea or its fulfillment? Were they working to create a system only for themselves or struggling to create an entire "pioneering" society?[12] They made little distinction between pioneerism as an ideological value in itself and member-

---

*Zionism made frequent use of military terminology. There was the "labor army," the "labor battalion," the "the battalion in defense of the language," the "conquest of the language," the "conquest of the land," the "conquest of the sea," the "conquest of labor," and so on. David Ben-Gurion spoke of "conquering pioneers."[10]

ship in HeHalutz, the Zionist political movement that settled young Jews on farming communities in Palestine.

In the Zionist vision agriculture was seen as a cure for the Jewish people, who had "degenerated" and become "sick" in the Exile. Reclaiming the land would fortify them militarily and was also considered a moral obligation.[13] In its fierce rejection of the traditional Diaspora way of life, Jewish pioneerism was revolutionary. Indeed, many of the pioneers adopted the slogans of Bolshevik socialism, speaking of a "new world" and a "new man." But the yearning to "return to nature" was also rooted in romantic European nationalism, and in this sense the pioneering phenomenon was antimodernist, even manifestly reactionary, a complement to the Zionist longing for the glory days of the biblical era.

As part of the exultation of the land, city life in general was vilified. The writer and farmer Moshe Smilansky described Tel Aviv as a giant hotel and warned that its "shopkeeper's commercialism" would lead the city's inhabitants to "gypsiness, assimilation, and loss of identity, not to national revival." Tel Aviv was nothing but a Jewish town from the Pale of Settlement, griped another commentator. "Store on top of store . . . hotel on top of hotel, beauty parlors, soda fountains, kiosks"* There is almost no building that does not have a stand selling soft drinks, complained Y. Ch. Rabnitzky in Ha'aretz, taking note also of the "horrible scourge" of moneylenders charging interest and "all sorts of other bloodsucking leeches." When labor movement spokesmen wanted to invoke the most dire, horrible future imaginable, they predicted that some day Tel Aviv would have a stock exchange. Their goal was to "obliterate the memory of the city."[15]

Here and there were a few champions of the city, speaking in the spirit of Herzl, who had dreamed of a modern urban Jewish society. Mordechai Ben-Hillel Hacohen, one of Tel Aviv's founders, had written back in 1919 that one could assume that the world's Jews, once in Palestine, would prefer to live in cities, and so urban centers should be developed. Another writer in Ha'aretz claimed that cities were more important than rural settlements because they gave the country its cultural character. Meir Dizengoff, the mayor of Tel Aviv, stood out in his fight for the city's rightful place in the national experience and in the Zionist budget. Chaim Weizmann stated that the communal method of agricultural work was not beneficial.[16] These were, however, isolated voices.

---

*Soft-drink vendors were a popular symbol used to deride the easy city life.[14]

The agricultural ethos prevailed as a patriotic symbol; the labor movement succeeded in identifying its rural, pioneering worldview with the
entire Zionist movement. Most of the urban population who belonged to
the "civil camp" lacked ideological fervor. Nor were they good at organizing their interests into political power; they seemed drab, pale, and indi-
vidualistic compared to the esprit de corps and romance of the
communes and kibbutzim.[17] They could not offer a powerful alternative
to the pioneering methods of the labor movement. So the people of Tel
Aviv, imbibing the agricultural zeal of national regeneration, decorated
the walls of their homes with quasi-biblical scenes—wheat harvesters,
dancing girls, and shepherd boys playing their pipes—all painted on colorful tiles from Vienna.

Moshe Glickson, the editor of *Ha'aretz* and a resident of Tel Aviv, tried
to find a place in the national ethos for the growing number of Jews living
in the new garden suburbs of Jerusalem and Haifa. People were buying
their houses rather than renting them, welcome proof that they were
"tying their fate to the land," a positive trait that was not to be found
among the Jews of the Exile. Glickson identified in the new suburban
dweller "something of the psychology of the farmer and the man of the
land," he wrote in wonder, referring to that "feeling of solid traditional
cultural life that the Germans call *Bodenständigkeit* (a foothold in the
land)." Glickson was not alone in his attempt to display loyalty to the prevailing ideology. Meir Dizengoff, a rich man, wrote against "the pursuit of
wealth," and Mordechai Ben-Hillel Hacohen, a successful businessman
himself, complained of "national laziness and indifference to work."[18*]

3.

The image of the ideal pioneer was largely congruent with the image of
the "new man" supposedly being created in Palestine. He appears on
period posters and in photographs as a muscular, light-haired, joyous
youth. The ideal was part of the Zionist movement from its beginnings.
Max Nordau was famous for his call for a revival of "muscular Judaism."
Arthur Ruppin praised the pioneers as members of "a new Jewish race."[20]
Ze'ev Jabotinsky said, "There is a need to create a new Jewish frame of
mind, I am almost prepared to say a new psychological race of Jews." Ben-

---

*There were some attempts to copy the socialist communal ideal in the city. Workers' neigh-
borhoods and "hostels" were constructed, inspired by the workers' housing then being
erected in "Red Vienna."[19]

Gurion dreamed of a "new type of Jew who will be an exemplar for tourists." The inspiration for this ideal came largely from the Soviet Union, but also from Weimar Germany and Fascist Italy.[21]

Chaim Shalom Halevi, formerly Yefim Gordin, adopted the image as part of his new identity. His father and mother should know, he wrote to them, that when they came to Palestine they would find a new generation, "a proud Hebrew generation, healthy in flesh and mind, aware of its own value, a healthy soul in a healthy body." Life in the Diaspora was, in contrast, "a dog's life" and "beggary."[22]

The forge in which the new man was created was the Hebrew Zionist school. The education system was fairly heterogeneous from an ideological and political point of view, but all schools worked to shape a kind of new Jew free of the characteristics attributed to the Exile. A young person in the land of Israel has important advantages over his peers in the Diaspora, wrote a leading educational figure, listing them one after another, cliché after cliché: "He is erect, brave, handsome, physically well-developed, loves work, sports, and games; he is free in his movements, devoted to his people and its patrimony." An article published in *Ha'aretz* hailed the graduates of the Ben-Shemen agricultural school: "They will bring pure and clean blood to our national enterprise, working the land." Young people who chose to dedicate themselves "to simple, dirty work" were praised as "wonderful human material." In a letter to his wife, Chaim Weizmann described these children in a letter to his wife: "A sheer delight! You'd be indescribably thrilled, these youngsters are absolutely blooming . . . beautiful, natural, cheerful, they love the land." The children in the farming villages represented "independent Jewish life," no longer a fairy tale, Weizmann wrote to his Vera, "but a potent and splendid truth!"[23]

In schools close to the labor movement there was an anti-intellectual tendency to dismiss the value of general humanistic education, and even of education all together. "Minimize books, maximize hikes and talks," teachers were told, the reason being that "we are meant to raise simple farmers here . . . not philosophers." This instruction expressed, among other things, the fear that a broad, general education would encourage students to leave the country. "A direct, spiritual, deep connection to every clod of earth, to every stone and every boulder, to every plant and to every tree, to all living things" was meant to ensure loyalty and patriotism. The "return to nature" was thus further identified with the "return to the nation."[24]

In kibbutzim and other agricultural settlements, a manifestly conservative element was at work: children were meant to follow in their parents' footsteps. But for most of the schoolchildren, sons and daughters of immigrants who lived in the cities, the attempt to create a new man involved rejecting their parents' value system and mentality. Poet David Shimoni wrote, "Do not listen, my son, to the instruction of your father, and do not give heed to the teaching of your mother . . . a man should listen to the song of his son."[25] The Hebrew youth culture then developing in Tel Aviv looked beyond the city to the labor battalion for its ideal.

The battalion's full name was the Yosef Trumpeldor Labor and Defense Battalion. Most of its members, high school graduates in their late teens and early twenties, had originally come from Russia; almost all were single. Many had been followers of Trumpeldor; their leader, Menachem Elkind, had been his friend. They worked very hard, generally on jobs such as road building funded by the administration, and they earned very little. At best, the battalion managed to obtain tents, but in many cases its members slept in the open, at their work sites.[26]

"We ran into them each morning, on our way to the Gymnasium," wrote Tziona Rabau from Tel Aviv, whose parents had come from Russia before the World War. "Boys with tangled hair, wearing Russian shirts, and slender girls, dressed in flowered tunics tied tight around the waist, their curls flowing down their necks. They worked on the streets using hammers to shatter the stones to gravel, and paved the road. When I'd pass them I'd hang my head and feel ashamed because I, the daughter of a well-off family, was still studying, living in a stone house with a shower, eating my fill, while these beautiful, upright young people were, with their own hands, fulfilling the obligation to build the land." When Rabau was fourteen she founded a secret "commune" of her own together with three boys and two other girls. They aspired to a shared life of agricultural labor. "Each morning one of us would bring some anemones, which we tucked into our collars as a sign of fraternity and equality," Rabau wrote.

Some young people left their parents' homes in the cities to join agricultural settlements, at least for a time, and those sojourns became a Hebrew rite of passage. Those who went for "fulfillment," as working the soil of the homeland was called, did so in the framework of ideological youth movements. Many more only fantasized about it: Tziona Rabau made do with the gymnasium's flower garden; Berl Katznelson believed that his vegetable garden in Jerusalem had Zionist value, too.[27]

But the real world and the grandiose values dictated by the national ethos were bound to collide. In Europe and the United States, the 1920s were a time of intense urban growth, and most Jews lived in cities. Naturally, they expected to live an urban life when they came to Palestine. Yet kibbutz members, committed to the religion of labor, were the nobility and priesthood of the national ideology. They called themselves the "laboring Yishuv," as if they had a monopoly on labor, as if no one in the cities worked. In fact, the communal agricultural settlements could not have survived without financial support from the national Zionist institutions.[28] In this sense they were closer to the "Old Yishuv" of Jerusalem and its dependence on *chalukkah* money than to the new society they were claiming to create.

Even as contradictions surfaced in the national ethos, its proponents glorified it with lofty language and sought to impose it on the rest of the Jewish community. Moshe Smilansky complained that many immigrants were unwilling to work hard and were "poisoning the air." People were coming with dreams of a good life, wrote *Ha'aretz;* they were hoping to "find a position" and wanted to live in comfortable houses, "like in Tel Aviv." This was wrong, the newspaper insisted. All were welcome, but they should know that "there is space in Palestine for a thousand philosophers, no more. No more! The rest—if they wanted to live and build—need not a mind but a pair of hands." Even Chaim Weizmann thought there were too many intellectuals, including doctors and lawyers, among the immigrants.[29] Pioneerism was being debased, complained David Ben-Gurion from his residence in Tel Aviv; like most labor movement leaders, he preferred to live in the city. He wasn't the only urban resident to complain about dwindling pioneer zeal. Ben-Zion Dinaburg, a teacher living in Jerusalem, complained that too many farmers were seeking bourgeois pleasures rather than working the land. "One farmer bought a piano," Dinaburg declared with moral indignation.[30]

The wide gulf between ideal and reality led to many disappointments. The labor battalion got tangled up in a web of heartbreaking intrigues and disputes, split, then disbanded. Menachem Elkind and several dozen of his followers returned to Stalin's Russia, where they dispersed to unknown destinations. Elkind apparently managed to work for a time on the staff of *Pravda;* he later disappeared in one of Stalin's purges. "They were drawn to 'the world of tomorrow' as a moth is drawn to a flame, and like the moth they went up in flames," wrote historian Anita Shapira.[31]

But of the immigrants who left the country, most went for a more prosaic reason: they couldn't make ends meet in Palestine.

4.

Chaim Shalom Halevi had discerned signs of an incipient economic crisis within a few days of his arrival, which was why he had urged his parents to hurry while they could still obtain immigration permits. From another point of view, he saw the crisis as an advantage: the rent on rooms was going down.[32] Like the intoxicating illusion of plenty, the despairing shock of the economic depression belongs largely to the history of Tel Aviv: at its peak, one out of every two unemployed people in the country lived in the city; the Jewish unemployment rate rose to over 17 percent.[33] Halevi explained to his parents how this had happened: "The fourth aliya put up buildings on the sand and it is known that sand is a shaky foundation."[34] Not long after this letter, the Casino went bankrupt. It was demolished and disappeared among the dunes.

In 1925, 64 percent of all investment was in construction. Investors put up rental housing on the assumption that immigrants would continue to come.[35] Apart from direct employment, the building industry also supported a large circle of factories and businesses. The construction boom depended on an inflow of overseas capital; foreign investors transferred their money to the local office of the Zionist Organization or to their local bank, which was then transferred to banks in Palestine. Contractors often worked on credit, using capital that was on the way as collateral.

In 1926 the Polish economy went into recession and Polish currency was devalued. Many people in Palestine were saddled with debts they could not pay and were forced to stop building. As construction companies and associated industries collapsed one after another, jobs disappeared. The British administration expanded public works unwillingly and to a limited extent; its inclination was not to intervene. Neither the Histadrut labor union nor the Zionist movement was prepared to handle such a profound crisis.

A sense of despair spread throughout the country. Many left. In 1926, the number of emigrants was close to half the total of immigrants; in 1927 emigration exceeded immigration, and in 1928 the two figures were equal. Overall, during these three years, fifteen thousand Jews left Palestine.

But the crisis did not last long and left no permanent scars. The citrus industry soon began to take off, largely because new export markets opened up. Small factories, more like workshops, were replaced by larger plants using more sophisticated methods of production, management, and marketing. The Zionist movement overseas soon got back on its feet and poured in assistance. Within a year or two the crisis was forgotten; immigration rose, emigration decreased.[36]

In the midst of the crisis, the politicians took advantage of the moment to attack one another. It was the middle class's fault, David Ben-Gurion wrote. The bourgeoisie had come and failed, inevitably, because instead of bowing to the new values, they had insisted on pursuing the same occupations in Palestine as they had in Exile. The failure of the "soft drink vendor and the property speculator" had filled the bourgeoisie with despair, said Ben-Gurion, and their despair had "poisoned the Zionist soul."[37] Businessmen and entrepreneurs, for their part, accused the Zionist movement of not having invested sufficiently in the development of industry.*

The Zionist approach to the economy remained unchanged: its purpose, first and foremost, was to promote a Jewish state, regardless of economic logic. From time to time calls went out to community leaders to work more efficiently, more rationally. The demand came principally from the American Jewish community. But, in general, nationalist interests took priority over financial ones. "If we are to be guided by economic considerations only," said Menachem Ussishkin, "then we ought to give up Palestine altogether. Better opportunities exist elsewhere."[39]

Halevi wrote to his parents that settling in Palestine involved sacrifice and that the country needed more sacrifice. "At every step and inch we must push ourselves past our limits, sacrifice ourselves, do without." The country is unique, he explained: "It loves only those who bind themselves to it with all their heart and soul. Only someone who comes here without looking back, who burns behind him all the bridges leading to Constantsa and Trieste and Marseilles"—the ports from which the European immigrants departed—"only he puts down roots, and gains a foothold in the country." The country needs soldiers, Halevi wrote: "There is a war ahead of us, long and hard—a war against the Arabs and the English, against the sea and the rivers, the mountains and the valleys, the cold and the heat, the sand and the desert, the rocks and the boulders, a war that may go on for perhaps hundreds of years, may my grandchildren be privileged to see its end."[40]

---

*In the first ten years of British rule, Jewish capital imports to Palestine totaled 44 million Palestinian pounds, about twice the government's outlays; 12 million (27 percent) was institutional investment, and the rest (73 percent) was private capital.[38]

Halevi warned his parents, "Overseas, Palestine is romanticism . . . but people who like romance should stay there . . . the moment you arrive in the country, all romanticism evaporates, the haze of dreams disperses and what remains is a rough land, full of rocks and boulders, half-wild and undeveloped."[41] From time to time, Halevi criticized his parents for not being ready for the necessary sacrifice. His conclusion, inspired by the Book of Deuteronomy, was "What man is there that is fearful and faint-hearted? Let him go and return to his house." Halevi proposed adding the impatient man and also those who love money to the list: "What do we have in common with the people of the Exile who go to the Palestinian California to fill their pockets with yellow metal?" he wrote. "We have no precious metals and no precious stones."[42]

Halevi expressed the prevailing Zionist attitude. Emigration was considered flight, desertion, and treason. "The nation's very existence is in danger," wrote author A. Z. Rabinowitz, "and all those whose hearts are touched by the good of the nation will not desist from the campaign. We will live here until we rot. We will not move from our country. This is the duty of the Hebrew labor army." In tandem, people began to develop a siege mentality, evident in Takhi's commune diary: those who stay are strong and good; those who leave are weak. "Please leave quickly and do not taint the air," *Ha'aretz* wrote contemptuously. The same sentiment was expressed in a statement issued by one of the political parties: "We need pioneers, not deserters and refugees. Better they not come at all than come and go back."[43]

The ferocity of the rhetoric reflected a breach between the great collective dream and a sense of personal disappointment, a basic and widespread feeling that life abroad was better and more fulfilling than life in Palestine. Halevi first encountered that feeling at his aunt's home in Haifa. He responded by seeing himself as a soldier in the war for the ethos of natural rebirth and Hebrew pride. In Jerusalem he enlisted in one of the war's great battles: the struggle between the two languages of the Jewish people—Hebrew and Yiddish, or "Jargon," as it was called. For Halevi, the cause of Hebrew became his way of being a pioneer.

5.

In May 1927, Martin Buber came to Jerusalem as a guest of the Hebrew University. Halevi, a student and member of an organization called the Battalion for the Defense of the Language, tried, together with his friends, to dissuade Buber from lecturing in German. "You will consider this horrible insolence, unheard-of discourtesy," he wrote to his parents, "but we, who champion a great and sacred ideal, did this bold deed and today everyone acknowledges that we were right."

The group met Buber at his hotel. They spoke Hebrew, which he understood; he responded in German. He explained that he was insufficiently fluent to lecture in Hebrew. They asked that he read his text from a written Hebrew translation. Buber refused, saying that he would speak in German or not at all. They did not dare respond to Buber's face, but afterward they wrote to him that it would indeed be better if he canceled his speech. Buber considered doing so, but the university's rector, Judah Magnes, was able to mollify him. Buber spoke in German; the Battalion for the Defense of the Language made do with issuing a protest. After thirty years of Zionist activity, anyone who cannot express himself in Hebrew should remain silent in German, they proclaimed.[44]

The Battalion for the Defense of the Language was founded by pupils at the Herzliya Hebrew Gymnasium in Tel Aviv, Tziona Rabau among them. Its slogan was "Jew, speak Hebrew." The group made an effort to organize Hebrew lessons for new immigrants and campaigned against the use of other languages. Once they handed a leaflet to a man sitting on a park bench conversing in Yiddish. The man turned out to be Hebrew poet Chaim Nachman Bialik.[45] The Tel Aviv branch included several dozen activists, most of them students. At the largest party the battalion ever managed to organize, held at the Tahkamoni school to celebrate its third anniversary, there were perhaps a hundred people, close to half of them guests. Among the battalion's prominent supporters were Mordechai Ben-Hillel Hacohen and Tzvi Yehuda Kook, the son of the chief rabbi.[46]*

Similar "battalions" were established in other places. Attorney Yisrael Amikam headed the battalion in Haifa; the Jerusalem branch was led by Judge Mordechai Levanon.[48] Chaim Shalom Halevi joined the Jerusalem branch a short time after arriving in the city. Its activities were an important part of his life; each day he devoted two or three hours of his time to the movement. In a letter to his parents he explained why. First of all, he was an idealist, he wrote; this was why he had settled in Palestine, and even when he lived in Vilna he had fought against using Jargon. But this

---

*Use of the Hebrew language was one of the trademarks of the "new man." A. D. Gordon once wrote that the Jews were parasites not only in the sense that they had no land of their own but also in the spiritual sense, as they had no language of their own, no literature.[47] Like the return to the land, the return to the language of the Bible was an expression of a manifestly conservative element in Zionism.

was not all. While still in Haifa, soon after arriving in Palestine, he had gone crazy from boredom and not been able to find anyone of his own age to chat with, just to pass the time. He did not make friends easily, as his parents certainly knew, and he did not find friends at the university, either. But he found them in the battalion. There were three or four young men he became close to. "The battalion gave me friends!" he wrote. He did not yet have a girlfriend.

The battalion gave him another advantage. Through it he found a job tutoring a schoolboy, for which he earned one pound a month. He was not being paid for teaching Hebrew. "The principle of the battalion is that Hebrew is taught for free," he wrote. If a pupil was willing to pay, the money went into the battalion's kitty, and Halevi voluntarily donated ten or fifteen piastres of his tutoring fee. He enjoyed working for the battalion after long hours of studying and felt he was doing something important. He wrote letters and gave instructions. The battalion won him respect, and people looked up to him. Every once in a while he would give a short talk, which brought him into contact with important people, even more influential than Judge Levanon, he wrote. He mentioned Leo Motzkin, an important Zionist official, Buber, and Bialik.

Such details were necessary to convince his parents that what they had heard in Vilna about the Battalion for the Defense of the Language was not true. The Jewish press, most of it in Yiddish, generally portrayed the battalion as a gang of fanatic, insolent hoodlums.[49] In fact, the battalion acted as patriotic watchdog, barking loudly and baring its teeth but seldom actually biting. Even when there was violence, it was never more than a nuisance.

The battalion's stationery listed its activities as "culture, dissemination, teaching, art, propaganda, fund-raising." The group tried to recruit Hebrew teachers and collect contributions here and there, but worked with less method and organization than the letterhead would have one believe.[50] The words "Defense Squadron—Sign Patrol," which appeared on battalion stationery, referred to the members' practice of going from store to store demanding that shopkeepers write their signs in Hebrew and display them prominently. Annie Landau complained of the flood of threatening letters she received from the battalion demanding that she change the sign on her school, on which the Hebrew name followed the English. The name should first appear in Hebrew, the battalion members wrote, also pointing out a Hebrew spelling mistake. They threatened to conduct a "public war" against her school.[51]

They sent letters to individuals and institutions, threatened to boycott businesses, and pestered passersby. Once or twice they heckled at public lectures given in other languages and even threw a stink bomb at a lecture by a well-known Yiddishist. Twice they disrupted Yiddish film screenings, throwing bottles of ink and rotten eggs at the screen until the police were called. When battalion activists tried to prevent students from entering the French-language Alliance school in Tel Aviv, they were arrested, tried, and fined. The high commissioner was shocked. If this is how Jews behaved toward one another, we can imagine what they will eventually do to the Arabs, he wrote.[52]

Some members of the Zionist movement were disturbed by these expressions of chauvinism. The Zionist enterprise depended on restraint and patience, one of them wrote to Colonel Kisch. Once, in a public speech, Menachem Ussishkin had his audience raise their left arms and take an "oath" of loyalty to the Hebrew language.[53] Kisch thought this was the kind of thing an Arab fanatic would do, not a Jewish leader, but he tended to treat the battalion with indulgent paternalism; they were making some childish mistakes, he reassured his colleagues, but in general they were good boys and their work was beneficial. He even sent the battalion small contributions.

Chaim Arlosoroff, the head of the Jewish Agency's political department, was outraged when Halevi protested because he was writing letters in English. The battalion demanded that Arlosoroff desist and threatened to make its protest public if he did not give in to its demands. Arlosoroff described the battalion as "a secret linguistic police" and prepared a sharp letter of response. Moshe Shertok, also of the Jewish Agency, toned the letter down.[54]

The battalion itself considered Buber's lecture delivered in German a setback. For its next campaign, Halevi and his comrades stockpiled stones in the university yard. If the university decided to establish a chair in Yiddish, they threatened, they would smash windows. This new cause had begun with a festive dinner in honor of Magnes and the university held by David Shapira, the publisher of *Der Tog,* a New York Yiddish newspaper. During the course of the dinner Magnes announced that Shapira had offered to raise $50,000 for an endowed chair in Yiddish. He had given Magnes a down payment of $10,000. The chair was intended to provide an impetus for the Yiddish language, but also to generate good publicity for the donor's newspaper and the new university. The story took off. *Davar* reported that the gift would total $100,000. There was an outcry at the university. Joseph Klausner told his students, among them Chaim Shalom Halevi, that he intended to resign in protest.

Magnes made a great effort to keep the dispute behind closed doors, to no avail. Halevi went to speak with a reporter from *Do'ar HaYom*, offering him the following quote: "Shylock sold a pound of his flesh for money and we are selling our entire soul for money." The battalion mounted a demonstration in front of Magnes's house and handed out leaflets with a black frame around the words "The chair in Jargon, the end of the university" and "The chair in Jargon, an idol in the sanctuary." This was considered extremely harsh language.[55]*

Fifteen years previously, the small Jewish community in Palestine had been shaken by a battle over the use of German and Hebrew in schools. Now, too, the campaign against the chair was conducted as if a total war were being fought over the very existence of the nation. Given the attenuated status of the Jewish religion, the Hebrew language remained the last bastion of Jewish nationalism, and the proposed chair in Yiddish put the unity of the nation at risk, one of its opponents wrote.[57]

Halevi wrote to his parents about the student assembly called to discuss the matter; it ended in a fistfight. "What a disgrace," he wrote, referring to the many students who supported the chair.[58] Reports had claimed that all the students were in favor. No, Halevi told his parents, the reports were wrong. One had to distinguish between quantity and quality—most of the students came to the university only out of boredom and idleness, to pass the time, or to get a cheap meal at the student union cafeteria; those were in favor of the chair. The others, who came to study seriously, were against it. He was not deterred by being part of the minority; he would not betray what was dear and sacred. The whole world was lies, politics, and diplomacy.[59]

Some labor leaders, Berl Katznelson among them, did not oppose the chair. Here and there a few people dared suggest the use of other languages in schools, for example in science instruction, and even discussed granting official status to English and Arabic. Hebrew ideologues were afraid, however, that these languages would "compete" with Hebrew; they wanted to consign foreign languages to oblivion, along with city life.[60] Somewhere

---

*Something similar had happened once before. Sarah Thon reported on an incident in 1919 in Jerusalem's Hurva Synagogue. Chief Rabbi Kook began to deliver a sermon in Yiddish. Menachem Ussishkin, who happened to be there, left the hall in protest. A few young people heckled, and Rabbi Kook switched to Hebrew. Another part of the audience protested against that, and Kook switched back to Yiddish.[56]

among all these proposals was a debate over whether to write Hebrew in Latin letters; Halevi, of course, thought the idea was "ridiculous."[61] The fight rolled on and on in tense arguments all over the world; furious antagonists traded stinging insults, causing wounds that never healed.

None of those who supported the Yiddish chair defended their cause with the same patriotic fervor that characterized its opponents. Notable in this respect was the timid stand of Chaim Nachman Bialik. Eliezer Ben-Yehuda and Ahad Ha'am, the two towering figures of the Hebrew revival, were no longer alive, and Bialik, the national poet, was one of the major figures at the university. Naturally, great importance was attached to his position on the issue: "Magnes believes in Bialik as he believes in God," wrote Joseph Klausner.[62] Bialik favored endowing the chair in Yiddish but was afraid to say so. He was bold enough to condemn the Battalion for the Defense of the Language in public, calling its members "untutored and headstrong boys" and referring to their campaign as "impudent sputum." But when people in his audience protested, he retracted his words.

Halevi was present at the occasion and recorded Bialik's speech. Bialik opened with the thesis that Hebrew owed its survival to Yiddish, which had served as a sort of surrogate for Hebrew. Had the Jews spoken Hebrew in the lands of the Diaspora, the language would have evolved in a different way in each country and would have been lost forever. Thanks to Yiddish, which temporarily replaced Hebrew, the national language was preserved in its original form. Bialik explained that Yiddish had no future, that it was doomed to die, that the future belonged to Hebrew, but Halevi was not satisfied. Bialik was equivocating, he complained. When Bialik proposed that the chair concentrate on the study of the language rather than on its instruction, Halevi responded that this was a morphine injection for Jargon. Bialik conceded. In internal university discussions, he voted to table the issue.[63] Magnes also judged that the controversy was liable to hurt the university and thus preferred, unwillingly, to give in. The chair in Yiddish was postponed for better days.

Battalion member Yisrael Amikam continued fighting for another cause: the right to send telegrams in Hebrew. The British authorities permitted sending telegrams in the Arabic alphabet, but Hebrew cables could be sent only in Latin letters. Amikam corresponded with the postal authorities in Palestine for fifteen years, as well as with the high commissioner and with the Mandate Commission of the League of Nations. While working in the telegraph office of the Jerusalem postal service he had invented a Morse code for the Hebrew alphabet for use in cables, but his superiors told him to stop dabbling in politics. Amikam resigned, turned to law, and settled in Haifa. Time and again he went to court in an attempt to impose his demand on the government, lost his case, and appealed.

Amikam did manage to garner the support of several Zionist leaders. The National Council of the Elected Assembly joined his lawsuit, receiving a thoroughly technical answer from the administration's chief secretary, Wyndham Deedes: telegrams in the Hebrew alphabet could not be sent to foreign countries, because international postal treaties did not allow it, and telegrams in the Hebrew alphabet could not be sent within Palestine because there was no great demand for this service, Hebrew telegrams in Latin letters constituting only 11 percent of all telegrams sent. Furthermore, most workers in the telegraph service knew Arabic, but only a few knew Hebrew. Every telegram is handled by thirteen workers and telegraphists, and the authorities should not be required, "at this time of crisis," to hire the number of new workers necessary to allow sending telegrams in the Hebrew alphabet.[64]

Amikam, a tireless pest, did not give up. His fight produced thousands of pages, countless memorandums and petitions, signed declarations of support from leaders of the Zionist movement, as well as a letter to the London *Times*. In the end he defeated the British Empire and was allowed to send, from the Afula post office, "the first Hebrew telegram since the creation of the world."[65]*

The relentless struggles of people like Amikam led Zionism to victory; Chaim Shalom Halevi was also among its soldiers. When he was twenty Halevi went out with a girl. Simcha was pretty and interesting, he wrote home. When his mother demanded to know everything, he explained that Palestine had changed him with regard to women as well. In Vilna, he had blushed every time he spoke with a girl. He did not know if that was normal in Vilna, he wrote to his mother, but here in Palestine it was different. In Palestine he could speak with a girl without blushing.[67]

---

*Amikam financed the fight out of his own pocket; naturally, he hoped the Zionist Executive would reimburse him. Moshe Shertok wrote that the executive held him "in great esteem" but it could not support the right of every citizen to act at his own discretion and then unload his expenses on the public purse. This was the beginning of a long correspondence. Amikam said that his fight cost 268 pounds, Shertok offered 50, and in the end they agreed that the Zionist Executive would contribute 100 pounds toward the costs of a book in which Amikam documented his campaign. Years later, when his son's death in the 1948 War of Independence completed his heartbreak, Amikam killed himself and was forgotten.[66]

12

Negotiations with Friends

1.

A few minutes after three in the afternoon of Monday, July 11, 1927, four-year-old Dumia al-Sakakini was playing with her doll when Palestine quaked. Thousands of homes collapsed, about 250 people were killed, and close to 1,000 were injured. Dumia's aunt managed to extricate her from the windmill that then served as her family's living quarters, at the edge of the Rehavia neighborhood in Jerusalem; Dumia extricated her doll.

A year earlier, Khalil al-Sakakini had returned from a long spell in Egypt. Herbert Samuel was still in office, and Sakakini had refused to resume working for the administration's department of education. He had returned to Jerusalem only because the climate in Cairo was not good for his son Sari's health, and proceeded to make a living by publishing articles and giving Arabic lessons.

By the time of Sakakini's return, the first manifestations of the Zionist revolution were visible; the country's appearance was being transformed. Yet little had changed for the Arabs. At least seven out of ten continued to live in villages, of various sizes, of either Muslim or Christian persuasion. The British authorities had done some things: they had offered the farmers new agricultural methods, improved health services, built schools, and connected villages to new roads. The improvement in transportation enabled contact between people who had not previously had any and expanded their circle of identification beyond the bounds of the village. To some extent, the village was now exposed to new ways of life and new ideas that would in time fracture the traditional frameworks of authority.[1]

But all told, the British did very little to bring the Arab villages into the twentieth century. In general, their inclination was to preserve traditional village life—the same colonial attitude that had guided the British throughout the empire. Their stance had a certain political logic: it was designed to promote stability and tranquillity, not social revolution. The same logic led the administration to recognize the status of the mukhtars and work with them. All this was very different, though, from the support the administration gave to the Zionist revolution.

The daily routine of the Arab village went on in its sleepy way, in keeping with a tradition that was stronger than time. Children could expect to lead lives very similar to those of their parents. They too would not go to school or learn how to read and write. They too would experience a very short childhood; boys quickly became men, and girls mothers. A man would work in the field; a woman would cook, launder, and care for the children and, when necessary, she would also work in the field. A wife would obey her husband, and both would obey his father and the village mukhtar. The cycles of nature and religious ritual would prescribe their days of rest and celebration and mourning, their prayer days and fast days, when to plow the fields and when to harvest the crops, how to commemorate births, weddings, and deaths. Locals would seldom venture to the city; some never left their villages. National politics reached them slowly, if at all.

Sakakini, a member of the Arab national movement, had already gained fame as an educator and writer. He participated as a delegate in the national Arab congresses convened from time to time, and though a Christian, he was invited to ascend the pulpit in Jerusalem's Al-Aqsa Mosque to protest a visit by Lord Balfour. He would soon be involved in an initiative to establish a "new national school" that would be run in the spirit of his educational philosophy. In the meantime he had become a vegetarian. He frequented a coffeehouse not far from the Jaffa Gate, which had after World War I become a popular meeting place for Arab journalists and writers. They called it the Poor People's Coffee House. Sakakini liked to refer to the clientele as the Poor People's Party and even wrote a kind of party platform.[2] The place was a magnet for exiled intellectuals, refugees who had fled Damascus after the fall of Prince Faisal's short-lived reign. The dream of Greater Syria had been shelved for the time being, since Damascus was now under French control, and Palestinian Arabs, threatened by the Zionist program, began to develop a distinct and separate identity. They spoke of the need to organize themselves, debated whether to direct their struggle against the British or against the Jews and whether terrorism was productive or counterproductive. Arguments that had begun years earlier continued with greater urgency. By 1926 about a dozen Arabic periodicals were being published, twice as many as five years previously.[3] But they had relatively few readers—even in the cities, most Arabs could not read.

Beyond this swell of discussion, Arab politics lay dormant during the 1920s, essentially limited to relations between clans, which competed over economic interests, influence, and honor, rather than ideology. Some politics revolved around animosity between Muslims and Christians, although Muslim-Christian associations, the first organizational expression of Palestinian Arab nationalism, did begin to assume the form of political parties. While central to Zionist thinking, the aspiration for national independence still took second place among Arabs. The British authorities helped perpetuate the tribal-familial rivalries, navigating between clans and bestowing money, jobs, and other perks on all parties. They also nurtured Haj Amin al-Husseini, the mufti of Jerusalem. As head of the Supreme Muslim Council, the mufti enjoyed a great deal of control over Muslim property and considerable influence over the Arab judicial and educational systems, including the power to make appointments and hand out jobs. Husseini also drew authority from the Executive Committee, an Arab secular body established in 1920 that claimed to represent the Arab population to authorities.[4]

While the mufti was accruing power and emerging as the leader of his community, David Ben-Gurion experienced a parallel rise. The mufti used Islam to promote Arab nationalism, organizing an international fund-raising campaign to renovate the mosques on the Temple Mount. Ben-Gurion, for his part, leader of the Histadrut labor federation, used socialism to push the Zionist agenda. Each man had to shore up his position against a rival center of power: the mufti elevated Jerusalem's status above that of Damascus, whereas Ben-Gurion worked to strengthen his base in Tel Aviv against the Zionist movement's center in London. Each of them also grew stronger as the British authorities came to recognize him as a legitimate leader. Both encouraged aggressive nationalism but remained acceptable to the British because they were able to keep at bay even more extreme political challenges.

Admired by their countrymen, and soon to become national symbols, Husseini and Ben-Gurion would ultimately lead the country to war. They never met.

2.

During the 1920s, Jews and Arabs came into contact predominantly through the Jews' efforts to buy the country from its owners. And the Arabs were willing to sell. Generally, more land was available than the Zionist movement could afford to buy. Some of the landowners lived outside Palestine: some of the sellers were land agents, and some were farmers offering their property directly to prospective buyers. Among those who sold were leaders of the Arab national movement—patriots on the outside, traitors on the inside.

The Zionist movement had always planned to buy Palestine with money. In the early days of the movement, Herzl had wanted to purchase land from the Turkish sultan. At the turn of the century, the Zionists had established the Jewish National Fund (JNF), whose main activity was acquiring property. The JNF was engaged in a national enterprise; the working assumption was that the land bought would not be handed over to "gentiles," that is, it would not be returned to the Arabs. Besides the JNF, other Zionist organizations allocated money for acquiring land for Jewish settlement and private buyers invested as well. The term used was "redemption" of the land, another quasi-religious word laden with emotion and ideology.[5]

The JNF sketched out a master plan; it drew up budgets, convened regular meetings, and kept minutes. But, in fact, the land deals did not proceed according to any organized strategy; rather, they happened through chance, luck, improvisation, fraud, bribery, risk, violence, and vision. No one displayed these traits and employed these practices more than Joshua Hankin, a Russian-born Zionist, a legendary figure who "redeemed" perhaps a third of all the land that came into Jewish hands. Still, by the end of the Mandatory period, the Zionists had purchased a total of only two million dunams. They had hoped to buy much more. At the beginning of the British occupation the Zionists had expected to acquire five million dunams within five years. They ended up owning a mere 10 percent of the country, and of the land included in the Zionist wish map submitted to the Paris Peace Conference their holdings constituted much less than 10 percent. However, excluding the land considered unfit for habitation—that is, the Negev Desert—the Zionists' property came to about 25 percent of Palestine.[6]*

The questions of where to buy and how much to pay were a source of endless debate among those in charge of Zionist policy; the dispute reflected the struggle between advocates of urban and agricultural life. According to one opinion, urban settlement was the more worthwhile and prudent way to begin; the assumption was that this would neutralize the opposition of the Arab population. Ideological considerations, however, won out. "Our principal goal is to return our nation to working the land," stated a 1923 report submitted by the JNF to the Zionist Congress. Agricultural land was cheaper; in the end, though, cost was not always the central factor.[8] Most of the land purchased by the Jews was in the expensive and fertile regions of the coastal plain, the eastern Galilee, and the valleys. The aim was to create a contiguous area of Jewish settlement.

Arabs had opposed Jewish land purchases in Palestine from the beginning of the century. In the early 1920s, the Al-Manashia Theater in Nablus presented a play written by Mohammed Izzat Darwazza called *Land Agent and Landowner*. The agent of the title has a daughter who seduces a landowner's son in order to sell his land to Jews.[9] The Arab press frequently published articles decrying the sale of land, but market forces were stronger—demand pushed prices up, and the Jews made good offers.

Some of the land purchased by the JNF was sold directly by the farmer-owners, but much of it was occupied by tenant farmers. It is very difficult to determine how many tenants were evicted, which of them were removed by force, how many received compensation and how much, and what happened to them after they left. The questions of eviction and compensation came up repeatedly before various British commissions of inquiry. When at the end of the 1930s the evictees were granted the right to demand assistance from the administration, some 3,000 claims were submitted, representing approximately 15,000 people, but this figure is probably inaccurate: a number of the claims proved to be groundless, while some farmers no doubt failed to come forward.[10]

There were Arabs who sold land because of financial difficulties; some

---

*The exact percentage of the country included in the Zionist holdings is complicated. Palestine was divided into different types of land—habitable and nonhabitable—according to legal definitions that changed every so often from region to region and from one period to another. The surveying methods and units of measurement also shifted, as did the various kinds of holding, ownership, and methods of registration. Nor were the registrations accurate.[7]

were enticed, like the farmer in Darwazza's play; yet others sold land so they could invest the money in urban enterprises. One way or another, the plight of the farmers provided grist for the mill of national politics. A dynamic formed: the Arabs accused the Zionists of dispossessing them, and the Zionists denied it. Time and again, however, the Zionists promised that once the Jews formed a majority, the Arabs would not suffer: "Just as our forefathers learned to treat both citizen and stranger with justice and honesty because they 'were strangers in the land of Egypt,' so we will remember as we move from the lands of the Exile to the land of our liberty not to persecute or oppress, because we ourselves were persecuted and oppressed," one JNF official wrote.[11] Arab landowners were not forced to sell. They cooperated with the Zionists against the national interest of their own people.

Attorney Aouni Abd al-Hadi, a well-known Arab figure, helped Joshua Hankin purchase land in Wadi Hawarat—Hefer Valley in Hebrew. The transaction involved evicting tenant farmers. While the affair was still in progress, Abd al-Hadi went to the high commissioner and demanded that he prohibit all land sales to Jews.[12] "What a great discrepancy there is between what people say and what they do," Khalil al-Sakakini wrote. "They sell land and speculate in it . . . and afterward shout and protest and demand that the government pass a law that forbids them to sell land. They are like someone addicted to opium who asks people to prevent him from taking the drug, and then when they do so, complains, 'Good God, they are violating my liberty!'"[13]

Zionist officials took careful note of Arab nationalists who sold land, and when the Jewish-Arab conflict intensified they prepared special lists of the relevant names, perhaps for purposes of extortion, perhaps for psychological warfare, or both. A 1937 list included Musa Kazim al-Husseini, the former mayor of Jerusalem, for years an acknowledged leader of the Arab national movement. Several other members of the Husseini family also appeared on the list, among them the father of mufti Haj Amin al-Husseini and attorney Jamal al-Husseini, also a prominent nationalist. Eight other mayors are listed as well, including Jerusalem's Ragheb al-Nashashibi and mayors of Jaffa and Gaza.[14] Additional lists reveal the names of civic leaders, political activists, religious figures, businessmen, and other notables, including Muslims and Christians and scions of respected families such as the Dejanis of Jerusalem and the A-Shawa family of Gaza. Musa Alami, one of the most influential Arabs in Palestine, sold the land on which the Zionists established Kibbutz Tirat Zvi, named for an Orthodox Zionist rabbi.[15]

3.

The Arab leaders' willingness to sell land to the Jews heightened the contempt Zionist figures felt for the Arab national movement. After a meeting with Arab dignitaries, Chaim Weizmann concluded, "They are ready to sell their souls to the highest bidder." The compact Weizmann reached with Prince Faisal in 1918 had also been based on the assumption that the prince would make money off his peace with the Zionists. One of Faisal's aides had received a down payment of £1,000 and then demanded more.[16] This experience contributed to the Jews' conclusion that the national consciousness of the Palestinian Arabs could be bought. Indeed, politicians and petty thieves, dignitaries as well as hoodlums—all offered the Zionists their services in espionage and sabotage, in rumormongering, defamation, extortion, and all kinds of intimidation; the supply often outstripped the demand.

The information passed on sometimes led to land purchases, but the Zionists were also interested in Arab thinking and political currents, as well as power struggles within the national movement. On occasion they received extremely specific and up-to-date intelligence: this person had visited so-and-so, this one had met with that one, this one said this, and that one said that. A certain man had sold a rifle, another had bought a horse. Occasionally Jewish Agency officials paid for Arab signatures on petitions they sent to the authorities, including declarations of support for Zionism. Here and there the agency funded provocative incidents meant to embarrass the Husseinis.[17]

Some of these Jewish-Arab connections were established in the Turkish period and continued to develop under the Mandate, thanks largely to a Jewish agronomist, the legendary Chaim Margalit Kalvarisky, who had purchased land in the upper Galilee on behalf of the movement.[18] A Zionist and a man of peace, an idealist and a cynic, Kalvarisky had an almost mystical faith in the corruption of the Arabs; indeed, he saw it as the key to coexistence. A man identified by Kalvarisky only by his initials, who was almost certainly Musa Kazim al-Husseini, complained about not having received his money. People told him that the Zionists don't keep their word, he'd said, but he'd heard that Kalvarisky was different. Now it turned out that Kalvarisky was just like the others. For his part, the man claimed he'd done what he'd promised. He'd guaranteed peace and quiet, and since the Jaffa May Day events things had, in general, been calm. He'd promised to moderate the extremists in his camp, and he'd done so. What else did they want from him?

Kalvarisky responded that the Zionist movement wanted to reach an understanding with the Arab population on the basis of the Balfour Declaration and continued British rule. "No," Husseini had answered forcefully. "No. I will not sell my homeland for money." Kalvarisky had argued that as a political person he should recognize reality and historical facts. The Balfour Declaration was included in the Mandate, which in turn was part of an international treaty, not likely to be revoked through propaganda. Husseini had cut him off suddenly: "Before we start talking politics, the Zionists must keep their promises," he'd said.

Summing up, Kalvarisky wondered whether Husseini would have the courage to go over to the Zionist side openly. He felt this was improbable—and unnecessary: "Better he should remain a leader of our opponents and try to undermine their activity behind the scenes, in this way preparing the ground for mutual understanding." Kalvarisky went on to consider establishing a Muslim Arab organization "that would be putty in our hands and take orders from us." But such a venture would require money, he wrote.[19]*

The Arabists, as the Zionist movement called its specialists in Arab relations, tried to set up a network of ostensibly nationalist Muslim clubs to compete with the Muslim-Christian associations, which were gradually consolidating into a national movement. The Zionists' "Arab secretariat" reported that it had "given advice" to the leaders of these clubs and had "shown them the way to go." At the same time, Colonel Kisch, the head of the Zionist Executive, planned to found a "moderately pro-Zionist" Arab party and also looked into the possibility of putting out an Arabic newspaper. An ongoing rivalry between the country's main Arab families—particularly the more moderate Nashashibis and the vocally nationalist Husseinis—should be exploited, he noted, estimating optimistically that the Husseini family's standing was already in decline.[21]

One day Kisch received a call from a man asking to meet with him. The man refused to identify himself, and Kisch hung up. But the anonymous caller phoned again and again, and in the end Kisch agreed to receive him

---

*A nonconformist and a dreamer, Kalvarisky bribed people indiscriminately, as he saw fit, even paying out monthly salaries. This got him into trouble. From time to time he made promises he could not keep, because the Zionist movement did not give him the necessary funds. He would then finance his activities out of his own pocket, even going into debt. Kalvarisky, feeling that he bore a heavy responsibility, was certain his expenses would be refunded. Some were, but in negotiations with Zionist leaders he was often treated with suspicion, as if he were asking them to overlook an act of fraud.[20]

at home. The man turned out to be Taher al-Husseini, the mufti's nephew. He had come to Kisch in the hope that the Zionists and the British might help him stage a coup; he wanted to depose his uncle and take the mufti's post himself. He brought new information, telling Kisch that it was the mufti who had organized the demonstration against Balfour in Damascus, providing money for this purpose. The sum, between four and five hundred pounds drawn from the Supreme Muslim Council treasury, had been sent via Bedouin messengers.

The mufti, Taher al-Husseini claimed, had also plotted the disturbances in Jaffa and Jerusalem, which were meant to have sparked a revolution. The mufti intended to set up an Arab nationalist government with himself at its helm, his nephew related. To this end he had established a military wing, whose men were training in the mountains, with weapons smuggled over the border and assistance from Jerusalem's Latin patriarch. The mufti was counting on aid from France, in exchange for which he would support French rule in Syria. He was planning to send a delegation to the United States soon, to be headed by Musa Kazim.

Kisch believed his informer. The man wanted no money; he said, correctly, that in coming to Kisch he had placed his life in Kisch's hands. He could overthrow his uncle within a month, he maintained—he intended not to destroy him but to banish him. The move would not cause any disturbances; while the Arab public would not tolerate the post of mufti being taken from the Husseini family, no one would get upset if it passed from one Husseini to another. Kisch concurred in the assessment and agreed to speak with the high commissioner. Husseini wanted government support but asked that Ronald Storrs not be informed. He did not, however, object to Norman Bentwich's involvement. He described himself as a friend of the Jews, in the spirit of his late father, who had also served as mufti. Kisch confirmed that the previous mufti had indeed been sympathetic to the Jews. Kisch went to Samuel; Bentwich was also present. The high commissioner promised to check out the story, but that's as far as the whole affair went. The mufti remained in power and at one point got himself into an embarrassing situation over dealings with Jews: he signed an agreement with a Jewish contractor, Baruch Katinka, to build a luxury hotel in Jerusalem.

The Palace was to be built across from the large Muslim cemetery in Mamilla. Katinka had reasoned that a Jew would not get the job, so he entered into a partnership with an Arab contractor. The two of them, together with Tuvia Dunia, another Jewish builder and Chaim Weizmann's brother-in-law, concluded their deal with the Supreme Muslim Council, which was backing the project, and got to work. The mufti demanded that preference be given to Arab workers and that any day of rest during the course of the work would be on Friday. But when he was forced to choose between religious piety and business interests, he chose the latter and made Katinka, the Jewish contractor, his confidant.

A short time after excavation began on the hotel's well, it turned out, as it often does in Jerusalem, that there were graves under the hotel lot—the excavations had turned up several skeletons. Katinka asked the mufti what he wanted to do about the discovery of what seemed to be a Muslim burial site, and Haj Amin ordered that the matter be kept secret. He feared that the matter would become known to Mayor Nashashibi, who, seeking to discredit a rival Husseini, would take the opportunity to halt construction. The skeletons were carted away secretly, and work continued. Nashashibi nevertheless did manage to outmaneuver his great enemy by refusing to link the building to the city sewage system. Katinka suggested to the mufti that an alternative system of pumps and pipes could direct the hotel's sewage, after partial treatment, into the Mamilla cemetery. The mufti agreed, again on condition that the pipes be laid in total secrecy, at night. Under no circumstances should anyone find out.

The Supreme Muslim Council invested £70,000 in the building, which had four stories and was decorated with carved stone arabesques. The foyer had a colossal staircase and huge majestic marble columns. A modern bathroom adjoined each room, and the beds came with elaborate canopies and bedside telephones. The mufti was a frequent guest.[22]* He was a pretty easygoing man, Katinka wrote, bright, intense, and polite. He tried to engage Weizmann's brother-in-law in political conversations of the kind he occasionally held with prominent Jewish figures. Any compromise acceptable to the Jews, the mufti once said, would be seen by the Arabs as betrayal. Therefore, there was no possibility of an agreement. The two Jewish contractors were careful not to get drawn into this sort of discussion. Katinka told the mufti about a Jew who sold pretzels at the entrance to a bank in New York. They had an agreement: the Jew didn't

*Several Jews met with the mufti for political discussions. Judge Gad Frumkin knew him well. David Hacohen, a labor activist in Haifa and the son of Mordechai Ben-Hillel Hacohen, once had a friendly chat with him, and the Jewish Agency's intelligence operative Eliahu Sasson also met with the mufti. Zionist Executive members, however, generally avoided contact with him; Kisch never had any. Chaim Arlosoroff once found himself next to Husseini at the tea table at the high commissioner's residence.[23]

interfere with the bank's business, and the bank didn't sell pretzels. The two contractors built a house for the mufti for a low price spread out in yearly payments, the contractor later wrote; he didn't mention whether the mufti paid.*

Apart from fanning inter-Arab rivalries, Kisch devoted much of his time to fostering relations with "moderate Arabs." The "moderate Arab" did not have to be a Zionist; he was required merely to get his compatriots to recognize that Zionism would win. Kisch's activities were eventually institutionalized; some of his contacts with informers were put in writing. A collaborator from Ramle, Ibrahim Abadin, asked to receive the political platform he was supposed to distribute in his community and also inquired after some articles the Zionists had intended to send him for publication in the Arab press under assumed names. He had already found a home for the Muslim club; "Business here is going well," he reported. He asked that he be sent £10 at once. In the Zionist budget these expenses were recorded under the heading "negotiations with friends" and were partly covered by money donated by Baron Rothschild in Paris. The sums were relatively small—about £20,000 a year, according to Weizmann. The collaborators were required to sign receipts.[25]

Kisch felt uncomfortable with these dealings; he wrote about them in his diary. He recorded "an unpleasant hour" spent in the Muslim National Club in Tiberias, where club members demanded £560 for their loyalty. After "a great fight" Kisch managed to lower the sum to £200. That same day he also left some money for the mayor of Tiberias, an "intensely stupid" man, he wrote.[26] He also succeeded in reducing the "wages" of the mayor of Beisan from £30 pounds to £10. The mayor had been very reluctant to accept the new terms.[27] A big quarrel broke out in the Jerusalem branch of the Muslim National Club, and Kisch had to mediate between the two factions. The warring members came to his home and sat in separate rooms as he went from one side to the other to broker an agreement. In the end he got rid of the club's president for £50 and appointed someone else to replace him. According to Kisch's diary, he managed at the same time to cut the club's monthly budget from £250 to £100.[28] His "clients" frequently came to his house. "In the afternoon Khalid Bey from

---

*When the hotel was completed, it was handed over to the management company belonging to George Barsky, who also ran the Fast Hotel in Jerusalem. The hotel did not last long. It had no chance against the King David, which opened soon afterward. The mufti's opponents accused him of waste and fraud.[24]

Nablus came to collect the 100 pounds I promised," he wrote. The man demanded £400 for general expenses, but Kisch would only pay for specific assignments.[29] On occasion he refused to pay altogether: he dismissed one sheikh from Jenin as a rogue who obviously only wanted to fill his pockets.[30] An Arab from Lebanon turned up to demand £600 "for political work" but went away with £100 as an advance. Kisch ended their meeting after ten minutes. "Most unpleasant," he noted.[31]

A man named Ibrahim Najar, a journalist, demanded that his monthly retainer be raised from £75 to £100. Kisch was angry. "*Chutzpah!*" he wrote. "He was quite offensive and treated me as if I had robbed him. He did not get any change out of me." Sometime later the man returned and gave Kisch some worthless information about the resumption of war between Britain and Turkey. Kisch gave him £50. "He is a tiger for money," he remarked in his diary. A few months later Najar threatened that unless he received £275 he would find someone else to work for. "I refused to be thus blackmailed," Kisch wrote. Two months later he nevertheless advanced the man a sum from the following month's pay. Given the political situation, he thought, it was not a good idea for Najar to leave empty-handed.[32]*

Kisch also helped arrange government appointments for Arabs, his assumption being that a steady job would foster moderation. For this reason the Jewish Agency encouraged the appointment of Aref al-Aref, considered an extremist, as governor of Jenin.[34] The same premise lay behind Kisch's payments to several Arab representatives who sat on Herbert Samuel's advisory council. By attending council meetings, the Arabs were implicitly giving recognition to British rule and the national-home policy, and so the Zionists had an interest in supporting them. These representatives' political rivals applied heavy pressure on them to resign, Kisch wrote to Weizmann, and they wanted money in exchange for remaining.

Kisch offered one representative, Arif Pasha Dajani, £100 a month, but he claimed that he would not sit on Samuel's council for even £200. Instead, he demanded £500. Mayor Ragheb al-Nashashibi asked for a similar sum,

*Najar was the editor of the daily newspaper *Lisan al-Arab*, "The Arab Tongue." When the newspaper first came out, in 1921, it was the only daily in Arabic. A Zionist Commission report described it as an important and serious publication, European in form, with many readers. According to the report, *Lisan al-Arab* represented a modern Arab Muslim line and distanced itself from the war against Zionism. Najar came again and again, and once proposed to make his newspaper into an organ of the Zionist Farmers Party, another creation of Kisch's. Hebrew newspapers, among them *Ha'aretz*, also received assistance from the Zionist Organization, through Kisch.[33]

adding that in order to hold on to his influence he would sometimes have to take extremely anti-Zionist positions. It was difficult to work with people who used such methods, Kisch complained in some distress, but he understood their logic. He believed he could satisfy both men with £400. "I think we should give it to them," he wrote.[35]

At the beginning of 1923, Kisch sent a letter to Chief Secretary Wyndham Deedes containing a serious accusation: the authorities were encouraging Arab nationalist fanaticism, he claimed. Most of the Arabs understood, Kisch claimed, that Zionism was bringing economic benefits, and they wanted good relations with the Jews. Many were prepared to cooperate with the Jewish Agency, but the mufti's men were deterring them through intimidation, and the authorities were providing no protection. One village sheikh who had refused to cut his ties with Jews was denounced to the police for having married two minors, and then thrown in jail. Then there was a *kadi,* a religious judge, who had been deposed by the authorities on the basis of a groundless accusation; other Muslim clerics had defamed the *kadi* because of his friendship with Jews. And there was the case of a man who had been accused of stealing a herd of cattle, only because of his positive attitude to Zionism. A former mayor of Haifa, Hasan Shukri, was another friend of the Jews and Zionists who had been abandoned by the British and lost his job.

Deedes put the government to work. The police, the district governors, and the attorney general all provided detailed reports about the men Kisch had cited. Together, the reports form a kind of collective profile of the Arab collaborator: "loves money," "changeable, without principles," "bad character," "deceives the Government and other people," "known to figure in every village intrigue," "unreliable." According to Deedes's information, one of the men named by Kisch was "a thorough rascal, thief, liar, criminal, convicted for forgery, an out and out scoundrel trying to make friends with the Jews whom he really hates in the hope of making money." Another man was "a leader of a gang of highway robbers," had been accused of attempted murder, had spent time in jail for assaulting a government official, and was an "insincere moral pervert and violently anti-British." Of Hassan Shukri, the reports said coldly that he served as president of the Muslim National Association, "which is believed to be subsidised by the Zionists."

On the basis of this material, one of Deedes's men suggested giving Kisch instruction in proper administration, politics, and ethics, the most important lesson being: Do not bribe. Kisch needed to be told that the effect of enticing collaboration through money, presents, or hints about government favors would surely "alienate" the most positive elements among the Arabs and lead them to associate Zionism with corruption. The Zionists would then be left with only "the support of those whose support is not worth having." The document continues: "[T]o consider a party recruited by these means a 'moderate' party" is to fool oneself. Asking the government to support such a party or to show any sympathy is to ask the government "to associate itself with methods it cannot approve" and in whose efficacy it does not believe.

Had Kisch received this document, he would no doubt have known to take it with a grain of salt. He was familiar with the kinds of bribes the British Empire gave to Arab rulers. While serving as a British intelligence officer he had himself been responsible for the monthly retainer, in gold, paid to the ruler of Mecca and the Hejaz. Storrs and his men also bribed local leaders. But the effort the administration put into drafting Deedes's response to Kisch was for naught—the document was never sent to him. "I do not think that any good will result from further correspondence respecting the characters of the individuals . . . it might be well to let the correspondence drop," one of Deedes's staff decided, and there the matter ended.[36]

David Ben-Gurion also believed there was no benefit to be gained from negotiating with Arabs who could be bought. "Every Arab" would take money, he thought. For this reason, the only negotiations with any lasting value were those with truly patriotic Arabs. Ze'ev Jabotinsky also warned that the bribery policy would not pay in the end. "They take the money and behind our backs they laugh at us," stated one memorandum. Someone complained that bribes were buying only "platonic love." The American consulate in Jerusalem, which followed the discussions in the National Council, quoted the view that the payoffs were a waste of money—the British were offering much more than the Jews.[37] Indeed, the money was a political write-off: it neither quashed nor moderated Arab nationalism.

4.

One day, a German newspaper reported that Sir Ellis Kadoorie, a Jewish Iraqi millionaire who had just died in Hong Kong, had left £100,000 for the development of education in Palestine. There was great rejoicing in the Zionist Organization; naturally, everyone assumed the money was intended for Jewish education. Herbert Samuel set up a committee to plan how the money would be spent. Only some time later was Kadoorie's will read carefully, and then it turned out that the beneficiary was not specifically the British administration in Palestine but the British government in London, and Kadoorie had granted it the choice of whether to invest in Palestine or Iraq. There was no indication in the will that he intended the money to be used for Hebrew education. In the ensuing commotion, Weizmann trotted out the deceased man's brother and managed at least to obtain a decision that the sum be invested in Palestine. Humphrey Bowman, the director of the education department in Jerusalem, then suggested that the bequest be used to set up an elite school, a sort of local English public school, for both Jewish and Arab boys.

The idea was that the lower grades would study in Hebrew and Arabic and the intermediate and higher grades largely in English. Students would board at the school, creating a small, binational community meant to foster "true Palestinian spirit." The Zionist movement immediately launched an energetic campaign against the plan. Kisch conducted quasi-diplomatic negotiations with Bowman, arguing that at this stage of its development, the Jewish national home needed Jewish national education. Bowman did not hide his disappointment. "Here was an opportunity of bringing Jews and Arabs together on common ground," he wrote in his memoirs. He had hoped the school would be his legacy to Palestine; he was soon to complete his service and return home.

The government gave in. An academic high school would be established for the Jews, together with a separate agricultural school for the Arabs, the assumption being that the Arabs did not need the sort of instruction that would prepare them for college. The Zionist Organization agreed to this at first, but then issued a demand to set up a Jewish agricultural school as well, lest anyone think their foothold in the land of their fathers was weaker than that of the Arabs. Kisch thought that the agricultural school could be a joint Jewish-Arab venture, like a government-sponsored law school that had been established in Jerusalem, but he kept his opinion to himself. In the end, after interminable difficulties, two agricultural schools were established, not far from each other, one in the Arab city of Tulkarem and the second in the Jewish village of Kfar Tabor; both were called Kadoorie. Segregation carried the day. Jabotinsky had already begun speaking of an "iron wall" that had to be raised between the Jews and the Arabs.[38]

The principle of segregation was accepted by all parts of the Zionist movement, with a very few exceptions. Occasionally there was still talk of

Palestine being part of a large Arab federation, but even Ahad Ha'am said he would not remain in Palestine if that were to happen. "Better to die in the Exile than to die here and be buried in the land of my fathers, if that land is considered the 'homeland' of the Arabs and we are strangers in it," he wrote. Weizmann sent Kisch to the high commissioner with a clear warning: the Jews in Palestine would violently resist any effort to implement the federation idea. The principle of segregation also guided the Zionists' strategy of purchasing land to create a single contiguous area of Jewish ownership, even at the price of giving up property in other parts of the country. Segregation had led to the establishment of Tel Aviv, and at one point there was talk of dividing Jerusalem into submunicipalities, one of them solely Jewish.[39] Segregation was at the heart of a fight over the orange trees of Petach Tikva.

5.

It was mid-December 1927. Petach Tikva was a small Jewish town where many residents were citrus growers. As a rule they sold their fruit while it was still on the tree. This meant that the buyer, usually an Arab merchant, would also pay for the crop to be picked. Obviously, he would try to keep his labor costs low, and therefore would employ Arab laborers. But this year was a time of economic crisis, and hundreds of Jewish workers demanded that they be employed instead, which would raise the cost of the harvest. At the end of the 1920s the accepted pay for a day's labor was 1.75 piastres for a Jewish man and 1.50 for a woman; an Arab man received one piastre, a woman even less. The Jewish laborers also clamored to be out in the fields as well as in the orchards. The farmers calculated that this would reduce their income by between 30 and 40 percent.[40]

In reality, the struggle that ensued was between employer and employees, not between Jews and Arabs. Still, at the height of the season the Jewish laborers set up pickets in the Petach Tikva citrus groves and prevented the Arab workers from doing their job. The Jewish farmers called the British police, and mounted officers, armed with clubs, dispersed the picketers with considerable violence. People were wounded and arrested.

The campaign for Jews to employ "Hebrew labor" had begun in the Turkish era. Thus farmers in the Jewish villages were placed in the position of having to choose between economic interest and national loyalty. Like Arabs who sold their land to Jews in contradiction to their patriotic obligations, many Jewish farmers preferred to employ Arabs, who were not only cheaper but also more experienced and obliging. The pioneers, mostly graduates of academic high schools in Russia, had not engaged in hard physical labor before and tended to slack off. They also brought with them youthful impudence and a socialist ideology that the farmers perceived as a threat.

Labor leader Berl Katznelson noted the psychological difficulty of being a boss to Jewish workers who were partners in the national struggle. He quoted a proverb: "He who buys a Hebrew slave buys himself a master." Overall, it was easier to handle an Arab laborer than a Jewish one. Jewish Agency executive Chaim Arlosoroff explained the situation to a guest from England, comparing Arab workers to Indians: they obey instructions and do not know enough to talk about reasonable hours, protection for women and children, and such.[41] Jewish laborers demanded not only higher wages but also better treatment.

More than once the farmers felt the need to defend their actions. The editor of *Ha'aretz*, Moshe Glickson, a confirmed capitalist, called on the farmers to ignore "small change" in favor of "national change." The farmers rejected his plea: Glickson lived in the city, among the private "mansions" that had been built with private money. What right did he have to preach to them about the national mission? Glickson responded that Zionism was founded on two major aspirations: the return to Hebrew culture and the return to the land. He could take justifiable credit for his newspaper's contribution to Hebrew culture. The farmers, for their part, should give up some of their profits, because without Hebrew labor there was no hope for the Zionist program.[42] The Petach Tikva "Boazes," as the farmers were called, after the rustic Boaz of the Book of Ruth, were also censured for having called in the British police, which was tantamount to "informing" and comparable to treason.

Negotiations commenced. The farmers appreciated the patriotic principle but refused to fund it. On the other side, the Jewish workers were unwilling to take a cut in their pay and work for Arab wages. Beyond patriotism and profit, there were other forces in play: the farmers were afraid that an influx of Jewish workers would threaten their control in the villages. The Histadrut, which represented the workers, was concerned with politics; its interest lay in strengthening the labor movement.

The Histadrut was caught in an awkward situation. It was fighting to protect the Jewish workers' wages and safeguard their political interest, but socialism did not condone discrimination against Arab workers. Histadrut leaders had already been forced to decide whether to accept Arab workers into the labor federation. If the union was open to all, the Jews would quickly lose control, they reasoned, and this would be counterproductive, since the struggle of the Jewish laborer was identified with the struggle for national independence. The Histadrut, which was fast developing into one of the power centers of the Jewish community, was first and foremost committed to the national goal. Thus segregation won out over socialism. Ben-Gurion proposed that the Arabs set up their own organization, though he did not reject the possibility of an "alliance" between the two labor unions.[43]

Characteristically, the Zionists never stopped debating the contradiction between nationalism and socialism and were constantly seeking formulas to assuage their socialist consciences. This balancing act demanded no small amount of ideological contortions. At one point labor leaders considered the following idea: If they helped Arab workers organize and stand up for their rights, in keeping with socialist values, the Arabs would eventually demand equal wages. When that happened, Jewish farmers would no longer have reason to employ Arabs, and Hebrew labor would prevail.[44]

Some people toyed with the idea of importing Jews who would be willing to work for Arab wages, which led to interest in a few hundred Bedouin living in Baghdad who claimed to be of Jewish extraction. One prominent Zionist, Yitzhak Ben-Zvi, located a Bedouin tribe in the Galilee that wanted to convert to Judaism, and he urged Colonel Kisch to handle the matter. Kisch applied to the chief rabbinate. Previously, Jewish laborers had been imported from Yemen. The Yemenites received higher wages than the Arabs, but lower than European Jews. The justification was that they had fewer needs.[45]

There were those who argued that employing Arab workers would bring Palestinian Jews and Arabs closer together, while shutting off the Jewish economy would intensify Arab opposition to Zionism. Norman Bentwich would later go so far as to call the principle of Hebrew labor "economic apartheid."[46] Ben-Gurion responded that most of the violent conflicts had actually broken out in places where Arabs were employed. He linked the phenomenon to Jewish history: "The bitter experience of the Jews in all lands has proved that the employment of non-Jewish workers by Jewish masters has not only failed to prevent antisemitism but has actually done the opposite—it feeds and augments this hatred." The need for Hebrew labor was also linked to the need to train Jewish farmers; they could hardly train with Arabs because, Ben-Gurion noted, the Arab economy was closed to Jews.

One by one, he refuted the practical reasons for employing Arabs, but Ben-Gurion's main argument focused on Hebrew labor as the essential foundation for "building the land"—promoting the Zionist program. "Without Hebrew labor there is no way to absorb the Jewish masses. Without Hebrew labor, there will be no Jewish economy; without Hebrew labor, there will be no homeland. And anyone who does anything counter to the principle of Hebrew labor harms the most precious asset we have for fulfilling Zionism."[47]*

In principle, the Jewish population agreed with Ben-Gurion, but from time to time there were violent incidents.[50] Zionist ideology did not stop Jews from employing Arabs. The free market was a decisive factor, as was the general level of tension in the country: when it rose, Arab workers stopped showing up, and when it subsided, they returned.

6.

"We had quite an earthquake," Chaim Shalom Halevi wrote to his parents. He had been on the bus on his way to Mount Scopus when Palestine trembled. He had felt nothing during the trip. "I'm really sorry I didn't feel it," he said. "Everyone says it was a very interesting feeling and who knows if it will happen twice in a lifetime?" One of the university's buildings was destroyed, and others were seriously damaged. Halevi's class met that day under a wild pepper tree. Judah Leib Magnes showed up to photograph them; he said that the pictures might help raise a little money to cover the damage, Halevi told his parents.[51]

The earthquake also hit Kibbutz Degania. The damage was estimated at £5,000. Degania applied to a government fund established to assist victims of the earthquake and asked for aid. The government refused, saying that Degania was supported by funds from the Zionist movement; it had no need of a loan. The incident is indicative of the evolving relations between the Zionist movement and the administration. Kisch believed that the government's response was a characteristic attempt to humiliate the Zionist movement; the man behind the refusal was Chief Secretary Stewart Symes, a veteran of the military administration, later to be governor-general of Sudan. "He does not like Jews," Kisch wrote.[52]

---

*Industrial enterprises also employed Arab workers; a large part of Jewish production was meant for Arab consumers, and that market was receptive only as long as manufacturers employed Arab labor. Firing the Arabs would lead to closing the factories, which would deprive Jews of work as well.[48] The Zionists often called the employment of Arabs *"avoda zara,"* literally "foreign labor" but also a rabbinic term referring to idolatry.[49]

If the Zionist Organization itself were to request aid following the earthquake, it would be admitting publicly that its financial situation was desperate. The very British Kisch decided against bargaining with the government. However, Berlin-born Arthur Hantke, the director of Keren Hayesod, the Zionist Organization's building fund, insisted that the Zionists had a right to aid; it was a matter of principle. Kisch referred the whole issue to the central Zionist office in London, who also felt that it was undignified for the Zionist movement to beg the British Empire for a loan that amounted to a mere £5,000.[53]

The high commissioner was now Lord Herbert Charles Onslow Plumer, a celebrated field marshal. In the five years that preceded his appointment, he had served as governor-general of Malta; a few months before the earthquake he had turned seventy. A short, solid man, he typically wore a blue serge suit and a black bowler hat and carried a rolled umbrella. Edward Keith-Roach thought he looked like a benevolent grandfather. Helen Bentwich, the attorney general's wife, took note of his twinkling blue eyes. His white, drooping walrus mustache was legendary. Police officer Douglas Duff wrote that Plumer looked the way American caricaturists like to draw English generals.[54] Plumer's term was a quiet one; he managed to stay out of politics.

The fact that the second high commissioner was not Jewish allayed some of the resentment that had built up during Samuel's administration. In parallel, Jewish immigration during this period sharply declined; the economic crisis that had hit the Zionist movement made it seem less threatening. Arab leaders, among them the mufti Haj al-Husseini, were not at this stage considering countrywide violent resistance or capable of organizing it. They feared that any rebellion was liable to harm them as well. The grand mufti, as the British courteously referred to him, owed his position to the authorities, and it was conditional on him keeping the peace. The British had appointed him and could remove him. Similarly, they could dismantle the Supreme Muslim Council, which functioned under their sponsorship.[55] Thus the mufti opposed the Balfour Declaration as if he were not dependent on the British, but restrained himself and cooperated with the British as if there were no Balfour Declaration.

Some Arab leaders had over the years begun to realize the importance of British public opinion. They traveled to London, where they were received as the authorized representatives of their population. In contrast to the Zionists, they were amateurs in the field of public relations, and they lacked the international support, infrastructure, and financial backing available to the Zionist movement. But they tried to behave like the Zionists. In London they stayed in an expensive suite at a prestigious hotel and worked to make political connections and create positive public opinion. Miss Frances Newton went with them. Wyndham Deedes described a public assembly arranged by several supporters of the Arabs in Parliament. A lord by the name of Lamington served as chairman, but the audience was largely composed of old ladies and retired army officers. Not a single statesman of influence attended.[56] The Arabs did manage to find attentive ears in a few newspapers, but good press also depended on political restraint; public support was contingent on Palestine not burning.

High Commissioner Plumer tended to assume that the tranquillity he enjoyed was permanent. A short time after arriving in Palestine he proposed to London that he stop sending the monthly reports he received from the district commissioners. He also planned to reorganize the military forces in Palestine, dismantling some of the units. Admired by his staff and accepted by both Jews and Arabs, the elderly field marshal could report to London that all was calm and that existing policies were perfectly adequate. Officials in London were pleased; they were still hardpressed to explain to themselves how they had gotten into Palestine in the first place. Plumer's peaceful tenure led them to conclude that there was no reason to leave.[57]

Ruling Palestine, like ruling Malta, was for Plumer an administrative task. When he granted land to the Arab population, as he did in the area of Beisan, he saw this as agricultural development only, and when he initiated public works, he did so to lower the unemployment rate, especially among Jews. Similarly, apolitically, he recommended sending away new immigrants who had not found a livelihood, and, free of political considerations, he cooperated with the representative institutions of the Jewish community. He instituted local municipal elections, which he saw largely as a practical step, a stage in preparing the population for self-government, as the Mandate required, not as an arena for political struggle. When the Arabs indicated willingness to reconsider an idea they had rejected in the past, a general Palestinian legislative assembly, Plumer simply avoided addressing the issue, considering it a "political" matter and outside his jurisdiction. Unlike other British officials, he was not excited by the notion that such an assembly would imply Arab acceptance of the Mandatory regime. An enlightened governor, he let the press criticize him personally but forbade it to attack the prestige of his office. In another practical, apolitical measure, he instituted Palestinian citizenship and a local currency, replacing the Egyptian lira.[58] Above all, Plumer shared London's primary concern: Palestine was not supposed to cost money.

The Plumers invited the Bentwiches to tea. "We found them both charming," related Helen Bentwich in a letter from Jerusalem. Lady Plumer, taller than Mrs. Bentwich and thin, tended to dress "in the old style, with long skirts reaching mostly to the ground." When she went out she wore a huge feathered hat. "They have already refurbished their rooms and laid out his trophies and her objets d'art and made Government House look like an old-fashioned country house belonging to a retired public servant," Mrs. Bentwich wrote. Judge Gad Frumkin was impressed by Lady Plumer's collection of fans, some made of silk, others of ivory, feathers, or shells; she also collected miniatures.

Helen Bentwich helped Lady Plumer wend her way through the city's web of diplomatic sensibilities: the French high commissioner in Syria could not be hosted together with certain Arabs because the French had bombed Damascus. The former prime minister of Belgium could not be invited with the Italian consul because the Belgian was a socialist and the Italian a fascist.

The high commissioner entertained a great deal. Dame Millicent Fawcett came for a second visit, along with her sister. While staying at the Bentwiches', she received a cable from London: the bill to give women the vote had passed a second reading in the House of Commons. The two women waltzed around the room in joy. Plumer was not much impressed. An officer molded by the previous century, he refused to accept the honorary presidency of the Palestinian scout movement because girls were allowed to participate in its activities. Colonel Kisch, also an officer and a gentleman, refused to accept the appointment for the same reason.[59] Plumer brought with him strict ideas on education: he thought its purpose should be to firm up the pupil's character. In general, he believed the Jews invested too much money in education; better to put more money into agriculture.

Plumer played cricket; his wife liked bridge. They enjoyed the musical evenings the Bentwiches held at their house, and they once hosted the Tel Aviv opera company. The mufti and the Latin patriarch were also invited to the party. "We enjoyed watching these bitter anti-Zionists listen to songs sung in Hebrew in the official home of the British High Commissioner," Helen Bentwich later wrote. When the earthquake damaged Government House on Mount Scopus, the Plumers moved to a house on Bethlehem Road.

The city of Safed also suffered serious damage in the earthquake, but the worst destruction was in the Arab town of Nablus, where hundreds of houses collapsed.[60] Chaim Shalom Halevi read in the newspaper that many of Nablus's inhabitants were leaving. Who knows, he wrote to his parents, maybe a Jewish city will rise over the ruins. He wondered why the Jews in Tel Aviv, many of whom were unemployed, were so quick to send three truckloads of bread to Nablus. The Arabs, Halevi noted, had applied for help to the Jew hater Henry Ford, but a Jewish millionaire named Nathan Straus had sent them $5,000 without even being asked. "This is the way we are," Halevi remarked, in either sarcastic bitterness or self-congratulation.[61] In the end, rather than seek a meager loan, the Zionist movement contributed £100,000 to the government reconstruction fund.[62] The earthquake was an opportunity to prove that Zionism was good for the whole country. Earlier, Kisch had encouraged Ronald Storrs to fund a nutrition project for Arab children in Jerusalem. In his diary, the colonel noted the public relations value of such gestures.[63]

There were no Jews among the 250 people killed by the earthquake. The chief rabbinate announced a special prayer of thanksgiving for the following Sabbath.[64] One of the mosques on the Temple Mount had been damaged, but the Western Wall was not affected; Halevi attributed this to "the hand of God."[65] In contrast, Judge Horace Samuel expressed his regret that the earthquake had not obliterated all the holy shrines, which had over the centuries been the source of so much hatred.[66]

PART II

TERROR

(1 9 2 8 - 3 8)

———•◦•———

"For more than six years I've been living in Jerusalem, growing medicinal plants," wrote Miss Jane Lancaster. "This work of mine isn't a hobby. It is my life-work, and I am doing it as a service to the country, both for Jews and for Arabs. I do not make a living out of it, but it is my life. . . ."

—•—

13

The Nerves of Jerusalem

1.

On Sunday afternoon, September 23, 1928, Constable Douglas Duff was patrolling the Old City when he ran into Jerusalem's current district commissioner, Edward Keith-Roach. The pasha of Jerusalem, as he was known, was on his way to the *mahkameh,* the Muslim religious court, and he invited Duff to join him. One of the court building's windows looked out over the Western Wall. Yom Kippur, the Jewish day of atonement, was to begin that evening, and people were gathering for the Kol Nidre service marking the start of the fast. Suddenly Keith-Roach saw that a screen had been set up in front of the wall—an ordinary collapsible screen, of the type that people sometimes use in their bedrooms, Duff later wrote, a few wooden frames covered with cloth. The screen was being used to separate male and female worshipers. Duff had noticed it earlier that day but had given it no thought. Keith-Roach remarked that he had never seen it there before. This comment was the opening shot for the tumultuous battles that raged in the following months. Hundreds of people would be killed, leaving absolutely no doubt: the conflict over Palestine was going to lead to war.

Duff suggested after the event that had the district commissioner kept quiet, the day might have passed peacefully. A commission of inquiry set up later heard that the Muslims had known about the screen in advance; they had learned of it by chance, the result of an argument between the wall's Sephardic and Ashkenazic beadles. Whatever the case, Keith-Roach pointed out the screen, and the sheikhs hosting him at the *mahkameh* launched into an emotional protest and demanded that it be removed. Any physical alteration to the site, even the temporary addition of furniture, prompted the Muslims' suspicion that the Jews were trying to find a way to give the wall the status of a synagogue, as a first step in taking it over. Unless the screen was taken down, the sheikhs said, they would not be responsible for what happened. In fact, keeping the peace wasn't their responsibility, but the vague threat was the sheikhs' tactic for getting their way.[1]

Keith-Roach tried to make light of the issue and cheerily promised that he would remove the screen himself. He went down to the wall, together with Duff, where they found the Ashkenazic beadle, Noah Baruch Glasstein, an old man with a noble appearance. Keith-Roach was blunt: the screen had to go because the Arabs demanded it. The beadle asked to leave the screen standing until the end of the prayer service. Then he would find some non-Jewish workers to take it down. Keith-Roach agreed and proceeded to pay what Duff described as a "courtesy visit" to the Hurva Synagogue.

The two men found Attorney General Bentwich among the worshipers, and told him about the screen. Bentwich asked that nothing be done until after the fast was over, but the district commissioner stood his ground and maintained that the Arabs should not be provoked.[2] Duff returned to the wall; the beadle, in tears, promised to take the screen down during the night. The constable went to report to Keith-Roach at his home in the Old City's Christian Quarter. Keith-Roach had guests, and Duff's impression was that the wall was no longer on his mind. He poured Duff a glass of whiskey and told him only to make sure the screen was gone by morning.

From his memoirs, Duff emerges as a violent man, a racist, a misogynist, and a fool, but he seemed to sense that the screen meant trouble. He took out his pad, wrote down an order in the spirit of Keith-Roach's instruction, and had the commissioner sign it. Afterward Duff even went to his office to have the order officially stamped. He then returned to the wall, where the screen was still in place. He warned the beadle that if he found it there at seven A.M. the next day he would destroy it. At six-thirty on Monday morning, Duff went into action. First he called in reinforcements. His men reported immediately, he later wrote, because they knew from experience that when Duff called, there was action. About ten armed policemen assembled; Duff told them to take steel helmets. "We stormed down the narrow alley of David Street," he wrote, as if going into battle. Arab residents urged them on, calling "Death to the Jewish dogs!" and "Strike, strike!" At the wall the police found a small group of old men and women—and the screen. Duff grabbed the beadle by the shoulders and shook him. The old man, alarmed in the extreme, could not get word out; apparently he hated violence in all its forms, Duff noted dryly.

Duff ordered one of his sergeants to destroy the screen. In the meantime, worshipers had gathered; Duff complained of "the smell of overheated and underwashed femininity" that hung in the air. In his description, what ensued seemed like a battle of the sexes: the women screamed hysterically, banged the policemen's heads with parasols, and tried to tear their clothing. He described them as "angry ladies," as if he were at a demonstration of suffragettes. One worshiper, dressed in a black caftan and a broad-brimmed hat trimmed with fur, gripped the screen and shouted in English that he would never let it go, even if they killed him. Duff and his troops dragged the man out of the Dung Gate and threw him into Kidron Valley still gripping the remnants of the screen. The man was unhurt except for a few scratches, Duff wrote.

His superiors were furious, with good reason. Duff had used excessive force without good judgment. The storming of the Western Wall and the violent clash with worshipers on the morning of Yom Kippur caused, not surprisingly, a great deal of tension. Now Duff brought out his written orders, congratulating himself on his foresight. He was not dismissed and was allowed to remain in his position. The Arabs considered him a hero, he wrote, while the Jews marked him as a target. He recorded three attempts to murder him: once they'd tried to drop a boulder on him, once to run him over, and on another occasion they'd shot at him. Luckily, he said, he lived, otherwise he would have been buried in Bishop Gobat's cemetery on Mount Zion. It was a "most unsatisfactory resting place" in his view—one day archaeologists would surely dig there to uncover the walls of Jebusite Jerusalem.[3]

2.

Jews had prayed at the Western Wall since the Middle Ages. They considered the wall, one side of a narrow alley, to be the sole remnant of the Second Temple. It was holy to the Muslims as well, considered part of the Al-Aqsa Mosque, where, according to the Islamic faith, the prophet Muhammad had tied his horse, Al-Buraq, before setting off on his night journey to heaven. For Jews, the wall is the most sacred place in the world for prayer; for Muslims the two mosques on the adjoining Temple Mount are of lesser importance than the holy cities of Mecca and Medina. As part of the Temple Mount, the Western Wall was under control of the Waqf, the Muslim religious trust.

Under the Turks, the Jews were allowed to pray by the wall more or less undisturbed. They longed for the coming of the Messiah, when the Third Temple would be built on the Temple Mount, in place of the two great mosques, but the messianic age did not seem to be close. The Jews of the *chalukkah* days, mostly helpless old people with no interest in claiming ownership of the wall, never posed a real threat. Thus, over the years, a fairly flexible modus vivendi had evolved. Officially, the Jews were subject to a whole series of prohibitions; in practice, a wink and a bribe eased relations with the Waqf, and on special days, especially the High Holidays, the Jews were allowed to blow the ram's horn, or shofar, at the wall and set up an ark and benches. Annie Landau told Colonel Kisch that, to the best of her memory, the Jews had from time to time put up a screen to separate the men from the women.[4]

Keith-Roach knew all this, so he was a little perplexed by the sheikhs' insistence that the screen be removed. The sheikhs, however, connected the screen to the Zionist program and the Balfour Declaration and feared that in the new climate, treating the wall as a synagogue was but a first step in expropriating it from the Muslims. Similarly, the Waqf's leaders had once explained to Ronald Storrs why they refused to let the Jews install chairs at the wall on a permanent basis: first they'll put out chairs, they'd said, then wooden benches, then stone benches. The next thing would be walls and a ceiling to keep out the sun and the cold, and suddenly the Muslims would have a building on their property. This was the Palestine conflict in a nutshell. Ah, what does the world know about the nerves of Jerusalem? Ronald Storrs sighed. The collision of passion and politics lit a dreadful fire—few knew this as well as he did.[5]

The Palestine conflict was more than a struggle for land; it was also a battle for myths, religious faith, national honor, and history. Jews and Arabs fought it out with a primal fervor that led inevitably to violence; on many occasions they failed to distinguish between reality and words and symbols; more than once they preferred to believe in fictions and fantasies.

The battle was never-ending, conducted in every arena. One of its theaters was a committee appointed to reach a consensus on place-names in Palestine—an impossible task, of course. Not only did the Jews and Arabs have different names for the towns in which they coexisted—the Arabs called Jerusalem Al-Quds and Hebron Al-Khalil—but the Jewish committee members also demanded that exclusively Arab areas be given Hebrew names: they wanted Jenin and Tantura to be called Ir Ganim and Doar. The minutes of committee meetings frame these disputes as scholarly, devoid of politics. In truth, these arguments were over sovereignty. The committee was a subcommittee of a colonial body that established the English spelling of geographical names all over the world. One of its British members wrote, "I have now been a member of the Permanent Committee on Geographical Names for nearly fifteen years and I think it is fair to say that Palestine has given the Committee more trouble not only than the rest of the Colonial Empire but than the whole rest of the world together."[6]

The Jews wanted the government to use the country's Hebrew name, Eretz Israel, or "the Land of Israel," but they settled for the strange formulation of Palestine E.I., which appeared on all official documents, including coins and banknotes. One Arab leader, Jamal al-Husseini, petitioned the Supreme Court to eliminate the letters E.I. from the country's stamps, but his suit was rejected. Colonel Kisch suggested getting people to call the fifty-piastre coin by the biblical name of *shekel*. If the expression took hold the authorities would have no choice but to recognize it, he thought. The idea didn't work.[7]

Anthems and flags were also inflammatory issues. The Hebrew press was full of reports of British soldiers, officers, and administrators who did not stand up when the "Hatikva," the Zionist anthem, was played at public events.[8] Miss Landau once sat down demonstratively when the song was played, together with officers of the military administration. "We have known traitors, but not many traitoresses," *Ha'aretz* wrote, comparing Landau to Jacob de Haan.[9] On the other hand, when administration officials did stand up for the Zionist anthem, they could expect a protest from Frances Newton.

Indefatigable Newton, a one-woman lobby, once discovered that the *Encyclopaedia Britannica* included the Zionist flag—two blue stripes on a white background with a blue Star of David—among the flags of the world and defined it as the flag of Palestine. She dashed off a letter of protest; the editor responded that the encyclopedia indeed seemed to have been "somewhat premature"; in the next edition it corrected itself.*

---

*The design of the Zionist flag went through several stages and was not finalized until after World War II; the "Hatikva" also went through a number of versions.[10]

The Zionist movement, for its part, protested to the publisher of an American encyclopedia in which the Nebi Musa riots were attributed to a chain of events that began when a Jew defaced a Muslim flag.[11]

Both Jews and Arabs made great efforts and invested no little money in shaping history to their tastes. The Jewish Agency took it upon itself to fund a book in English, its object being "to put an end to the false concept that the Jewish exile from its land was absolute and that the Arabs found here a land empty of Jews." The author, Ben-Zion Dinaburg (later Dinur), came from Russia; from 1921 on he was an instructor at the teachers college run by David Yellin in Jerusalem. There is probably no one who did more than he to adjust the history of the Jewish people to fit the Zionist argument. He stressed Jewish historical continuity and its uniformity throughout the world, as if there were a single Jewish narrative and a single chronology. He dated the beginning of the exile from Palestine to the seventh or eighth century C.E., far later than other historians and scholars; only then, he argued, when the Arabs occupied Palestine, did the country lose its "Jewish character." Thus Dinur cut the Exile down to little more than a thousand years.[12] The Zionist Organization also initiated research projects designed to prove that many of the Arabs had arrived in Palestine only recently.[13]

The Arabs also went to great lengths to promote their national culture and construct historical arguments aimed at denying the Zionists' claim to the land.[14] They borrowed some of their symbolic initiatives from the Zionist movement, including forestation activities. The Arabs realized the importance of propaganda and urged every citizen to purchase a small Arab national flag to finance the struggle and every Arab child to learn to say, "Down with Herbert Samuel." George Antonius established the Arabic Language Academy.[15]

When the Arabs were permitted to bury Mohammed Ali, the brother of the leader of India's Muslims, in the Al-Aqsa Mosque, the Zionists brought to Jerusalem the furnishings of Theodor Herzl's study in Vienna. They had failed to arrange for Herzl's reburial in Jerusalem. On the other hand, the movement succeeded in purchasing a rocky cliff by the Dead Sea where a small band of Jewish rebels had made a last stand against the Romans—Masada. It cost £3,000.[16]

The Zionists also continued to pursue the possibility of acquiring the Western Wall. In May 1926 Judge Gad Frumkin, who had contacts in the Arab community, was put to work on the matter. He began negotiations with owners of several nearby houses, with the aim of opening a new access road to the wall from David Street. The operation was delicate; as a British-appointed judge, Frumkin was not supposed to be involved in such things. Kisch addressed his letters to the judge as "personal and confidential" and paid him with a personal check for £25, which could be interpreted as expense money, an agent's fee, or a bribe.

At the same time, Kisch managed to persuade the Jewish millionaire Nathan Straus of New York to provide £5,000 to buy a single house in the area. The owner, from the Khalidi family, was prepared to sell. Kisch told Straus that he was privileged to be involved in this national enterprise, and proposed that the deed to the house be made out in Straus's name to provide some cover. Under no circumstances should Judge Frumkin's involvement be revealed, Kisch warned.

Frumkin wrote to Straus directly, relating how Jewish philanthropists, among them Moses Montefiore and Baron Rothschild, had tried to purchase the wall in the previous century but had failed. There was now a historic opportunity, he explained, asking for $100,000 to "secure the goodwill" of the owners of the houses adjacent to the wall. Straus feared he was being misled; the Arabs were demanding "fantastically exaggerated prices," he complained, and there his interest ended. The Western Wall was too expensive for him.[17] He preferred to invest his money in a health center that bore his name. But Kisch would not give up. As a central, national shrine the Western Wall would energize the Zionist movement and strengthen its position vis-à-vis the ultra-Orthodox and world Jewry, as well as the British and the Arabs.

The British were committed to preserving the status quo of the holy places as they found it on their arrival, but they could not decide whether to follow the status quo set by law or by practice. The question produced a prodigious correspondence and a myriad of legal and historical opinions.[18] The Western Wall was only one of such holy places. The authorities were also called in to settle disputes between different Christian sects at the Church of the Holy Sepulchre and at other sites. There was the monk who placed a ladder in someone else's cell, the nun who lit a candle at an hour assigned to another nun, a wall erected without permission, a passage opened without consultation. Every case was extremely sensitive and sometimes led to an altercation.[19]

More than once the authorities had to intervene in conflicts between Jews and Christians, particularly in Jerusalem. Only there would the deputy district commissioner be required to resolve a conflict caused by young Russian immigrants and the bodies of two pious women of the tzar's household. One was the Grand Duchess Elizabeth, Queen Victoria's granddaughter and the tzarina's sister. Her husband, Grand Duke Sergei, had been murdered in 1905, after which his widow had joined a convent and devoted her life to good works. She was murdered during the revolution, together with her servant, also a nun. Their bodies were spirited out of Russia, first to China. After many adventures, they turned up in the Holy City to be buried. Deputy District Commissioner Harry Luke had seen many religious ceremonies in Jerusalem, he wrote, but had never attended one as moving as this. Two simple wooden caskets arrived at Jerusalem's tiny train station, two weeping Russian nuns broke out in a sweet mournful song, and the small Russian fellowship set out slowly in the direction of the Orthodox cemetery on the Mount of Olives.

Suddenly a messenger approached on horseback and reported to the deputy commissioner that a group of Jewish pioneers from Russia with revolutionary fervor still hot in their veins were planning to disrupt the tzarist princess's funeral procession on Jaffa Street. With diplomatic dexterity, Luke redirected the procession to a path running along the southern slope of Mount Zion.[20]

In another incident, the editor of *Do'ar HaYom,* Itamar Ben-Avi, was put on trial for slandering the Christian religion. The story began with an embarrassing item: Hans Herzl, the son of the founder of the Zionist movement, had converted to Christianity. *Do'ar HaYom* commented that, unlike Jesus of Nazareth, Herzl's son was at least not a bastard. The ensuing trial threatened to turn into a Jewish-Christian scandal of international dimensions, but it ended with the imposition of a small fine. When Jewish archaeologist Eliezer Sukenik announced the discovery of an ossuary inscribed with Jesus' name—Yehoshua or Yeshua ben Yosef in Hebrew—Colonel Kisch immediately demanded that he deny the story, to avoid giving the impression that Zionists were challenging the status of Jesus' traditional burial site.[21]

At one point, the Latin patriarch lodged a protest with Ronald Storrs against a production of *The Jewess,* an opera by Fromental Halévy. One of the opera's protagonists is a cardinal, and his portrayal upset the patriarch. Storrs himself was obliged to intrude between the two parties and bring about peace, which he did with great delight. Experienced, intelligent, carefully suppressing his disdain, Storrs suggested turning the cardinal into a judge; the patriarch was pleased. But the compromise set off a debate in the Hebrew press. *Ha'aretz* wrote that whether the cardinal appeared on stage in a red gown with a cross hanging from his neck or in a black robe without a cross was of no significance. The militant *Do'ar HaYom* argued, however, that the governor's intervention had brought a "new inquisition" to Jerusalem.[22]*

On occasion the Jews complained about violations of the status quo at the Western Wall. Hebrew linguist Eliezer Ben-Yehuda noticed, on one of his walks around the Old City, that Arab workers were doing some sort of repair work there. He rushed to inform the Zionist Commission, which sent Ronald Storrs an emotional letter. Storrs called in his engineers, who proposed that instead of the Waqf the government should make the necessary repairs, as part of the work of the antiquities department. Thus Storrs navigated between the official status quo and actual practice. Once he proposed that the Waqf install benches for the Jewish worshipers, so demonstrating its ownership of the wall.[24]†

3.

The incident on Yom Kippur 1928 eventually led to a wave of violence, not only as a result of Keith-Roach's gaffe or Duff's disastrous handling of the affair. The horrifying proportions were rooted in the building tensions in internal Arab and Jewish politics. Political rivals within both camps were competing to demonstrate their patriotism, each side accusing its opponents of being overly submissive on the national issue. Both Arab and Jewish politics made demagogic use of religious symbols; both were easily drawn into extreme positions and lost control of events. Among the Arabs internal politics were driven largely by the ongoing rivalry between the Nashashibis and the Husseinis; among the Jews, the competition was between the followers of Ben-Gurion and of Jabotinsky.

The mufti was accused by his opponents of despotism and corruption. Unlike the Zionist leaders, Husseini could not point to any real progress toward Arab independence, and felt threatened. At one point the mufti's camp split, and some of his followers joined forces with his rivals.[26] He benefited from the screen incident and accused the Zionists of plotting not only to take over the wall but also to destroy the mosques on the Temple Mount and rebuild the Temple. This, he said, was part of a larger plan

---

*Jews made similar objections to a production of *The Merchant of Venice* in Gaza, in which Shylock was portrayed as an offensive and sinister figure and the audience shouted, "Jew, Jew." Several British police officers were present.[23]

†Storrs missed the big conflict over the wall. He had been transferred to Cyprus two years previously. In his diary he wrote, "There is no promotion after Jerusalem." He was considered hostile to Zionism even after he published his memoirs.[25]

to seize control of the country and expel the Arabs. Setting himself up as the chief defender of the Islamic holy places, the mufti was able to reinforce his image as a national leader.

The Zionists had no plans to destroy the mosques, and building the Third Temple was not on their agenda, but they certainly exploited the religious yearnings for a temple, especially in their fund-raising efforts. Zionist publications around the world used images of a magnificent but imaginary domed structure on the Temple Mount to symbolize the national dream. The American consulate in Jerusalem sent Washington a drawing distributed by Arabic propagandists, who had taken it from a Zionist publication in the United States, *Das Yiddishe Folk.* The illustration shows Herzl gazing out over a vast stream of people, all on their way to Jerusalem, which appears as an Arab city, although a Zionist flag waves atop a building looking much like the Dome of the Rock. Zionist propaganda also appropriated as a symbol a Muslim minaret the Turks built on the Old City Wall, which Jews call David's Tower.[27]

The term *national home* made allusions to the Temple, because the Hebrew word for home, *bayit,* is also traditionally used to refer to "the House of God." A few months before the Yom Kippur incident, the Yeshurun Synagogue in Jerusalem held a post-Passover celebration. The main speaker was Menachem Ussishkin, who banged his fist on the table and declared, "The Jewish people wants a Jewish state without compromises and without concessions, from Dan to Be'ersheva, from the great sea to the desert, including Transjordan." At that moment in his speech he looked like a prophet, Chaim Halevi wrote to his parents. Ussishkin concluded by saying, "Let us swear that the Jewish people will not rest and will not remain silent until its national home is built on our Mt. Moriah," referring to the Temple Mount.[28] Avraham Yitzhak Hacohen Kook, the Zionist chief rabbi, had intervened in the screen uproar, strengthening the impression that religious yearnings and the Zionist plan were one and the same.

All this provided a foundation for the popular Arab belief in the Jewish threat. The fear was authentic, and the mufti exploited it. He played with a smoldering fire that suddenly flared into a great conflagration.[29] Zionist politics had a very similar dynamic.

4.

As the head of the Zionist movement, Chaim Weizmann continued to concentrate power and prestige in his own hands, but as the years went by he had to cope with internal opposition on two fronts, one led by David

Ben-Gurion, the other by Ze'ev Jabotinsky. Over time, Jabotinsky's Revisionists had become Weizmann's main opposition.[30] Ben-Gurion worked to consolidate his position as the leader of the Jewish community in Palestine; he thought in organizational terms. Jabotinsky divided his efforts between the larger Zionist world and politics in Palestine; he was more a man of words. Jabotinsky promoted heroism and symbols of independence; as in the past, he frequently complained that the British regime was evading its obligation to assist the Jews and was discriminating in favor of the Arabs. He drew his power from Zionist indignity.

A few days after the screen incident Jabotinsky arrived in Palestine to begin a new career as an insurance agent. He settled in Jerusalem and soon became the editor of *Do'ar HaYom,* replacing Itamar Ben-Avi. He worked on organizing the Revisionist Party, which established a youth movement called Betar, an acronym for the Yosef Trumpeldor Alliance and also the name of the last outpost of the Jewish uprising against the Romans. Betarists wore paramilitary uniforms, and, like the Revisionists and their leader, they claimed to be more patriotic than all the other parties and youth movements.

Summing up the public response to the situation at the wall, Jabotinsky wrote, "Other than ourselves, who have broken away from the majority, everyone has forgotten to be insulted." True, the leftists made very fine speeches, Jabotinsky noted, but it was hard to fool an experienced firebrand like himself: "Behind the elegant words one feels no sense of urgency."[31] Ben-Gurion had stated that the wall should be "redeemed," predicting that this could be done perhaps "in another half a year," but he rejected the emotional phraseology and hysteria he attributed to Ussishkin and Jabotinsky. He recalled publicly that Jabotinsky had opposed sending reinforcements to support the settlers at Tel Hai. He warned against confrontation with the Arabs, urging instead a confrontation with the government.[32] Still, Jabotinsky won this particular round of the patriotism contest; the wall affair was good for him, just as it was good for the mufti.

5.

The screen incident sparked a series of protests on the part of the Arabs, including proclamations, telegrams to the League of Nations, and a one-hour general strike.[33] In the days that followed, Arabs assaulted the wall's beadle. The Zionist Executive in Jerusalem also petitioned the League of Nations and complained to the district commissioner about construction work the Muslims were carrying out nearby. A few days later the beadle was attacked again because he tried to put out chairs. Two of the Arabs involved were sentenced to six months in prison in a lightning trial. The mufti sent a cable of protest to the king of England. Rabbi Kook followed up with a similar telegram.

Throughout October Palestine was without a high commissioner; Plumer had left in July 1928, and his replacement, Sir John Chancellor, was not due to arrive until November. Chancellor was an impressive man; Edward Keith-Roach compared him to "a good-looking Shakespearean actor."[34] He was strikingly handsome in his uniform. Born in Edinburgh, he was fifty-eight years old when he came to Palestine, with a career as an army officer behind him and twenty-five years of colonial service in Mauritius, Trinidad and Tobago, and Southern Rhodesia.

The Zionist Organization prepared a dossier on Chancellor; it attributed to him the belief that the Zionists had unlimited cash. A gracious man, ignorant of the complexities of Palestine, he expressed astonishment that no philanthropist had yet been found to buy the Western Wall. The Zionist delegation that met with him before his departure from London received the impression that he might help purchase it. Chancellor told the Zionists that he felt particularly privileged to assist their great ideal, although he asked that this comment not be made public. He brought many hopes and plans with him, but three years later he admitted sadly that the people of Palestine were no happier than they had been when he came. He'd had no luck—the tranquillity he found upon his arrival turned out to be an illusion. As the mufti wrote, "Although the surface of the waters are now quiet the deep waters are in a very troubled condition. I regret to see the wicked fire of abhorrence is blazing under this layer of ashes."[35]

Once in Jerusalem, the high commissioner frequently met with the mufti; at times they spoke for hours. The two discussed the details of Jewish worship at the wall, whether the Jews should be allowed to blow the shofar, whether there should be lights and a rug, and, if so, a large rug or a small mat. The mufti complained of the noise the Jews made; the high commissioner replied that he could not dictate to anyone how to pray to God or how loudly. Chancellor had the impression that the mufti was a bit scared and was being pushed by young extremists.[36] Husseini had said so himself, the high commissioner noted. He had no control over some of his men. The atmosphere was tense, with more provocative articles, leaflets, and speeches.

In the months that followed the tension swelled. The mufti convened an international conference for the protection of the wall, and four hundred delegates attended. The British government issued a statement defending Douglas Duff's actions. In May 1929 Arab ruffians threw stones at Jewish worshipers at the wall; one of them was hurt. The next day the beadle was beaten yet again. In June Arabs disturbed a Friday night service at the wall, banging on drums and playing flutes, in accordance with an old religious custom, and they continued to do so the next week, despite the district commissioner's demand that they desist.

In July Rabbi Kook protested that the Arabs were demolishing a wall near the Western Wall. More assemblies were held, more protests were issued, more articles were published. At the beginning of August Jewish worshipers were pelted with stones once again. The Zionist Congress, which had convened in Zurich, protested that the authorities were allowing the Muslims to build a new mosque at the site. It was "an absurd dispute," wrote Edwin Samuel.[37]

6.

More than just political manipulation, the fight over the Western Wall created very real turmoil among the Jews. Chaim Shalom Halevi often wrote about the tension in letters he sent to Vilna. Private letters written by a son to his parents, they excel at documenting the force of the Jews' pain and anger, indignity and hatred, more than any statement written for publication. Halevi, now on summer recess from his university studies, was still waiting for his parents and sister to immigrate. He was still working as a clerk at the Hadassah hospital and giving private lessons. He found it very difficult to concentrate on his work. "My brain and my heart," he wrote to his parents, "my mind and my feelings" were preoccupied with the "horrible acts" carried out by District Commissioner Keith-Roach and police officer Douglas Duff. "My heart hurts too much and the wound has not yet healed so it is still impossible for me to evaluate the matter," he wrote; but the incident's significance went, he thought, far beyond the wall itself.[38]

A few weeks before the tension turned into outright violence, Halevi wrote his parents something the public would understand only later: the conflict in Palestine was about the hatred between two nations. "They hate us and they are right, because we hate them too, hate them with a deadly hatred," he said. This was the truth, he insisted, behind the Zionist movement's nice language and goodwill. Realizing the Zionist dream would lead to pushing the Arabs out of the country, Halevi believed that one day "Nothing will be left of them."[39]

Halevi thought he knew best how to deal with Jew haters, and he resented the Zionist establishment's conciliatory response. A few days after the screen incident the Yeshurun Synagogue received police permission to conduct a large procession marking the Sukkot and Simchat Torah holidays, but the Zionist Executive objected. "Kisch fears a demonstration," Halevi wrote. "He believes in working peacefully, by persuasion, by pleading and receives—nothing." The procession was intended to be a religious event, but Kisch was afraid that it would turn into a political provocation. He instructed Yeshurun to cancel the gathering, and it agreed to his request. Kisch, Halevi said to his parents, had also agreed to switch the new ark at the wall with the previous one; the new ark was larger than its predecessor and so violated the status quo. Halevi imagined him groveling and begging to be allowed to keep even the old ark. "And yesterday, the insult happened and the new ark was taken away. . . . Mr. Kisch is a diplomat and has to live in peace with the government, concede to it, concede and concede." For this reason, Halevi believed that the Jews should demonstrate not against Keith-Roach, but against Kisch.[40]*

Halevi imagined the Arabs and the English laughing at the Jews for their weakness, and nothing infuriated him more. Ridicule was much worse, much more painful and disgraceful than the Arabs' hatred, he wrote, quoting the Roman emperor Caligula: "Hate me but fear me." In general Caligula was insane, Halevi thought, but in this case he expressed a profound truth that was vouchsafed only to lunatics. The Jews had lost their dignity: "Up until now I could meet an Englishman or an Arab and look him straight in the eye—we were worthy opponents. He hated me and I him and we fought each other. Now that's not the case. I would blush on meeting a non-Jew. He has seen us at our worst, in our weakness, and I no longer see hatred in his eyes. This little puppy, the Jewish Yishuv, knows only how to squirm and bark loudly; he cannot arouse hatred. He is not worth hating." For Halevi, the events at the wall were "the most horrible defeat of our Zionist government."

Halevi comforted himself with dreams of revenge. "History knows no mercy," he wrote. "It does not understand politics and diplomacy. It will avenge this nation whom they—the top men—humiliated and scorned. It will avenge the people who became pawns in their hands." His parents

---

*Ironically, Kisch himself expressed similar sentiments. When the Jewish high commissioner, Herbert Samuel, would greet the mufti without the latter bothering to get off his horse, Kisch wrote, "my blood used to boil."[41]

apparently had a difficult time identifying with the force of emotion that Halevi conveyed. "That is the distance from the Exile to the Land of Israel," he wrote, but unfortunately even some of the country's residents had lost their "free spirit" and "proud gaze." He was referring to, among others, Chaim Kalvarisky, who was running around trying to mitigate the tensions with the Arabs. "This worm," Halevi wrote, "this detestable provocateur walks through the streets of Jerusalem and no one goes up to him in Jaffa Street to give him a slap on the face that will make his ears ring. No one! So what can we say? Are we a nation, a living nation? No! We are not! We are a dead carcass, decomposing, rotting, stinking, a carcass with which everyone does as they wish." These were harsh words, and Halevi knew it. "My hair stood on end and a shiver ran through me when I wrote this, but the things I see around me are so horrible, so terrible and frightening, that I cannot hold back the anger, so close am I to despair."[42]

In this mental state Halevi joined the Committee for the Western Wall established by his beloved teacher Joseph Klausner. He thus became a rebel, as Klausner planned to use his disciples without regard for the Zionist Executive's policy.[43] Halevi's decision to join was not easily made. He told his parents that he had given it much thought. "Yes!" he decided in the end. "We should rebel against the Zionist Executive and the National Council, we should come out against them and defy their order to hold back. We should shout and make the earth shake. Blessed be the ones whose blood still throbs and boils, who raise their voices against their leaders and say, Make way, because, in its thousands and tens of thousands, the nation is going to redeem the wall, which you sold in your apathy and abandoned in your politics!"

The events of the summer reached a climax on August 14, 1929, on the eve of the Ninth of Av, the fast day marking the destruction of the Temple. The Committee for the Western Wall debated what to do. Halevi reported "fear, abjectness, and servility" among the committee's members, but after much argument his position and that of his friends triumphed. "There will be action," he wrote. "I cannot do otherwise," he explained, inspired by a verse from the Psalms: "It is time for thee, Lord, to work, for they have made void thy law."[44]

7.

That night thousands congregated at the wall. Halevi was an usher. The mood was very angry, he told his parents, but order was kept and the police did not intervene. Joseph Klausner went home; Halevi remained at the wall until after midnight. The next day, the fast day itself, Halevi went to Klausner's house to report on the situation. Later several hundred young people demonstrated at the wall.[45] Most of the protesters belonged in one way or another to the Battalion for the Defense of the Language; some were probably also from Betar. A few had come from Tel Aviv. The police allowed the demonstration to proceed, but the protesters then violated the conditions of their permit: they made political speeches, waved the Zionist flag, and sang the "Hatikva."[46]

The Muslims responded two days later with a counterdemonstration, which they held on the prophet Muhammad's birthday. At the end of the Friday services in the mosques, a number of worshipers left the Temple Mount and broke into the wall area, beating Jews and defacing Torah scrolls. In the evening they held a torchlight procession. The next day they attacked the wall once again and interfered with the worshipers. Chaim Shalom Halevi organized several dozen young people to defend the people praying. "The situation in the city has gotten out of hand," he wrote. "Every day there are attacks and stabbings."[47]

In this atmosphere a small incident was enough to set off a conflagration. Avraham Mizrahi, seventeen years old, seems to have been murdered because the soccer ball he was playing with, not far from the Arab village of Lifta, rolled into an Arab family's tomato patch. A girl grabbed the ball and hid it among her clothing. When Mizrahi and his friends tried to get it back, the girl started screaming. Within minutes a fight developed. Someone hit Mizrahi on the head with an iron rod and shattered his skull. That same evening another fight broke out, and an Arab pedestrian was injured. "It was most desirable for the maintenance of the status quo that they should both die," the high commissioner's aide-de-camp wrote in his diary.[48] Mizrahi died of his wounds; the Arab recovered.

The police imposed a series of restrictions on Mizrahi's funeral, but it nevertheless turned into a demonstration. The police used force to quell the protesters—Douglas Duff again. When he returned from the funeral, Halevi wrote to his parents, "Even though our Jews are a bit to blame, the police were immeasurably cruel and a shiver runs through me when I recall the scene of savagery and beatings that I saw four hours ago."[49]

High Commissioner Chancellor and some top figures in the British administration, as well as a few Jewish leaders, were out of the country at the time—to escape the summer heat, they had gone off on vacations or to the Zionist Congress in balmy Zurich. Kisch quickly flew to London to warn the Colonial Office. Sir John Shuckburgh, assistant undersecretary of state, cut his vacation short and returned to London to handle the crisis; he sent a firm telegram to Jerusalem. Filling in for the high commissioner was Harry Luke. The problems he faced were not new, wrote Edwin Samuel, his secretary. "If military reinforcements are called for in time, trouble often does not break out and the man who called for them gets a reputation for being 'windy.' If, on the other hand, as in Luke's case, he does not call for them until too late, he is blamed for the subsequent disorders."[50]

8.

Sir Harry Charles Luke was then forty-five years old. Born in London, he had studied at Eton and Oxford. His career in the Colonial Service had taken him from Sierra Leone to Barbados and Cyprus. From Palestine he would go to Malta, topping off his service as governor of Fiji. In 1921 he had sat on the commission of inquiry looking into the events in Jaffa and had participated in its dubious report. Thoroughly English and colonial, he tried to conceal his origins, but everyone gossiped about them: his father was a Hungarian-born American Jew named Lukach, they said erroneously. Ben-Gurion described Luke as a coward.[51]*

With hindsight, Luke tended to attribute the British failure in Palestine to the Balfour Declaration, as if it were an original sin, but he believed that like a Greek tragedy, the war for the country was predestined. There was no point in the dialogue between Jews and Arabs that he initiated in the summer of 1929, but at least Luke could tell himself, as everyone else did, that he had done his best. He invited the mufti for lunch and urged him to maintain the peace. Afterward he also spoke with Chief Rabbi Kook.

He went to great lengths to organize a kind of cease-fire; according to his diary, the initiative came from the Jews. He managed to bring together the three men who represented the Zionist Organization in Kisch's absence and several senior Muslims. Yitzhak Ben-Zvi was the most prominent Jewish political figure; the ranking Muslim representative was Jamal al-Husseini, a close associate of the mufti. They went to Luke's home on

---

*Luke left behind a fine diary; like many men in colonial service, who tended to be members of the upper class and graduates of Oxford, he could appreciate a good conversation. In March 1929 he hosted the author Rudyard Kipling in Jerusalem; Kipling was then primarily interested in military cemeteries. In May that year Luke hosted Chaim Weizmann and recorded an "admission" from him: the driving force behind the Bolshevik revolution had been and still was Russian Jewry. Apparently Weizmann had not tired of disseminating the legend of Jewish power in the world.[52]

Thursday afternoon, August 22, 1929, the day after Avraham Mizrahi's turbulent funeral.

Luke served tea and suggested that he absent himself, but the men insisted he remain. Somewhat ceremoniously, he expressed his pleasure in convening the meeting, and said that he would like it to end with an agreement on a soothing announcement to be issued in advance of the Muslim prayer services on Friday, the next day. Then he left for his office and told the group to telephone him when they had reached an agreement.

On the face of it, the meeting was merely a conversation between community leaders, but it was conducted like any diplomatic conference of representatives of two national movements, a summit conference in a sandbox. First, the Arabs and the Jews blamed each other for the situation—an established rite in most talks between the two groups; they always began with an exchange of historical accusations. Then they got down to a practical discussion. In principle, everyone agreed to issue the announcement Luke had requested. The draft submitted by the Arabs said that the Jews recognized Islam's right to Al-Buraq, as they called the wall, and the Muslims recognized the right of the Jews to visit the site, in keeping with the status quo that had preceded the recent tension.

But the Jews objected that the term Al-Buraq was not sufficiently clear. Did it mean just the wall itself or also the area in front of it? And besides, they said, they were not authorized by the Jewish people to sign a historical agreement regarding the status of the wall. They had come only to arrange a kind of cease-fire. They wanted a general declaration that would attribute the events to an unfortunate misunderstanding and call for peace. An argument ensued.

Toward evening the men called Luke and notified him that an agreement had been reached. He came home and found there was no agreement. They all continued to talk until 9:30 P.M. and achieved nothing. Luke pressured them to at least announce that they had met; he thought that such a statement would be sufficient to calm tempers on Friday. According to Luke's diary entry, the Jews agreed but the Arabs refused. They set another meeting for the following Monday. Luke called Amman and asked for reinforcements to be at the ready.[53] Had the Arab and Jewish leaders published a call for restraint that night they could, perhaps, have prevented the bloodbath that began just a few hours later. Perhaps not. Luke deserves to be remembered as the first peacemaker in the history of the Israeli-Palestinian conflict.

The previous day, Chaim Halevi had told his parents that they were not coming to a land of peace. "We must conquer the land," he wrote, "and every conquest requires sacrifices, so anyone who comes to participate in the conquest needs to be prepared to make sacrifices."[54] In Hebron all was quiet that night; three weeks earlier the local police force had received a new chief.

14

—•·•—

Hebron, 1929

1.

In the early-morning hours of Friday, August 23, 1929, thousands of Arab villagers began streaming into Jerusalem from the surrounding villages. They had come to pray at the Temple Mount; many were armed with sticks and knives, and the city was filled with a sense of tension and violence. Harry Luke, as acting high commissioner, requested reinforcements from Amman. Toward 9:30 the Jewish merchants began closing their stores. About an hour and a quarter later, the mufti promised the Jerusalem police commander that the worshipers were carrying sticks and knives only out of fear that the Jews might try to create some sort of provocation. When one of the preachers made a nationalist speech calling on the Islamic faithful to fight against the Jews to the last drop of their blood, mufti al-Husseini urged his community to keep the peace.[1]

At roughly 11:00 A.M., twenty or thirty gunshots were heard on the Temple Mount, apparently intended to work up the crowd. Several hundred worshipers swarmed through the alleys of the marketplace and began attacking Jewish pedestrians. Edwin Samuel, Luke's secretary, was in his office, not far from the Nablus Gate. The sound of the mob was indistinct and seemed to come from far away; Samuel at first thought he was hearing the buzz of a swarm of bees.[2] A crowd had gathered beneath his window. Luke quickly got the mutfi on the phone and demanded that he take control of his people. The mufti came to talk to the mob, but

Luke's impression was that the religious leader's presence was not calming people down—in fact, it seemed to be having precisely the opposite effect. Later, the mufti explained that by the time he'd arrived, the crowd had been joined by Arabs injured by Jews, which made keeping the peace very difficult. Edwin Samuel remembered the flash of the rioters' daggers glinting in the noonday sun.[3]

At midday, Edward Keith-Roach was on a tour of the Old City. Near the Jaffa Gate, he saw a Jew running for his life, followed by a crowd of Arab thugs waving sticks. Yitzhak Ben-Zvi also saw a man fleeing from a gang—he may have been the same one. Ben-Zvi had been sitting in the Zionist Executive office on Jaffa Street. At first he was told that the worshipers were dispersing quietly; then he heard there were problems. He rushed to the Jaffa Gate, where he met the man, bloody and injured. Before being rushed to the hospital, the man managed to tell Ben-Zvi that he had been sitting in the doorway of his son's shop when the first of the worshipers came down from the Temple Mount and pounced on him.[4]

While this was taking place, the tensions had reached the Jewish Mea She'arim neighborhood, and two or three Arabs were murdered there. A report from the American consulate, which documented the events in nearly minute-by-minute detail, determined that the killings occurred between 12:00 and 12:30. Afterward there was much controversy over whether the day's first victims had been Jews or Arabs.[5]

Violence spread quickly throughout most of the city and into its suburbs. "Shots could be heard from both sides of the house," wrote Shmuel Yosef Agnon, a resident of Talpiot. In all the noise he heard a voice calling, "*hawajah*," "sir" in Arabic, and realized the Arabs were close. He later recalled, "The shooting grew louder. I rubbed my ears; I wondered whether my sense of hearing had been impaired. Suddenly came the alarming awareness that we were all alone in Talpiot, there was no one to defend us . . . there was no answer to the Arabs' gunfire from the English side. The English had deceived us."[6]

The police were, for all intents and purposes, helpless. The force had only 1,500 men in the entire country; the great majority were Arab, with a small number of Jews and some 175 British officers.[7] Since the general situation had shortly before been judged peaceful, a larger police force was deemed unnecessary; in fact, as later noted by an aide-de-camp to High Commissioner Chancellor, the country's internal security was maintained largely through the force of Lord Plumer's personality. The Arabs in the force were reluctant to act for another reason: they were afraid of killing rioting Arabs and then becoming the target of vendettas by the victims' families. While waiting for the reinforcements Luke had requested, many administration officials were required to attach themselves to the police force, even though they were not trained; the Jews among them were called up but then sent back to their offices.[8] At some point, several English theology students from Oxford who happened to be in the city were deputized. Until extra troops arrived, Luke had the city's telephone lines disconnected and declared a curfew.

While only Jews were being attacked, the British police held back from the mob. The same aide-de-camp to Chancellor later judged this was a wise decision. Had they shot into the Arab crowd, he reasoned, the Arabs would have turned their anger on the police, and the British force would have faced the mob defenseless. The police were very tired the first day of the riots, having slept little the previous night.[9]

In the Yemin Moshe neighborhood some residents greeted the Arabs with gunfire, although most of Jerusalem's Jews did not defend themselves. The Haganah defense organization, set up in the aftermath of the Jaffa riots, was still only a loose confederation of local cells, not all of which obeyed the central command; it had no real ability to take action. In Jerusalem's Rehavia quarter, the Haganah met in Ben-Zvi's backyard. Margery Bentwich, the attorney general's sister, lived not far away; she described a parade conducted by a few youngsters in the neighborhood's streets. They carried sticks and looked to her like the rabble in some Shakespearean play. At the outbreak of violence, Yitzhak Ben-Zvi demanded that weapons be distributed to the Jews but was turned down. In the days to follow he repeated the demand and was again refused.[10]

2.

When Superintendent Raymond Cafferata received an order to leave Jaffa and assume command of the police force in Hebron and the surrounding area, he considered the post a challenge. "Divisional work especially in an area like this is awfully interesting and full of experience and incident," he wrote to his mother. He had about forty villages under his control, he said, and "some of them are dashed bad ones and there is always tons of crime." Bandits would cross the border from Transjordan to attack camel caravans; every other man was armed to the teeth, Cafferata remarked. The environment stimulated his love of adventure.[11] There were about 20,000 people living in Hebron then, mostly Muslim Arabs, with a few hundred Jews—800 according to the Jewish Agency; Cafferata put the number at 600.

Cafferata came from a good home—his father was a Liverpool solicitor—but he had been lax in his studies. In an unpublished memoir, most of which was burned, Cafferata wrote that he was frequently beaten by his teachers; once or twice he was expelled. Apparently, he excelled at soccer, a talent noted many years later by his commanders in his personal file. At the age of seventeen he began working as a railroad clerk and hated every minute of it. Then, he wrote, fate smiled upon him and World War I broke out. Like many young men, he lied about his age, claiming to be twenty-one, and enlisted in the army. He took part in the battle of Flanders; his commander described him as an excellent officer—energetic, efficient, bold, and capable, winning the confidence of his fellow officers and men. The king of Belgium decorated him. After the war Cafferata joined the Royal Irish Constabulary and took part in suppressing the riots in Ireland. From 1921 on he served in the Palestinian police. When he was transferred to Hebron in early August 1929, he was thirty-two years old and a bachelor. His friends called him "Caff."

The transfer had happened very quickly: Cafferata's predecessor had to return home suddenly, leaving barely enough time for Cafferata to pack his personal belongings. There was another problem as well: he had just met the love of his life. "It is a bit hard having to leave," Cafferata told his mother. Peggy Ford-Dunn was visiting Palestine, and the two had met at the Jaffa hockey club. He felt lonely in Hebron—there were no British people in the town except for two elderly missionaries. He spent his first days getting organized, renting the house that had served his predecessor. He had to pay the rent in advance, which also came as an unpleasant surprise, but at least the house was furnished; except for linens, it had everything. The house was large, and Cafferata felt a little odd living there alone after so many years of army camps. He also had to buy an automobile. A five-horsepower Citroën cost him fifty-five Palestinian pounds; it was more economical than American cars, he remarked. He hoped the bad roads in the area would not wreck it.[12]

His many preoccupations may explain why Cafferata did not have more time to devote to Hebron's problems. He would later tell a commission of inquiry that he had managed to meet only a few local Arab leaders, and had not yet become closely acquainted with the small Jewish community. When news of the escalating tensions in Jerusalem reached

Hebron, Cafferata sent plainclothes men into the streets to find out what was going on; the Hebron police had no intelligence network. He himself visited some nearby villages and met with the mukhtars to get a sense of which way the wind was blowing. His impression was that the Arabs in the region had no serious grievances. The harvest was good; with the exception of some minor brawls here and there, everything was fine, they told him. They did not mention the Jews.

Cafferata spoke to the city's Jews as well. He learned that they had been living in Hebron for generations, that they knew their Arab neighbors well and regarded many of them as friends. In fact, the Sephardic community had been living in Hebron for eight hundred years, the Ashkenazim for perhaps one hundred. Some were connected to the Slobodka Yeshiva; others engaged in trade, crafts, and the dairy business or made their living as moneylenders. The Zionist Anglo-Palestine Bank had a branch in the city. A few dozen Jews lived deep within Hebron, in a kind of ghetto where there were also several synagogues. But the majority lived on the outskirts, along the roads to Be'ersheba and Jerusalem, renting homes owned by Arabs, a number of which had been built for the express purpose of housing Jewish tenants. The rent they paid was a significant component of the town's economy, and relations between the landlords and their tenants were generally good.

After the British conquest, as Jewish immigration increased and the Zionist program progressed, and as the Arab national movement developed, tensions arose in Hebron as well. Arabs harassed Jews on a daily basis, cursing them on the streets and even on occasion waylaying and beating them. On the face of it, the incidents were mostly minor, boys throwing stones at Jewish houses and breaking windows, or a few young Arabs disturbing Jewish prayers at the Cave of Makhpela, Abraham's burial site. But by 1923 the local Jewish committee believed the episodes were political in nature and attributed them to the Muslim-Christian Association, which, the Jews claimed, was spreading hatred. The association was teaching the Arabs unpleasant songs about Jews and inciting them against their neighbors. The Jews had made several complaints that the Hebron police force was not doing enough to protect them.[13]

The force under Cafferata's command was quite limited: there were eighteen constables on horseback and fifteen on foot. Of these, eleven were elderly and in bad physical condition; only one was Jewish. Cafferata had consulted with Abdallah Kardous, who was acting district commissioner, and with the deputy commander of the Gaza police, who visited him a few days before the violence broke out in Jerusalem. Both assured him there was no cause for concern; regardless of events elsewhere, Hebron would remain quiet. Being new in the city, he had no reason to doubt these assessments, and, indeed, all was peaceful in Hebron—until the early afternoon of Friday, August 23.[14]

At 2:45 Cafferata reported nothing unusual, but having heard of the trouble in Jerusalem, he decided at 3:00 to station three of his men at the outskirts of the town; their task was to search for weapons in the cars coming back from prayers in Jerusalem. The passengers who stopped spoke of what was going on there, and the rumor that Jews were killing Arabs spread quickly. People soon began gathering at the municipal bus station, intending to travel to Jerusalem. One man, Sheikh Talib Markha, made a speech. Cafferata went to the station to persuade the crowd that the rumors were baseless; as he approached, Sheikh Markha fell silent. Everything was quiet in Jerusalem, Cafferata lied, estimating the crowd at around seven hundred. He sent some men to patrol the Jewish houses and went along as well, taking eight mounted policemen with him. Cafferata noted that many Jews were standing on their roofs or balconies. He ordered them into their homes, but they ignored him.

Near the small hotel run by the Schneurson family Cafferata encountered Rabbi Ya'akov-Yosef Slonim and his daughter. By one account they were on their way to Cafferata's house. Cafferata's own impression was that they were running back and forth in the street shrieking for no apparent reason. Slonim harangued Cafferata and demanded protection, interrupting himself to trade shouts with the crowd. This drew showers of stones. A Jewish woman screamed at Cafferata from her balcony. In the meantime he managed to persuade Slonim to go back into his house. The exchange between the two men was later the subject of much debate; the principal charge was that Cafferata had spoken rudely. No one disputed that he had done everything to ensure that the Jews remained in their homes.

After getting the rabbi and his daughter off his hands, Cafferata turned his attentions back to the crowd. On horseback, he and his men, using only their clubs, tried to disperse the people. At around 4:00 Arabs began gathering at the Hebron yeshiva and hurling stones. The only people inside the yeshiva were the sexton and a student, Shmuel Halevi Rosenholz, twenty-four years old, born in Poland. Hit by a stone that came in through one of the windows, he attempted to leave the building and found himself facing a group of Arabs. He tried to retreat back into the yeshiva, but it was too late: the Arabs grabbed him and stabbed him to death. The sexton managed to hide in a well and escaped. The Jews prepared to bury Rosenholz immediately, before the onset of the Jewish Sabbath. Cafferata feared that the funeral would inflame the rioters, so he ordered the attendance limited to six people.

Cafferata then proposed to Abdallah Kardous that he summon all the mukhtars in the area and assign them responsibility for preserving the peace. The Arab officer objected; he believed that passing the burden to the Arab leaders would only ignite more violence. By 6:30 Hebron was quiet again. Cafferata nevertheless asked for reinforcements from Jerusalem; he was told that none were available. He tried his colleagues in Gaza and Jaffa, who promised to help.[15] Some two and a half hours later several mukhtars from the region visited Cafferata. They had heard that Jews were slaughtering Arabs in Jerusalem; apparently the mufti was demanding they take action and threatened to fine them if they refused. Cafferata promised that everything was now peaceful and instructed them to go home and stay there.

Indeed, Jerusalem had calmed down by that time. The day's dead amounted to eight Jews and five Arabs. Fifteen Jews and nine Arabs had been injured. During the night the residents of Talpiot were evacuated, after having spent four hours entirely unprotected. One of them was the Hebrew University's Joseph Klausner. His neighbor, Agnon, later remembered that while they were crouching, bullets flying around them, Klausner said with great pathos that he would choose to remain in Talpiot except that his wife was ill. But they were soon rescued and sent to join refugees evacuated from other neighborhoods. Before leaving his house, Agnon hastily packed several manuscripts into a leather briefcase, but in the crush and panic he lost them. "It had already occurred to me that I should leave my writings and trust them to God's mercies, as all these distraught people could not stand and wait for me," he wrote. But then a neighbor lit a candle, and they found the manuscripts.[16]

The Jews from Talpiot were brought to a community building on HaHabashim Street. Rehavia's residents spent the night in Ratisbonne Monastery. According to Margery Bentwich, the wretched events of the day were all because of the wall. "This business of the wall, how pitiful it is indeed. Is it a symbol of former glory? Much more of present humiliation. To see a man fling himself on the stones, kiss them, isn't it revolting? Like praying to an idol—as if a stone had ears. The best thing that could happen . . . were to raze it to the ground. . . . Strange that such a great number of people can die for an untrue idea and so few can live for a true one." Raymond Cafferata slept in his office that night.[17]

3.

On Saturday, August 24, 1929, at around 7:00 A.M., the Sabbath morning-prayer service was about to begin at the home of Eliezer Dan in Hebron. Dan was Rabbi Slonim's son. The previous night, a few dozen Jews had huddled there, too afraid to stay in their own homes. Among those present at the morning service was Y. L. Grodzinsky, a tourist from Poland who had arrived in Hebron on the Thursday before. The prayers had just begun when Grodzinsky looked out the window and saw several cars packed with Arabs bearing sticks, swords, knives, and daggers driving in the direction of Jerusalem. As the vehicles passed the house, the Arabs spied the Jews and drew their fingers across their throats to signify slaughter.

A short time later Sheikh Markha walked past the Schneurson hotel. Schneurson invited him inside and served him a glass of tea. According to the hotel owner's son, Markha said there was no reason for concern. Nothing would happen. They could leave the hotel door open. The sheikh himself testified that Schneurson had even escorted him to the door, arm in arm. They were friends, the sheikh said. The previous day he had chased away several Arab boys who were trying to harm Jews.[18]

Masses of Arabs from the surrounding villages had in the meantime begun to stream into Jerusalem. At the Dan house, an argument ensued. Though he was a tourist, Grodzinsky was angry at the police order to remain indoors. If the police could not protect the Jews outside, they would not be able to protect them inside either, he said, and proposed that the group go to Cafferata immediately. Some of the men then went out to look for the police commissioner, but on the way they encountered a hail of stones. One of the Jews claimed that when they reached Cafferata he sent them away; they were forbidden to leave their homes, he repeated over and over again. Cafferata himself denied that he had seen them that morning, and Grodzinsky backed him up: after going halfway, the delegation returned to Dan's house.

Cafferata had, however, also observed the convoy of armed Arabs setting out for Jerusalem. Being short of policemen, he did not try to stop them—in fact, he was pleased they were leaving the city. At around 8:30, Arabs began throwing rocks at Jewish homes. The police chief together with all eighteen mounted policemen tried to chase away the rioters. At this stage, they were still not armed with rifles. Then he noticed several Arabs attempting to break into an isolated Jewish house, the Heichal home. Two young Jews emerged from the house, and Cafferata and his men tried to protect them with their horses, but one of the young men was hit by a stone and the second was stabbed, right by Cafferata's horse. Both died. Next the rioters attacked Cafferata himself; he fell off his horse but was not hurt. He went to fetch another horse and a rifle and took the opportunity to call again for reinforcements from Jerusalem.

As prayers continued at the Dan house, Grodzinsky noticed a group of attackers approaching. "Here come the Arabs," he said, and the worshipers halted the service. "We went to reinforce the door and ran around the room like madmen," Grodzinsky recalled. "The shrieks of the women and the babies' wailing filled the house. With ten other people I put boxes and tables in front of the door, but the intruders broke it with hatchets and were about to force their way in. So we left the door and began running from room to room, but wherever we went we were hit by a torrent of stones. The situation was horrible. I can't describe the wailing and screaming.

"In one room my mother was standing by the window shouting for help. I looked out and saw a wild Arab mob laughing and throwing stones. I was afraid my mother would be hit, so I don't know how, but I grabbed her and shoved her behind a bookcase in the corner. I hid another young woman there, as well as a twelve-year-old boy and a yeshiva student. Finally I went behind the bookcase myself.

"Suffocating, we sat on top of one another and heard the sound of the Arabs singing as they broke into the room, and the shouting and groaning of the people being beaten. After about ten minutes the house grew still except for some stifled groans. Then there was loud gunfire, apparently from the police."

Outside, Cafferata found himself facing a huge throng attacking Jewish homes. He ordered his men to shoot directly at the mob and began firing himself. One man was hit, but Cafferata continued to shoot because he saw no one fall; another two or three Arabs were hit, and the crowd began to disperse. Cafferata galloped to Jews Street, where he had stationed some of his men to keep the rioters at bay. In spite of the police presence, the mob was running amok. Cafferata shot again and knocked down two Arabs, his report stated. People tried to escape through the marketplace, and in their flight looted both Arab and Jewish stores.

A scream came from one of the houses. Cafferata entered the house and later described what he saw: "an Arab in the act of cutting off a child's head with a sword. He had already hit him and was having another cut but on seeing me he tried to aim the stroke at me but missed; he was practically on the muzzle of my rifle. I shot him low in the groin. Behind him was a Jewish woman smothered in blood with a man I recognized as a police constable, named Issa Sherrif from Jaffa. . . . He was standing over the woman with a dagger in his hand. He saw me and bolted into another room, shouting in Arabic, 'Your honor, I am a policeman.' I got into the room and shot him."

Grodzinsky: "I barely managed to get out of my hiding place. It was difficult to move the bookcase because of the bodies that lay piled up against it. My eyes were dark from the sight of the dead and the wounded. I was overcome with terror and trembling. I could find no place to put my foot. In the sea of blood I saw Eliezer Dan and his wife, my friend Dubnikov, a teacher from Tel Aviv, and many more. . . . Almost all had knife and hatchet wounds in their heads. Some had broken ribs. A few bodies had been slashed and their entrails had come out. I cannot describe the look in the eyes of the dying. I saw the same scene everywhere. In one room I recognized my brother's wife, who lay there half-naked, barely alive. The entire house had been looted, it was full of feathers and there were bloodstains on the walls. . . .

"I approached the window and saw policemen. I asked them to send a doctor. That same moment some Arabs passed by carrying a dead man on a stretcher. When they saw me they set down the stretcher and threatened me with their fists. I returned to my hiding place. A moment later I heard voices. They were the voices of the wounded who had gotten up and also of people who had been miraculously saved by hiding in the shower room behind the toilet. Apparently the Arabs had gotten as far as the toilet and killed one of the people there.

"I recognized my brother among the injured. He had a hatchet wound on his head and a large bruise on his forehead, probably from a rock. I threw water on him and he stood up, but died of his wounds a few hours later. Dubnikov had apparently died of suffocation. His murdered wife lay next to him. I again approached the window and asked for doctors, because many people could have been saved with prompt medical help. One of the policemen outside answered me in Hebrew—soon, he said. About a quarter of an hour later some cars came to take us to the police. We began taking care of the wounded."[19]

In a letter to the high commissioner, the Jews of Hebron described other atrocities: sixty-eight-year-old Rabbi Meir Kastel and seventy-year-old Rabbi Zvi Drabkin, along with five young men, had been castrated. Baker Noah Imerman had been burned to death with a kerosene stove. The mob had killed pharmacist Ben-Zion Gershon, a cripple who had served Jews and Arabs for forty years; they had raped and killed his daughter as well. Yitzhak Abujzhdid and Dovnikov had been strangled with a rope. Yitzhak Abu Hannah, seventy years old, had been tied to a door and tortured until he died. Two-year-old Menachem Segal had had his head torn off. The letter detailed other acts of rape and torture. There are photographs of hands and fingers that had been cut off, perhaps for their rings and bracelets. Houses, stores, and synagogues had been looted and burned. Some people had survived only because they had lain under bodies and pretended to be dead. Toward 10:30 A.M. the riot ended and the Arab villagers returned to their homes.

Sixty-seven Jews had been killed. Most were Ashkenazic men, but there were also a dozen women and three children under the age of five among the dead. Seven of the victims were yeshiva students from the United States and Canada. Dozens of people had been wounded, about half of them women, and quite a few children, including a one-year-old boy whose parents had both been murdered. The American consulate reported that nine Arabs had been killed.[20] The Hebron Jews were buried in mass graves; the survivors, including the wounded, were taken to Jerusalem.

While the atrocities were taking place in Hebron, several Arabs from the village of Kolonia attacked the Maklef family in their home in Motza, a Jewish village just outside Jerusalem. They murdered the father, mother, and their son and two daughters, as well as two guests staying in the house. After the murders they looted the house and set it on fire. Only one son, Mordechai, was saved; years later he became chief of staff of the Israeli army. "A dreadful week has passed," Chaim Shalom Halevi wrote to his parents. He found it hard to return to his daily routine, and could not understand how other people managed to do so. He felt that life would never be the same again.[21]

4.

David Ben-Gurion compared the massacre in Hebron to the Kishinev pogrom, and he would later use the Nazi expression *Judenrein* to describe Hebron after the Jews left. "The pogrom was committed by Hebron's

Arab masses," wrote Rehavam Ze'evi, who edited a book on the event. "All the Arabs of Hebron did this," he noted, "[w]ith the exception of individuals who provided shelter for their Jewish neighbors." He added the Hebron massacre to the historic roster of anti-Jewish persecutions. "Pogroms, slaughters, and massacres have been part of our nation's history in their Diaspora and now this horrifying spectacle has been repeated in the Land of Israel," he wrote.[22] But he was wrong.

The murder of Jews in Hebron was not a pogrom in the historic sense. Unlike attacks on the Jews of Eastern Europe, the authorities did not initiate the Hebron riots, and the police did not simply stand aside. Raymond Cafferata did his best, but the Hebron police force was just too weak to be effective. Thirty years later David Ben-Gurion wrote, "What can a lone British officer do in a city like Hebron?" He could have been writing about British rule in Palestine as a whole. The British could do very little.

The riots struck at the professional honor of the men responsible for law and order in the country and also violated their sense of fairness. Eric Mills, assistant chief administrative secretary, said that one of the bitterest moments of his life was when he, an Englishman, saw what had happened under the British flag. At the same time, the police forces' actions to save the Jews did not necessarily reflect sympathy for the Zionist enterprise. Cafferata wrote to his mother that he would not be surprised if there was another outbreak of violence and Palestine became a "repetition of the Irish show," unless the government accepted some of the Arab demands. He believed the Arabs would not be satisfied with anything less than a revocation of the Balfour Declaration, and he criticized the government for refusing to do this.[23]

The attack on the Jews of Hebron was born of fear and hatred. The Muslims believed the Jews intended to violate the sanctity of Islam, and that the Zionists wanted to dispossess them of their country. According to the American consulate, the Jews were also murdered for economic reasons, as merchants and as moneylenders.[24] The Arabs hated them as foreigners—most had come from Europe and America. And a few probably attacked Jews out of some appetite for murder, without any clearly defined reason. Many of the rioters were not from Hebron but from the surrounding villages.

Most of Hebron's Jews were saved because Arabs hid them in their homes. The community confirmed this, writing, "Had it not been for a few Arab families not a Jewish soul would have remained in Hebron." The Zionist Archives preserves lists of Hebron Jews who were saved by Arabs;

one list contains 435 names. Over two-thirds of the community, then, found refuge in twenty-eight Arab homes, some of which took in dozens of Jews. "Arabs were hurt defending their neighbors," one Jew testified afterward. Dr. Abdal Aal, an Egyptian doctor, received a letter of gratitude from Colonel Kisch for the assistance he rendered the Jews of Hebron; in addition to the care he gave the wounded, he himself protected an entire family.[25]*

Some of the saviors may have expected a reward in exchange for their help. Still, most saved the Jews out of human decency, putting themselves at risk, acting in the tradition of hospitality that had induced Khalil al-Sakakini to open his home to Alter Levine so many years earlier. In any case, Jewish history records very few cases of a mass rescue of this dimension.

In Jerusalem, the violence continued. Shmuel Yosef Agnon feared for the historical archive he had left in his home. He went from person to person, trying to enlist help; people had other concerns, however. "People laughed with broken hearts at this man who came to tell them of crumbling manuscripts at a time of such terrible trouble," he wrote. In the end Avraham Krishevsky, a member of the Haganah, declared, "An archive like that is worth even human lives," and went with Agnon to Talpiot. The papers were scattered throughout the house and yard; Agnon did not know what to save first, and Krishevsky pressed him to hurry. He quickly gathered up some manuscripts and went back to the city. Joseph Klausner's house had also been ransacked and his library vandalized.[27]

Among those wounded in Jerusalem that day was insurance agent Alter Levine. Soon after the disturbances began, several Arabs from the village of Lifta entered Romema, Levine's neighborhood, and opened fire. Levine, his wife, and his daughters lay on the ground for hours until British policemen beat back the rioters. The house was damaged. Levine sued for compensation.[28]

The violence spread across the country; Arabs even tried to penetrate Tel Aviv. The British called in reinforcements from Egypt and Transjordan, but despite the additional forces the atrocities continued. Events in Safed were much like those in Hebron. Colonel Kisch met five girls who

---

*Attorney S. Horowitz, who collected the information, wrote to Kisch that one name should be removed from the list of survivors: a Jewish woman who had found refuge with a mukhtar. She was in fact a prostitute. She remained in Hebron after the massacre, while the rest of the Jews left.[26]

had seen their parents murdered.[29] Arab spokesmen reported acts of terror perpetrated by Jews, including the lynching of Arab passersby and the
murder of women and children. In a few cases, the Arabs claimed, Jews
attacked people who had given them refuge. The Jewish Agency investi-
gated some of these charges and concluded that "in isolated cases" there
were Jews "who shamefully went beyond the limits of self-defense." One
memorandum reporting that Jews had broken into a mosque and set
sacred books on fire bears a scribbled note: "This unfortunately is true."
When the violence finally subsided, 133 Jews and 116 Arabs were dead: 339
Jews and 232 Arabs were injured.[30]

Shmuel Yosef Agnon changed his attitude toward the Arabs in the wake
of the Hebron events. "Now my attitude is this," he wrote. "I do not hate
them and I do not love them; I do not wish to see their faces. In my humble opinion we should now build a large ghetto of half a million Jews in
Palestine, because if we do not we will, God forbid, be lost."[31]

High Commissioner Chancellor returned to Palestine on August 31.
Colonel Kisch returned the same day; he had been in London for the
birth of his son. Chancellor considered the possibility of bombing some
Arab villages from the air, but decided against it. A few days later, his aide-
de-camp wrote in his log that all was quiet in Palestine.[32] Chancellor published a statement condemning the violence against the Jews and found
himself, like Raymond Cafferata, caught in the middle; the Arabs decided
to be insulted. Chancellor issued a second, more diplomatic statement,
and then the Jews decided to be insulted.[33] After a visit to Hebron, Chancellor wrote to his son, Christopher, that he could not express the sense of
revulsion that had gripped him. "I do not think that history records many
worse horrors in the last few hundred years," he said.[34] He wanted to go
home. "I am so tired and disgusted with this country and everything connected with it that I only want to leave it as soon as I can," he wrote.[35]

15

• • •

Breakfast at Chequers

1.

John Chancellor's term in Palestine frayed his nerves; almost every day brought a new aggravation. The prime minister didn't like him, and the Colonial Office meddled in his work instead of assisting him. When the high commissioner wanted to expand the police force, London spoke about the cost, as if there had been no trouble in Palestine. Perhaps he could make do with policemen from the Sudan, Colonial Secretary Passfield suggested.[1]*

Chancellor also found himself in conflict with the army, and was even required to intervene in internal disputes between officers and between the army and the air force. Every party involved was convinced that it knew best how to maintain law and order. Officers were constantly insulting each other and feeling offended. "His views as to the defense of Palestine are idiotic and a danger to the Empire," the high commissioner wrote of a top RAF commander.[3]

With considerable reluctance, Chancellor ordered trials for the Arabs

---

*Sidney Webb, Lord Passfield was a founder of the Labour Party and a well-known economist. Weizmann noted "the depth and persistence" of his hostility to the Zionist cause. When the 1929 disturbances broke out, Weizmann went to visit him. Only his wife, Beatrice, was at home; Beatrice Webb was a well-known writer. In his memoirs, Weizmann quotes her as saying, "I can't understand why the Jews make such a fuss over a few of their people killed in Palestine. As many are killed every week in London in traffic accidents and no one pays any attention."[2]

who had murdered Jews, as well as for the few Jews who had killed Arabs. On the face of things, the entire process was carried out in accordance with the law and proper criminal procedure, couched in strictly legal language. But in fact the high commissioner was asking the judiciary to make manifestly political decisions by demanding that the courts maintain at least the appearance of holding Jews and Arabs equally culpable. Chief Justice of Palestine Sir Michael Francis Joseph McDonnell cooperated, but in exchange asked that Norman Bentwich be replaced; the attorney general had functioned as chief prosecutor as well. The Arabs also wanted the Zionist Bentwich to be dismissed. Chancellor valued Bentwich's professional skills and believed that getting rid of him was unfair. Still, he understood that Bentwich would have to go. The high commissioner would have been happy had the attorney general resigned of his own volition, but Bentwich did not make the unpleasant task easy. Chancellor offered to arrange for a chief justiceship of Cyprus or Mauritius; Bentwich wanted to remain in Jerusalem.

The problem was resolved according to local custom: one day when Bentwich left his office to have lunch, he was approached by an Arab court employee. The young man drew a pistol and shot him in the knee. Bentwich went home to England, ostensibly for medical treatment, and never resumed his post. Chief Justice McDonnell felt "great relief"; the impression is that he detested Bentwich. Weizmann arranged a lectureship at the Hebrew University for him, although as a former colonial official, he was not received with enthusiasm there either.[4]*

Some 700 Arabs were put on trial for violence and looting. Of these, 124 were accused of murder, 55 were convicted, and 25 were sentenced to death. About 160 Jews were also put on trial; 70 were accused of murder, and 2 were convicted and sentenced to death. Their sentences were commuted to life imprisonment.[6]

Chancellor then had to decide whether to execute the Arabs who had received the death sentence. This was one of the most painful decisions of his life, he wrote to his son; it was also difficult from a political point of view. The courts had not given him enough help, he complained; for some legal reason they had not decreed the death sentence for the two worst

---

*While still in his post, Norman Bentwich had on occasion been forced to defend himself against Jewish charges that he was treating Arab criminals too lightly. "[The Jews] can't forgive us for being English any more than the British can forgive us for being Jews," his wife wrote, adding, "It's a hard world." Bentwich took it upon himself to serve as defense attorney for the young man who had shot him.[5]

murderers, one Arab and one Jewish. Chancellor asked himself whether, in the light of this, it would be fair and just to hang the rest of the condemned men. If he carried out the sentence, he feared losing all connection with the Arab population. On the other hand, commuting it might make him seem weak. Either decision would be bad for him, he knew; the question was just how bad. He ordered three Arabs hanged and commuted the other sentences to life in prison. Colonel Kisch visited him on the day of the hangings; the high commissioner was in great distress. Arab psychology required a strong hand, Kisch tried to reassure Chancellor.[7]*

Only the psychology of the conflict can explain the macabre story of how the graves of the Hebron dead were opened. The Hebrew press claimed that the Arab murderers had mutilated their victims' bodies; Arab spokesmen denied the charge. Kisch tried his best to stop this gratuitous dispute, without success. Finally, the two sides decided to find out the truth by exhuming the bodies. Kisch thought this was a very bad idea but felt he had no choice—there was too much pressure on him to agree. The high commissioner also opposed the idea, but could do nothing to stop it.[9]

So Jewish, Arab, and English doctors, as well as Jewish and Arab grave diggers, gathered around the mass graves in Hebron and began to dig up the bodies one by one. They were in an advanced state of decay, and there was no way to determine whether they had in fact been mutilated. When Kisch arrived at the cemetery he was told that the first twenty bodies had produced no clear conclusion; he instructed the doctors to cease their examinations. He hoped that this would be the end of the matter, but the Arabs claimed the exercise had proved them right: the bodies had not been mutilated. There was much bickering over the significance of a single arm, found without a body, although there was no way of knowing whether the arm had been severed before or after the victim's death. Kisch had been right to oppose the exhumation: the Zionists came out of the affair looking rather graceless. "It seems curious that this should be a matter of so much concern," Norman Bentwich commented.[10]†

---

*Kisch would soon suggest that Chancellor bribe the mufti to sell the area in front of the Western Wall; money was no object, he promised. Chancellor wrote that Kisch was a "shifty character."[8]

†Kisch attributed the mutilation debacle to the political leanings of several of the doctors who had urged the exhumation. They were Revisionists and Anglophobes, he wrote.[11] He was more successful in his efforts to prove that Arab propaganda was making use of *The Protocols of the Elders of Zion*. He also made some small political capital from a report that Christians had, in advance of the riots, marked their homes with crosses to distinguish them from Jewish houses; this implied that the riots had not been spontaneous.[12]

In the weeks that followed, Kisch put a great deal of effort into rehabilitating Zionist-British relations, no easy task: "The hatred of the Jews for the English is now greater than the hatred they had for Russia," Shmuel Yosef Agnon wrote to Zalman Schocken, his publisher in Germany. The feeling was mutual; the British resented being blamed for the riots. Helen Bentwich noticed the hostility at her tennis club: every time she missed a ball, the wives of the British officials would break out in applause. She frequently heard the expression "bloody Jews." The high commissioner forbade soccer matches between British soldiers and Jewish teams, out of fear that they would turn violent. "What folly," he wrote.[13]

In his determination to shore up goodwill, Kisch traveled from city to city, making a point of meeting with the district commissioner and senior police officers to thank them personally for their efforts to save Jews; in some cases they had risked their own lives, he noted. Police officer Douglas Duff also got his share of gratitude. Kisch was quite concerned by the accusations Jews made against Arab policemen. Most of the charges were surely groundless, he thought; had they been true the number of Jewish victims would have been much higher.[14] Kisch protested, however, the award of a medal to Raymond Cafferata, who had, since the riots, become a famous hero. All of Britain was proud of him, and the Liverpool newspapers trumpeted his glory, calling him "a man of lead": he had faced 20,000 people alone and had saved Jewish children, they wrote. His picture and family history appeared in the press, and he received many admiring letters. In awarding Cafferata the king's Police Medal, the government, Kisch thought, was attempting to paper over the security blunders that had led to the murder of so many Jews.[15]

At the same time, Kisch, always navigating between necessity and sentiment, sent a secret memorandum to editors of the Hebrew newspapers demanding that they moderate their critical tone, lest the Zionist movement lose British support. Without that support, he warned, Zionists had no chance of realizing their plans. Personal criticism of officials who could not defend themselves should be avoided, Kisch instructed the newspapers; the British considered it a violation of the rules of fair play.[16]

The inclination to blame the British for what had happened led High Commissioner Chancellor to conclude that the Jews were an "ungrateful race." Others in the administration thought likewise; Kisch agreed. "It is politically important that we try to assimilate something of the Englishman's attitude toward the Tommy as a cheerful simple fellow and toward the policeman as a friend of the public," he wrote in his diary.[17]

While Chancellor found himself caught between Jews and Arabs, Kisch was caught not only between the Jews and the British but also between the labor movement and the Revisionists. In the wake of the events of the summer of 1929, the competition and animosity between the two Zionist branches grew far more intense.[18] David Ben-Gurion gained strength. By the following winter, he had forged various left-wing and union groups into one party, the Party of the Workers of the Land of Israel, or Mapai. The party, along with the Histadrut and, eventually, the Haganah, formed Ben-Gurion's power base. For the Revisionists, the events of 1929 only seemed to deepen their nationalist sentiments. Predictably, Jabotinsky took an "I told you so" attitude and fruitlessly demanded that the Zionist leadership be replaced.[19] For his part, Ben-Gurion charged Jabotinsky and his militant followers with responsibility for the massacres.

Chaim Shalom Halevi felt deep pain about the political situation in the country. The Yishuv had learned nothing, he complained. Instead of melding into a great force of Zionist unity, people were preoccupied with petty partisan quarrels. In his eyes, this was the worst thing of all. "We are always singing that it's good to die for one's country. But it's horrible to realize that this death is superfluous." The politicians behave as if a glass of water has been spilled, not blood, Halevi wrote; yet blood is "the grease on the wheels of history." Jabotinsky himself could not have put it better.[20]

2.

Once again, a commission of inquiry was appointed. Headed by Sir Walter Shaw, a former chief justice of Singapore, it included three members of Parliament, one from each of the three main parties. The commission had a quasi-judicial purpose, but inevitably its proceedings turned into a battleground of politics and propaganda.[21]* Everyone devoted a great deal of time to the fundamental problems of the Mandatory regime and the Zionist program, but ultimately, the commission's report was not meant to uncover some historical truth. The main question was whether it would be "pro-Zionist" or "pro-Arab." Other investigations were

---

*In anticipation of Raymond Cafferata's appearance before the commission, his superiors made changes to his original report. "You will note that the report differs in many ways from the original," his commanding officer wrote, "but this was necessary in order that it should conform to the general lines on which . . . it was agreed that the enclosures to the main report should be framed." Cafferata was shocked but kept his silence.[22]

launched after the massacre, and this was the principal question hanging over them all. The League of Nations sent a committee to examine the problem of the Western Wall; the British sent Sir John Hope-Simpson, a colonial official, to investigate how many more Jews could be settled in the country.[23]*

These many inquiries produced piles of documents and data and arguments and reports, every word of which was carefully weighed, their authors always under pressure from the Zionists and the Arabs and British politicians. Overall, the reports convey a widely shared sense that Britain's national-home policy in Palestine was misguided, unjust, and impossible to carry out. John Chancellor played a large part in projecting this impression.

He continued to do his job, hosting garden parties and appearing at public events. "Mummie and I went to a flower show this afternoon at the Citadel of the Old City," he wrote to his son. "It was a rather grim affair, but it is well to have these functions to make people believe that things are normal."[25] Palestine did nothing but irk him, though. Pinhas Rutenberg, a Jerusalem Revisionist, repeatedly demanded that Chancellor arrest the mufti for instigating the wave of violence. The mufti had distributed written instructions among village mukhtars, Rutenberg claimed. The mufti insisted that these letters were forged, and Chancellor demanded that Rutenberg provide proof. Rutenberg had none, yet he refused to back down. As an old revolutionary, he said, he knew that in a situation like this one you arrest everyone who is liable to make trouble. The high commissioner responded that such methods might do very well in Russia, but he was sworn to govern Palestine in accordance with the law.[26]†

---

*Hope-Simpson was one of those colonial administrators who thought about the human significance of their work. Before coming to Palestine he had been involved in the tragic population exchange between Greece and Turkey; Hope-Simpson was concerned with protecting the Arab farmers from a similar fate. He was not surprised that many British officials came to Palestine with pro-Jewish sympathies and left with pro-Arab inclinations, he wrote. During their time in Palestine, he believed, they learned to identify with the plight of the Arab farmer.[24]

†David Ben-Gurion believed that the mufti would never have signed such orders, for fear of incriminating himself. The mufti's dependence on the British continued to dictate restraint on his part and, in turn, the events of 1929 reinforced the administration's need of him as a channel to the Arab population.[27] The status of "grand mufti," as the British called him, entitled him to special deference, and so he was not required to appear before the commission of inquiry—the commission came to him.[28]

Chancellor felt besieged on all sides. He was annoyed with the Arabs because he had to wring out of them condemnations of the summer's events almost by force; they also sent him letters he returned unanswered because they were, to his mind, too "impertinent." Then he learned from the American consul in Jerusalem that the Jews had organized an intelligence network—all the secret reports he sent to London were reaching the Zionists first.[29]

In the meantime, the Jews and the Arabs continued to squabble over the status of the Western Wall area. With the approach of the High Holidays, the question arose of whether the Jews would be able to blow the shofar. The Arabs objected; the Jews threatened the high commissioner that they would not pray at the wall if they could not use the shofar. Chancellor responded that Jerusalem would be much better off if the Jews kept away from the wall. They finally agreed that at the end of the prayer service they would enter a nearby synagogue to blow the shofar. The high commissioner saw the whole issue as a needless irritation. "How childish it all is," he wrote to his son.[30]*

On occasion, though, Chancellor himself was roused to defend the sanctity of national symbols. During a visit to St. George's Cathedral in Jerusalem, he became quite offended when "God Save the King" was omitted at the end of the service. Chancellor protested: the anthem was always played in all the imperial colonies. The vicar explained that he had decided to play it only from time to time, because he did not want to upset the many Americans in his congregation. The high commissioner was furious, as people in Jerusalem often were in response to such issues: "What! Are the British people not to be allowed to pray for their own King in a British cathedral and a territory of which he is sovereign for fear that a few foreigners might not like it?" He ordered the anthem to be played every Sunday morning.[32]

Chancellor soon reached the conclusion that the Balfour Declaration had been a "colossal blunder," unfair to the Arabs and detrimental to the empire's interests. He was gradually overcome with despair. The situation is "pretty black," he wrote to his son.[33] His letters to Christopher, a kind of personal diary, may have helped him organize his thinking. He proposed four possibilities: to expel the Jews, to expel the Arabs, to cancel the Balfour Declaration, or to maintain the regime by military force. Chancellor

---

*He frequently referred to the Arabs as "children" and "fools." They were unteachable, Chancellor wrote with colonial sorrow.[31]

most feared that he would be required to carry on with the policy dictated by the Balfour Declaration without having an army at his disposal. In January 1930 he sent a long, detailed memorandum to London. He wanted to extricate Britain from the Balfour Declaration and he hoped to deal a blow to Zionism.[34]

The only way to preserve Britain's position in Palestine was to give its inhabitants a measure of self-government, he wrote; by "inhabitants," he meant the Arab majority. The Jews could view Palestine as their national home without having a state. He proposed restricting their right to purchase land and taking greater care to match immigration with the country's economic capacity to absorb newcomers. From the day he arrived in Palestine Chancellor believed his predecessors had erred in allowing so many Jews to settle there in the 1920s—the country could not support them, he argued. His proposal was given a respectful hearing in London; the king asked for a copy.[35] Together with the reports produced by the various investigations in Palestine, Chancellor's memorandum led to an attempt at codifying a new policy.

3.

The main innovation proposed by the White Paper issued by Colonial Secretary Passfield in October 1930 was expressed in the thesis that the Balfour Declaration imposed on Britain a binary and equal obligation toward both Jews and Arabs. This meant a redefinition of the country's capacity to absorb immigrants. Up until now the administration's quotas had largely been fixed according to the state of the Jewish economy. From this point on Jewish immigration would be allowed only at a rate that would not put Arabs out of jobs. In the spirit of Chancellor's position, Passfield assumed that the Jews would remain a minority, and that at most they would enjoy some measure of autonomy, largely in the cultural sphere. The White Paper promised to develop Palestine so that it could take in another few tens of thousands of people, some of them Arabs. To this end, the government would invest several million pounds in the country.

British officials in Palestine were very pleased. The White Paper, they told Chancellor, finally clarified the situation. They felt that from now on they would be able to perform their jobs with greater confidence. Chancellor was gratified by his men's response, and the Arabs were pleased as well.[36] The Jews, however, claimed that Britain had betrayed them. "Poor Passfield found himself pilloried as the worst enemy of the Jewish people since Haman," the British historian A. J. P. Taylor wrote.[37] The Passfield White Paper never went into effect; indeed, it is notable only because the Zionist movement was able to get it revoked.

The story is remarkable. The new policy had been adopted after several discussions in the cabinet, as well as the preparation of countless position papers, memorandums, and drafts.[38] From the British point of view, linking immigration to the Arab as well as the Jewish economy and making a statement of equal support for Palestine's Arabs was a logical move. The events of the summer of 1929 had made clear the costs of supporting Zionism. Yet within a few months the new policy had disappeared. The Zionists had won again.

To a large extent, the victory was Weizmann's—a tribute to his charm and craftiness, his diplomatic astuteness, his conviction, audacity, and luck. Weizmann spoke to the British in the name of their interests, and he spoke as a lover betrayed. He was disappointed with the limits of British patriotism, he said gravely, and resigned from the presidency of the Zionist movement in protest. Then Weizmann began marshaling his forces as he knew best, networking, lobbying, applying pressure. His telephone book looked like a Who's Who of London.*

Three members of the Conservative opposition were persuaded to write a letter to the *Times* protesting the government's White Paper—former prime minister Stanley Baldwin, former foreign secretary Austen Chamberlain, and former colonial secretary Leopold Amery. Chancellor ascribed great importance to this letter; everything would have worked out had it not been printed, he wrote. David Lloyd George, Winston Churchill, and Herbert Samuel were also enlisted to object to the new policy. Ernest Bevin, another ally, was put to work. Bevin was concerned with the outcome of a forthcoming election in Whitechapel, where there was a large Jewish population.[40]

Weizmann's campaign coincided with a moment when the government was weak, primarily preoccupied with the economic crisis following the 1929 stock market crash. The crisis also served to strengthen Chancellor of the Exchequer Philip Snowden's opposition to one of the key elements of the new policy: the investment of millions in Palestine's development. Snowden and especially his wife were sympathetic to the Zionist movement and were on Weizmann's list of friends. Within a short

---

*The Weizmann Archive preserves a fairly short list of names under the heading "Anti-Zionist MPs."[39]

time, treasury officials were demanding that the whole matter be reconsidered. Prime Minister Ramsay MacDonald sent his son Malcolm to reopen the issue in discussions with Weizmann; the younger MacDonald was an old friend of labor Zionists.[41] Foreign Secretary Henderson was also involved in the negotiations.

Within a few months, Weizmann received a letter from the prime minister containing a new "interpretation" that for all practical purposes canceled the White Paper. The empire bowed its head, almost in apology. It was a humiliating defeat, running against the best political thinking and Britain's own interests.

There is no rational explanation for this stunning turn of events. The government's panicked retreat from Passfield's White Paper reflected fear. MacDonald had been intimidated by the Jews, Chancellor wrote to his son, and he was right. The world economic crisis required special caution; who wanted at this juncture to get in trouble with "world Jewry"? Chancellor, for his part, was not surprised. From the day of his arrival in Palestine he had complained that it was difficult to govern a population whose representatives enjoyed free access to the prime minister and his cabinet. The Zionists had even enlisted a special man, Chancellor wrote, whose job was to ensure that the prime minister continue to be nice to them.[42] He was referring to Josiah Clement Wedgwood.*

The Zionists' victory was particularly notable given that the movement had no army and little money at this point, and it was riven by internal conflict. Weizmann's opponents in Tel Aviv and New York were endlessly harassing him and challenging his leadership; he resigned frequently. The Jewish Agency had expanded to include non-Zionist Jewish organizations, although it was far from representing all the world's Jews. The Jewish community in Palestine was entirely dependent on the willingness of the British administration to protect it and aid its development. The Jews' power to impose themselves on the British Empire, against its own interests, thus derived from a false image that was conditional on the willing belief of the British.

---

*Labour MP Wedgwood would tell anyone who listened that Palestine should be made into the seventh dominion; that is, it should be given preferred status within the empire, like Australia, Canada, and South Africa. The goal was, he said, that the Jews in Palestine become English. "Comrade Wedgwood," David Ben-Gurion wrote, was "the best of our friends," but his Zionist fervor threatened to endanger the movement's cautious activity. Once Wedgwood asked Ben-Gurion to name a street after him in Palestine. Ben-Gurion replied that it was not the practice to name streets after living people. This was not true: Allenby, Balfour, and others had had streets named after them before they passed away.[43]

Pinhas Rutenberg told High Commissioner Chancellor that the White Paper pitted Britain against 15 million enemies around the world from Moscow to Washington. Chancellor believed him. The Jews had already activated the American State Department, he wrote to his son. A few years later, Chancellor cited pressure exerted by American Jews at the top of a list of factors involved in the White Paper cancellation. A senior official in the Foreign Office, Sir George Randall, also attributed great importance to the influence of the United States on British policy in Palestine: "The Americans could not afford to antagonize the extremely important Jewish vote in New York, Detroit, Chicago, and other cities, and therefore pressed the purely Zionist point of view on us in and out of season." In various places Jews demonstrated against the White Paper. They received a great deal of coverage; Chancellor believed they controlled the press as well.[44]

Weizmann summed up the affair like a general surveying a battle: "The attack was successfully repulsed," he wrote. He assumed that Prime Minister MacDonald had incorrectly evaluated the forces involved, but even many years later Weizmann was hard put to explain how he had succeeded in scaring the British; in the wake of the White Paper's demise the country eventually received from 40,000 to 60,000 Jewish immigrants a year. Even Jabotinsky the extremist had limited his demands to 30,000, Weizmann noted with amazement, barely believing himself the success of the Jewish bluff.[45]

This was Chaim Weizmann's final personal victory. In the summer of 1931 he was in effect deposed from the presidency of the Zionist movement. His success in getting Passfield's White Paper repealed had not helped him. His removal, on the grounds that he was taking an overly moderate line toward the British and the Arabs, was initiated by the Revisionists and led by Ze'ev Jabotinsky.*

In this context, David Ben-Gurion recorded a story that was very telling about the Zionist movement's standing with the British government. A few days before Weizmann was ousted, he made a final attempt to save his position. He sent Ben-Gurion to London to persuade the prime minister to establish "parity" in Palestine: Arabs and Jews would partici-

---

*The Zionist Congress, which convened in Basel, rejected Jabotinsky's proposal to declare that the "final goal" of the Zionist movement was a Jewish state; officially, the Zionists still spoke of a "national home." Jabotinsky, furious, tore up his delegate's card and walked out with his faction. Nachum Sokolow was elected in place of Weizmann, but until Weizmann was reinstated a few years later, the movement was left without any real leadership.[46]

pate in government; their strength, however, would be determined not on a proportional basis but as if they were two populations of equal size. Up until then the British had rejected this idea; if they could now be persuaded to accept it, Weizmann would be able to present the Zionist Congress with a diplomatic coup.

Weizmann entrusted this mission to Ben-Gurion because of the feelings of socialist solidarity Ramsay MacDonald and his son bore toward him. Traveling with Ben-Gurion was a confidant of Weizmann's, the historian Lewis Namier. Ben-Gurion's plane was late, and he was unable to notify London of the delay. The prime minister waited and waited. No damage was done, however. The next day, Saturday, MacDonald invited Ben-Gurion and Namier to breakfast at his residence, Chequers, a two-and-a-half-hour drive from London. The Jewish millionaire Israel Sieff put his Daimler at their disposal.

Present at breakfast were MacDonald, his two sons, his daughter, his grandchildren, a friend, and "two old ladies" whom Ben-Gurion was unable to identify. He sat to the prime minister's left, Namier to his right. "The food was put on the second table and each of us had to go and choose for himself what he wanted," Ben-Gurion related. In fact, this was his second visit with MacDonald at Chequers. The house itself, which had been built in the eleventh century, made little impression on him. The prime minister showed him Cromwell's sword and Napoleon's pistol, the library, and a painting attributed to Rembrandt. Then the two went for a walk around the gardens. Ben-Gurion marveled at the view and the ancient trees. The prime minister said that the Jews were making terrible trouble for him, but then added that he would never forget his visit to Palestine a few years earlier. Ben-Gurion had felt back then that the Zionist movement had gained a friend, and apparently he had not been mistaken.[47]

The guests spoke freely, as equals, as people who trusted each other. Namier complained that the high commissioner had changed the name of Nathan Straus Street in Jerusalem to Chancellor Street. The prime minister responded that he was aware of the high commissioner's hostility to the Jews and would have dismissed him long ago, if he could. Chancellor would soon be leaving the post, MacDonald said, expressing his concern that on his return to London the former high commissioner would involve himself in pro-Arab activity. He asked whether Ben-Gurion knew the identities of the high commissioner's contacts in London, and took down a volume of Who's Who to peruse the names of people likely to link up with Chancellor.

Namier said that Chancellor was not the only British official in Palestine hostile to Zionism, and mentioned one by name. The prime minister had heard of the man and agreed that his contract should be canceled but, sadly, he had no control over the Colonial Office. No matter, there would soon be a more sympathetic high commissioner. The prime minister himself would speak with him, he promised. Together they all disparaged Colonial Secretary Passfield with considerable relish, and then went on to the matter of parity. The Jews should not be content just with parity, MacDonald said—some method must be devised to give them preference. Ben-Gurion and the prime minister's son Malcolm put MacDonald's words in writing and the prime minister signed the memo. Now all that remained was for Ben-Gurion to return to the congress in Basel.

Ben-Gurion had missed that day's flight; the next day, Sunday, there was no flight. Malcolm MacDonald called his father's office. Downing Street discovered a special flight that would cost sixty pounds, but Ben-Gurion could not pay that much. MacDonald called again. The prime minister's office made further inquiries and called back saying that it had found a flight costing only fifty pounds. Ben-Gurion replied that this was still too expensive. MacDonald called the Air Ministry, as the prime minister wished to fly Ben-Gurion to Basel on a special RAF plane. He eventually decided against this idea—someone in Parliament was liable to submit a vexing question on the matter. Downing Street made more inquiries and finally located a train to Basel. However, the train went through France, and Ben-Gurion did not have a French visa. So MacDonald disturbed the weekend leisure of the French ambassador and a visa was arranged. MacDonald's son accompanied Ben-Gurion to London; Ben-Gurion called him Malcolm.[48]*

The American consul in Jerusalem, Paul Knabenshue, was not surprised that Colonial Secretary Passfield had failed to appreciate the power of the Jews. All the people in the Labour Party were naive types, he thought. They trusted the system and believed in the position papers submitted to them. In a report sent to the U.S. secretary of state, Knabenshue described the 1930 White Paper as an amateurish document, and wrote, "Lord Passfield, a very precise and laborious investigator, is a great believer in facts and figures. Were he to be told that the Moon is made of green cheese he would doubtless be skeptical; were he to be shown statis-

---

*Ben-Gurion wrote sometime later, "We've got to get our own airplane."[49]

tics of green cheese exported from the Moon to Mars and Venus he would unquestionably accept them."[50]

MacDonald's note to Weizmann provoked outrage. The Arabs called it the "black letter." John Chancellor felt himself to be in an impossible position. "The feeling among the Arabs against [the government] and the Jews is boiling," he wrote. He believed that now they would launch a rebellion against the British.[51] He had done his best to be impartial, he claimed, and neither side had been grateful. But the Jews were the worst, he said, because they saw no point of view other than their own, nor did they recognize anybody else's rights or claims. He sensed that the Jews did not like him, he wrote. Despite his prime minister's letter, Chancellor was convinced that the Jews in Palestine were a minority with no future. They maintained their presence through the protection of British bayonets— only the British were saving them from Arab knives and bullets, and the Jews wanted that protection to continue. But the day would come when the British taxpayer would tire of this and the British soldiers would leave. The bloody retribution that would accompany their exit would be worse the longer they remained. Again and again he thought of Ireland, and toward the end of his term wrote that in Palestine only God in heaven would make a good high commissioner.[52]

His wife did not like life in Palestine either. She suffered from the heat, and their residence was not comfortable. The high cost of living did not allow them to save money. Quite the opposite: the high commissioner calculated that he had put out £1,200 of his own money for official and entertainment expenses. Still, he would complete his service that summer, making him eligible for retirement on the maximum pension, and a businessman had offered him a job developing connections in Rhodesia. These were all good reasons for Chancellor to end his long career in the empire's colonies, and he decided to do so. Toward the end of his term Chancellor oversaw the construction of a magnificent new residence for the high commissioner, but he himself lived there for only a very short time. "Life is full of disappointments," Chancellor wrote, and went home.[53]

James Pollock, a district commissioner, had taken it upon himself to arrange the wedding of the year. Raymond Cafferata, the "hero of Hebron," was marrying Peggy Ford-Dunn. The ceremony was held in Jaffa, and Caff and his Peggy spent their honeymoon at home; if the newspapers are to be believed, all Liverpool celebrated with them.[54]

Hamlet in Bir Zeit

1.

The new high commissioner's residence, or Government House, stood on the Hill of the Preacher in the south of Jerusalem, erroneously identified by some as the New Testament's Hill of Evil Counsel. Offering a breath-taking view, surrounded by a pine grove and gardens containing a hand-some fountain, the stone mansion exhibited architectural elements carefully selected from the West and the East. It exuded majesty and per-manence, and one glance left no room for doubt: the British Empire had come to stay. Adjacent to the building was a dog cemetery: Boots came into the world in June 1938 and met his maker in May 1941; Judy was also born in June 1938 but went to her eternal rest in July 1944.

On the ground floor, next to the dining and the billiard rooms, was a ballroom whose parquet floor was famous throughout the Middle East; part of it was covered with Persian rugs. There was also a resplendent fire-place, inlaid with blue and white Armenian tiles. The curtains, the furni-ture, the fixtures—all were imported from overseas. The walls were covered with oil portraits of the kings of England, hung in heavy gold frames. A crystal chandelier illuminated the ballroom, and there was a minstrel's gallery for the police band. There were separate bathrooms for the British and for natives.[1]

Arthur Wauchope, the high commissioner who replaced John Chan-cellor in November 1931, was a fatherly general, a bachelor who loved to entertain. The American consulate in Jerusalem once reported to Washington that in a single month Wauchope hosted no less than six hundred people. He was a rich man. "Money and champagne flowed like water," wrote one of his senior officials.[2]

Jerusalem was their Camelot, a myth of splendor—and self-delusion. The British talked about "the government" as if it were the nerve center of a huge empire, not a clutch of officials manning a smallish bureaucracy in a remote province. A head of department was respected as if he were a minister, a consul an ambassador; every woman was a duchess; the high commissioner was addressed as "your excellency." This inflation of status was the key to British social life, one of them later suggested. The sweaty constrictedness of colonial existence, the way they lived on top of one another, seemed to magnify each of them to an extravagant size. The smaller the pond the bigger the fish, Horace Samuel commented.[3] They dressed and spoke and entertained each other properly, in accordance with strict social conventions.

Beatrice Magnes, wife of the university chancellor, recalled an incident of minor social rebellion that almost caused a scandal. The ladies, almost all of them wives of senior administration officials, were expected to appear at the high commissioner's balls dressed in décolletage, their shoulders bare. Despite the chill of Jerusalem evenings, they never dared to wear anything else. Magnes violated this rule by appearing in public with a watermelon-colored shawl over her shoulders. Once, it got caught on the medals on a guest's official uniform; by the time the high commissioner's aide-de-camp had rushed over to separate them, the two had become acquainted. He was Prince Ras Tafari of Ethiopia, soon to be the emperor Haile Selassie, and someone to talk about.[4] People were always hungry for someone to talk about. Everyone gossiped about everyone else, with great delight and sweet viciousness: "Major Bentley bought a silver bracelet for General Parker's secretary. Lady Nolan changed cooks. Mrs. Sherwood leaves in revulsion any room that Captain Boulder enters."[5]

Arab leader George Antonius, by this time a senior official in the British administration, wrote to his daughter in Paris about a "do" in the garden of a local society woman. The guests sat around little tables, like at an Arab coffeehouse. There was a dance band. Antonius provided a precise rundown of who danced with whom; he danced with Mrs. Knabenshue, the American consul's wife. Champagne was served, but Antonius revealed that his hostess had given the waiters instructions to economize with the expensive drink. He invented a game: he would soon give a party of his own, he announced to the company. He would invite ten couples, but on one condition: each man must come with a woman not his wife and every woman with a man not her husband.

A wave of whispers and giggles passed through the crowd; eyes winked and hints were dropped. Everyone began guessing who would want to go with whom. One woman said she did not care who accompanied her "so long as it isn't K.R." Formerly a military censor, Antonius was careful to use initials in his letter, as if he feared that even this piece of gossip would be scrutinized by another pair of eyes before it reached his daughter. Perhaps K.R. was Keith-Roach.[6]

The pasha of Jerusalem, Keith-Roach himself, recalled the many excellent meals, the Sodom and Gomorrah Golf Club by the Dead Sea, the brothel established by the military authorities in a Jerusalem hotel for the use of their soldiers. He claimed to object to the latter institution, even though the women who worked there underwent periodic medical examinations. William Dennis Battershill, the high commissioner's chief secretary, waxed sentimental in his own memoir over the police ponies, which he and his friends used for polo matches. He recalled with nostalgia the grouse hunts on the grounds of Government House; the high commissioner himself sometimes went out to hunt game birds. Later, when tensions increased and British officials, fearful of attacks, stopped going out for fun or outdoor sports, Battershill was miserable. He seems to have had no greater enemy than boredom; only the heat bothered him as much.[7]

Chaim Arlosoroff once summed up an evening at the Officers Club: "The conversation revolved largely around duck hunting," he wrote in his diary. Lord Reading, who once sat next to him at dinner, at least talked about tiger hunting in India. When Arlosoroff needed to locate administration officials urgently, on weekends, he had trouble finding them, which he found annoying. "If a revolution were to break out in Jerusalem one fine Sunday morning," he wrote in his diary, "it would be pretty far along by the time the government returned to the capital."[8]

Arlosoroff replaced Kisch as head of the Zionist Executive and chief of the Jewish Agency's political department in 1931. Kisch, a Weizmann protégé, left in the wake of his mentor's ouster. Like Kisch, Arlosoroff spent his days at receptions, dinners, afternoon teas, and concerts. One day he would meet the army commander, another the director of education or the postmaster general or perhaps the chief justice; they all spent a lot of time in the lobby and bar of the King David Hotel. Arlosoroff was as adept as Kisch at settling matters over a glass of whiskey, but unlike his predecessor he often found this part of his work very tiresome. Kisch was an English officer and gentleman; Arlosoroff had grown up in Germany and was an ideologue and a socialist, with a Ph.D. in economics. Chief Secretary Battershill had never heard of Chaim Nachman Bialik, Arlosoroff wrote, feeling most disturbed; he asked himself how it was possible to expect sympathy and understanding from people who knew nothing about the Zionist movement and its major figures.[9]*

The Jewish Agency formulated a detailed program for developing close relations with government officials through encounters at sports clubs and parties. Part of the plan involved building tennis courts and encouraging the British to live in Jewish neighborhoods, and even subsidizing their rent.[11] The strategy did not work: most of the British in Palestine preferred to live among themselves or in Arab neighborhoods. "The Jew is addicted to politics," wrote a top police officer, "and in the Holy Land that is a subject it is well to keep clear of." So he always spoke about boxing, he wrote.[12]

Just as administration officials were living on the very margins of the empire, many Jews felt as if they, too, had landed at the outer limits of the cultural world. Most still considered themselves European. What they found in Jerusalem, the opera included, was a poor substitute for real culture. A product of the vision and energy of Mikhail Golinkin, a conductor from the Ukraine, the opera was one of those things that no one else had done before. Golinkin managed to produce *Aïda, The Barber of Seville,* and other great works, but the crises and disappointments he suffered are themselves worthy of an opera. The productions were staged at the Eden Theater in Tel Aviv and the Zion Theater in Jerusalem: instead of an orchestra there was a piano. *Ha'aretz* wrote that pianist Professor Avi-Lea played so wonderfully that the lack of an orchestra was not felt at all.[13] *Ha'aretz* reminded its readers that Theodor Herzl himself had fantasized about a Jewish opera in his book *Altneuland,* the great utopian Zionist novel.†

---

*High Commissioner Wauchope did, however, show interest in *Auto-Emancipation,* the major work of the pre-Herzlian Zionist Leon Pinsker. Arlosoroff sent him the book, and the two exchanged a series of letters about it.[10]

†Ronald Storrs, who liked to whistle arias while accompanying himself on the piano, sneered at the audience of pioneers who attended the opera. Young people in heavy shoes, short pants, and "Bolshevik shirts" would wander the rows of seats cracking pistachios, he wrote. The British came in evening dress.[14] When the Tel Aviv municipality sent out invitations to a production of *Twelfth Night* at the Habima Theater, evening dress was specified.[15]

Nothing thrilled members of the new Jewish society, so sensitive to their place on the margins of European culture, more than visits by famous Europeans. Beatrice Magnes listed them one by one, including Jascha Heifetz (twice), Arturo Toscanini, and Thomas Mann, who came for a few days. Their arrival seemed to bolster the Jewish elite's self-image, cut off as it was from its cultural center. The Zionists often tried to impress their guests, as Menachem Ussishkin did with Magnus Hirschfeld, a well-known sexologist from Berlin and a Jewish evangelist of homosexuality. "Hirschfeld arrived in Palestine with a fey and foppish Chinese assistant," Chaim Arlosoroff observed. Ussishkin told Hirschfeld the story of a Jewish shepherd he had met, somewhere off in a field, reading a book. Ussishkin had asked the shepherd what he was reading. Oh, the shepherd had replied, it's just Schopenhauer's *Die Welt als Wille und Vorstellung*.[16] Hirschfeld had believed him and, who knows, it might actually have been true.

Palestine's Jewish intellectuals had a far more complex attitude toward Europe's centers of Jewish culture. The European legacy was embraced as part of the new Hebrew milieu; Jewish culture was supposed to remain in the Exile. Yet many intellectuals in Palestine felt a strong emotional need to preserve their ties to the places they had left—often by trying to persuade the place to move to Palestine. Mordechai Ben-Hillel Hacohen made desperate efforts to convince the great historian Simon Dubnow to settle in, or at least visit, Palestine. The two conducted an agonized correspondence on the subject. Dubnow did not oppose the "rebirth" of Palestine, he wrote, but he also believed in the future of Jewish life in Europe. Hacohen needled him to come, just as Zionists had earlier tried to persuade Albert Einstein to stay. Even as the Jews in Palestine rejected the Exile morally and nationally, and held it in contempt and disdain, they still badly wanted the Exile's recognition. Hacohen swore he would not rest until he brought Dubnow over. "We'll still get him here," he wrote in his diary. "He'll come. He'll come."[17]*

The new high commissioner, Lieutenant General Arthur Grenfell Wauchope, was fifty-seven years old when he arrived in Palestine. A Scotsman from Edinburgh, he was a professional soldier. He had fought in the Boer War and in World War I, served in Australia and New Zealand, and gained diplomatic experience as chief of the British section of the Military Inter-Allied Commission of Control in Berlin. He also brought experience in

---

*Dubnow did not come. Toward the end of his life he settled in Riga, Latvia, and was murdered when the Nazis invaded the city.

antiterrorism: before coming to Palestine he had been commander of the British forces in Northern Ireland.[18]

His men described him as an arbitrary despot. Wauchope would blow up at them rudely, insult them to the point of tears, and then do anything to mollify them, including awarding a medal he had designed himself. Edward Keith-Roach described him as Jerusalem's own Dr. Jekyll and Mr. Hyde. He radiated power and totalitarian resoluteness, but in fact changed his decisions by the minute, wrote Chief Secretary Battershill. A master of intrigue, he was generally persuaded by the opinion of the last adviser who spoke to him; everyone in his employ was suspicious of everyone else. Wauchope demanded that his people agree with him, but behind his back they hated him. Battershill compared the high commissioner to Adolf Hitler: his green study was known as the "torture chamber"; Battershill thought he would be "a very Hitler if only he knew something of administration." Wauchope was also endlessly going out to the field, making decisions himself, sometimes contrary to the army's position and even in violation of the law. His administration was run like a comic opera, the chief secretary complained.[19]

Unlike Chancellor, Wauchope liked the country, although there was nothing he hated more, he said, than the lies, anger, and ill will that threatened the happiness of its people, both Jews and Arabs. From time to time he would make contributions out of his own purse to charitable projects. Norman Bentwich described him as a man who loved culture and was close to the Labour Party. "He liked to have heretics and artists around him," Bentwich wrote. Wauchope believed in the goodness of man. In a fourteen-page letter he once sent to the colonial secretary he quoted John Milton: "Time will run back and fetch the Age of Gold."[20]

Together with his mercurial temperament and love of Palestine, the new high commissioner projected a welcome illusion: everything would go back to the way it was before the massacre, as if nothing had happened. Some of the Jewish property looted in the riots was restored to its owners, and the refugees received government compensation.[21] In the spring of 1931, some 160 of Hebron's Jews, led by Rabbi Chaim Bagaio, returned to their homes.[22]* The police force was fortified and reorganized. In the view of one government minister, Palestine was now "a well-guarded zoo."[24]

---

*Ben-Gurion opposed the resettlement of Hebron. "People and money should not be wasted on the city," he wrote; at best, Hebron could only ever become "a Jewish point of exile," where a Jewish minority lives among an Arab majority.[23]

Touring the country with guests—George Bernard Shaw and Gene Tunney, the heavyweight boxing champion—Edwin Samuel observed that "the country is outwardly normal," happily reporting to his father that in many places Arab and Jewish laborers were again working side by side.[25] Jewish contractor Baruch Katinka resumed construction of the Palace, the luxury hotel ordered by the mufti; he had been forced to stop building during the riots, but only for ten days.[26] In April 1933 General Allenby returned to Jerusalem to dedicate the YMCA tower; after the ceremony, the YMCA had a quote from Allenby's speech engraved at the stone entrance: "Here is a place whose atmosphere is peace, where political and religious jealousies can be forgotten and international unity be fostered and developed."

The imperial optimism radiated by the new Government House, the sleeping lion guarding the city, was, however, illusory.[27] While British society was dancing on that splendid parquet floor, another wave of violence was building, and the regime began counting its days. Senior officials started disparaging the administration, doing so in the way they knew best—by making fun of it. One of them recalled the story of an official in his department who wore a homburg when he went to a Jewish neighborhood and a red tarbush in an Arab one. When the man once found himself in the middle of a street fight between Jews and Arabs, he ran to the nearest telephone booth and called his department to ask for instructions: Which hat should he wear, the homburg or the tarbush? Wear both, he was told.[28]

The American consul in Jerusalem sent a situation report to Washington. "The real question at issue is whether Palestine is to become an Arab or a Jewish state," he wrote. Jewish Agency leader Arthur Ruppin took his Browning automatic pistol, loaded it, and placed it on his desk; for ten years the pistol lay there untouched. "But you never know . . ." Ruppin wrote in his diary.[29] This was the political lesson he had learned from the events of 1929.

Meanwhile, Alter Levine was fantasizing about international commerce. At the end of October 1929 he proposed that the Anglo-Palestine Bank invest £10,000 in two grand new insurance companies to be called Jerusalem and Jordan. "They will be a great and valuable thing for Palestine and in time also for the neighboring countries," he wrote in the fervor of his vision. Eliezer (Siegfried) Hoofien, the bank's director-general, took only three days to reply. Cautious and dry, he rejected the idea with a single sentence.[30]

Levine was now composing heartfelt love letters, in French, to a mysterious woman who apparently lived in Beirut. He loved her madly, he said, and wrote her poems. He told her about Rivka, his daughter, who had died in a foreign land and been brought back to Jerusalem for burial in the shade of an ancient olive tree. He wrote with chivalrous restraint, controlling his passion with dignity; it seems his love was never consummated. The letters were composed on a typewriter, presumably one he had imported himself. There is no way of knowing whether the letters found among his papers are copies or the originals, never sent. If Levine's beloved ever replied to him, he did not save her letters. Maybe she never answered; maybe she never existed, except in his imagination.

Over the previous few years, Levine had endured great tragedy. His wife and daughters had fallen sick, and as was the practice in Palestine, he had sent them for treatment to the best doctors in Europe. Levine demanded that his family be given the finest care but haggled over the price. His eldest daughter, Rivka, had died in a private hospital in Berlin.[31] A haze of mystery surrounds his relationship with her. There were rumors in Jerusalem that Rivka had fallen in love with a man by the name of Laniado. Levine had objected to the match because the man was Sephardic, not "one of ours." So he had sent his daughter to Europe, to separate her from her beloved, and she had died there of sorrow. Perhaps she had even died at her own hand. Also in Europe, Levine's wife had suffered a breakdown. Before he brought her back to Jerusalem, she had been wandering the streets of Berlin, muttering the word of God. She may never have recovered from her torture by the Turks ten years earlier.

In the final episode of this urban tale, Levine's second daughter, Rachel, fell in love with the same Laniado who had captured Rivka's heart. The two married and left Jerusalem. In the poems of this time that Levine stashed away in his desk drawer, he wrote about nightfall and "the dying day."[32] As the tenth anniversary of Rivka's death approached in 1933, Alter Levine hanged himself on the date tree in his garden. He left behind no letter, only a poem in which he asked that a date palm be planted on his grave: "And may a palm spread its sanctuary of peace over me, and guard me day and night / and its dates drip honey on my grave, under the skies of my land / and I will taste eternity!"[33]

Khalil al-Sakakini read about Levine's suicide in the newspaper and was very sad. "Poor man," he thought. "Had the English entered Jerusalem just a little later both my fate and his would have been to hang. Here this man, who was saved from the Turkish gallows, has hanged himself by his own hand. He fled death but fell dead. There is no power and no might but God. May God have mercy on him." From time to time Sakakini thought about Levine; despite all that had happened, he never regretted taking him into his home.[34]*

2.

The violence that began in 1929 became persistent.[35] Political terrorism was now part of daily life; in the years leading up to the next outbreak of riots, in 1933, both Jews and Arabs were killed.

Most Arab acts of political violence were directed at Jewish farmers, but in July 1932, for the first time, a senior British official was the target of an assassination attempt. He escaped death, but his wife did not. The Arab national movement had gathered momentum; within a month of the events of 1929 no less than five political conventions took place, representing different sectors of the Arab population. These included a students' congress and a women's congress. Chaim Arlosoroff estimated that within fifteen to twenty-five years, the Arab national movement would be the equal of the Zionists'.[36]

As part of this development a radical nationalist Arab party emerged. The Istiqlal (Independence) Party failed to mobilize the masses and did not last for long. But like the Revisionists within the Zionist movement, the Istiqlal Party forced Arab community leaders to demonstrate their loyalty to the national cause.[37] The strength gained by the mufti in the wake of 1929 depended on his ability to maneuver between the demands of his people and the expectations of the authorities—a delicate enterprise, which became harder by the day.

In October 1933, the mufti brought out several thousand demonstrators in cities across Palestine, mainly to protest the government's immigration policy: nearly 30,000 Jews had entered the country by the end of the year. During the weeks that followed, Arab demonstrators clashed with the police in Jerusalem, Jaffa, Nablus, and Haifa. At the end of the violence, the official count was thirty dead, including one policeman and a six-year-old boy, and more than two hundred wounded.[38] "Today Palestine became a battlefield," wrote Khalil al-Sakakini to his son Sari.

---

*At the time of Levine's death, two of the most outstanding attorneys in Jerusalem, Shalom Horowitz and Daniel Auster, were still handling Levine's suit for damages for the suffering he had endured in the Damascus jail. By the time payment—about $2,000—arrived, Levine was no longer alive.

"Demonstrations everywhere, attacks on police and railway stations, hundreds of dead and wounded. The hospitals are overflowing and tempers are hot with anger. What tomorrow may bring, God only knows."[39]*

Once a year, on the anniversary of his arrest with Alter Levine, hours before the British occupied Jerusalem, Sakakini turned his thoughts to the changes wrought by time. In December 1933, the sixteenth anniversary of the British conquest, he wrote that he owed them nothing, because his people had not been liberated. The country was no better off than it had been in the Turkish era, he maintained.[41] To Sakakini the bloody disturbances were part of a single chain of events. "Whoever investigates the rebellions in Palestine during the English period will see them as an ongoing development. . . . The first was local and limited to Jerusalem; the second was a little broader, but limited to only a few cities; the third was even broader and the entire country, people in the cities and villages, and the nomads, all participated."

The protests were directed at the Jews and at the government, because it was aiding the Jews. "The entire world will see that the Arab nation is not easy prey," Sakakini declared. He could not predict how the events would affect the government, but he believed the Jews were panicking. And this was just the beginning: "Either people will suppress their anger, which will make them go mad, or they will rebel and placid, beautiful Palestine will become a land of insurrections. In either case, life will be too hard to bear," Sakakini wrote.[42]

In the taut atmosphere, all crime took on a nationalist tinge. In one story, twenty-three-year-old Yohanan Stahl, a new immigrant from Germany, and twenty-two-year-old Salia Zohar met up in Tel Aviv, went for a walk, and disappeared. As it later turned out, they had been attacked by several Bedouins, who stabbed Stahl to death and then raped and murdered his companion. The police launched an investigation, publishing a notice that included their pictures, but the bodies were not found. The Revisionist newspaper *Do'ar HaYom* presented the lagging investigation as yet another Jewish Agency blunder, saying that if the Jews stopped groveling before the authorities, then the British might pay more attention to security, and two young Jewish people might be able to walk unmolested in their own country. At the very least, the police would be making a greater effort to find the murderers. The newspaper played on

---

*About half of the dead were killed at Jaffa's Clock Square; the police commander there was Raymond Cafferata.[40]

questions of tribal unity, presenting the incident as a crime against the entire Yishuv. The Jewish Agency also demanded that the authorities expedite their investigation, as if the whole matter were a national issue.*

Nationalist fervor played a considerable role in the widening gap between the labor movement and the Revisionists, or between the "left" and the "right," as people began to say. The tension between the two forces reached its peak when Chaim Arlosoroff, a key figure in David Ben-Gurion's Mapai Party, was murdered in Tel Aviv in June 1933. The murder was never solved, but Mapai accused the Revisionists of the crime.[44]

At that point, some Revisionists were openly talking of the need to throw the British out of the country, and they would soon sound out Fascist Italy and Nazi Germany as partners for this purpose. Chief Secretary Battershill warned his superiors not to dismiss the possibility that Jewish terrorists might also try to murder British officials.[45] Radicalization and violence, then, were a direct outgrowth of the events of 1929, among Arabs and Jews alike. Both sides began to train terrorists. Britain sent reinforcements.

3.

Alex Morrison, a seventeen-year-old "Tommy" from Liverpool, liked serving in Palestine. "I think I spent here some of my happiest days of my army life," he later wrote. While still in England he had brought his unit honor as a boxer, so his commanders were reluctant to let him go, but Morrison had seen a notice on the army bulletin board calling for volunteers to serve in Palestine—and he could not resist the magical lure. "I had heard many romantic stories of the mystic east," he explained.

Morrison had just arrived in Palestine on the deck of the *California*, together with two thousand other soldiers, when he was shot at by Arab snipers. One of his comrades was killed, and his body disappeared into the waves. Duty in Palestine promised a unique kind of excitement, and Morrison looked forward to adventure and comradeship.[46] He had three pals, and they did everything together.

He was assigned to a supply unit as a lorry driver; his base was Gibraltar Camp in Haifa. The soldiers slept in wooden barracks. Reveille was at 6:00 A.M., followed by washing and shaving. At 6:30 there was inspection and an hour of morning exercise. Then they all ran to the beach, swam, returned to camp, and had a quick shower. Breakfast was at 8:00. The

---

*Eventually, *Do'ar HaYom* hired private detectives, who found the bodies of the couple. Subsequently, the murderers were arrested.[43]

food was excellent, Morrison wrote; they ate lots of oranges, and if they wanted more, they could go to the camp greengrocer, Ali. This Arab arranged all kinds of matters for them, both legal and dubious. The men had an Indian tailor who sewed their uniforms.

They got to work at 9:00. First there was maintenance: the vehicles had to be kept in good working condition, sparkling and spotless. An officer came to inspect them. He would crawl under the lorry, run his finger over the chassis, the transmission, and the engine; if he found any dirt, the driver was in trouble. The soldiers spent three days a week on the road, carrying water, provisions, and supplies to units on the northern border. Within a short time Morrison felt he knew the roads of Palestine better than the streets of his own Liverpool. The soldiers worked hard but were content. From 4:00 P.M. on, they were at liberty. They played football and tennis, and had a swimming pool as well. Morrison and his three friends studied Arabic; they dreamed of finding work with the Iraq Petroleum Company.

Haifa was good to them. A white city perched on the slopes of Mount Carmel with golden beaches and green palm trees, Haifa looked so peaceful. It surely resembled the promised land of the Bible, Morrison imagined.[47] He loved the Hadar Hacarmel neighborhood, with its busy shops, coffeehouses, and cinema. Many of the Jews who lived there were immigrants. The Arab part of the city was "out of bounds"—Morrison and his comrades were allowed there only while on duty. Sometimes they would sneak into the forbidden area and wander the alleys of the marketplace, between the little nargileh and coffee shops and the mosques. There was also a large club where girls danced the cancan every night, but the entrance fee was very expensive, and only rich Arabs were allowed in.

Haifa had undergone a revolution. By the end of the 1920s the city had become the most important industrial center in the country; one out of ten factories in Palestine were located there, employing 16 percent of the country's industrial workforce, Jewish and Arab, and producing about a quarter of its industrial output. Haifa's factories represented 35 percent of the capital invested in industry.* When the elderly Mordechai Ben-Hillel Hacohen came to town to visit his son David, he could not contain his

---

*Between 1929 and 1939 the number of inhabitants in Palestine nearly doubled, approaching 1.5 million, 1 million of them Arabs. During this period, Haifa's population more than doubled, from some 30,000 to 65,000. This means that one out of every two residents of the city was new; two out of every three were Arab.[49]

enthusiasm. For the first time in his life he saw a five-story building: "Please rise, Theodor Herzl, from your grave, to see your vision in Haifa," Hacohen wrote in his diary.[48]

Most of Haifa's Jews came from Europe; many were from Germany. They had been forced to flee their homes by the rise of Nazism, and on the whole they were not Zionists. The story of the German immigrants is a sad one; most would have preferred to remain at home. They arrived as refugees and felt strange and out of place in Palestine.[50] A great many of Haifa's Arabs were newcomers as well. Some 30,000 young men had moved there from three hundred surrounding villages. Their story was a sad one, too.

They left their villages because the family farms could no longer support them. A demographic drama was at work: ten years after the British entered the country, the infant-mortality rate declined and life expectancy increased. The growing population of the villages could have been sustained by modern farming methods, but most farmers were reluctant to depart from venerable traditions. Many villages suffered widespread hardship.[51] The tax burden was heavy; farmers often took loans. They were strongly tempted to sell land to the Jews, directly or through Arab middlemen, but when they did it further reduced their ability to provide for their families. Altogether, there were compelling reasons for a young man to leave home and go to the city. A report composed by the Zionist Organization found that some villages in the Nablus area had been almost emptied, their inhabitants having moved to the city.[52] New roads shortened the distances, so relocating did not mean complete separation from the village. A young Arab could work for a time in Haifa, return to his parents' house, and then go back to his job. Many began using bicycles. Quite a few had never left home before. Like Alex Morrison and many of the British soldiers, and like the new immigrants, these young men often felt displaced and were forced to grow up very quickly. The great majority did not know how to read or write.

4.

In early 1929 Rudyard Kipling came to Palestine. He visited the Arab teachers college and told the students that if, as he hoped, they became good teachers, they would realize how little they knew.[53] Indeed that is more or less what happened.

Upon arriving in Palestine the British found that the Turkish educational system had been destroyed during the war; even before that it had been woefully inadequate. Only four out of ten Arab children attended school, almost all of them boys. About half of these studied in foreign-run Christian schools. The rest studied in a *kutab,* a Muslim elementary school where the curriculum consisted largely of the Koran and the teaching method of rote learning. In this area, as in so many others, the British had to begin almost from scratch. It was not easy.[54]

The British quickly decided that the language of instruction would be Arabic, not Turkish. This was a radical move, a gesture to Arab identity, going against the long-standing British reluctance to change the status quo. Herbert Samuel made a goal of establishing a school in every Arab village, and in his time hundreds of schools were set up.[55]

The senior men in the administration's education department tried to broaden the school system in accordance with their departmental interest, often supporting their program with cultural and political arguments. Jerome Farrell, one department director, tried to persuade his superiors not to treat the Arabs in Palestine like the bushmen in Africa or the wild tribes of Papua. High Commissioner Wauchope demanded that the colonial secretary increase the schools budget.[56] Still, despite the profusion of memorandums, position papers, minutes, and reports investigating the structure, goals, and content of the schools system, little was done to extend Samuel's first efforts. The British neglected Arab education because they did not want to finance it and feared its political effect.

The Mandatory government's education budget amounted to between 4 and 7 percent of its total expenditures; more than two-thirds was spent on Arab education—this proportion would grow over time—and the rest on the Jewish system. The Jews funded most of their own educational needs, while the Arab pupils studied largely at government expense.[57] From time to time the British asked themselves whether they received a good return on their investment. In 1931, a committee examining the benefits to the British administration determined that much of village education was "money thrown away." The committee was inclined to blame the villagers: as in India, it concluded, people take their children out of school and put them to work. Some of the children then forget how to read and write.[58] "Why teach the children of the peasantry at all?" a department director wondered. "Schools are the bane of the East, little else than nurseries for agitators," he maintained.

Humphrey Bowman, another director of education, formulated a rule: "Make your peasant happy and prosperous and agitation will cease." The practical translation of his idea was to give children some measure of schooling, especially vocational training, but not to go beyond literacy. The administration did not want literate farmers leaving their villages and streaming into the cities with hopes of getting government jobs, as had happened in Egypt and India.[59]

An Arab child was to begin studying at the age of seven and remain in school for five years. The major subjects taught in the villages were religion, Arabic (reading and writing), arithmetic, personal hygiene, history, geography, nature, physical education, drawing, handicrafts, and practical agriculture—that is, raising vegetables and flowers in the school garden.[60] Schools inspector Khalil al-Sakakini was pleased. Returning from a visit to three village schools near Ramallah, he wrote, "The pupils can read and write and speak politely." They knew no more than that, apparently. Sakakini organized them into "health detachments," whose job was to convey to the villagers the principles of hygiene they had learned in school, and "reading and writing detachments," to read newspapers and books to the villagers and write letters for them.[61]

Education in the city was designed to perpetuate the difference between urban and village Arabs. City children studied basic geometry and were taught some elementary science instead of agriculture. Beginning in the fourth grade, they also studied English. Most of the pupils were boys, and few would continue to secondary schools. Of those who graduated from high school, even fewer would go on to college. Girls learned sewing and home economics, which would save them, as women, from the fate of their predecessors, the director of education wrote: "A woman will be no longer a chattel and a drudge, but a wife capable of bringing up her children in clean and healthy surroundings."[62]

Different grades often studied together in the same room with the same teacher, who taught all subjects. Many parts of the curriculum were omitted, often because the teachers did not know how to teach them. A school that used a blackboard and chalk was considered innovative; one with a world map was an advanced institution.[63] Pupils were frequently absent for several hours a day, or they left school before completing their years of education. Thus, the system served a kind of baby-sitting function: its main purpose was to preserve the population's ignorance and society's traditional structure, in the hope of preventing trouble. Arab spokesmen often accused the British of imposing illiteracy upon them. But, unlike the Jews, they invested little in their own education. Schooling was not compulsory.[64]

Some schools were noted for their standards, such as the private high school in the village of Bir Zeit, north of Ramallah. Most of the students were Christian, and some of the teachers had studied at the American University of Beirut. All the pupils, girls included, were expected to graduate. Hilda M. Wilson, an English teacher who taught there, remembered the students as very sharp. Once, when her class read John Milton's famous speech on freedom of the press, Khalid, a boy sitting in the front row, asked why Britain had freedom of the press but not Palestine. Khalid was a redhead.

The pupils studied *Hamlet* and identified with the prince. In fact, Wilson wrote, Hamlet was nearer to the Arab mentality than to that of the twentieth-century Englishman. She was thinking of the duty of revenge and Ophelia's utter obedience to the men in her family. In her view, the Arab tendency to cloak everything in dramatic eloquence was present in *Hamlet,* and the play also had the figure of a young fellow who had been to university and returned to a distasteful place with backward social customs. Wilson assumed that her pupils identified Wittenberg with the university in Beirut.

Her pupils were very nationalistic. Once Miss Wilson read a poem in class on the heroism of Great Britain's soldiers in World War I: "They went with songs to the battle, they were young . . . they fell with their faces to the foe," she quoted. The pupils cried out "Palestine!" and Fuad, a good-looking boy whom Miss Wilson imagined as a reincarnation of King David, wanted to know where she stood on the Palestine question. They identified with the guerrillas who were fighting the British. And she? Miss Wilson said that she mourned the British soldiers who fell in battle and suggested that they all join each other in sorrow.[65] Her impression was that the class accepted that.

Wilson's diary of Bir Zeit, a charming document, shows how much a dedicated teacher could achieve, and the opportunities an entire generation of Arab children would miss. The waste seems all the worse in light of the massive demand for Arab education—the number of registrants each year for the schools available was almost twice the number of places.[66] Britain's meager investment in education is especially notable given the resources that were invested in supervising the curriculum: according to one report, schools supervisors sent an average of 130 letters a year to each school, one letter every other day, a total of many thousands.[67] The education department, and High Commissioner Wauchope himself, took a special interest in history. Director of Education

Jerome Farrell considered the existing history textbooks too "chauvinist." The department had the authority to censor them, he wrote, but he doubted that censorship would be worthwhile. Any vetting system would probably be inefficient; furthermore, it would cost too much.[68]* Most Arabs thus remained ignorant—but tens of thousands left their villages anyway.

5.

A country boy arriving in the city would go first to family or friends from his village who had come before him. In this way he would find a job and a place to live. He would probably work in the quarries or in construction, as a stevedore at the port or as a factory laborer. Or he might work in the market, trying his hand as a peddler. Small groups of villagers slept in metal shanties, in tiny rooms they rented from Haifa's Arabs, on roofs, in yards, or even in caves or on mats on the beach. Their lodgings often had no showers or toilets. They ate in the market or cooked for themselves. Quite a few got married in Haifa, generally to girls from their villages; the city Arabs considered the villagers inferior and tended to look down on them. A village laborer rarely married a Haifa girl.[70]

Many migrants understood their situation as a direct result of the fact that their family homesteads had been sold to Jews. Not infrequently they found themselves working on the construction of new Jewish residential neighborhoods. The homes built for Jews were not luxurious, but they probably roused the envy of the laborer who, after a day's work, went back to a cave or a shack at the edge of the city. The Jews who worked with them received higher wages; they had a labor organization that looked after their interests and sometimes even brought them in to replace Arab workers.

When work began on construction of the Haifa port during John Chancellor's term, Jewish community representatives, David Ben-Gurion among them, went to the high commissioner to demand a commitment that a percentage of jobs be given to Jews. They also wanted the Jewish laborers to receive higher pay than the Arabs, in the form of a special five-piastre daily bonus, which meant a 30 percent supplement above an Arab

---

*Once, Farrell approved lashings for several children because they missed school on the anniversary of the Balfour Declaration. In his memoirs he wrote that the pupils were not punished for taking part in an anti-Zionist demonstration but because they had been absent from school without the principal's permission.[69]

laborer's pay. They justified their request on the grounds that the Jews' standard of living was higher than the Arabs'.*

The young villagers, torn from their homes, found compensation in the pleasures the city had to offer: alcohol and the cinema, ice cream and prostitutes and card clubs. At the coffeehouses they listened to the radio, and here and there they talked politics.[72] Loneliness and alienation led some of them into the Communist movement and into any of a number of social-political clubs linked, though often only loosely, to the Arab national movement. As in their villages, many were also attracted not to political protest but to the house of God. The Istiqlal Mosque in the lower city had a preacher with a great talent for offering these young men hope and faith. He provided a refuge from urban anonymity, from distress and resentment. His name was Sheikh Iz-al-Din al-Qassam.

---

*Chancellor objected to the Jews' demand; it reminded him of discrimination in South Africa, he said. He assumed, perhaps only for the purposes of the discussion, that the Arabs were better workers but the Jews more intelligent. So he suggested that the Jews not do the dirty work, which also meant they would earn more. The Jewish representatives rejected his proposal. Their people did not want to be an "aristocracy of labor"; they wanted to do their share of the dirty work, but their wages had to be higher. Chancellor knew that any concessions he made would not remain secret, and he expected that the Arabs would protest. The discrimination demanded by the Jews violated the law, he feared. He devoted a great deal of time to the problem, and in the end raised the pay of all workers to a sum that fell between the Arab wage and the one the Jews requested. His compromise increased the wage component of the construction budget by about 20 percent.[71]

17

Khalil al-Sakakini Builds a Home

1.

Muhammed Iz-al-Din al-Qassam came to Haifa from Syria. He was born in Jablah, a village near the Syrian town of Latakiah, sometime in the early 1880s. His father was a teacher and belonged to one of the mystical orders of Sufi Islam. Like Haj Amin al-Husseini, the mufti of Jerusalem, al-Qassam studied at Al-Azhar University in Cairo. Upon returning to his village he became a teacher and also served as imam of the local mosque. He called on the villagers to return to God.

In 1911, Italy invaded Libya and al-Qassam declared a jihad, a holy war, against the infidel Catholics defiling a Muslim nation. He collected funds for the Libyan resistance and wrote a victory anthem. He enlisted dozens of volunteers, and they all set out for Libya, but the Ottoman authorities detained them and ordered them home. When World War I broke out, al-Qassam enlisted in the Turkish army. He received military training and then was attached to an army camp near Damascus as chaplain. Toward the end of the war he returned to his village and set up a local defense force to fight the French, who were designated to take over the area. However, the locals began to fight among themselves, incited by the French; al-Qassam left the village, headed for the mountains with several of his followers, and prepared for guerrilla war.

The whole area was in the grip of lawlessness after the war, and everyone was fighting everyone else—this was the time of the attack on

Tel Hai. When Prince Faisal declared his kingdom in Damascus, al-Qassam went to join the prince's cause, but fled as the French besieged the city. Using false passports, he and his men were able to reach Beirut, and from there went to Haifa. Al-Qassam's wife and daughters later joined him. He was already in his forties.

In Haifa he first taught school, but within a short time he was appointed imam of the Istiqlal Mosque. He radiated charisma, mysticism, and nationalist fervor. Taking an interest in the laborers from the villages, he sought them out on street corners and in their shanty neighborhoods, even in the hashish dens and the brothels. At the same time, al-Qassam organized a local youth movement. His fame spread, and he was admired by many. Close to the Istiqlal Party, al-Qassam was supported by several well-off businessmen, who financed his activities.

At some point, al-Qassam was appointed regional registrar of marriages for the Supreme Muslim Council, and was thus in the service of the mufti of Jerusalem. In his new capacity he would go from village to village, making connections and gaining influence. Everywhere he went he gave religious and political sermons, and he gradually began encouraging people to organize terrorist cells to strike at the British and the Jews. Al-Qassam's followers learned to equip themselves with firearms and bombs and began to attack Zionist targets: on one occasion three members of Kibbutz Yagur were killed, and then a father and son were murdered at Nahalal. Both Yagur and Nahalal were Zionist symbols, cornerstones of the national home. The cells also vandalized trees planted by the Jews and the railroad tracks laid by the British, both symbolic targets.[1] The popular and near-spontaneous outbreaks of violence, fostered by al-Qassam, were expressions of social unrest, national rage, and the dark mood of a generation that had matured under British rule. He tried to persuade al-Husseini to join him and to issue a joint call for a jihad against the British, perhaps a mass rebellion, but the mufti refused.

In November 1935, al-Qassam left Haifa with several men and holed up in the hills around Jenin. The pressure was building in Palestine, partly as a result of mass Jewish immigration. "Every day the ships bombard us with hundreds of Jewish immigrants," Khalil al-Sakakini noted. "If this immigration continues," he wrote, "Palestine's future is very black . . . there is no choice but to rouse ourselves, there is no choice but to shake ourselves, there is no choice but to act."[2] At the port of Jaffa officials discovered a stash of weapons and ammunition the Jews had tried to smuggle through in barrels of cement. This news made the atmosphere even more tense. The political situation in the surrounding Middle Eastern countries and in Europe also had an effect. Saudi Arabia, Iraq, Syria, and Egypt were all on their way to gaining independence. In Germany the Nazis had come to power, and there was already talk of war. Italy's Fascist regime was growing ever stronger; when Mussolini's army invaded Ethiopia, Britain did very little.[3]

Al-Qassam's time in the mountains is shrouded in the mystery of legend; it is said that he wandered with his men from cave to cave, studying suras from the Koran. No one knows exactly how many people were with him—perhaps only a dozen—or how much support he really had—perhaps the backing of a mere few hundred. Nor is it certain that he left Haifa with the intention of fighting or whether he simply went into hiding. He was over fifty years old; most of his followers seem to have been about the same age. Whatever the case, they spent about ten days in the mountains, receiving food from nearby villages. The authorities knew more or less where they were hiding, apparently through informers. Then two of al-Qassam's men clashed with a police patrol searching for fruit thieves. One policeman, a Jew, died in the exchange of fire. The security forces launched a manhunt; within days they found al-Qassam in a cave near the village of Ya'bad. A gun battle ensued, and al-Qassam was killed.[4]

This event was the Arab Tel Hai, David Ben-Gurion said, and it portrayed al-Qassam as a fanatic warrior willing to face martyrdom.[5] Indeed, al-Qassam was the Arab Yosef Trumpeldor. Like Trumpeldor, al-Qassam had come from another country and had brought military experience with him. The Zionist nationalism of the dentist from Russia was mixed with Marxism; the Arab nationalism of the teacher from Syria was interlaced with Islam. Each of them had built his support among working people: Trumpeldor's followers were urban Russian students who had left their homes to work the land in Palestine; al-Qassam's were farmers who had left their villages to find work in the city. The veneration in which both men were held in life intensified after their deaths in battle; they each gave their national movements a heroic myth, a far more useful contribution than anything they had done in life.

Like Trumpeldor, al-Qassam bequeathed a few exalted last words, a prayer to God to strengthen him in his struggle. They were written on a scrap of paper apparently found in the folds of his headdress. Thousands attended his funeral, which turned into a massive demonstration of national unity; the figure of Iz-al-Din al-Qassam became an inspiration to fighters.[6] In Berl Katznelson's view, the killing of al-Qassam was a "bad thing"; the authorities should have let him live. "What could he have done? At most he would have killed ten Jews," Katznelson said.[7] The author of Trumpeldor's memorial prayer knew the value of a dead national hero.*

2.

The Arabs acted in small groups, or "gangs," as the Jews called them. Khalil al-Sakakini noted that many of the guerrillas were young, about seventeen years old, and there were even boys of twelve. Did the English know that these fighters were still in school, he wondered?[9] Miss Hilda Wilson knew. When she was on the road, the teacher from Bir Zeit would sometimes discern boys directing pieces of glass at the sun. Perhaps they were signaling to fighters hiding in the mountains; Wilson wrote of them with affection.[10]

Some of the guerrillas were nationalist idealists, some were unemployed young men with criminal backgrounds, and many were both. A few had enlisted full-time; others only joined in sporadic operations. They wandered the villages, sleeping in the mountains and in the woods, every night somewhere else. They carried their gear on mules, receiving food on demand from the villagers; lists have been found that note what and how much they took: sugar, rice, flour, barley, cigarettes, dates, tea, cheese, olives, soap. Their demands were often accompanied by threats: what was not given would be taken by force. The fighters confiscated weapons that had been in the villages from Turkish times and also collected money—part rebellion tax, part protection insurance. Some city mayors also gave them money to purchase arms. Fairly well-ordered financial records remain, showing the names of contacts in the cities who managed the cells' bank accounts.

There was some regional coordination among the terrorist bands, but they had no national headquarters. Weapons, money, and a number of the fighters, notably Fawzi al-Qawuqji, had come from Iraq; a few were equipped with French-made machine guns designed to hit aircraft; once they shot down a British plane.[11] Generally they staged ambushes, but there were occasional open battles, face-to-face, with British troops.

---

*Years later, the al-Qassam myth continued to provide inspiration for Palestinian terrorism. Airplane hijacker Leila Khaled wrote that she was taking up the struggle where al-Qassam had left off: "His generation started the revolution; my generation intends to finish it," she said.[8]

Lorry driver Alex Morrison from Liverpool was part of a supply convoy that set out from Haifa to Safed.The convoy included ten trucks, several escort cars, an ambulance, and six donkeys, needed to transfer supplies to isolated army outposts. "The Palestine situation is worse today than ever," one of the administration's men wrote. The roads were passable only in convoys.[12]

Morrison's group took a difficult mountain road; down below was a cleft they called Death Valley. Suddenly there was a terrific explosion. When the cloud of dust settled, Morrison saw a deep hole in front of him where a lorry had been. Pieces of the vehicle that had tripped the mine hit Morrison's lorry, but most flew over him and disappeared deep into the valley. The only trace of the driver was a boot with a foot inside. "Lawrence of Arabia certainly taught the Arabs how to make bombs," Morrison thought. He also thought about the driver, Snowy; they had slept in the same barracks. As he drove on, all he could think was "Glad it wasn't me!"

They unloaded supplies and resumed their trip. On the ascent up to Mount Canaan, near Safed, they suddenly encountered a roadblock of stones. They halted the convoy, jumped out of their vehicles, took up positions, and waited. For a few minutes nothing happened. All was quiet. Then, as if someone had given a sign, a massive burst of gunfire erupted from all directions. Morrison quickly took cover under his lorry.

"I was afraid of death," he wrote in his diary, "and then I found the excitement warming me up. I plucked up enough courage to peer out from under the lorry to scan the hills on one side. I saw nothing to fire at, and felt I wanted action. Then I saw a flash from behind a large rock. I kept my eyes on this spot, sighted my rifle and waited, no longer afraid. After a moment or two came another flash as I saw something white move. I fired. To my amazement an Arab stood up in full view, before dropping face down. My first kill and I felt nothing but excitement. . . . I was no longer scared. I had shot my first Arab, and I was only seventeen years old!" He continued to shoot at anything that moved. The exchange of fire went on for about an hour, until British infantry arrived from the Canaan outpost. "We were very lucky with only three men slightly wounded," Morrison summed up, "incredible after so much gunfire. However, we left many dead Arabs behind us as we proceeded."[13]

Hilda Wilson used to stop army vehicles and ask for rides to Jerusalem. Two soldiers who once gave her a ride said they were sixteen and seventeen years old. Although she could not quite believe them, they looked no older. She had taught students their age, Arabs, she said. One of them replied gaily, "I killed a couple of Arabs yesterday."

Wilson was drawn to the Holy Land, captivated by its magic in a way that certain Englishwomen were, and she identified with the Arabs. She fell in love with the carpet of red, blue, pink, and cream-colored anemones that stretched from Bir Zeit to Jalazun, on the outskirts of Ramallah, almost apologizing to every flower she trampled as she walked among them. Riding in the army truck with the two young soldiers, Wilson sank into a reverie as she was jolted from one pothole to the next. The Arabs are accused of exploiting minors, who are not liable for the death penalty, when they send boys out on murder operations, she thought. What was the difference, she asked herself. The British also used teenaged boys for deadly missions. There was no use trying to solve the country's problems by force, she told the soldiers. They grinned sheepishly but said nothing.[14]

Alex Morrison had his own opinion about the situation. Ostensibly, the British had been sent to Palestine to keep the peace and punish terrorists, Arabs and Jews. In practice, the authorities discriminated in favor of the Jews, never punishing Jewish terrorists with the severity they used on Arabs. He thought that was not right. "The Arabs always seemed to get a raw deal," he wrote.[15]

3.

Arab terrorists acted in the cities as well. On Saturday night, May 16, 1936, three Jews were killed as they left the Edison cinema in Jerusalem. Dr. Zvi Shevhovsky, thirty years old, was a doctor from Poland who had been in Palestine for half a year and worked as a volunteer at Hadassah. He left a pregnant wife. Yitzhak Yalovsky, twenty-seven, was a baker. Born in Poland, he had immigrated a year earlier and had married a month and a half before his death. Alexander "Sasha" Polonsky was twenty-three years old, a university student, also born in Poland, one year in the country. He worked as a plasterer and was waiting for his girlfriend to receive an immigration permit. The film at the Edison that night was *The Song of Happiness,* a Soviet movie. The murderer fled; High Commissioner Wauchope expressed his deep abhorrence of the crime. Khalil al-Sakakini admired it: "There is no other heroism like this, except the heroism of Sheikh al-Qassam," he wrote to his son Sari.[16]

A few weeks later a young Arab opened fire on the car of a Jerusalem police officer, wounding him. A British soldier returned fire; the Arab was hit and later died. Sakakini knew him personally—his name was Sami al-Ansari, a cousin of Musa Alami. The boy had been talented. Before reaching nineteen he had been an English teacher. "A tall boy, wiry, slender, sharp and adept, handsome, mad about sports, well-dressed. He had only just started to live." The British police officer al-Ansari had tried to kill had harassed Arabs, Sakakini wrote. "The people" had frequently made complaints to the high commissioner about this particular policeman, but to no avail. So al-Ansari had volunteered "to free the people from his evil."

Before al-Ansari died, Sakakini related, he managed to call his brother. "Don't be sorry, I have done my duty," he said. The next day, Sakakini continued, "the people" went to the house of the dead boy's father, the man "who brought this hero into the world." They went to offer not consolation but congratulations. The father spoke proudly of his heroic son. "He had good reason to be proud," Sakakini wrote. The heroism of terror expressed the spirit of the nation, he meditated, revealing to his son Sari another detail he had learned: Sami al-Ansari had been the terrorist at the Edison cinema.[17]*

In October 1935, Sakakini submitted a request to bear a weapon. Asked on the form for his reasons, he wrote, "Whereas the Jews are armed and since they wish ill of the Arabs, and every time an Arab falls into their hands they attack him, and whereas the government protects them, discriminates in their favor, and instructs them and this brings them to denigrate the law, for all these reasons I request a license to bear a weapon."[19]

What the Jewish community called "the events" and the Arabs referred to as their "rebellion" began on April 19, 1936, in Jaffa, when nine Jews were murdered and four wounded. Four days earlier, though, on April 15, Yisrael Hazan, a Greek-born poultry merchant, seventy years old, had been killed in an ambush while driving his car near Tulkarem. Soon after, stores in Tel Aviv began selling a book emblazoned with the name of the Jewish memorial prayer Yizkor, containing "pictures and facts about the martyrs of the month of Nissan 5696"—the month and year in the Jewish calendar approximating April 1936. Yisrael Hazan's portrait appeared on the book's cover, above the caption "The first victim." A different volume, published by the Histadrut, began its list of victims with Moshe Rosen-

---

*The Edison was the most luxurious of the city's cinemas. A few years after the murder that so roused his father's admiration, Sakakini's son Sari purchased a subscription to the Palestine Philharmonic concerts, held in the same hall. At the beginning of each concert the orchestra played the Zionist anthem, the "Hatikva." Sari Sakakini and his sisters remained seated as the rest of the audience gave them dirty looks.[18]

feld, the Jewish policeman killed in the encounter with al-Qassam's men.[20] So competition was under way for the title of "first victim." In truth, the opening shot for the terror that killed all these victims had occurred in the summer of 1929. From then until the beginning of World War II, more than 10,000 incidents were recorded, in which at least 2,000 people were killed, at least half of them Arabs. More than 400 Jews were killed in the terrorist attacks, and some 150 Britons.*

Most of the attacks involved land mines, bombs, gunfire, and ambushes on the roads or in isolated settlements. But even a person leaving home in Tel Aviv was at risk of being injured by a bomb hurled through the window of the train to Jaffa. A person taking the children to school had to weigh the possibility that the school building would be set on fire. Sitting in a coffeehouse, a man could not be sure there was not a bomb under his chair.

Jewish Agency leader Moshe Shertok announced to members of the Zionist Executive that, according to information at his disposal, the Arabs had decided to create a state of terror aimed at Jewish leaders and British officials.[22] Chief Secretary Battershill sent a similar evaluation to the Colonial Office in London.† They were soon proved right.

Now the conflict between the two peoples became a threat to the security of every individual, every day of the week and every hour of the day; life was a routine of total horror. "We sleep to the sound of whistling bullets and wake to the sound of whistling bullets," Sakakini wrote to his son. "They throw bombs, shoot, burn fields, destroy Jewish citrus groves in Jaffa, blow up bridges, cut telephone cables, topple electric poles. Every day they block roads and every day Arabs display a heroism that the government never conceived of."[24]

He thought about the rebellion's public relations: the problem was that the Jews controlled the newspapers and the radio. But the sword was

---

*The official record includes all the British victims and most of the Jewish dead. The number of Arab casualties is much higher than those documented: thousands were killed in clashes with the military forces, and hundreds, perhaps thousands, were killed in inter-Arab skirmishes. Assessing the Jewish victims presents its own problems: one account includes a number of cases of Jews who were killed in accidents, three who were murdered in Baghdad, two who died on their way to Palestine, and one who committed suicide while still in Poland, apparently in sorrow on hearing "the first terrible news from Palestine." These are described as "the fallen of the Exile."[21]

†Chief Secretary Battershill made up a list of officials who, in his evaluation, were targets for assassination, himself included. Lewis Andrews, the governor of the Galilee, who was later murdered in Nazareth, did not appear on the list.[23]

mightier than the book, he wrote, praising to Sari even the following act of terror: "Two anonymous heroes," he wrote, threw a grenade at a passenger train full of Jewish civilians and the British soldiers who were escorting them. "Who would believe there are such heroes in Palestine? What a great honor it is, my Sari, to be an Arab in Palestine." Sometime later he depicted the clash as a personal conflict between Chaim Weizmann and Haj Amin al-Husseini, contending that Weizmann would like to be the mufti.[25]

As the wave of violence spread, the political leadership under Husseini wished to take control of events and channel them to meet its own needs. To this end, the Arab Higher Committee was established, a kind of national-unity government of Palestinian Arabs. The mufti had long tried to play a double game with the British authorities and the national movement, but in the mid-1930s he had to come down firmly on one side or the other; apparently without much enthusiasm, the mufti decided for the rebellion. He placed himself at its head and organized fund-raising and weapons shipments.[26]* In response to a demand by Nablus members of Istiqlal, among others, the new committee declared a general strike, giving the violence the appearance of organized nationwide protest.

4.

Forcing normal life to shut down was an accepted form of protest. The Jews had also used it from time to time. In a general strike, people kept away from work, stores remained shuttered, transportation stopped running, and the schools stayed closed. A strike usually lasted only a few hours, occasionally an entire day. An Arab strike in 1933 had led Sakakini to write in astonishment, "Who would have ever thought that Palestine would strike for eight days!"[28] The Arab strike that began in April 1936 lasted for half a year.

A population of one million people cannot live in idleness for six months, and in fact not everyone participated in the strike. Government and municipal workers continued to report to their jobs, which seems to have prevented the administration's collapse.[29] Khalil al-Sakakini contin-

---

*Sakakini supported the mufti but complained that the national struggle was being swamped by politics: "Party X objects to Party Y, not to save the country from danger, but to deny the other party honor and influence," he wrote. These squabbles brought him to despair: "We are a nation that does not want to live and that is that."[27]

ued his work as a school supervisor, but when asked to participate in broadcasts of the government's Arabic radio station he refused because the announcers identified the station as being in the land of Israel, rather than Palestine.* To Sakakini, boycotting the station was a way of boycotting the authorities. When he received an invitation to dinner with the high commissioner, he declined, writing sarcastically, "Your humble servant is a poor man and asks nothing of life but to work and eat whatever comes to hand together with his family."[31]

The Haifa port also continued to function; the employees feared that Jewish workers would be brought in to replace them. Most farmers did not let their fields lie fallow, and the school strike happened to coincide in part with summer vacation. Certain people received exemptions from striking and contributed money instead, and some secretly violated the strike.

Oversight committees were established in every city and in many villages, as were committees to aid the needy. In certain places, the rebellion took the form of the poor rising up against the rich, and some leaders of the rebellion were portrayed as Robin Hoods. In the name of patriotism, there were also threats, intimidations, blackmail, and other forms of hooliganism, and at times the rebellion seemed more like a civil war than a national uprising. Several Arab leaders were murdered, including some mayors, having been accused of collaborating with the British and the Jews, but often the cause was just internal politics.[32] A number of Arabs took advantage of the rebellion to pursue feuds with other families, under the cover of anti-British agitation. One young man was engaged to his cousin; two other cousins objected to the match, so the groom turned them in to the authorities; in revenge, their brother murdered him.[33]

Indeed, the rebellion quickly deteriorated into internecine fighting; Judge Anwar Nusseibeh called it "a bitter and self-consuming abomination." Ostensibly, the rebels were subordinate to a higher authority, the mufti, but he had gone to Damascus. The rebel leaders became the lords of the land, with exclusive authority over people's lives and property, especially in the villages. They suppressed their opponents blindly, cruelly, and

---

*The government radio station, which operated out of the Palace Hotel in Jerusalem beginning in 1936, broadcast in English, Arabic, and Hebrew. Initially the station was called the Voice of Palestine Eretz Israel, but the Arabs protested, and its name was eventually changed to the Voice of Jerusalem. In fact, the announcers had not even used the full Hebrew name, only the initials EI, pronouncing them as one word. The Jewish community had considered this a great affront.[30]

very often foolishly, Nusseibeh wrote. Many Arabs lost their lives at the hands of other Arabs.[34]

Sakakini told his son that the strike leaders were forcing storekeepers to close their shops, locking the stores and taking the keys. City dwellers who wore red tarbushes were told by the rebels to wear the traditional Arab *hatta* or kaffiyeh instead. Urban Arab women were told to cover their faces with scarves, as was the custom in the villages.[35]

Patriotic symbols became part of the struggle, similar to periodic battles within the Zionist movement. The *hatta*, a white cloth with a black headband, or *akal*, represented the Arab people and consequently their national struggle; the tarbush had, from Turkish times, been a mark of the comfortable urban class. The importance of the head covering indicated that class conflict was in play as well. Eventually tarbushes took on a political aspect as well; those who wore them were identified as supporters of the opposition led by the Nashashibi family.*

The general strike hurt the Jews, but it also weakened the Arabs and failed to shut down the economy.[37] It did, however, reflect an unprecedented nationwide organizational effort that conveyed a very clear message: the Arab community in Palestine was demanding independence. Identifying the British regime with the Zionist program, the Arabs asked the British to leave. The strike finally came to an end when several Arab kings intervened—at least according to the official, diplomatic version. The real story was simpler. "I have children," said a strike organizer. "If I don't support them they will die."[38] Israeli historian Yehoshua Porat has tried to establish a connection between the strike's trajectory and the citrus crop; common wisdom had it that when laborers were needed, the strike stopped. Moshe Shertok linked the waves of terror to the hour of the moonrise. "Don't laugh," he wrote to Chaim Weizmann. "It's a very important factor. Even rebels can't ignore it."[39]

The rebellion cast the Arabs in a new light. Instead of a "wild and fractured mob, aspiring to robbery and looting," Ben-Gurion said, they emerged as "an organized and disciplined community, demonstrating its national will with political maturity and a capacity for self-evaluation." Were he an Arab, he wrote, he would also rebel, with even greater intensity, and with greater bitterness and despair. Few Zionists understood the Arab feeling, and Ben-Gurion found it necessary to warn them: the rebel-

---

*The *hatta* business boomed. Sellers of the headdress adopted a rhyming slogan: "*Hatta, hatta* for ten *grush*, damn those who wear the tarbush."[36]

lion was not just terror, he said; terror was a means to an end. Nor was it simply politics, Nashashibi against the mufti. The Arabs had launched a national war. They were battling the expropriation of their homeland. While their movement may have been primitive, Ben-Gurion said, it did not lack devotion, idealism, and self-sacrifice. This, he said, was what he had learned about the Arabs in the days of al-Qassam.[40]

5.

As he reported and interpreted the progress of the rebellion in letters to his son Sari, Khalil al-Sakakini devoted most of his time to building his new house in Jerusalem's Katamon neighborhood. He documented the project as if he were establishing his national home—perhaps no coincidence. The work on the house began in May 1934; Sakakini and a few friends set out in a kind of procession, maps in hand. "We surveyed the land on the heights, in the valleys, and on the plain," he later wrote.

He had no money, but if he waited until he did, he would never buy land. So he decided to take a loan of £100 or £150, to be paid off in installments. The project fired his imagination. At first he thought about a modest house, he wrote to his son, but then decided that the family needed a grove for the animals and birds and a tennis court. Then the thought occurred to him to plant coconut palms to raise monkeys of all sizes and build a swimming pool where the water would be changed daily. The greater his fantasies, the greater his despair—after all, he had no money. Maybe he should abandon the whole idea and continue to live as he had always done, wandering from house to house. He encountered difficulties purchasing the land as well, but in the end he was able to buy a plot in Katamon.[41]

He was about to celebrate his silver wedding anniversary. His Sultana, called Um Sari after the Arab custom of referring to parents by the name of their eldest son, was his great love: "The joy of my life, the source of my happiness, soul friend." He was now fifty-eight years old and wondered how his life would have been without her; he probably would have aged quickly and might already have been senile.

Two years went by; the builders began digging the well and the foundations. Sakakini hoped to complete construction before Sari returned from studying in America; he began planning a party for his son. He wanted to celebrate not his new house but the higher education his son had gained in America, as well as the brightness of his youth. He discerned in Sari his own optimism: "I hope, I hope, I hope that peace and brotherhood may prevail among human beings, that all mankind be happy, and that our celebrations mark the beginning of an age of peace, brotherhood, and happiness, may God will it."

Then came the great strike, halting construction of the house for about six months. This was followed by the holy Muslim month of Ramadan, and then the rains began. But Sakakini continued to dream: "To build a modest house—that is the essence of happiness," he wrote.[42] In the meantime he inspected many schools; he liked his work better than vacation.[43] "Education must be first and foremost nationalist and only afterward education for its own sake," he declared, urging teachers to instill in their pupils a national consciousness. They should know they belong to a noble, honorable, and advanced nation, he explained; they should be proud of being Arabs. He dictated a slogan to the schools, in the spirit of the words of a Baghdad poet, Ibn al-Rumi: "A homeland have I that I have sworn not to sell / And never to see it in another's hands." Rudyard Kipling's famous poem "If" inspired Sakakini to write another national anthem.

Like the Hebrew nationalists, Sakakini knew the importance of cultural patriotism in daily life and condemned the tendency of people in Jerusalem to adopt British manners. Once, when invited to tea, he made a point of demanding coffee, Arab coffee. When offered a cigarette, he asked for a nargileh. "A nation with a sense of inferiority, one that is ashamed of itself, is a dying nation," he wrote. His travels around the country deepened his love for its landscape: "Were someone to buy it for all the money in the world, he would profit; if someone were to sell it for all the money in the world, he would lose," he wrote. Palestine was for him like the Garden of Eden.[44]

But on this subject, as on so many others, Sakakini was ambivalent; in his own way he was a most skeptical nationalist. "I will not hide from you that whenever I travel in the country I want to be blind and not see, to be deaf and not hear, to stop up my nose and not smell," he wrote to Sari. More than anything else, he was pained by the thought that his children would live in Palestine. He would like them to live in a country with a nobler culture. People told him, Sakakini wrote, that he should not have sent his son to America but to Al-Azhar University in Cairo. He wondered what they would say if they knew he preferred Beethoven to the popular Egyptian Abdel Wahab or Um Kultum. Or that he considered the literary value of the Bible greater than that of the Koran. Or that he supported allowing young men and women to mix freely.[45]

Palestinian culture, he asserted, was a culture "of honor and family connections, of let us eat and drink and grow strong and attack . . . not of let us sacrifice and forgive and respect and have compassion." If he only could, he would emigrate. In one letter, he told Sari about a visit to Nablus. "Every time I visit there I feel like I've gone back to the Middle Ages," he wrote. "It looks to me as if Nablus has never heard of electricity and cinema and theater and concerts and tennis courts." Along with nationalism, Sakakini tried to instill in the schools the principles of advanced education he had embraced in the past—liberation of the students, sex education, humanist and socialist ideas.[46]

Terrorism also bothered him. "Don't ask, Sari, how much I suffer from this situation," Sakakini wrote. "I feel the pain of the troubles, whether they fall on Arabs or on the English or on the Jews. For that reason you will sometimes find me on the side of the Arabs, at other times on the side of the English, and still other times on the side of the Jews. And if there were animals who suffered from even a faint whiff of these troubles, I would sometimes be on the side of the animals."[47]

Another three years went by. Construction on the house was proceeding satisfactorily, Sakakini wrote. He went every day to check its progress, "stone by stone." He measured the height, the length, the width. "This will be the bedroom, we'll put the bed here, the wardrobe here, and the chair here. This is the kitchen, we'll put the oven here, the sink here. This is the study for Dumia and Hala, we'll cover the wall with shelves, and we'll put Dumia's desk here and Hala's desk here." One day, while he was at the site, his wife brought him a letter from Sari. The salutation read "My Dear Khalil!" Sakakini was ecstatic. "I don't think anyone has ever done that before," he wrote to his son, encouraging him to carry on calling his father by his first name. "You will be Sari and I will be Khalil; let us set aside the titles of father and mother."

People began to gossip. Where was he getting the money to build such a house? Sakakini was building with no thought to the cost: the builder was the best in town, as was the carpenter, the ironmonger, the tiler, and the painter. Who knows, he wondered, perhaps the thirteenth-century poet who wrote, "I will leave if they say not to invest and will accept only the best" was referring to him.

Sakakini decided to call his house the Island, because it was surrounded by streets except on one side, like the Arabian peninsula. Each room had a name: San'a and Damascus, Cordoba, Baghdad, and Cairo. The house's gates were called the Gates of Eternity. When Sari returned from America, "victorious and conquering, enlightened and educated," they would circle the house as if it were the Holy Kaaba in Mecca, and would go from room to room as if they were going from city to city. Afterward they would crown him with a wreath of laurel or olive branches.

The family moved in May 1937. The house was a one-story building, pleasant but not outstanding, with a red shingled roof and a small garden surrounded by a low wall. "We all feel as if we were born yesterday," Sakakini wrote, and everyone who saw him wondered at the source of his youthful exuberance. All his guests received a tour: this is the bedroom, here is the study, the living room, and the rest of the house. Sakakini decided to create a map for visitors. "The house, the house, all we talk about is the house," he told Sari. "Our house is a universe, and we are all in it, eternity is our slave." When his telephone was connected, he was beside himself with wonder. "We have been linked to the world and to each other," he philosophized. "The telephone, the telephone. I do not understand how people can live without a telephone!" Sari returned that summer. The rebellion was still in full swing. "If we live, let us live with honor, and if we die, let us die with honor," Sakakini had written sometime before.[48]

Zionist poster calling on Jews to join the agricultural settlements (Central Zionist Archive)

Tel Aviv, 1948: "They have four-story buildings!" wrote Mordechai Ben-Hillel Hacohen. (Central Zionist Archive)

Jerusalem, 1931: High Commissioner Arthur Grenfell Wauchope (William Dennis Battershill)

Wauchope and his men at the hunt (Zvi Oron)

A garden party at Government House: ". . . surrounded by a pine grove and gardens, the stone mansion . . . exuded majesty and permanence, and one glance left no room for doubt: the British Empire had come to stay." (Zvi Oron)

1939: Arab soldiers in the
service of the British
(Central Zionist Archive)

London: David
Ben-Gurion, a guest of His
Majesty's Government
(Central Zionist Archive)

Berlin, 1941: the mufti, Haj
Amin al-Husseini, a guest
of the Third Reich
(Central Zionist Archive)

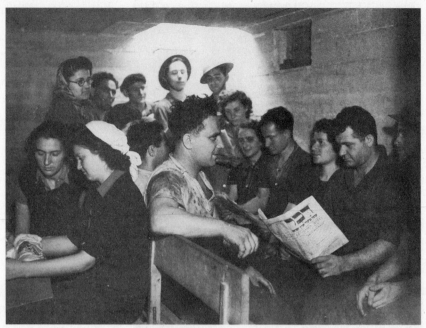

Tel Aviv, 1941: in shelters as Italian aircraft bombed the city (Central Zionist Archive)

British patrol: "Palestine is a millstone around our necks"—the colonial secretary (Central Zionist Archive)

Jerusalem, June 1947.
"The English have
betrayed us ..."
—Nathan Alterman
(Central Zionist Archive)

1948: A Haganah fighter in Jerusalem, with a picture of Abed al-Khader al-Husseini. "The Jews have won," wrote James Pollock, "What else is there to say?" (Imperial War Museum)

"I must be my own master"—Sari al-Sakakini
(State Archive)

General Evelyn Barker (Central Zionist
Archive)

Katy Antonius (State Archive)

"These plants are my life," wrote Jane Lancaster. (Ricarda Schwerin)

Lod, 1948: "It's time to be going." (Imperial War Museum)

—•◦•—

18

Made in Palestine

1.

In August 1934, David Ben-Gurion made the trip to Shuafat, the home of Musa Alami, a small Arab village south of Jerusalem. A Cambridge gradu- ate and an advocate in the British attorney general's office, Alami was a close associate of the mufti's. He hosted Ben-Gurion in his yard under an oak tree, which he claimed was the oldest tree in Palestine. Ben-Gurion had brought two ideas to put before Alami. The first involved Jewish- Arab self-government on the basis of parity, giving equal status to both communities regardless of their relative sizes. The second was the inclu- sion of Palestine in a regional Arab federation; the Jews would become the country's majority and would rule it, but the federative link with neigh- boring countries would make the Arabs of Palestine part of a regional majority.

Echoing the usual Zionist claim, Ben-Gurion insisted that the develop- ment of the country, as the Jews were implementing it, would benefit all its residents, Arabs included. Alami answered that he would prefer that the country stay poor and desolate for another hundred years, until the Arabs could develop it themselves. He suggested an autonomous Jewish canton around Tel Aviv as part of an independent Arab country under British suzerainty. This canton would constitute the Jewish national home. Alami promised to arrange a meeting between Ben-Gurion and the mufti. The meeting never took place.[1]*

Ben-Gurion held talks with other Arab leaders as well. He found George Antonius, also a graduate of Cambridge, to be a pleasant and erudite man. Ben-Gurion said that the Zionists aspired to a state within the borders of biblical Israel with a population of four million Jews. He went on to meet Aouni Abd al-Hadi, an attorney and a member of the Istiqlal Party, who, with his "malicious snicker," made an unpleasant impression on Ben-Gurion. "If I were in your place," al-Hadi is quoted as saying, "I would be a Zionist, and if you were in my place you would be an Arab nationalist like me."

Wauchope received reports of these conversations and reached the same conclusion that Ben-Gurion reached: the gulf between the Arab national and Zionist movements was unbridgeable. Talks between other Zionist and Arab leaders all led to the same impasse.[3]

When, in November 1936, Ben-Gurion considered the causes of the Arab rebellion, he wrote, "The main factor is the numerical weakness of the Jews." Secondary, in his view, was "the violent doctrine of Islam." Ben-Gurion believed that a murderous mentality and intolerance of minorities were inherent in the Arab nature. If there were no Jews in the country, he thought, the Arabs would attack the Christians.[4] From the Arabs' point of view, the rebellion had come a little too late, Ben-Gurion wrote. From the Jewish point of view, it had come a bit too early.[5] He was right: by the late 1930s the Arabs no longer had the strength to threaten the national home. The institutional foundations laid by the Zionists in the first twenty years of British rule and under Britain's sponsorship were firmly established. But the Jews were still a minority in Palestine and not strong enough to defend themselves. Advancing the national home still involved dependence on the British. A senior official once asked Ben-Gurion when, in his estimation, he would feel able to say that the national home was in place. Ben-Gurion evaded the question—there was no fixed point in time, he said, it was a historical process. Arthur Wauchope played a role in this process; he was a Zionist. Both Ben-Gurion and Jabotinsky still believed in the British. Still, the situation demanded a response, and two pivotal discussions would emerge over the next few years: one centered

*Many years later, Alami said that the mufti and Ben-Gurion were similar in that neither hid their nationalist intentions. In a conversation with a Jewish acquaintance, he made the generous comment that, unfortunately, the Arabs had never produced a Ben-Gurion of their own.[2]

on how to react to Arab terror, the other on whether to divide Palestine into two states. Some proposed setting up a binational state for both peoples; others advocated expelling the Arabs from the country.

2.

During the second decade of British rule, more than a quarter of a million Jews settled in Palestine, twice as many as in the previous ten years. In 1936 the number of immigrants exceeded sixty thousand; never had so many arrived in a single year.[6] The rise of the Nazis thus proved advantageous for the Zionist movement; for the Arabs, the developments in Germany eroded their strength.

The immigration process had not changed since the early days of the Mandate. The authorities assigned the Jewish Agency a specific number of immigration permits, which the agency then distributed more or less as it saw fit. However, Jews with capital, their relatives, and certain other categories of Jews were for all practical purposes allowed to come without restriction. As before, the Jewish Agency asked for more permits than the authorities granted; the quotas were a subject of constant negotiation with the high commissioner and an endless source of complaint for the Jewish Agency, which argued that the British were discriminating against the Jews. At times the discussions became heated. If the government continued to deny the Jews permits and put obstacles in their way, Weizmann told Wauchope, then they would just swim over. Zionist leaders more than once complained of the immigration officials' contemptuous attitudes. Some immigrants found ways to enter Palestine without permits. Most of them came to the country as tourists and simply stayed. The great majority of illegals were allowed to remain; only a few dozen were deported.[7]*

Women could obtain permanent resident permits via fictitious marriages. Mordechai Ben-Hillel Hacohen told of a love story that had begun at the Haifa port. A man went up to a taxi driver and asked whether he was available. The driver answered in the affirmative and started his engine. "No," the man said, "I mean, are you available? Are you single?"

---

*An old friend of George Antonius's, a British banker living in Poland, told him that many Jews without money were able to use "capitalist" immigration permits by means of a round-robin scam. One person would show that he had sufficient resources to qualify as a capitalist, immigrate to Palestine, and then send the money back to Poland to be used by another Jew. Antonius's friend, the director of the Anglo-Polish Bank, was resentful: the immigrants had once used his bank but were now using another bank with ties to the Zionist movement. The Arabs frequently complained of the round-robin arrangement.[8]

The driver gave a positive answer to this question as well and agreed to board a boat that had just docked to marry a young woman trying to enter the country. The young woman was allowed to disembark with the driver. He knew only Russian and Hebrew, while his new wife spoke only German. But the couple remained together. At first, Hacohen wrote, they communicated with gestures, through "movements of the fingers and kisses on the lips." Little by little, she learned Hebrew, he began to understand German, and they grew to live in peace, harmony, and love. The administration knew about the fictitious marriages and eventually amended the law to prevent a husband's citizenship from automatically extending to his wife.[9]*

But these negotiations with the authorities were part and parcel of what David Ben-Gurion called the "constant wrangling." More important was the ongoing cooperation between the Jewish Agency and the government, based on the consensual principle of limiting immigration to accord with the Jewish community's ability to support the newcomers.[11]

Many of the immigrants, particularly the refugees from Germany, brought money with them. Their arrival gave impetus to the Zionist program and stimulated the Jewish economy, which, in turn, eased pressure on the British treasury, a consideration of particular interest to the colonial secretary. Wauchope himself identified with the plight of the refugees from Nazi Germany. Opening the country to mass immigration was consistent with his politics, his sympathy for Zionism, and his innate humanitarianism. At the beginning of the 1930s the Jews were about 17 percent of the total population; by the mid-1940s they were 30 percent—almost half a million.[12]

3.

In the ten years between the 1929 disturbances and the outbreak of World War II, the Zionists persisted in their efforts to purchase land in Palestine.

---

*In the summer of 1934, the Zionists began organized efforts to land immigrants without permits on the shores of Palestine. Both the labor movement and the Revisionists bought ships to bring the illegal immigrants. The Revisionists complained about discrimination in the Jewish Agency; the labor movement gave expression to their patriotic impatience; and both were spurred on by the competition between them. The illegal immigration, ha'apala in Hebrew, embarrassed the Jewish Agency, as it ran counter to cooperation with the British. In response the authorities deducted a certain number of legal permits to account for the illegal immigrants. In other words, a Jew who entered the country without a permit came at the expense of another Jew. By the end of Wauchope's term, the number of Jews who had arrived this way was less than two thousand.[10]

Even during the Arab rebellion they had no trouble finding sellers; as before, the supply of available land exceeded the Zionists' budget. In fact, the Jewish National Fund refused to buy some of the land on offer. On the other hand, the Arab rebellion made it harder to evict the Arab tenant farmers, whose resistance had stiffened. On several occasions the farmers refused to budge.[13] From time to time the courts ruled in favor of the buyer and the authorities sent soldiers to carry out the evictions. The JNF offered the tenant farmers other land and financial compensation. But as time went by the question of legal right was increasingly beside the point. What people saw was Jews dispossessing Arabs.

The Zionist movement went to great lengths to prove that the tenants had not suffered for losing their land. A survey of several hundred villagers who had been moved from the Jezreel Valley found that most had managed to resettle and were no worse off.[14] For purposes of compensation, the British tried to establish the number of Arab farmers who were left without land or work as a result of the sale of their property to Jews. Louis French, a colonial official who had served in India, was appointed to investigate compensation claims; he received over three thousand inquiries but certified less than seven hundred. Partly, the small quantity of accepted claims was due to the procedure by which the applications were processed. First they had to be vetted by officials at the Jewish Agency, as if the agency were a branch of the government bureaucracy, rather than a party to the dispute.[15]

At the same time, the British initiated legislation to restrict Jewish purchases of land, which caused the Zionists some concern. Nonetheless, the authorities allowed the Jewish Agency's settlement program to continue apace. During the 1930s, some 130 new settlements were established; most of them were agricultural outposts, including fifty-three new kibbutzim.[16]

Some of these settlements were constructed in the middle of the night, which gave them a clandestine, heroic aura. The settlers, nearly all of them young people with ties to the labor movement, would arrive at the site, build a fence around the land, and erect a watchtower, which is why these settlements were called *homa u-migdal*, or "stockade and tower." At first they were meant to prevent Arab farmers from continuing to work land bought by the Zionist movement. But the *homa u-migdal* system also allowed the settlers to feel patriotic and rebellious, as if they were engaged in secret military operations.[17] The overnight projects thus became a way for the labor movement to channel and control the nationalist fervor of its members.

On occasion there were run-ins between the settlers and the district commissioners, but on the whole the settlements were established with the authorities' consent. So, for instance, the Jews negotiated with the government over the creation of Hanita, a kibbutz that became a Zionist symbol. The British wished to postpone the project, but after a few days of discussions Chief Secretary Battershill notified Moshe Shertok that the government had agreed to settlement on the site. To Shertok, the explanation for the British decision was obvious: the authorities were simply fulfilling their obligation to establish a Jewish national home.[18]

"During my years in Palestine," Wauchope wrote to Moshe Shertok a short time before his retirement, "one of my chief sources of encouragement has been the Jewish settlements and it is perhaps my chief hope now that by the time I leave their security may be permanently assured." In a letter to Ben-Gurion, Wauchope wrote that he would remember the settlement enterprise as "a most inspiring experience."[19]

The kibbutzim continued to believe they were fulfilling a national mission, and were generally considered a political and ideological elite. But, in fact, the center of Zionist life was Tel Aviv. In the 1930s, its population rose almost fourfold, from 45,000 to 165,000.[20] Toward the end of the decade, one out of every three Jews in Palestine lived in Tel Aviv. They were the real elite.

When Mordechai Ben-Hillel Hacohen descended from Jerusalem, where he lived, to the city he had helped found, he felt like a stranger. The place seemed to him like something out of a dream. There are buildings of four stories, the elderly writer noted in his diary, crowds fill the streets, automobile traffic threatens the pedestrians, and people spend entire nights in dance halls. Several members of the administration also described Tel Aviv with wonder; the police commander wrote that he had spent the happiest years of his life there, in part because of the jazz bands playing in the city's hotels. Tel Aviv, the man wrote, expresses the inherent possibilities of the Jews as a nation.[21]

From time to time Hacohen would visit his old home on Herzl Street, which he still owned. He was dumbfounded when he was offered £20,000 for it. He did not want to sell, and his banker advised him that one did not let go of a house on Herzl Street—its price would only rise.* Hacohen

---

*District Commissioner Stirling regretted that he had not purchased land in Tel Aviv. He could have brought a plot for £90; by the time he published his memoirs he could have sold it for £300,000.[22]

recorded the offer as a landmark in Tel Aviv's history. Once Hacohen went to the city's Allenby Cinema; he saw a film on the nineteenth Zionist Congress.[23]

When authorities consented to new settlements, they were taking on the responsibility for protecting them. The deputy commissioner of the southern district, James Pollock, received high praise from the Union of Farmers for the protection he offered. According to the annual report of the union's central committee, Pollock responded to their calls day and night. The union reserved special praise for Pollock's wife, Margaret, who acted "untiringly" to locate her husband when he was traveling among the district's Arab villages and Jewish settlements. "Thanks to the central committee's regular contacts with the authorities and the police, it was in a number of cases able to obtain the necessary help for one settlement or another at moments of the greatest danger, or transfer army and police detachments to endangered locations," the report declared. Jews who wished to serve in the police force were accepted only after the Jewish Agency recommended them. Thus the agency had a role in the police as well.[24]*

The authorities made no objections to the establishment of the Jewish defense organization, the Haganah. They sought, however, "in total secrecy, in the manner of a conversation between friends," to reach a "gentleman's agreement" on the matter.[26] Thus close and fairly effective cooperation was achieved in the three most important areas of Zionist activity: immigration, settlement, and security.

Wauchope was certain that Zionist and British interests were allied. "I am a whole-hearted believer in the success of the National Home," he wrote. "I have the deepest sympathy not only with the Jews who settle in Palestine, but also with the ideals that inspire them." Colonel Kisch compared Wauchope's Zionism to Balfour's. "He is the best high commissioner we have had," David Ben-Gurion wrote; he told Wauchope directly that the Jews had never felt more secure than in the days of his administration.[27] Wauchope was also the first high commissioner to recognize Ben-Gurion's leadership status. He once invited Ben-Gurion to Government House, and the two talked long into the night, about the spiritual roots of Zionism and about its aspirations and needs. The movement was

---

*The Jewish Agency also bribed police officers. The deputy inspector general of the Palestine Police, Alan Saunders, received a loan from the Anglo-Palestine Bank, and the Jewish Agency promised to pay the bank back if Saunders was unable to.[25]

grateful to Britain and identified with its culture, Ben-Gurion said. As a boy, he told the high commissioner, he had read George Eliot's *Daniel Deronda,* which gave profound expression to the vision of Jewish redemption. And ever since, Ben-Gurion knew that the Jews had friends in England. Wauchope said he may well have read the book too.

Privately, Ben-Gurion called the high commissioner "the old man." He once asked Wauchope for advice: teach me how to fight against you, he requested, and was promised a memorandum on the subject.[28] Ben-Gurion and his associates frequently met with the high commissioner and other administration officials and coordinated almost every matter with them. On occasion Wauchope made Jewish Agency officials party to secret information. He spoke with them freely; once he vilified Palestine's chief justice, calling him an antisemite. When the Arab rebellion broke out, ties between the Jewish Agency and the administration became even stronger, as the two joined forces to suppress the uprising.[29]

4.

At first Arab terrorism was directed principally at the British. When attacks on Jews became more frequent, there were increasing cries for retribution and revenge—mainly a psychological reaction. The Jews killed in terrorist attacks were described as "pure and innocent souls" who had fallen as "martyrs"; the Jews in Palestine were being destroyed in a "Holocaust," it was said.[30] In keeping with the inclination to describe the events of the 1920s as pogroms, Zionist spokesmen tended to link the terrorism of the 1930s to the persecution of European Jewry. This interpretation confirmed the Zionist doctrine that the Jews had "no choice" but to return to Palestine and stand their ground there. "Our blood is as water on all the lands of the earth," wrote poet David Shimonowitz, "But here . . . not as lambs will we go to our deaths. . . . The destruction wrought by evil men will not prevail or make us fear / A people for whom only one way is left / Only one way—in its own land to be redeemed! / In its only land, the Land of Israel!" Arab terrorism would unite and fortify the people. "There are moments in which the nation is forged," moments in which "man is invigorated," in which history is made, Berl Katznelson wrote, warning, "Woe to the generation that falters at such moments."[31]

The first acts of revenge were spontaneous: pedestrians in Tel Aviv beat up two Arab shoeshine boys. Immediately Ben-Gurion grasped the potential of the event to lead to an escalation of violence. He called the attack a "defilement of something very holy" and urged restraint. A few weeks later came the murder in the Edison cinema. Ben-Gurion was in his office that evening. The Haganah command demanded permission to retaliate, but Ben-Gurion refused. The Haganah repeated its request. Finally, late at night, he warned that he would resign if the Haganah did not obey him. "We must not act on momentary impulses," he said, but admitted that he'd come close to departing from his own rule of nonretaliation that night. The psychological need for revenge was very strong.[32]

Ben-Gurion denied feeling the desire for vengeance. "I never felt hatred of the Arabs and none of their actions ever awakened vengeful emotions in me," he wrote in his diary. But at the same time, he thought Jaffa should be obliterated: "The destruction of Jaffa, the city and the port, will happen and it will be for the best," he commented. "This city, which grew fat on Jewish immigration and settlement, is asking for destruction when it swings a hatchet over the heads of its builders and benefactors. When Jaffa falls into hell I will not be among the mourners."[33]

The main question was whether counterterrorism would help or damage the Zionist cause, and whether it was ethical or unacceptable. The people clamoring for action argued that restraint would be interpreted as weakness; if the Arabs believed the Jews to be weak they would only increase their violence. Weakness might also lead the British to abandon the Jews. The Haganah was not yet a real army; for the most part, its members guarded settlements and received arms from the authorities. Some Haganah units attacked Arab villages while on patrol, but they were usually breaking with the Zionists' strategy. The Haganah's national leadership was more like a board of representatives from the various political parties than a hierarchy of professionals. Until the outbreak of World War II the Haganah had no chief of staff.[34]

There were two major reasons for maintaining restraint. First, counterterrorism was liable to set off blood feuds and an endless cycle of revenge and counterrevenge, in keeping with Arab tradition. From the beginning of Zionist immigration the specter of an Arab blood feud had acted as a deterrent to the guards who had defended the first Jewish settlements. Second, a policy of retribution might well harm the Zionists' cooperation with the British.

There were moral considerations as well. Committed to the values of European humanism, those who opted for restraint argued that innocent Arab citizens should not be hurt. The notion of "an eye for an eye" was in conflict with "thou shalt not kill." In 1939, a group of intellectuals and politicians issued a declaration against terror. "The imperative [not to kill], present at the infancy of an ancient people, applies today," they stated. Shmuel Yosef Agnon signed the declaration, as did Shaul Tchernikovsky, Martin Buber, Berl Katznelson, and Golda Myerson, later Israeli prime minister Meir.[35]

Imbued with the national ethos, Zionist leaders saw themselves as moral people fighting the forces of evil. "We did not do as they did," wrote Bracha Habas in a children's weekly founded by Berl Katznelson. "We did not set fields afire, we did not cut down trees . . . and we are proud of it."[36] Most of the newspapers opposed acts of vengeance, in keeping with the law and with the leaders' policy of restraint.*

Others favored counterterrorism. They argued that traditional Jewish morality sanctified revenge, citing the biblical command to the Israelites to obliterate their enemies, the Amalekites, even though there were certainly innocent people among them. The British had instituted a blockade against Germany during World War I, starving women and children. "No one thought that was immoral," these newspapers wrote. The conclusion: "Choose life! Choose the path of honor, the path of response, the path of defense and active combat, because that way lies your only hope of deliverance and a life of honor in the homeland."[38]

Ben-Gurion and his followers, and even Jabotinsky, were faced with the same difficulty that the outbreak of Arab violence had posed for the mufti. They did not want to jeopardize the British-Zionist alliance, but they were worried about their image as proud patriots; self-restraint would be seen as weakness. This imperative to defend the Jews' national honor motivated many, including Revisionist Chaim Shalom Halevi. "Two ways lie before us," a Revisionist broadside declared, "the way of life and the way of death, the way of honor and the way of shame, the way of surrender and slavery to Ishmael and the way of war and total victory."[39]

For some time, the Revisionists had considered setting up their own defense organization, which was eventually known as the National Military Organization, or Etzel—its Hebrew acronym. The British called it the Irgun, Hebrew for "organization." Chaim Shalom Halevi was among

---

*The Histadrut newspaper, *Davar,* edited by Berl Katznelson, had begun to appear in 1925. In the second half of the 1930s, Zalman Schocken, a Jewish millionaire from Germany, became the owner of *Ha'aretz* and his son became editor. There were several other daily newspapers and political weeklies in Hebrew. The first evening paper, *Yediot Aharonot,* was launched in 1939.[37] The English-language Zionist daily, the *Palestine Post,* began publication in 1932. In general, the newspapers saw themselves as part of the Zionist struggle, partners in the effort to consolidate the Jewish community's national, cultural, and political identity.

its founders. One of his classmates at the university, Avraham Stern, had by then composed his song "Anonymous Soldiers," later to become the anthem of the Freedom Fighters of Israel, or Lechi, which the British called the Stern Gang.[40] Earlier, poet Uri Zvi Greenberg had written a poem calling for the Jews to act like the Sicarii, a Jewish terrorist faction that had fought the Romans. He inspired the establishment of a short-lived organization called Brit HaBirionim, or Covenant of the Strong-man. As the urge to revenge and the arguments of counterterrorism grew stronger, they breathed life into Etzel and later into a terror unit established within the Haganah.*

Etzel members ambushed and killed Arabs; they threw bombs into Arab coffeehouses and marketplaces, causing dozens of deaths. Like the Arab terrorists and the Haganah, Etzel often acted without any nationwide coordination. This seems to have been the case when its members shot at an Arab bus traveling from Safed to Rosh Pina in April 1938. The action was taken to avenge the murder of four Jews in a car near the same spot a few days earlier; the victims included a child and two women. No one on the bus was hurt, but the three perpetrators were caught and tried. One, Shlomo Ben-Yosef, was the first Jewish terrorist to be executed.[42] Now Etzel had its own mythic hero. Ben-Gurion believed this had been the organization's goal; the Revisionists had wanted Ben-Yosef hanged, he maintained.

The Revisionists tried to drag the Jewish community into a display of mourning for Ben-Yosef. Someone flew a black flag over the Histadrut building, and Ben-Gurion ordered it removed. This is not a day of mourning, he said, but a day of mortification. "I am not shocked that a Jew was hanged in Palestine. I am ashamed of the deed that led to the hanging," he added. He rejected the claim that no Jew should ever receive the death penalty, which would mean that rapists and child killers would be considered immune. He thought it a catastrophe that people were attempting to turn Ben-Yosef into a martyr. No, he said, this was not authentic "Jewish sentiment" but an emotion "fabricated" by the Revisionists.

---

*The man who founded Etzel was Avraham Silberg-Tehomi, Jacob de Haan's assassin. A member of the Haganah, he broke away with several of his comrades. While the Haganah functioned as a kind of popular militia affiliated with the labor movement, Tehomi and his men wanted a more rigid military organization. In 1937, about half of his followers—some 1,500 men—returned to the Haganah. The rest continued to act under the sponsorship of the Revisionists.[41] Jabotinsky was not at first enthusiastic about a separate Revisionist military unit, but he bowed to pressure and gave it his backing.

Just as young Arabs on strike forced store owners to close their shops, Revisionists also tried to force tradespeople to close their businesses as a gesture of mourning and protest.[43] Violent encounters occurred between Haganah and Etzel supporters; a meeting between Haganah leader Eliahu Golomb and Ze'ev Jabotinsky was not successful. "He hopes to create a cult of Ben-Yosef among the Jewish people," Golomb concluded. Jabotinsky saw Ben-Yosef as a more important figure than Trumpeldor. "With the help of this cult he hopes to create discord and factionalism among our youth," Golomb wrote. "To this end, he is prepared to continue acts of retaliation without any regard for the consequences."[44] Ben-Gurion referred to Jabotinsky as the "Fascist Satan" and described the Revisionists as "a party of Nazis."[45]*

Local leaders repeatedly condemned counterterrorism, as did the Zionist Congress.[48] But Ben-Yosef's execution gave Etzel momentum, and, as it increased its activities, young people in the labor movement also began to demand revenge. On more than one occasion they, too, were drawn into acts of retribution. Ben-Gurion feared that the Revisionists were co-opting patriotic sentiment and that he was losing control of his men. "The pressure from the ranks forced the chief commanders to find an outlet for the anger and vengeance that filled their men's hearts," says the official *Haganah History Book*.[49] In 1939, Ben-Gurion agreed to set up a revenge organization, the Special Operations Units, subordinate to him—at this point he was chairman of the Jewish Agency.

According to Nachum Shadmi, a unit commander, the Special Operations Units were established to strike at Arabs who had killed Jews, but also at the British administration and at Jewish informers and traitors. He described one operation in the Arab village of Lubia in the Upper Galilee. The unit's men sneaked into the village at night, silently, in tennis shoes, pouring gasoline behind them to keep dogs from tracking them. Once in the village, they chose a house with its lights on. They peered in and saw three men and two women seated around a dead body laid out on the floor. The unit's men fired their weapons into the room through the window. One member of this unit, Yigal Allon, would go on to become a

---

*In the wake of an explosion that killed dozens of Arabs in the Haifa marketplace, Ben-Gurion told the high commissioner that in his opinion the act had been carried out by Nazi agents. The British had failed to halt anti-Jewish terrorism, yet Ben-Gurion was almost forgiving, telling the authorities that one's life was in danger even in Chicago and New York.[46] Chief Secretary Battershill did not rule out the possibility that the Revisionists would also act against British officials.[47] But in its early years, Etzel targeted only Arabs.

famous Israeli soldier and politician. There had also been children in the house, it turned out. Three people were killed, two men and a woman, and three were wounded, including a two-year-old boy and a ten-year-old girl.

A few days after the action Berl Katznelson published a sharp condemnation in *Davar*. Restraint, he said, meant "purity of arms"—that is, there were moral and immoral uses of force. Shadmi and his comrades, stung by the criticism, considered going to Tel Aviv to explain their position to Katznelson. Then they concluded that there was no point; there was a division of labor—Katznelson wrote on morality for the newspaper, and they did what was necessary in the field.[50]*

Shadmi once witnessed the violent interrogation of an Etzel man who was an informer. The interrogator, David Shaltiel, later a general in the Israeli army, "handled him in a horrible way," Shadmi wrote. As was the case with Arab terror, the Jews' revenge operations attracted criminal types as well. Moshe Shertok recorded a "base act," the murder of an Arab by a Jew because of a private dispute. "In the past no one would have believed that a disagreement of this type would lead to gunfire," he wrote. He proposed a "bold act" to his colleagues: they should be willing to hand "crazy young men" to the authorities. He also compared Jewish terror to Arab terror: "The filth that rules the Arab population has gotten into certain groups in the Jewish population," he wrote.[52]

5.

The violence, the Arab strike, and Arab attempts to boycott the Jewish economy made daily contact between the two peoples difficult and advanced the notion of separation. Ben-Gurion considered segregation essential to Jewish economic independence, an important step on the road to political independence. To that end, he supported building a port in Tel Aviv, a symbolic gesture as much as an economic one.

The port was built in 1936, in response to the strike at the Jaffa port. The trade dimension did not interest Ben-Gurion. He knew nothing of imports and exports—shipping of so many crates of oranges was not the issue. He identified the port with the Zionist vision itself: "We have finally conquered the path to the sea and that is equal in my eyes to a new Balfour

---

*Martin Buber once demanded that Moshe Shertok write an article condemning one such retaliation operation, in exchange for which Buber would not issue a condemnation of his own. Shertok, who had replaced Chaim Arlosoroff as chief of the Jewish Agency's political department, arranged for a critical statement to be published.[51]

Declaration," he wrote. His use of military terminology in this context was no accident: "Nations go to war for an outlet to the sea," he noted. "I want a Jewish sea," he told his colleagues. "The sea is a continuation of Palestine," he said, and "we must enlarge the country."[53]

High Commissioner Wauchope had called on the Jewish Agency to keep the Jaffa port operating by using Jewish workers; in this way he hoped to break the strike. The agency rejected his demand. Ben-Gurion saw the Arab strike as a blessing; it encouraged the principle of "Hebrew labor" and provided work for the Jews.[54] "In this sense we are not interested in stopping the strike," he said. Some Jews warned against building a separate port in Tel Aviv, lest it launch an economic war that the Jews were liable to lose. Ben-Gurion responded by saying that anyone who shirked any effort to create the port "ought to be shot."[55]

The new port, at the northern edge of Tel Aviv, was a simple wooden wharf, but Ben-Gurion took great pride in it. "The wharf is a wharf," he wrote, "and our boys, with their bare tanned skin, work in the water, loading and unloading and pulling the boats like born stevedores." Ben-Gurion could hardly remember when in his life he had felt such great joy. Someone had once come up to him and asked in Yiddish whether there would really be a port in Tel Aviv, he recalled. "Both a port and a kingdom," Ben-Gurion had replied. "We ought to reward the Arabs for giving us the impetus for this great creation," he wrote in his diary, and a while later he said, "The mufti performed a great service for the Jewish people."[56]

As terrorism increased, many Jews chose to leave Jaffa and other Arab towns, and Tel Aviv filled up with thousands of refugees. "They cannot leave Palestine but they cannot live in it," Khalil al-Sakakini gloated.[57] Many of Tel Aviv's newcomers were housed in tents on the beach. They had come from Tiberias, Haifa, and Jerusalem's Old City. Zionist leaders spoke with the commissioner of Jerusalem about dividing the city into boroughs. The Hebron Jews who had returned to their homes a short time after the 1929 riots again fled the town.[58]

In this context, the Jews resumed their debate about using "Hebrew labor" exclusively, and now security factors entered into the discussion. One intelligence report painted a "frightening picture," revealing that some of the leading Arab terrorists had previously worked for Jewish employers. "Arab workers in our fields will always serve as spies," the report stated. There was a continued effort to spread the Hebrew language and strengthen Hebrew education, and the Zionists initiated a campaign to buy only products "made in Palestine," meaning goods pro-

duced by farms and factories under Jewish ownership.[59] In the mid-1930s
the Association for Palestinian Products was established in Tel Aviv—its
name was misleading, as the association sought to promote not products
of Palestine but of the Jewish economy. Like the Battalion for the Defense
of the Language, the organization was an attempt to impose national loyalty on people as part of their daily routine. "Every man and woman in
the Yishuv, without regard to faction or party, must lend a hand to this
important effort, directed at strengthening the economy and against the
enemies of our rebirth," one declaration stated. The group would soon
change its name to the Product Loyalist Alliance; buying agricultural and
industrial products from Jewish farms and factories was described as a
"commandment."

The organization's volunteers patrolled the markets and on occasion
threatened merchants who sold Arab products. They "denounced traitors" in published announcements or with graffiti painted on shop doors.
They also broke display windows. The Product Loyalists did run into
some opposition—they were accused of using gangster tactics and turning Tel Aviv into a second Chicago—but like the defenders of the language, the Jewish products faithful were mostly lauded as patriotic
pioneers.[60] The editor of the children's newspaper *Davar LeYeladim*
encouraged his young readers not to eat foreign products, even if they
had to disobey their mothers. "Tell mother," he instructed, "always to buy
products of the Hebrew economy."[61]*

The "Buy Hebrew" campaign was an extension of the struggle for the
status of the Hebrew language. "We should impress upon the public to
refrain from buying merchandise produced in Palestine if it has no labels,
wrappers, or tag in Hebrew," wrote the Central Council for Instilling
Hebrew in the Yishuv, one of the many bodies concerned with language.
Thousands of people replaced their European-sounding family names
with Hebrew names.[63]

But the principal effort to consolidate a separate national identity was
reserved for education. A British commission of inquiry studying the

---

*From its beginnings, the Zionist enterprise had struggled for the supremacy of "Hebrew"
goods. Shortly after the British entered Palestine, the Zionist Commission asked for a permit to import machinery for a soap factory. Jabotinsky quoted what one British official had
told him: "Don't forget that there is a flourishing soap factory in Nablus. If the Jews also
open a soap factory, perhaps better and cheaper, what will happen to the Arab factory?"
Ha'aretz ran an advertisement promising locally produced soap made from pure olive oil,
"free of any Arab admixture, and of higher quality than the soap of Nablus."[62]

Hebrew school system found that Jewish parents in Palestine expected more of their children's education than parents in England—they saw education as a national enterprise. Most schools, the commission wrote, made great efforts to imbue the pupils with a deep attachment and sense of belonging to the land of Israel. Hebrew schools fostered Hebrew culture, especially the Bible and literature. Lessons on the geography of Palestine were described as "homeland" classes and included many field trips, aimed at inculcating Zionist ideology. Commission members found something "puzzling" in all this, which was a restrained way of saying what British education officials in Jerusalem were saying in stronger language: director Jerome Farrell compared Hebrew education to Nazi education.[64]*

In early 1940, a storm over a children's playground in Safed seemed to represent the entire conflict over Palestine. The playground, in the yard of a Jewish school, was paid for by the Guggenheimer Foundation, a branch of Hadassah, the American Zionist women's organization. There were a few swings and a sandbox. Arab children soon started coming to the playground, and the Jewish parents decided to prevent them from playing there. The head of Safed's Jewish community, Moshe Podhortzer, supported them.

There followed a flurry of correspondence about issues of principle. Representatives of the Guggenheimer Foundation wrote that closing the playground to Arab children violated the philanthropist's will, and besides, something larger was at stake, of importance to "the entire Yishuv": contact between Jewish and Arab children would bring the "two communities" closer. The foundation's letter referred to the happy fact that the Arab children had come to the playground of their own volition. "This, in our opinion, is the correct and natural way and it is not right to close the doors in their faces." After all, the Zionist movement's declared policy was one of peace. Therefore the playground should remain open at least to small Arab children, up to the age of thirteen.

Podhortzer, later the town's mayor, also addressed the question of principle. "If you are concerned with keeping the will of the late Bertha Guggenheimer, we are no less concerned with keeping a will more ancient and more important: to educate our children in the spirit of the Torah

---

*Director of Education Bernard de Bunsen noted derisively that the Jews taught Shakespeare in Hebrew. De Bunsen was also dissatisfied with the role played by the Hebrew University; there were no more than two or three Arab students there, he said.[65]

and Jewish ethics, and to keep them away from bad companions so that they not learn their ways." He refused to allow small Arab children to play in the sandbox, citing "the corrupt character of these children from the very beginning of their childhood. . . . Even in the ages between zero and ten not only are their mouths always full of filthy and rude language, but they are also capable of perverted acts."

Podhortzer saw no reason to celebrate the fact that the Arab children had come to the playground of their own volition: "We can assure you that these 'children' will always be willing to come on their own—not only to the playground but also to any place that you give them an opportunity to come into contact with our children." He knew the value of the contact between the two communities, he wrote, but he would not allow the corruption of the morals of impressionable children. "That is too dear a price for us," he stated. There were enough realms for contact, in accordance with the decisions of the Zionist Congresses, and he saw no reason to include his sandbox among them. The Guggenheimer Foundation turned to the Jewish Agency. Moshe Shertok hesitated and then decided not to intervene.[66]

British education director Jerome Farrell disliked the practice of segregation as much as he disapproved of the Jewish school curricula and their focus on Zionist ideology. Moreover, he found the schools' teaching methods outdated and medieval and their management inefficient. Furthermore, some Jewish children, especially those whose parents came from Arab countries, did not attend school at all.[67] The Hebrew school system did face many difficulties, including budgetary constraints. From time to time there were teachers' strikes. The system was far too heterogeneous—schools differed in their level and their approach; most of them, in fact, belonged to one or another political stream within Zionism and developed their curricula accordingly. But unlike the Arab schools, the Hebrew system reflected a national and community-wide effort that the Arabs could not have made.[68] A commission that inspected the schools a few years later noted with some amazement that the Jewish schools had too many teachers—one for every twenty-two pupils. The proportion was far higher than that in English schools.

A large share of the Hebrew schools' budget came from overseas contributions and an education levy that the Jewish community imposed on itself. The government contributed a relatively small part of the budget; from time to time the Jewish Agency argued that the authorities were giving Jewish education less than its due.[69] Unlike Arab children, almost

every Jewish child, boy or girl, went to school. This was the great difference between the two national movements; along with the revival of the
Hebrew language, education was Zionism's greatest accomplishment.

6.

Parallel to segregating Jews and Arabs, David Ben-Gurion also worked to
separate the Jews in Palestine from the World Zionist Organization, striving to transfer the center of decision making from London to Jerusalem.
No principle was at stake in this dispute; both he and Weizmann were aiming for independence, and both believed in cooperating with the British.
They did have tactical differences, though: Ben-Gurion wanted to take a
firmer line with the British and demand increased immigration, but he
was aware of the limits of the possible; he, too, was careful not to bring
relations with the British to a point of crisis. Nor did Ben-Gurion aspire to
replace Weizmann as the head of the Zionist movement. His goal was to
direct affairs from within Palestine and to concentrate power in his hands.

In 1935 Weizmann was reelected president of the Zionist movement,
with Ben-Gurion's support. But Ben-Gurion insisted on having oversight
of Weizmann's activities to prevent him from becoming "a kind of political dictator." Ben-Gurion suggested that Weizmann be "first among
equals." He made a show of his independence and power. "In speaking of
official policy, one should distinguish between Chaim's policies and mine
and Moshe [Shertok]'s," he wrote.[70] Ben-Gurion's demands infuriated
Weizmann. "We are being reduced to an Embassy," he complained. Jewish
Agency leaders in Jerusalem would soon ask to review Weizmann's letters
to the British before he sent them. Weizmann is dangerous to Zionism,
Ben-Gurion declared.[71]

Like Ben-Gurion, Wauchope was also inclined to control all decision-
making power regarding Palestine. He succeeded in doing so not only
through the force of his dominant personality but also because, unlike his
predecessor, he was close to the British prime minister and because during his tenure the post of colonial secretary changed hands four times.
"The center of gravity has passed from London to Jerusalem," Ben-
Gurion told his associates, referring both to his own position and that of
the high commissioner. He was pleased: this made his relations with the
authorities much easier.[72]

As the Jews in Palestine became more of a power in their own right,
Ben-Gurion began to modify the Zionist agenda. In theory, his obligation
to the Jews of the Exile remained unchanged. In 1938 he wrote, "The pur-

pose of the Jewish state will be to absorb a maximum number of Jewish immigrants and help solve the question of the Jewish people in the world." An independent state would serve to "redeem" world Jewry and enable Jews to return to their homeland.[73] But in practice, Ben-Gurion's priorities were different: first and foremost, a state would strengthen the Jewish community in Palestine against the Arabs. The new Zionist rationale coincided with the growing awareness that war with the Arabs was inevitable.

Paradoxically, the deteriorating situation of the Jews in Europe hastened the shift. Suddenly there were millions of people who needed refuge, but Palestine could not take them all in. Ben-Gurion often fantasized about numbers. In 1934 he said there was room in Palestine for four million Jews; two years later he spoke of eight million, "at the least."[74] Sometimes he mentioned an immigration rate of 50,000 a year; at other times he cited a figure of 100,000. In any case, he believed that bringing Europe's Jews to Palestine was a process that would take between fifty and one hundred years. Even then, no more than half the world's Jews would be living in Palestine.[75] In other words, even at the most optimistic estimate, only a small fraction of Europe's increasingly beleaguered Jews could have immigrated to Palestine during the 1930s. Tragically, Zionism predicted the catastrophe, but the solution it offered the Jews was inadequate just when it was most needed.*

As Ben-Gurion and the rest of the Jews in Palestine came to realize that the country could not take in all persecuted Jews, they ceased to see the state as a means of saving the Jewish people and focused on their own needs instead. When in 1937 Ben-Gurion spoke of bringing a million and a half Jews to Palestine over fifteen years, he was thinking predominantly of the necessity to create a Jewish majority.[77] Ben-Gurion also began to view the rise of the Nazis in Germany as a means to advance Zionism.[78] "We want Hitler to be destroyed," Ben-Gurion said, "but as long as he exists, we are interested in exploiting that for the good of Palestine." Consequently the Zionists took action to ensure that Europe's Jewish refugees would come to Palestine rather than go elsewhere. On one occasion Ben-Gurion told the high commissioner that he would support the transfer of

---

*Even Ze'ev Jabotinsky, who campaigned loudly for a massive influx of Jews, spoke in terms of numbers that were small in comparison with the dimensions of the approaching cataclysm. In 1936 he proposed a plan to "evacuate" a million and a half Jews from Europe and settle them in Palestine. But even this figure would have to be spread over ten years.[76]

Poland's Jews to America or Argentina, "despite our Zionist ideology," if such a step were possible.[79] Nonetheless, he saw other endeavors to help European Jews as harmful competition. Among the targets of his anger was the Joint Distribution Committee, the worldwide Jewish-aid organization that functioned independently of the Zionist movement.[80]

Ben-Gurion's sense of competition explains his reaction to the international conference that convened in Évian, France, to discuss the problem of the Jewish refugees. He warned that opening other countries to Jewish immigrants was liable to weaken the Zionists' demand that they be evacuated to Palestine. The Yishuv depended on immigration, he wrote, expressing his fear that the persecution in Europe would adversely affect the Zionist movement's ability to raise development funds. "While myriads of Jewish refugees are languishing and suffering in concentration camps, even Zionists will not respond to the needs of Palestine," he noted.[81]

A few years earlier, Ben-Gurion had made the following statement about the rescue of German Jewish children: "If I knew that it was possible to save all the children in Germany by transporting them to England, but only half of them by transporting them to Palestine, I would choose the second—because we face not only the reckoning of those children, but the historical reckoning of the Jewish people."[82] He was speaking in December 1938, a short time after *Kristallnacht.* To make sure he was not misunderstood, Ben-Gurion added, "Like every Jew, I am interested in saving every Jew wherever possible, but nothing takes precedence over saving the Hebrew nation in its land."[83]*

The tendency to see the Jews of Europe as "human material" necessary to establish the state, rather than seeing the state as a means to save the Jews, guided the Zionist leadership in setting its immigration policy. Given the choice, Ben-Gurion said, he would opt for young immigrants, not old ones and not children—children would be born in Palestine. He preferred workers.[84] Indeed, most immigration permits issued in the 1930s were assigned to unmarried male "pioneers" in their twenties; only 20 percent of the permits were assigned to young women. While a small number of permits were allocated to children, the Jewish Agency stipulated that no

---

*The Zionist movement frequently grappled with the question of whether it should try to improve living conditions of Jews in other countries or restrict itself to settling Jews in Palestine. In fact, on many occasions the Zionists did work to improve the lot of Jews around the world.

retarded children should be permitted to come, because it would be difficult to make appropriate arrangements for them in Palestine.[85]*

Three years after the Nazis came to power in Germany, with World War II on its way, a special fund was established in Palestine to finance the return of incurably ill Jews to Europe. The justification was that these immigrants "had become a burden on the community and its social institutions." The Histadrut and the Tel Aviv municipality helped set up the fund. By the end of December 1936 it had arranged the return of several dozen immigrants.[87]

While local leaders tried to pick and choose potential immigrants, they were upset that Europe's Jews seemed to be in no hurry to come to Palestine. Moshe Shertok complained that Polish Jews were not rushing to take advantage of the immigration permits the Jewish Agency sent them. He estimated that thousands already had permits but kept putting off their departure. "The Jews of Poland apparently do not know that a sword is hanging over our necks," he said, referring to the dangers faced in Palestine. He suggested creating a panic in Poland to encourage the Jews to leave.[88] Other leaders continued to demand that the Exile provide funding for the Zionist program. "They are contributing too little," wrote Arthur Ruppin during a tour of the Jewish communities of Poland; this was in March 1938, a year and a half before the Nazis invaded Poland and began murdering the Jews.[89]

Less than two weeks before the outbreak of war Ben-Gurion complained, "It is the fate of Palestine that lies in the balance." In a sharp attack on the Jews of Europe, he added, "Call me an antisemite but I must say this. . . . We are choking with shame about what is happening in Germany, in Poland, and in America, that Jews are not daring to fight back." Commenting on the psychology of life in the Exile, he declared: "We do not belong to that Jewish people. We rebel against that kind of Jewish people. We do not want to be such Jews." A few months earlier, Ben-Gurion had said, "Pleading is fit for rabbis, for women; our way is not to plead but to spread political propaganda."[90]

Ben-Gurion was impressed by the power of the British Empire. While he frequently vilified British officials and statesmen, even lashing out at the "bloody British," he admired British democracy. After a visit to the Houses of Parliament he joked that he might as well have been at the

---

*Men married to non-Jewish women encountered special problems in receiving immigration permits from the Jewish Agency.[86]

Zionist Congress, the speakers had been so sympathetic to Zionism.[91]*
He continued to believe that the British supported Zionism because it
was in their interest, but also because they honored the commitment
made in the Balfour Declaration and sympathized with the plight of the
Jews. Ben-Gurion reprimanded Menachem Ussishkin in this regard. "We
have some naive belief that Great Britain is under our thumb and has to
obey our every whim," he wrote. The political situation made it necessary
to preserve Britain's goodwill, Ben-Gurion warned, because "the greatest
catastrophe the world has ever seen" was about to take place, and who
knew which army would end up in Palestine. The country could be occupied by Hitler, Stalin, or Ibn Saud or remain Great Britain's. Even then, so
late in the day, the Zionists in Palestine were preoccupied with how they
would fare when the war broke out.[92]

---

*Ben-Gurion reserved special fury for Jewish politicians in Britain who were unwilling to
adopt his positions down to the last detail. He called Herbert Samuel a "traitor and slave"
and James Rothschild "cowardly and foolish."

19

The Story of a Donkey

1.

The connections Chaim Weizmann had made and cultivated over the years continued to open almost every door in London to Zionist leaders. One Foreign Office official claimed that the Jewish Agency virtually had the status of a foreign embassy.[1]

In turn, top British officials continued to treat Weizmann with honor, despite the erosion of his position in the Zionist movement. Sir Archibald Sinclair, leader of the Liberal Party, hosted him at his home for dinner; Winston Churchill was among the guests. Churchill got drunk, called Prime Minister Stanley Baldwin an "idiot," and promised Weizmann that he would support the Zionists even if they did horribly stupid things. Churchill turned to Clement Attlee, who would himself become prime minister, and, pointing at Weizmann, declared, He is your teacher, he is my teacher, he was Lloyd George's teacher—we will do whatever he tells us.[2]

The Zionists often knew what was said behind closed doors as well. Lord Balfour's niece, a devout Christian and a Zionist like her uncle, volunteered to be a spy. Blanche Dugdale had an intimate friendship with a government minister, whom David Ben-Gurion and Moshe Shertok identified in their diaries only as "a friend." This was Walter Elliot; he served in the government in various posts during most of the 1930s. The information he leaked to his "Baffy" was of no small assistance to the Zionist movement's endeavors; she spoke to him at least once a day. Walter came at about 10:30, she once recorded in her diary, "and stayed till 1 A.M. Part of the time we talked about the Palestine situation." Ben-Gurion compared her to the prophetess Deborah. Dugdale was an intelligent woman, and Weizmann and Ben-Gurion did more than just exploit her personal connections. They made her a true partner in their diplomatic labors.[3]*

Support for Zionism was still seen in many British circles as a matter of fairness. The *Times* of London was the leader in this approach, which cut across party lines and was shared by all kinds of members of the political establishment. Some of them seemed almost addicted to Zionism; as in the past, this strange and intimate attraction was a combination of awe and fear, admiration and revulsion. One evening Moshe Shertok went to the theater in London and, to his surprise, found Palestine there as well. The play being performed told the story of a top Foreign Office official in charge of Palestinian affairs who was forced to resign because he had cheated on his wife. The man was extremely frustrated; had he not been fired, he believed, he could have ended the riots in Palestine. One of the women on stage asked, "What do they really want, those Arabs?" The official's mistress responded, "All I know about Arabs is that a piece of soap would do no harm to each and every one of them." Shertok reported that the audience laughed.[5]

Occasionally, Palestine came up for discussion in the cabinet, in Parliament, and in the press, but the ongoing economic crisis in Britain, Nazi Germany's threat to Europe, and especially the trauma suffered by the political system when the king fell in love with an American divorcée pushed Palestine out of the center of discourse. Ben-Gurion estimated that in England there were perhaps a hundred people—members of Parliament and newspaper editors—who took an interest in events in Palestine. Were all of them to set sail in a single boat and sink, no one in Britain would know what was happening in Palestine, Ben-Gurion thought. At most they might find a letter from 1917 containing some sort of obligation.[6]

As the Arab protest continued, as terrorism increased, and as the winds of war began to blow in Europe, the growing feeling in London and among the British in Jerusalem was that Palestine had become a burden there was no longer any reason to bear. This shift did not happen all at once, nor was it the result of rational analysis. More than anything else, it reflected discomfort and impatience; Britain was getting sick of Palestine.

---

*George Antonius and his wife, Katy, also maintained friendly relations with Blanche Dugdale and her Walter, the minister.[4] But in general the Arabs did not enjoy the unmediated access to British leaders that characterized the Zionist movement.

The country was a long-standing and near-insoluble problem, a Foreign Office official wrote: "it is hard to see" how a solution might be found. The pledges and promises received by the Jews and Arabs could never be reconciled, at least not as interpreted by the two parties to the dispute. Terror was forcing Britain to send reinforcements to Palestine, and that cost money. Wauchope threatened to raise local taxes to cover military expenses, but his power to do so was limited.[7]

In the summer of 1936 the authorities destroyed several hundred houses in the Old City of Jaffa—Arab spokesmen said eight hundred, the *Times* said three hundred. Some of them were blown up. The few thousand residents, all Arab, were given twenty-four hours' notice and ordered to evacuate their homes; some of the evacuation orders were dropped from an airplane. The authorities promised compensation, but did not provide alternative housing. At first, people crowded into schools and store cellars and flocked to the beach.[8]

The demolished homes stood in a tangle of narrow alleys that had provided cover for stone throwers and snipers, making the area a danger zone for security forces. A correspondent for the *Times* praised the authorities. The neighborhood was a poor one, he said, with alleys full of filth, violence, and crime. Its destruction enabled the correspondent to walk freely where previously even a policeman would not have dared walk alone.[9] But Chief Justice Sir Michael McDonnell directed scathing and embarrassing criticism at the government because it had lied to the residents. Instead of telling them the truth—that the demolition of the houses was for security purposes—the authorities had pretended the work was part of an urban renewal project, as if their intention was to spruce up the neighborhood's appearance and promote public health. The government had thrown dust in people's eyes, the judge wrote. During court proceedings the different government authorities evaded responsibility for the demolition, and the judge criticized this as well. Wauchope was livid at McDonnell's behavior; the chief justice had stabbed the administration in the back, he claimed. The incident damaged the government's standing, Wauchope said, and further fueled the Arabs' complaints. The judge was soon removed from Palestine.[10]*

---

*During this period several other prominent judges were replaced. Some of the new appointees pursued a more equitable, less arrogant approach on the basis of the common law and "the doctrines of equity in force in England." Like the rest of the administration, the judges acted according to their personal background and outlook, and their political position on events in Palestine.[11]

The demolition of the houses in Jaffa revealed the authorities' willingness to pursue an iron-handed policy against terror, but their foolish attempt to conceal the true purpose of the operation was a reflection of the many difficulties that policy entailed. Wauchope demanded that the supervision of counterterrorism remain in his hands, but at the same time he did not want his administration identified with specific acts. Better to appear as a "kindly father" rather than as the commander of "bloody soldiers," he wrote. After all, it was the civil administration, not the army, that would have to live with the country's inhabitants after public order was restored. The Jaffa incident had inflamed the wrath of the Arab community. Concerned abut an escalation of the violence, the high commissioner tried to delay for as long as he could the decision to impose martial law.[12]

Eventually, Wauchope admitted that he had been mistaken in his approach to governing Palestine. When he had arrived he had hoped to meld Jews and Arabs into a single civil society. To that end, he had tried to institute an idea that had been circulating in Palestine since Herbert Samuel's term—a Jewish-Arab legislative council. But this did not work out. No one wanted a council: both Jews and Arabs were striving for victory, not compromise.[13]*

The Arab rebellion convinced Wauchope that there was no chance of creating a single community of Jews and Arabs, because neither side wanted it. So he reached the conclusion that Palestine's future depended on dividing the country. The deterioration in Arab-Jewish relations was threatening the prestige of the entire empire. "The British Empire is not going down!" the colonial secretary declared, somewhat pathetically. The senior official in the Foreign Office, Sir Robert Vansittart, even raised the possibility that the Mandate for Palestine be given to a different power.[15] As usual, the British appointed a commission of inquiry to study the situation. The decision was made in the summer of 1936; by the time the commission reached Palestine, winter had arrived.

The commission was most respectable, "royal" by definition, headed by a distinguished peer, Lord Peel, former secretary of state for India. Four of the commission's five members bore the title "Sir"; they included a for-

---

*The high commissioner established correct relations with mufti al-Husseini and with his opponent, Raghib Nashashibi. He took an interest in agriculture and from time to time went to visit Arab villages to demonstrate his interest. He was inclined to accept as authentic the Arabs' fears of the Jews, and believed that they should be taken into account. But his real sympathy was for Zionism.[14]

mer governor and a High Court judge, a former ambassador, and a professor of history from Oxford. All of them were highly experienced people equipped with the necessary background for such a weighty inquiry.[16] They arrived in Palestine wearing top hats and tails.*

The commission's hearings were treated with the utmost seriousness. Weizmann, Ben-Gurion, Jabotinsky, the mufti, Winston Churchill, and the elderly Lloyd George all testified, as did many others; some testified in closed-door sessions. Ben-Gurion told the commission that the Bible was the Jewish people's "Mandate." According to accepted Zionist practice, Ben-Gurion was careful not to use the term *state,* explaining that what the Jews desired was a national home. The mufti said there was no chance for coexistence in one country between two such different nations and that any attempt to force coexistence was liable to harm both parties.[18]†

The Peel Commission was the most thorough inquiry into the Palestine conflict carried out thus far, but there was something misleading about it. The royal commission had not, of course, come to "study" anything; it had come to help the government divest itself of Palestine. Lord Peel seems to have brought with him a foregone conclusion: "The social, moral and political gaps between the Arab and Jewish communities are already unbridgeable," he wrote to the colonial secretary. The report issued at the end of the investigation quoted an English proverb—half a loaf is better than none—and tried very hard to persuade the Jews and Arabs to agree to Palestine's partition.[20]

The proposal was not an original one. In the three preceding decades, there had been some ten plans to divide the country between Jews and Arabs, into regions, "cantons," autonomous areas, or independent states; at least two of the plans had been prepared by Arabs.[21] But the Peel Commission composed an impressive document, 404 pages in length, well-written, containing a wealth of useful information and intelligent analyses. It remains one of the most important sources for the study of

---

*Eleanor Rathbone, MP, was furious that there was no woman on the commission. The colonial secretary responded that he had been told that religious Jews and Muslims would refuse to cooperate with the commission if there was a woman among its members.[17]

†David Ben-Gurion told his colleagues in the Jewish Agency about his exchange with Lord Peel. Even if a million Jews live in Palestine, the lord asked, what will that give the seventeen-million-strong Jewish nation? Ben-Gurion said that in the western part of Palestine alone there was room for four million Jews. Peel believed that most Jews would remain in the Diaspora.[19]

the period. The report also contains maps, one tracing possible borders between the two states: the Jews would receive Tel Aviv, the coastal plain, the northern valleys, and part of the Galilee, while the Arabs would receive the west bank of the Jordan River, the mountainous region, and the desert in the south. The British would retain Jerusalem and a narrow corridor linking it to the sea.*

The British government accepted the commission's recommendations.[23] After twenty years of rule in Palestine, the British seemed to have given in to Arab pressure, proposing to retain only Jerusalem, a largely sentimental gesture. By ceding the land link between Egypt and Iraq and leaving Haifa in the hands of the Jews, Britain for all intents and purposes had dismissed the strategic worth of Palestine.

This interpretation of the commission's recommendations was widely shared. Moshe Shertok heard it from, among others, Sir Basil Henry Liddell Hart, a well-known and influential expert on the theory of war and military strategy. "He adheres to the theory that minimizes the value of our corner of the Imperial scale," was Shertok's impression. Baffy Dugdale reported that she too had heard people discounting Palestine's military value.[24] Sir Robert Vansittart also considered Palestine a military burden, consuming valuable British forces that would be needed for the war in Europe, he told Chaim Weizmann. Above all, the prevailing tendency, as in the past, was to measure Palestine's strategic value in money; the cost of keeping order there was the major factor in the government's considerations.[25]

Most Arabs did not want partition, nor did many Jews, so the idea was not feasible. Edward Keith-Roach haughtily summed up the reaction: "The Jews, Christians and Muslims are like three bewildered, disconsolate children at a party. 'We don't want jam; we don't want honey; we don't want cake. We want jelly.' Alas, there is no jelly."[26] The Jewish and Arab response was shaped by the internal political dynamic in their respective camps. Among the Arabs, the leadership under the mufti opposed partition and silenced a small group of people who were inclined to support it.[27] Among the Jews, the leadership under Weizmann and Ben-Gurion was inclined to support the idea, but under pressure from opponents, some of them from the "right" and some from the "left," they were forced to express reservations. The Arab opposition was unbending; the Jews were uncertain and argued a lot.

---

*Minister Walter Elliot showed his Baffy a secret early copy of the report when they met for a midnight meal at the Savoy Grill.[22]

The Arabs could not agree that part of their country be handed over to Jewish sovereignty; the Peel Commission had also recommended transferring several thousand Arabs from their homes in the territory within the proposed Jewish state to the Arab area. In this context, the commission cited the population exchanges between Turkey and Greece that had begun in 1923; one commission member, Sir Horace Rumbold, had been involved in that enterprise.[28] Frances Newton wondered what would happen to the Arabs' citrus and olive groves; trees could not be transferred as easily as their owners, she wrote. She summed up the Arabs' feelings about the report: "Everyone is simply poleaxed by the recommendation for partition. A friend of mine said to me, 'The report is just like toxic fly killer and we are the flies on the floor.'"[29]

The Zionist movement did not reject partition on principle but disagreed with the proposal's details. The Jews expended great energy on a very dramatic debate. Partition would bring about a Jewish state, thereby realizing the Zionist dream, but the proposal's opponents argued that the territory offered was too small. The discussion acquired the air of a truly historic decision. The Zionists pondered whether they could take upon themselves the decision to concede part of the country, including Jerusalem. At the same time, they wondered whether they could afford not to. Future relations between the Jews and Arabs concerned them, as did the future of the Jewish people. The debates over partition sounded like the world's greatest seminar on the fundamental problems of Jewish history.[30]

Ben-Gurion favored partition. He did not accept all the details, but he saw the proposal as the first step in a plan to gradually lay claim to the entire country, on both sides of the Jordan River. "A partial Jewish state is not the end, but the beginning," he explained to his son Amos, "a powerful impetus in our historic efforts to redeem the land in its entirety." Ben-Gurion set down the advantages and disadvantages of the proposal and found that one point outweighed all the drawbacks: "forced transfer."[31]

2.

At first Ben-Gurion could not believe his eyes. Initially, he had overlooked the recommendation to transfer Arabs out of the territory designated for Jews. When, on his second reading, he grasped the implications, he could barely contain his enthusiasm. "This will give us something we never had, even when we were under our own authority, neither in the period of the First Temple nor in the period of the Second Temple," he wrote in his diary, underlining the two decisive words: "forced transfer." The proposal was of "huge consequence," he continued. For the first time in history a "really Jewish" state was on the verge of becoming a reality. He underlined the words "really Jewish" as well. The Jews would have an "undreamed of possibility, one which we could not dare to imagine in our boldest fantasies." He described the commission's report as "our declaration of independence" and prophesied that the Balfour Declaration would dim by comparison.[32]

The idea of transfer had accompanied the Zionist movement from its very beginnings, first appearing in Theodor Herzl's diary. "We shall try to spirit the penniless populations across the border by procuring employment for them in the transit countries, while denying them employment in our own country," Herzl wrote in June 1895. For the next twenty-five years the question had no practical relevance, but when the British occupied Palestine, the idea was raised at regular intervals.[33] Yosef Sprinzak, a leader of HaPoel HaTzair, once said, "We must receive Palestine without any reduction or restrictions. There is a known quantity of Arabs living in Palestine and they will receive their due. Whoever wants to will cultivate his plot. Whoever does not want to will receive compensation and seek his fortune in another land."*

At the beginning of the 1920s the idea found a well-known advocate: Israel Zangwill, the writer. The Arabs should be persuaded to "trek," Zangwill wrote. He formulated an argument the Zionist movement would repeat many times: the Arabs had the whole Arab world, while the Jews had only Palestine. There were only two possible outcomes to the conflict, he wrote: either the Jewish minority would dominate the Arab majority, which would be undemocratic, or the other way around. Neither outcome was desirable. His conclusion: the Arabs must go.[35]

Zangwill was a queer fish—he thought that the Jewish state could be established anywhere on the globe and need not be in Palestine. His proposal to expel the Arabs is worthy of note only because Arab spokesmen frequently cited it as proof that the Zionists meant to expropriate their country, and because Zionist leaders learned an important lesson from Zangwill's frankness—under no circumstances should they talk as though the Zionist program required the expulsion of the Arabs, because this would cause the Jews to lose the world's sympathy. In fact several Zionists distanced themselves from Zangwill and denied that he had

---

*That the full implications of this statement were understood by all is indicated by the fact it is crossed out in the meeting's minutes.[34]

expressed the movement's position. "In Palestine there is room for you and for us," they told the Arabs, and decided that the less talk about transfer, the better.[36]

In practice, the Zionists began executing a mini-transfer from the time they began purchasing land and evacuating the Arab tenants. "Up until now we have accomplished our settlement in Palestine by population transfer," Ben-Gurion said in one discussion of the issue.[37] In the summer of 1931, Colonel Kisch had written to Weizmann that the Zionists should formulate a clear policy on the matter, and he asked the opinion of several people. Jacob Thon, who had been active in settlement affairs before World War I, responded that "of course" transferring the Arabs to Transjordan was desirable, for the Arabs as well as the Jews; with the money they received for a hundred dunams in Palestine the Arabs could purchase at least five hundred dunams in Transjordan. Thon warned, however, that if the Zionists talked about transfer openly their chances of accomplishing it would diminish. Any steps would have to be taken "privately."[38]

"Disappearing" the Arabs lay at the heart of the Zionist dream, and was also a necessary condition of its realization. According to Menachem Ussishkin, starting the Jewish state with nearly half the population of Arabs living on their own land, and with most of the Jews packed into Tel Aviv and its environs, would mean the death of the Third Jewish Commonwealth even before it began. The Jewish Agency spoke about transferring at least 100,000 Arabs; Ussishkin thought in terms of 60,000 families. "I do not believe in the transfer of an individual. I believe in the transfer of entire villages," Arthur Ruppin said.[39]

With few exceptions, none of the Zionists disputed the desirability of forced transfer—or its morality. "I am prepared to stand and defend the moral aspect before God and the League of Nations," Menachem Ussishkin said. "I do not see anything immoral in it," Ben-Gurion asserted.[40] He did bring himself to consider "the horrible difficulty" of forcibly uprooting 100,000 Arabs who had been living in their villages for hundreds of years, but principally he was worried by the "slackness of thought and will" of those Jews who believed that expulsion was an unlikely scenario. Even Menachem Ussishkin thought transfer was improbable. "Suddenly Mohammed will leave our country? Why should he?" he asked, and he warned that "polygamy will multiply their numbers swiftly." Ben-Gurion insisted that "transfer is definitely possible." Above all, they questioned whether Britain would dare carry out the deportations.[41]

Clearly, transfer was feasible only if the proposal came from the British, and if their forces carried it out: "We cannot and must not propose such a thing, because we never wanted to expropriate Arabs," Ben-Gurion wrote to his son Amos. But in the event of England giving an Arab state part of Palestine promised to the Jews, "it would be only right for the Arabs in our country to move to the Arab part."[42]

Beginning in the 1930s the Zionist leaders made preparations for a population transfer, setting up a special committee for the task. Occasionally they recognized the suffering the Arabs would endure if they had to leave their homes. They also addressed the question of whether the transfer would be forced or voluntary. But even "voluntary" transfer referred not to the will of the individual but to an agreement between states.[43]

In general the sessions of the Committee on Population Transfer were businesslike and practical, dealing with who would be deported first, villagers or city people (preferably the farmers); the rate of the deportations (probably over a period of ten years); where the deportees would go (as far away as possible, Gaza or Baghdad); and the cost of the whole operation (close to £300 million).[44] Ben-Gurion supposed that the Zionist movement would pay for the transfer. There was also a proposal to allow only Arabs bearing special work permits, which would be issued in limited numbers, to be employed in Palestine, in the spirit of Herzl's idea. One member of the Jewish Agency suggested raising taxes, "so that they flee the taxes."[45]

The committee examined the possibility of obtaining the Arabs' agreement through the Zionists' old and trusted method: bribery. In his diary, Ben-Gurion fantasized about paying Iraq £10 million sterling in exchange for that country absorbing 100,000 Arab families from Palestine—some 500,000 people.[46] Chaim Weizmann was charmed by a man named Harry St. John Philby, a soldier, Orientalist, eccentric, and charlatan. While sitting at the Athenaeum club in London, the two mused on the possibility that Arabia's king Ibn Saud might be given "between ten and twenty" million pounds sterling in exchange for accepting all the Arabs of Palestine; their idea seemed to be that the United States would help fund the program.[47]

During the 1940s the idea of transfer continued to circulate in the Zionist movement, bolstered by discussions at the outbreak of World War II about mass population transfers in territories occupied by the German army. "The world has become accustomed to the idea of mass migrations and has almost become fond of them," Ze'ev Jabotinsky wrote, adding that "Hitler—as odious as he is to us—has given this idea a good name in the world."[48]

Toward the end of World War II, Roberto Bachi, a statistician and demographer, wrote a secret report in which he sounded an alarm on the demographic danger presented by the birthrate of the Arabs in Palestine, the highest in the world. For the Jews to reach a majority of 2 or 3 percent within five years, they would need to bring in about a million immigrants, 200,000 a year. But their majority would hold for only a short time; by 2001, Bachi forecast, only 21 to 33 percent of the population would be Jewish, given the Arab birthrate. In order to achieve the Zionist objective, he proposed transferring "a large part" of the country's Arabs to Arab countries, "peacefully."[49]

Later, there were attempts to misrepresent Ben-Gurion's position on the transfer question. A letter preserved in his archive includes the sentence "We must expel the Arabs," but the sentence is a counterfeit. Ben-Gurion's biographer Shabtai Teveth has gone to great lengths to distance Ben-Gurion from the idea of population transfer, and several historical documents have also obfuscated his interest in expelling the Arabs.[50] Both interpretations are unprincipled: Ben-Gurion's stand on deportations, like that of other Zionist leaders, is unambiguous and well-documented. The notion of population transfer is deeply rooted in Zionist ideology, a logical outgrowth of the principle of segregation between Jews and Arabs and a reflection of the desire to ground the Jewish state in European, rather than Middle Eastern, culture. The Arabs' refusal to allow the Zionist movement to establish a state with a Jewish majority in any part of Palestine also fostered thoughts of transfer, as did the Arab terror campaign.*

All these ideas reflected not only Zionist ideology but also the fact that there was no basis for compromise between the national movements, as the Royal Commission learned. One of the mufti's associates, Jamal al-Husseini, said, "The Arabs do not wish to get rid of the Jews, but if the Jews want to leave, so much the better." There were already 400,000 Jews in Palestine, Husseini said, so "it is time that another place was found for

---

*When the Jewish Agency planned to get rid of the Arabs, it also discussed those who would remain. The Zionist movement, which did not believe that Jews could live as a minority in Europe, also had trouble digesting the existence of an Arab minority in a Jewish state. Ben-Gurion leaned toward giving the Arabs equal rights, but not everyone thought this way.[51] The Zionists once discussed the possibility that Arabs would be allowed to serve in the army.[52]

the Jewish national home." According to him, "The Jews [have] made a hell of Palestine."[53] This position left no room for hope even among those Jews who sought a "binational" solution.

3.

Writer and journalist Yehoshua Hatalmi (Radler-Feldman), who was known by his pen name, Rabbi Benjamin, once proposed to do away with the Jewish-Arab conflict through intermarriage between the two peoples. "And type shall find its countertype and become one," he wrote. Years earlier Arthur Ruppin had initiated the establishment of an organization called Brit Shalom, meaning "covenant of peace." The new movement called on both peoples to give up their national aspirations: "We do not want a Jewish state but rather a binational commonwealth," wrote one of its sympathizers.[54]

Ruppin and his colleagues came largely from central Europe, and many were university graduates. Liberal in their outlook, they often spoke to each other and corresponded in German. Most of them lived in Jerusalem. They held public meetings, wrote articles, and issued statements.[55] They also had sympathizers overseas: Martin Buber and Zalman Schocken in Berlin, Herbert Samuel in London.*

In the summer of 1930 Brit Shalom formulated several dozen practical proposals designed to bring Jews and Arabs together. These included the joint marketing of oranges, cooperation among firefighters, joint campaigning against malaria and against changes in the country's rent-control laws; common censorship of films; shared labor unions, education, and political parties. These proposals reflected a mood more than a feasible plan.[57]

Brit Shalom came to be identified with Judah Leib Magnes, but in fact he was neither a founder nor a member. Magnes believed that Ruppin would support Arab deportation if only an opportunity were to present itself, and he turned out to be right.[58] Magnes was active in a similar society established later, called Ihud, or "Unity."

The members of Brit Shalom and other such organizations tried at the same time to hang on to their Zionist ideology; they made a great effort to

---

*Edwin Samuel, a district commissioner, received special dispensation from the British administration to join Brit Shalom. He sent at least some of its statements to his father in advance of their publication. The former high commissioner, who had resumed his political career in London and served for a time as home secretary, read the drafts and returned them to Jerusalem with his comments and suggestions.[56]

win the blessing of the Zionist movement. Sometimes being cast out of the Zionist camp seemed to trouble them more than the fear that Zionism was leading to war. "We are all good Zionists," Martin Buber asserted. [59] But had the members been true to their beliefs, they would have had to admit that they had parted ways with Zionism. According to their plan, Jewish immigration would continue, but at a rate that would ensure the Jews would never become more than half the population.[60]

The Zionist Organization rejected Brit Shalom and its ilk. "While it is true that you pay lip-service to the establishment of a strong national Jewry in our land," Colonel Kisch wrote, "your work and programme tend regularly to deny such aims."[61] In the Jewish Agency the common wisdom was that the peace initiatives of Magnes and his associates should be treated gingerly, lest they reveal the fact that the Zionists were not united. Any evidence of a schism could lead the Arabs to take an even tougher line. One document referring to the binationalists' proposals for a settlement with the Arabs is entitled "The Danger of the Jewish Moderates."*

They never numbered more than a hundred people, but the Zionists invested a great deal of energy in downplaying the impression that peace with the Arabs was dearer to the binationalists than it was to the Zionist establishment. Brit Shalom elicited a great deal of interest in Britain and the United States, and found considerable sympathy among administration figures there. Hebrew University president Magnes enjoyed international prestige as a humanitarian. But what was at stake was not merely an issue of public relations: Brit Shalom confronted Zionist ideology with its conscience.

Unlike many other revolutionary movements, the Zionist movement did not espouse a moral code of its own. Its values were those of Western liberalism, and when Zionist leaders spoke of justice, they meant human and civil rights according to the concept of democracy that had developed in Europe and the United States, especially after World War I, including the right of all peoples to national self-determination. The conflict over Palestine sincerely troubled many Zionists—they wanted with all their hearts to be not only strong and victorious but also good and just. The binationalists brought to the fore the contradiction between the national aspirations of the Zionists and the standards of universal morality they aspired to. This dilemma explains the willingness of the move-

*Magnes was involved in several other private attempts to reach a peace agreement with the Arabs.[62]

ment's leaders, David Ben-Gurion included, to engage in numerous and lengthy discussions with the members of Brit Shalom, Ihud, and the other binationalist organizations. These talks were agonizing and painful. The Zionist politicians spoke a lot about morals, and the binationalists spoke a great deal about politics; the former wanted moral approval, the latter wanted political recognition. Both sides seem to have had a psychological need for these talks, but they could not find common ground.[63]

The binational idea also necessitated formulating an approach to Arab culture, something that presented difficulty for most of the binationalists because they had come from Europe, cherished its culture, and had no desire to give it up. They shared this feeling with most of the Zionist establishment. Even Rabbi Benjamin called on the Zionists to "educate the Arabs" and "prepare them" for "a life of culture." They also talked about accepting Arab children into Jewish schools.[64]

Magnes knew many Arabs and sometimes believed he had found some who shared his binational stance. In fact, most Arabs responded negatively to the idea. Like the majority of Jews in the country, they were wedded to their national identity and committed to victory. Once attorney Aouni Abd al-Hadi hosted a tea party and, as was customary in Jerusalem, invited several foreigners, including a well-known American journalist, Lewis Fisher. The visitors talked about the future of Palestine. Fisher got into a long argument with one of the other guests, Khalil al-Sakakini. The conflict between the Arabs and the Jews would be solved in one of two ways, Sakakini had written: "Either the country will remain ours or it will be taken from us by force," and he expressed this view at the tea party.

When Abd al-Hadi told Fisher that Sakakini was a Christian, another guest, also an American, commented that the Christians, like minorities in any country, tended to be extremists because they feared the majority. The Christians, he said, did not represent the majority of Arabs. Sakakini asked the man how he knew so much and learned that the guest had been living in the country for twenty years. "How is it that we don't know you?" Sakakini wondered. "Who are you?" The rest of the company were astonished by his question—this is Dr. Magnes, president of the Hebrew University, they told Sakakini, who said that he had heard of him. Until that point , the two had not met face-to-face. Magnes said he was familiar with Sakakini's books; he had used them to study Arabic. He paid Sakakini a number of generous compliments.

Sakakini refused to be impressed. "Come, let us speak frankly, Doctor," he said, and told him a story. A man was riding on his donkey and saw another man walking. He invited the man to ride with him. Mounting the donkey, the stranger said, "How fast your donkey is!" The two rode on for a while. When the stranger then said, "How fast our donkey is!" the animal's owner ordered the man to get off. "Why?" the stranger asked. "I'm afraid," said the owner, "that you'll soon be saying, 'How fast my donkey is!'"

A lengthy debate ensued. Unlike most Zionists, Sakakini wrote after the encounter, Magnes did not think that Palestine belonged to the Jews: he even thought that the country should remain in the hands of the Arabs but stay open to Jewish immigration. "That is precisely the danger we fear," Sakakini told Magnes, and with that the conversation ended.[65] The tragedy of such Jewish men of peace was that there was no demand for their goodwill. When the Nazis came to power in Germany, the gap between Jews and Arabs became even wider.

Before moving to their new home in Katamon, the Sakakinis lived in the German Colony. Their two daughters attended a German school. When the Nazis seized power, the school adopted the new regime's educational principles. Only the German children actually joined the Jerusalem branch of the Hitler Youth, Hala Sakakini recalled, but all the children sang *"Deutschland Über Alles"* and "Raise the Flag," the Nazi Party anthem.[66] Sakakini, the humanist educator, came to believe that Nazi Germany might weaken Britain and thereby liberate Palestine from the Jews. So he supported the Nazis.[67] He expressed his sympathies in his diary several times.

Hitler had opened the world's eyes, Sakakini wrote. Before he came to power, people feared the Jews; they were thought to have boundless influence. Hitler had showed the world that the Jewish rifle was not loaded. The Germans had been the first to stand up to the Jews and were not afraid of them. In fact, Sakakini wrote, there were two nations that had fooled the world: the Jews and the British. Hitler had come and put the Jews in their place; Mussolini had occupied Ethiopia and put the British in their place. When word reached Jerusalem that a majority of the Saarland's inhabitants had voted to annex the region to Nazi Germany, Sakakini celebrated the news together with the Husseinis' victory in the Jerusalem municipal elections. He saw the two victories as one.[68]

Frances Newton fed the Nazi press information on the repression of the Arabs. This vexed the British intelligence service. The Jewish Agency believed that the Arabs were being incited by foreign elements—the French, the Italians, or the Germans.[69] Khalil al-Sakakini would have been happy had that been the case, but after fifty days of the Arab strike, he wrote, "Up until now we have received no help from either Italy or Germany. All we have heard from them is fine words."[70]* There was also a great deal of sympathy for Nazi Germany among Miss Wilson's pupils in Bir Zeit. When they were given Disraeli's novel *Coningsby* to read, the children were up in arms, as Wilson had expected in advance. "But he was a Jew!" they protested about the author. Wilson tried to divert the discussion to the question of what makes a great man—one who influences the spirit of his generation, Wilson suggested. Most of the students, she wrote, then put Adolf Hitler at the head of their list of great men.[72]

Here and there contact between Jews and Arabs continued: they bought goods from each other, Arabs worked for Jews, and Jews rented their apartments from Arabs. There were cases in which Jewish and Arab workers even went on strike together. A Jew and an Arab were joint leaders of a transport strike.[73] The Histadrut also published a newspaper in Arabic, which included, among other things, translations of Gerhart Hauptmann's *The Weavers* and stories by Maxim Gorky, Oscar Wilde, and Avraham Reizin, a Yiddish writer.[74]

The Jewish Agency continued to hand out bribes, as well. "Mr. Shertok happened to meet with Ragheb Nashashibi," Ben-Gurion reported. "The conversation took place at a diplomatic reception in Jerusalem. Mr. Shertok learned that Ragheb had approached a certain Jew in Jerusalem and asked for a loan because his financial situation is deteriorating. We may have to help him get the loan, with some reliable security, of course. There is no doubt that if the country is partitioned, Ragheb will be the top man in the Arab government."[75] They also fostered the collaboration of Emir Abdallah, ruler of Transjordan. "Abdallah asked for two thousand, Rutenberg gave him one," Ben-Gurion recorded in his diary.[76]

In the main, however, Jewish-Arab encounters were hopeless. Mordechai Ben-Hillel Hacohen recorded in his diary a story told to him by David, his son. David had been driving to Haifa when he saw an Arab family on the road, a husband and a wife, who was holding a baby in her arms, and a small girl hanging on to her mother's apron. They asked for a ride and Hacohen inquired whether they had any money. The man gave him ten piastres. The family got in the car and, Hacohen related, there was a real stench.

Along the way, the two men got into conversation. The Arab came from

---

*Hitler issued a statement that the world would do better to condemn the repression of the Arabs in Palestine than to condemning Germany.[71]

a small village in the Tulkarem area. He had six children. His property amounted to a few fig and olive trees so he worked near Petach Tikva as a foreman of a road team and earned twelve piastres a day. He had organized a tent and mats at his work site so he could stay there. Then the baby had become ill, so he had paid fifty piastres for his treatment in Petach Tikva, and now the family was returning to their village. Hacohen gave the family some food he had brought with him. "The ten piastres he had received from the poor Arab felt like it was burning a hole in his pocket," Mordechai Hacohen wrote. Near Tulkarem, the Arab asked to get out, but Hacohen volunteered to take him to his village.

The Arab was "overwhelmed by the good treatment" and revealed a secret: the baby was in fact dead and they were going to the village to bury him. The rest of his children had stayed near Petach Tikvah; only their eldest had come with them; she was eight years old and was terribly upset to part with her baby brother. Hacohen took them to the village, returned the money he had taken at the beginning of the journey, added several more shillings to it, and went on his way.[77] The encounter reflected the distance, compassion, arrogance, and guilt that characterized the attitude of many Jews toward the Arabs, as well as the noble self-image cultivated by many Jews. These sentiments received much expression in Hebrew literature.[78]

Separatism remained the dominant thrust of Zionist thinking, and in the wake of the Peel Commission the Jewish Agency set up committees to begin planning for the state. The partition plan had given the Zionist dream a very practical dimension, in the short and foreseeable range. Ben-Gurion had questions: How do we do this? How do we set up a new state?[79] And so a team of Zionists got together to map out the embryonic nation. But while the Zionists were busy planning, the British reneged on the proposal. By 1938, the partition plan had sunk into oblivion, its only trace being the paper mountain it left behind. The idea of a population-transfer proposal had been shelved even earlier. A senior official in the British Foreign Office said that deportations "might have been the position adopted by the Germans or the Russians, but it was unthinkable that the British should do so."[80]

The British dismantled the partition plan just as they had created it, with the ritual procedure of a commission of inquiry. The Woodhead Commission heard many witnesses and put together a fine book, 310 pages long, full of useful information and wise evaluations. The commission was charged to examine how its predecessor's recommendations might be carried out. Inevitably, the commission reached the conclusion that partition could not be implemented because the Jews and Arabs did not want it.[81]

Twenty years later Ben-Gurion wrote, "Had partition been carried out, the history of our people would have been different and six million Jews in Europe would not have been killed—most of them would be in Israel."[82] The statement was unfounded even on the basis of Ben-Gurion's own predictions: the Jewish community in Palestine was not able to absorb millions of Jews. Nor was there any question of a missed opportunity. By the time the principle of partition had been put on the table, there was no chance of resolving the conflict peacefully.

The whole discussion was a waste of time, wrote Chief Secretary William Dennis Battershill, feeling that the British in Palestine had taken several steps backward. "Everyone here is living on their nerves," he wrote. From the outbreak of the Arab rebellion the British no longer occupied Palestine because they thought it was the right thing to do; they stayed even though they knew they should go home. They just did not know how to pull out. No one knows what to do, Battershill wrote; he himself never went anywhere without his pistol.[83] The Arabs escalated their terror. After murdering Lewis Andrews, district commissioner of the Galilee, in September 1937, Arab rebels took control of large swaths of the country—roads, villages, and cities; government forces had to evacuate Be'er-sheba and Jericho, and the rebels besieged Jaffa. For a few days in October 1938 the rebels had de facto control of the Old City of Jerusalem.[84]

At the beginning of that same month Arabs raided the Jewish neighborhood in Tiberias and murdered nineteen people, including eleven children. Truck driver Alex Morrison arrived in the city shortly after the attackers had withdrawn. "They had left behind them one of the worst sights I ever saw in my life," he later wrote. The place was strewn with the bodies of men, women, and children. "The naked bodies of the women exposed the evidence that the knives had been used in the most ghastly way," Morrison wrote. In one building, apparently a nursery, the burnt bodies of children were still smoldering; the attackers had poured gasoline over them and then set them alight.[85]

—•—•—

20

Ireland in Palestine

1.

Sometime after the beginning of the Arab rebellion, the British sent one of their great experts on counterterrorism to Palestine. Sir Charles Tegart had gained his experience as one of the top figures in the British police force in India and came to Palestine to coordinate the various security services. In addition, some 25,000 soldiers and policemen also arrived in Palestine. Moshe Shertok told his colleagues that, according to reports from England, no military force of this size had left that country's shores since World War I. In the autumn of 1937, a short time after the murder of Lewis Andrews, the British began operating military courts in the Galilee, in an intensified effort to suppress Arab terror with a very strong hand.[1]

The British government would soon decide to replace Arthur Wauchope. At the end of a six-and-a-half-year term, the high commissioner was sixty-three years old, tired, and overworked, with mostly failures to his credit. Like his predecessors, Wauchope had come to understand that no high commissioner could succeed in Palestine, but he wanted to stay nonetheless. "You can imagine how I hate retiring, especially at this juncture, when Palestine is in so bad a way," he wrote to William Battershill. "If Weizmann had not so constantly used the word, I'd say I was heartbroken." There were still many things he wanted to do in Palestine; he asked the Jewish Agency to write out for him, as a farewell present, the words to the "Hatikva."[2]

His successor, Harold MacMichael, was a chilly, cynical, introverted bureaucrat who treated Palestine as merely another station in his colonial career; he came from the Sudan and Tanganyika and went from Palestine to Malaya. The former foreign secretary Lord Curzon was his uncle. Prior to MacMichael's arrival, Ben-Gurion recorded the opinion of an acquaintance: MacMichael is a snob, pro-Arab, inefficient, and corrupt; apparently in the Sudan he had an Arab mistress, the daughter of a sheikh, and for this reason had diverted a rail line unnecessarily to pass through the sheikh's territory. Not everyone agreed with this evaluation.

MacMichael was an Orientalist; Ben-Gurion's impression was that he held the Arabs in contempt. But at their first meeting, the new high commissioner also expressed doubt as to whether Palestine could solve the problem of the Jews. Everyone was rushing into things too quickly, he said. Ben-Gurion formed the opinion that the Zionists had run into another wall. The Englishman, he said, does not understand what time means to us. Still, after their meeting Ben-Gurion estimated that MacMichael was neither particularly pro-Arab nor pro-Jewish; he was British, and acted in accordance with the interests of his administration.[3]

Unlike his predecessors, MacMichael evinced no great interest in meetings with people in Palestine. Whatever he needed to know he learned from his officials or from the files. Had he not enjoyed reading the *Palestine Post*, he once said, he would have ordered it shut down. The daily English-language newspaper took a moderate Zionist line that upset many of its readers, most of them officials in the British administration. Why, the high commissioner complained, did the newspaper mention the Jewish origins of Suzanne Lenglen, the legendary tennis star who had passed away?[4] He summed up his feelings about the job as follows: "I shall be lucky if I leave with one hair that is not white on my head."[5]

2.

Charles Tegart had a security fence erected along the northern border to prevent the infiltration of terrorists; he built dozens of police fortresses around the country and put up concrete guard posts, which the British called pillboxes, along the roads. He imported Doberman dogs from South Africa and established a special center in Jerusalem to train interrogators in torture.[6]

Suspects underwent brutal questioning, involving humiliation, beating, and severe physical mistreatment, including the Turkish practice of hitting prisoners on the soles of their feet and on the genitals. Jerusalem police chief Douglas Duff described the interrogation methods in his memoir. Beatings often left marks, Duff wrote; the "water can" method, however, left no traces. The police would lay the suspect down on his back, clamping his head between two cushions, and trickle water into his nostrils from a coffeepot. A member of Etzel, Mordechai Pechko, related that he had been tortured in this way. Some subjects were forced to stand under icy showers for extended periods.[7]

Military law made it possible to hand down swift prison sentences. In 1939 the number of Arab detainees rose to over nine thousand, ten times the figure of two years previously.[8]* Thousands were held in administrative detention, without trial, in extremely overcrowded camps with inadequate sanitation. At one point the overcrowding was so bad that it became necessary to release veteran detainees whenever new ones were arrested.[10]

From the beginning of 1938 to the end of 1939 more than one hundred Arabs were sentenced to death—an average of one a week—and more than thirty were executed, or more than one a month.[11] It occurred to Edward Keith-Roach that he had seen scores of people die but he had never witnessed a natural death.[12] On occasion the British hung two or three men on the same day. Northern District Commissioner Kirkbride described such a day.

Alec Seath Kirkbride loved the Galilee in the springtime. The wildflowers made traveling a pleasure, and in his memoirs he listed their names: irises, asphodel, ranunculuses, narcissi, cyclamen, and anemones, in red, white, and magenta. He had grown up and been educated in Egypt, where his parents had settled when he was a boy; in World War I he had enlisted in the Royal Engineers, and in 1918 he was sent with Lawrence of Arabia to deploy Prince Faisal's army against the Turks. After that he served in the British administration in Transjordan. When Lewis Andrews was murdered, Kirkbride replaced him as district commissioner of the Galilee and Acre; there was an attempt on his life, too, but he escaped. The carpet of flowers rolled out its spectrum along the roads, he later wrote, tempting him to forget for a time how close he was to death, how close to bloodshed.

---

*Two Jewish Agency officials who dealt with Arab relations devised a proposal to bribe Arab witnesses appearing before military courts. A payment of twenty-five pounds per witness was conditional on the outcome of the trial; there would be no payment for a sentence of less than fifteen years in prison. There was no danger that the plan would make the Arabs hate the Jews, the officials believed. On the contrary, they wrote, the Arabs would consider this a Jewish version of the vendetta, a natural thing to them.[9]

On the morning of the day that took him to Acre prison, Kirkbride woke to the green and gold of a wonderful spring. How could you hang people on such a nice day, he thought, but set out on his way. An armored police car drove ahead of him. He was scheduled to attend three executions; the first hanging had been set for 8:00 A.M.

Acre prison was located in an eighteenth-century stone fortress. Kirkbride arrived fifteen minutes early. He stood on the bridge that spanned the fortress's moat and chatted with the warden and the local medical officer, who had come out to greet him. A Muslim clergyman passed by, on his way to prepare the first of the condemned men. He greeted the district commissioner, and Kirkbride thought he saw the blackest hatred in his eyes. Kirkbride felt guilty and mean and was plagued by a sense of remorse; he had to remind himself that he had not been the one who had pronounced the death sentences.

The gallows room was a kind of alcove in the fortress's inner wall; its walls were whitewashed, the windows narrow, sinister slits. The setting looked medieval to Kirkbride. On the floor was a wooden platform with a trapdoor at its center; above was a beam from which three ropes dangled. The district commissioner had no sooner entered the room and taken his place in a far corner than two jailers entered with the first of the condemned men, an Arab in his twenties. He was accompanied by the policeman who had been present at the young man's trial, and who now had to identify him, right under the gallows.

The prison warden began reading the sentence out loud, but the prisoner cut him short. "Get it over with, for God's sake," he shouted. His hands were handcuffed behind his back. The jailers tied his elbows together as well and covered his head with a black sack. At least he would not have to see the man's face, Kirkbride thought. The man was placed on the trapdoor; Kirkbride noticed that the precise spot was marked in chalk. The jailers tied his ankles and took a few steps back. The warden slammed a lever, the trapdoor dropped, and the young man fell forward and down through the opening, rebounding when the rope reached full extension. The entire platform trembled from the force of his fall.

The young man lost consciousness but did not die immediately. His body continued to jerk for several long minutes, and his feet spread despite their having been tied. Blood dripped from beneath the black hood. The jailers said he had hit his head when he fell, but the warden corrected them with all the force of his superior knowledge: the blood came from a burst vein in the nasal cavity. The medical officer tore open the man's shirt and listened to his heart, which was still beating at a good rate. He waited a little longer and then pronounced the man dead. Kirkbride went out to the sunny courtyard, and there, he noted with relief, the odors of mildew and antiseptic were less penetrating than inside. Until the next hanging, at nine, the district commissioner sat in the warden's office, where he ate breakfast.

The second hanging was like the first, with the exception that the condemned man made a mess of the procedure. When the jailers placed him on the trapdoor, he fainted and had to be held up to ensure a clean fall. This time the assembly waited twenty minutes before the medical officer pronounced the man dead. The wait seemed interminable to the district commissioner.

In the time remaining before the next hanging, at ten, Kirkbride toured the prison. He hated visits to prisons, he wrote, but anything was better than sitting idly and waiting. As he walked past the cells the inmates fell silent. All eyes followed him. Everyone knew why he had come. Through the bars of one of the cells he noticed a prisoner running back and forth. He asked who the man was; he was the next victim. The feeling that had accompanied the district commissioner throughout the morning grew stronger. People were killed in wars, he knew, but what he had come to do in Acre prison was an abominable deed. He was swamped with "an overwhelming feeling of pity," partly for the condemned men and partly for himself. He hoped he would be able to face his own death bravely when it came, as these men had, he wrote, somewhat pathetically.

In one cell at the end of the corridor there were several Jewish prisoners accused of belonging to terrorist organizations. Their eyes were also full of hatred. "Not, of course, because I had come to hang a few Arabs," Kirkbride wrote. "The fact that I was British was enough." Only one man did not look at him. The prisoner was leaning on an embrasure, staring out to sea. Kirkbride felt an odd need to thank him for not staring.

After the third hanging the district commissioner still had one more job to do: filling the role of coroner and holding an inquest. This was largely a formality, but it involved viewing the three bodies lying on a marble slab, their faces swollen and purple. Their deaths solved nothing, Kirkbride thought, and told himself that it might be a good idea to require judges to be present when their sentences were carried out.[13] Others shared this sentiment: "I wish that some of those more directly concerned with giving the sentences or approving them were in my shoes," wrote Edward Keith-Roach.[14] Kirkbride signed several documents and drove home. "You look green," his wife said when she saw him. He felt green.[15]

Young criminals were often sentenced to lashings. These were boys of seven to sixteen; they were beaten with a birch or pliable cane. Boys of up to fourteen were given six lashes; over the age of fourteen they received up to twenty-four lashes. If the sentence called for more than twelve, they were divided into several sessions, each of six lashes, spaced at three-day intervals. The punishment was not carried out in public but in the prison, in the presence of the warden; if the sentence was more than twelve lashes, a doctor's presence was required.[16]

3.

The laws and regulations under which the authorities conducted their counterterrorism operations placed responsibility for crimes on the entire community—whole villages, neighborhoods, sometimes even cities. The guiding principle was that everyone was guilty until proven otherwise and everyone was to be punished. Judge Gad Frumkin believed that he had initiated the practice of collective punishment in response to the Nebi Musa and Jaffa riots in the 1920s.[17]

Hilda Wilson, the teacher in Bir Zeit, described several searches in the village where she lived. First a plane would appear in the sky and someone would throw down a curfew order. Then the soldiers would come, sometimes in the hundreds, with dozens of vehicles. Once Wilson counted two hundred men. She never knew whether they had really come to conduct a search or whether the operation was aimed just at punishing, intimidating, and humiliating the villagers.[18] Wilson loved the people of Bir Zeit, and when the army entered the village to conduct searches or mete out punishment she felt ashamed and tried to restrain the soldiers. On occasion the British closed the village off and then she walked to Jerusalem in a roundabout way, through the mountains.

In his diary, truck driver Alex Morrison described an operation in Tulkarem, a small village, "a picture out of the Bible," he wrote. Morrison "assumed" that the army had entered the village to capture a wanted terrorist. But upon arriving, the soldiers found that all the men had departed, leaving only women and children and a few old men, one of them the mukhtar. The commander demanded, through an interpreter, to know where all the men were, but the mukhtar refused to say. That was typical of Arabs, Morrison commented, adding, "I always admired them for their courage, for I have seen them die before they would betray anyone." In this case the man was not required to die, but all the women were forced to stand in a line and bare their breasts to the soldiers to ensure that none of them were men dressed as women, Morrison explained. They were indeed all women. Afterward, the soldiers searched the houses and found nothing.[19]

Such operations were routine; almost every village might be searched at any time. In such situations, the men were gathered in an improvised enclosure or "cage," as the British called it. While the men were detained, the soldiers went from house to house, searching for weapons. They would break down doors, smash furniture, and ransack pantries, ripping open sacks of rice, flour, and sugar and strewing the contents all over the floor. They would also empty cans of oil. Their assumption was that people were hiding weapons in sacks of food or cans of oil. But the soldiers also acted maliciously: "They deliberately mixed the flour and oil and poured it all over the beds," one villager remembered. The Arab rebels advised villagers to keep their olives on the trees for as long as possible.[20]*

A British doctor named Elliot Forster documented in his diary an operation in the village of Halhoul, near Hebron, in May 1939. Several women who escaped from the village reported that all the villagers had been put into open-air pens, one for men and one for women, and were deprived of food and drink. The women told the doctor that twenty people had already died. "This is obviously a wild exaggeration," he wrote, "but where, oh where is the light conscience with which I declared (up to a year ago) that the British Army didn't do such things and that these terrible yarns must be a complete fabrication."

Five days later, the doctor received more information from an eyewitness. The women had been allowed to leave the pens after two days, but the men were still being held. Most of them were elderly; the bolder young men had managed to slip away. Someone reported that the detainees were under medical supervision and that all was well, but during the course of the day it turned out that six men had died. Afterward, the doctor wrote, four more expired: they had been forced to sit in the cage for seven days, under the fierce May sun, during a heat wave, without

---

*Correspondence among the army chiefs confirmed that soldiers stole money and valuables during the searches and invented all kinds of abuses and humiliations. In a personal letter, the Anglican bishop in Jerusalem wrote to the colonial secretary that he could confirm this, on the basis of "personal knowledge."[21]

water. The British could probably teach Hitler something he didn't know about running concentration camps, Dr. Forster wrote in his diary.

High Commissioner MacMichael confirmed that eight people had died from heat exhaustion in Halhoul. The village was "notoriously 'bad,'" he wrote; the search had uncovered twenty-six rifles and five revolvers. He explained that the eight had died because of "a combination of unfortunate circumstances"—the heat had been abnormally intense, and the victims were elderly. In other words, the incident was a work accident. No one had killed the Halhoul villagers deliberately, and there had been no deed that could be called an "atrocity," the high commissioner wrote. Nevertheless, because of the unfortunate circumstances, the families of the deceased would receive a total of £2,065 in compensation.[22] Similar operations were carried out in other villages.[23]

The British frequently discussed the principles of collective punishment; they seemed to have sincerely tried to prevent arbitrariness. They told themselves that unlike Westerners the Arabs placed greater value on the collective than on the individual; the obligation to avenge the blood of a murder victim lay on the family, not on any one of its members. The Turks had frequently disciplined clans and tribes, the British noted; they had arrested entire tribes for unlimited periods and flogged sheikhs and mukhtars. These methods were very efficient, one officer remarked, regretting, apparently, that the British did not do the same. "The defeatist spirit needs overcoming," wrote General Robert Haining, commander of the army in Palestine.[24] The British also imposed collective fines, mostly on Arab villages. The district commissioners were empowered to oversee these fines, and in their writings they talk about the measure as a peculiar blend of discipline and pedagogy; some officers sound like Scout leaders improving their flock. They always sought to preserve an appearance of "fairness."

In one village near Jenin, one hundred olive trees were set on fire, apparently by a local criminal. The district commissioner ruled that some people in the village had not done all they could to prevent the crime. He imposed a fine of £115: £100 would be divided among the tree owners as compensation, and £15 would go to the government.

In another village the district commissioner ruled that a fine would be used to prepare a plot of land where children would learn that it was not "manly" to destroy fruit trees. He added some platitudes about the role of fruit trees in the lives of those who claim to belong to the human race. Elsewhere, the district officer ruled that the money from a collective fine would be invested in improving the access road to the village; from a moral and psychological point of view, he explained, this was the best way to treat primitive villagers. Sometimes the authorities accepted appeals, agreeing that the fines had not been just or were too high, or that they should be imposed on the rich and not the poor.

Moshe Shertok suggested that when it was difficult to identify the village terrorists had come from, all the villages in the area should be penalized and held responsible.[25] Hilda Wilson once overheard a briefing before an army operation. The forces were to cordon off one village, the sergeant said, and then drive the people out of their houses onto the hillside. He said the word "drive" with a ferocity that she would never forget, she wrote in her diary. Wilson frequently spoke with soldiers. Once she took cover from the rain in a pillbox guard post. She noted that the thing most worrying the soldiers was their breakfast; they kept a large cache of eggs on the upper level of the post. They were always tired and looked like sleepwalkers, she wrote.

Her acquaintance with soldiers brought her to the conclusion that they went on their rampages largely out of monotony. "The men are bored stiff," she observed. They were stuck in a lonely outpost where there was no cinema and no recreation. Searching a village was the only excitement they had. Soldiers are by nature careless of other people's property; even in England they had wrecked requisitioned houses during the war, Wilson wrote, so what could be expected of them in a distant country, among villagers whom they have been told are enemies?[26]

At times the army would enter a village and stay there for several months. Some villages were entirely emptied of their inhabitants. As part of the counterterrorism campaign, the authorities also destroyed houses. James Pollock, district commissioner of Samaria, once received a letter thanking him for the "punitive demolition" of fifty-three houses in the village of Baka al-Gharbieh.[27] Between 1936 and 1940, the authorities destroyed 2,000 houses, according to one estimate.[28] Judge Anwar Nusseibeh maintained that lynching was less heinous than the British repression of the Arab rebellion; while all violence springs from the same emotions of fear and hatred, at least lynching was not sanctioned by law.[29]

The villagers were caught in impossible dilemmas. If they gave cover to terrorists, the army was liable to impose dreadful punishment; if they turned in a terrorist, his comrades would take revenge. Both the rebels and the army would enter and leave villages, sometimes within a few hours of each other. Both made demands of the villagers, threatening to take retribution for any aid to the enemy. The rebels conducted quasi-legal inquiries and disciplined those who did not fall in line.

At one point, the authorities required anyone leaving his village to carry a transit pass; the rebels threatened to punish anyone who cooperated with this demand. Thus the villagers could either remain home in a self-imposed curfew or risk the rebels' revenge. Bus drivers were hobbled by these conflicting demands too. The pupils in Miss Wilson's class did not know how they would get to soccer matches outside their village, and the women had a problem with the village cats. In Bir Zeit, Wilson explained, there were huge numbers of cats. Every so often they would be caught in sacks and set free close to Neve Ya'akov, a nearby Jewish neighborhood. "We, the falaheen, are caught between the devil and the deep blue sea," stated a letter sent from a village near Ramallah to the high commissioner. The letter contained a description of life trapped between the rebels and the soldiers. Still, there were greater criminals among the latter, the villagers wrote.[30]*

Similar actions took place in the cities as well. In Nablus in August 1938 close to five thousand men were held in a cage for two days and interrogated one after another. When they were finally released, each man was marked with a rubber stamp. While they had been held, the city was searched. Some wanted men were discovered, as was a workshop for producing bombs and two pairs of khaki pants that were considered army property. At one point a night curfew was placed on most of the cities.[32]†

The authorities were very sensitive to allegations of wrongdoing, in part because they produced repercussions in the British and American press. "Things are being published in Palestine and Britain and brought before Parliament and newspaper editors and . . . they are influencing public

---

*Making life more complicated, the security forces also employed the mufti's opponents. These "Nashashibi units," as they were called, imposed their own reign of terror on villages. Furthermore, people were sometimes at the mercy of warring factions within the villages and among the rebels.[31]

†Police officer Geoffrey Morton tried to force the people of Jenin to wear tarbushes to prove they were law-abiding citizens.[33] One army chief even proposed putting anyone who wore a *hatta* into the "cage" until they gave up their national symbol, but his superiors objected. The Jewish Agency also thought of demanding that the government forbid wearing the traditional headdress outside the villages, but Moshe Shertok believed there was no chance of enforcing such a law.[34] Some Zionist leaders were "extremely disturbed" that the laws on collective punishment, including fines, applied to Jewish settlements as well. "This is not just a financial issue," they wrote. "It is a political issue of the first order." Soon the Jews would also be complaining of the iron hand of the police and soldiers.[35]

opinion," wrote Moshe Shertok on the suppression of the Arab revolt. "The use of strong measures, such as imposing fines on entire communities, or destroying houses, or shooting and killing people, even if only during the course of a confrontation, foments discontent among the British. The measures cause suffering to good people along with bad, and are all the more troubling when British officials and soldiers are killed." Nazi Germany exploited news of the repression in its propaganda.[36]

The authorities generally denied that they were violating civil rights, or described such violations as "exceptional." They claimed that cases of mistreatment "could not" reflect a widespread policy, as abuse was not in keeping with the character of the British soldier.[37] But one top army commander complained of "unnecessary violence," vindictiveness, and cold-blooded murder. He insisted that soldiers be court-martialed if they overstepped the bounds of the permissible. Soldiers who were tried for abuse and even murder of civilians were given extremely light sentences.[38]

Chief Secretary Battershill wrote that suppressing the revolt required measures that were "drastic in the extreme." He recorded an ideological justification in his diary: "I doubt whether any Arab really has any ethical feeling against murder, and I am sure Arabs look upon murder as a justifiable and satisfactory weapon to use not only in private feuds but in political controversies. We shall never get them to change their fundamental belief on this point and so our only hope is to make murder and disturbances as unpleasant and expensive for them as possible or, in a word, make them see that it does not pay. Then they will stop." No, this was not pleasant work, Battershill wrote, but it was essential.[39]

General Haining expressed his regret that the army was not allowed to use tear gas in order to deter terrorists from the northern border; Britain was signatory to the international convention forbidding the use of gas. Gas was permitted only in operations intended to save human life, as in the case of terrorists who were holding out inside a house. "It is a pity that teargas is called gas," Haining remarked. "That is the whole trouble."[40]

The British encountered no international objections, however, when they burned the bodies of dead terrorists. They did this to prevent the terrorists' funerals from turning into mass demonstrations.[41] Nor did they have any problems forcing Arab civilians to drive at the head of their convoys to prevent terrorists from mining the roads or railway tracks; they would even seat them in special cars attached to the train engines. One such hostage related, "We would sing in loud voices to warn the rebels of the approaching convoy and let them know that Arabs had been used as bait." This idea had come from another colony; it was regularly employed in India.[42]*

4.

Arab terrorism helped the Jewish Agency make the point that the Zionist movement and the British Empire were standing shoulder to shoulder against a common enemy, in a war in which they had common goals. The British administration was now inclined to recognize this.

The Arabs, for their part, were left without any real leadership. A few weeks after the murder of Andrews the authorities deposed mufti al-Husseini and he fled to Lebanon, disguised as a Bedouin; the Arab Higher Committee was outlawed, and several Arab leaders were deported to the Seychelles Islands.[44] In fact, Husseini had burned his bridges to the British long before they forced him to flee the country—the inevitable outcome, according to Judge Anwar Nusseibeh, of an unnatural friendship. The mufti was not anti-British—indeed, many considered him a friend, even an agent, of the authorities. But at some point he was no longer able to maneuver between his dual loyalties and preferred to adhere to the Arab cause.[45]

As efforts to suppress the terror intensified, relations between the Jewish Agency and the authorities tightened. During this period the Jewish Agency almost seemed like a security branch of the administration, serving, as it did, as informer, subcontractor, and client. At several points the British army might almost have been acting under orders from the Jewish Agency, something like a mercenary force or security service. The agency even helped fund some of the security costs.

Arab terror necessitated police reinforcements; a good portion of the force was made up of Arabs whose loyalty was now in doubt. Thousands of Jewish policemen enlisted, some of whom were attached to special guard

---

*The British consul general in Egypt proposed what he described as a "checkmate" to terrorism. For every person killed by Arab terror, the authorities would issue another 100 immigration permits to the Jews, and for every death attributed to Jewish terrorism, the British would rescind 100 permits. At least part of this idea had occurred to Ben-Gurion three years previously. In his version, though, the Jewish Agency would receive 1,000 additional immigration permits for every Jew killed. He thought this was a "fantastic idea" and laid out its advantages: "There is no more convenient and effective means of tying the terrorists' hands. It is easier than maintaining ten battalions and demolishing houses and pursuing the gangs in the mountains. This method will work automatically." Shertok passed the idea on to Wauchope; the high commissioner said politely that he would think about it.[43]

and various auxiliary units. A Jewish settlement police force was also established. All these additional units functioned in theory as part of the administration; in practice they were under the command of the Jewish Agency
and intended to form the backbone of a Jewish military force set up under
British sponsorship, in preparation for the inevitable clash with the Arabs.[46]
"We have told the government clearly," Moshe Shertok said. "This entire
defense enterprise will not work unless it is run by the Jewish Agency." The
conscripts were to be loyal to the agency: "You must follow all orders you
receive from the government," Shertok explained, "but you have another
moral obligation . . . to accept not only the government's discipline, but
also that of the Jewish leadership. . . . You have not hired yourselves out
merely as mercenaries . . . you belong to a Jewish organization that may
come to you with demands. It is your leader." Shertok stated that the existence of a future Jewish army depended on success. Thus they had a duty
"to behave in a responsible Zionist way from a political point of view." The
assistance the Yishuv was giving the administration, Shertok said, was a
kind of "promissory note" signed by the authorities. Once the revolt was
repressed, he noted, the Yishuv's role "will have to be taken into account."[47]

Jewish and British officials coordinated manhunts and collective
actions against villages, and discussed the imposition of penalties and
sentences. Once, Moshe Shertok proposed sending out a bus filled with
soldiers instead of passengers as a decoy to Arab rebels. "Ah, a mobile
trap!" Chief Secretary Battershill glowed. Some of the contacts over security affairs, including operational details and the exchange of intelligence,
were conducted by Shertok directly with the high commissioner himself.
"The high commissioner told me in confidence and for my knowledge
only that we must be prepared to enlist 3,000 more men," he wrote. He
passed on information about weapons smuggling by the Arabs.[48]

In a conversation with one top British official, Shertok promised the
Jewish Agency's cooperation to prevent Etzel terrorist attacks against Arab
civilians. When Shertok learned that the authorities were about to arrest
the militant professor Joseph Klausner, he urged them to refrain because
of possible negative repercussions. The British followed his advice.[49]

Shertok reported on a discussion that would have been unimaginable
only a few years previously. In June 1936, the government demanded that
the Yishuv bear part of the costs of the police force. Fifteen years earlier, the
British had objected to the Jews' efforts to "top up" the salaries of Jewish
policemen, having seen this as a kind of bribery. And now the authorities
were insisting that the Zionists share the burden of the policemen's salaries

and also pay for their uniforms; the British would supply only weapons. Shertok demurred, and the British began to bargain—they would pay for the uniforms. Shertok was still not satisfied; he proposed splitting salary and upkeep costs equally. The high commissioner agreed. At one point the Jewish Agency seemed to run into trouble trying to fund all the Jewish police the government was willing to enlist.[50*]

The administration provided security services to commercial concerns as well. "I have the honour to refer to your application for the appointment of 3 supernumerary police constables to guard the property of Ruhama colony," the police chief wrote to the Gan Shlomo company, which had citrus groves in the Ruhama area. "I shall be grateful if you would deposit a sum of £72 to cover the cost of the maintenance of these supernumerary police for a period of 3 months." The company was not satisfied with the service it received and sent the police letters drafted in the form of a consumer complaint.[52]

Charles Tegart believed in Zionism and encouraged close cooperation with the Jewish Agency, even engaging the Histadrut's construction company, Solel Boneh, to build the fence he designed along the northern border.[53] Solel Boneh also built the new police fortresses, popularly known as the Tegart Fortresses.

Solel Boneh official David Hacohen described Tegart as a tall Irishman, old and gaunt with white locks crowning his head. His face was etched with lines, and his long nose was crooked like the beak of a hawk. Hacohen first met Tegart in his room at the King David Hotel in Jerusalem. There were no hangers in the closet, and Tegart told Hacohen just to throw his coat on the bed. Without ceremony, they began discussing the fence project. Hacohen enumerated various difficulties. He would have to import the barbed wire from Mussolini's Italy, and the British government was liable to object. He would need a large number of Jewish guards to defend the workers, which had to be considered part of the cost.

Tegart wanted quick action without open bidding or other bureaucratic delays. He did not bicker over the price. According to Edward Keith-Roach, he spent £2 million on his fortresses and the fence.[54] Hacohen estimated that building the fence brought Solel Boneh a profit of more than £60,000. Some one thousand workers, almost all Jews, were

---

*According to information given to the British Parliament, the maintenance costs of the additional forces in Palestine to suppress the Arab revolt reached some £175,000 a month.[51]

taken to the distant northern border for a spine-tingling national construction project. Hacohen called the fence an epic undertaking, similar to the laying of the railroad tracks to America's Wild West. Author Bracha Habas, Hacohen's wife, commemorated the heroic operation in a book.

Hacohen had frequent contact with top British military officers; several of them helped him, often in violation of both the civil administration's instructions and the law. [55] They considered him an ally and trusted him. Tegart once sent Hacohen a letter in which he compared the leaders of the Revisionists to Hitler and Mussolini. As he was writing, he sensed that he was getting caught up in local politics, which was forbidden. Irishmen often get carried away, he wrote, expressing his confidence that Hacohen would know to keep his words in confidence. Someone, perhaps Hacohen, wrote on the letter "top secret" in Hebrew.[56]

5.

If Tegart's cooperation with the Zionists was based largely on calculated recognition of mutual interest, Orde Wingate was another matter. Wingate, an intelligence officer, was a radical believer in Zionism; he adopted it as his religion. "He looked like a man devoured by a kind of inner fire," Moshe Shertok wrote, "addicted to a single idea that had captured his imagination." Wingate's biographer was hard put to explain the obsession of his subject, who seemed, by his background, far more likely to be influenced by the pro-Arab atmosphere that characterized certain parts of the army. He had been born in India, the son of a family of colonial officers. His cousin, Sir Reginald, was a former high commissioner of Egypt who believed that the Jews had dragged the Ottoman Empire into a war against the British Empire.[57] Wingate attended a prestigious school, specialized in Arab affairs, and served in the Sudan. He spoke some Arabic. All indications are that he discovered Zionism only after arriving in Palestine in 1936 as an intelligence officer, a captain.

He knew the country from his familiarity with the Bible; David Hacohen, one of the first local figures he met, took him for a tour. Near Ein Harod, the site of a biblical battle, Wingate criticized King Saul's strategy. He should have set up his base at the top of the hill instead of down by the spring, and then everything would have turned out differently, Wingate maintained. Hacohen heard emotion, wrath, and even pain in his voice, as if Saul had been defeated only the day before. Wingate then went on to establish his base at the site that King Saul should have chosen.[58]

Basil Liddell Hart described Wingate as a kind of Lawrence of the Jews. Shertok called him "an imperialist of the idealistic school," a man with moral ambition who was able to rise to self-sacrifice and bravery.[59] A special prayer in his memory composed after he was killed in an airplane crash in Burma compared him to Gideon in the Book of Judges. Ben-Gurion and others called him simply "the friend." A lexicon issued by the Israeli Ministry of Defense many years after his death states, "The teaching of Orde Charles Wingate, his character and leadership were a cornerstone for many of the Haganah's commanders, and his influence can be seen in the Israel Defense Force's combat doctrine." The men who served under him portrayed him with a mixture of admiration and disgust; behind his back they said he was mad.[60]

On his own initiative, Wingate set up virtually a private army that specialized in pursuing terrorists in the night. He began organizing the unit independently; only after the fact did he receive permission from his superiors. The Special Night Squads operated in the Galilee; they comprised four platoons, altogether about 200 troops, including some 150 Jews.[61] They guarded the oil pipeline from Iraq as well as Tegart's security fence, and countered terrorism with terror of their own.

One of Wingate's men, Tzion Cohen, wrote, "We would get close to a village where the oil pipeline had been sabotaged. We'd wait there until dawn and then enter the village, rounding up all the men and forcing them to stand with their faces to the wall and their hands behind their backs. Wingate and his Englishmen would inflict the punishment because he did not want to fan the Arabs' hatred for us." Cohen was referring to whip lashings on the villagers' bare backs, "a horrifying sight," according to one member of the company. First, Wingate would stand on a rock and give the villagers a scolding in broken Arabic. As time went on, Tzion Cohen wrote, the punishments became more severe. Sometimes Wingate would make the villagers smear mud and oil on their faces. On occasion he would shoot and kill them. "Wingate taught us to be good soldiers with values," Cohen noted.[62]

Cohen described the retaliation against the massacre of fifteen Jews in Tiberias. The action took place in a village called Hitin. Wingate and his troops rounded up all the village's men, chose ten, and ordered them to step forward. Cohen served as his interpreter. You killed women and children and old people in their sleep, Cohen said in Wingate's name. You had no mercy. You are cowards. I sentence you to death so that you may atone

for your transgressions. Then the soldiers shot the ten men. One participant in the operation was Yigal Allon.*

One of Wingate's officers was Humphrey Edgar Nicholson Bredin.
According to testimony in the Zionist Archive, Bredin passed a "death
sentence" on two Arabs after they had been "tried" before him. Another
report says that he rounded up all the men in a village and demanded that
they hand over ten rifles. When they did not respond, Bredin counted
them off, taking every fifteenth man out of the line—a total of three—
and ordered them shot. At times British soldiers went out on operations
drunk; they tortured Arabs and looted the villages.[66]

Once, Wingate considered creating provocation in the Haifa marketplace. His men, Jews, were supposed to dress up as Arabs, enter the market with pistols, and shoot to kill, all in order to sow confusion—the
operation was never carried out. Once he thought of scaring terrorists by
blowing rams' horns. The previous night he had been reading how Joshua
had brought down the walls of Jericho.[67]

The Jewish Agency participated in the Special Night Squads' costs, as if
they were in its service. The agency paid some of the soldiers' salaries;
funded a training course; gave a supplement to the company commanders; helped with provisions, vehicles, and horses; and covered the costs
of constructing barracks and stables. An internal report states that the
agency also supported collaborators and informers; this was called "fostering good relations."[68]

The actions of Wingate's Special Night Squads ran counter to what
Shertok described as the "innate inhibitions of the best of our people."
Behavior of this type "does not befit us," he believed, fearing that any
chance of living together with the Arabs would be ruined forever. Consequently, Shertok reported, some Zionists had even made common cause
with administration officials who opposed Wingate. But service in the
special unit enhanced the self-image cultivated by some of the young
men, especially those from the kibbutzim. "It has been proven to the

---

*Yigal Allon wrote about the operation. With extreme caution, as if he were giving testi-
mony or recording history, he wrote, "When the villagers sensed the army's presence they
began to flee. . . . We opened fire and the estimate is that three were killed." Allon was careful
to write in the plural, using passive construction. The only comment written in the first person singular was "I ordered the shooter shot." Wingate himself is not mentioned in the
report. Five other people, Allon wrote, were also killed after opening fire on the army, or
while trying to flee.[63] General Haining, commander of the British forces in Palestine, once
wrote that the phrase "'shot while attempting to escape' grates on British ears."[64] A report
on another operation, in which Moshe Dayan participated, states that "our men" pillaged,
tortured one prisoner to death, and tried to do the same to others.[65]

British army that the young Jew can be a good soldier and good comrade and that the Hebrew Yishuv is not made up only of money-grubbing storekeepers," one report stated.[69]

6.

At the beginning of November 1938 William Battershill recorded in his diary, "A new star has burst into our firmament." He expected trouble. Major General Bernard Montgomery, who had come to put down the revolt, would try to take control of the entire country, Battershill feared.[70] In his diary, he made a long list of disagreements between the military and government officials; there had been loud arguments, insults exchanged, and one attempt to depose High Commissioner MacMichael in a kind of palace coup. The source of the conflict was that the army not only wanted a free hand to suppress the uprising; it also demanded that the police force's operations be stepped up. The civil administration was not doing anything to help itself, army commander Haining complained. Its officials, he said, expected God to do all the work for them.[71]

"Monty" brought an opinionated haughtiness to Palestine. In his reports he leveled harsh criticism at the Palestinian government, especially at the police force. He thought that its top staff should be sent home and their powers given to Tegart instead. He received command of a division and set out to beat the enemy. As he saw it, the clash with the Arabs was a war: the rebels wore uniforms, Montgomery emphasized over and over again, and he rejected the civil administration's judgment that the revolt was the expression of an indigenous national movement. Most of the Arab population was sick of the revolt, Monty maintained; his adversaries were "gangs of professional bandits."[72]

The war was a rather curious one, he wrote. You don't see the enemy, but you are always exposed to the risk of being murdered or blown up. He gave his men simple orders on how to handle the rebels: kill them. He introduced the Bren gun, an improvement on the old Lewis machine guns the British had used previously. Montgomery knew how to imbue his men with combat spirit and believed that this war would create superior soldiers for the next war in Europe. He wrote as if Palestine were a sandbox and his men tin soldiers. Montgomery believed that his troops should receive a special decoration, and so they did.[73]

The reports Montgomery sent could have just as easily come from any other country. He was a professional soldier, short-tempered, with no inclination to study the particular details of the conflict in Palestine. He thought the army would be wrong to free prisoners in an attempt to improve the atmosphere for the upcoming political negotiations. "We adopted such a policy during the Sinn Fein war in Ireland in 1920/21," Montgomery wrote. "It produced the most dreadful repercussions and prolonged the war for many months."[74]

The comparison to Ireland was a common one.[75] Many of the military and police men serving in Palestine had previously served there.[76] When administration figures said "Ireland" they meant terrorism and failure. David Ben-Gurion feared that such a comparison would harm Palestine's image and hinder the Zionist movement's efforts to attract investors. The country should therefore not be identified as a second Ireland, as a land of terror and anarchy, he warned.[77] But this is exactly what happened. "I remember you predicted all this some years ago . . . if the Colonial Office did not alter its policy, you said we shall have another Ireland on our hands," an acquaintance of John Chancellor's wrote to the former high commissioner as terrorism intensified. "We have one, and so bad has this second Ireland now become that we must deal with it as we did with the other. . . . After all that has happened we can never hope to govern . . . either Jews or Arabs."[78]

The parallel between Palestine and Ireland is "singularly complete," wrote Colonial Secretary Ormsby-Gore, comparing the Jews in Palestine to the Protestants in Ulster. The country should be partitioned between its inhabitants, he believed. Foreign Office officials debated whether the mufti was like Michael Collins and Gandhi: "It was the Arab movement which made him rather than he who made the Arab movement," wrote one official, adding, "He does not seem to be a leader with the dynamic qualities of Collins or Gandhi."[79]* To Khalil al-Sakakini the future of the Arab national movement depended on one of two possibilities: either there would be a holy war, a jihad on a national scale, or the Arabs would fight as isolated terrorist cells, as the rebels in Ireland had done.[81]

Jewish nationalists also drew hope and inspiration from the story of Ireland. When Lechi operations chief Yitzhak Yezernitsky, later Israeli prime minister Yitzhak Shamir, needed a nom de guerre, he chose Michael. David Hacohen also admired Collins. He had been living in England when the disturbances broke out in Ireland, at the beginning of

---

*One of Chancellor's acquaintances, Major General John Glubb, made another comparison. We have a real war on our hands, he said, and it needs four or five divisions, like the Boer War.[80]

the 1920s, and he identified with the Irish. "I read about the English lords taking the best land in Ireland, about the exploitation of their tenants, the death of hundreds of thousands of Irish farming families in the famine, the persecutions, trials, and hangings of Irish patriots, the flight and emigration of a large part of the Irish."[82]

With all his sympathy for the British and his gratitude for their support, Hacohen was nonetheless ambivalent toward their colonial presence in Palestine. While serving as a member of the Haifa city council, Hacohen applied for a permit to build an additional road from the lower city into the Merkaz Hacarmel neighborhood higher up. Edward Keith-Roach, now district commissioner of Haifa, kept striking the plan from the city's budget, year after year. One day, at a cocktail party on the deck of a British warship, Hacohen managed to persuade Keith-Roach to endorse the project. The district commissioner, feeling good from the whiskey, agreed to the road on condition that it be named after him.

When the road was completed, small enamel signs were installed along its length, bearing the commissioner's name in English, Arabic, and Hebrew. Not long after, someone began vandalizing the signs. The city engineer, a man called Weston, told Hacohen that Keith-Roach had ordered an investigation to find the culprit. Hacohen admitted that he himself was the vandal: he regretted having named the street after Keith-Roach. "Sometimes, when I drove up to Mount Carmel at night," he wrote, "I would stop near the signs and dig a deep rut in them with a heavy monkey wrench." The city engineer was astounded by Hacohen's frankness but understood his feelings. Weston was a good man, fair and a Zionist, Hacohen wrote.[83]

This story illustrates the Zionists' growing sense of power and impatience. In 1938 members of the Mapai Party wanted to call for immediate independence. Moshe Shertok thought the idea was mad. What did they intend to do? he asked his colleagues. To begin killing Englishmen? Two years previously Shertok had said, "We see the British government as a permanent element in this country." And Ben-Gurion had stated, unambiguously and without any reservations, "We must not give up the Mandate."[84]*

Charles Tegart liked to compare Palestine to India as well as Ireland.

---

*The continuation of the Mandate was so important to the Yishuv leaders that they participated in a meeting of the League of Nation's Mandates Committee that took place on the eve of Yom Kippur.[85]

Wauchope had also been reminded from time to time of the situation in India. The British army commander in Palestine, General Haining, once warned Tegart that David Ben-Gurion was liable to adopt Gandhi's policy and stop cooperating with the authorities.[86] The Zionist movement made great efforts to establish a link with Gandhi to garner his support. Gandhi expressed his sympathy for the persecuted Jews in Nazi Germany but rejected the Zionist program, partly because it involved the use of British force against the Arabs. He expressed a qualified understanding for Arab terrorism and suggested that the Jews of Palestine not fight the Arabs even if they tried to throw them into the Dead Sea; the world's sympathy would save the Jews in the end, he believed. In turn, Ben-Gurion made some noncommittal statement about the liberation of India. Just as Gandhi could not support Zionism because he opposed British rule in his country, so Ben-Gurion could not support freedom for India because he favored the continuation of British rule in Palestine.[87]

7.

While the British were suppressing the Arab revolt, in cooperation with the Jewish Agency and the Haganah, war in Europe had become more and more likely. British officials in the Middle East began sending warnings to London. In the framework of preparations for war, they cautioned, the Arabs should be taken into account. "When we have trouble in Europe they will seize the opportunity to embarrass us here, in every possible way," warned one official in Amman. To gain the Arabs' friendship, he proposed offering them independence. "That would keep them friendly: if they do not actually help us, they will not go against us in the next war," he wrote. In the meantime, one view gaining currency was that Britain had been wrong to allow so many Jewish refugees from Nazi Germany to settle in Palestine. "Hence the tears and blood," wrote one official, suggesting that the Jews not be allowed to force the pace of immigration. Thus began a proposal to "suspend" immigration—to stop it entirely, at least for the duration of the coming war.[88]

As the war grew closer, Jewish power obviously weakened, and with it the influence of the Zionist movement; consequently, the importance of the Arabs increased. Even those Britons who still believed the Jews ruled the world took note that the Nazis had destroyed at least one of "world Jewry's" centers of power. The German Jewish community had been decimated, and the Zionist movement had been powerless to prevent it.

Chaim Weizmann, who had twenty years previously been credited with demonic, world-encircling powers, was now a rather frazzled, marginal figure. He had been undermined by Ben-Gurion's battle for the supremacy of the Yishuv in Palestine over the movement's center in London, and by Ben-Gurion's fight to increase his personal standing over Weizmann's.

Unlike Weizmann, the king of the Jews, the incarnation of Jewish history, Ben-Gurion was regarded by the British as a life-size local political activist with growing strength, to be sure, but not the leader of the Jewish people. Ben-Gurion's close relationship with Malcolm MacDonald, now the colonial secretary, was not of much help. On the contrary—MacDonald, an old acquaintance, let Ben-Gurion call him by his first name, but when the two were in conflict, MacDonald treated him as merely the chairman of a distant Labor Party branch.

British policy makers repeatedly discussed the influence of American Jews. All their evaluations affirmed that Jewish influence was still considerable; at one point, Britain even initiated an extensive public relations campaign in the United States to counter Zionist propaganda. But there was general agreement that in this war Jewish influence was insufficient to sway U.S. opinion. Indeed, attempts by American Jewish leaders to prompt President Roosevelt to act were not successful.[89]

"The Jews?" wrote the British ambassador to Egypt. "Let us be practical. They are anybody's game these days. But we need not desert them. They have waited 2,000 years for their 'home.' They can well afford to wait a bit until we are better able to help them get their last pound of flesh. . . . We have not done badly by them so far and they should be made to realise that crying for the moon won't get them anywhere—especially if we are the only friends they have left in the world." To remove any remaining doubts about British leanings, the ambassador to Egypt, Charles Harold Bateman, emphasized that he was neither pro-Arab nor anti-Jewish. "I think them each as loathsome as the other. There is only one people on earth that I am thoroughly 'pro' and that's British, and I can't see any justification for the loss of a single British soldier in the faction fight between those d———d Semites." A Foreign Office official in London suggested notifying the ambassador that the office supported everything he said.[90]

"If we must offend one side," Prime Minister Neville Chamberlain said, "let us offend the Jews rather than the Arabs."[91] His choice was not an easy one to make, but on the eve of the war it was not unreasonable. As war approached, statesmen were inclined to think that holding on to

Palestine and Egypt and preserving the link with Iraq were vital. The Jews had no alternative other than to support Britain; the Arabs, in contrast, could choose to support the Germans. Thus, to secure the Arabs' allegiance MacDonald proposed halting all Jewish immigration for the entire period of the war, with a plan to review the future of Palestine once it was over.[92]

Before announcing this new policy, the British called Arab and Zionist leaders to a conference at St. James's Palace, performing a superfluous but inevitable diplomatic ritual similar to the many commissions of inquiry sent to Palestine.[93] The St. James's conference was not needed to formulate the new policy, nor was it convened with the hope of bringing the Jews and the Arabs to an agreement. The intention was to demonstrate that the British were still playing fair. This didn't work.

A great many people sat around an overlarge table in an oversized room whose walls were covered with large, imposing oil paintings, portraits of kings and queens. Moshe Shertok observed that Henry VIII, a tyrant with terrifying eyes, glared at good Queen Victoria, herself all contentment and tranquillity.[94] Prime Minister Chamberlain attended the talks, as did Foreign Secretary Lord Halifax, Colonial Secretary MacDonald, ministers, parliamentary secretaries, undersecretaries, and lesser officials. Everyone came in formal dress and top hats. Discussions with the Arabs and the Jews were conducted separately; they entered and left the palace from different gates. The Arab delegation represented both the Arab states and the inhabitants of Palestine; some of the rebel leaders were brought over from exile in the Seychelles. The rebels had named Haj Amin al-Husseini to head their delegation, but the British rejected their proposal, so the deposed mufti did not come to London.*

Jamal al-Husseini, a veteran political activist, was the senior member of the Arab delegation from Palestine; the most important liaison between the Arabs and the English was Musa Alami. The most interesting speaker was George Antonius. He had brought his wife, Katy, who aided the delegation by collecting information about Britain's iron-hand policy toward the Arabs; to this end she included testimony by women from Jerusalem and other Arab cities.[96] The Arabs "see themselves as victors," Ben-Gurion

---

*Ben-Gurion believed that the Zionist interest would be best served if the Palestinian Arabs were represented solely by the mufti's men. "It will be much easier for us to counter their claims," he explained. "We can say that they stand for terrorism and represent only a small part of the Arab population. A broad delegation including 'moderates' will display the Arab public's general resistance to the Jews."[95]

said, "and they really have won—first they practice terror and then they are invited to negotiate with the government."

The Zionists made dozens of telephone inquiries prior to their conference to confirm the order of the proceedings. They were concerned that their delegation look big and sit precisely opposite the British representatives; Ben-Gurion even made a point of touring the palace before the talks began. Chaim Weizmann headed the Zionist delegation, which included some twenty members. Yitzhak Ben-Zvi spoke a few words in Hebrew. "Not just the seven ministers of the crown, but also the many generations of English sovereigns on the walls were amazed to hear the strange language," Moshe Shertok marveled. The British took care to memorialize the opening sessions with official photographs; stenographers noted that tea was served.[97]

The meetings' minutes make fascinating reading, in their mix of political science seminar, diplomatic training, and courtroom proceeding. The records reveal considerable agonizing over historic justice and injustice—and strenuous efforts by the Jews and the Arabs to prove that the country belonged to them. The Arabs kept referring to written commitments Britain had made during World War I contained in the "McMahon Letters." These documents were then still classified; the government foolishly tried to resist the Arab demand that they be published, but finally gave in. The affair proved embarrassing for the government, but at most the Arabs won on a technicality; the letters did not decisively confirm that Palestine would be included in the independent state the British had promised the Arabs.

Despite MacDonald's earlier proposal to halt Jewish immigration altogether, he tried, at the conference, to persuade the Arabs to consent to its continuation, at least during the war. MacDonald demanded, and even pleaded, that the Arabs make concessions. In his eagerness to please them he made a gaffe, explaining why the Jews were asking for more than they deserved: "Such a claim is in the nature of the Jewish people," he said.[98] He tried to discuss setting the number of immigrants and their rate of arrival, and he offered all kinds of assurances, but the Arabs demanded full control of immigration policy after the war. They continued to demand independence and majority rule, in line with the principles of democracy, but they did not want the British to leave immediately.

The Arabs brought their internal strife to London and spoke in multiple voices; MacDonald ran back and forth between the Carlton, where the

Nashashibis were staying, and the Dorchester, where the Husseinis were lodging. Baffy Dugdale noted that Malcolm MacDonald had changed since meeting the Arabs. They had made a profound impression on him. Nonetheless, he tried to explain the Jews' position. A minority wherever they lived, they aspired to have one country in which they would govern their own affairs.[99] He tried to play on a sense of pity for the plight of the Jewish refugees; the Arabs responded that somewhere in the length and breadth of the British Empire there must be other places to settle Jewish refugees from Europe.*

At one point the delegates talked about absorbing several thousand refugees in Arab countries; MacDonald liked the idea.[101] Musa Alami had discussed the idea with Norman Bentwich, who, a little naively, ran to tell Ben-Gurion. The Zionist movement, Ben-Gurion reminded him coldly, was not interested in Jews immigrating to Arab states. The Jews and Arabs also met face-to-face at St. James's; nothing came of it.[102]

In view of the great turbulence in Europe, the British expended remarkable energy on the question of Palestine. During the seven months preceding the promulgation of the new policy, the cabinet discussed the issue at least twenty-eight times, and the relevant cabinet committee convened another eleven times.[103] Prime Minister Chamberlain tried to be nice to the Zionists; when his father had served as colonial secretary, Chamberlain reminded them, he had received Theodor Herzl and had suggested settling the Jews in the Sinai Desert or in East Africa. Ben-Gurion believed that Chamberlain's sympathy was sincere. The prime minister, who spoke a great deal about the empire's power, exuded confidence, unlike MacDonald, who seemed irritable and pessimistic and gave the impression of being an office clerk with no authority, Ben-Gurion remarked. Nonetheless, Chamberlain would not defend the Zionists in the cabinet, and they were not made party to any real negotiations. Most of their time in London they waited to see what concessions MacDonald would manage to extract from the Arabs. Baffy Dugdale attempted to exert moral and psychological pressure on MacDonald,

---

*By the time the war broke out, Great Britain itself had taken in 50,000 refugees from Germany. Thousands were also accepted by other countries in the British Commonwealth—Australia, Canada, and South Africa. And Britain continued to search for alternative places of settlement for persecuted Jews, from Guyana to Africa. President Roosevelt asked Benito Mussolini to allow Jews to move to Ethiopia, which was under Italian rule; Il Duce wondered why the refugees could not be settled in the United States.[100]

sometimes of a very personal kind. She even accused him of treason, but to no avail.[104]*

In May 1939, after endless consultations and negotiations, Britain announced that within ten years an independent, binational state would be established in Palestine. This statement was issued in the form of a "white paper," or legislative proposal. The White Paper also placed restrictions on the transfer of Arab property to Jewish ownership and limited Jewish immigration to 75,000 over the next five years. This figure was calculated to ensure that the Jews would constitute no more than a third of Palestine's population. Any increase was made conditional on Arab consent.[106] The principle that had guided immigration policy up until then—the country's economic ability to absorb newcomers—had finally been rescinded.

The St. James's conference frayed Ben-Gurion's nerves. "I don't think I could have suffered another two weeks with that horrible tension," he wrote to his wife, "not even one week." He described the White Paper as a severe, almost mortal blow. "A more evil, foolish, and shortsighted policy could not be imagined," he wrote; the government had essentially revoked the Balfour Declaration. In private, he used even harsher language. "Satan himself could not have created a more distressing and horrible nightmare," he wrote in his diary. MacDonald was deemed a charlatan, a liar, a deceiver, a counterfeiter, a traitor. How could the rulers of Britain tolerate such an "inadmissible scoundrel"? MacDonald was full of the hypocrisy and intrigue of a cheap lawyer, fit only to represent gangsters and racketeers.[107]

As a politician, though, Ben-Gurion was impressed by MacDonald's tactics. "His pleading, his type of persuasion, his way of doling out promises, the way he soothed us and then attempted to make us afraid . . ." There could be no doubt, he summed up, that MacDonald was one of the greatest "crooks" in England.[108]† Ben-Gurion had known Mac-Donald for ten years and considered him a personal and political friend. The two had often spoken about the future Jewish state.

The new policy embittered Jews everywhere. There were hostile news-

---

*As the new policy was being formulated, one Foreign Office official remarked to Moshe Shertok that the Zionist position was well represented in the government by Walter Elliot, who was "in contact" with Mrs. Dugdale. Baffy was extremely alarmed by this comment and decided not to tell anyone about it, even Walter himself. A few days later Shertok wrote in his diary that Baffy had suspended her Zionist activities for a time; her sister, a member of the royal family, had killed herself.[105]

†When Ben-Gurion caught a cold during the talks, MacDonald sent flowers to his hotel. Ben-Gurion reminded himself to beware of British courtesy: "Even when they put you on the gallows they stand by politely."[109]

paper articles, declarations, strikes, and demonstrations, and some were suppressed violently. The British army chief in Palestine reported that banners carried by the demonstrators compared the White Paper to the Nuremberg laws and MacDonald to Hitler. Shertok recorded that when the White Paper was issued, a Jewish girl from Poland, a student at Oxford, appeared in his office. She proposed to go to Parliament, murder Chamberlain, and kill herself as well. A young man came to Weizmann offering to kill himself in Parliament as a gesture of protest.[110]

In the months between the publication of the White Paper and the outbreak of war, Etzel carried out several attacks against British government installations, blowing up telephone booths and planting mines in the central post office in Jerusalem. At the same time, Etzel continued to carry out attacks against Arab civilians in marketplaces and coffeehouses. By its own account, Etzel murdered more than 130 people during those months. Commander David Raziel and several dozen associates were arrested; broadsides described severe torture. One police agent accused of mistreating a woman prisoner was murdered on the street, along with a colleague.[111] The labor movement was pushed to respond.

Ben-Gurion's answer to both the British restrictions on immigration and the Revisionists' terrorism was an "immigration rebellion." He explained, "We will bring thousands of young people from Germany, Austria, and other countries and confront the English with the necessity of either shooting the refugees or sending them back." He thought that such an operation would have the world up in arms, led by public opinion in the United States, and that it would "rouse the humane conscience" in Britain itself. He copied into his diary a poem by W. H. Auden, given to him by Edwin Samuel, the story of refugees without a passport or country: "The Consul banged the table and said / 'If you've got no passport you're officially dead.' / 'But we are still alive, my dear, but we are still alive.'"[112]

8.

In June 1939, High Commissioner MacMichael noticed that people in Jenin were once more wearing tarbushes.[113] A few weeks later Bernard Montgomery said, "The rebellion is definitely and finally smashed; we have such a strong hold on the country that it is not possible for the rebellion to raise its head again on the scale we previously experienced."[114] Alex Morrison, the lorry driver, was about to finish his tour of duty in Palestine. On the eve of his departure he fulfilled a longtime dream: he dressed up as an Arab and went, together with a pal and a local escort, to the Arab Can-Can Club in the heart of the Haifa marketplace. The club was off-limits to British soldiers, and had he been caught he would have been court-martialed. Even worse, had people in the club discovered that he was British, they might have killed him. But nothing happened. He drank arak, and at midnight an Armenian girl danced stark naked among the tables. She was worth the danger, Morrison wrote.[115] Not many British officials would have said that at the time.

Despite Britain's success in defeating the Arab rebellion and despite the White Paper, the British had a growing feeling that there was nothing left for them to do in Palestine. Montgomery observed that "the Jew murders the Arab and the Arabs murder the Jew. This is what is going on in Palestine now. And it will go on for the next 50 years in all probability."[116] The British were stuck in a dead end, and they knew it. "The Arabs are treacherous and untrustworthy, the Jews greedy and, when free from persecution, aggressive. . . . I am convinced that the Arabs cannot be trusted to govern the Jews any more than the Jews can be trusted to govern the Arabs," wrote Colonial Secretary Ormsby-Gore. High Commissioner MacMichael thought that even a million soldiers could not prevent terrorism in Palestine.[117]

The British complained that the Arabs hated them. One official wrote, "Even had there been no Zionist policy we should eventually have got up against the Arabs if we had attempted to govern them. The new generation would demand the right to rule themselves and we should have to have given in." And they complained that the Jews hated them as well: "They hate all Gentiles," wrote Sir John Shuckburgh of the Colonial Office.[118] "We became natives in his eyes, and he resented the difficulties we created for him," Chaim Weizmann wrote.[119]

Had William Dennis Battershill known what awaited him in Palestine, he would not have come. He was sick of it all. His job was impossible: "One works all day and half the night and gets nowhere in the long run. Social life, family life, exercise, and mental relaxation—there is none. Even in one's house at night one is pursued by chits and telephone calls. One is tempted to say, How long O Lord how long?" He thanked God for leaving him at least a shred of his sense of humor, and then mused on a theological explanation for the troubles. Palestine has known no peace for the last two thousand years, he thought. Perhaps this was God's way of punishing the country for crucifying his son. Battershill dreamed about Cyprus, and when he received an unexpected transfer, he could barely contain his joy.[120]

   The Arabs' great achievement then, greater even than the White Paper, was to have made the British sick of Palestine. Only a catastrophe, High Commissioner MacMichael wrote, might change anything in the country—an earthquake or two, or a great war, or a plague. James Pollock, who had come to Palestine a few days after its conquest, wrote to his father, "Everything seems to be just as bad as it can be."[121] That same day, World War II began.

PART III

RESOLUTION

(1 9 3 9 – 4 8)

— • ◆ • —

As the violence grew worse, the authorities ordered all British citizens to leave the country. Jane Lancaster was worried about the care of her garden. "I have to go away, probably for some months," she wrote to Golda Meyerson, "and there is a danger that things might be stolen, as there are some costly plants in the garden." She asked Meyerson to find someone to guard her flowers. This was very important to her, she wrote. In one of the most dramatic periods in the history of the Jewish people, the head of the Jewish Agency's political department set aside all her other business and assigned a member of her staff to see that no harm came to Miss Lancaster's garden.[1] Thus the garden remained as it was.

—•◦•—

21

Hunting Season

1.

When World War II broke out, Ya'akov Cohen had fallen in love for the first time. He was a student at Balfour High School in Tel Aviv. Barbara ("Bebs") Fuld had beautiful eyes. Ya'akov first met her at a Scout troop, where he was giving a talk on the situation in Palestine. She was in the audience. His eye caught hers, and he could not stop looking. After the lecture she pulled him into the dance circle and he joined her in the hora. He thought the attraction was mutual, but he was wrong. Bebs did not return his love.

Four weeks after the war began Sultana al-Sakakini passed away. Her husband was inconsolable. Each day he went up to the Greek Orthodox cemetery on Mount Zion to lay flowers on her grave and weep. Characteristically, he described his grief in language that could easily apply to his nationalist feelings. Pondering the notion of accepting God's will and praising him, Sakakini asked the stonemason to engrave the words "We will never accept the judgment" on his wife's tombstone. He considered adding the phrase "We shall be the first to declare a rebellion against earth and heaven." His son Sari played the piano to comfort him, a selection from Beethoven that Sultana had loved, but Sakakini broke down crying.[1]

Sari Sakakini had returned from America with a master's degree in political science from the University of Michigan. He found work at the American consulate in Jerusalem. His sister Hala, who had gone to study at the American University in Beirut, recalled that her brother also brought home a great fondness for cornflakes and for *Life* magazine, whiskey, and iced tea. In many ways, he had realized his father's American dream.[2] He soon found a friend in Jerusalem—Omran, a taxi driver. Theirs was an impossible love.

Michael Bryant, the director of the British electric company in Jerusalem, loved Lotte Geiger, but their love was another short-lived illusion. She was Jewish; he was English and married. General Evelyn Barker, commander of the British forces in Palestine, also married, fell in love with Katy Antonius. This too was an all-consuming passion, doomed to fail.

2.

Ya'akov Cohen was a good boy, very attached to his parents; he sometimes went to the movies with his mother. His was a "bourgeois" house—his father worked in an office. The family had come from Lodz, in Poland, where Ya'akov's father had been in commerce. He had moved first to Germany and France, and when he lost his money, he settled with his family in Palestine. That was in 1934, when Ya'akov was ten. A year previously the boy had begun writing a diary, and he kept it for the rest of his life.

The diary is an important document. It tells the story of a generation in Palestine; the first pages are written in German, but then it switches to Hebrew to describe an adolescence in Tel Aviv. "I like school life," Ya'akov wrote. He worked hard at his studies; his goal was to graduate from high school. Being in the Scouts was also important to him. He read, swam, and kept a stamp collection, participated in an Arabic-language club, and visited relatives. When Aunt Yetta received an immigration permit there was great happiness. Uncle Eliezer built a house, and they made a small party when the roof was completed. Aunt Yetta arrived in Palestine, and now they all waited for the rest of the family, still in Lodz. Tel Aviv celebrated its thirtieth anniversary in 1939; its population had reached 200,000. Ya'akov broke his hand leaping over a vaulting horse but his cast came off after only three weeks.[3]

Bebs, who came from Berlin, was Ya'akov's ideal. He thought of her day and night. "It was a very childish love," he wrote later. "I was nothing to Bebs and she meant nearly everything to me. But sometimes a person needs a one-sided love like that. Months passed before I could free myself of that feeling." He believed he had only stayed in the Scouts because of her; he never forgot that he had once picked an anemone for her but she refused to accept it.[4] In September 1939, Ya'akov Cohen started his second year of high school.

When the war broke out Palestine was in the grip of a recession that had begun with the Arab revolt and the subsequent decline in immigration. Then the war slowed citrus exports and halted construction work. In August 1940, unemployment reached a record high. However, the country was soon transformed into a huge supply depot for the British army; the economy took off and dozens of new factories were built. Palestine supplied the British with ammunition and mines, gasoline, tires, and spare parts. It dressed and shod the soldiers and fed, lodged, and entertained them when they passed through on leave. Palestine flourished in the war; tens of thousands of people owed their livelihoods to it. Only butter became too expensive, Arthur Ruppin wrote, and margarine was used instead.[5]

Cohen lived the war. He read the newspaper each day and copied headlines into his diary. He frequently listened to the news on the radio. Once or twice his school staged air-raid drills, and occasionally the air-raid sirens went off in Tel Aviv. A nightly blackout was instituted, and Ya'akov's father enlisted in the civil guard. Others joined the army or special police units. "Everyone supports Britain," Cohen wrote.[6] In September 1940, the Italian air force bombed Tel Aviv and more than one hundred people were killed; many fled the city. Cohen was in Jerusalem that day; nothing happened to his family. He soon wrote that life had returned to normal. He thought that the bombing was an exceptional event and that people should get on with their lives.

3.

The White Paper was not meant to be long-lived, and Ben-Gurion knew it. "This is not the last word," he wrote in his diary. His feeling was apparently based on more than just intuition. He later told the high commissioner that Prime Minister Neville Chamberlain had told him explicitly that the new policy would last at most for the duration of the war; the government could hardly set itself a plan for ten years in advance. So he was not afraid of the White Paper, Ben-Gurion said, because it would not be implemented.[7]

The idea of binational independence was indeed filed away immediately, along with a thousand other ideas; like them, there was little chance of the proposal being realized. New regulations aimed at restricting the transfer of Arab land to the Jews also existed only on paper; both Jews and Arabs found a thousand ways of circumventing them, as they had done under the Turks. The White Paper could not be revoked for the time being; Ben-Gurion thought the Zionists should oppose it as if there were no war, but help the British army as if there were no White Paper, which is what they did.[8] As in World War I, the Zionists saw opportunities to advance their cause. "They all seem to think that the defeat of Germany will necessarily entail the establishment of a Jewish state in Palestine," stated a Foreign Office memorandum.

This was indeed the fundamental assumption that guided David Ben-Gurion.[9] He recorded in his diary what he had heard from Edwin Samuel, who would soon be chief censor in the Post Office: There were "army circles" friendly to the Zionist cause who believed the White Paper was an error. "We will not fight England," Ben-Gurion determined, explaining that "the best in the English nation" opposed the new policy and considered it a breach of trust. The most prominent of these friends was Winston Churchill, soon to be prime minister.[10]

Still, British-Jewish relations were tense. The beginning of this new campaign was not good. A few weeks after the war began, forty-three members of the Haganah were arrested not far from the town of Beisan (Beit She'an); they were returning from maneuvers and carried illegal weapons. The group included Moshe Dayan. They were court-martialed; one was sentenced to life imprisonment and the rest to ten years. But the chief of the imperial general staff, Field Marshal Sir Edmund Ironside, thought the sentence was "savage and stupid" and ordered that it be revoked. Other prison terms imposed on Haganah members were also reduced and revoked from time to time.[11] This flexibility was notable, given the court's severe treatment of the Arabs, who were sometimes sentenced to death. There was, of course, a difference: the Arabs were acting against the British, while the Haganah was preparing, for the time being, to strike only at the Arabs.

Within four months of the outbreak of war, the Jewish Agency gave the authorities a list of 134,000 Jews who wanted to serve in the British army—one out of every two men of military age and 20,000 women. By the end of the war some 30,000 soldiers had actually enlisted.[12]

The Zionist movement, however, tried to convince the British to establish specifically Jewish army units to defend Palestine. The initiative came from Ze'ev Jabotinsky, who had worked to set up the Jewish Legion in World War I. To this end, Chaim Weizmann also tried to exert pressure on the authorities, but with no success. There was no reason to treat Jews differently, any more than "special arrangements should be made for the recruitment of Scotchmen or bus conductors or people with red hair," one official declared. By the time a Jewish brigade was established, the war had ended; the brigade's 5,000 men heard only the final shots.[13*]

Ze'ev Jabotinsky announced from New York, where he was living, that the Revisionist movement would stand beside the British in its war against the Nazis. Etzel also ceased its terrorist activities. The organization's commander, David Raziel, was released from prison and was sent on a British commando operation in Iraq, where he was killed.[15] However, some Etzel members, led by Avraham Stern, refused to halt their campaign of violence and set up a splinter organization in a dispute as much over power as principle.[16] When Jabotinsky died, in 1940, the Revisionists were left without a leader.

4.

On Thursday, January 23, 1941, Ya'akov Cohen began a new notebook for his life history, as he called his diary. This was his custom at the start of each year. In the weeks that had passed since he had finished the previous notebook, a number of events had taken place, in particular the bar mitzvah of his younger brother Gabriel. On the night before the party, at one in the morning, the air-raid sirens had suddenly gone off. Everyone was extremely alarmed; until then there had been no sirens at night. The family went down into the bomb shelter.

But the bar mitzvah was a success; Gabriel read the haftarah very well. About seventy guests came, and Gabriel's friends dropped by in the afternoon, bringing gifts of books and games. Ya'akov labored until midnight washing dishes in the kitchen, and when he finally went to sleep there was another siren. At school the teachers stopped using the top floor, and one day a week, in addition to Saturday, there were no classes at all. Ya'akov's latest pastime was rowing on the Yarkon River, sometimes long distances. He continued to go to the movies; he liked Leslie Howard and Ingrid Bergman. Once he went to the HaOhel Theater to see Hašek's *The Good Soldier Schweik*. The play made *Ha'aretz* furious. God only knew how this foolish, primitive pacifist had become so popular with the public when

---

*During the course of the war Weizmann made any number of fairly pathetic attempts to revive the bluff of Jewish power that had brought the Zionists success during World War I. Once he even went to Switzerland to demonstrate an invention for desalinating seawater. He and Baffy Dugdale fantasized about who would receive the patent, the British or the Americans. Nothing came of Weizmann's efforts; Ben-Gurion continued tirelessly to sabotage his position. Before the war was over, Weizmann drafted an extremely sharp letter, which he never sent, in which he described Ben-Gurion as a "petty dictator" who shared characteristics with Adolf Hitler.[14]

everything depended on success in the war, it wrote. But Ya'akov Cohen thought the play was great.[17]

In June 1941 Tel Aviv was again bombed from the air. One shell hit an old-age home, and several residents were killed. Now a volunteer fireman, Ya'akov was called to help; the bombing severely interfered with his studies for his final exams in English grammar and mathematics. As the summer vacation approached, high school students were called on to "enlist" in the villages and kibbutzim to help with work. This campaign reflected the assumption that there was something "parasitic" about life in the city and that the kibbutzim were doing more to promote the Zionist cause. Ya'akov Cohen opted to go to the Galilee. He enjoyed his time at the kibbutz, getting up at four in the morning to drive the hay wagon; he was able to swim in the Sea of Galilee and to go on hikes. "We marveled at the beauty of our land the whole way," he wrote.[18]

The British used Jews for intelligence and sabotage missions in Lebanon and Syria, which were then under the control of the Vichy government, and in their war against the Germans in the western desert. Moshe Dayan, who lost an eye in a British army operation, proposed enlisting "Aryan types" to serve as spies in the German prison camps. He also suggested that Jews disguised as Arabs and trained in the Arabic language and Islamic ways of life carry out secret missions for the British. The German unit and the Arab unit, along with a few others, served as the founding nucleus of the Palmach, the Haganah's crack military force. Thus the Zionists' principal combat units were established in full cooperation with the British authorities and functioned initially under their sponsorship.[19]

Until the fall of 1942 there was still the possibility that the Nazis might conquer Egypt and advance on Palestine. People were in a terrible panic; some tried to arrange refuge in monasteries, while others equipped themselves with cyanide. The British army offered its Jewish soldiers the option of leaving the country; Jewish Agency leaders considered going into exile and tried to organize the evacuation of Jewish community figures in Egypt. The agency feared that the Nazis, once in Palestine, would make common cause with the Arabs. One ultra-Orthodox spokesman even prepared an emotional plea to the Arabs to have mercy on those Jews who had not supported Zionism.

The specter of a Nazi invasion ignited a fierce debate about survival and patriotism. Should the Jews surrender to the Nazis and live in disgrace or should they fight and die with honor?[20] But the British halted the

German army's advance at the battle of El Alamein; one of the casualties in North Africa was Frederick Kisch. Bernard Montgomery, who led the British to victory, won everlasting glory and the gratitude of the Jews in Palestine. Already indebted to Monty for suppressing the Arab revolt, the Jews were now doubly indebted to him for saving them from the Nazis. Against this background of mutual interests, military cooperation between the Yishuv and the British authorities grew even closer.

5.

When Ya'akov Cohen was in his senior year of high school, he copied into his diary slogans from posters calling on young people to enlist in the army; he also copied quotes from Churchill and put the "V" for victory symbol at the top of each page. He read the Hebrew edition of *Der Fuehrer,* a biography of Hitler by Konrad Heiden, and learned how to imitate the fuehrer's speeches, to the hilarity of his friends. His class was engaged in argument; the question was whether to enlist in the British army or the Haganah. Twenty-two students, Ya'akov Cohen among them, vowed to "hand themselves over to the national institutions" when they finished their studies; only one decided to enlist in the army. In June 1942, after he graduated from high school, Ya'akov joined the Palmach. A year had gone by since the Palmach's beginnings, and it now comprised some one thousand people, about half of them from kibbutzim.[21] Mostly, the conscripts worked in the agricultural settlements; part of the time they received military training.

Palmach commander Yitzhak Sadeh, formerly Landoberg, had emigrated from Russia. An adventurer, music lover, art trader, and artists' model, Sadeh was also a wrestler and a womanizer, a bohemian romantic who sought the friendship of literary and theater people. He had grown up during the Communist revolution and had served in and deserted from the Russian army. He had known and admired Yosef Trumpeldor. Upon arriving in Palestine he had joined the labor battalion, working as a stone breaker and writing articles. Sadeh radiated militancy and revolutionary ardor; a founder of the Haganah, he took his patrols beyond the borders of their settlements, considered a bold innovation at the time. When Chaim Weizmann visited Palestine during the Arab revolt, Sadeh served as his bodyguard. One of Sadeh's relatives, the philosopher Isaiah Berlin, recalled that Weizmann had been fond of Sadeh and had called him "Reb Yitzhak."[22] In the Palmach he was known as "the old man"—in 1940 he turned fifty—and was a much-admired, charismatic figure.

The Palmach never numbered more than six thousand soldiers, including some one thousand women, but its troops were seen as the very incarnation of the "new man." Fiercely patriotic, the Palmachniks also identified with the Red Army and admired Joseph Stalin. They displayed youthful arrogance and were tough, headstrong, elitist, and seemingly free of all inhibition. But they imposed their style and way of life on one another with ideological fanaticism, as if participating in a secret cult. The men's hairstyle, with its tousled forelock, their *tembel,* or fools' hats, their sandals, shorts, and slang, their emotional rigidity and sexual asceticism, their nightly campfires and songs and particular sense of humor, their political and ideological idioms—every aspect of the Palmachniks was prescribed by strict, precise rules. No exceptions were allowed; the group was everything.

Ya'akov Cohen's two years of service in the Palmach took him to various kibbutzim—Ein Ha-Horesh, Givat Brenner, Hulda, and Dafna. He cultivated bananas, fertilized fields, grazed cows, and worked as a plumber. He learned to shoot a Bren gun and engage in hand-to-hand combat. "A lesson on grenades and a lecture on Arabs," he wrote in his diary one day. He also heard talks on the Arab disturbances and took part in bayonet drill, reconnaisance training, infiltration, and "espionage exercises." He read the Bible with his comrades and joined in lots of folk dancing. His impressions of Hitler continued to amuse his friends. Once he participated in setting up a new settlement—during the war some sixty new settlements were established.[23] On Saturday nights the group listened to records.

From time to time, Cohen would go home on visits, where he would shower, sleep, and drink soda at Witman's. Tel Aviv was full of young men evading military service, he noted. Occasionally he saw Bebs; they went to a movie together. *Gone With the Wind* was playing in Tel Aviv. "I failed again with Bebs," he wrote in his dairy, "perhaps it was my fault."[24] Quite a few nationalist clichés appear in his diary, echoes of what he had internalized at school. He visited Masada and left with a sense of respect and admiration for the Jewish heroes who had died rather than surrender to the Romans. He believed that the Negev could be settled. Hebrew labor and Hebrew energy would overcome all obstacles, he wrote.

The Palmachniks claimed to symbolize not only their generation but also an ideal that was cherished by the entire Yishuv.[25] In this sense, they were very conservative, very much part of the establishment. Etzel, on the other hand, declared a "revolt."

6.

"The revolt sprang from the land and from the blood," wrote Menachem Begin, Etzel leader.[26] Despite its name, though, Etzel's action was not a revolt, but rather a decision to resume terrorist activities, largely against the British. Etzel made this decision at a point when the Left seemed to be gaining a monopoly on heroism. The Warsaw Ghetto rebellion of April 1943 was depicted in Palestine as the achievement of Zionist socialists; the role Revisionist youth had played was suppressed. A series of events in Palestine expressed solidarity with the ghetto fighters, all under the sponsorship of the labor movement.*

Then, in September 1943, after a sensational trial, two Haganah men were sentenced to ten and seven years in prison, convicted of having stolen hundreds of rifles and some 100,000 rounds of ammunition from the British army. The men denied the charges and the Jewish Agency sent Golda Meyerson to testify in their favor. Nevertheless, the Haganah did seem to have been behind the operation. Although the weapons accumulated were intended for a war against the Arabs, not the British, the Haganah was breaking away from the authorities' tutelage: a large portion of its training was now taking place without the authorities' permission.

A few weeks after the trial, when tensions were running high, a violent clash took place at Kibbutz Ramat HaKovesh. Close to eight hundred soldiers surrounded the kibbutz to conduct a weapons' search. The police arrived in some forty vehicles; airplanes supervised the operation from the air. The police were under the command of Raymond Cafferata. They rounded up all the men into the kind of cage used in the Arab villages and began searching the kibbutz houses, causing a large amount of damage to the buildings. The kibbutz members threw stones, and the policemen responded by beating people with rubber truncheons and rifle butts. Cafferata shot into the crowd but, according to an official statement, aimed at people's feet. One kibbutz member died from a skull fracture. In a report, the commander of the operation stated, "I have had considerable experience of

---

*In October 1943, two Haganah soldiers, kibbutz members, were parachuted into Romania from an RAF plane. The object of their mission was to start a myth to the effect that the labor movement had gone to the rescue of Jews in the Holocaust. A few months later, paratroopers were sent behind enemy lines on a similar mission.[27]

internal security work in Ireland and India but I have never before witnessed a more violent or fanatical reaction to those engaged in the search."[28]*

Menachem Begin had been a close associate of Ze'ev Jabotinsky in Poland. When he arrived in Palestine in 1942 he was twenty-nine. He brought with him the same brand of nationalism that had guided Jabotinsky, including a belief in the Jewish people's right to the entire territory of the biblical land of Israel, "from the Nile to the Euphrates." Begin urged the "redemption of the land," convinced that it would be accomplished by force. Etzel publications also spoke of building the Third Temple.[30] He also adopted Jabotinsky's statesmanlike self-image and something of his distinguished style—he too harnessed the power of words and drama.

In February 1942, Avraham Stern, the leader of the Etzel breakaway group Lechi, had been shot and killed by a British police officer in controversial circumstances.[31] Some of his followers had defected to set up yet another organization, which concocted an improbable plan to kidnap the high commissioner. Some of the leaders of Lechi managed in the meantime to escape from a detention camp where they were being held. Only Etzel appeared to be doing nothing. A bold gesture was needed. Thus, in February 1944, Begin issued a "declaration of war" against the British, "war to the end." At the top of the declaration appeared the organization's symbol: a rifle within a map of Palestine reaching to the Iraqi border, and the words ONLY THUS. Begin thought of opening his revolt by taking control of the Western Wall; the plan did not work out.[32]

During the period of Etzel's revolt, the organization had about six hundred members, but only two hundred were capable of going out on operations. None of the members served in the organization full-time, and only very few received any kind of pay. Almost all continued with their regular civilian work, which provided ideal cover for their activities. Etzel's funds came from robbing banks or extorting money from local businessmen; the organization received contributions as well, mostly from America. Etzel's revolt began with attacks on government office buildings in several cities, and its success spurred Lechi to redouble its own operations.[33]

In August 1944, Lechi operatives tried to assassinate High Commissioner Harold MacMichael. They threw a bomb at his car, near Givat Shaul in Jerusalem; the high commissioner was slightly wounded, his wife was not hurt. His driver was seriously injured. This was Lechi's second attempt to kill the high commissioner. A few months later, in November

---

*Cafferata also commanded a search operation at Kibbutz Givat Haim; seven residents were killed. Other kibbutzim also had violent confrontations with the police.[29]

1944, Lechi men murdered Lord Moyne, Britain's senior representative in Egypt, an act that lost the Zionists the friendship of one of their most important supporters, Winston Churchill.[34]

"This is a great blow to Zionism. . . . We cannot even conceive the extent of the damage this thing is going to cause us," Ya'akov Cohen wrote in his diary. "If the gangs don't stop their escapades once and for all, our chances of a pro-Zionist decision on the question of Palestine will disappear." Moyne's murder, Cohen wrote, had thrust the Yishuv into a decisive political struggle.[35] He was right.

Like the illegal immigration operations initiated by Ben-Gurion in response to the 1939 White Paper, anti-British terrorism was part of the struggle for control of the Jewish community, and almost brought the Jews to the point of civil war. Etzel's underground radio broadcasts, its broadsides, and the Revisionist newspaper attacked Jewish leaders in general and figures in the labor movement in particular, vilifying them as false, cowardly, imbecilic, and traitorous. Etzel called on Jews to join its ranks, and this was the organization's main message. Its operations were aimed not only at the British; they were designed to magnify Etzel's standing in comparison with the labor movement. At the same time, Etzel and Lechi also competed with each other. Menachem Begin was not enthusiastic about Moyne's assassination.[36] As for the Haganah, it intensified efforts to help the authorities capture members of the Revisionist organizations. In English this period was called "the season"—the hunt was on for Jewish terrorists. Moshe Shertok suggested that the high commissioner set up a special anti-Jewish terrorism unit,[37] a classic example of the mutual interests of the Zionist establishment and the authorities.*

Begin's revolt placed Ben-Gurion in a difficult position. He tried to explain to High Commissioner MacMichael that political concessions to the Zionists, especially loosening the immigration restrictions, would strengthen the Jewish Agency and help it fight terrorism, but MacMichael was inclined to blame the Jewish Agency for Etzel's campaign of terror. Ben-Gurion reported on one conversation in which MacMichael had been "furious"; at one point he had "boiled over" and gone red with rage, his whole body shaking with fury. The Jews are a strange nation, he said. They are bad psychologists as well, because they do not understand the

---

*One of the top men in the British establishment later denied that the mainstream Zionists provided this kind of assistance. "The truth is that no Jew will ever inform to a Gentile on another Jew," lied Chief Secretary Sir Henry Gurney.[38]

British. Only one nation in the world was helping them, only one country was doing anything to save them, and the Jews were incessantly sullying and slandering and humiliating that very nation. Not a word of thanks.*

In October 1944 the Haganah's chief of staff, Moshe Sneh, met with Etzel commander Menachem Begin and warned him against trying to capture the community's "soul." The labor movement led the Yishuv and had no intention of abdicating its leadership. The labor movement, he claimed, represented the Jewish people; any attempt by Etzel to usurp power would "necessarily lead to confrontation." The two men were rivals, old acquaintances from their days as political activists in Poland. Begin responded that he had lived through Siberia and the NKVD's dungeons, and his comrades were battle hardened as well. Sneh could not frighten them. Begin denied, however, that he wanted to take over the leadership. Sneh did not believe him.[40]

Baffy Dugdale recorded a conversation with some labor movement activists who were concerned that the Revisionists might step up their actions against the British. She suggested some sort of grand national counteraction—like bringing in a ship of illegal immigrants in broad daylight.[41]

7.

Most of the illegal immigrant ships operated by the labor movement sailed from the port of Constantsa in Romania; some sixty journeys were made altogether. Each one was a great human and operational drama, a saga of bravery and passion for life. Ships and crews had to be found and readied for sailing, and equipped with food, water, and medical supplies; passenger documents and a national flag had to be obtained. The passengers had to be collected and transferred to the port of departure. They were frequently smuggled across borders in truck convoys or through mountain paths and thick forests, even as the war raged. The Nazis did their best to intercept them.

The immigrant operations demanded faith, courage, organizational talent, contacts, and money to bribe police and secret service chiefs, government ministers, and foreign consuls. The Mediterranean Sea was a

---

*British officials frequently leveled this charge. General Evelyn Barker wrote to Chaim Weizmann that the military cemeteries were full of the graves of soldiers who had fallen liberating Palestine during World War I, making it possible to lay the foundations of the national home. North Africa was also strewn with dead soldiers who had repelled the Nazi invasion of Palestine, which had saved the Jews there.[39]

battlefield and dangerous for civilian ships, all the more so for the shoddy vessels the Zionists used. Conditions on board were abominable: the ships were overcrowded, and there were insufficient provisions, water, and sanitary facilities. Some of the boats were large, bearing hundreds of refugees; others were tiny, carrying but a few. Most reached Palestine's coast at night, where the Palmach helped the refugees cross the last stretch of sea to dry land.

By the end of the war, close to 20,000 people had entered the country this way. Another 40,000 immigrants had arrived with legal permits.[42] However, the illegal operation did not in the end enable more Jews to flee the Holocaust, because the British deducted an estimated number of illegals from the 75,000 permits promised in the White Paper. And even this quota was not fully utilized.* The British had a difficult time fighting illegal immigration. Some of the boats were caught at sea, towed to the Palestinian shore, and their passengers arrested. The illegals were then often deported to detention camps in Mauritius.†

On more than one occasion the immigrants resisted arrest, either passively or violently. The colonial secretary wrote to the prime minister complaining that militants were deliberately provoking violent confrontations with the security forces and it could well be that the Nazis were infiltrating secret agents among the immigrants. British police and soldiers dealt with the detainees harshly, women and children included. The Haganah sent several agents to sabotage a ship called the *Patria,* which was about to deport several hundred illegal immigrants from the country. The operation was hasty and bungled and cost the lives of nearly three hundred immigrants.[45]

Some of the boats sank at sea, and their passengers drowned. The *Struma* sank with nearly eight hundred illegals on board. That was in February 1942. The ship sailed from Constantsa and anchored for several months at Istanbul. Historian Ronald Zweig has shown that the Turkish authorities compelled the ship to return to the high seas at the initiative

---

*There are contradictory counts of the number of Jews who immigrated to Palestine during the war years, based on different methods of computation and conflicting data. According to one source, on March 31, 1944, some 20,000 legal immigration permits had not been used. Another source puts the number at 8,000 at the most. Either way, the White Paper quota was exhausted only in December 1945. In one calculation, a total of 75,031 immigrants had arrived by December 31, 1944, 31 over the quota. Close to 50,000 had come legally.[43]

†Churchill opposed keeping the deportees behind barbed wire. His private secretary, John Martin, warned against imprisoning them in a "British Dachau."[44]

of Foreign Secretary Anthony Eden, who deliberately misled Prime Minister Churchill and the cabinet as to the ship's seaworthiness. After this catastrophe the British decided to divert as many ships as possible to Cyprus. The government was obliged to return to the problem over and over again; its decisions reflect increasing flexibility, including the inclination to permit those people who succeeded in reaching Palestine to remain there. The refugees emerge from the saga looking like soldiers who succeeded in defeating an empire.[46]

The British continued to agonize and vacillate over the future of Palestine. In November 1940 John Martin, Churchill's principal private secretary, wrote that instead of hunting down the refugees at sea it would be better to give the Jews an independent state. Martin called Palestine by its Hebrew name, Eretz Israel. He imagined a Jewish state joined in a federation with the Arab countries. Churchill himself supposed that after the war it would be necessary to establish a Jewish state for the absorption of millions of Jews.[47]

The discussion of a state came up as part of a reassessment of the White Paper, which began almost immediately after the paper's publication, just as Ben-Gurion had predicted. "Palestine is a mill-stone around our necks," the colonial secretary wrote. In 1941 the British already had begun to think about the postwar Jewish refugee problem and wonder how this would affect the situation in Palestine. As always, one official wrote a position paper, and another put forward an opposing argument. Then, in the summer of 1943, the officials returned to the thought that it might be best to partition Palestine into two states. No less than ten position papers on the subject landed on the cabinet table.*

Essentially, the renewed debate over what to do with Palestine arose largely from the fact that Churchill opposed the White Paper. He saw it as a gross violation of an obligation Britain had taken upon itself. He did not rescind the White Paper, but he allowed it to sink into oblivion. From time to time he approved exceptions to policy.

---

*Determining policy remained principally in the hands of the Foreign and Colonial Offices. The many officials' position papers reflect different perceptions of the status of Palestine in the Middle East and the status of the Middle East itself. They all share one quality, however: their authors were battling not only for the interests of the British Empire, but also for their personal, political, and departmental egos. Many of these statesmen, diplomats, and military experts were graduates of prestigious universities, and seemed to be competing to deposit the most articulate document in the historical archive. Their linguistic sparkle and wit often seemed to shape rather than serve their views.

The restriction on immigration levied a price in human life, but the White Paper's role in the Holocaust is, in the end, relatively small. In the summer of 1941, Chaim Weizmann estimated that when the war ended it would take twenty years to bring a million and a half Jews to Palestine; Ben-Gurion argued that three million could be brought in ten years.[48] Palestine, then, was not the solution for the Jewish people; the only way to save them and millions of non-Jews was war. Most of the Jews who survived in Europe were in fact saved thanks to the defeat of Nazi Germany. Britain lost more than a quarter of a million soldiers in this struggle, as well as tens of thousands of civilians.[49] One of those soldiers was Chaim Weizmann's son Michael, a pilot.

Before and during the war, as well as toward the end, when the genocide of the Jews had become well known, opportunities apparently arose to buy Jewish lives from the Nazis. In a few of these cases British officials acted to frustrate the negotiations; some expressed antisemitic sentiments in the process.[50] Perhaps Jewish Agency leaders should have struck a deal behind the backs of the British. They were reluctant to do so, however, because, among other reasons, they continued to regard themselves as part of the British administration. Large question marks hang over several major rescue initiatives. In any case, while more Jews might have been rescued, neither the British nor the Zionist movement could have saved millions during the war.

Both parties were more interested in events in Palestine than in the fate of the Jews of Europe. "I was not well-versed on matters of saving the Jews of Nazi-occupied Europe, even though I was chairman of the Jewish Agency," Ben-Gurion wrote a few years later. "The heart of my activity was enlisting Jewry in the demand to establish a Jewish state."[51] The British, for their part, were mostly concerned with the reaction of the Arabs.

8.

Khalil al-Sakakini could never forgive the British, even after they adopted the White Paper, nor did he forgive the Jews, even when he learned that the Nazis were killing them. He continued to feel that they could come to Palestine to die there, as they had done in Turkish times, but not to live there under British protection.[52]

When he read of the sinking of the *Struma*, Sakakini wrote that the incident saddened him. Still, the eight hundred passengers who were lost were not refugees but invaders, Sakakini wrote. If the Arabs had self-government, they would have fought the ship even before it set out and might even have laid mines along its route to prevent it from reaching Palestinian shores. He described the passengers as adventurers, more fanatical than brave; he compared them to people who threatened to throw themselves into the sea unless he gave up his house.

Sakakini ridiculed the public day of mourning the Jews in Palestine declared after the boat sank. Why not mourn every boat that sank? Why cry only when Jews drowned? No, he wrote, don't expect the world to love you. The world was one thing, and the Jews were another. As part of his campaign against Jewish immigration, Sakakini published an article in the newspaper *Falastin;* printed on the front page, it included a sarcastic attack on David Ben-Gurion. "Welcome, cousins," Sakakini sneered. "We are the guests and you are the masters of the house. We will do everything to please you. You are, after all, God's chosen people." When he went into town he received much praise. Wonderful! people said. An acquaintance in Jaffa sent him a telegram of congratulations: "May your teeth grow strong," he wished. Sakakini, sixty-six years old, felt he had grown old and that the praise was coming too late. He had not expected such an enthusiastic response to the article, he wrote. At one bookstore he was told that dozens of people had come to buy the newspaper.[53*] Sakakini liked to sit at the Piccadilly Café on Mamilla Street, where he would meet Arabic-speaking Jewish intellectuals and discuss the events of the day with them.[55] His writings did not reflect personal animosity toward individual Jews; they reflected the widening gap between the Zionists and the Arab national movement.

The Arab position on the war was the subject of much speculation. The Jewish Agency's sources stressed the Arab inclination to support the Nazis for mostly obvious political reasons but also, at times, out of ideological identification. The Zionist intelligence services reported a few German secret agents working among Palestine's Arabs but assumed that no single organization could really be considered a fifth column. By one estimate, some 60 percent of the country's Arabs supported the Nazis.[56]

Britain's evaluation of the Arab position was more complex. According to its sources, the Arab tendency was to support whoever was going to win. At the beginning of the war, the high commissioner reported to London that fortune-tellers in Jerusalem were predicting Hitler's death. As

---

*A few years earlier, Sakakini had written that the Jews were paranoid. They were always wailing about being persecuted by the Germans and Arabs, he scoffed, dismissing them as incurable. Anyone who tried to heal the Jews, he maintained, was just as mad as they were.[54]

the German army advanced, Hitler's popularity increased, and at the height of his success he was being described as an Arab hero.[57] The American consulate in Jerusalem also tracked Arab opinion, using in part reports written by Sari al-Sakakini. In one of his first memorandums, Sakakini tried to refute the general view that Nazi Germany had taken over the Arab national movement through secret agents and bribes. He compared the Arabs to the American revolutionaries: the Germans were helping the Arabs but were not taking over their cause, just as the French had helped the American revolt against the British but did not run affairs in the United States a result.

The American independence fighters had not made common cause with the French because they liked them but because the French were the enemy of their enemy, Sakakini noted. So the Arabs had turned to Germany; they were prepared to receive support from any party. There was a simple way to keep the Arabs from the Nazis: Britain could end its support for the Zionist cause and transfer its patronage to the Arabs. Palestine's Arabs were willing to take Britain's side; so was the mufti, Sakakini wrote.[58] Haj Amin al-Husseini in the meantime had paid a visit to Adolf Hitler.

While living in Beirut, where he had gone after fleeing Jerusalem, the deposed mufti had disseminated Arab nationalist propaganda, organized political activities, raised money, and purchased arms. The French Mandate authorities stationed guards around his house; every day he went out for an afternoon walk. One day, in October 1939, he did not appear—the guards assumed he had remained at home because of the Ramadan fast. He was not seen the next day either, and then the guards recalled having noticed several women leaving the house in a car. At the time, they had simply thought that the women were the mufti's wives, but now they realized their error. The mufti himself had been in the car, wearing a dress, his face covered by a veil. The intelligence services of half a dozen countries began hunting for him; he was apparently hiding out in Baghdad or perhaps in Tehran.[59] In any case, on November 30, 1941, he was sitting in the fuehrer's office in Berlin.

Reaching Hitler had not been easy for the mufti, and he did not get what he wanted. The minutes of their conversation are reminiscent of the talks between the Zionist leadership and the British during World War I. Husseini asked for two things: a declaration of support for the Arabs in Palestine and the establishment of an Arab legion under Wehrmacht sponsorship. The mufti had previously met with Mussolini; he hoped that

Hitler would agree to issue a joint statement with Il Duce. The Arabs were "natural friends" of Germany, he argued; they were both facing the same enemies—the English, the Jews, and the Communists. He expressed his confidence that the Germans would win the war and offered the Arabs' help in exchange for Germany's promise to help them after the war.

Hitler agreed with Husseini's fundamental assumptions. He was fighting two countries controlled by the Jews, Britain and the Soviet Union; he would of course not agree to the establishment of a Jewish state in Palestine. Nevertheless, he would not issue a declaration of support; at this point he did not want to anger the French government, which still controlled Lebanon and Syria.[60*]

Berlin was the mufti's base until after the war. He was invited to give lectures and from time to time sent the authorities various operative suggestions, including a plan for bombing Tel Aviv and dropping paratroopers in Palestine. None of his proposals were included in the Germans' war plans, although the Nazis did show some interest in the idea of establishing an Arab legion. In the end they used the mufti in an initiative to set up a Muslim-Balkan unit in the framework of the Waffen-SS. As part of this project, Husseini entered into close contact with Heinrich Himmler.

Sari al-Sakakini believed that even after the White Paper was issued, the British failed to understand that the Arabs' position in World War II was very similar to that of the Jews in the previous war: they could choose to side with the British or the Germans. Their decision was only a matter of which alliance would be more worthwhile.[62†]

George Antonius's papers preserve the draft of a letter an Arab doctor in Jerusalem apparently intended for the president of the United States. The letter contains the essence of the position Arab spokesmen would

---

*The mufti spoke French; Johann Eppler, his interpreter, told the fuehrer that courtesy required serving coffee. Hitler angrily responded that he did not like coffee. The mufti, noting Hitler's anger, asked what had happened—perhaps the fuehrer was not pleased to see him. Eppler reassured the mufti and explained to Hitler that a conversation without coffee would leave a bad impression on the guest. Hitler jumped up from his seat, shouting that he did not allow anyone to drink coffee in the high command and stalked out of the room, slamming the door behind him. A few minutes later he returned with an SS man, who brought two glasses of lemonade.[61]

†At the same time that the mufti was asking for the Nazis' help, Avraham Stern, the Lechi commander, suggested establishing a Jewish alliance with Nazi Germany to end British rule in Palestine. He was guided by the same principle: my enemy's enemy is my friend.[63] However, Stern operated on the margins of the opposition to the Zionist leadership, while the mufti represented the entire Arab national movement in Palestine. Furthermore, Stern's plan existed on paper only.

adopt after the Holocaust, that the Arabs should not have to pay the price for Europe's persecution of the Jews. "We all sympathize with the Jews and are shocked at the way Christian nations are persecuting them. But do you expect Moslems of Palestine . . . to be more Christian or more humanitarian than the followers of Christ: Germany, Italy, Poland, Romania, etc. etc.? Have we to suffer in order to make good what you Christians commit?"[64] Antonius wrote in a similar vein: "The treatment meted out to Jews in Germany and other European countries is a disgrace to its authors and to modern civilization but . . . the cure for the eviction of Jews from Germany is not to be sought in the eviction of the Arabs from their homeland."[65]*

Toward the end of the war High Commissioner MacMichael was driven to the same frustration his predecessors had evinced. He was so despondent about his role in Palestine that he became careless, failing to watch his tongue even with David Ben-Gurion. He had no idea what the British wanted from him, he said. No one had told him what measures they expected him to carry out. The government's policy was constantly changing, there were countless interpretations, countless commissions of inquiry, no end of white papers. For twenty-five years London had not known what it wanted. He himself had no clue what he was doing in Palestine. As far as he was concerned, everything was possible, if someone would only tell him what to do. If they wanted partition, there would be partition. If they wanted a state, there would be a state. It was all the same to him. MacMichael had no interest in politics; he did not understand it. That was not his business, and it was not his job. His job was to keep order.

At the end of this remarkable conversation, when Ben-Gurion was standing by the door ready to leave, the high commissioner said, "You have much more power than we do." He did not understand what Ben-Gurion wanted from him, either, he added, but he supposed that Ben-Gurion had something in mind. After all, there was always some kind of intrigue in what the Jews said and did. The fact that the prime minister opposed his own government's official policy made MacMichael's life even more difficult. MacMichael himself proposed dismantling the Jew-

---

*A short time after the defeat of the Arabs in 1948 Anwar Nusseibeh wrote that the mufti had not gone beyond the principles of Arab patriotism by collaborating with the Nazis. The mufti, he thought, had erred only in thinking he could achieve more with Italy's or Germany's help. "People in despair are apt to commit mistakes and the British had driven him to despair," Nusseibeh wrote.[66]

ish Agency—after the war there would be bloodshed in Palestine, he warned. But his suggestion was filed away.[67]

Ben-Gurion estimated that the high commissioner would be pleased to be released from his position and given some remote colony where he could rest. "A small man," Ben-Gurion commented; talking to him, he told his colleagues, was "torture." Golda Meyerson also reported difficulties talking to leaders of the British establishment; their conversations all came down to the same thing: the chief secretary and the high commissioner demanded that the Jewish Agency take more determined action against Jewish terrorism, while the Jewish Agency wanted concessions on immigration that could be presented to the public as an achievement.[68]*

9.

Sometime after meeting Omran in Jerusalem, Sari al-Sakakini wrote to his sisters, "He is my best friend. His manliness impresses me." Omran was absolutely devoted to him, he said.[69] A few months later Sari published an article in a mimeographed bulletin put out by the YMCA in Jerusalem under the heading "My Best Friend," whom he identified only by an initial. "We like to be together, to do things together," he wrote. "Both of us think of the other. Both of us would do anything to please the other. We know each other's virtues and shortcomings. We trust each other, we take refuge in each other. The moment we part we start longing for each other. Each considers all expressions of beauty and poetry as rising from his heart for the other. . . . We understand each other to the point of reading one another's thoughts. Neither dares speak out to the other the love that is in one's heart."[70]

This last sentence was not quite true. Omran sent Sakakini a series of long, passionate, erotic love letters on the stationery of the cab company that employed him, Orient Taxi on Princess Mary Avenue. He often wrote in the morning, upon returning to work after a night spent with his friend. Sakakini composed a love poem for him.[71] In addition to adopting his father's nationalist worldview and cultural values, Sari al-Sakakini seems also to have absorbed his father's concepts of masculinity. "I would like you to be so strong that if you fought a bull you would throw him over," Khalil al-Sakakini had written to his son. "I would like you to have

---

*MacMichael completed his term of duty in the winter of 1944. His replacement, Lord Gort, died about a year after arriving in Palestine. Sir Alan Cunningham, the seventh and last high commissioner, began his term of service in November 1945.

great stature, taut muscles, a vast chest, sinewy arms." He wished to give his son an appreciation of strength. In one letter he wrote, "Strength, strength. If you must worship anything, then worship strength. Make of your body a perfect statue for this god." Once, when Sari al-Sakakini had to fill out a form, in the space for status he wrote, "single, thank you"; next to the question marked "dependents" he wrote, "in no way and never."[72]

In March 1944, Ya'akov Cohen turned twenty. "Now I am certain I have entered the age of maturity and know my duties to God, my people, and my parents," he wrote in his diary. He had finished his term in the Palmach. "Two years of service for the homeland," he noted, asking himself if the time spent had been worthwhile. "Yes, definitely yes!" he responded.[73]

Toward the end of the war, Cohen moved to Jerusalem and enrolled at the Hebrew University. He also worked as a counselor in an institution for children. On May 8, 1945, the day of Germany's surrender, he wrote, "The whole city got up and went out to the streets, to take part in our shared celebration." David Ben-Gurion did not share the general happiness. The war had killed six million Jews. "It is a sad day," he wrote in his diary, "very sad." Khalil al-Sakakini was not pleased with Germany's defeat: "If any one of the combatants has reason to be proud, it is Germany, because it fought the entire world for six years," he wrote.[74] Meanwhile, the Jewish terrorist organizations escalated their activity against the British.

—•—

22

"Give Me a Country
Without Wars"

1.

One morning, sometime after General Sir Evelyn Barker had arrived in Palestine to suppress the Jewish terrorist organizations, he heard Irving Berlin's "Dancing Cheek to Cheek" on the radio program *Musical Clock.* That was in the summer or autumn of 1946, at 7:15 in the morning. The general immediately sat down to write to Katy Antonius: "You are the first woman I've ever done it with," he wrote, referring apparently to dancing cheek to cheek. "I enjoyed every moment and wished it could have gone on." She had told him that he had, perhaps, fallen in love with her. Barker appreciated her comment more than anything, he wrote, because in fact he had been in love with her for months.[1]

Their love story is revealed in close to one hundred letters that the general wrote on official army stationary and sent by special messenger, his driver, to his beloved's house in east Jerusalem, a few blocks from his own home on the city's west side. The letters tell a story of ecstasy and tragedy, pathos, mystery, and deception, danger, hope, and disappointment, romance, tears, and kisses—all against the background of nationalist terror, the crumbling of an empire, the birth of one nation and the devastation of another.

Barker was forty-two, married, and the father of a son. Before arriving in Palestine in May 1946 he had enjoyed a celebrated military career that began when he decided in his youth, a short time before World War I, to enlist in the army and become a professional soldier like his father. In the 1930s, Barker was sent to Palestine for the first time to help the army suppress the Arab rebellion. In World War II, he participated in the invasion of Normandy. He distinguished himself in the battle to liberate Le Havre, as a result of which the king granted him a knighthood. Afterward he joined the VIII Corps, which crossed the Rhine under General Montgomery and advanced through northern Germany. On April 15, 1945, his men liberated the Bergen-Belsen death camp. An officer of the old school, he exuded colonial arrogance—tall, thin, slightly bent, with a steely, penetrating gaze devoid of emotion. Yet in his letters to Katy Antonius he sounds like a schoolboy in love.*

The widow of George Antonius, Katy was the daughter of Dr. Faris Nimr Pasha of Alexandria, senator, expert on the Arab language, and owner of the prestigious newspaper *Al-Muqadam.* From a young age she had been taught that her culture was European. She kept company with Western diplomats and spoke a number of their languages as if they were her own. Her sister married Sir Walter Alexander Smart, a high official in the British embassy in Cairo.† "Katy Antonius was an intelligent, bright, and witty woman, full of humor and charm," Anwar Nusseibeh said of her, "always up-to-date on the intricacies of political events, pretty, good-hearted, and generous." She lived in a house that was owned by the mufti and was a high-society hostess; her guests included everyone who was anyone in the British administration—Western politicians, journalists, artists, notables from around the world, as well as many leaders from the Arab countries.[5]

One of her guests, British journalist and politician Richard Crossman, described her house as a political salon in the French style. He wrote of one magnificent party: "Evening dress, Syrian food and drink, and dancing on the marble floor." As far as he could make out, the guests were a mix of Arabs and Britishers. "It is easy to see why the British prefer the Arab upper class to the Jews," Crossman went on. "This Arab intelligentsia has a French culture, amusing, civilized, tragic and gay. Compared

---

*George Antonius had died in 1942, after having gained fame as the author of *The Arab Awakening,* published in 1938, the most important book written to date on the history of the Arab national movement in Palestine.[2] Khalil al-Sakakini was one of his pallbearers, as was Musa Alami. When Sakakini began to eulogize Antonius by his grave on Mount Zion, tears welled up in his eyes and he was almost unable to speak.[3]

†George Antonius's love for Katy also produced a large collection of letters written in English, some of them on official Mandatory Education Department stationary. A supporter of the mufti, he nonetheless preferred to tie the fate of the Arab national movement to the British Empire. His love letters indicate that the relationship was fairly tormented.[4]

with them the Jews seem tense, *bourgeois,* central European." In the car that took Crossman back to the King David Hotel, a British official explained that there were two societies in Jerusalem, not three—one Anglo-Arab, the other Jewish, and the two could not mix.[6]

Barker seems to have fallen in love with Katy Antonius at one of those parties. When they saw each other at social events they would keep a discreet distance; the following day he would write how hard he had found being in her company without touching her. He frequently visited her home in the evenings, and the next morning would write to her how much he enjoyed her company, how important she was to him, how much he loved her. "I am not sentimental," he wrote once during a flight home, "but am sensitive to love and kindness. I could not keep the tears away from my eyes as I drove off this morning—stupid as you may think me."[7] By the time Barker's plane had landed he had written Katy another letter.[8] He promised over and over again that he was on the Arab side and made her party to several military secrets, including some dealing with the fight against Jewish terrorism.

2.

With the war in Europe over, Ya'akov Cohen was now a pessimist, he told his diary. "How will peace be established in the world?" he wondered. He also worried that he was too preoccupied with politics and not enough with life itself. On Saturdays he would go on hikes with the children from the institution where he worked. "There is nothing finer than the season of cyclamens and anemones," he wrote, but he was lonely and bored and longed for love.[9] Once, by chance, he ran into Bebs on Ben-Yehuda Street in Tel Aviv. As usual, nothing came of it. Bebs had also enlisted in the Palmach; they called her Bracha now. A short time later she was killed. Ya'akov Cohen read about it in the newspaper.

Tel Aviv had been waiting for a ship that had sailed from Italy, bringing close to 250 illegal immigrants. In commemoration of the second anniversary of Orde Wingate's death, the boat was named the *Wingate.* The operation was especially large: hundreds of people—thousands, according to one source—were deployed by a special staff under the command of Yitzhak Sadeh himself, and his deputy Yigal Allon. People were stationed at key posts along the shore; many roads were blocked by trucks and cars to prevent army and police from approaching. Hundreds of families were standing by, ready to house the passengers. But the British discovered the boat at sea and intercepted it before the immigrants reached the shore.

There was an exchange of fire between Palmach members and the British. Bracha Fuld was wounded and died in the hospital; six months later an illegal immigration ship was named after her.[10]

The day after her death Ya'akov Cohen wrote, "My day will come as well. I will not hesitate even for a moment. I will do my duty." A few days later the British captured another illegal immigration ship, called the *Tel Hai*. No, people were not dying because it is good to do so for one's country, Cohen wrote, invoking Yosef Trumpeldor's legendary last words. They were dying to make life secure. Sacrifice was unavoidable; there were no alternatives. One heretical thought did come into Cohen's mind, however: Was it all absolutely necessary? He quickly repressed the question, almost in alarm. "There must be no wavering," he warned himself.[11]

By the first anniversary of "Wingate night," as the clash came to be called, Bracha Fuld had become a national symbol. This bothered Cohen: up until then Bebs had been his alone, a secret love. How he had admired her, how he had longed to serve her, how he had wanted to be like her, he wrote. At times, he felt, she had seemed almost to be making fun of him, as if saying, "He knows he will not succeed, because I am not just his, I belong to everyone." Which is exactly what had happened. "Bebs gave me a stinging blow," Cohen wrote. In the months since her death the forbidden thought had recurred: "We should ask ourselves if this is worthwhile," he recorded in his diary. "Should we risk the lives of young men and women just for prestige? After all, the immigrants will come anyway."[12]

Ben-Gurion was troubled by the possibility that Holocaust survivors would not want to come to Palestine but would choose to settle elsewhere. "I think we should not treat this danger lightly. It is the greatest danger not only to Zionism but to the Yishuv," he wrote, even before the war was over.[13] The competition between the labor movement and the Revisionists continued to occupy his thoughts. Terror was deployed, among other reasons, to forcibly take control of the Yishuv and the Zionist movement as a whole, he claimed.[14] The conflict might even lead to civil war, he believed. "We must take up our rifles against them," he declared. "Whoever tries to have their way with guns—I will answer him with guns." He was convinced however, that unlike the Germans, the Jewish community in Palestine would not capitulate to the right wing.

This was no chance comparison. He continued to call Etzel a "Nazi gang" and "Jewish Nazis." The Revisionists are liable to murder each and every one of us sitting here, Ben-Gurion told his colleagues in the Histadrut. He compared Begin to the fuehrer. "Hitler also had boys who joined his movement and were killed to sanctify their ideal. Certain Nazis had pure, idealistic motives. But the movement as a whole was reprehensible and destroyed the German people. "Etzel was similarly liable to destroy the Yishuv, Ben-Gurion argued, describing the organization and its supporters as a bubonic plague.[15]*

The labor movement was also divided internally. Some advocated operations against the British, including terrorist attacks, particularly members of the kibbutzim and the Palmach. Unwilling to limit themselves to illegal immigration operations, they put pressure on the leadership, which ultimately led, in October 1945, to the establishment of the Hebrew Resistance Movement, a joint Haganah venture with Etzel and Lechi. The labor movement's cooperation with Etzel and Lechi lasted for only eight months but represented a general acceptance by the Jewish leadership of the principle that the British should be fought militarily; for the Revisionists this was an important achievement. The two organizations received recognition and a role in the national decision-making process; the Jewish Agency and the Haganah also stopped turning their members in to the authorities. The Hebrew Resistance Movement provided an outlet for the growing activist agitation in the Palmach, which now allowed its men to carry out a few attacks on railroad tracks and bridges.

The period of cooperation between the Haganah and the competing organizations endangered relations between the Jewish Agency and the authorities but gave the Haganah a certain amount of control over the two other groups, enabling it to restrain them.[17] During this period an attempt was made to murder Raymond Cafferata, and an attack on the King David Hotel was planned.

3.

Cafferata was chief of police in Haifa at the time. His name continued to appear in the British press. At the end of 1942, Lord Wedgwood claimed that the British policemen in Palestine were dyed-in-the-wool anti-semites; they had even cheered when Italian warplanes bombed Tel Aviv. Noting the "Fascist spirit" prevalent among the police, Wedgwood referred sarcastically to "these gentlemen with the good old Anglo-Saxon names," citing Cafferata in particular.[18] In response, Raymond Cafferata sent a sharp letter of protest. Only the Nazi enemy could benefit from

---

*Ya'akov Cohen also called Etzel and Lechi Nazis: "They are leading us straight to a Holocaust," he wrote.[16]

Wedgwood's charges, he wrote. The comment on his family name was more appropriate to a Hyde Park tub-thumper, he said, though perhaps he was being unjust to the tub-thumpers, since they at least had some decency.[19]

In fact, Cafferata was sympathetic to the tragedy of the Jewish refugees. At one point, probably just after he completed his service in Palestine, he wrote down a sad memory of an encounter, during the war years, with a fifty-year-old man named Kupperman. Cafferata had met him at a café in Tel Aviv, and Kupperman had told his story. He had come from Germany alone, leaving his family behind. He described the harsh conditions on board the illegal immigration ship. When the ship came in to dock, it ran up on a sandbar not far from the Tel Aviv shore. The passengers were told to jump into the water. Kupperman jumped. He didn't mind leaving his baggage behind—he was wearing a belt around his waist in which there were several diamonds. He managed to reach the shore, and together with several other people he stood there, soaked and shivering in the cold and the dark. Suddenly a boy of sixteen or seventeen appeared and led them to a wooden hut where there were several bunks, eating utensils, and a dirty kerosene stove. The boy told the refugees to stay there and gave them food. After some time they dared venture out. Some of them had relatives in Palestine.

Kupperman went into Tel Aviv. At a coffeehouse he struck up a conversation with several people, who realized he was an illegal immigrant. Kupperman was alarmed, but they reassured him. Kupperman said he had to get his family out of Germany and bring them to Palestine, and the people he had met promised to help but demanded money. Kupperman gave them one of the diamonds from his belt. Later he gave them another and then another. It turned out that his new acquaintances were confidence men and extortionists. When he refused to give them more diamonds they threatened to notify the Gestapo chief in Frankfurt whom he had fled. He would never see his wife and children again, they threatened. He gave away the last of his diamonds and was left with nothing. At this point he encountered Cafferata, who was not surprised by the story. He had been in the country for ten years—everything cost money.

He tried to give Kupperman some encouragement, buying him a sandwich and a cup of tea. The British did not send Jews back to Nazi Germany after they had fled, Cafferata explained, and he promised to try to arrange an immigration permit for Kupperman's wife and children. The two were supposed to meet at the same café the next evening. A few hours before setting out, Cafferata was handed a summary of the day's events. Several burglaries, a knife fight or two, and the arrest of two small-time hashish pushers. The body of a man, about fifty years old with gray hair, had been found on the beach. Cafferata went to the morgue and identified Kupperman. He had drowned himself.[20]

Several Jewish community leaders in Haifa testified that they had a correct working relationship with the city's police commander. But the members of the Haganah remembered their clash with Cafferata at Ramat HaKovesh and Givat Haim. Those from Etzel remembered the Hebron massacre and accused the police chief of killing one of their men, Asher Trattner, an eighteen-year-old student from Breslau. Some Haifa policemen had run into Trattner while he was pasting up Etzel broadsides in the street. He had tried to flee, and the policemen had shot and hit him in the leg. He had been arrested for interrogation and taken to Acre prison, where apparently he did not receive proper medical care. Three weeks later he was brought to the hospital, where his leg was amputated. Two days after that he died. Etzel claimed that Trattner had died of sadistic torture and held Cafferata responsible. Trattner himself had managed, before dying, to tell his brother that he suffered from pain in his leg, but his interrogators had not tortured him.[21]

The initiative for Cafferata's murder came from Lechi; the commanders of the Hebrew Resistance Movement knew of the plan in advance—they neither approved it nor forbade it. In the spirit of unity that prevailed among the terrorist organizations at that time, members of Lechi and Etzel worked together. Cafferata lived with his wife, Peggy, and their two children on Mount Carmel; his office was on Kingsway in the lower city, not far from the entrance to the port. His driver took him to his office every morning in a blue Ford. The plan was to block the car not far from the Herzliya Court Hotel, at the entrance to the Hadar HaCarmel neighborhood; there was a sharp turn in the road and trees to provide cover. The attackers planned to shoot Cafferata or throw a bomb into his car. Nehemia Ben-Tor of Lechi, who was assigned to carry out the assassination, wrote, "I was happy to accept the job and proud to be among those who avenged the blood of the victims of 1929." Ben-Tor recalled his orders: if Peggy Cafferata was in the car with her husband, the operation should be canceled.

The day of the attack was stormy; rain had emptied the streets, which was good, but the plan failed anyway. The driver of the car supposed to block Cafferata's vehicle was not quick enough, and Cafferata's driver managed to maneuver his way out of the trap. Ben-Tor emptied his revolver into the car's back window; one bullet backfired and hit Ben-Tor in the leg. Inevitably, the incident led to an exhaustive debate over the details of the operation and the apportionment of blame for its failure. Many years later Ben-Tor wrote, "More than once I have been overcome with curiosity to know what happened to the man whose life I was ordered to take, what kind of man was he?" They had at least one thing in common: Cafferata had also once been hit in the leg by a bullet that had backfired from his pistol.[22]

Cafferata escaped unharmed. He proceeded to his office as if nothing had happened. His secretary noticed that he was a bit upset, but she knew nothing about what had happened. In the days that followed the police chief was in a bad mood; he had long known that his life was in danger, but had always felt that nothing would happen to him.[23]*

Cafferata's secretary described him as a generous man, devoted to his family. He had few friends and seldom went to pubs. She never heard a bad word about the Jews escape his lips; her impression was that he had no political views. As it turned out, she was a secret agent for the Zionists: she copied every letter he dictated to her and sent it to the Haganah.[24]

A few weeks after the attack, Cafferata was shipped home. He claimed that he had submitted his resignation before the assassination attempt. The Jews had done everything to ruin him, Cafferata wrote, explaining that some Jewish friends had made him aware of the intensity of the opposition he roused in Palestine. The hostility toward him made it impossible for him to do his job, he maintained, citing Wedgwood's remarks in the House of Lords. So he decided to go. But had Cafferata not gone of his own initiative, he would have been forced to leave. He was shocked, he wrote. He was not antisemitic—he had played soccer for many Jewish football teams, which was more than most officials in Palestine had done. Most of his contacts with Jews had been in connection with saving their lives, he wrote. He did not want to leave Palestine—had he stayed six years longer he would have received a full pension.[25]†

In June 1946 terrorist attacks intensified, and at the end of the month General Barker ordered Operation Agatha: more than 100,000 soldiers and policemen surrounded dozens of Jewish settlements throughout the

*In an unpublished autobiography, Cafferata wrote that he and his comrades lived with the constant feeling that the terrorist organizations were liable to liquidate them; he described Menachem Begin as a ruthless thug who made Al Capone look like a novice.

†Lechi operatives also tried to kill General Evelyn Barker near his house. "I was dressed as a nanny and went for a walk with a baby carriage on the sidewalk facing Barker's house," a

country and imposed a curfew that included Tel Aviv and Jerusalem. To the Jews, the event became known as "Black Sabbath." Some 3,000 people were arrested, among them members of the Jewish Agency Executive; a large cache of weapons was found at Kibbutz Yagur.[27] Four weeks after Black Sabbath, Etzel operatives blew up the south wing of the King David Hotel, which housed the government secretariat. As the country was in flames, General Barker shared a fantasy with Katy Antonius that should he ever find himself single again he would return to the Middle East to help the Arabs fight for their rights. "We might even combine," he suggested to her.[28] Soon, however, he got himself in trouble, and was forced to leave his Katy.

4.

Black Sabbath was the most extensive and violent operation against the Jews of Palestine; the attack on the King David had killed more than ninety people and was the largest action against the British.[29] Both events were exceptional—the Jews and the British tended to restrain themselves and not fight at full force.

One evening in the winter of 1946 Etzel men attacked a police station in Jerusalem, having previously laid mines in several surrounding streets. The action failed, and the mines were discovered and dismantled. In the wake of the incident the high commissioner canceled a formal dinner, since the mines in the city streets made it difficult for the guests to get to his residence. Canceling the dinner was the most dramatic response the authorities made that evening. A meeting to discuss the attack was called only the following day. Viscount Montgomery, now chief of the Imperial General Staff, was furious. Had the matter been handled properly, mobile army forces would have been sent to the scene within ten minutes and the terrorists would have been captured, he wrote. He also criticized the local police: they did not function in a tolerant and good-natured way, as they did in England; they did not enjoy the confidence of the community. In

---

Lechi woman recalled. "The baby in the carriage was a doll. The bomb's fuse was concealed in the handle of the carriage. Time after time I went to Barker's house and each time a motorcycle driver waited some distance away. The intention was to set off the booby-trapped baby carriage as soon as Barker left his house and get away quickly, but the plan did not work. Barker never appeared on time. After a few days, the neighbors started taking notice. 'Isn't it a bit cold, on a day like this, to be walking outside with a baby?' they asked. We had to give up the plan."[26]

Palestine they were armed to the teeth and often drove in armored cars. Instead of being first-class policemen they were third-class soldiers. And the population hated them because Jews in general hated policemen.[30]

The legendary Monty had returned to Palestine to repress Jewish terrorism with an iron hand, just as he had done with the Arab rebellion. Years before, Orde Wingate had told Ben-Gurion that Montgomery hated the Yishuv. The situation in Palestine infuriated him—the government had for all practical purposes lost control of the country; the real rulers, in his view, were the Jews, who were telling the authorities "Don't you dare touch us."[31] Things could not go on like this, Montgomery told Prime Minister Clement Attlee; there were 100,000 soldiers stationed in Palestine with their hands tied. Two of them were being killed each day. He, Montgomery, would not allow this state of affairs to continue. "If we are not prepared to maintain law and order in Palestine, then it would be better to get out," he said.

The army and the civilian government were caught in yet another confrontation: the army demanded freedom of action, while the high commissioner's inclination was toward restraint. In the back of everyone's mind was concern with how history would portray them. The army was readying its argument that Palestine had been lost because Britain was not prepared to use the force at its disposal. Indeed, the official version in the end was that the government and the high commissioner had been too weak.[32]

Their hands were not stayed by weakness, however, but by a powerful sense of moral limitations on harsh behavior toward Jews. The British had both operational and legal justifications for action and were well aware that terrorism was dealing a blow to the empire's prestige elsewhere in the world. But even after the murder of Lord Moyne they held their force in check. When they went to search for weapons they acted not on mere hunches but only on the basis of authoritative intelligence information, and they worked in parallel to disarm the Arabs.[33]

The authorities did institute draconian emergency laws; the Jewish Bar Association complained that the regulations were worse than those imposed in Nazi Germany.[34] A general night curfew lasted for many months. On four occasions the British declared a total curfew in Tel Aviv while they conducted house-to-house searches. They arrested and tortured suspects, deported people to Africa, and hanged prisoners. But they never acted against the Jews with the determination and harshness that characterized the suppression of the Arab rebellion.[35] Judge Anwar Nusseibeh pointed out that the residents of Yemin Moshe, the Jewish neighborhood adjacent to the King David Hotel, had not been punished for the explosion in the hotel. Likewise, the population of Givat Shaul had not been held in any way responsible for the nearby attack on the high commissioner. Yet punishing entire Arab neighborhoods or villages for crimes that occurred in their vicinity, he noted, was common British practice.

There were some differences in the two situations, though. Many Jews opposed anti-British terrorism, so collective punishment would have proved counterproductive. During the Arab rebellion, the authorities acted on the assumption that most Arabs supported the terror campaign. Also, the Jewish terrorists acted largely in the cities rather than in the villages, which made it difficult for the British to locate and act against them. But mostly, the Jews were Europeans, not "natives," allies in the war against the Nazis and Holocaust survivors. The British were acutely aware of the limitations these circumstances imposed: "Every honorable member will agree that we are not prepared when we use the phrase 'at all costs' to resort to mass extermination of the population in the way that the Nazis did," said one parliamentarian; Winston Churchill echoed this sentiment.[36] In addition, the Jewish Agency and the Haganah continued to see themselves as part of the regime in Palestine, despite the terror, and the British recognized their allegiance until the very last day of the Mandate.*

The unified Hebrew Resistance Movement did not last beyond the explosion at the King David Hotel. The Haganah condemned the bombing and claimed it had taken no part in the action. This was not quite accurate: the joint Jewish command had approved the attack, but in the wake of the huge number of deaths that resulted there was a heated debate over the details of how it had been carried out.†

After the united underground movement was dismantled, rivalry between the different Zionist organizations resumed. When the British sentenced an Etzel operative, Dov Gruner, to death, Ben-Gurion

---

*Incredibly, but perhaps typical of the confusion that marked Britain's Palestine policy, in at least one case the Haganah received informal permission from the administration to carry out an attack against it. Richard Crossman, Labor MP and a great friend of Zionism, told the undersecretary of state for air, John Strachey, that the Haganah was considering blowing up the bridges over the Jordan River. He requested "advice." Strachey, a member of the Cabinet Defense Committee, asked for time to look into the matter, and the next day gave Crossman his consent.[37]

†Ben-Gurion was in Paris at the time. Among the people he met there was the leader of the Vietnamese national movement, Ho Chi Minh. They stayed at the same hotel for some two weeks and saw each other nearly every day.[38]

responded the same way he had to the earlier sentences against Revisionists. He didn't want anyone hanged, he said, but he would do nothing to prevent the execution. Nor would he fly a black flag. Begin and his men were playing fast and loose with the Yishuv and had to be stopped once and for all. Otherwise the labor movement might as well just hand him the keys.[39] Begin was Ben-Gurion's number one enemy, more important than any Englishman.

Etzel continued its operations, however. The most famous of these were an attack on the officers' club in Goldschmied House in Jerusalem, a breakout from Acre prison freeing some major Revisionist prisoners, and the hanging of two British sergeants in retribution for the deaths of Etzel men.[40] Ben-Gurion was particularly angry about the hanging because the deed coincided with the arrival of the illegal immigration ship the *Exodus,* and diverted attention from it. The *Exodus* was planned as dramatic propaganda, the boldest illegal immigration operation yet, "one of the greatest displays of the Jewish struggle, of Jewish pride, and of the connection with the Land of Israel," according to Ben-Gurion. Now Etzel had stolen the show from the Jewish Agency. Who in the world would pay any attention to the *Exodus* after a deed like this, he wondered. He called the hanging a "Nazi act."[41]

The Mandatory government was focusing most of its security efforts on protecting its personnel, not on maintaining the regime. Montgomery instructed Evelyn Barker to stress to the soldiers that they were facing a cruel, fanatical, and cunning enemy, and there was no way of knowing who was friend and who foe. There were female terrorists as well, so all fraternizing with the local population would have to cease.[42]

In the wake of the King David bombing, Barker translated these instructions into an order declaring all Jewish establishments, including restaurants and places of entertainment, off-limits to British soldiers. He knew this would be difficult, Barker wrote to his men, but the Jews had to learn just how much the British despised them, and the best way to punish them was by striking at their pockets, which the race particularly disliked. His choice of words was unfortunate. They were interpreted as antisemitic and caused an uproar. Katy Antonius preserved among her papers a caricature that appeared in England showing Barker brandishing his statement while standing on a copy of Hitler's *Mein Kampf.* Barker was soon returned to England. Many years later he claimed, in a conversation with Lord Nicholas Bethell, that it had been "a rotten letter written on the spur of the moment."[43]

But Barker's disclaimer was false. Sometime after returning to England, he wrote to Kate Antonius. "They do hate having their pockets touched, as I said in my letter," he noted, adding, "I hope the Arabs will no longer think we are afraid to hang Jews." Two terrorists had committed suicide in prison before being executed, and Barker commented, "So that's two more less." His hostility to the Jews was clearly an inseparable part of his love for his Katy, and that love was part of his hostility. He would gaze at her picture, his eyes growing damp: "Katy, I love you so much, Katy," he wrote her. "Just think of all this life and money being wasted for these b—y Jews. Yes I loathe the lot—whether they be Zionists or not. Why should we be afraid of saying we hate them—it's time this damned race knew what we think of them—loathsome people."[44]

A few months after returning from Palestine, Barker received a package. "The smell was strange," he wrote Antonius that same day. He discerned greenish powder, silver paper, and two wires, and then was certain what it was. He called a sapper, who dismantled the device, a letter bomb. Two Etzel men had also planned to mine the road leading to his home in England. One of them was Ezer Weizman, the Zionist leader's nephew, who would follow in his uncle's footsteps to become president of Israel. At the time Barker received the bomb, Weizman was checking out the possibility of killing Raymond Cafferata.[45]

Barker was not the only one to make antisemitic comments. Another officer, Lieutenant Colonel Richard Webb, summoned reporters and gave his pejorative views of the Jewish race. One intelligence evaluation stated that "making money is almost a second religion with the Jews." The Jewish Agency was constantly filing complaints about soldiers who had used antisemitic expressions: they frequently said "bloody Jew" or "pigs," sometimes shouted *"Heil Hitler,"* and promised they would finish off what Hitler had begun. Churchill wrote that most British military officers in Palestine were strongly pro-Arab.[46]

This hostility was largely a problem of morale. Most of the soldiers, a British intelligence officer reported, had come to Palestine with sympathy for the Jews, partly because of the suffering they had endured in World War II.[47] As a British paratrooper named Wilson wrote, the men of the Sixth Airborne Division had seen the persecution of the Jews with their own eyes when they fought the Nazis in Europe. But when these same soldiers arrived in Palestine, they found themselves facing large, hostile groups of Jewish demonstrators chanting "Free immigration," and "a

Hebrew state." The men of the Sixth Airborne Division were "mystified" by the Jews' enmity, Wilson wrote. The terror campaign angered and often humiliated them; once, Etzel agents kidnapped two of the division's men, pulled down their pants, and gave them a whipping, retribution for a lashing received by one of their own members.[48] Wilson complained about what seemed to him a violation of fair play. The men were revolted and frustrated by Lechi's methods, he wrote, and he termed one operation, an attack on soldiers guarding a military parking lot in Tel Aviv, "mass murder."[49] Many of the soldiers would soon consider all Jews terrorists.

The members of the Sixth Airborne arrived in Palestine in 1945 under the command of Major General E. L. Bols, the son of Allenby's chief of staff, who had had Herbert Samuel sign the famous "receipt" for Palestine. They were first stationed in Gaza and then deployed to suppress the terrorist organizations.[50] The paratroopers wore red berets, leading the Jews to call them "anemones."

Nathan Alterman, a Hebrew poet who wrote about the struggle against the British, penned a pretty love song called "Anemones." Its most political lines are "Oaths of love may be forgotten/Anemones will always blossom/Like smoke the oaths have come and gone/Anemones go on and on."[51] The song was hardly political, but the "anemones" themselves considered it a stinging insult, one of the many they had to endure. Jews would shout "Gestapo" at them, or call out "English bastards," and children would taunt them by singing the song's chorus, "Anemones, anemones." In writing his chronicle, Wilson quoted a line from the song that, he claimed, compared anemones to the paratroopers—their heads were red but their hearts were black. These words hurt them more than anything, he said, because British troops were renowned for their love of children.[52] Their pride was wounded gratuitously; while the metaphor might have been popular, there is not a trace of it in Alterman's lyrics.

Once the soldiers were restricted to their camps, to strike the Jews "in their pockets" and protect the lives of the men, they were sentenced to a "fairly monastic" life. They played bridge and poker and read books. They saw movies and played cricket and football, but had few other forms of recreation.[53] So they liked going out on missions. Some were very young and considered the action in Palestine compensation for what they had missed in World War II. There were also soldiers who wanted to use stronger measures than those permitted. From time to time, soldiers went out on their own to take revenge on civilians. Wilson made note of one of the soldiers' major obstacles: the international press, in the form of reporters and photographers, was around all too often. The soldiers frequently felt they had gotten caught up in a propaganda war, especially when they had to arrest illegal immigrants.

Wilson wrote of the refugees with compassion, without rancor, even though some of them acted, he said, with fanatical violence. There was something tragic and touching in their yearning to remain in the Holy Land, he thought. The Holocaust survivors were miserable and pathetic, another officer noted, and the orders to arrest and deport them troubled many of the soldiers.[54] Nathan Alterman wrote of one such soldier, "It is not easy to drag orphans and mothers / Or to tussle on one's knees with mourning fathers / And be loyal and worthy of the homeland / That sent him off with its flags." What it came down to, one paratrooper concluded, was that the soldiers had an unpleasant job often requiring them to deal with unpleasant people.[55]

A Jewish Agency emissary in London, Teddy Kollek, reported that he had seen letters sent by soldiers serving in Palestine in which they clearly recognized there was no purpose and no justice in the war they were fighting. Parents and friends often sent these letters to the press, but the newspapers did not print them. Abba Eban, another Zionist representative, also reported from London that the soldier's low morale was of much concern to the army's officers; they had trouble explaining to the soldiers why they were in Palestine. Many were again inclined to minimize the country's strategic importance. In Jerusalem antipathy to the British was growing ever stronger. A Jewish Agency official expressed his fear that the Yishuv's leadership might lose control of the community.[56]

5.

Hostility to the British focused on the Labour government's foreign secretary, Ernest Bevin. The party's platform had promised free Jewish immigration to Palestine and even transfer of the Arabs.[57] But the party did not keep its promises; the number of immigrants was limited to fifteen hundred a month. This was reprehensible, a base betrayal, Ya'akov Cohen wrote in his diary. "We came out of World War I with the Balfour Declaration," he said. "We came out of this war with nothing."[58]

Cohen went on, "The Egyptians, Babylonians, Assyrians, Greeks, Romans, Persians, and others have all been here, they've all been here and now they are gone. You will also be thrown out. England, know what your end will be if you persist in your mistreatment and your provocations.

God will take his revenge on you as he took revenge on the Germans. There is justice in the world. Neither the airborne division nor the atom bomb will quell us. We know where we are going. Justice is with us. The day will come, whether you want it or not, that you will leave this country. It is not your country." To prove the justice of their presence in Palestine, the British were deliberately inciting the conflict between Jews and Arabs, Cohen wrote, expressing a common belief.[59] He proposed disobedience to the authorities. Foreign Secretary Bevin was, in his eyes, an anti-semite.[60] This view was also widely shared. Bevin was considered one of the great nemeses of the Jews, like Haman, Titus, Hitler, and Himmler, wrote Alan Bullock, his biographer. Golda Meir (Meyerson) wrote: "I don't know (nor really does it matter any more) whether Bevin was a little insane, or just anti-Semitic, or both." Hers was a relatively mild assessment.[61] The postwar hostility to "Nazi Britain," as it was often called, clouded the collective memory of the entire Mandatory period. The strength of anti-British feeling nourished a patriotic surge, but it did not last—many people were not anti-British at all. The anti-British terror and illegal immigration operations were prompted more by the battle between different Zionist parties than by a genuine national struggle against a foreign ruler.[62] The Revisionists and the labor movement, and various factions within the labor movement, were competing for control of the state that would soon be established. The "resistance" against the British was thus to a large extent a political and psychological fiction. The British were not the real enemy; the Arabs were.

In January 1947, a Jewish Agency official, Yehezkel Sahar, went to the police inspector general and complained, as Jewish leaders had done countless times in the previous thirty years, that the authorities were employing too many Arab policemen. The inspector-general, Colonel William Nicol Grey, explained that Sahar would have to understand that the war between the British and the Arabs was over. Now the British were at war with the Jews. Sahar, who would soon replace Grey as head of the police force for the State of Israel, promised there was no war between the Yishuv and the British but rather between two Jewish terrorist organizations and the British. He proposed cooperating in the struggle against the terrorists, "with the exception of steps liable to lead to civil war." The high commissioner was inundated with letters, some in German, from citizens proposing how to fight terrorism.[63]

A few months later, the Jewish Agency published a broadside in which it called on parents to turn in members of terrorists organizations, even their own children. The demand was based on Deuteronomy 21:18–21: "If a man have a stubborn and rebellious son," he should be handed over to the city's elders, to be taken to the city gate and stoned to death. The British would not do that, the Jewish Agency promised; at most the authorities would hold the prisoners for a year or two, and then release them.[64] As late as February 1947, Golda Meyerson reminded the high commissioner of his promise to assist the Jewish Agency in its fight against the Revisionists. She raised the issue in the context of a request to allow several hundred illegal immigrants being detained in Cyprus to enter the country legally, "as an advance on next month's quota." Such a concession would help enormously in the fight against the terrorist organizations, she wrote. Meir's request reveals the joint interests of two parties sharing government responsibility, not resistance to a foreign ruler.[65] Intercepting illegal ships and diverting them to transit camps in Cyprus was now carried out with the consent of—indeed in coordination with—the Jewish Agency.

Most Jews continued to view the British administration as a legitimate authority and did not join in a general boycott. People obeyed the law and heeded the government until its final day. Thus, the chairman of the Hefer Valley regional council asked the authorities to release several prisoners on the grounds that they were innocent; his letters tacitly assume the government's legitimate right to arrest real criminals. Hannah Ben-Eliezer and Yaffa Tamarkin, wives of imprisoned Etzel men, met with the chief secretary and asked that the government provide financial aid to their families; afterward, they protested that the British were sending them on a wild goose chase from one office to another. Laja Faitlowicz contacted the authorities through the agency of the Ethiopian consulate in Jerusalem, requesting that the valuable library belonging to her brother, a scholar of Ethiopian Jewry, not be harmed during the search actions in Tel Aviv. A few days after the attack on the King David Hotel a search operation was conducted in Tel Aviv called Operation Shark. The searches prompted a series of complaints, all of which reflect the same assumption: the security forces had gone beyond the proper behavior expected of them.[66]

The council of the Beit Yisrael neighborhood in Jerusalem petitioned his excellency the high commissioner to prevent soldiers from molesting people "in violation of British tradition." Thus, with obedient courtesy, Kibbutz Shefayim asked his excellency to conduct an investigation into the beating of a kibbutz member by policemen. The unstated assumption of the letter was that the act was exceptional and that the policemen would be punished.[67]

Dr. Georg Beer of Haifa sent his excellency a long and touching letter that might have made General Barker happy. Before escaping to Palestine, apparently from Germany, Beer had been a judge. He had brought all his savings and had invested them in a small pub at 67 Jaffa Street in Haifa, called the Nelson. Most of the patrons were members of the British security forces. Now the military authorities had declared his bar off-limits, simply because it was owned by a Jew. So he was being punished for crimes committed by other Jews. His family had lost its livelihood and was on the verge of starvation, all because of the new policy. In his three-page letter, Beer pleaded for justice: soldiers should be allowed to return to the Nelson.*

The Friends of the Palestine Folk Opera asked the government for financial assistance in January 1947. During the war, they claimed, more than 600,000 people had attended opera performances. They had seen, among other works, Puccini's *Madama Butterfly* and Verdi's *Rigoletto*, as well as an opera called *Dan the Guard* by Mark Labri, a local composer. The chief secretary responded that he greatly appreciated the importance of music, but "in the present circumstances" government help was inconceivable, since the authorities did not have enough money even to eliminate illiteracy. In fact, a long list of Hebrew cultural institutions received assistance from the government. The Hebrew University was awarded a grant of £14,500 in the spring of 1948, an act described as one of the last decisions of the British administration.[69]

For a long time the British tried to preserve an appearance of normalcy, as if there were no threat of terror. The army tried to persuade the media in Palestine and in England not to use the term *terror,* lest it give the impression that the authorities were frightened—the media were not convinced.[70]† In June 1947 a big parade was held in honor of King George VI's birthday. Special programs were printed in English, Arabic, and Hebrew, including a large map for the convenience of guests, showing the parade route around the Old City, along Julian's Way, and past the King David

*Beer received a curt answer, to the effect that the high commissioner could not intervene in the matter. Internal correspondence reveals that the bar was closed because it had frequently been the site of altercations between soldiers and policemen, all British.[68]

†Out of similar considerations, Jewish opinion makers once debated whether Arab terrorism should be termed a "rebellion." Ben-Gurion believed that the term used was immaterial.[71]

Hotel. The hotel was still in ruins, but the map made the city out to be a colorful, gay place; it showed the locations of all the hotels and cafés—the Regent, the Savoy, the Trocadero, the Empire, the Queens Restaurant, as well as a bar called Fink's.[72] The celebration was somewhat grotesque—just a half year earlier the authorities had evacuated some two thousand British subjects from Jerusalem for their own safety, most of them women and children.

David Ben-Gurion was making great efforts to persuade the British to stay in Palestine; but despite their best efforts to carry on as normal, the British wanted to go home.

Jock Jardine, of the British Council, was sick of the country. He had no idea where the government would send him next, and he did not care—just as long as it was somewhere else. "Give me a country without wars and fighting and threats and barbed wire," he wrote. "I want a rest from war and talk of war and above all from emotionalism and nationalism and all the isms which go with immaturity and youth and muddled education!" Yes, he admitted, he was dreaming of paradise, or perhaps simply about England.[73] "And so we left," the last high commissioner wrote.[74]

One British company commander considered his service in Palestine the high point of his military career. "Excellent climate, lovely flowers, a spice of danger, but a lot of fun—riding, shooting and trips to Jerusalem and the Holy Places," he recalled. His memories were included in an official British publication that sums up thirty years of British rule with the words, "Little has been achieved."[75] That was true, of course, only for the British. The Jews, for their part, had achieved independence.

————•◦•————

23

The Last Salute

1.

At the beginning of 1946 the Jewish Agency received a report on the tragic story of a young woman who had come to Palestine from Austria, met a British soldier in Jerusalem, and married him. A while later he abandoned her; she murdered their baby and tried, unsuccessfully, to kill herself. "You should give this case maximum publicity," the agency's man in London wrote back to Jerusalem. He didn't want any mention made of the fact that when the baby was born the couple had still not married, so as to avoid sullying the girl's reputation. "But it is essential," he wrote, "to play up the negative aspects of the story as a warning," since the case was hardly an exception. Romantic attachments between Jewish girls and British soldiers had long been the object of scorn even before the Jewish Agency considered putting them to use in aid of the Zionist cause.

"On the face of it, you can see her point," the editor of *Yediot Aharonot* wrote sarcastically of one exemplar. "She went out once with a Jewish boy, but he left her. You all know our boys—they are very ill-mannered. And then she met the English boy. He was so different. What a gentleman. You couldn't begin to compare him to our boys. A real lord!" She dreamed of foreign climes, the editor went on; he promised her a life of pleasure, luxury, and respectability. She followed him home, but in England everyone humiliated her and made fun of her. Finally she understood that she would never be a lady in England because her mother-in-law hated her and in church they made fun of her foreign accent. The girl from Tel Aviv would always be a provincial outsider. The article, headlined "Liberated

Darling," mentioned twenty women, the mothers of twenty children, whose British husbands had left them. "I would like to have a photograph of these forty lost souls and paste it up on all the notice boards in Palestine." That would "deter Jewish girls from relations with gentiles," he wrote.[1]*

When Lotte Geiger came to Palestine from Germany, in 1933, she was eighteen and expected to find a liberal country without class and social divisions. She worked in a number of offices, including the Public Works Department and the British military censor. Many *yekkes,* as Jewish immigrants from Germany were called, as well as lawyers and businessmen from the old, pre-Zionist Sephardic community in Jerusalem, mixed socially with the British, unlike most other Jews in Palestine.[3] Lotte Geiger's friendship with Michael Bryant, the British director of the Jerusalem Electric Corporation, blossomed against the backdrop of a city that seemed to have become ever more cosmopolitan as the days of the British in Palestine neared their end.

Geiger, Bryant, and their friends used to meet at the Salvia Hotel, near Salameh Square in Talbieh. They were immigrants and escapists, do-gooders, plotters, terrorists, poets, and British officials, foreign correspondents from anywhere and everywhere, connoisseurs of whiskey and war stories—all spinning romance among the pines and geraniums and addicted to the intoxicating times. The final anarchic days of the British regime were much like those of the winter of 1917 when the winds of war were blowing through the city; Jerusalem is "at war with itself," a British official wrote.[4] The city of eternity had sunk into twilight, much as it had thirty years earlier. The British were leaving, and no one had taken their place. For a brief while, there were no norms, no binding rules. Free from the grip of history, people lived only for themselves. These were fine days for a forbidden and impossible love between an Englishman and a Jewish woman.

But it was not easy for Bryant and Lotte. He was kidnapped by Etzel, which suspected him of aiding the Arabs. "I always knew," he wrote to her, that "an Englishman would never really be accepted here unless he identified completely with the Jews." He did identify with the Jews, but his

---

*Once, some Jewish boys in Tel Aviv got into a fight with Jewish girls who had gone out with foreign soldiers. The boys had handed out leaflets protesting these liaisons, signed "the Sons of Pinchas." The biblical Pinchas, the son of Aaron, had killed an Israelite man and a foreign woman who were found consorting together. Five participants in the fight had to be hospitalized.[2]

interrogators did not believe him. "Maybe I should just tell them that I stayed because I was in love with a Jewess," he wrote.[5] Bryant's colleagues were packing up; the fate of their suitcases concerned them more than the fate of the Holy City.

2.

Along with evacuating some seventy-five thousand people and a quarter of a million tons of possessions, the British also had to decide what to do with their desks, who would get the horses, when to release criminals from the prisons, and how much food to leave behind in the mental hospitals. "The administration's task was to cut off the branch on which it was sitting," Chief Secretary Henry Gurney wrote.[6] As their departure approached, the British were unsure what to do with the dogs the police had used in their counterterrorism operations. "They 'speak' Afrikaans," one government document states—the dogs had been brought from South Africa. Several alternatives were considered, and finally the police decided to destroy the dogs rather than subject them to possible starvation.

They also destroyed documents, stamps, and paper money. Still, the British planned to take most of the equipment, from their locomotives to the last of the paper clips. Some supplies and a few buildings were put up for sale. One official proposed making a list and simply hanging it on the door before they all left, but bureaucratic tradition required a certain protocol: every rifle and typewriter had to be accounted for, with remarks on the condition of each item and its monetary value. Special forms were printed up for the purpose and had to be filled out in octuplicate. The operation was rather complex—the authorities discovered that it was easier to establish an administration than to dismantle one.[7]

The British left the country because more and more of them had come to realize that the Balfour Declaration had been a mistake—something various officials had said twenty years earlier. Sir John Hope Simpson of the Foreign Office shared the following thought with former high commissioner Chancellor: "What a lot of Jews are now in authority. . . . The world is no pleasant thing to contemplate these days."[8]

This was a widespread feeling. In both Jerusalem and London people once again thought that the Jews had influence on American policy, as in World War I. Then the feeling had spurred the British to conquer Palestine; now they were inclined to leave it. "The American press and American Zionists are responsible more than anyone else for the present troubles in Palestine," Chief Secretary Gurney wrote in his diary, adding,

"The sooner we go the better." Soon after, Sir Henry was left with but a single word to account for the British presence in Palestine: stupidity.[9]

The pro-Zionist lobby in the United States had in fact grown stronger since the end of World War II, and wielded greater influence than ever before. At one stage America seemed to be trying to force Britain to remain in Palestine and reaffirm its support of the Zionist movement, against its will. This additional pressure from abroad convinced the British that in leaving the country they were saving themselves from sinking even deeper into a quagmire.

For many years thereafter, Israelis conducted an agitated and sensitive debate over the question of who had really gotten rid of the British. Former members of Etzel, Lechi, the Haganah, and the Palmach vied with each other to claim credit for "ejecting" the British; all invested considerable energy in the argument, enlisting historians, educators, journalists, and other shapers of memory and myth. The political stakes were high, the assumption being that whoever had expelled the British had thereby won the moral and national right to lead Israel's government. All the warring parties completely ignored the role played by the Arabs in sending the British packing.

The Arab rebellion of the late 1930s had been cruelly suppressed, but it had brought home to the British that compromise between the Arabs and the Jews was impossible. Only war would decide the issue; whoever won would control the country, or as much of it as they could conquer. The British had drawn the right conclusion. Once the Zionist movement came to Palestine with the intention of creating an independent state with a Jewish majority, war was inevitable. All indications pointed toward a long war that would end without a clear victory. This projection greatly reduced the country's strategic value and increased the risks to the British themselves. With hindsight they could—justly—say to themselves that they had erred in allowing the Zionist movement to drag them into this adventure. Twenty years after the Balfour Declaration, they could even claim that they had kept their commitment: at least the foundations of the Jewish national home were in place.

The Arab rebellion had made the British sick of Palestine. World War II had delayed their exit, but during the war they continued to discuss how to rid themselves of the country when the war ended. Terrorism and illegal immigration only served to intensify a feeling that had crystallized among many of the British by the end of the 1930s. After three decades of Zionism in Palestine, there was still no clear timetable for the Jewish state, but no doubt remained that Jewish independence was on the horizon. The social, political, economic, and military foundations of the state-to-be were firm; and a profound sense of national unity prevailed. The Zionist dream was about to become reality.

There is therefore no basis for the frequent assertion that the state was established as a result of the Holocaust. Clearly, the shock, horror, and sense of guilt felt by many generated profound sympathy for the Jews in general and the Zionist movement in particular. That sympathy helped the Zionists advance their diplomatic campaign and their propaganda, and shaped their strategy to focus efforts on the survivors, those Jews in displaced-persons camps demanding that they be sent to Palestine. All the survivors were Zionists, the Jewish Agency claimed, and they all wanted to come to Palestine. The assertion was not true.

The displaced persons were given the choice of returning to their homes in Eastern Europe or settling in Palestine. Few were able or willing to return to countries then in the grip of various degrees of hunger, anti-semitism, and communism, and they were never given the option of choosing between Palestine and, say, the United States. In effect, their options were narrowed to Palestine or the DP camps. Many, but not all, wanted to settle in Palestine; others came because there was nowhere else for them to go or in response to the exhortations of Zionist emissaries. A secret report on the first immigrants to reach the country after the war stated that a considerable number felt let down. "The disappointment derives from the lack of a Zionist outlook and Zionist education, on the one hand, and from the hasty, even dishonest promises, of our overseas emissaries. . . . The [immigrants] believe in no vision."[10] Mutual disappointment was one of the causes of a great schism between the Jews of Palestine and the Holocaust survivors.*

---

*Sometime after the Holocaust, and as a result of the decimation of Europe's Jews, the Zionist movement discovered the Jews of the Arab world and brought them to Palestine. The country needed people to work and fighting hands in the war against the Arabs, which had begun in the final months of British rule. The war over Palestine would soon make it impossible for Jews to continue to live in Arab countries—this was a casualty of the Zionist vision. A secret report written by a top Jewish Agency official contains extremely harsh descriptions of the absorption of the Jews from the Arab countries, especially those from Yemen. Housed in tent camps, the immigrants lived in conditions that were mortally dangerous. The report warned that "we are starting to build slums." A tent cost £40, the report noted. At the beginning of 1945 the Jewish Agency began building transit camps with apartment buildings in which each unit cost £350. But those buildings were meant for immigrants from Europe. This is one of the sources of the ethnic gap that would later characterize Israeli society.[11]

The problem of the displaced persons required a solution; one of the loudest voices demanding they be allowed to settle in Palestine was that of Herbert Samuel, the high commissioner Ben-Gurion had once described as a "traitor."[12] President Truman also supported sending the refugees to Palestine. Foreign Secretary Bevin was angry: Truman wanted to settle them in Palestine to keep them out of America, he said, in one of the acerbic comments that earned him his reputation for antisemitism.

Bevin seems, in fact, to have sincerely believed that the Jews could be repatriated, and he considered this to be part of Europe's moral rehabilitation. His view of the world contradicted the foundations of Zionist ideology: he had been brought up as a pacifist and considered Judaism a religion, not a nation. That did not make him an antisemite; on the contrary. The speech in which he proposed that the refugees be reabsorbed in Europe expressed a deep abhorrence of all kinds of racial discrimination and a genuine concern for the future of the DPs. An Anglo-American commission of inquiry would soon be established to study the problem and recommended, among other things, that 100,000 refugees be settled in Palestine.[13]

Khalil al-Sakakini was angry at the suggestion that Palestine take in Holocaust survivors. "If this is a human problem, then let humanity solve it," he wrote; the Jews were exploiting the Holocaust parasitically, by demanding Palestine as a homeland. When they got it, Sakakini believed, the Jews would say, "Throw the Arabs out so we can take their places!" He was aware of the Jews' influence in the United States. Were he able, he wrote, he would divest the American Jews of their right to vote.[14]

For a brief moment, the possibility of making the United States a partner in ruling Palestine made a renewed appearance in the diplomatic world, as it had after World War I. The British were thinking principally of the financial burden involved in continuing their control of the country.[15] The idea of establishing an American administration in Palestine was fascinating but improbable; unlike the British, the Americans generally knew to keep themselves out of such a predicament. Helplessly, seeing no way out, the British again tried to bring the two peoples of Palestine to some sort of accord, and as expected, failed.

3.

In early 1947, David Ben-Gurion held a series of talks with Ernest Bevin in which he tried to persuade the foreign secretary to turn the wheel back to the period preceding the White Paper of 1939. He entered discussions as if the various Zionist parties in Palestine were not at the same time doing their patriotic best to throw the British out. The talks with Bevin and other cabinet ministers were not merely a diplomatic trick as some of Ben-Gurion's admirers said later, trying to prove that he too had worked to get rid of the British. The Zionist movement had nothing to gain from such a deception, and Ben-Gurion could only have been hurt by it politically. Ben-Gurion wanted British rule to continue because the Haganah was not ready for a war with the Arabs. His goal was to gain time. In July 1947 he was still talking about the possibility of "international supervision" instead of independence, estimating that this supervision could last for "years."[16]

Ben-Gurion must have known that the chances of persuading the British to remain were poor, but the minutes of his conversations with Bevin reflect how hard it was for him to grasp that the British were really ready to leave. Ben-Gurion seems not to have understood the depths of Britain's postwar economic, social, and psychological crises. For many years thereafter he tended to attribute the difficulty in his relations with Britain to Bevin's personal hostility to Zionism.[17]

Ben-Gurion already felt that the focus of world decision making had passed from London to Washington, but he continued to cling to the colonial myth. Zionism had hitched itself to the British Empire, advancing under its sponsorship to the verge of independence, and Ben-Gurion wanted to revive the old alliance. In fact, he even tried to convince the British to remain in Palestine on the basis of the original mandate. Bevin, however, proposed dividing the country into quasi-autonomous cantons and restricting immigration. The Zionists rejected the plan; the Arabs rejected it also.[18] The British were left with only one alternative: to go home.

The talks were, however, interesting, delving as they did into the roots of the Palestine conflict. Ben-Gurion maintained that a man could walk for days through the country without meeting a living soul, echoing the platitude that Palestine was a land without people for a people without a land.* He kept praising the historic friendship of the Jewish and British peoples; he spoke of the two nations' common values and even at that late stage tried to tempt Bevin with Chaim Weizmann's old promise of a European foothold in the Middle East—the Jews were the sole represen-

---

*Bevin later compared the expulsion of the Arabs to the expulsion of the Indians in America. The claim was problematic, as the Zionists could retort that they were only doing in Palestine what the British had done in America. But when Bevin talked about the conquest of America, he obscured the British identity of the conquerors and spoke only of "the white man."[19]

tative of Europe in a Muslim world, he argued, and always would be. Bevin, pessimistic and occasionally downright hostile, compared Palestine to twins sired by different fathers.

Bevin devoted many hours to his talks with Ben-Gurion. In one set of minutes he is quoted as saying, "Palestine is not vital to England but England does not want to have to admit failure," thus articulating the crux of Britain's position. He did not know how to explain to his people what their sons were doing in distant Palestine, two years after the end of the World War, he explained. Feeling was running high all over England.[20] Everywhere people were demanding that he bring the boys home. Their voices were being heard in the press, in Parliament, and in the cabinet.

"Rule or Quit," one newspaper declared; a second asked, "Must Our Boys Die?" And a third simply said, "It's Time We Get Out." The headlines reflected, among other things, the psychological effect of terrorism. Internal government correspondence also mentions public opinion as a reason for giving up Palestine.[21] One MP recounted a memory from his military service in Ireland. Putting a twist on the enlistment slogan "Join the army and see the world," the soldiers had joked, "Join the Royal Irish Constabulary and see the next world." The same slogan was now applicable to Palestine, he suggested.[22]

The man who raised the loudest voice in favor of getting out of Palestine was Winston Churchill. He had no lack of arguments for his position but, as in the past, the thing that seemed to bother him most was the price: the 100,000 soldiers deployed there were costing the British taxpayer £30 million a year, Churchill said over and over again—£30 million in order to keep 100,000 men away from home. This huge force was necessary not only to suppress Jewish terrorism but to check the growing tension between the Jews and the Arabs. The continued British presence in Palestine would seem doubly grotesque once Britain left India. "To abandon India . . . but to have a war with the Jews in order to give Palestine to the Arabs," Prime Minister Clement Attlee told the cabinet, "appears to carry incongruity of thought and policy to levels which have rarely been attained in human history."[23]

Churchill at one point addressed the claim that Palestine was needed to defend the Suez Canal. This was "a very wrong idea," he said, declaring, "Let us then stay in the Canal Zone and have no further interest in the strategic aspects of Palestine." For his part, he had never believed that Britain had any strategic interest in Palestine. The army and War Office continued in the meantime to compose position papers on the country's strategic value, which the government then chose to ignore. Like Winston Churchill, the government thought that controlling Palestine cost too much: "British troops . . . have been the British taxpayers' liability throughout," Sir Henry Gurney noted in his diary.[24]

Attlee, Bevin, and Colonial Secretary Arthur Creech Jones did not always see eye to eye. Attlee was skeptical of Britain's economic and military ability to preserve its status as a great power in the Middle East. Bevin feared Soviet penetration and still thought in terms of international greatness and prestige; he still believed in the military value of the Middle East and was also interested in Arab oil. In the final analysis, however, he agreed with the prime minister that Palestine should be dropped. Creech Jones was inclined to support the moderate branch of the Zionist movement, but not so fervently that he would argue for the continuation of the Mandate. This was a rare moment of consensus on Palestine.[25]

The most conclusive formulation of Britain's position on Palestine was written by one of the ministers in a letter to Attlee. "The present state of affairs is not only costly to us in manpower and money," he wrote, "but is, as you and I agree, of no real value from the strategic point of view—you cannot in any case have a secure base on top of a wasps' nest—and it is exposing our young men, for no good purpose, to abominable experiences and is breeding anti-Semites at a most shocking speed."[26] Not coincidentally, the letter's author, Hugh Dalton, was serving as chancellor of the exchequer. Economics had not motivated Britain to enter Palestine or to remain there, but it was a major factor motivating them to leave.

Dalton's letter bears the date August 11, 1947. Four days later, India's independence was declared, a profound trauma for Britain; if India was the jewel in the empire's crown, Palestine was hardly more than an anemone in the king's buttonhole. The Holy Land had brought joy to British hearts, but not for long. "The people are fed up with the whole business," the high commissioner told Ben-Gurion.[27]

In February 1947, the British government had decided to turn the Mandate over to the United Nations, the League of Nations' successor. The U.N. set up its own commission. Surveys and reports were prepared and witnesses were summoned and their comments recorded, producing yet more impressive documentation of positions and historic claims set down in meticulous detail. Finally, the commission decided, by a majority, to recommend to the General Assembly that Palestine be partitioned.

This decision prompted a worldwide diplomatic campaign involving pressure, threats, promises, and bribes. The Jewish Agency budgeted a million dollars for its own campaign of bribery; in official parlance the money was allocated to "irregular political activity."[28]*

Until the actual vote in the United Nations there was no way to be certain how the General Assembly would decide. But on November 29, 1947, the U.N. voted to divide Palestine into two states, one for the Jews and one for the Arabs; Jerusalem was to remain under international control.

The Arabs were as unprepared for battle as the Jews, and thus also had an interest in the continuation of British rule. But they may have believed that ultimately they would win. In any case, still hostage to the rejectionist position they had adopted in 1917, they opposed partition and continued to demand independence in all of Palestine, promising to respect the rights of the Jewish minority. The partition boundaries proposed by the U.N. assigned the Jewish state almost twice as much territory as the British partition plan of ten years previously, and the Arabs had turned down that proposal as well. "They refused at any time to sign their own death warrant," Anwar Nusseibeh wrote.[30] But in rejecting the partition plan, the Arabs missed a chance to gain time to prepare for war. They had made a tactical error.

There were Jews who opposed partition as well. Revisionist "hawks" would not agree to give up the territories assigned to the Arabs; the binationalist "doves" decried the principal of separation, believing in one or another form of coexistence. The Zionist movement accepted the partition plan, in a wise tactical step. Even then all the players understood that geographically and demographically the U.N.'s partition plan could not be implemented. The border between the two states was long and contorted, impossible to defend; the Jewish state would include more than half a million Arabs, slightly more than the number of Jews then living within the proposed boundaries. Some ten thousand Jews, including the inhabitants of the city of Nahariya, would find themselves within the Arab boundaries. Furthermore, there was no reason to trust that interna-

---

*The Zionist Organization and the British government continued to bribe influential Arabs. President Roosevelt told Chaim Weizmann that, in his opinion, the Arabs could be bought; Weizmann responded that he had heard something to that effect. In the minutes of their conversation the Arabic word *"baksheesh"* appears. The Jewish Agency's biggest client seems to have been Prince Abdallah of Transjordan.[29]

tional control of Jerusalem was viable.[31] No one believed in the U.N.'s map; everyone knew there would be war.*

The proposal was passed by a majority of thirty-three—including the United States and the USSR—against thirteen, with ten abstentions, including Britain. The victory was largely due to the work of the Zionist lobby. David Lloyd George would not have been surprised—he had always known that the Jews controlled the world. Sir Henry Gurney, the chief secretary, followed and analyzed the components of the Zionist movement's propaganda carefully; his analysis was hostile, but not unintelligent. He noted that the Zionists had successfully equated anti-Zionism with anti-semitism. Gurney supposed that the Americans would have been unenthusiastic about helping the Jews had they wanted to establish an independent state in New York. The pressures "the Zionist" creates, he wrote, makes the world hate him, but apparently he does not care. He has a suicidal urge. That was what made him so desperate and self-centered, Gurney wrote.[33]†

Ya'akov Cohen sat glued to the radio all night, listening to the progress of the historic vote in New York. When he heard the result, he could hardly contain himself: "The ear cannot comprehend it, the heart does not believe it—a Hebrew state! Unbelievable!" Once again, he wrote, "the people of Jerusalem have taken to the streets, just like the time of the victory over Germany, old and young danced, sang, drank, and cheered en masse all day." The British policemen and soldiers even danced with them, he noted. No, this was not the state the Zionists had hoped for. "After all, the entire country was in our sights," he remarked. Now the Jews had a territory that did not include Jerusalem.‡

But when the vote was counted, there was no room for doubt. "I was happy to the depths of my soul," Cohen wrote. He ran through the streets all day, as if there were no university, as if he did not teach school. "A

---

* In preparation for the struggle over partition, Ben-Gurion strove to ensure that the Jews present a united front to the U.N. He initiated an agreement with the Orthodox community, which became the basis of a status quo on religious legislation that would affect relations within the State of Israel for many years thereafter.[32]

† Ernest Bevin also seemed to believe in the power of "international Judaism." Like his predecessors in the government thirty years earlier, he discerned a link between the Jews and the Communists aimed at bringing Israel into the Soviet circle of influence. The Soviets, surprisingly and rather inexplicably, supported the Zionist movement at the time.[34]

‡ Sometime later the mayor of Herzliya proposed that his city be made the capital of the Jewish state. His justification was that it was the only city named after Herzl. Ben-Gurion gave some thought to names: the Arab state would be called Abdalia, the Jewish state Judea.[35]

light has risen for the future, mass immigration, the liberation of the oppressed, intensified building, independence and freedom," he noted in his diary. At the time he was in love with a girl named Dolly. They went to concerts starring Shoshana Damari; they especially liked to hear her stirring rendition of "Anemones."[36]

4.

General Evelyn Barker felt obliged to apologize. His government had not been fair. It should not have returned the mandate to the U.N. in New York, since the atmosphere there was so pro-Jewish. On the other hand, he wrote to Katy Antonius, he could not blame the British—even Haj Amin al-Husseini, the former mufti, thought only of his own interests and not of his people, and had done the Palestinian Arabs a great disservice. The mufti sought only to augment his political power. The Arabs had only dissension and petty jealousies. Their tragedy was that they had no real leadership.*

The U.N. debate might have been avoided had the Arabs come forth with constructive suggestions instead of turning down all the British ideas, Barker wrote. The Arabs needed to use a Western approach in evaluating their problems, he added, and he imagined himself serving as political adviser to the Arab Higher Committee. Katy Antonius seems to have agreed with at least some of his criticism. It was too bad the Arabs didn't listen to her, he said—maybe they dismissed her because she was a woman.[38]

Barker was serving as commander in chief, eastern command, in May 1947; Antonius had left her home in Jerusalem and moved to Egypt. "I shall always love you for your own sweet self and for your grand fighting spirit which I so much admire," he wrote her.[39] He was pained that the British were imposing such a situation on their Arab friends, he wrote a short time after the General Assembly had adopted the partition plan; he was angry at President Truman for selling himself to the Jews. But as a military man he had no doubt: the Jews would not be able to withstand the force of the entire Arab world, and in the end they would all be eradicated. They could blame their destruction only on the Zionist policy they had adopted, and on Lord Balfour, of course. Even though Barker had not been appointed

---

*The former mufti had managed to extricate himself from the ruins of Berlin at the very last moment. He reached France, where he was arrested as a Nazi collaborator, but he managed to escape and make his way to Cairo. "There was great joy," Khalil al-Sakakini wrote in his diary when he heard of this.[37]

adviser to the Arabs, he offered them advice through his lover. They had to unite, to be more cunning, to work according to a plan. He would willingly fight at their side in order to exterminate Zionism, he reiterated.[40]

A year had gone by since Barker had last seen his Katy, yet his heart was full of her. A lot had happened in the meantime, but his deep affection for his dear little love remained constant. He recalled one evening in particular, when they had consummated their love. Yes, he wrote, perhaps she had been right in saying he loved her more than he should, but he was so happy to have had those rapturous months in Jerusalem—her friendship was a pearl of great price. He thought of her at night when he went to sleep and in the morning when he woke, when he was in the bathtub and at work—always always he thought only of his Katy, with the white streak of hair, whom he loved and still loved.[41]

One day Barker was nearly caught. He left some letters on his desk, and his wife noticed the Egyptian stamps. Luckily, another letter from Egypt was in the pile and he was able to explain away the correspondence somehow. But the moment was very alarming for him. Now he asked Katy to send him, along with her real letters, something formal for him to show his wife. Please, do this even if you think it is cheating, he wrote her.[42] Sometimes he had friends over who also knew Antonius, and her name would come up in conversation. One evening he had supper with Musa Alami. Barker held him in high esteem, and would have liked to see him leading the Arab movement in Palestine, despite some concern that Alami would be too uncompromising.[43]* Alami was connected to the Husseini family by marriage; for a time he had indeed been considered the chief representative of Palestine's Arabs.

Alami had been expelled from Palestine during the Arab rebellion but had since been allowed to return to Jerusalem, where he worked as a lawyer. For a time he coordinated Arab public relations in diplomatic circles, setting up liaison offices in London, New York, and Washington. This venture was financed by the Arab League, which had been established in

---

*During their meal, Barker wrote, he and Alami discussed a recently published book by Richard Crossman containing a description of a party at Katy's house. Alami liked the book, while Barker was angry about several inaccuracies and was wondering whether to write to the author. Crossman is such a nasty little man that I hardly feel it's worth the trouble, he wrote to Katy.[44] Not long after his meal with Alami, Barker heard on the BBC news that the "bloody Jews" had blown up Antonius's house in Jerusalem. He had always feared that would happen, he wrote her, but he had hoped that she would at least be able to remove her belongings in advance. He did not know that the Jews had taken a large quantity of documents from the house, including his love letters.

1945 by several Arab states, with its headquarters in Cairo. Sari al-Sakakini, who had left his job at the American consulate, was asked to direct the Arab League's office in Washington, which was in need of new and better management. He was just right for the job. While working at the consulate, he had learned how to explain Palestinian Arab politics to the Americans and how to explain American politics to the Arabs. His father was correct when he wrote in his diary that "a person like Sari has what it takes to do this work and may it be for his good and for the good of the Arab nation."[45] But the proud father seems not to have known about the powerful love that kept his son tied to Palestine.

In an effort to remain in Jerusalem, Sakakini drew up a detailed proposal for the American consulate to establish an Arab department, which he wanted to head. His letters to the consul are intimate in tone, evincing a measure of personal attachment. "I want to stay with you no matter what," Sakakini wrote, whether his preference served the Arab cause or not.[46] A similar mix of subservience and ambition marks Sari al-Sakakini's letters to Musa Alami. Again and again Alami tried to persuade him to take the job in Washington, but Sakakini made grandiose demands. He wanted a luxurious home, an unlimited entertainment budget, and freedom of action to do as he saw fit. "I have to be my own master," he wrote. Alami ran into various difficulties that also served to delay Sakakini's departure, but the impression is that Sakakini was being evasive, both wanting and not wanting to go. In one letter he said he was remaining in Jerusalem "for personal reasons"; in another he claimed to have begun working as an English teacher and explained that his students needed him.[47]

In the end he remained with Omran and assisted Alami in the Arab office in Jerusalem. When the U.N. General Assembly decided to partition Palestine into two states, Alami believed that the plan should be accepted as a starting point for negotiations with the Jews. Alami would soon fall out with Haj Amin al-Husseini, resulting in Alami's dismissal from all official activity.[48] One of the first Zionist diplomats, Eliahu Eilat, would later describe him as a humanist, a man of justice and peace.[49]

5.

The first shots were fired at a bus on its way to Jerusalem. Six Jewish passengers were killed. The attack occurred a few weeks after the U.N.'s vote on partition; the assailants were Arabs. Many of the city's Jews were still celebrating the U.N. decision. In the weeks that followed, more than eighty Jews and ninety Arabs were killed.[50]

The Arab forces facing the Haganah, Palmach, Etzel, and Lechi were made up of volunteers, some of whom had participated in the Arab rebellion ten years previously. There were also youth organizations that received military training and were linked, like the Jewish youth movements, to competing political parties. Thousands of other volunteers had received military training and combat experience in the British security forces, including the police, which again employed many Arabs. There was also the Arab Legion of Transjordan, a unit the British used against Jewish terrorists similar to the Special Night Squads, which had enlisted Jews to provide protection from Arab terrorism.

In the first stages of the conflict, the Arabs attacked Jewish stores and set off bombs in city centers. The Haganah attacked Arab villages, sometimes without orders from the top command, as in the case of Khasas, a village in the Hula Valley, where two men and five children were killed in retribution for the death of a Jewish settler. Although some observers dubbed the conflict a "civil war" the outbreak of hostilities was clearly, at that stage, a war between two distinct peoples. Soon, forces serving in the regular armies of the neighboring Arab countries joined the fighting; for some time the Arab states had been in the process of taking control of the conflict, in effect neutralizing Palestine's Arab leaders, including the former mufti.[51]

The situation in Jerusalem was particularly difficult. At one point the Jewish part of the city was under siege by the Arabs and cut off from the rest of the city. During a stay there in April 1948, Ben-Gurion recorded in his diary that morale in the city was very low. There was "great agitation," he wrote, noting that "everyone" was blaming the Haganah for the city's predicament. The extreme ultra-Orthodox Neturei Karta faction wanted to surrender, while the yekkes in Rehavia were helpless. People were stealing water from wells and stockpiling food; some had become war profiteers; and many were evading military service.[52] Against this background there is something grotesque in the patriotic platitudes Ya'akov Cohen recorded in his diary. He had returned to the Palmach and was stationed at Ma'aleh HaHamisha, a kibbutz near Jerusalem named after five young men who had been killed there during the Arab rebellion. Cohen belonged to the Harel Brigade, whose operations officer was Yitzhak Rabin.* Once, returning from action in an Arab village, Cohen wrote,

*Like Bols, commander of the anemones, and Sari al-Sakakini, Rabin belonged to the second generation of the war over Palestine. His parents had met and fallen in love during the Nebi Musa riots, twenty-seven years earlier.

"The operation did not always go well, but we quickly found solace . . . happy is the nation that has sons like these, exemplary sons, and I was proud because I was and am one of them." He also wrote, "The road to independence is strewn with alternating sorrow and joy, so we will prepare for what is to come with confidence and faith in the justice of our cause and our noble movement." There was also a girl with the soldiers, Michal. "She has captured my heart because of her great similarity to the late Bebs," Cohen wrote.[53]

From time to time, Cohen went back to Jerusalem for a quick visit to the children's institution where he had worked, in the Arnona neighborhood, located somewhere between the homes of Jane Lancaster and Shmuel Yosef Agnon. The Arab siege of the city had brought the Jewish neighborhoods close to starvation. There was no certainty the Jews would be able to hold out. Access to distant neighborhoods like Talpiot and Arnona was becoming more and more difficult. Cohen often thought of the children who remained there and tried to reach them for a game of football. Occasionally he wondered what would become of his university studies, but wrote that he had no reservations about "devoting himself to the homeland."[54] On January 11, 1948, he wrote, "There is no way of knowing where death lurks." Five days later he was killed, one of thirty-five men who set out on a night march to the Etzion bloc, beyond Bethlehem.

6.

A few days after Cohen's death Khalil al-Sakakini turned seventy. "This is the age of senility," he wrote, but he noted that his health was excellent. He continued to take a cold shower every morning and feel as if he had been reborn. The Arab Language Academy in Cairo had elected him to membership and he decided to change his famous calling card. Instead of the motto "Human being, God willing" under his name, he would now write "Member of the Language Academy, God willing."

In the winter months of 1947–48 Sakakini's diary sounded more and more like his diary of the winter of 1917. Once again, the war was at his doorstep; his neighborhood of Katamon was a target of Yitzhak Rabin's forces. Once again, his sleep was disturbed by explosions, just like the days of the British approach to the city. In early January Sakakini wrote, "The Jews slipped into Katamon on a dark and rainy night, at two in the morning, when people have let down their guard, and blew up the Samiramis Hotel, which collapsed on top of its guests and many were killed." The building served as headquarters for the Arabs; among the casualties was the Spanish consul, Count Antonio de Ballobar's successor.[55]*

Sakakini's neighbors organized guard duty, gathering for lengthy discussions at his home. They tallied the weapons at their disposal and collected money to buy more and to hire guards. They positioned sand-filled barrels at the neighborhood's entrance. There were several doctors and nurses in the vicinity, Sakakini noted proudly, and engineers checked the houses to locate their weak points and determine from which direction they might be attacked. The neighborhood became a fortress, Sakakini wrote with sad irony; "the fortress of Gibraltar is nothing in comparison."[56]

In a more serious mood, he despaired of withstanding the Jewish attacks. The Jews were organized, united, and well equipped, while the Katamon residents had no such advantages. "Has the time not come for us to understand that unity wins over factionalism, organization over anarchy, readiness over neglect?" Sakakini asked. To a large extent, he was telling the story of the Arab defeat. When Lechi agents penetrated Katamon and blew up several houses, Sakakini and his neighbors went to the Arab Higher Committee and demanded arms. There aren't any, they were told. The Katamon residents demanded guards. There aren't any of those either, they learned. "Where are the trained volunteers?" Sakakini wanted to know. "Where is the money collected from all the Arab and Islamic countries?" It occurred to him that he was witnessing the fulfillment of Proverbs 25:14: "One who boasts of gifts that he does not give is like clouds and winds without rain."

In the midst of the siege, Sakakini hosted Abu Musa, also known as Abd al-Kader al-Husseini, one of the top Arab commanders. Sakakini set out for him some moral rules of war: the wounded must be cared for, prisoners must be treated properly, soldiers' bodies must be returned. He quoted the words of the first Arab *khalif:* "Thou shalt not kill a child, an old man, or a woman, thou shalt not burn a tree nor destroy a house, thou shalt not pursue one who flees and thou shalt not mutilate bodies, thou shalt not harm he who is occupied in the worship of God." He made no record of the commander's response, but apparently Abu Musa did not encourage his host to continue. Sakakini would have liked to tell him, "Return your

*Ballobar himself, an official in the Spanish foreign ministry, would soon be packing his bags. Almost thirty years after leaving the city, he returned to serve as his country's consul in Jerusalem, soon to be divided between Israel and Jordan.

swords to their scabbards, there is enough room in the world for everyone." But Sakakini assumed that no one would listen to him, so he comforted himself with the words of Jesus: my kingdom is not of this world. Husseini was a revered hero, the son of Musa Kazim al-Husseini and a leader of the Arab national movement and the Arab rebellion.

Abd al-Kader al-Husseini fired the imagination of many, including a student at the Arab high school for boys in Haifa, Adnan al-Yehiya. Adnan liked to correspond with boys and girls in the United States and Australia; he received a 98 in English. He got good grades in his other subjects as well—only a 77 in math ruined his average. Also, he liked to write to his brothers and cousins studying in various places around the country. They told each other about their teachers and classmates, about soccer and cinema. Once Adnan told a cousin about a movie he had seen called *Love Letters* and mentioned a song from the movie called "How Would You Like to Kiss Me in the Moonlight?" Adnan wanted to find the words to the song and hinted mysteriously that he would explain why he needed them when he saw his cousin. They wrote a lot about girls they dreamed of meeting and loving, and shared the vicissitudes of adolescence. But like Ya'akov Cohen in Tel Aviv, Adnan al-Yehiya lived the conflict over Palestine. Like Cohen, he internalized all the platitudes of his people's cause and regurgitated them in his letters as if they were his own invention.

Sometimes Adnan wrote poems, love poems and patriotic poems. He called on his people to unite and repel the Zionist enemy. In another poem he praised his teacher for saying that the Arabs would not allow the Jews to remain in Palestine and that Jerusalem would not fall. In a third poem, the boy thundered against Arabs who sold their land to the Jews, calling them mad dogs. His brother Mohammed, who studied in Safed, castigated him for spending entire nights at the nationalistic Muslim Brothers club instead of preparing for his exams. Mohammed also said that snow had fallen in Safed.

A friend from Jerusalem wrote that the British had closed off entire neighborhoods, out of fear of terrorism. The Jews called these areas "Bevingrads." A friend from Tulkarem reported that the Jews were shooting in all directions, as if they were having target practice with human beings. The friend was afraid, but when the time came, all his brethren would report as one to defend their country; there was no greater honor than to fall as a *shaheed*, or martyr, in a holy war for the homeland. In March 1948 a friend wrote, "I am happy, Adnan, that you know some Hebrew, so you can understand the murderous Jews."*

A pen pal from Lebanon sent good news: the Arab army is advancing, he informed Adnan, and you will soon see it before you; he was a soldier and at that moment was training in Damascus, serving in one of the battalions established by the Arab states. He would soon arrive as well, he wrote. His battalion was named after a battle Salah a-Din had waged against the Crusaders on the Yarmouk River. From time to time, Adnan's letters mentioned the hero Abd al-Kader al-Husseini, who was fighting in the Jerusalem area.[57]

Judge Anwar Nusseibeh also admired Abd al-Kader al-Husseini; the two had gone to school together. "Even while still a student," Nusseibeh wrote, "Abd al-Kader stood out as a rebel, protesting the injustices of Western imperialism as expressed in Zionism." A natural leader, he had given up all the benefits of his origins, education, and status and had lived in the mountains among the farmers during the days of the rebellion. His comrades love him and would gladly die at his bidding, Nusseibeh wrote.

In April, Abd al-Kader fought in the battle for the Kastel escarpment and the village at its top, on the way to Jerusalem, one of the most important theaters of the war. Nusseibeh's reflections on the battle fit his thesis about the entire war: the Arabs were too few, and their equipment was minimal and outdated. Abd al-Kader fell in the battle, although the Arabs gained a temporary victory, in which they managed to capture Jewish positions. But the death of the soldiers' admired commander stupefied them; they streamed into Jerusalem for his funeral, leaving the Kastel undefended. Nusseibeh described the hysteria and madness of the mourners—people fired shots in the air as a sign of bereavement. "It sounded as if a major battle was on," Nusseibeh wrote. Some mourners were even killed at the funeral. In the meantime the few men who had remained to guard the Kastel panicked when they saw Jews approaching and abandoned their posts. "It appeared that the men could not resist the attraction of Abu Musa's funeral and had left the village to attend it," Nusseibeh wrote.

Sakakini also took part in Abd al-Kader al-Husseini's funeral. "The entire country walked behind his casket," he said.[58] District Officer James H. H. Pollock wrote to his wife that more people had been hurt during the

---

*The Yehiya family seems to have had some social contacts with Jews; among the letters sent to Adnan by some pen pals in New Orleans, he saved an invitation to a Jewish wedding: Tova Zoldan married Uriel Schitzer in the garden of the Noga Café on Balfour Street.

funeral than in the battle in which Abd al-Kader had died.[59] One of Adnan al-Yehiya's pen pals, Fawzi, wrote, "He was a hero. He filled the Jews' hearts with terror and fear. The Jews murdered him. The Arabs bow their heads. He blazed a trail for us. Our duty is to go in his footsteps." Fawzi composed a poem in this spirit, which he recited in class; he received a prize, a nice book of poetry. He was certain Adnan would also write a poem in memory of their hero and asked him to send a copy.[60]

Abd al-Kader had died as a patriot and idealist and as such perhaps his death had been inevitable, Anwar Nusseibeh wrote, but he also died a victim of the politicians' cynical careerism and intrigue. "The entire operation was thus for nothing," Nusseibeh reflected, referring either to the battle for the Kastel or the entire war. "All and entirely for nothing—a complete waste." Nusseibeh left the funeral and sadly went home.[61]*

The battle over Katamon grew ever more fierce. "The whistle of the bullets and the thunder of the shells do not stop day or night; we heard nothing like this in the past world wars," Sakakini wrote. Every time he entered his home he expected it to explode, and on the streets he stayed close to the walls, afraid that a stray bullet might find him. Sakakini's telephone did not stop ringing. Relatives and friends in other parts of the city were worried because everyone knew that Katamon was like the crater of a volcano. Lava was flowing, smoke was blowing, and the flames were rising. "In this situation it is no wonder the residents are thinking of moving to another area or another city," Sakakini wrote, listing the names of neighbors who had already gone. On April 7 Sakakini found a bullet on his balcony. It had hit the right doorjamb, leaving a faint mark, he noted, adding that had anyone had been sitting on the balcony at the time, he would have been killed. He tried to comfort himself, saying, "The believer is not hit twice by the same stone."

On April 13, Sakakini felt like he was on a battlefield. "Night comes and we cannot close our eyes. We say that if we live to see the day, we will leave this neighborhood, Katamon, for another, or leave this country completely." A week later he and his two daughters left, taking only their clothes. They thought they would be coming back.

"Every time I recall that horrible hour when we left the house like thieves in the night, with the shells falling around us and bullets flying over our heads," he wrote a few months later, "I hit myself and think: How

---

*One Israeli historian was highly critical of the Hebrew army's handling of the battle, describing a series of errors in a book chapter entitled "Accident at the Kastel."[62]

could we have forgotten to take all the bottles in the cupboard?" He imagined the Jewish soldiers finding his liquor and saying that a good drink made all the fighting worthwhile. He had forgotten his nargileh as well, but above all he mourned the loss of his books. "Are you safe, my books?" he wrote. "I don't know what your fate was after we left. Were you ruined? Were you burned? Were you respectfully transferred to a library, public or private? Or did you end up at a corner grocery store, your pages wrapped around onions?"[63]*

Hala Sakakini later wrote that her father's decision to leave Katamon was influenced not just by the shells that fell on his home but also by the massacre in the Arab village of Deir Yassin, an hour's walk from the Sakakini home, in April 1948.[65] In coordination with the Haganah, an Etzel and Lechi force attacked the village, killing dozens of civilians, including women and children. The Jewish Agency condemned the action, and a senior British official described the atrocities at Deir Yassin as a "beastly Holocaust." Chief Secretary Gurney wrote that Belsen "pales" beside the bestialities of Deir Yassin.[66]

In contrast with his previous exile to Damascus, Sakakini left for Egypt in an automobile, with his two daughters; Sari had gone earlier. They drove to Cairo. Being a refugee was painful for him, but he lodged comfortably in the Victoria Hotel. "We are living in Egypt as we lived in Jerusalem," he wrote. He liked to sit at Groppi, a well-known café, and was visited in Cairo by Haj Amin al-Husseini. Sometime later his son Sari wrote to a friend from his college days in America, "Living in Cairo is rather pleasant and has its advantages. There is quite a season of opera, ballet, theater and music during the winter. But this is quite expensive entertainment and we are compensated with the many movie theaters we can go to."[67]†

A few days after the death of Abd al-Kader and the massacre at Deir Yassin, Arab forces attacked a convoy of vehicles traveling from the Jewish side of the city to Mount Scopus. Most of the passengers were Jewish civilians, employees of the Hebrew University and Hadassah hospital, including doctors and nurses. The ambush took place not far from the

---

* In the summer of 1967, Hala and Dumia al-Sakakini went to the National Library in Jerusalem and found their father's books there. The Hebrew University sometimes attached members of its staff to Haganah forces; they would collect books from abandoned Arab houses.[64] Prior to his departure, Sakakini had managed to deliver his diaries, which covered some forty years, to his sister.

† Sari al-Sakakini died in May 1953 of a heart attack. He was thirty-nine. His father died about three months later.

Antonius house. Of the 112 passengers in the convoy, 78 were killed.[68]* Anwar Nusseibeh claimed that the convoy had been taking arms and military gear to the Haganah outpost on Mount Scopus.[70]

The Zionists' plans for the new state were based on the assumption that a large Arab minority would remain.[71] But the tragedy of the Arab refugees from Palestine was a product of the Zionist principle of separation and the dream of population transfer. The tragedy was inevitable, just as the war itself was inevitable. The number of refugees reached approximately 750,000. Some planned their departure, some fled, and about half were expelled.[72] "People left their country," Sakakini wrote, "dazed and directionless, without homes or money, falling ill and dying while wandering from place to place, living in niches and caves, their clothing falling apart, leaving them naked, their food running out, leaving them hungry. The mountains grew colder and they had no one to defend them." As always, Sakakini did not shrink from self-criticism. "What breaks our hearts is that the Arab countries see and hear and do nothing," he said.[73] Luckily—and in some ways catastrophically—they had places to flee to, which weakened their resolve. Possibly, the lives of many Arabs were saved because they fled their homes, but the mass flight destroyed their national fabric for many years to come.

Anwar Nusseibeh also wrote about the refugees. First the rich left, in part because they feared being forced to finance the war, as they had in the rebellion. Jews who could afford to also left when the war broke out, Nusseibeh remarked. As the war escalated, so did the stream of emigrants. In many places, their departure was necessary. One family in Nusseibeh's own neighborhood, Sheikh Jarah, left only after their home was shelled and collapsed. The Deir Yassin massacre prompted more people to flee, and Arab leaders could not halt the process. They had no right to do so, Nusseibeh believed, since they lacked the ability to protect civilians, including women and children. Nusseibeh found no fault with the Arabs who left: no one thought the war would last so long or end as it did. Everyone believed they would be able to go home after the victory of the Arab armies, and take control of the country, he wrote.[74]

By the end of the Mandate, May 15, 1948, the Haganah, Palmach, Etzel, and Lechi forces had won a series of victories, including the conquest of

---

*One of the people then on duty at the hospital was Chaim Shalom Halevi; he had been working there since his student days. He had gone to Mount Scopus two days before the attack on the convoy.[69] Halevi, one of the founders of medical economics in Israel, died in 1988. The square in front of Jerusalem's Yeshurun Synagogue was later named after him.

Tiberias, Safed, and Haifa. By the time Ben-Gurion visited Haifa, the city had emptied of most of its Arab population. It was "a frightening and fantastic sight," Ben-Gurion wrote of his tour of the abandoned Arab neighborhoods. "A dead city, a carrion city . . . without a living soul, except for stray cats." He wondered what had happened that tens of thousands of people had left their homes "without good reason."[75] Apparently, the Yehiya family was among those who fled, because Haganah forces entered their home and confiscated Adnan's letters. A few days later Jaffa was conquered, and it, too, emptied of its Arab inhabitants.

The battle for Jaffa produced an absurd document, typical of the last days of British rule. Chief Secretary Gurney wrote to Ben-Gurion that if the fighting in Jaffa did not cease, the RAF would bomb Tel Aviv. Ben-Gurion did not even bother to answer; the chief secretary received his reply from a junior Jewish Agency official.[76]

7.

The war caught the Arabs unorganized and leaderless. They had not recovered from their defeat during the rebellion, and they had fewer combatants than the Jews and those they had were inadequately equipped.[77] Anwar Nusseibeh described a supply of weapons the Arab Higher Committee sent to Jerusalem from Cairo. The rifles were secondhand. Most were junk, Nusseibeh wrote. Efforts were made to repair them in Jerusalem but the rifles came from a large variety of sources—England, Germany, Italy, France, and other countries that could not be identified. There was no ammunition in Jerusalem that fit all these types of rifles. Often soldiers were left without ammunition, making their rifles useless.[78] At one point, the Arabs in Jerusalem decided to purchase weapons at their own expense and took up a collection for this purpose. Compared to the success of the Jewish appeal in New York, the results of the Arab collection were pathetic, according to Nusseibeh.[79]

Scion of one of the most respected families in Jerusalem, Nusseibeh had read law at Cambridge and served as a magistrate upon his return. He had gone on to work in the government lands department, but resigned in 1945 to join Musa Alami's Arab office in London. In 1946 he returned and worked as a lawyer, and in May of that year was brought into the Arab Higher Committee. When the fighting broke out he was a prominent leader in Jerusalem, whose activities included organizing local defense initiatives. He was then in his mid-thirties. At the beginning of the 1950s he composed a book of memoirs, in English, but his political involvement—

he was soon to serve as a senior minister in the Jordanian government—apparently induced him to file his manuscript away, and it was never published. Nusseibeh wrote openly about the incompetence, corruption, and treason of the Arab politicians. He also took the British to task: they had weakened the Arabs and strengthened the Jews, who, Nusseibeh believed, were plotting to take over the world.

The Arab Higher Committee, he argued, had been too centralized, which hurt the local population largely because the committee was located in Cairo. The Arabs of Palestine were for all intents and purposes left to flounder alone. Attempts to organize local defense began too late. The committee's leaders, as well as the top Arab League officials, were at odds with one another and preoccupied with internal rivalries. None of them were aware of the real situation in Palestine. "Obviously, they thought of the Palestine adventure in terms of an easy walkover for the Arabs, and the only point that seemed to worry them was credit for the expected victory. Neither group was anxious to share the credit with the other and both were determined that the Palestine Arabs should at all costs be excluded." Indeed, historical research reveals that at the height of the war Arab leaders were bickering about the size of their salaries, among other things.[80] They besmirched Haj Amin al-Husseini and left him without influence. The mufti had succeeded as a symbol, Nusseibeh wrote, but failed as a leader. There was also rivalry and personal, family, and political competition between the two principal leaders of the war against the Jews, Fawzi al-Qawuqji, who fought in the north, and Abd al-Kader al-Husseini, who fought in the Jerusalem area. Almost every Arab plan was leaked to the Jews by traitors, Nusseibeh noted. The Jews were also good at psychological warfare. They deployed noisy machines to frighten the Arabs.

Nusseibeh believed that some of the commanders of the local army thought in terms of the revolt against the British in the 1930s. The rebels had often retreated to the mountains, which made sense, as the British had not sought to take control of the country. But the Jews were fighting for complete domination, so the fighters had erred in withdrawing from the villages instead of defending them, Nusseibeh wrote. He blamed himself as well. "I underestimated the strength of my enemy and overestimated the strength of my own people," he wrote. He had believed in the glory of the past and had ignored the difficulties of the present. His central thesis, however, was that the Palestinian Arabs could have won the country had their leaders not sabotaged the war effort and known how to cooperate. He also believed that had supreme authority of the Arab army been given to a local commander instead of officers from the Arab countries, the Palestinian tragedy might have been averted.[81]

Sometime after the war, during which he lost one of his legs, Nusseibeh considered the larger historical context of the conflict between the Jews and the Arabs. He had read *The Protocols of the Elders of Zion* and knew the book had been discredited as a fabrication, but he, Nusseibeh, could not determine that with certainty. In any case, it could not be disregarded, he wrote.

Nusseibeh had read Chaim Weizmann's autobiography. Was it only a coincidence that Weizmann was of Russian origin and that communism was first adopted in Russia? Nusseibeh wondered. So many Jews were implicated in the Russian Revolution. Had Zionism and communism sprung up independently or were they two branches of the same tree? And was it just coincidence that the *Protocols* had been fabricated, so it was said, in Russia?

Either way, Nusseibeh wrote, if the *Protocols* really were a plan for the domination of the world, the methods it advocates could be successful. True, Zionism was a national movement and communism international, but perhaps the two were part of a single plan, that of the elders of Zion. Thus there was no room for compromise between Arab nationalism and Zionism. Like Nazism, Nusseibeh wrote, Zionism is an aggressive, dynamic movement. However much the Arabs might try to appease it, they will always fail.[82] Like the pro-Nazi sentiments that Khalil al-Sakakini recorded in his diary, and along with some other antisemitic remarks in Nusseibeh's book, his theories document the vast gulf separating the two national movements.*

---

* "Had the mufti attacked the Old City of Jerusalem he would have slaughtered all the Jews," David Ben-Gurion said in one of the first meetings of the Israeli cabinet, mentioning the Holocaust. In a strange outburst, he suddenly began talking about the Arabs of Palestine in the second person plural, as if they were present in the cabinet room: "You made war—you lost." In another meeting Ben-Gurion stated, "We decided to clean out Ramle." Sometime later Ben-Gurion proposed the conquest of the Galilee as a means of expelling 100,000 Arabs. Here he used the verb "to clean" again. By the end of the war some 6,000 Jews had fallen, about one out of every hundred Jews living there at the time.[83]

8.

The British were supposed to bear responsibility for preserving law and order until midnight, May 14, 1948; on several occasions they defended Jewish settlements and neighborhoods, among them the Jewish Quarter in the Old City of Jerusalem.[84] They did not, however, attempt to prevent the advance of the Haganah or the flight and expulsion of the Arabs; in some cases they even helped the Arabs leave their homes. At the same time, they coordinated the transfer of many aspects of government with the Jewish Agency. This effort at a smooth handover was Britain's final contribution to the Jewish national home.

Evacuating the army and dismantling the administration were both as carefully planned as a military operation, and were carried out in stages.[85] Sometime before the U.N.'s partition vote Ben-Gurion asked Chief Secretary Gurney to transfer a series of services, such as the telephone exchanges and Jerusalem's water supply, to the Jewish Agency. The agency had equipped itself with a precise list of thirty-seven government departments, divided them into groups according to their importance—from the auditor general and the radio station to the statistics, surveys, and urban planning offices—and constructed a detailed system for taking control. The agency believed the best policy would be to continue employing the existing officials.[86]

Gurney replied to Ben-Gurion that Britain could not set up a state for the Jews. He was very angry, according to Ben-Gurion, who declared, with all the munificence of the victor, that the Jewish Agency was interested not only in an "honorable" parting of the ways but also in a "cordial" one. The Jews wanted to maintain friendly relations with the British, he insisted; perhaps this is not important for you, he told Gurney, but for us it is.[87]

The Jewish Agency then considered two scenarios: either the British would transfer control in an orderly way to ensure continuity, or they would leave in sudden panic, creating chaos in their wake. In the latter case there would be a Jewish-Arab race to grab control, with the prize going to the swiftest. The Jews' working assumption was that the British would choose the second option. One of the agency's intelligence operatives stated that clearly the British would do everything to keep the Zionists from taking over; he predicted a scorched earth policy.[88]

The British were thinking in other terms. Their concern was to notify government employees of their dismissal and guarantee that they would receive an advance on their continued employment elsewhere, and to organize the shipment of furniture and other equipment to England. Making arrangements for the widows' and orphans' pension fund was at the top of their list of sixty-two tasks, set down in a fourteen-page document.[89]

They could, of course, have left without giving any thought to what would happen after—but their bureaucracy was too dear to them. Edward Keith-Roach wrote, "High commissioners come and high commissioners go. To them Palestine is an incident in their official careers; to me and other officials here it is our lives."[90] Having been in the country for twenty-five years, having invested considerable work in building the administration, they could not watch its demolition without pain and distress, James Pollock wrote. Pollock and others like him wanted the state administration to continue to function properly, and so they did in fact make a great effort to transfer it to the Jews. Some functions were handed over to the municipalities, others to the Jewish Agency.[91] In addition, the evacuation plan, from south to north, left responsibility for Jewish population centers in British hands almost to the very last minute, thus impeding Arab war plans.[92]

It was not sympathy that motivated the British to perform this service for the Zionist movement—it was their mentality as rulers. The day after they left someone would have to remain in charge of the courts and the veterinary service and the antiquities department and the train schedule.[93] How the administration would have acted had the Arabs also had a government-in-waiting remains an open question.

9.

Chief Secretary Gurney felt as if he were sitting on a razor's edge. In the twilight days of the Mandate, he was in a rather lunatic mood, making nonsensical remarks on the situation in his diary. He cabled Isaiah 37:32 to the Colonial Office in London: "For out of Jerusalem shall a remnant go out, and they that escape out of Mount Zion: the zeal of the Lord of hosts shall do this."[94] In the midst of the general collapse of order and murderous violence raging through the city, administration officials held tightly to their work routines; the situations that resulted were often absurd. Bernard De Bunsen, director of the education department, found himself conducting a heroic operation to receive the government high school examination papers. They were being held at the home of Juda Leib Bloom, an official in the education department, who lived in the

Rehavia neighborhood. At that point, getting around the city was no longer easy; barbed-wire fences sectioned off different areas, and permits were required to move from one to the other. De Bunsen managed to get from his office on Princess Mary Street as far as Gaza Street in Rehavia, near where Bloom lived. The two men met at a sandbag-and-barbed-wire barrier and soldiers helped Bloom pass the forms from one side to the other.[95]

This reverence for exams was doubly absurd because, after thirty years of ruling Palestine, the British had still not instituted compulsory school attendance. Education standards differed for city and village children and for boys and girls, and only three out of every ten Arabs went to school. The other seven, mostly in the villages, grew up illiterate.[96] They were a lost generation. The result of this loss for the Arab community was catastrophic. A nationwide system of education would have forged national cohesion. But the war of 1948 found the Arabs rent by regional, social, and economic divisions, with profound differences between city dwellers and villagers.[97] The Hebrew education system, by contrast, formed the Jews into a national community, prepared them for their war of independence, and led them to victory. Had Britain limited its support for Zionism to nothing other than perpetuating Arab illiteracy, His Majesty's Government could still claim to have kept the promise enshrined in the Balfour Declaration.*

The British had come with good intentions and had set the country on a course to the twentieth century, Chief Secretary Gurney claimed. Palestine had become rich. It had first-class roads and water supplies, schools, hospitals, and electric power. There were agricultural research stations, ports, and railways. There was a judicial system unique in the Middle East for its freedom from corruption. "In spite of mistakes we have done an extremely good job," said one member of Parliament. High Commissioner Cunningham had only to look out his window to see what had been accomplished in Jerusalem in the last twenty-five years. He regretted, however, that out of a yearly budget of £24 million he had had to spend £8 million on security, and he never stopped thinking about what might have been done with this money for the betterment of the country.

---

*Chief Secretary Gurney cited the Zionist schools' requirement that students perform a year's voluntary national service as an example of the narrow, militaristic patriotism those schools produced. Referring to the Haganah's order forbidding Jerusalem's Jews to leave the besieged city, he wrote, "The Jews are becoming more and more Nazi and ruthless in their treatment of their own people."[98]

Chief Secretary Gurney believed that the problems in Palestine were more fundamental. From the outset, the British edifice had been built on sand. "I thought today," he wrote, "if Palestine has to be written on my heart, must it be written in Arabic *and* Hebrew?"[99]

James Pollock, now stationed in Haifa, weighed a crucial decision—whether to send his china and silver in a separate shipment or have them packed together with the furniture. During the thirty years since his arrival in Jerusalem in the wake of Allenby's army, he had spent a short time in Nigeria, but had been back in Palestine for some time. As always, he wrote home every day. His wife had left a few months previously, with the rest of the civilians, and Pollock made her party to his dilemma. If he sent the silver and china separately, he was liable to incur greater costs, because the rest of their belongings, including the furniture, were going at government expense.

He wrote to his wife about a ceremony to mark the thirtieth anniversary of the British conquest. Everyone was there, Pollock related, in their colorful robes and elaborate headgear, just like the first ceremony. He added details about the gang warfare going on in the city.

"I think when we go there will be an almighty cheer," Pollock noted. He believed the British would be leaving on May 1, a day with a history of disturbances. And this year May 1 happened to fall on a Saturday; it was also the day of the holy fire ceremony at the Church of the Holy Sepulcher and the Nebi Musa procession. "It does not matter as we will not be responsible," he wrote with great relief. "Well," he concluded after the U.N. voted for partition, "the Jews have won. . . . What else is there to write about?"[100]

From time to time, he provided news of the terrorist campaign as well, telling his wife that this person had been killed and that one wounded, the Rex cinema had been set ablaze, the city was under curfew. He told her about a golf game in Jerusalem, British civilians versus the army, with gunfire from Kibbutz Ramat Rachel in the background. One of the soldiers rode a horse over to see what was going on. He returned, on foot, very frightened, muttering only, "Isobel has been shot." With some effort, the players were able to make out that he meant his horse.

On another occasion in Jerusalem a shock wave from a huge explosion that shook Ben-Yehuda Street nearly threw Pollock out of bed. Ten people were killed. "The Jews firmly believe it was done by British police," Pollock wrote to his wife. He did not rule out the possibility, merely noting that the event had overshadowed the news that Palestine had been removed from the bloc of countries whose currencies were linked to sterling. The *Palestine Post* editorial office had been attacked a few days previously, and the Jewish Agency building was a target some weeks later—all three occurrences could have been British acts of retaliation, but they could just as well have been carried out by Arabs or even by Jews seeking to create provocation; Jewish agents sometimes operated in British uniform.[101]*

Absurdities abounded. One policeman, D. Drakeford, asked the Jewish Agency to write him a letter of recommendation, pointing out that during the previous seven years he had worked "in close cooperation" with the agency. He did not know what he would do next—perhaps move to New Zealand or South Africa. The Jewish Agency gave him the letter of recommendation and wished him all the best. A British soldier wrote to Golda Meyerson that he had decided to remain in Palestine and become a farmer. He was 100 percent pro-Jewish, he said; his duty as a believing Christian demanded nothing less. One day Palestine would be all Jewish, because that is what the Bible says and he believed in the Bible, he wrote.[103]

Michael Bryant also wanted to tie his fate to Palestine. Like General Barker, the director of the Jerusalem electric company seems to have shaped his political views under the influence of his love. Bryant had settled in Jerusalem in 1936, with his wife and son, when he was twenty-five. During his twelve years at the electric company, he had become well-assimilated in local society, and when he was accused of spying for the Arabs, he wondered why. After all, he had sympathy for the Jews and was known to both the Haganah and the Jewish Agency.

In a diary that came into the hands of Lotte Geiger, Bryant documented his efforts to ensure a steady supply of electricity to Jerusalem under siege, no easy task. His fuel reserves began to diminish, and he had no way of replacing them. The electricity company also began to run out of money because Jerusalem's residents had stopped paying their bills. In addition, Bryant worried about the security of the company's facilities and the safety of its workers, most of whom were Arabs. On May 12, he summed up a meeting with Dov Yosef, appointed by the Jewish Agency as governor of the city's western sector and an old friend of Bryant's. To save electricity, Bryant suggested immediately instituting "double summer

---

*Anwar Nusseibeh described these three attacks proudly; he was hurt by the fact that the Jews had doubts as to whether they were the work of Arabs.[102]

time," but Yosef, a sour-faced attorney, dressed, as always, in a pin-striped suit, said that he could not move the hands of the clock because the Jewish Agency would be accused of trying to advance the end of the Mandate by two hours.

On May 13 Bryant searched for a country or organization that would allow him to fly its flag above the electric company's facilities to symbolize its neutral status in service of the public. The representative of the International Red Cross immediately acceded, and then tried to put the Red Cross in charge of the whole city. Both the Jewish Agency and the Arab Higher Committee rejected the idea. So Bryant went to the U.N., which gave him permission to fly the international organization's flag but recommended against it. The U.N. flag was blue and white, and the Arabs were liable to think that it was Israeli. Bryant did not want to fly the Union Jack because he knew that both Jews and Arabs detested it. In the end, several foreign consuls in Jerusalem gave permission for Bryant to fly their flags together. Once again, thirty years after the British conquest, the siege of Jerusalem was also the hour of the consuls.[104]*

The Haganah held a farewell dinner for the last of the British officials; the atmosphere was gloomy.[106] The government's offices were already empty; the police had locked up the last of its gear, valued at £1 million, in a warehouse and wanted to hand the keys over to the U.N. The U.N. refused to accept them. So on his last evening Chief Secretary Gurney went to U.N. headquarters and placed the keys on the steps. He didn't sleep that night; gunfire began at midnight and continued, as usual, until 4:00 A.M.; he thought the fighting foolish.

At 7:15 A.M., Gurney left the King David Hotel with seventeen members of his staff. One of them lowered the flag on the roof of the damaged hotel and raised the Red Cross flag in its place. The BBC correspondent was there, as were many other journalists and photographers. Then Gurney and his staff left in a convoy of two civilian vehicles, a bus, and four armored police cars. Tanks were stationed at Allenby Square and all along the way to nearby Kalandia airport. A few people were out on the streets; some of them waved good-bye.

---

*Michael Bryant and several of his employees were defendants in Israel's first criminal trial. They were accused of espionage, under the emergency laws Israel carried over from the British. Lotte Geiger made great efforts to free Bryant, running from ministry to ministry, speaking with anyone who was willing to listen. Bryant was finally released for lack of evidence and went home. The British consul in Jerusalem, who followed the affair closely, was careful in his reports to place the words "State of Israel" in quotation marks.[105]

At Government House, the high commissioner surveyed his last honor guard; with the raising of the Red Cross flag he left also, a few minutes after 8:00 A.M. In Kalandia he bade farewell to the rest of his people and left for Haifa, where he attended a few other parting ceremonies; he was to be at sea by midnight.[107] Bernard De Bunsen was in another convoy that departed the country from the airport at Lydda. The passengers boarded their plane and were about to take off when someone noticed the Union Jack still flying over the airport building. One of them ran over to fetch the flag. "We were quite worn out," De Bunsen wrote, "and not even the eggs and bacon at 4:00 A.M. in Malta could rouse us until we stumbled half-awake into England."[108]

That is the end of the story, although there is a postscript, one that is somewhat absurd. On Friday, May 14, 1948, James Pollock wrote in his diary, "A very sad day, the Jews . . . have proclaimed their independent state."[109] He was to remain in Palestine for a while longer, along with a British general named MacMillan. For several weeks after David Ben-Gurion read the Jews' declaration of independence, the British continued to control a small enclave around the Haifa port to ensure the evacuation of their equipment and final personnel. In his papers, Pollock, who managed the enclave, sounds as if he were setting up a little country of his own. He divided his officials into departments: one for finance, one for justice, one each for transport and ports, in the plural, as if he were planning a second. His staff included two special advisers, for Arab and Jewish affairs. General MacMillan issued a historic statement declaring the enclave's jurisdiction, as if he were General Allenby himself.[110]*

Pollock's own title was "chief civil adviser." He and his men helped the last of Haifa's Arabs leave the city, but spent most of their time directing the dissolution of the administration and the sale and packing of equipment. A report summing up his activity indicates that the operation was carried out well and without mishaps. Pollock revealed the calamities he suffered only to his diary: at the very last minute someone managed to make off with three Cromwell tanks that were parked at the Ramat David airfield. One was found abandoned, but two disappeared. "A real flap," Pollock noted. He also had to bear one final ignominy: in honor of the departure of the army commander, a battleship fired a fifteen-gun salute,

---

*The Israeli government tended to treat these last few British officials leniently, almost fondly. Once in London, Pollock received an invitation to a cocktail party at the legation Israel had established there.[111]

followed by another ship firing an additional, superfluous round. "The final salute was a mistake," Pollock noted. He hated slips like that. With great relief, he finally cabled his wife that he was looking at "a perfect sea, with Palestine fading into a haze behind us."[112]

The war for Palestine went on at full force. One day, in the midst of the battle at Kibbutz Ramot Naftali, a small airplane appeared in the sky. A woman sat beside the pilot: Lorna Wingate, the widow of Orde, "the friend." She circled for a time above the Hebrew boys fighting for their lives and their homeland, and then, to raise their spirits, she tossed down her husband's Hebrew Bible. Arthur Koestler loved the story and included it in his book about Israel's independence, in a chapter called "David and Goliath." Perhaps the story is nothing but wishful thinking; there are those who say Mrs. Wingate was persuaded at the last minute to forgo her aerial adventure.[113] But among the dreams and illusions, the fictions and myths, this story, too, has its place.

NOTES

————•◦•————

ABBREVIATIONS

ISA: State Archive
CZA: Central Zionist Archive
FRUS: Papers relating to the Foreign Relations of the United States
H.C. Debs: Parliamentary Debates, House of Commons
H.L. Debs: Parliamentary Debates, House of Lords
HMSO: His Majesty's Stationery Office
IWM: Imperial War Museum, Department of Documents
JTS: Jewish Theological Seminary
KCL: King's College, London. Liddell Hart Center for Military Archives
MEC: Middle East Center, St. Antony's College, Oxford
PCL: Pembroke College Library, Cambridge
PRO: Public Record Office
PRONI: Public Record Office of Northern Ireland
RCS: Royal Commonwealth Society, Cambridge University Library
RHL: Rhodes House Library, Oxford
ULL: University of Liverpool Library, Special Collections and Archives
USNAM: United States National Archive Microfilm

INTRODUCTION: UNTIL WE MEET AGAIN

1. Gabriel Barkai, "The Archaelogical Remains in the Area of the Gobat School" (in Hebrew) in *The Old City of Jerusalem*, ed. Eli Schiller and Gideon Biger (Jerusalem: Ariel, 1988), p. 152ff.
   Gideon Hermel, "The Protestant Cemetery on Mt. Zion," in Schiller and Biger, *Old City*, p. 174ff.

2. Milton O. Gustafson, "Records in the National Archives Relating to America and the Holy Land," in *With Eyes Toward Zion*, ed. Moshe Davis (New York: Arno Press, 1977), p. 133.
   Miriam Borla, "The Dutch Galilean," *Davar*, 10 Dec. 1976, p. 10.
   Ya'akov Shavit, Ya'akov Goldstein, and Haim Be'er, *Lexicon of People of Palestine, 1799–1948* (in Hebrew) (Tel Aviv: Am Oved, 1983), pp. 124, 186, 251, 262–63, 291, 293, 309, 362, 435.

3. Antonius collection, ISA P/329, no. 813; P/330/864.

4. Michael Asaf, *The Relations Between Jews and Arabs in Palestine, 1860–1948* (in Hebrew) (Jerusalem: Tarbut Ve-Hinuch, 1970), p. 132.

5. Ruth Baki, *Russian Roulette* (in Hebrew) (Tel Aviv: Ministry of Defense, 1992).

6. Weizmann to Curzon, 2 Feb. 1920. *The Letters and Papers of Chaim Weizmann*, ed. Jehuda Reinharz (New Brunswick, NJ, and Jerusalem: Transaction Books, Rutgers University, and Israel Universities Press, 1977), vol. IX, p. 306.

7. Estelle Blyth, *When We Lived in Jerusalem* (London: John Murray, 1927), p. 230.
   Yehoshua Ben Arieh, *A City in the Mirror of an Era: New Jerusalem at Its Beginnings* (in Hebrew) (Jerusalem: Yad Ben-Zvi, 1979), pp. 371ff.

8. Bertha Spafford Vester, *Our Jerusalem: An American Family in the Holy City* (Beirut: n.p., 1950).

9. Meron Benvenisti, *City of the Dead* (in Hebrew) (Jerusalem: Keter, 1990), p. 112
   Margaret S. Drower, *Flinders Petrie: A Life in Archaelogy* (London: Victor Gollancz, 1985), p. 424.

10. P. J. Marshall, ed., *Cambridge Illustrated History of the British Empire* (Cambridge: Cambridge University Press, 1996), p. 82.
    Correlli Barnett, *The Lost Victory: British Dreams, British Realities, 1945–1950* (London: Macmillan, 1995).

11. C. R. Ashbee, *Palestine Notebook, 1918–1923* (London: Heinemann, 1923), p. 276.

12. Isa Khalaf, *Politics in Palestine* (Albany: State University of New York Press, 1991), p. 135.

13. Lecture by Arthur Wauchope, 1 Nov. 1932, CZA S25/1006.

14. Weizmann to the JAE, 7 Mar. 1939, CZA Z4/303/32.

15. Wauchope to Battershill, 27 Sept. 1937, RHL, "Battershill Papers," Box 10:4: ff 11–13.
    Moshe Sharett, *Political Diary* (in Hebrew) (Tel Aviv: Am Oved, 1971), vol. II, pp. 146, 184, 247ff.
    Anwar Nusseibeh, "Pattern of Disaster: Personal Note on the Fall of Palestine," p. 29, with the kind permission of his son.

16. Natan Yellin-Mor, *Freedom Fighters of Israel* (in Hebrew) (Shakmona, 1975), p. 197ff.
    Yehuda Koren, "The British Officer's Lover," *Davar Ha-Shavua*, 28 Nov. 1986, p. 12ff.

17. David Kroyanker, *Jerusalem Architecture: Building in the British Mandate Period* (in Hebrew) (Jerusalem: Keter, 1991), p. 310.

18. Edwin Samuel to his mother, 29 Nov. 1930, ISA, P/653/85.
    Edmund Peleg, *My Land of Israel* (Tel Aviv: Am Hasefer, 1957), p. 69.
    Nasser Eddin Nashashibi, *Jerusalem's Other Voice* (London: Ithaca Press, 1990), p. 15.

19. Kroyanker, *Jerusalem Architecture*, p. 231.

20. Edward Keith-Roach, *Pasha of Jerusalem* (London: Radcliffe Press, 1994), p. 89.
    E. C. Hodgkin, ed., *Thomas Hodgkin: Letters from Palestine, 1932–36* (London: Quarter Books, 1986), p. 91.
    Walter Francis Stirling, *Safety Last* (London: Hollis and Carter, 1953), p. 232.
    Ronald Storrs, *Orientations* (London: Ivor Nicholson and Watson, 1939), p. 446.
    Stirling, *Safety Last*, p. 116.

21. Moshe Sharett, *Political Diary* (in Hebrew) (Tel Aviv: Am Oved, 1971), vol. II, p. 292.

22. Memoirs of Aharon Danin, *Urgent Dreamers* (in Hebrew), ed. Shimon Halfi (To be published). Quoted with the kind permission of Rachel Halfi.

23. Ronald Storrs, *Orientations*, p. 446.

24. Edward Keith-Roach, *Pasha of Jerusalem*, p. 90.

25. Herbert Samuel, "The Future of Palestine" (Jan. 1915), ISA P/649/1.

26. Herbert Samuel on Wyndham Deedes (undated), ISA P/650/1.

27. Congreve to Wilson, undated [apparently April 1920], IWM HHW/2/52a/16.
    Bateman to Oliphant, 30 Aug. 1938, PRO FO 271 21881.
    Cafferata to Martin, 17 July 1946, Cafferata Papers. With the kind permission of his daughter.
    David Ben-Gurion, *Memoirs* (in Hebrew) (Tel Aviv: Am Oved, 1971), vol. I, p. 365.

28. Gurney diary, 19 Mar. 1948, MEC, GUR 1/1.
    Henry Gurney, "Palestine Postscript," p. 21, MEC, GUR 1/2.

29. Gurney, "Palestine Postscript," p. 21.

30. Gurney diary, 14 May 1948, MEC, GUR 1/1.
Sir Alan Cunningham, "Palestine: The Last Days of the Mandate," *International Affairs*, vol. XXIV (1948), p. 490.
31. David Ben-Gurion, *Memoirs* (in Hebrew) (Tel Aviv: Am Oved, 1973), vol. III, pp. 416, 418.

1: KHALIL AL-SAKAKINI RECEIVES A VISITOR

1. Khalil al-Sakakini, *Such Am I, O World* (in Hebrew) (Jerusalem: Keter, 1990), p. 69.
2. Mordechai Ben-Hillel Hacohen, *The Wars of the Nations* (in Hebrew) (Jerusalem: Yad Ben-Zvi, 1985), vol. II, p. 767.
David Lloyd George, *War Memoirs* (London: Odhams Press, 1938), p. 1,089ff.
3. Spanish Vice-Consul Jona Kuebler to Alter Levine, 7 Sept. 1917, Levine Papers. With the kind permission of the Munin family.
4. Aziz Bek, *Intelligence and Espionage in Syria, Lebanon, and Palestine in the World War 1913–1918* (Ramat Gan: Bar-Ilan University, Ma'arachot, 1991), p. 25ff.
5. "Jerusalem Diary" (in Hebrew), *Hadashot Mi-Ha-Aretz*, 18 Dec. 1918, p.7.
"The Cruel Deportation of American Citizens from Jerusalem to Damascus," undated memorandum, signed by Alter Levine and 150 others, Levine Papers. With the kind permission of the Munin family. See also: Hacohen, *The Wars of the Nations*, vol. II, p. 791.
6. Asaf Halevy ish Yerushalayim, *Ancient Scroll* (Tel Aviv: Dekel, 1915).
7. Memorandum by Shulamit Levine, undated, Levine Papers. With the kind permission of the Munin family.
8. Memorandum by Shulamit Levine [apparently from 1920]; memorandum by Consul Ballobar, 22 June 1920. Levine Papers. With the kind permission of the Munin family.
9. Asaf Halevy ish Yerushalayim, "Geschichte fun a Martir," *Yidishes Tageblat* (Jewish Daily News), 11 May 1919, p. 4.
10. Sakakini, *Such Am I, O World*, p. 73.
11. Ballobar diary, 18 Nov. 1914. With the kind permission of his daughter.
Meir Dizengoff, *With Tel Aviv in Exile* (Tel Aviv: Omanut, 1931), p. 13; Mordechai Naor, ed., *Tel Aviv at Its Beginnings, 1903–1934* (Jerusalem: Yad Ben-Zvi, 1984), p. 71.
12. Sakakini, *Such Am I, O World*, p. 56.
13. Shabtai Teveth, *The Burning Ground* (in Hebrew) (Tel Aviv: Schocken, 1997), p. 36ff., 298. See also: Matiyahu Mintz, "The Historical Conception: A Clarification of Ben-Gurion's Political and Zionist Position at the Time of the First World War, Before the Balfour Declaration," *Ha-Tsionut*, vol. XIII (1988), p. 69ff.
14. Mordechai Eliav, *Palestine and Its Settlement in the Nineteenth Century* (in Hebrew) (Jerusalem: Keter, 1987), p. 335; Yisrael Kolat, ed., *The History of Jewish Settlement in Palestine Since the First Aliya, the Ottoman Period* (Jerusalem: National Academy of Sciences, Bialik Institute, 1990).
15. Kisch to Brodetsky, 24 May 1931, and correspondence, CZA S 25/2726.
16. David Ben-Gurion, "On the Question of the Old Yishuv," *Ha-Ahdut*, Sept. 1910, p. 55.
Menachem Friedman, *Society and Religion: Non-Zionist Orthodoxy in Palestine, 1918–1936* (in Hebrew) (Jerusalem: Yad Ben-Zvi, 1977), p. 33.
17. Hacohen, *The Wars of the Nations*, vol. I, p. 127.
Ballobar diary, 31 May 1915, 7 Sept. 1915, 21 June 1916. With the kind permission of his daughter.
Diary of Mohammed Adel Al-Saleh, National Library, Jerusalem, Manuscript Division, AR80.46, p. 93.
18. Ballobar diary, 26 Aug. 1915, 19 May 1916. With the kind permission of his daughter.
George Antonius, *The Arab Awakening* (London: Hamish Hamilton, 1938), p. 189.
19. Eduardo Manzano Moreno, ed., *Diario de Jerusalem, 1914–1919* (Madrid: Nerea, 1996), p. 13ff.

20. Rachel Elyashar, *Family Album* (in Hebrew) (private publication), 1990, p. 30.

21. Hacohen, *The Wars of the Nations*, vol. II, p. 745.

22. Ballobar diary, 7 and 18 Jan. 1915, 4 May 1915, 21 Dec. 1916, 11 Jan. 1917. With the kind permission of his daughter.

23. Ya'akov Gross, ed., *Jerusalem, 1917–1918: Destruction, Miracle, Redemption* (in Hebrew) (Tel Aviv: Koresh, 1992), pp. 20, 48.
    Ballobar diary, 20 Mar. 1915. With the kind permission of his daughter.

24. Bertha Spafford Vester, *Our Jerusalem: An American Family in the Holy City* (Beirut: n.p., 1950), p. 246.

25. Yehuda Walch, "The Military Engagement in Palestine During the First World War," in *The History of the Jewish Yishuv in Palestine from the Time of the First Aliya (The British Mandate)* (in Hebrew), ed. Moshe Lissak (Jerusalem: Israel Academy of Sciences, Bialik Institute, 1993), part I, p. 97ff.

26. Moshe Smilansky, *Memoirs* (in Hebrew) (Tel Aviv: Hitahdut Ha-Ikarim, 1935), vol. X, p. 196.
    Aref al-Aref, *A History of Gaza* (in Arabic) (Dar Al-Itam Al-Islamiyya, 1943), p. 251. See also: Michael Asaf, *The Relations Between Arabs and Jews in Palestine, 1860–1948* (Tel Aviv: Tarbut Ve-Hinuch, 1970), p. 131. Gerald Butt, *Life at the Crossroads: A History of Gaza* (Nicosia: Rimal, 1995), p. 109ff.

27. Hacohen, *The Wars of the Nations*, vol. II, p. 548.
    Uziel Schmaltz, "The Reduction of the Population of Palestine in World War I" (in Hebrew), in *In Siege and in Suffering: Palestine During World War I*, ed. Mordechai Eliav (Jerusalem: Yad Ben-Zvi, 1991), p. 17ff.

28. Ballobar diary, 4 Mar. and 2 Apr. 1917. With the kind permission of his daughter.

29. Ben-Zion Dinur, ed., *The Haganah History Book* (in Hebrew) (Tel Aviv: HaSifriya HaTzionit, Ma'archot, 1954), vol. I, p. 392ff.
    Yitzhak Olshan, *Din U-Devarim* (Dispute) (in Hebrew) (Jerusalem: Schocken, 1978), p. 45ff.

30. Yitzhak Lufben in *HaPoel HaTzair*, qtd. in Ilan Shchori, *Dream That Became a City* (in Hebrew) (Tel Aviv: Avivim, 1990), pp. 3–20.
    Smilansky, *Memoirs*, vol. X, p. 211.

31. Smilansky, *Memoirs*, vol. X, p. 215.
    Ilan Shchory, *A Dream that Became a City* (in Hebrew) (Tel Aviv: Avivim, 1990), p. 105. See also: Tsiona Rabau, *In Tel Aviv on the Sands* (in Hebrew) (Tel Aviv: Masada, 1973), p. 60ff.

32. Hacohen, *The Wars of the Nations*, vol. II, pp. 540, 573–74.

33. Yosef Chaim Brenner, "The Way Out" (in Hebrew), in *Writings: Stories, Novels, Plays* (Tel Aviv: Sifriyat Poalim, Hakibbutz Hame'uhad, 1978), vol. II, p. 1693. See also: Menachem Brinker, *To the Tiberian Alley* (in Hebrew) (Tel Aviv: Am Oved, 1990), p. 43. Hillel Yafeh, *The Way of the Ma'apilim* (in Hebrew) (Tel Aviv: HaSifriya HaTzionit, 1971), p. 385.
    Moshe Smilansky, *Memoirs*, vol. X, p. 216.

34. Moshe Smilansky, *Memoirs*, vol. II, p. 664; vol. X, p. 110ff.
    Ballobar diary, 19 May 1916, 31 May 1916. With the kind permission of his daughter.
    Boris Schatz, *They Built Jerusalem: Daydream* (in Hebrew) (Jerusalem: n.p., 1924), pp. 91, 174.
    Helena Kagan, *My Early Time in Jerusalem* (in Hebrew) (Jerusalem: WIZO, 1983), p. 64ff.
    Bertha Spafford Vester, *Our Jerusalem: An American Family in the Holy City* (Beirut: n.p., 1950), pp. 257, 264.
    Izzat Darwazza, "95 Years of Life—Memories and Musings" (in Arabic), in *Arab Thought Forum* (Jerusalem: 1993), p. 294.

35. Schmaltz, "The Reduction of the Population of Palestine in World War I," p. 38.

36. Captain C. H. Perkins, Nov. 1917, IWM, 87/18/1.

Brian Gardner, *Allenby* (London: Cassell, 1965).

A. Wavel, *Allenby: Soldier and Statesman* (London: George G. Harrap, 1945), p. 160ff.

Cyril Falls, *Military Operations Egypt and Palestine* (London: HMSO, 1930), p. 395ff.

Walch, "Military Deployment," p. 97ff.

Gideon Biger, *Crown Colony or National Home: The Influence of British Rule on Palestine, 1917–1930, a Geographical-Historical Examination* (in Hebrew) (Jerusalem: Yad Ben-Zvi, 1983), p. 5.

37. Richard R. Meinertzhagen, *Army Diary, 1899–1926* (Edinburgh: Olivier and Boyd, 1960), p. 222ff.

    Friedrich Freiherr Kress von Kressenatein, *Mit den Tuerken zum Suezkanal* (Berlin: Otto Schlegel, 1938), p. 249. See also: Yiagel Shefi, "The Conquest of Palestine in World War I: The Element of Deception," in *In Siege and in Suffering: Palestine During World War I*, ed. Mordechai Eliav (Jerusalem: Yad Ben-Zvi, 1991), p. 219ff.

38. Captain William Hine to Hilda Gosling, 5 Sept. 1917, IWM, Con. Shelf, Gosling Papers.

39. Walch, "The Military Deployment in Palestine During the First World War," pp. 1–120.

40. Hacohen, *The Wars of the Nations*, vol. II, pp. 774ff., 779ff., 796, 1,000.

    Rabau, *In Tel Aviv on the Sands*, pp. 75ff., 78.

41. Smilansky, *Memoirs*, vol. III, p. 357.

    Ilana Bet-El, "A Soldier's Pilgrimage: Jerusalem 1918," *Mediterranean Historical Review*, vol. VIII, no. 2 (Dec. 1993), p. 218ff.

42. Captain C. H. Perkins, Nov. 1917, IWM 87/18/1.

43. C. H. Dudley Ward, *History of the 53rd (Welsh) Division* (Cardiff: Western Mail, 1927), pp. 152, 163ff.

    Vivian Gilbert, *The Romance of the Last Crusade* (New York: D. Appleton, 1926), p. 139. See also: George de S. Barrow, *The Fire of Life* (London: Hutchinson, n.d.), p. 170ff.

    W. T. Massey, *How Jerusalem Was Won* (London: Constable and Company, 1919).

    Walch, "The Military Engagement in Palestine During the First World War," p. 125.

44. Smilansky, *Memoirs*, vol. X, p. 222.

45. Ballobar diary, 16 Feb. 1917. With the kind permission of his daughter.

46. *HaHerut*, 7 Mar. 1917, pp. 1, 3; *HaHerut*, 23 Mar. 1917, p. 1.

    G. Karsel, *The History of the Hebrew Press in Israel* (in Hebrew) (Tel Aviv: HaSifriya HaTsionit, 1965), p. 135.

47. Ballobar diary, 11 June 1917. With the kind permission of his daughter.

48. Sakakini diary, 17 Nov. 1917. With the kind permission of his daughters.

    Sakakini, *Such Am I, O World*, p. 68.

    Ballobar diary, 26 June 1917. With the kind permission of his daughter.

49. Sakakini, *Such Am I, O World*, p. 74.

50. Fund-raising agreement, yeshiva letter, permit from the American consul in Jerusalem (1881), naturalization papers, 6 May 1897, and other documents, Levine Papers. With the kind permission of the Munin family.

    David Tidhar, *Encyclopedia of the Pioneers and Builders of the Yishuv: The First Ones* (in Hebrew) (1947), vol. II, p. 920.

51. Gideon Shiloh, "The Life and Diaries of a Palestinian Educator of Jerusalem," in Sakakini, *Such Am I, O World*, p. 9ff. See also: Sakakini Bibliography, p. 270.

    Anton Shammas, "This Story Has No Headline" (in Hebrew), *Kol Ha'ir*, 2 Sept. 1983, p. 29ff.

    Anton Shammas, "Uncle Alter Takes Off" (in Hebrew), *Kol Ha'ir*, 30 Sept. 1983, p. 18ff.

    Hala Sakakini, *Jerusalem and I* (Amman: n.p., 1987).

    Elie Kedourie, "Religion and Politics: The Diaries of Khalil Sakakini," *St. Antony's Papers*, No. 4 *(Middle Eastern Affairs, No. 1)* (London: Chatto and Windus, 1958), p. 77ff.

52. Sakakini, *Such Am I, O World*, pp. 33, 44ff., 82. See also Hala Sakakini, *Jerusalem and I*, p. 23.

53. Documents in Levine Papers. With the kind permission of the Munin family.

54. Sakakini, *Such Am I, O World*, pp. 156, 160.

Shiloh, "Life and Diaries," p. 11. See also: Yehoshua Ben-Hanania, "On the History of Arab Education in Palestine" (in Hebrew), *Hed Ha-Mizrah*, no. 12 (26 Nov. 1943), p. 5 (part of a series).

55. Levine to Zehavi, 1 Oct. 1924, Levine Papers. With the kind permission of the Munin family.
   Asaf Halevy ish Yerushalayim, *Ancient Scroll* (Dekel, 1915), p. 243.

56. Sakakini, *Such Am I, O World*, p. 47.

57. Sakakini, *Such Am I, O World*, pp. 50–51ff.

58. Sakakini, *Such Am I, O World*, p. 73ff.
   Asaf Halevy ish Yerushalayim, p. 5.

59. Sakakini, *Such Am I, O World*, p. 74ff.

60. Tom Segev, *Soldiers of Evil* (New York: McGraw Hill, 1987), p. 196.

61. Aliza Gidoni, "The End of the War" (in Hebrew), in *Jerusalem 1917–1918: Destruction, Miracle, Redemption,* ed. Ya'akov Gross, p. 193.
   Ballobar diary, 8 Dec. 1917. With the kind permission of his daughter.
   Gad Frumkin, *The Way of a Judge in Jerusalem* (in Hebrew) (Tel Aviv: Dvir, 1954), p. 194.
   "The Last Days of Jerusalem Under the Turkish Government" (in Hebrew), *Hadashot Mi-Ha-Aretz Ha-Kedosha*, vol. 1, no. 1 (4 Apr. 1918), p. 3.

62. Sakakini, *Such Am I, O World*, p. 76ff.
   Ballobar diary, 8 Nov. 1917. With the kind permission of his daughter.

63. Walch, "The Military Engagement in Palestine During the First World War," p. 127.
   Franz von Papen, *Memoirs* (London: Andre Deutsch, 1952), p. 76.
   Steuber, *Jilderin: Deutsche Streiter auf heiligem Boden* (Berlin: Gerhard Stalling, 1925), p. 120.
   Mordechai Eliav, "The Involvement of German and Austrian Representatives in the Events of 1917 in Palestine" (in Hebrew), *Kathedra* 48 (June 1988), p. 90ff.

64. Ballobar diary, 15, 20 Nov. 1917; 8 Dec. 1917. With the kind permission of his daughter.
   Zvi Shiloni, "Changes in the Jewish Leadership in Jerusalem During the Period of World War I" (in Hebrew), *Kathedra* 35 (Apr. 1985), p. 87.

65. "The Last Days of Jerusalem under the Turkish Government," p. 3.
   Ballobar diary, 5, 8 Dec. 1917. With the kind permission of his daughter.

2: "A CONTRACT WITH JEWRY"

1. Herbert Samuel, *Memoirs* (London: Crescent Press, 1945), p. 3ff.

2. Mayir Verete, "Kitchener, Grey and the Question of Palestine in 1915–1916: A Note," *Middle Eastern Studies*, vol. IX, no. 2 (May 1973), p. 226.

3. Jehuda Reinharz, *Chaim Weizmann: The Making of a Statesman* (New York: Oxford University Press, 1993), p. 131.

4. Samuel in a discussion on the Balfour Declaration, 7 Feb. 1917, ISA P1/650/99. See also: Weizmann to his wife, 31 Jan. 1919. *The Letters and Papers of Chaim Weizmann*, ed. Jehuda Reinharz (New Brunswick, NJ and Jerusalem: Transaction Books, Rutgers University, and Israel Universities Press, 1977), vol. IX, p. 107ff.
   Samuel to Weizmann, 29 Nov. 1920, CZA Z4/16/15445.
   David Ben-Gurion to his wife, 25 Oct. 1938 (in Hebrew), in David Ben-Gurion, *Memoirs* (Tel Aviv: Am Oved, 1982), vol. V, p. 360.

5. Bernard Wasserstein, *Herbert Samuel: A Political Life* (Oxford: Clarendon Press, 1992), p. 210.

6. Herbert Samuel, *The Future of Palestine* (Jan. 1915), ISA 649/1.
   Weizmann to Ahad Ha'am, 14–15 Dec. 1914, in *The Letters and Papers of Chaim Weizmann*, ed. Leonard Stein (Jerusalem: Israel Universities Press, 1975), vol. VII, p. 82.
   Wasserstein, *Herbert Samuel*, p. 206ff.
   Devorah Barzilai, ed., *The Letters of Chaim Weizmann* (Jerusalem: Bialik Institute, 1977), vol. VII, p. 16.

7. Samuel, *The Future of Palestine*, ISA P/649/1.

David Fromkin, *The Last Peace: Creating the Modern Middle East, 1914–1922* (New York: Henry Holt, 1989), p. 146.

Elisabeth Monroe, *Britain's Moment in the Middle East, 1914–1971* (Baltimore: Johns Hopkins University Press, 1981), p. 11.

8. Regina Sharif, *Non-Jewish Zionism* (London: Zed Books, 1983), p. 79.

9. David Lloyd George, *Memoirs of the Peace Conference* (New Haven: Yale University Press, 1939), vol. II, p. 720.

David Ben-Gurion, *Memoirs* (in Hebrew) (Tel Aviv: Am Oved, 1973), vol. III, p. 261.

Sharif, *Non-Jewish Zionism*, p. 79.

10. Barbara Tuchman, *Bible and Sword* (New York: Macmillan, 1956), p. 223.

Barouh Mevorah, *The Love of Israel and the Return to Zion Among the British in Modern Times* (Jerusalem: Hebrew University, 1987).

Wasserstein, *Herbert Samuel*, p. 211.

11. Lloyd George, *Memoirs of the Peace Conference*, vol. II, p. 720.

Verete, "Kitchener, Grey," p. 223.

12. Verete, "Kitchener, Grey," p. 223.

13. Wasserstein, *Herbert Samuel*, p. 136.

14. Wasserstein, *Herbert Samuel*, pp. 8, 211.

15. Lloyd George, *Memoirs of the Peace Conference*, p. 721ff.

16. Mayir Verete, "The Balfour Declaration and Its Makers," *Middle Eastern Studies*, vol. VI, no. 1 (Jan. 1970), p. 69. See also: Mayir Verete, "On the Balfour Declaration and Its Makers" (in Hebrew), *Ha-Uma*, vol. 6 (Nov. 1967), p. 306.

Fromkin, *The Last Peace.*

Reinharz, *The Making of a Statesman*, p. 92ff.

17. Fromkin, *The Last Peace*, p. 247.

18. Reinharz, *The Making of a Statesman*, p. 219ff.

19. Ronald Storrs, *Orientations* (London: Ivor Nicholson and Watson, 1939), p. 432.

Fromkin, *The Last Peace.*

20. Fromkin, *The Last Peace*, p. 274.

21. Chaim Weizmann, *Trial and Error* (London: Hamish Hamilton, 1949), p. 144.

22. Sharif, *Non-Jewish Zionism*, p. 76.

Stenographisches Protokol der Verhandlungen des VII Zionisten-Kongress (Berlin: Juedischer Verlag, 1905), p. 85.

23. Weizmann, *Trial and Error*, p. 144.

L. S. Amery, *My Political Life* (London: Hutchinson, 1953), p. 114.

24. Weizmann to Ahad Ha'am, 14–15 Dec. 1914.

Leonard Stein, ed., *The Letters and Papers of Chaim Weizmann* (Jerusalem: Israel Universities Press, 1975), vol. VII, p. 81ff.

Reinharz, *The Making of a Statesman*, vol. II, p. 145.

25. Weizmann to Aaron Aaronsohn, 3 Dec. 1917, in *The Letters and Papers of Chaim Weizmann*, Meyer W. Weisgal, general ed. (Jerusalem: Transaction Books, Israel Universities Press, 1977), vol. VIII, p. 16.

26. Weizmann to Brandeis, 21 Dec. 1917; Weizmann to Rosov, 21 Dec. 1917; Weizmann to Sir Ronald Graham, 23 Dec. 1917; *The Letters and Papers of Chaim Weizmann*, Meyer W. Weisgal, general ed., vol. VIII, pp. 30–34.

27. Balfour to Louis Brandeis, 24 June, no year, CZA Z4/16009.

28. Howard Sacher, *A Jewish Palestine* (London: Zionist Organization, 1919), p. 16.

Reinharz, *The Making of a Statesman*, p. 137.

Fromkin, *The Last Peace*, pp. 41, 79, 247, 317ff.

29. Reinharz, *The Making of a Statesman*, p. 137.

30. Kerr to Derby, 22 Aug. 1917, PRO 20/4452. With the kind permission of the Jabotinsky Archive.

Shmuel Katz, *Jabo* (in Hebrew) (Tel Aviv: Dvir, 1993), p. 200.

Yigal Elam, *The Jewish Legion in the First World War* (in Hebrew) (Ma'arahot, 1984).

31. Lawrence James, *The Rise and Fall of the British Empire* (New York: St. Martin's Press, 1994), p. 353ff.

32. David Lloyd George, *War Memoirs* (London: Odham Press, 1938), p. 586.
    Chaim Weizmann, *Trial and Error*, pp. 191–92.

33. Reinharz, *The Making of a Statesman*, p. 151.

34. George Antonius to Jeffries, 17 Nov. 1936, ISA P/330, no. 866.

35. *Parliamentary Debates House of Lords*, 21 June 1922 vol. 50 H.L. Deb. 55 col. 1118.
    E. L. Woodward, ed., *Documents on British Foreign Policy, 1919–1939* (London: HMSO, 1952), 1st series, vol. IV, p. 345.

36. *The Interests of the Commonwealth in the Middle East* (Three papers by a study group of the Cairo Group at Chatham House, 1945), CZA S25/7573.

37. Antonius files, ISA P/382 file 2731. See also: Yeshayau Friedman, *The Palestine Question Between the Years 1914–1918* (in Hebrew) (Jerusalem: Magnes, 1987), p. 83ff.
    George Antonius, *The Arab Awakening* (London: Hamish Hamilton, 1938).
    Fromkin, *The Last Peace*, p. 173.

38. Reinharz, *The Making of a Statesman*, p. 219.

39. *The Interests of the Commonwealth in the Middle East*, CZA S25/7573.
    Lloyd George, *Memoirs of the Peace Conference*, vol. II, p. 724ff.
    Edward Keith-Roach, *Pasha of Jerusalem* (London: Radcliffe Press, 1994), p. 67.

40. Theodor Herzl, *Diary* (in Hebrew) (Tel Aviv: Neumann, 1930), vol. I, p. 12.

41. Ronald Sanders, *The High Walls of Jerusalem* (New York: Holt, Rinehart and Winston, 1983), p. 564ff.
    Reinharz, *The Making of a Statesman*, vol. II, p. 198.

42. Reinharz, *The Making of a Statesman*, p. 172.
    Weizmann to C. P. Scott, 13 Sept. 1917, in Leonard Stein, ed., *The Letters and Papers of Chaim Weizmann* (Jerusalem: Israel Universities Press, 1975), vol. VII, p. 510.

43. Yeshayahu Friedman, "The Question of Palestine in the Period of the First World War" (in Hebrew), in Moshe Lissak and Gabriel Cohen, eds., *The History of the Jewish Yishuv in Palestine from the Period of the First Aliya and the British Mandate* (Jerusalem: Bialik Institute, 1993), part I, p. 16ff.

44. Herbert Samuel on Zionism, 15 Oct. 1917, PRO CAB 21/58.
    Reinharz, *The Making of a Statesman*, vol. II, p. 199.

45. The Royal Institute of International Affairs, *Great Britain and Palestine, 1915–1936* (London: Royal Institute of International Affairs, 1946), p. 15.

46. Samuel Archive, ISA P/1 649/4.
    L. S. Amery, *My Political Life* (London: Hutchinson, 1953), vol. II, p. 117.

47. Robert Graves and Alan Hodge, *The Reader Over Your Shoulder* (London: Jonathan Cape, 1943), p. 21.

48. Reinharz, *The Making of a Statesman*, vol. II, p. 205.

49. Sanders, *The High Walls of Jerusalem*, p. 615.

50. Arthur Koestler, *Promise and Fulfilment: Palestine 1917–49* (London: Macmillan, 1949), p. 7.

51. Weizmann to Balfour, 19 Nov. 1917. Dvorah Barzilay and Barnet Litvinoff, eds., *The Letters and Papers of Chaim Weizmann* (New Brunswick, NJ, and Jerusalem: Transaction Books, Rutgers University, and Israel Universities Press, 1977), p. 9.

52. Nachum Gutman, *A Small City of Few People* (in Hebrew) (Tel Aviv: Am Oved, Dvir, 1959). See also: Tsiona Rabau, *In Tel Aviv on the Sands* (in Hebrew) (Tel Aviv: Masada, 1973), p. 76ff.
    Eliahu Elishar, *To Live with Jews* (in Hebrew) (Tel Aviv: Marcus, 1980), p. 101ff.
    Moshe Smilansky, *Memoirs* (in Hebrew) (Tel Aviv: Hitahdut Ha-Ikarim, 1935), vol. X, p. 229.

Mordechai Ben-Hillel Hacohen, *The Wars of the Nations* (in Hebrew) (Jerusalem: Yad Ben-Zvi, 1985), vol. II, p. 796.

53. Ballobar diary, 9 Dec. 1917. With the kind permission of his daughter.

54. Bertha Spafford Vester, *Our Jerusalem: An American Family in the Holy City* (Beirut: n.p., 1950), p. 273.

Ya'akov Gross, ed., *Jerusalem, 1917–1918: Destruction, Miracle, Redemption* (in Hebrew) (Tel Aviv: Koresh, 1992), p. 148ff.

Dov Gavish, "On the History of the American Colony and Its Photographers" (in Hebrew), in *The Ze'ev Vilnai Book,* ed. Eli Schild (Jerusalem: Ariel, 1984), p. 127ff.

55. Gisele Levine to Count de Ballobar, 14 Dec. 1917, Levine bequest. With the kind permission of the Munin family.

56. Khalil al-Sakakini, *Such Am I, O World* (in Hebrew) (Jerusalem: Keter, 1990), p. 76. See also: Feigenbaum to Ruppin, 11 Jan. 1918, CZA Z3/74.

57. Ballobar diary, 9 Dec. 1917. With the kind permission of his daughter.

Helena Kagan, *My Start in Jerusalem* (in Hebrew) (Jerusalem: WIZO, 1983), p. 74.

C. H. Dudley Ward, *History of the 53rd (Welsh) Division* (Cardiff: Western Mail, 1927), p. 158.

58. Gad Frumkin, *The Way of a Judge in Jerusalem* (in Hebrew) (Tel Aviv: Dvir, 1954), p. 195.

59. Ballobar diary, 9 Dec. 1917. With the kind permission of his daughter.

60. Gross, *Jerusalem 1917–1918*, p. 180.

Ballobar diary, 11 Dec. 1917. With the kind permission of his daughter.

61. Ron Fuchs, "The History of the Planning of British Cemeteries in Palestine" (in Hebrew), *Kathedra* 79 (Mar. 1996), p. 114ff.

A. Wavel, *Allenby: Soldier and Statesman* (London: George G. Harrap, 1945), p. 233.

Brian Gardner, *Allenby* (London: Cassell 1965), p. 161.

62. Gavish, "On the History of the American Colony," p. 139.

63. Gross, *Jerusalem, 1917–1918*, p. 235.

Wavel, *Allenby*, p. 170. *The Palestine News,* 6 Dec. 1918, p. 12.

64. Vivian Gilbert, *The Romance of the Last Crusade* (New York: D. Appelton, 1926), p. 171. See also Lloyd George, *Memoirs of the Peace Conference,* vol. II, p. 720.

65. James Pollock to his father, 16 Dec. 1917, PRONI B 37908.

James Pollock to his parents, 12 Apr. 1918, PRONI D 1581/2/3. See also: Ilana Bet-El, "A Soldier's Pilgrimage: Jerusalem 1918," *Mediterranean Historical Review,* vol. 8, no. 2 (Dec. 1933), p. 218ff.

66. Gardner, *Allenby,* pp. 145, 161ff.

3: SELF-SERVICE

1. Yosef Eliahu Shlush, *The Story of My Life, 1870–1930* (in Hebrew) (published by the author, 1931), p. 365.

2. Rachela Makover, *Government and Administration in Palestine, 1917–1925* (in Hebrew) (Jerusalem: Yad Ben-Zvi, 1988), p. 73ff.

Gideon Biger, "The Administrative Organization of Palestine During the Period of the Military Rule, 1917–1920" (in Hebrew) in Mordechai Eliav, ed., *Siege and Distress: Palestine During the First World War* (in Hebrew) (Jerusalem: Yad Ben-Zvi, 1991), p. 17ff.

3. Ronald Storrs, *Orientations* (London: Ivor Nicholson and Watson, 1939), p. 303.

Ballobar diary, 8 Apr. and 8 July 1918. With the kind permission of his daughter.

4. "Memorandum on the Provisional Administration of Palestine," 22 Jan. 1917, CZA A16/32.

5. Gideon Biger, *Crown Colony or National Home* (in Hebrew) (Jerusalem: Yad Ben-Zvi, 1983), p. 5.

Storrs, *Orientations*, p. 297ff.

Edwin Samuel to his father, 5 May 1918, ISA P/653/76.

6. Makover, *Government and Administration in Palestine*, pp. 36ff., 142.
   Storrs, *Orientations*, pp. 287, 296, 329.
7. Storrs to Herbert Samuel, 6 July 1920, ISA P/649/7.
8. Ya'akov Gross, ed., *Jerusalem, 1917–1918: Destruction, Miracle, Redemption* (in Hebrew)
   (Jerusalem: Koresh, 1992), p. 289ff. See also: Anita Shapira, *Berl Katznelson* (in Hebrew)
   (Tel Aviv: Am Oved, 1980), vol. I, p. 112ff.
9. Mordechai Ben-Hillel Hacohen, *The Wars of the Nations* (in Hebrew) (Jerusalem: Yad
   Ben-Zvi, 1985), vol. II, p. 962.
10. Undated memorandum, PCL, Storrs Papers, III/2, 1918 folder.
    Storrs, *Orientations*, p. 451.
    Prostitution regulations, *Ha'aretz*, 1 Aug. 1918, p.2.
    Herbert Samuel to Mugras, 1 May 1925, ISA P/649/12.
11. Storrs, *Orientations*, p. 329.
12. David Kroyanker, *Architecture in Jerusalem: Construction in the Period of the British
    Mandate* (in Hebrew) (Jerusalem: Keter, 1991), p. 28ff.
13. Storrs, *Orientations*, p. 456.
    C. R. Ashbee, *A Palestine Notebook* (New York: Doubleday, 1923), p. 156ff. See also: C. R.
    Ashbee, ed., *Jerusalem, 1918–1920* (London: John Murray, 1921).
    Harry Luke, *Cities and Men* (London: Geoffrey Bles, 1953), vol. II, p. 216.
14. Storrs, *Orientations*, p. 336.
    Luke, *Cities and Men*, vol. II, p. 216.
15. Douglas V. Duff, *Bailing with a Teaspoon* (London: John Long, 1953), pp. 18ff., 35.
16. Storrs, *Orientations*, p. 375.
    See also: PCL, Storrs Papers, III/2, 1918 folder.
17. Edward Keith-Roach, *Pasha of Jerusalem* (London: Radcliffe Press, 1994), pp. 1ff., 47.
18. Pollock to his mother, 23 Jan. 1919, PRONI B 37908.
    PRO CO 733/175/64711, part I.
    Pollock to his father, 5 June 1920, PRONI D/1581/2/5.
19. Horace Samuel, *Unholy Memories of the Holy Land* (London: Hogarth Press, 1930),
    p. 38.
20. Eviatar Friezel, *Zionist Policy After the Balfour Declaration, 1917–1922* (in Hebrew) (Tel
    Aviv: Tel Aviv University, 1977), pp. 36ff., 419.
    Chaim Weizmann, *Trial and Error* (London: Hamish Hamilton, 1949), p. 269.
    Chaim Weizmann, 8 July 1920, Weizmann Archive.
21. Jehuda Reinharz, *Chaim Weizmann: The Making of a Zionist Leader* (London and New
    York: Oxford University Press, 1985), p. 151.
    Shmuel Katz, *Jabo* (in Hebrew) (Tel Aviv: Dvir, 1993), vol. I, p. 148.
22. J. B. Hobman, ed., *David Eder: Memories of a Modern Pioneer* (London: Victor Gol-
    lancz, 1945), pp. 9, 21, 81, 119ff. See also: Friends tell about Eder, 19 Nov. 1936, CZA
    K11/354/1.
    James T. Boulton and Andrew Robertson, eds., *The Letters of D. H. Lawrence* (Cam-
    bridge: Cambridge University Press, 1984), vol. III, p. 353.
    John Carswell, *The Exile: A Life of Ivy Litvinov* (London: Faber and Faber, 1983), p. 37ff.
23. Weizmann to his wife, in *The Letters and Papers of Chaim Weizmann*, ed. Dvora Barzilay
    and Barnett Litvinoff (New Brunswick, NJ, and Jerusalem: Transaction Books, Rutgers
    University, and Israel Universities Press, 1977), vol. VIII, p. 99.
24. Minutes of the first meeting of the Zionist Commission, 11 Mar. 1918; minutes of the
    second meeting of the Zionist Commission, 14 Mar. 1918, CZA L3/285.
25. CZA L3/629; L3/26 II; III.
    CZA L3/33–37.
    Weizmann to his wife, 9 Aug. 1918, in Barzilay and Litvinoff, *The Letters and Papers of
    Chaim Weizmann*, vol. VIII, p. 252.
    Hacohen, *The Wars of the Nations*, vol. II, p. 903.
26. Minutes of the Zionist Commission, 2 June 1918, CZA L3/285. See also: Hagit Lavsky,

Elements of the Budget for the Zionist Enterprise: The Zionist Commission, 1918–1921 (in Hebrew) (Jerusalem: Yad Ben-Zvi, 1981), p. 173.
Report on the Zionist Commission to Palestine (undated), CZA L3/657, p. 40.

27. Weizmann to de Haas, 18 Apr. 1918, in Barzilay and Litvinoff, *The Letters and Papers of Chaim Weizmann*, vol. VIII, p. 132.
Lavsky, *Elements of the Budget*, p. 54.

28. The Center of Zionist Organizations in Jerusalem to the Zionist Commission (undated), CZA L4/966.
The Zionist Palestine Office to the Zionist Commission, 24 Jan. 1919, CZA L3/411. See also: Minutes of the Zionist Commission, 11 Mar. 1918, CZA L3/385; 5 Nov. 1919, CZA L4/966.

29. *Impressions on the Jerusalem Situation*, 1 Apr. 1919, CZA A18L/86/I. See also: CZA L3/655, L3/285.
Lavsky, *Elements of the Budget*, p. 167ff.
Y. L., "The Public and the Management" (in Hebrew), *Ha-aretz*, 25 June 1919, p. 1. See also: "Zionist Commission or Executive Committee" (in Hebrew), *Ha'aretz*, 6 Aug. 1919, p. 1.
Y. L., "Support," *Ha'aretz*, 28 Aug. 1919, p. 1.
Edwin Samuel to his father, 16 Feb. 1918, ISA P/653/76.
Weizmann to his wife, 1 July 1918, in Barzilay and Litvinoff, *The Letters and Papers of Chaim Weizmann*, vol. VIII, p. 218.
Hacohen, *The Wars of the Nations*, vol. II, p. 927.

30. Minutes of the Zionist Commission, 2 June 1918, CZA L3/285.
Weizmann to his wife, 18 Apr. 1918, in Barzilay and Litvinoff, *The Letters and Papers of Chaim Weizmann*, vol. VIII, p. 132.
Weizmann at the Zionist Commission, 23 Sept. 1918, CZA L4/434. See also: Weizmann at the Zionist Commission, 16 May 1918, CZA L4/28.
Weizmann to Sokolow, 22 May 1918, in Barzilay and Litvinoff, *The Letters and Papers of Chaim Weizmann*, vol. VIII, p. 193ff.
The Zionist Commission to the press, 13 May 1918, CZA L3/385. See also: Ussishkin to Yitzhak Ashkenazi, Frankfurt, 19 May 1920, CZA L3/5.
Hacohen, *The Wars of the Nations*, vol. II, p. 938.

31. Weizmann to Brandeis, 25 Apr. 1918; Weizmann to his wife, 30 May, 1 July, 1 and 9 Aug. 1918, in Barzilay and Litvinoff, *The Letters and Papers of Chaim Weizmann*, vol. VIII, pp. 158ff., 197ff., 218ff., 245ff., 252ff.
Weizmann to Money, 26 Jan. 1919, in Jehuda Reinharz, *Chaim Weizmann: The Making of a Statesman* (New York: Oxford University Press, 1993), p. 105.

32. Menachem Friedman, *Society and Religion* (in Hebrew) (Yad Ben-Zvi, 1977), p. 33.
Hacohen, *The Wars of the Nations*, vol. II, p. 927.

33. Weizmann to his wife, 9 Aug. 1918, in Barzilay and Litvinoff, *The Letters and Papers of Chaim Weizmann*, vol. VIII, p. 252.
Ruth Walichtenstein to the military governor, 12 Feb. 1919, CZA L3/91. See also: Eder to General Weston, 14 Aug. 1919, CZA L4/297.
Zionist Commission with the chief administrator, 25 Aug. 1919, CZA L4/947.
Eder to the governor of Jaffa, 31 Aug. 1918, CZA L4/25.

34. Weizmann to his wife, 18 Apr. 1918, in Barzilay and Litvinoff, *The Letters and Papers of Chaim Weizmann*, vol. VIII, p. 132.

35. Hacohen, *The Wars of the Nations*, vol. II, pp. 916, 941. See also: Shoshana Halevi, *Affairs in the History of the Yishuv* (in Hebrew) (n.p., 1989), p. 193ff.
Minutes of the second meeting of the Zionist Commission, 14 Mar. 1918; minutes of the 13th meeting of the Zionist Commission, 29 Apr. 1918, CZA L3/285; minutes of the 19th meeting of the Zionist Commission, 1 Sept. 1918, CZA L4/293.
Ronald Storrs, *Orientations*, p. 360.
B. Z. Kedar, "The Cornerstone-Laying Ceremony for the Hebrew University," in *The*

History of the Hebrew University in Jerusalem (in Hebrew), ed. Shaul Katz and Michael Hed (Jerusalem: Magnes, 1997), p. 93.

Bernard Wasserstein, *The British in Palestine* (Oxford: Basil Blackwell, 1991), p. 227. Weizmann to Ormsby-Gore, 1 May 1918.

Weizmann to his wife, 9 Aug. 1918, in Barzilay and Litvinoff, *The Letters and Papers of Chaim Weizmann*, vol. VIII, p. 176ff.

Weizmann to Balfour, 30 May 1918; Balfour to Weizmann, 26 July 1918, CZA L3/310. See also: *Report on the Zionist Commission to Palestine* (undated), p. 11.

Hacohen, *The Wars of the Nations*, vol. II, p. 941. See also: Edward Keith-Roach, *Pasha of Jerusalem*, p. 70.

36. Hacohen, *The Wars of the Nations*, vol. II, p. 918.

37. Reinharz, *Chaim Weizmann: The Making of a Statesman*, p. 22.

Weizmann to his wife, 13 Mar., 16 Mar., 23 Mar. 1913, in *The Letters and Papers of Chaim Weizmann*, ed. Gedalia Yogev, Shifra Kolatt, Evyatar Friesel, and Barnett Litvinoff, vol. VI, pp. 12ff., 15ff., 20ff.

Our Festive Day: The Details of the Cornerstone Laying for the Hebrew University Building, Hebrew University, central archive. See also: Ya'akov Gross, ed., *Jerusalem 1917–1918: Destruction, Miracle, and Redemption* (in Hebrew) (Koresh, 1993), p. 338ff.

Hacohen, *The Wars of the Nations*, vol. II, p. 951.

38. Hacohen, *The Wars of the Nations*, vol. II, pp. 940, 952ff. See also: *The Day of Our Rejoicing: The Details of the Celebration for the Laying of the Cornerstone of the Hebrew University Building*. See also: Gross, *Jerusalem, 1917–1918*, p. 338ff.

Ballobar diary, 29 July 1918, with the kind permission of his daughter.

Weizmann, *Trial and Error*, p. 295.

39. Hacohen, *The Wars of the Nations*, vol. II, pp. 804, 846, 864.

40. Weizmann to Bella Berlin, 20 June 1920, in *The Letters and Papers of Chaim Weizmann*, ed. Jehuda Reinharz (New Brunswick, NJ, and Jerusalem: Transaction Books, Rutgers University, and Israel Universities Press, 1977), vol. IX, p. 375.

Hacohen, *The Wars of the Nations*, vol. II, p. 863.

41. Yigal Elam, *The Jewish Legion in the First World War* (in Hebrew) (Tel Aviv: Ma'archot, 1984), pp. 174, 245ff.

Report on the Zionist Commissioner to Palestine (undated), p. 38, CZA L3/657. See also: J. H. Patterson, *With the Judeans in the Palestine Campaign* (London: Hutchinson, 1922).

42. *A Brief Record of the Advance of the Egyptian Expeditionary Force Under the Command of General Sir Edmund H. H. Allenby* (London: HMSO, 1919), p. 101.

Ron Fuchs, "The History of the Planning of British Cemeteries in Palestine" (in Hebrew), *Kathedra* 79 (Mar. 1996), p. 114ff.

43. Ballobar diary, 5 Oct. 1918. With the kind permission of his daughter.

44. Khalil al-Sakakini, *Such Am I, O World* (in Hebrew) (Jerusalem: Keter, 1990), pp. 70, 89.

45. Levine to Kurt Silman, 28 Feb. 1918, and to an unidentified friend, undated, Levine papers. With the kind permission of the Munin family.

Sakakini, *Such Am I, O World*, p. 87

Sakakini diary, 30 Dec. 1917, with the kind permission of his daughters.

46. Hanoch Bartov, *I Am Not the Mythological Sabra* (in Hebrew) (Tel Aviv: Am Oved 1995), p. 88ff. See also Yehoshua Porat, *A Dagger and Pen in His Hand: The Life of Yonatan Ratush* (in Hebrew) (Tel Aviv: Mahbarot Le-Sifrut, Zemora, 1989); Ya'akov Shavit, *From Hebrew to Canaanite* (in Hebrew) (Jerusalem: Domino, 1984).

Untitled poem, Levine papers, with the kind permission of the Munin family. See also: Asaf Halevy ish Yerushalmi, *Scroll of the East (Megilat Kedem)* (in Hebrew) (Dekel, 1915), pp. 287ff., 183.

Rachel, "Megilat Kedem," *Hashelah*, vol. 37, books 217–22 (Summer 1920), p. 595. For other reviews, including those by R. Benyamin, Ezra Hamenahem, Moshe Smilansky, A. A. Kabak, Dov Kimche, Y. Rabinowitz, D. Shimonowitz, see Levine papers, with the kind permission of the Munin family. See also: "A Soul for Asaf Halevy ish Yerushalmi (Alter Levine)," *Ha'aretz*, 28 Sept. 1934, p. 9.

47. Notes from New York, Levine papers, with the kind permission of the Munin family.

48. Sakakini, *Such Am I, O World*, pp. 27, 72, 81, 89, 162. See also: Khalil al-Sakakini to his son, 12 Dec. 1932, 7 Jan. 1933, and 12 Jan. 1933, ISA 378/2646/P.

49. Sakakini, *Such Am I, O World*, pp. 81, 84.
Levine to Kurt Silman, 18 Feb. 1918, Levine papers. With the kind permission of the Munin family.

50. Levine to his wife, 15 Aug. 1918; Levine to an unidentified friend, undated; Levine to Kurt Silman, 28 Feb. 1918; Levine to Chaim Kalvarisky, undated. CZA J15/6484; Levine to Ruppin, 8 May 1918; Secretary of the Joint Distribution Committee to Samuel Harkabi, 18 June 1918, Levine papers. With the kind permission of the Munin family. See also: Memorandum on the situation of the refugees in Damascus, 17 Jan. 1919, CZA L4966.

51. Sakakini diary, 13 Feb., 17 Mar. 1918, quoted from the original with the kind permission of his daughters.
Sakakini, *Such Am I, O World*, pp. 101, 107, 129, 220. See also: Geoffrey Furlonge, *Palestine Is My Country: The Story of Musa Alami* (New York: Praeger, 1969), p. 46.
Spanish consul in Jerusalem, CZA L/33–37. See also: Memorandum on the situation of the refugees in Damascus, 17 Jan. 1919, CZA L4/966.

52. Khalil al-Sakakini, *Such Am I, O World*, pp. 106, 220.

53. *Ha'aretz*, 28 Dec. 1919, p. 1 (advertisement).

54. Ballobar diary, 6 Aug. 1918, with the kind permission of his daughter.
Keith-Roach, *Pasha of Jerusalem*, p. 59.

55. Helen Bentwich, *If I Forget Thee* (London: Elek, 1973), pp. 159, 164. See also: Beatrice L. Magnes, *Episodes* (Berkeley: Judah L. Magnes Memorial Museum, 1977), p. 94.

56. Margaret Pollock to her mother, 6 Oct. 1919, 19 Apr., 7 May, 4 Sept. 1920, PRONI D/1581/2/4.

57. Margaret Pollock to her mother, 24 Sept. 1919, PRONI B/37908.

58. Pollock to his father, 17 Apr. 1921, PRONI D/1581/4/10.

59. Ronald Storrs, *Orientations*, p. 460.

60. Pollock to his parents, 1 Mar. 1919, and Pollock to his mother, 8 June 1919, PRONI B/37908.
Margaret Pollock to her mother, 6 Oct. 1919, PRONI D/1581/2/4.

4: EGO VERSUS EGO

1. Chaim Weizmann, *Trial and Error* (London: Hamish Hamilton, 1949), p. 275.

2. Weizmann to his wife, 6 Apr., 19 May, and 20 May, 1918, in *The Letters and Papers of Chaim Weizmann*, ed. Dvora Barzilay and Barnett Litvinoff (New Brunswick, NJ, and Jerusalem: Transaction Books, Rutgers University, and Israel Universities Press, 1977), vol. VIII, pp. 118ff., 187ff.
Weizmann, *Trial and Error*, p. 289.

3. Weizmann, *Trial and Error*, p. 322.
Weizmann to his wife, 6 Apr. 1918, in Barzilay and Litvinoff, *The Letters and Papers of Chaim Weizmann*, vol. VIII, p. 118.

4. Weizmann to his wife, 26 May 1918, in Barzilay and Litvinoff, *The Letters and Papers of Chaim Weizmann*, vol. VIII, p. 196.
Report on the Work of the Zionist Commission to Palestine (undated), CZA L3/657, p. 35.
Eder to Sokolow, 27 Nov. 1918, CZA Z4/538. See also: "Allenby in Rishon l'Zion," *Palestine News*, 11 April 1918, p. 7.

5. Allenby to Rosov, 16 June 1919, CZA L3/427.
Weizmann to Samuel, 22–23 Nov. 1919, in *The Letters and Papers of Chaim Weizmann*,

ed. Jehuda Reinharz (New Brunswick, NJ, and Jerusalem: Transaction Books, Rutgers University, and Israel Universities Press, 1977), vol. IX, p. 255.

Memorandum to Clayton, 31 Dec. 1918, PRO FO 371 4170/105.

Officers to their superiors, 12, 16 Aug. 1919, CZA Z4/16044.

6. Ballobar diary, 18–29 July 1918. With the kind permission of his daughter.

   Report on the Work of the Zionist Commission to Palestine (n.d.), p. 51, CZA L3/657.

   Norman Bentwich, "The Legal System of Palestine Under the Mandate," *Middle East Journal*, Jan. 1948, p. 33ff.

   Gad Frumkin, *The Way of a Judge in Jerusalem* (in Hebrew) (Tel Aviv: Dvir, 1954), p. 210ff.

7. Mordechai Ben-Hillel Hacohen, *The Wars of the Nations* (in Hebrew) (Jerusalem: Yad Ben-Zvi, 1985), vol. II, p. 763.

   CZA L4/25; L3/5.

   W. F. Stirling, *Safety Last* (London: Hollis and Carter, 1953), pp. 112, 228.

   Ronald Storrs, *Orientations* (London: Ivor Nicholson and Watson, 1939), pp. 354, 358, 382.

8. The Jewish Legion to the Jewish Agency, 14 June 1931, CZA S 25/6733.

   Stirling, *Safety Last*, p. 115ff.

   Lt. Col. A. C. Parker to Jacob Thon, 29 Dec. 1917, CZA L2/183 II.

9. Eder to Muni, 22 June 1918, CZA L3/9V-VA. See also: *Report on the Work of the Zionist Commission to Palestine* (undated), CZA L3/657, p. 50. Ussishkin in the Zionist Commission, 4 Dec. 1919, CZA L4/297.

10. Fast Hotel, CZA L3/300; L3/286.

    Storrs to Allenby, 25 Feb. 1920, ISA P/649/16.

11. Weizmann to Sir Louis Mallet, 18 June 1919, ISA M/1/37.

    Vriesland to Zionist Organization, 7 Mar. 1921, CZA Z4/13631.

    Report on the Work of the Zionist Commission to Palestine (undated), CZA L3/657, pp. 36ff., 59.

12. *Report on the Work of the Zionist Commission to Palestine* (undated), CZA L3/657. CZA L3/9/VA. See also: CZA L4/966.

    CZA L4/297.

    Eder, Bianchini, and Jabotinsky with Deedes, 18 Nov. 1918, CZA L4/294.

    Eder to Sokolow, 18 Feb. 1919, CZA L4/966.

13. Stirling, *Safety Last*, p. 118.

    Kisch diary, 25 Mar. 1925, CZA S 25/564. See also: F. H. Kisch, *Palestine Diary* (London: Victor Gollancz, 1938), p. 44.

    Bernard Wasserstein, *Wyndham Deedes in Palestine* (London: Anglo-Israel Association, 1973), p. 5.

14. Edwin Samuel to his father, 25 Dec. 1917, ISA P/653/75.

    Edwin Samuel to his father, undated, ISA P/653/76.

15. Clayton to Ormsby-Gore, 20 Apr. 1918, CZA L3/285.

    Clayton to Rosov, 16 June 1919, CZA L4/947.

    Hacohen, *The Wars of the Nations*, vol. II, p. 918.

    Chaim Weizmann, *Trial and Error*, p. 276. See also: Bernard Wasserstein, *The British in Palestine* (Oxford: Basil Blackwell, 1991), p. 49.

    Weizmann to his wife, 24 Mar. 1918, in Barzilay and Litvinoff, *The Letters and Papers of Chaim Weizmann*, vol. VIII, p. 148.

    Minutes of the Zionist Commission, 30 Oct. 1918, CZA L4/294.

    Weizmann to Clayton, 5, 27 Nov. 1918, in Reinharz, ed., *The Letters and Papers of Chaim Weizmann*, vol. IX, pp. 9ff., 40ff.

    Weizmann to Clayton, 7 July 1919, CZA L3/310.

    Jabotinsky to Weizmann, 12 Nov. 1920, CZA Z4/16135.

    Kisch diary, 12 Sept. 1929, CZA S25/838.

Arthur Ruppin, *Chapters of My Life in the Building of the Land and the Nation, 1920–1942* (in Hebrew) (Tel Aviv: Am Oved, 1968), p. 176.

16. Ronald Storrs, *Orientations* (London: Ivor Nicholson and Watson, 1939), p. 441ff.
17. Storrs report, 4 Nov. 1918, ISA M/4/1401.
18. Storrs, *Orientations*, p. 352.
19. Weizmann to Ormsby-Gore, 16 Apr. 1918, in Barzilay and Litvinoff, *The Letters and Papers of Chaim Weizmann*, vol. VIII, p. 128ff. See also: Storrs, *Orientations*, p. 374.
20. Congreve report (undated), IWM, HHW 2/52A/21.
    Weizmann at the Zionist Commission, 21 Oct. 1919, CZA L4/297.
    Congreve to the War Office, 21, 28 Apr. 1920, ISA government secretariat M/1/38.
21. Congreve to Wilson, 18 May 1920, IWM HHW 2/52B/17.
22. *Notes on Palestine and Syria*, IWM HHW 2/52A/21.
23. Minutes of the Zionist Commission, 13 Apr. 1918, CZA L3/285.
    Report on the Present Political and Economic Attitude of the British Administration in Palestine, 30 Apr. 1919.
    Report on the Work of the Zionist Commission to Palestine (undated), CZA L3/657.
    Weizmann, *Trial and Error*, p. 273.
    Wasserstein, *The British in Palestine*, p. 67.
24. Wasserstein, *The British in Palestine*, p. 19ff. See also: Money to Ormsby-Gore, 16 June 1918, CZA L3/285.
    Hacohen, *The Wars of the Nations*, vol. II, p. 912.
    Weizmann to Money, 26 Jan. 1919, in Reinharz, ed., *The Letters and Papers of Chaim Weizmann*, vol. IX, p. 104ff.
25. Money memorandum (1919), ISA M/10/239.
26. Horace B. Samuel, *Unholy Memories of the Holy Land* (London: Hogarth Press, 1930), p. 60.
    Douglas V. Duff, *Bailing with a Teaspoon* (London: John Long, 1953), pp. 36, 46.
27. Congreve to Wilson, undated, IWM HHW 2/52A/16.
28. *Report on the Work of the Zionist Commission to Palestine* (undated), CZA L3/657.
29. *Report on the Work of the Zionist Commission to Palestine* (undated), CZA L3/657.
    Meeting of the commissioners, 5 Dec. 1918, CZA L3/285.
    Weizmann to Sir Louis Mallet, 18 June 1919; Mallet to Weizmann, 7 June 1919, ISA, Government Secretariat, M 1/37.
30. *Report on the Work of the Zionist Commission to Palestine* (undated), CZA L3/657.
31. Zionist Commission to the Zionist Organization, 11 Aug. 1920, CZA L3/353.
32. *Notes on Palestine and Syria*, IWM HHW 2/52A/21.
    Organization of the Zionist Commission (undated), CZA L3/285.
    Chief Administrator to G.H.Q., 21 Apr. 1920, ISA Government Secretariat, 1/38/M.
33. Edward Keith-Roach, *Pasha of Jerusalem* (London: Radcliffe Press, 1994), pp. 70, 81.
    Pollock to his father, 15 May 1920, PRONI D/1581/5.
34. J. B. Hobman, ed., *David Eder: Memories of a Modern Pioneer* (London: Victor Gollancz, 1945), p. 197.
    Chaim Weizmann, 8 July 1920, Weizmann Archives.
35. Pollock to his father, 21 Dec. 1919, PRONI D 1581/5. See also: *Report of the Present Political and Economic Attitude of the British Administration in Palestine*, 30 Apr. 1919, CZA L4/977.
36. Pollock to his father, 21 Dec. 1919, PRONI D/1581/5.
37. Richard R. Meinertzhagen, *Army Diary, 1889–1926* (Edinburgh: Olivier and Boyd, 1960), p. 67.
    Weizmann to Balfour, 23 July 1919, in Reinharz, ed., *The Letters and Papers of Chaim Weizmann*, vol. IX, p. 188. See also: Weizmann to Sokolow, 11 July 1919, in Reinharz, ed., *The Letters and Papers of Chaim Weizmann*, vol. IX, p. 175.
    Weizmann to the Zionist Commission, 21 Oct. 1919, CZA L4/297.

Weizmann to the Zionist Bureau, 7 Nov. 1919, in Reinharz, ed., *The Letters and Papers of Chaim Weizmann*, vol. IX, p. 235ff.

38. Weizmann in the Zionist Commission, 4 Dec. 1919, CZA L4/297.
    Weizmann in the Zionist Commission, 21 Oct. 1919, CZA L4/297. See also; Kenneth W. Stein, *The Land Question in Palestine, 1917–1939* (Chapel Hill: University of North Carolina Press, 1984), p. 42.
    The Political Committee of the Zionist Commission, 6 Nov. 1919, CZA L3/310.
    Weizmann to Julius Simon, 22 July 1919, in Reinharz, ed., *The Letters and Papers of Chaim Weizmann*, vol. IX, p. 185.
39. Curzon to Balfour, 2 Aug. 1919, PRO FO 371/4233.
40. Congreve to the War Office, 21 and 28 Apr. 1920, ISA, Government Secretariat, M/1/38.
41. Bols to Allenby, 21 Dec. 1919, ISA P/650/102.
42. Bols report, 21 Apr. 1920, ISA, Government Secretariat, M/1/38.
43. Money to Eder, 26 June 1919, CZA L4/947.
    Report on the Work of the Zionist Commission to Palestine (undated), CZA L3/657, p. 38.
    Eder to Bols, 28 Jan. 1920, CZA L3/292.
    Tom Bowden, "Policing Palestine 1920–1936: Some Problems of Public Security Under the Mandate," in *Police Forces in History*, ed. George L. Mosse (London: Sage Publications, 1975), p. 115ff.
44. A. Almaliah, "Malignant Leprosy" (in Hebrew), *Do'ar HaYom*, 13 Nov. 1919, p. 1.
    Itamar Ben-Avi, *Dreams and Wars* (in Hebrew) (Public Committee for the Publication of the Writings of Itamar Ben-Avi, 1978), p. 36ff.
    Wasserstein, *The British in Palestine*, p. 58ff.
45. Proceedings of the Palestinian Council, 18 to 22 Jan. 1919, CZA J1/8766 I.
    Galilee settlers to the Zionist Commission, 5 June 1919, CZA L3/70.
46. Intelligence report, 1 Sept. 1919, CZA L4/761. See also: Minutes of the Zionist Commission, 20 Sept. 1919, CZA L4/297; CZA L3/9I.
47. Hacohen, *The Wars of the Nations*, vol. II, p. 979.
48. Center of the Zionist Organizations in Jerusalem to the members of the Zionist Commission from London (undated), CZA L4/966.
    Jabotinsky to Weizmann, 12 Nov. 1918, CZA Z4/16135.
49. Knesset Israel, National Council, *Book of Documents* (in Hebrew) (Jerusalem: n.p., 1949), p. 3.
50. List of books for translation, etc., CZA L3/411.
51. Jabotinsky dictionary, undated, CZA L4/697. See also: *Palestine News* (first year), no. 44 (2 Jan. 1919), p. 11.
52. Weizmann in the temporary commission, 22 Oct. 1919, CZA J1/8782. See also: Moshe Sharett, *Political Diary* (in Hebrew) (Tel Aviv: Am Oved, 1974), vol. IV, p. 157.
    Ben-Gurion in the assembly of the temporary commission in Jaffa, *Hadashot Ha-Aretz*, 21 Sept. 1919, p. 2. See also: David Ben-Gurion, *Memoirs* (Tel Aviv: Am Oved, 1971), vol. I, p. 198.
    Ussishkin versus the American members of the Zionist Commission, CZA L3/655.
53. Theodor Herzl, *The Jewish State* (in Hebrew) (Tel Aviv: Yediot Aharonot, 1978), p. 62.
54. J. H. Patterson, *The Man-Eaters of Tsavo* (London: Macmillan, 1914).
    J. H. Patterson, *With the Zionists in Gallipoli* (London: Hutchinson, 1916), p. 35ff.
55. Shmuel Katz, *Jabo* (in Hebrew) (Tel Aviv: Dvir, 1993), vol. I, p. 262ff. See also: *Hadashot Mi-Ha-Aretz*, 6 Dec. 1918, p. 3.
56. Report on the Zionist Commission to Palestine (undated), CZA L3/657, p. 60.
    Jacob Thon to General Allenby (undated), Knesset Israel, National Council, *Book of Documents* (publisher not noted), 1949, p. 9.
57. Hobman, *David Eder*, p. 156.
    Yigal Ilam, *The Jewish Legion in the First World War* (in Hebrew) (Ma'arahot, 1984), p. 290ff.
58. Shabtai Teveth, *The Burning Ground* (Tel Aviv: Schocken, 1997), vol. II, p. 22ff.

59. Tevet, *The Burning Ground*, vol. II, p. 26.

60. Minutes of the eighth assembly of the temporary commission, 22–23 Oct. 1919, CZA J1/8782.

5: BETWEEN MOHAMMED AND MR. COHEN

1. Khalil al-Sakakini, *Such Am I, O World* (in Hebrew) (Jerusalem: Keter, 1990), p. 111.

2. Sakakini, *Such Am I, O World*, pp. 65, 242, 220, 107ff., 110, 128ff., 167, 242, 88.

3. The Arab Legion, ISA, Antonius Archive, P/384, no. 3831.
George Antonius, *The Arab Awakening: The Story of the Arab National Movement* (London: Hamish Hamilton, 1938), p. 230.
Philip Mattar, *The Mufti of Jerusalem* (New York: Columbia University Press, 1988), p. 12.

4. Sakakini, *Such Am I, O World*, p. 115.

5. Police report, 19 Dec. 1920, ISA M/5/155.
Charter of the Christian-Muslim Association, CZA A/199/45.
Yehoshua Porat, *The Growth of the Palestinian Arab National Movement, 1918–1929* (in Hebrew) (Tel Aviv: Am Oved, 1976), vol. I.
Baruch Kimmerling and Joel S. Migdal, *Palestinians: The Making of a People* (New York: Free Press, 1993).

6. Sakakini, *Such Am I, O World*, p. 115.

7. Arieh L. Avneri, *Jewish Settlement and the Claim of Expropriation (1878–1948)* (in Hebrew) (Tel Aviv: Hakibbutz Hame'uhad, 1980), p. 64ff.

8. Ahad Ha'am, "Truth from Palestine," in *The Complete Works of Ahad Ha'am* (in Hebrew) (Tel Aviv: Dvir, 1949), p. 24.

9. Herzl–Al-Khalidi correspondence, Mar. 1899, CZA H III D. 13/H 197.
Yosef Lamdan, "The Arabs and Zionism, 1882–1914" (in Hebrew), in *The History of the Jewish Yishuv in Palestine from the Time of the First Aliya, The British Mandate* (in Hebrew), ed. Moshe Lissak (Jerusalem: Bialik Institute), p. 219. On this matter, see also reports from British representatives in Jerusalem, Cairo, and Istanbul Apr.–May 1911, PRO FO 371/1245.

10. Rashid Khalidi, *Palestinian Identity* (New York: Columbia University Press, 1997), pp. 28ff.

11. Mohammed Izzat Darwazza, *Ninety-Five Years of Life: Memoirs and Meditations* (in Arabic) (Jerusalem: Arab Thought Forum, 1993), p. 199.
Sakakini, *Such Am I, O World*, p. 47.
Khalidi, *Palestinian Identity*, pp. 158, 168.

12. Pesi, "From Imagination to Reality," *Ha-Olam* (second year), nos. 34, 38 (28 Aug., 25 Sept. 1908).
David Ben-Gurion, *Early Writings* (in Hebrew) (Tel Aviv: Ha'ahdut, 1962), p. 25. See also: the report of the Palestine Office on the Syrian Press, 24 June 1912, CZA Z3/1448 4. Report no. 17, 9 Dec. 1912, CZA L2/24 IV; Report no. 19, 28 Jan. 1913, CZA L2/24 V.

13. Minutes of the fifth assembly of the temporary commission, 9 June 1919, p. 112ff., CZA J1/8777. See also: CZA L4/769.

14. "A Show in Jaffa" (in Hebrew), *Hadashot Ha-Aretz*, 6 Mar. 1919, p. 12.

15. The Palestine Conference, 15 Feb. 1919, ISA M/5/155; CZA Z4/16078; CZA L4/767.

16. Arab protest, 1918, ISA M/4/1401-II.
Arab protest, Mar.–Apr. 1920, CZA M/1/30 I-II.

17. Sakakini, *Such Am I, O World*, p. 121.

18. Sakakini diary, 15 Apr. 1919. With the kind permission of his daughters.
Sakakini, *Such Am I, O World*, pp. 49–51ff.

19. Yaacov Ro'i, "The Zionist Attitude to the Arabs, 1908–1914," *Middle Eastern Studies*, vol. IV, no. 3 (Apr. 1968), p. 198ff.

Sokolow interview translated into German and the response of the Egyptian press Apr.–May 1914, CZA L2/24 VI.

20. Yitzhak Epstein, "A Question Has Been Lost" (in Hebrew), *Ha-Shiloah*, 1907, p. 193ff.

21. "Our Relations with the Arabs" (undated, apparently 1920), CZA L/353.

Ya'akov Yehoshua, *Childhood in Old Jerusalem* (Jerusalem: Re'uven Mass, 1966), pp. 215ff, 240.

Ronald Storrs, *Orientations* (London: Ivor Nicholson and Watson, 1939), p. 381.

Geoffrey Furlonge, *Palestine Is My Country* (New York: Praeger, 1969), p. 6.

22. Chaim Kalvarisky, "The Relations Between Jews and Arabs before World War I" (in Hebrew), *She'ifateinu*, vol. II, no. 2 (1931), p. 51.

Yosef Eliyau Shlush, *The Story of My Life, 1870–1930* (published by the author, 1931), p. 424ff.

Eliahu Elyashar, *Living with Palestinians* (in Hebrew) (Sepharadi Community Committee, 1975); Eliahu Elyashar, *Living with Jews* (in Hebrew) (Marcus, 1980).

23. Preparation Fund Account, 30 June 1918, CZA L3/285. See also: Jehuda Reinharz, *Chaim Weizmann: The Making of a Statesman* (New York: Oxford University Press, 1993), pp. 245, 287ff.

Weizmann to Bella Berlin, 8 Nov. 1919, in *The Letters and Papers of Chaim Weizmann*, ed. Jehuda Reinharz (New Brunswick, NJ, and Jerusalem: Transaction Books, Rutgers University, and Israel Universities Press, 1977), vol. IX, p. 251ff.

24. Weizmann to his wife, 24 Mar. 1918; Weizmann to Sokolow, 18 Apr. 1918; Weizmann to Ormsby-Gore, 21 Apr. 1918, in *The Letters and Papers of Chaim Weizmann*, ed. Dvora Barzilay and Barnett Litvinoff (New Brunswick, NJ, and Jerusalem: Transaction Books, Rutgers University, and Israel Universities Press, 1977), vol. VIII, pp. 107, 138ff., 151ff.

Minutes of the Zionist Commission, 25 Mar. 1918, CZA L3/285.

Report on the Zionist Commission to Palestine (undated), CZA L3/657, pp. 3, 13.

Weizmann in the Zionist Commission, 14 Mar. 1918, CZA L4/293.

25. Weizmann to Money, 26 Jan. 1919, in Reinharz, ed., *The Letters and Papers of Chaim Weizmann*, vol. IX, p. 150ff.

26. Reinharz, *Chaim Weizmann: The Making of a Statesman*, p. 257.

Weizmann to Ahad Ha'am, 3 Aug. 1918; Weizmann to Balfour, 30 May 1918, in Barzilay and Litvinoff, *The Letters and Papers of Chaim Weizmann*, vol. VIII, pp. 198ff; 257ff.

27. Weizmann to his wife, 30 Apr. 1918, in Barzilay and Litvinoff, *The Letters and Papers of Chaim Weizmann*, vol. VIII, p. 171.

28. Barzilay and Litvinoff, *The Letters and Papers of Chaim Weizmann*, vol. VIII, p. 198ff.

29. Sakakini, *Such Am I, O World*, p. 126.

30. Reinharz, *Chaim Weizmann: The Making of a Statesman*, p. 255.

31. Chaim Weizmann, *Trial and Error* (London: Hamish Hamilton, 1949), p. 290ff.

32. Weizmann to his wife, 17 June 1918, in Barzilay and Litvinoff, *The Letters and Papers of Chaim Weizmann*, vol. VIII, p. 210ff.

Clayton memorandum, 12 June 1918, PRO FO 371/3398/105824/F 27647. See also: Aaron Klieman, "The Weizman-Feisal Negotiations," *Chicago Jewish Forum*, vol. 24, no. 4 (Summer 1966), p. 297ff.

Weizmann, *Trial and Error*, p. 294.

33. Weizmann to Balfour, 17 July 1918, CZA L3/310.

34. Chaim Weizmann, *Trial and Error*, p. 298.

35. Kalvarisky to the Advisory Council, 7 Dec. 1920, CZA L3/9 II. See also: CZA L4/766 and L4/881.

36. Minutes of the fifth assembly of the temporary commission, 9–11 June 1919, CZA J1/8777.

37. Heads of Scheme for the Provisional Government in Palestine, Jan. 1919, CZA J1/8766 I.

Memorandum of the Zionist Organization on the matter of Palestine, 3 Feb. 1919, in Reinharz, ed., *The Letters and Papers of Chaim Weizmann*, vol. IX, p. 391ff.

38. Foreign Relations of United States, *The Paris Peace Conference 1919* (Washington:

United States Printing office, 1943), vol. IV, p. 169. See also: Reinharz, *Chaim Weizmann: The Making of a Statesman*, p. 299.

Weizmann to his wife, 28 Feb. 1919, in Reinharz, ed., *The Letters and Papers of Chaim Weizmann*, vol. IX, p. 118.

39. The Fifth Meeting of the Advisory Committee, 10 May 1919, CZA Z4/16009.

40. Martin Gilbert, *Atlas of the Arab-Israeli Conflict* (Tel Aviv: Ministry of Defense, 1980), p. 11. See also: Yigal Elam, "Political History, 1918–1922," in *The History of the Jewish Yishuv in Palestine from the Time of the Aliya (The British Mandate)* (in Hebrew), ed. Moshe Lissak (Jerusalem: Israel Academy of Sciences, Bialik Institute, 1993), part I, p. 158ff.

41. Chaim Weizmann, *Trial and Error*, p. 300.

42. Foreign Relations of the United States, *The Paris Peace Conference, 1919* (Washington: United States Printing office, 1943), vol. III, pp. 795–96.

43. "America's Place in World Government" (no author), *Round Table*, no. 33 (Dec. 1918), p. 34. See also: Yeshayahu Friedman, *The Palestine Question in the Years 1914–1918* (Jerusalem, Tel Aviv: Magnes and the Ministry of Defense, 1987), p. 70. Frank E. Manuel, *The Realities of American-Palestine Relations* (Westport: Greenwood Press, 1975), p. 273.

CAMP report, 15 Feb. 1919, ISA M/5/155.

Ballobar diary, 30 July 1918. With the kind permission of his daughter.

44. Ballobar diary, 27 May 1919. With the kind permission of his daughter.

Ha'aretz, 25 July 1919, p. 3.

45. Zaha Bustami, "American Foreign Policy and the Question of Palestine" (diss. submitted to Georgetown University, Washington, DC, 1989), vol. I, p. 237.

Weizmann, *Trial and Error*, p. 241.

46. Bustami, "American Foreign Policy," vol. I, p. 237.

Weizmann, *Trial and Error*, p. 241.

47. H. Sacher, *A Jewish Palestine: The Jewish Case for a British Trusteeship* (London: Zionist Organization, 1919), p. 17.

48. "Our Relations with the Arabs" (unsigned; apparently 15 Jan. 1920), CZA L3/353.

Edwin Samuel at the Palin conference (Apr. 1920), PRO WO 329616, p. 5.

49. Balfour memorandum, 11 Aug. 1919, in *Documents on British Foreign Police, 1919–1939*, ed. E. L. Woodward and Rohan Butler (London: HMSO, 1952), 1st ser., vol. IV, 1919, p. 343.

Weizmann, *Trial and Error*, p. 300.

Bustami, "American Foreign Policy," vol. I, p. 99.

CZA A 182/86/3.

CZA L3/340.

50. Charles Crane to Donald M. Brodie, 30 Nov. 1934, ISA (Antonius collection), P/381/2727.

Harry N. Howard, *The King Crane Commission* (Beirut: Khayats, 1963), p. 99.

CZA A 182/86/3.

CZA L3/340.

51. Sakakini, *Such Am I, O World*, pp. 121, 125.

52. *Editor and Publisher*, vol. 55, no. 27 (Dec. 22,), p. 1ff., ISA (Antonius collection), P/381/2727.

53. ISA P/1 650/103.

J. N. Camp, 12 Aug. 1919, in Woodward and Butler, vol. IV, p. 364.

Herbert Samuel with Emir Faisal, 15 Oct. 1919, CZA L3/27–29.

Jewish representatives with Faisal, 19 Oct. 1919, CZA Z4/1392 I.

Elam, "Political History, 1918–1922," p. 162.

Sakakini diary, 39 Mar. 1919, 15 Apr. 1919. Quoted with the kind permission of his daughters.

54. Weizmann to the Zionist Executive, 25 Mar. 1920, in Reinharz, ed., *The Letters and Papers of Chaim Weizmann*, vol. IX, p. 328ff.

Nakdimon Rogel, "Weizmann's Man in Damascus" (in Hebrew), *Ha-Tsionut*, VIII (1983), p. 292.

55. Samuel to his wife, 8 Aug. 1920, ISA, P/1 651/41.

Herbert Samuel, *Memoirs* (London: Cresset Press, 1945), p. 158.

Francis Emily Newton, *Fifty Years in Palestine* (Wrotham: Coldharbour Press, 1948), p. 143.

Weizmann to Eder, 8 Dec. 1921, in *The Letters and Papers of Chaim Weizmann*, ed. Bernard Wasserstein (New Brunswick, NJ, and Jerusalem: Transaction Books, Rutgers University, and Israel Universities Press, 1977), vol. X, p. 317.

Newton to *Ha'aretz*, 1 July 1921, p. 3. See also: Interview with Faisal, *Ha'aretz*, 18 Aug. 1920, p. 2.

56. Weizmann, *Trial and Error*, p. 294.

57. Mordechai Ben-Hillel Hacohen, *The Wars of the Nations* (in Hebrew) (Jerusalem: Yad Ben-Zvi, 1985), vol. II, p. 918.

58. Nakdimon Rogel, *A Front Without a Rear* (in Hebrew) (Yariv, 1979), p. 154.

Nakdimon Rogel, *The Tel-Hai Affair: Documents on the Defense of the Galilee, 1919–1920* (in Hebrew) (Tel Aviv: HaSifriya HaTzionit, 1994), p. 238.

59. Shulamit Laskov, *Trumpeldor* (in Hebrew) (Jerusalem: Keter, 1995).

60. Minutes of the Zionist Commission, 7 Mar. 1920, CZA L3/300.

61. Rogel, *A Front Without a Rear*, p. 190.

M. Glickson, "Memorial Day" (in Hebrew), *HaPoel HaTzair*, 22, 28 Mar. 1921, p. 5. *Ha'aretz*, 28 Mar. 1921, p. 3.

62. Y.L-N, "Tel Hai Day," *HaPoel HaTzair*, 22, 28 Mar. 1921, p. 3.

63. Yael Zerubavel, *Recovered Roots: Collective Memory and the Making of Israeli National Tradition* (Chicago: University of Chicago Press, 1995).

Arieh Pialakov, ed., *The Lesson of Tel Hai* (in Hebrew) (Tel Aviv: Hakibbutz Hame'uhad, 1980).

64. Yosef Chaim Brenner, "Tel Hai," in *The Collected Works of Y. Ch. Brenner* (in Hebrew) (Tel Aviv: Dvir, 1960), vol. II, p. 176.

65. Nahum Barnea, "The War over *Yitzkor:* From Berl Katznelson to Rabbi Goren," in *A Speech for Every Occasion*, ed. Tamar Brosh (Tel Aviv: Open University, 1993), p. 140.

66. Eder to Weizmann, 14 Mar. 1920, CZA Z4/16033.

67. *Ha'aretz*, 19 May 1920, p. 3.

6: NEBI MUSA, 1920

1. T. S. Eliot, "The Waste Land," *The Complete Poems and Plays of T. S. Eliot* (London: Faber and Faber, 1969), p. 61.

2. Khalil al-Sakakini, *Such Am I, O World* (in Hebrew) (Jerusalem: Keter, 1990), p. 137.

Intelligence report, 2 Apr. 1920, CZA L4/738.

Kamel Afandi at the court of inquiry, *Ha'aretz*, 9 May 1920, p. 4.

Statement on the Disorders in Jerusalem, Apr. 1920, p. 14, CZA A 145/102.

3. Sakakini, *Such Am I, O World*, p. 137.

4. Friends tell about Eder, 19 Nov. 1936, CZA K11/354/1.

Ussishkin with Husseini, 21 Oct. 1919, CZA I Z4/1392.

5. Intelligence report, 20 Mar. 1919, CZA Z4/16604; see also undated intelligence report, CZA L4/769.

Storrs to the court of inquiry, *Ha'aretz*, 1 June 1920, p. 4.

6. Petitions from the Arab population, ISA M2 I 1/30.

Zionist Commission to Ussishkin, 27 Feb. 1920, CZA L3/20 II.

Popham to the Zionist Commission, 8 Mar. 1920, ISA M/I 1/30/I.

Report on demonstrations in Jerusalem, 8 Mar. 1920; report on the events linked to the demonstration in Haifa, 8 Mar. 1920, ISA M/I 1/30.

Intelligence report, 9 Mar. 1920, CZA L4/738.

Press survey, 12 Mar. 1920, CZA Z4/16078.

City committee of the Jews of Jerusalem to Storrs, 10 Mar. 1920, ISA M/4/140 I.

Statement on the Disorders in Jerusalem, Apr. 1920, CZA A/145/102, p. 7ff.
Statement on the Disorders in Jerusalem, ISA M/2 1/30 II.

7. Jabotinsky to Weizmann, 12 Mar. 1920, in *The Haganah History Book* (in Hebrew), ed. Ben-Zion Dinur (Tel Aviv: HaSifriya HaTzionit, Ma'archot, 1954), vol. I, p. 913.
Ronald Storrs, *Orientations* (London: Ivor Nicholson and Watson, 1939), p. 316.
"The Holy Riots in Jerusalem," MEC, Adamson Papers.

8. Storrs, *Orientations*, p. 342.
Y. Schneurson, with Dr. Weizmann in Jerusalem in 1920, Weizmann Archive.
Chaim Weizmann, *Trial and Error* (London: Hamish Hamilton, 1949), p. 318.

9. Storrs, *Orientations*, p. 342.
Report of the Court of Inquiry, Apr. 1920, p. 27, Pro WO 32/9616, p. 5.

10. "Jerusalem Defense Scheme, 1919–1920," ISA M/1/43.

11. Ben-Zion Dinur, ed., *Haganah History Book* (in Hebrew) (Tel Aviv: HaSifriya HaTzionit, Ma'archot, 1954), vol. I, part 2, p. 626ff.
Sakakini, *Such Am I, O World*, p. 137.

12. General Money wrote of him. Jabotinsky had inundated top officers with imperious letters. He claimed that they were hostile to the Zionist movement: Money, 23 Mar. 1919, ISA, M/10/239.
Shmuel Katz, *Jabo* (in Hebrew) (Tel Aviv: Dvir, 1993), vol. I, p. 285ff.

13. Storrs, *Orientations*, p. 433.
Katz, *Jabo*, vol. I, p. 377.

14. Katz, *Jabo*, vol. I, p. 345.
Storrs, *Orientations*, pp. 441, 433.

15. Storrs, *Orientations*, p. 372.
Orientations drafts, PCL, Storrs papers, VI/II.

16. Sakakini diary, 7 Apr. 1920. With the kind permission of his daughters.

17. Migdal farm to Zionist Commission, 2 Apr. 1920, CZA L3/237.
Jaffa Jewish Committee to chief administrative officer, 8 Apr. 1920, CZA L3/278.
Rachel Yanait, Yitzhak Avrahami, and Yerah Etzion, eds., *The Haganah in Jerusalem* (in Hebrew) (Organization of Haganah Veterans, 1973), p. 10.

18. The Holy Riots in Jerusalem, 1920. MEC, Adamson Papers.

19. Report of the Court of Inquiry, Apr. 1920, p. 40, PRO WO 32/9616, p. 5.
Yanait, Avrahami, and Etzion, *The Haganah in Jerusalem*, p. 4.

20. List of immigrants on the *Ruslan*, 18 Dec. 1919, CZA 14/1000.

21. Yanait, Avrahami, and Etzion, *The Haganah in Jerusalem*, p. 10.
Yitzhak Rabin, *The Rabin Memoirs* (Boston: Little, Brown and Co., 1979), p. 4ff.

22. Statement on the Disorders in Jerusalem, Apr. 1920, p. 15, CZA A/145/102.
Sakakini diary, 6, 7 Apr. 1920. Quoted from the original with the kind permission of his daughters.

23. Yehuda Banari, "Field Marshall Allenby and the Riots in Jerusalem" (in Hebrew), *Ha-Uma*, vol. 7, no. 1 (25) (July 1968), p. 430.

24. De Sola-Pool report, 7 Apr. 1920, CZA Z4/16084.
Storrs to Ussishkin, 12 Apr. 1920, CZA L3/256.

25. Storrs, *Orientations*, p. 433.

26. Katz, *Jabo*, vol. I, p. 392ff.
Congreve to Wilson, 26 Apr. 1920, IWM, HHW/52a/18. See also: Report of the Court of Inquiry, Apr. 1920, p. 34, PRO WO 32/9616.
Times, 27 Apr. 1920, p. 17.

27. Report of the Court of Inquiry, Apr. 1920, p. 5, PRO WO 32/9616.
Edward Keith-Roach, *Pasha of Jerusalem* (London: Radcliffe Press, 1994), p. 71.

28. Testimony of an officer before the court of inquiry, *Ha'aretz*, 9 May 1920, p. 4.
Katz, *Jabo*, vol. I, p. 396.
Intelligence report, 20 Apr. 1920, CZA L4/738.

29. Report, 19 Apr. 1920, CZA L4/738.

30. Rashid Khalidi, *Palestinian Identity* (New York: Columbia University Press, 1997), p. 168ff.
"The Riots in Jerusalem" (in Hebrew), *Ha'aretz*, 6 Apr. 1920.

31. Joseph Klausner, "After the Riots" (in Hebrew), *Ha'aretz*, 8 Apr. 1920, p. 3.

32. Y.B.M., "Time for Action" (in Hebrew), *Igeret* (*Kuntress*) 39, 21 Feb. 1920, p. 19ff.

33. Richard Meinertzhagen, *Middle East Diary, 1917–1956* (New York: Thomas Yosellof, 1960), pp 3ff., 81.
Bernard Wasserstein, *The British in Palestine* (Oxford: Basil Blackwell, 1991), p. 71.

34. Meinertzhagen to the Foreign Office, 31 Mar. 1920.
Wasserstein, *The British in Palestine*, p. 71.

35. Citizens to Glazebrook, undated, Levin Papers, with the kind permission of the Munin family.

36. Statement on the disorders in Jerusalem, Apr. 1920, p. 10ff., CZA A/145/102.

37. Report on the Attitude of British officials, 30 Apr. 1919, CZA L4/977.

38. Report of the Court of Inquiry, Apr. 1920, p. 46, PRO WO 32/9616.

39. Eder to Weizmann, 21 June 1920, CZA Z4/16033.

40. Weizmann to his wife, 21 and 29 Mar. 1920, in *The Letters and Papers of Chaim Weizmann*, ed. Jehuda Reinharz (New Brunswick, NJ, and Jerusalem: Transaction Books, Rutgers University, and Israel Universities Press, 1977), vol. IX, pp. 324, 330.

41. Wasserstein, *The British in Palestine*, p. 65.
Weizmann to his wife, 19 Apr. 1920, in Reinharz, *The Letters and Papers of Chaim Weizmann*, vol. IX, p. 3.

42. Jehuda Reinharz, *Chaim Weizmann: The Making of a Statesman* (New York: Oxford University Press, 1993), p. 317.

43. J. B. Hobman, ed., *David Eder: Memories of a Modern Pioneer* (London: Victor Gollancz, 1945), p. 159.
Herbert Samuel, *Memoirs* (London: Cresset Press, 1945), p. 150.
Weizmann to his wife, 26 and 29 Apr. 1920, in Reinharz, *The Letters and Papers of Chaim Weizmann*, vol. IX, pp. 340ff., 343.

44. Weizmann to Eder, 8 June 1920, in Reinharz, *The Letters and Papers of Chaim Weizmann*, vol. IX, p. 356.
Demand for the Release of Jabotinsky—Knesset Yisrael, National Council, *Book of Documents* (in Hebrew) (n.p., 1949), p. 12.
L. Yafe, "Through the Grating" (in Hebrew), *Ha'aretz*, 22 Apr. 1920, p. 1.
Katz, *Jabo*, vol. I, pp. 387, 409.

45. Storrs, *Orientations*, p. 431.

46. Katz, *Jabo*, vol. I, p. 419.
Weizmann to Katznelson and Ben-Gurion, 8 June 1920; Weizmann to Eder, 8 June 1920, in Reinharz, *The Letters and Papers of Chaim Weizmann*, vol. IX, p. 364ff.

47. Weizmann to Eder, 8 June 1920, in Reinharz, *The Letters and Papers of Chaim Weizmann*, vol. IX, p. 354ff.

48. Weizmann to his wife, 26 and 29 Apr. 1920, in Reinharz, *The Letters and Papers of Chaim Weizmann*, vol. IX, pp. 341ff., 343.

49. Storrs to Samuel, 7 May 1920, ISA P/1 649/7.
Storrs, *Orientations*, p. 346.

7: A STEADY GAZE AND A FIRM JAW

1. Sakakini to Waters-Taylor and Bols, 21 June 1920, ISA P/354/1899.

2. Khalil al-Sakakini, *Such Am I, O World* (in Hebrew) (Jerusalem: Keter, 1990), p. 108.

3. Sakakini diary, 27 Apr., 26 May, 6 June 1919. Quoted from the original with the kind permission of his daughters.

4. *Ha'aretz*, 26 June 1920, p. 2.

5. Sakakini, *Such Am I, O World*, p. 138.
   Bernard Wasserstein, *The British in Palestine* (Oxford: Basil Blackwell, 1991), p. 83.
   Aref al-Aref, 25 June 1920, ISA M/1/32.
6. Pollock to his father, 6 May and 15 May 1920; Pollock to his mother, 30 May 1920, PRONI D/1581/5.
7. Wilson to Congreve, 12 July 1921, IWM HHW 2/52B/20.
   Wilson to Congreve, 11 Oct. 1921, IWM HHW 2/52B/34.
   Wilson to Congreve, 1 Apr. 1921, IMW HHW 2/52B/12.
8. Congreve to Wilson, 24 Apr. 1920, IWM HHW 2/52a/18.
9. Samuel to his wife, 3 July 1920, ISA P/1 651/41.
   Elisabeth L. McQueen: "A Historic Event in Palestine," *Current History*, vol. 14, no. 4 (1921), p. 583ff.
   Samuel to his wife, 3 July 1920, ISA P/1 651/41.
   Intelligence report, 7 June 1920, CZA L4/739.
   Eder to Weizmann, 21 June 1920, CZA Z4/16033.
10. Wasserstein, *The British in Palestine*, p. 231.
11. Balfour to Samuel, 31 Mar. 1919. ISA P/1 649/5.
    Samuel to his son, 27 Jan., 17 Mar., 9 June, 4 Aug., 18 Dec. 1919. Beatrice Samuel to her son, 25 Dec. 1919, ISA P/1 651/41.
12. Samuel to his son, 22 Feb. 1919. ISA P/1 651/41.
    Samuel to Curzon, 14 May 1920, ISA P/1 649/6.
13. Wasserstein, *The British in Palestine*, p. 88.
    Samuel to his wife, 4 Aug. 1920, ISA P/1 651/41.
    Samuel to his son, 16 Apr. 1920, ISA P/1 651/41.
    Bernard Wasserstein, *Herbert Samuel: A Political Life* (Oxford: Clarendon Press, 1992), p. 236ff.
14. Weizmann to his wife, 21, 29 Mar. 1920, in *The Letters and Papers of Chaim Weizmann*, ed. Jehuda Reinharz (New Brunswick, NJ, and Jerusalem: Transaction Books, Rutgers University, and Israel Universities Press, 1977), vol. IX, pp. 324, 330.
    Yitzhak Shirion, *Memoirs* (self-published, 1943), p. 203.
    ISA P/1 654.
15. Theodor Herzl, *The Jewish State* (in Hebrew) (Tel Aviv: Yediot Aharonot, 1978), p. 28.
16. Max Nordau, *Zionist Writings* (in Hebrew) (Tel Aviv: HaSifriya HaTzionit, 1960), book III, p. 44.
17. Mordechai Ben-Hillel Hacohen, *The Wars of the Nations* (in Hebrew) (Jerusalem: Yad Ben-Zvi, 1985), vol. II, p. 689.
    Yosef Gorny, *The Arab Question and the Jewish Problem* (in Hebrew) (Tel Aviv: Am Oved, 1985), p. 56ff.
    Hacohen diary, 9 Av 5695–8 Aug. 1935 (in Hebrew), National Library, manuscript division, C 514.
18. A. A. Kabak, "For the Repair of the Palestinian School," *Ha'aretz*, 2 Sept. 1920, p. 3.
    Baruch Ben-Avram and Henry Nir, *Studies in the Third Aliya: Image and Reality* (in Hebrew) (Jerusalem: Yad Ben-Zvi, 1995), p. 176.
19. Rafaela Bilsky Ben-Hur, *Every Individual a King: Ze'ev Jabotinsky's Social and Political Thought* (in Hebrew) (Tel Aviv: Dvir, 1988), p. 173.
20. Nurit Reichel, " 'Roots' or 'Horizons': A Portrait of the Desired Palestinian Pupil in the Years 1889–1933" (in Hebrew), *Katedra* 83 (Apr. 1997), p. 55ff.
21. Letters to Gittel, Rivka, Shlomit, and Rachel, Levine Papers. With the kind permission of the Munin family.
22. Advertisement, *Ha'aretz*, 7 Nov. 1923, p. 1.
23. Sakakini, *Such Am I, O World*, pp. 39, 129, 89, 81, 162, 201.
    Khalil al-Sakakini to Sari Sakakini, 12 Dec. 1932, 7 Jan. 1933, and 21 Jan. 1933, P/378/2646.
    Hala Sakakini, *Jerusalem and I O World*, (Amman: n.p., 1990), p. 73.
24. Sakakini, *Such Am I, O World*, p. 130.

25. Sakakini, *Such Am I, O World*, p. 162.
    Mordechai Ben-Hillel Hacohen, *The Wars of the Nations* (in Hebrew) (Jerusalem: Yad Ben-Zvi, 1985), vol. II, p. 689.
26. *England and the English* (in Hebrew), trans. M. Ezrahi Krishevsky (Tel Aviv: Sifria Amamit, HaPoel HaTzair, 1921), p. 3ff.
27. Hacohen, *The Wars of the Nations*, vol. II, p. 616.
    Weizmann to Balfour, 30 May 1918, in *The Letters and Papers of Chaim Weizmann*, ed. Dvora Barzilay and Barnett Litvinoff (New Brunswick, NJ, and Jerusalem: Transaction Books, Rutgers University, and Israel Universities Press, 1977), vol. VIII, p. 210.
28. Ben-Gurion to Wauchope, 29 to 30 July 1934, CZA S/25/16/1.
29. A. T., "Metullah and Deschanel" (in Hebrew), *Ha'aretz*, 22 Jan. 1920, p. 1.
    Z. Jabotinsky, "The Crisis in Palestine (Don't Exaggerate)" (in Hebrew), *Ha'aretz*, 28 Mar. 1920, p. 2.
30. Kisch to Brodetzsky, 3 Dec. 1928, CZA S25/1.
31. Kisch to Rothschild, 28 Aug. 1929, CZA S25/1.
32. L. S. Amery, *My Political Life* (London: Hutchinson, 1955), p. 116.
    Hacohen, *The Wars of the Nations*, vol. II, p. 881.
33. Humphrey Bowman, *Middle-East Window* (London: Longrams, Green and Co., 1942), p. 328ff.
    Shmuel Katz, *Jabo* (in Hebrew) (Tel Aviv: Dvir, 1993), vol. I, p. 275.
    Weizmann to Money, 26 Jan. 1919, in *The Letters and Papers of Chaim Weizmann*, ed. Jehuda Reinharz (New Brunswick, NJ, and Jerusalem: Transaction Books, Rutgers University, and Israel Universities Press, 1977), vol. IX, p. 106.
    Bernard Wasserstein, "British Officials and the Arab-Jewish Conflict in Palestine, 1917–1929" (thesis submitted to the Faculty of Modern History in the University of Oxford, 1974), p. 31.
    Chaim Arlosoroff, *Jerusalem Diary* (in Hebrew) (Tel Aviv: Mifleget Poalei Eretz Yisrael, 1949), p. 59.
34. *Hadashot Mi-Ha-Aretz Ha-Kedoshah*, 16 May 1918, p. 1.
    Weizmann to Samuel, 29 July 1920, in *The Letters and Papers of Chaim Weizmann*, ed. Bernard Wasserstein (New Brunswick, NJ, and Jerusalem: Transaction Books, Rutgers University, and Israel Universities Press, 1977), vol. X, p. 3.
    Wasserstein, "British Officials," p. 31ff.
35. Herbert Samuel, *Memoirs* (London: Cresset Press, 1945), p. 154.
36. Samuel to Turner, 5 Dec. 1959 and 16 Mar. 1960. ISA P/1 650/35.
37. Gad Frumkin, *The Way of a Judge in Jerusalem* (in Hebrew) (Tel Aviv: Dvir, 1954), p. 265.
    The Seventh Arab Congress to the Higher Commissioner (undated), CZA S/25 6651.
38. F. H. Kisch, *Palestine Diary* (London: Victor Gollancz, 1938), p. 121. See also: Arthur Ruppin, *Chapters of My Life in the Building of the Land and the Nation, 1920–1942* (in Hebrew) (Tel Aviv: Am Oved, 1968), p. 96.
    Ezriel Karlebach, *Book of Figures* (in Hebrew) (Tel Aviv: Ma'ariv, 1959), p. 349.
    Margery Bentwich to her sister, 7 June 1920. With the kind permission of Ari Shavit.
39. Samuel, *Memoirs*, p. 165.
    Samuel to his wife, June–Nov. 1920, ISA P/1 651/41.
40. Beatrice Samuel to her son, 2 May 1920, ISA P/1 651/46.
41. Samuel to his wife, 20 Aug. and 26 Sept. 1920, ISA P/1 651/41.
42. Samuel to his son, 14 July and 20 Aug. 1920, ISA P/1 651/41.
43. Ruppin, *Chapters of My Life in the Building of the Land and the Nation*, p. 14.
44. Zionist Organization to all Zionist federations, 18 Apr. 1919, CZA I L3/31.
    Samuel to Weizmann, 29 Nov. 1920, CZA Z4/15445. See also: M. Mossek, *Palestine Immigration Policy Under Sir Herbert Samuel* (London: Frank Cass, 1978).
    Weizmann to Samuel, 27 June 1921, in *The Letters and Papers of Chaim Weizmann*, vol. X, p. 209ff.
    Moshe Lissak, "Immigration, Absorption, and the Building of Society in Palestine:

Israel in the 1920s, 1918–1930" (in Hebrew), in *The History of the Jewish Yishuv in Palestine from the Time of the First Aliya (The British Mandate)* (in Hebrew), ed. Moshe Lissak and Gabriel Cohen (Jerusalem: Israel Academy of Sciences, Bialik Institute, 1994), part II, p. 215.

45. Samuel to his son, 4 Aug. 1920, ISA P/1 651/41.
Samuel to his son, 21 May 1922, ISA P1/651/47.

46. Samuel to Colonial Secretary, 4 Mar. 1925, ISA P/649/12.
Churchill memorandum, Aug. 1921, PRO CO733 14.
Sheila Hattis-Roleff, "Sir Herbert Samuel's Economic Development Policy: Rule and Implementation in the First Year of His Term as High Commissioner 1920–1921" (in Hebrew), *Katedra* 12 (1970), p. 70ff.
Norman Rose, *Churchill: An Unruly Life* (New York: Simon and Schuster, 1995), p. 156.

47. Norman Cohn, *Warrant for Genocide: The Myth of the Jewish World-Conspiracy and the Protocols of the Learned Elders of Zion* (New York: Harper and Row, 1966), p. 149ff.

48. Samuel, *Memoirs*, p. 169.
Bernard Wasserstein, *Herbert Samuel: A Political Life* (Oxford: Clarendon Press, 1992), p. 252.

49. Katz, *Jabo*, vol. I, p. 442ff.

50. Martin Gilbert, *Winston S. Churchill* (London: Heinemann, 1977), vol. IV, Companion part 2, pp. 860, 912, 1,010–12; part 3, pp. 1,110, 1,028–9.
Norman Rose, "Churchill and Zionism," in *Churchill*, ed. Robert Blake and Wm. Roger Louis (Oxford: Oxford University Press, 1993), p. 147ff. See also: Michael J. Cohen, *Churchill and the Jews* (London: Frank Cass, 1985).

51. Wasserstein, *The British in Palestine*, p. 97.
Presidium of the Va'ad Le'umi to Churchill, 21 Mar. 1921, Knesset Yisrael, Ha-Va'ad Ha-Le'umi, *Book of Documents* (in Hebrew) (n.p., 1949), p. 28ff.
To Ussishkin (unsigned), 5 Apr. 1921, CZA L3/413.
To Eder (unsigned), 21 Apr. 1921, CZA L3/413.
Ilan Shchori, *A Dream That Became a City* (in Hebrew) (Tel Aviv: Avivim, 1990), p. 380.
M. Glickson, "Churchill's Speeches" (in Hebrew), *Ha'aretz*, 5 Apr. 1921, p. 2.

52. Wasserstein, *The British in Palestine*, p. 266.
Samuel memorandum, 11 Apr. 1921, ISA M/10/245.

53. Frumkin, *The Way of a Judge in Jerusalem*, p. 285.

54. Samuel, *Memoirs*, pp. 161, 168.
See also the discussions of the Advisory Council, CZA II L 3/9.
Frumkin, *The Way of a Judge in Jerusalem*, p. 252.

55. Samuel to Curzon, 16 Dec. 1920, ISA P/1 649/7.

56. Ya'akov Reuveni, *The Mandatory Administration in Palestine, 1920–1948: A Historical Political Analysis* (in Hebrew) (Ramat Gan: Bar-Ilan University, 1993), p. 26.
Edward Keith-Roach, *Pasha of Jerusalem* (London: Radcliffe Press, 1994), p. 91.

57. Humphrey Bowman, *Middle-East Window* (London: Longrams, Green and Co., 1942), p. 236.

58. Samuel to Churchill, 4 Mar. 1925, ISA P/649/12.

59. Edwin Samuel, *A Lifetime in Jerusalem* (Jerusalem: Israel Universities Press, 1970), p. 64.

60. Baruch Kimmerling and Joel S. Migdal, *Palestinians: The Making of a People* (New York: Free Press, 1993), p. 18. See also: Ylana Miller, *Government and Society in Rural Palestine, 1920–1948* (Austin: University of Texas Press, 1985), p. 48ff.

61. Edwin Samuel, *A Lifetime in Jerusalem* (Jerusalem: Israel Universities Press, 1970), pp. 64ff., 74ff.
Harry Luke and Edward Keith-Roach, eds., *The Handbook of Palestine and Trans-Jordan* (London: Macmillan, 1930), p. 226.

62. Gideon Biger, *Crown Colony or National Home: The Influence of British Rule on Palestine, 1917–1930: A Geographical-Historical Examination* (in Hebrew) (Jerusalem: Yad Ben-Zvi, 1983), p. 160.

63. W. F. Stirling, *Safety Last* (London: Hollis and Carter, 1953), p. 114.

64. Samuel to Churchill, 4 Mar. 1925, ISA P/649/12.

65. Reuveni, *The Mandatory Administration in Palestine*, p. 111ff.

66. Reuveni, *The Mandatory Administration in Palestine*, p. 109.

67. Seventh Arab Congress to the High Commissioner, undated, CZA S25/665.

68. Robert Heussler, *Yesterday's Rulers: The Making of the British Colonial Service* (Syracuse: Syracuse University Press, 1963), pp. 74, 85, 216.

69. Reuveni, *The Mandatory Administration in Palestine*, p. 109ff.

70. Bramley memorandum, 14 Jan. 1925, RCS, Bramley papers.
Stirling, *Safety Last*, p. 118.

71. Harry Luke, *Cities and Men* (London: Geoffrey Bles, 1953), p. 213.

72. Heussler, *Yesterday's Rulers*, pp. 4, 205.

73. C. R. Ashbee, *A Palestine Notebook* (New York: Doubleday, 1923), pp. 156, 270.

74. E. C. Hodgkin, *Thomas Hodgkin: Letters from Palestine, 1932–1936* (London: Quartet Books, 1986), p. 127.

75. Sarah Ezriahu, *Chapters of My Life* (in Hebrew) (Neuman, 1957), p. 206ff. See also: Chaim Arlosoroff, *Jerusalem Diary* (in Hebrew) (Tel Aviv: Mifleget Poalei Eretz Yisrael, 1949), p. 283ff.

76. League of Nations Union to Rathbone, 6 July 1933.
ULL. RP XIV, Eleanor Rathbone Papers, 2.5.(33).
Colonial Office to Rathbone, 21 Feb. 1933.
ULL. RP XIV, Eleanor Rathbone Papers, 2.5.(8).

77. Luke, *Cities and Men*, p. 213.
Samuel, *A Lifetime in Jerusalem*, p. 85.

78. Keith-Roach, *Pasha of Jerusalem*, pp. 45, 110ff, 148.

79. Bowman, *Middle-East Window*, p. 296.

80. Reuveni, *The Mandatory Administration in Palestine*, p. 118ff. See also: Norman Bentwich, "The Legal System of Palestine Under the Mandate," *Middle East Journal* (Jan. 1948), p. 33ff.
Horace B. Samuel, *Unholy Memoirs of the Holy Land* (London: Hogarth Press, 1930), p. 177.

81. Frumkin, *The Way of a Judge*, p. 238ff.
Mordecai Sherman and the Palestine Electric Corporation Ltd. V. Feivel Danovitz, Civil Appeal No. 113 of 1940, *The Law Reports of Palestine*, vol. VII (1940), p. 303ff.
London Society for Promoting Christianity Among the Jews and Others v. Lionel Alexander William Orr and Others, Civil Appeal No. 29 of 1947, *The Law Reports of Palestine*, vol. XIV (1947), p. 218ff.
Asaf Lahovsky, "Colonial Images and English Justice in the Palestine Supreme Court of the Mandate" (in Hebrew), *Zmanim* 56 (Summer 1996), p. 87ff.
"No Confidence" (in Hebrew), *Davar*, 7 Feb. 1930, p. 1.
The Attorney General v. Zalman Rubashoff (H.C. No. 11/33), *Collection of Judgments of the Courts of Palestine, 1919–1933* (Tel Aviv: L. M. Rotenberg, 1935), p. 369ff.

82. Keith-Roach, *Pasha of Jerusalem*, p. 91.
Reuveni, *The Mandatory Administration in Palestine*, pp. 121, 133.

83. Samuel in his farewell message, 30 Apr. 1925, ISA P/649/12. See also: Speech by Samuel, 28 Nov. 1925, ISA P/649/12.
Palestine. Report of the High Commissioner on the Administration of Palestine, Colonial No. 15 (London: HMSO, 1925).

84. Nahum Gross, "The Economic Policy of the Mandatory British Administration in Palestine" (in Hebrew), *Katedra* 24 (June 1982), p. 153ff, and *Katedra* 25 (Sept. 1982), p. 135ff.

85. Weizmann and others to Samuel, 3 July 1920, CZA Z4/3766. See also: Barbara J. Smith, *The Roots of Separatism in Palestine: British Economic Policy, 1920–1929* (Syracuse: Syracuse University Press, 1993), p. 57ff.

86. Unsigned memorandum (Feb. 1923), ISA M/5/158II. See also: The Seventh Arab Congress to the High Commissioner (undated), CZA S/25 665.
M. F. Abcarius, *Palestine Through the Fog of Propaganda* (London: Hutchinson and Co., 1946), p. 105ff.

87. Ya'akov Metzer and Oded Kaplan, *Jewish Economy and Arab Economy in Palestine: Product, Employment, and Growth in the Mandatory Period* (in Hebrew) (Falk Center, 1990).

88. Smith, *The Roots of Separatism in Palestine*, p. 156ff.

89. Buckingham Palace to Samuel, 10 Aug. 1920, ISA P/649/7 1.

90. Samuel to his wife, 31 July 1920, ISA P/1.

91. Samuel to his wife, 26 Aug. 1920; Samuel to his wife, 7 Sept. 1920, CZA P/1 651/41.

8: JAFFA, 1921

1. Yitzhak Kafkafi and Uri Brenner, eds., *On Y. Ch. Brenner: More Memories* (in Hebrew) (Tel Aviv: Ha-Kibbutz Ha-Me'uhad, 1991), pp. 209, 213.

2. Mordecai Kushnir, ed., *Yosef Chaim Brenner: Selected Memories* (in Hebrew) (Tel Aviv: Ha-Kibbutz Ha-Me'uhad, 1944), pp. 151, 192.

3. "Yosef Chaim Brenner" (in Hebrew), *Ha'aretz*, 4 May 1921, p. 3.

4. David Ben-Gurion and Yitzhak Ben-Zvi, *Palestine in the Past and Present* (in Hebrew) (Jerusalem: Yad Ben-Zvi, 1979), p. 198.

5. *The Collected Works of Brenner* (in Hebrew) (Tel Aviv: Dvir, Ha-Kibbutz Ha-Me'uhad, 1960), vol. II, p. 323.
Y. Ch. Brenner, "From a Notebook" (in Hebrew), *Kontrass* 77, 28 Apr. 1921, p. 12ff.

6. Kafkafi and Brenner, *On Y. Ch. Brenner*, p. 215.

7. Testimonies of Wainright and Mohammed Abu Riali to the Haycraft Commission, CZA L3/483. See also: *Palestine. Disturbances in May 1921. Reports of the Commission of Inquiry with Correspondence Relating Thereto*, Cmd. 1540. (London: HMSO, 1921), p. 23. *Records of the United States Consulate in Jerusalem, Palestine*, Confidential Correspondence, 1920–1935 [Record group 84, USNAM].

8. *Palestine. Disturbances in May 1921. Reports of the Commission of Inquiry with Correspondence Relating Thereto*, Cmd. 1540 (London: HMSO, 1921), pp. 43, 44. Survivor testimony, *Kontrass*, 11 May 1921, p. 6 ff. See also: Tsiona Rabau, *In Tel Aviv on the Sands* (in Hebrew) (Tel Aviv: Masada, 1973), p. 95.

9. W. F. Stirling, *Safety Last* (London: Hollis and Carter, 1953), p. 114.
Letter to *Do'ar HaYom*, 1 Sept. 1921, CZA J1/78.

10. Stirling, *Safety Last*, p. 114.

11. Testimony of Rudenberg and Sandak before the Haycraft Commission, CZA L3/483.

12. Testimony of Meler before the Haycraft Commission, CZA L3/483.

13. Testimony of Wager before the Haycraft Commission, CZA L3/483.

14. Edward Keith-Roach, *Pasha of Jerusalem* (London: Radcliffe Press, 1994), p. 87.
Ha'aretz, 4 May 1921, p. 2.

15. M. Mossek, *Palestine Immigration Policy Under Sir Herbert Samuel* (London: Frank Cass, 1978), p. 20.

16. Yitzhak Ben-Zvi and David Yellin at the National Council, 5 May 1921, CZA J1/138.

17. Testimony of Eder before the Haycraft Commission, CZA L3/483.

18. Sokolow in the National Council, 8 May 1921, CZA J1/139. See also: Eder's notes, May 1921, CZA AK 41/2.
Y. L. Fishman in the National Council, 3 May 1921, CZA J1/7224.

19. Ben-Zion Dinur, ed. in chief, *Haganah History Book* (in Hebrew) (Tel Aviv: HaSifriya HaTzionit and Ma'archot, 1965), vol. II, part 1, p. 81.
Yehuda Erez, ed., *Book of the Third Aliya* (Tel Aviv: Am Oved, 1964), vol. I, p. 236.
Kalvarisky in the National Council, 3 May 1921, CZA J1/7224.

20. Kafkafi and Brenner, *On Y. Ch. Brenner*, p. 218.

21. Eder to the Zionist Organization in London, 15 May 1921, CZA L3/413.

Margolin testimony before the Haycraft Commission, *Ha'aretz*, 7 and 8 June 1921, p. 3.
Palestine. Disturbances in May 1921. Reports of the Commission of Inquiry with Correspondence Relating Thereto, Cmd. 1540. (London: HMSO, 1921), p. 30.
See also: Ben-Zion Dinur, ed., *Haganah History Book* (in Hebrew) (Tel Aviv: HaSifriya HaTzionit, Ma'archot, 1954), vol. II, part 1, p. 98.

22. Al-Asmar and Abu-Riali testimony to the Haycraft Commission, CZA L/483. Stirling, *Safety Last*, p. 115.
Dinur, *Haganah History Book*, vol. II, part 1, p. 103. See also: *Palestine: Disturbances in May 1921. Reports of the Commission of Inquiry with Correspondence Relating Thereto*, Cmd. 1540 (London: HMSO, 1921), p. 30.

23. Anita Shapira, *Berl* (in Hebrew) (Tel Aviv: Am Oved, 1980), part I, p. 169.
Mordecai Kushnir, "In the House of Brenner and the Yatzkers" (in Hebrew), *Kontrass*, 11 May 1921, p. 16.
Kafkafi and Brenner, *On Y. Ch. Brenner*, p. 221.

24. Avraham Ya'ari, *Memories of the Land of Israel* (in Hebrew) (Tel Aviv: Masada, 1974), pp. 1, 170.

25. Rabbi Benjamin, *Families, Writers, Faces* (in Hebrew) (The Public Committee for the Publication of the Writings of Rabbi Benjamin, 1960), p. 210ff.
S. Y. Agnon, *From Myself to Myself* (in Hebrew) (Tel Aviv: Schocken, 1976), p. 111.
Ze'ev Vilnai, *Tel Aviv-Jaffa: The Largest of Israel's Cities* (in Hebrew) (Ahiever, 1965), p. 276.
Shapira, *Berl*, part I, p. 169.

26. Nahum Shadmi, *A Straight Line in the Cycle of Life* (in Hebrew) (Tel Aviv: Ministry of Defense, 1995), p. 58.

27. *Palestine. Disturbances in May 1921. Reports of the Commission of Inquiry with Correspondence Relating Thereto*, Cmd. 1540 (London: HMSO, 1921), p. 60.

28. Ilan Shchori, *A Dream That Became a City* (in Hebrew) (Tel Aviv: Avivim, 1990), p. 324.

29. Shchori, *Dream*, p. 324.

30. Ezra Danin, *Zionist Under Any Condition* (in Hebrew) (Kidum, 1987), p. 42.

31. Shchori, *Dream*, pp. 388, 145.

32. Y.-Y., "Entrenchment" (in Hebrew), *Kontrass*, 20 May 1921, p. 7.
A.M.K., "In These Days," *Kontrass*, 21 May 1921, p. 11.
M. Glickson, "The Method," *Kontrass*, 20 May 1921, p. 3; M.S.-B., "On the Situation," *Kontrass*, 21 May 1921, p. 1.
The Collected Works of Brenner (in Hebrew) (Tel Aviv: Dvir, Ha-Kibbutz Ha-Me'uhad, 1960), vol. II, p. 323.

33. *Hadashot Mi-Ha-Aretz Ha-Kedosha*, first year, no. 11 (21 June 1918), p. 2.
Baruch Ben-Anat, "The Great Moment Found a Small Generation: The Nordau Plan, 1919–1920," *Ha-Tzionut* 19 (1995), p. 89ff.
S. Schwartz, "The Carlsbad Conference" (in Hebrew), *Ha'aretz*, 7 Sept. 1920, p. 1.
S. Schwartz, "Help for Ukrainian Jewry," *Ha'aretz*, 7 May 1920, p. 1.
Hadashot Mi-Ha-Aretz Ha-Kedosha, 19 June 1919, pp. 3, 4.
Ben-Zvi and others in the Zionist Executive, 22 Oct. 1922, CZA.
Conversation with Yisrael Belkind, *Do'ar HaYom*, 21 Mar. 1923, p. 4; Yisrael Belkind on the Ukrainian orphans, *Do'ar HaYom*, 28 Dec. 1923, p. 4.
"Arrangements for the Orphans" (in Hebrew), *Ha'aretz*, 22 Sept. 1922, p. 3; "Letter from Jaffa" (in Hebrew), *Ha'aretz*, 4 Oct. 1922, p. 2.
Ahad Ha'am, "Building," *The Complete Works of Ahad Ha'am* (Tel Aviv: Dvir, 1947), p. 334.

34. "To Inside and to Outside" (in Hebrew), *Ha'aretz*, 9 May 1921, p. 2.
"To all the House of Israel" (in Hebrew), May 1921, Knesset Yisrael, Ha-Va'ad Ha-Le'umi, *Book of Documents* (Jerusalem: n.p., 1949), p. 45.
S. Schwartz, "National Catastrophe and Insult" (in Hebrew), *Ha'aretz*, 13 May 1921, p. 2.

Shapira, *Berl*, part I, p. 172ff.

Shabtai Teveth, *The Burning Ground* (Tel Aviv: Schocken, 1997), vol. II, p. 81ff.

35. Yehoshua Porat, *The Growth of the Palestinian Arab National Movement, 1918–1929* (in Hebrew) (Tel Aviv: Am Oved, 1976), vol. I, p. 104ff.

36. Tewfiq Hammed and Shibly Jamel to the President of the League of Nations.

37. Khalil al-Sakakini, *Such Am I, O World* (in Hebrew) (Jerusalem: Keter, 1990), p. 140.

38. *Palestine. Disturbances in May 1921. Reports of the Commission of Inquiry with Correspondence Relating Thereto*, Cmd. 1540 (London: HMSO, 1921), p. 24.

   "In Blunderland," *Jewish Chronicle*, 11 Nov. 1921, p. 7.

   Bernard Wasserstein, *The British in Palestine* (Oxford: Basil Blackwell, 1991), p. 117. See also: Yerah Etzion, ed., *The Haganah in Jerusalem* (Tel Aviv: Haganah Veterans Organization, 1973), p. 21ff.

39. "Questions to the Government" (in Hebrew), *Ha'aretz*, 4 Nov. 1921, p. 1; Brutus, "Mr. Storrs and His Work in Jerusalem," *Ha'aretz*, 8 Nov. 1921.

40. Shabtai Teveth, *Ben-Gurion and the Arabs of Palestine* (in Hebrew) (Tel Aviv: Schocken, 1985), p. 86.

41. Ronald Storrs, *Orientations* (London: Ivor Nicholson and Watson, 1939), p. 378.

   Storrs papers, PCL, File VI/II.

42. Joseph Klausner, "On the Judgment" (in Hebrew), *Ha'aretz*, 27 Nov. 1921, p. 1.

   "Trial of the Defendants in the Murder of Y. Ch. Brenner and His Companions" (in Hebrew), *Ha'aretz*, 25 Jan. 1922.

43. S. A. Pen, "And for the Informers" (in Hebrew), *Ha'aretz*, 22 Jan. 1923, p. 2. See also: S. A. Pen, "And to All the Evildoers" (in Hebrew), *Ha'aretz*, 28 Jan. 1923, p. 3.

   David Tidhar, *In the Service of the Homeland, 1912–1960* (Hotza' at Yedidim, 1960), p. 99.

   "On the Trial of David Bar" (in Hebrew), *Ha'aretz*, 20 Mar. 1923, p. 3.

44. Ben-Gurion diary, 7 July 1926, BGHA.

   Avi Katzman, "The Life and Death of the First Hebrew Terrorist" (in Hebrew), *Koteret Rashit*, no. 136 (10 July 1985), p. 24.

45. Log of the events, 15 May 1921, ISA M/4/144.

   "Speech of the High Commissioner" (in Hebrew), *Ha'aretz*, 5 June 1921, p. 3; CZA Z4/16055. See also: Wasserstein, *The British in Palestine*, p. 89ff.

   Eder to the Zionist Executive in London, 4 June 1921, CZA A226/31/1.

46. Eder to the Haycraft Commission, CZA L3/488. See also: J. B. Hobman, ed., *David Eder: Memories of a Modern Pioneer* (London: Victor Gollancz, 1945), p. 162.

   Eder to Cohen, 9 May 1921, CZA Z4/16151.

47. Eder to the Zionist Executive in London, 4 June 1921, CZA A226/31/1. See also: Sofia Berger-Mohel memo, ISA P/649/25.

48. Arthur Ruppin, *Chapters of My Life in the Building of the Land and the Nation, 1920–1942* (in Hebrew) (Tel Aviv: Am Oved, 1968), pp. 17, 20ff.

   Ruppin and Sokolow in the National Council, 8 May 1921, CZA J1/139. See also: Correspondence between Grindle and Landman, 10–17 May 1921, CZA I L3/31.

49. The National Council to the High Commissioner, 10 and 20 May 1921; Yitzhak Ben-Zvi to the High Commissioner, 11 May 1921.

   Open letter by the National Council, 7 June 1921, Knesset Yisrael, National Council, *Book of Documents* (in Hebrew) (n.p., 1949), p. 39ff.

50. Weizmann to Deedes, 31 July 1921, in *The Letters and Papers of Chaim Weizmann*, ed. Bernard Wasserstein (New Brunswick, NJ, and Jerusalem: Transaction Books, Rutgers University, and Israel Universities Press, 1977), vol. X, p. 238.

   Evyatar Friesel, "Herbert Samuel's Reassessment of Zionism in 1921," *Studies in Zionism*, vol. 5, no. 2 (1984), p. 213ff.

51. Weizmann to his wife, 10 Aug. 1921, in Wasserstein, *The Letters and Papers of Chaim Weizmann*, vol. X, p. 250.

   Chaim Weizmann, *Trial and Error* (London: Hamish Hamilton, 1949), p. 343.

52. Weizmann to Ahad Ha'am, 30 July 1921, in Wasserstein, *The Letters and Papers of Chaim Weizmann*, vol. X, p. 234.
53. Kisch to Brodetsky, 3 Dec. 1928, CZA S25/1.
    Norman Bentwich and Michael Kisch, *Brigadier Kisch, Soldier and Zionist* (in Hebrew) (Tel Aviv: Ma'archot, 1978), p. 18.
54. Weizmann to Samuel, 12 and 27 June, in Wasserstein, *The Letters and Papers of Chaim Weizmann*, vol. X, pp. 202ff., 209ff.
    Weizmann to Eder, 13 June 1921, in Wasserstein, *The Letters and Papers of Chaim Weizmann*, vol. X, p. 203.
55. Shabtai Teveth, *Ben-Gurion and the Arabs of Palestine* (in Hebrew) (Tel Aviv: Schocken, 1985), p. 86.
56. Minute by HWG, 7 May 1921, PRO CO 733/17a24068.
57. Bernard Wasserstein, ed., *The Letters and Papers of Chaim Weizmann* (New Brunswick, NJ, and Jerusalem: Transaction Books, Rutgers University, and Israel Universities Press, 1977), vol. X, p. 254, editor's note.
58. Weizmann to Shmarya Levin, 15 July 1921, in Wasserstein, *The Letters and Papers of Chaim Weizmann*, vol. X, p. 217.
59. Jehuda Reinharz, *Chaim Weizmann: The Making of a Statesman* (New York: Oxford University Press, 1993), p. 355.
    Evyatar Friesel, "Herbert Samuel's Reassessment of Zionism in 1921," *Studies in Zionism*, vol. V, no. 2 (1984), p. 235.
60. Herbert Samuel, *Memoirs* (London: Cresset Press, 1945), pp. 225, 168.
    Samuel to his son, 25 Dec. 1919, ISA P1/651/45.
61. Sokolow with Samuel, 8 May 1921, CZA J1/139.
62. Friesel, "Herbert Samuel's Reassessment of Zionism," p. 224. See also: Elisabeth Monroe, *Britain's Moment in the Middle East, 1914–1971* (Baltimore: Johns Hopkins University Press, 1981), p. 142.
63. Wilson to Congreve, 1 Apr. 1921, IWM HHW 2/52B/12.
    Wilson to Congreve, 11 Oct. 1921, IWM HHW 2/52B/34.
64. Attachment, Wilson to Congreve, 16 Dec. 1921, IWM HHW/2/52B/42.
    Weizmann to Joseph Cowan, 13 Dec. 1921, in Wasserstein, *The Letters and Papers of Chaim Weizmann*, vol. X, p. 325.
65. Weizmann to Churchill, 22 July 1921, CZA Z4/16055.
    Friesel, "Herbert Samuel's Reassessment of Zionism," p. 224.
    C. R. Ashbee, *A Palestine Notebook* (New York: Doubleday, 1923), pp. 267, 277.
66. Weizmann to Balfour, 8 July 1921, in Wasserstein, *The Letters and Papers of Chaim Weizmann*, vol. X, p. 213.
67. Weizmann to Peter Schweizer and others, 8 Sept. 1921, in Wasserstein, *The Letters and Papers of Chaim Weizmann*, vol. X, p. 255.
68. Weizmann with Lloyd George and others, 22 July 1921, CZA Z4/16055.
    Weizmann to Ahad Ha'am, 30 July 1921; Weizmann to Deedes, 31 July 1921, in Wasserstein, *The Letters and Papers of Chaim Weizmann*, vol. X, pp. 233ff., 237.
    Wasserstein, *The British in Palestine*, p. 107.
69. Wilson to Congreve, 11 Oct. 1921, IWM HHW 2/52B/34.
    Wilson to Congreve, 1 Apr. 1921, IMW HHW 2/52B/12.
70. Bentwich and Kisch, *Brigadier Kisch, Soldier and Zionist*, pp. 89, 122.
    Weizmann, *Trial and Error*, p. 367.
71. Kisch diary, 14 Sept. 1925, CZA S25/3272.
    F. H. Kisch, *Palestine Diary* (London: Victor Gollancz, 1938), p. 213.
72. Kisch to Brodetsky, 3 Dec. 1928, CZA S25/1.
    Yigal Ilam, *The Jewish Agency: First Years* (Hebrew) (Tel Aviv: HaSifriya HaTzionit, 1990), p. 459.
73. Moody Papers, RHL, Mss. Brit. Emp. s382 3:3.
    Evyatar Friesel, "British Officials and the Situation in Palestine, 1923," *Middle Eastern Studies*, vol. 23, no. 2 (Apr. 1987), p. 194ff.

74. Minutes, Standing Defence Sub-Committee, 12 July 1923, PRO CO 537/809.
75. Stirling, *Safety Last*, p. 122ff.
   Philip Graves, *Palestine, the Land of Three Faiths* (London: Jonathan Cape, 1923), p. 233ff.
   Humphrey Bowman, *Middle-East Window* (London: Longrams Green and Co., 1942), p. 325ff.
76. Friends tell about Eder, 19 Nov. 1936, CZA K11/354/1.

9: CULTURE WARS

1. Aharon Tsarnivsky, "Albert Einstein, the Generation's Greatest" (in Hebrew), *Ha'aretz*, 9 Feb. 1921, p. 2.
2. Jehuda Reinharz, *Chaim Weizmann: The Making of a Statesman* (New York: Oxford University Press, 1993), p. 363.
   F. H. Kisch, *Palestine Diary* (London: Victor Gollancz, 1938), p. 166.
3. David Kroyanker, *Jerusalem Architecture: Building in the British Mandate Period* (in Hebrew) (Jerusalem: Keter, 1991), p. 251.
   C. R. Ashbee, *A Palestine Notebook* (New York: Doubleday, 1923), p. 150.
4. Einstein diary, 13 Feb. 1923. National Library, Jerusalem, Manuscript Division, Einstein Archive, 29–129.
   Norman and Helen Bentwich, *Mandate Memoirs, 1918–1948* (London: Hogarth Press, 1965), p. 89.
   "Einstein's Lecture on Mt. Scopus" (in Hebrew), *Ha'aretz*, 11 Feb. 1923, p. 3.
   Kisch, *Palestine Diary*, p. 29ff.
   Kisch diary, 7 Feb. 1923, CZA S25/564.
5. Einstein diary, 3 Feb. 1923. National Library, Jerusalem, Manuscript Division, Einstein Archive, 29–129.
6. Einstein diary, 5 Feb. 1923. National Library, Jerusalem, Manuscript Division, Einstein Archive, 29–129. See also: N. and H. Bentwich, *Mandate Memoirs*, p. 89.
7. Yossi Katz, "The Turning Point in the Attitude of Ussishkin and Hovevei Tzion to the Development of Jerusalem and to the Establishment of the Hebrew University Before the First World War" (in Hebrew), in *Jerusalem in Zionist Consciousness and Practice* (in Hebrew), ed. Hagit Levsky (Jerusalem: Merkaz Zalman Shazar, Hebrew University, 1989), p. 107ff.
8. David N. Myers, *Re-inventing the Jewish Past* (New York: Oxford University Press, 1995), p. 198.
   Jehuda Reinharz, "The Founding of the Hebrew University of Jerusalem: Chaim Weizmann's Role (1913–1914)" (in Hebrew), *Kathedra* 46 (Dec. 1987), p. 123ff.
9. Yosef Chaim Brenner, "From the Notebook" (in Hebrew), in *The Writings of Y. Ch. Brenner* (Tel Aviv: Ha-Kibbutz Ha-Me'uhad, 1960), vol. II, p. 143ff.
10. *Berl Katznelson on the Hebrew University* (Jerusalem: n.p., 1944), p. 31ff.
   Baruch Ben-Avram and Henry Nir, *Studies in the Third Aliya: Image and Reality* (in Hebrew) (Jerusalem: Yad Ben-Zvi, 1995), p. 128ff.
   Ber Borochov, *Writings* (in Hebrew) (Tel Aviv: Sifriat Po'alim, 1966), vol. III, p. 776.
   Ze'ev Sternhall, *Building a Nation or Rectifying Society?* (in Hebrew) (Tel Aviv: Am Oved, 1986), p. 330.
11. Weizmann to Ratnoff, in *The Letters and Papers of Chaim Weizmann*, ed. Bernard Wasserstein (New Brunswick, NJ, and Jerusalem: Transaction Books, Rutgers University, and Israel Universities Press, 1977), vol. X, p. 310ff.
12. Kisch diary, 5 Mar. 1924, CZA S25/564. See also: Myers, *Re-inventing the Jewish Past*, p. 50.
   ISA P/330 no. 864.

13. Memorandum of the Temporary Committee for the Opening of a Humanities Department of the Hebrew College in Jerusalem (1922), JTS, Ginsberg Papers, box 5.

14. *Day of Our Rejoicing: Details of the Cornerstone Laying Celebration for the Construction of the Hebrew University*, Hebrew University, Central Archive. See also: Ya'akov Gross, ed., *Jerusalem, 1917–1918: Destruction, Miracle, Redemption* (in Hebrew) (Koresh, 1992), p. 338ff.

15. Shimon Branfeld, "What Is Jewish Studies?" (in Hebrew), *Ha-Olam*, 5 June 1925, p. 419ff. Myers, *Re-inventing the Jewish Past.*

16. Bezalel Brashi, "Preparations for the Opening of the University in Jerusalem and Its First Years" (in Hebrew), *Katedra* 25 (Sept. 1982), p. 65ff.; Bezalel Brashi, "The Hebrew University in Jerusalem, 1925–1935" (in Hebrew), *Kathedra* 53 (Sept. 1989), p. 107ff.

17. David Yellin, *Writings* (in Hebrew) (Reuven Mas, 1976), vol. V (Letters II), p. 261. CZA XIII/A153/25.

18. Kroyanker, *Jerusalem Architecture*, p. 100ff. See also: M. D. Eder, *The Hebrew University of Jerusalem* (London: Zionist Organization, 1926), p. 3.

19. Baruch Ben-Avram, *Political Parties and Streams in the National Home Period, 1918–1948* (Merkaz Zalman Shazar, 1978).

20. Ze'ev Sternhall, *Building a Nation or Rectifying Society?*

21. Yosef Gorny, *Policy and Imagination* (in Hebrew) (Jerusalem: Yad Ben-Zvi, 1993), p. 76ff.

22. "The Second Session of the Elected Assembly" (in Hebrew), *Ha'aretz*, 8 Mar. 1922, p. 3. Yigal Drori, *Between Right and Left: The "Civil Circles" in the Twenties* (in Hebrew) (Tel Aviv: Tel Aviv University, 1990). See also: Hannah Herzog, "Women's Organizations in Civil Circles: A Forgotten Chapter in the Historiography of the Yishuv" (in Hebrew), *Kathedra* 70 (Jan. 1994), p. 11ff.

23. Chaim Weizmann, *Trial and Error* (London: Hamish Hamilton, 1949), p. 86ff.

24. *Ha'aretz*, 2 Jan. 1920, p. 3.
    Ben-Gurion in the Elected Assembly, *Ha'aretz*, 8 Mar. 1922, p. 3.
    Avigdor Hame'iri, "Religious to the Soul" (in Hebrew), *Ha'aretz*, 13 May 1923, p. 2.
    Do'ar HaYom, 16 Feb. 1922, p. 3; 22 Nov. 1922, p. 3.

25. Rabbi Benjamin, "Ya'akov De Han" (in Hebrew), *Ha'aretz*, 28 Nov. 1923, p. 4. See also: *Ha'aretz*, 14 May 1923, p. 4.
    Kisch, *Palestine Diary*, p. 51.
    Kisch diary, 2 July 1924, CZA S25/565.

26. Shlomo Nakdimon and Shaul Meizlish, *De Han: The First Political Murder in Palestine* (in Hebrew) (Tel Aviv: Modan, 1985), p. 11.
    Ronald Storrs, *Orientations* (London: Ivor Nicholson and Watson, 1939), p. 437.

27. The High Commissioner to the Colonial Secretary, 30 June 1922, ISA M/5/2/149/1. See also: Bramley to Foreign Office, 22 Nov. 1924, RCS, Bramley Papers.
    Zvi Meshi Zahav and Yehuda Meshi Zahav, *The Martyr: The First Zionist Murder in Palestine* (in Hebrew) (Jerusalem: Machon Ha-Yahadut Ha-Ultra-Ortodoksit, 1986).

28. Weizmann to Eder, 3 Mar. 1922, in *The Letters and Papers of Chaim Weizmann*, ed. Bernard Wasserstein (New Brunswick, NJ, and Jerusalem: Transaction Books, Rutgers University, and Israel Universities Press, 1977), vol. XI, p. 66ff.

29. Rachel Elboi-Dror, "Women in the Zionist Utopia" (in Hebrew), *Kathedra* 66 (Dec. 1992), p. 111ff.

30. Rafi Thon, *The Struggle for Equal Rights for Women* (in Hebrew) (published by the author, 1996), p. 31.
    "Announcement of the Zionist Commission Press Office," *Hadashot min Ha-Aretz*, 29 Sept. 1919, p. 3. See also: Moshe Smilansky, "Man-Woman" (in Hebrew), *Hadashot min Ha-Aretz*, 19 June 1919, p. 3.

31. Francis Emily Newton, *Fifty Years in Palestine* (Wrotham: Coldharbour Press, 1948), p. 21.
    Millicent Fawcett, *Easter in Palestine, 1921–1922* (London: T. Fisher Unwin Ltd., 1926), p. 80.

32. Sarah Azariahu, *Chapters of My Life* (in Hebrew) (Neuman, 1957), p. 159.
    Klausner at a women's rally (in Hebrew), *Ha'aretz*, 8 Apr. 1924, p. 4.

33. Draft of a notice, 24 June 1929, CZA J75/17, Press Summaries, p. 14, CZA J35/4.
    Itamar Ben-Avi, "Eve's Revenge" (in Hebrew), *Do'ar HaYom*, 11 Sept. 1919, p. 2. See also:
    Moshe Smilansky, "Man-Woman," p. 3.

34. Hannah Thon, "Thoughts on the Women's Movement" (in Hebrew), *Ha-Isha* 3 (May
    1926), p. 12.
    H. Galner, "Our Obligations Towards the Ascent of Woman," *Ha-Isha* 2 (Apr. 1925),
    p. 3ff.
    Statement, *Hadashot min Ha-Aretz*, 4 July 1919, p. 1.

35. Berl Katznelson, "To the He-Halutz Movement," in *The He-Halutz Book* (in Hebrew),
    ed. Moshe Basok (Jerusalem: Jewish Agency, 1940), p. 9ff.

36. Ben-Gurion in the executive committee of the Temporary Committee of the Jews of
    Palestine, 23 June 1919, *Hadashot min Ha-Aretz*, 4 June 1919, p. 2.
    Ben-Gurion at the sixth session of the Temporary Committee, 22–23 Oct. 1920, CZA
    J1/8782.

37. Ester Yavin to Sara Azariahu, 1 Nov. 1925, CZA J75/25, as well as Women's Union notice,
    1926, CZA J75/17.

38. Y.K., "We Must Concede This Time" (in Hebrew), *Do'ar HaYom*, 22 Oct. 1919, p. 1.
    "The Right of the Woman in Palestine" (in Hebrew), *Do'ar HaYom*, 26 Feb. 1922, p. 1.

39. Anita Shapira, "The Political History of the Yishuv, 1918–1939" (in Hebrew), in *The His-
    tory of the Jewish Yishuv in Palestine from the Time of the First Aliya (The British Man-
    date)* (in Hebrew), ed. Moshe Lissak (Jerusalem: Israel Academy of Sciences, Bialik
    Institute, 1993), part I, p. 11.

40. Sarah Azariahu, *The Union of Hebrew Women for the Equalization of Rights in Palestine*
    (in Hebrew) (HaKeren LeEzrat HaIsha, 1977), pp. 19, 51.
    Sarah Azariahu, *Chapters of My Life* (in Hebrew) (Neuman, 1957), p. 229ff.
    Notice, 15 Feb. 1930, CZA J75/17.

41. Colonial Office, ULL. RP XIV, Eleanor Rathbone Papers 2.5.(8).

42. Fawcett, *Easter in Palestine*, p. 87ff.

43. Gerda Arlosoroff-Goldberg, "Comments to the 'Palestinian' Women's Movement" (in
    Hebrew), *Ha-Isha* 2 (1929), p. 6ff.

44. Press summaries, p. 10, CZA J35/4 (in Hebrew), *Ha'aretz*, 8 June 1920, p. 2.
    Memo from Arab women of Palestine (1929), RHL, Chancellor Papers, Mss. Brit Emp.
    s284, 15:3 ff.28–29.

45. Storrs, *Orientations*, p. 435.
    Fawcett, *Easter in Palestine*, p. 72ff.

46. Dov Genihovsky, *Jerusalem Stories* (in Hebrew) (Jerusalem: Karta 1989), p. 79.

47. Fawcett, *Easter in Palestine*, p. 54ff. See also: CZA S25/1120.
    N. and H. Bentwich, *Mandate Memoirs*, p. 65.

48. Unsigned memorandum, 20 July 1936, CZA S25/3234. See also: CZA S 25/1461.

49. Weizmann to Eder, 8 Dec. 1921, in *The Letters and Papers of Chaim Weizmann*, ed.
    Bernard Wasserstein (New Brunswick, NJ, and Jerusalem: Transaction Books, Rutgers
    University, and Israel Universities Press, 1977), vol. X, p. 318.
    Kisch diary, 7 Feb. 1923, CZA S25/564.
    Newton to Szold, 5 Feb. 1937; Szold to Newton, 11 Sept. 1937, CZA S25/1120.
    Kisch, *Palestine Diary*, p. 214.

50. Dov Genihovsky, *Jerusalem Stories*, p. 79.

51. Herbert Parzen, "The Magnes-Weizmann-Einstein Controversy," *Jewish Social Studies*,
    vol. XXXII, no. 3 (July 1970), p. 187ff.

52. Kisch, *Palestine Diary*, p. 170.

53. Arthur A. Goren, ed., *Dissenter in Zion* (Cambridge: Harvard University Press, 1982),
    p. 233ff.
    Weizmann to Kisch, 14–16 Nov. 1923, in *The Letters and Papers of Chaim Weizmann*, ed.
    Joshua Freundlich (New Brunswick, NJ, and Jerusalem: Transaction Books, Rutgers

University, and Israel Universities Press, 1977), vol. XII, p. 22ff.

Kisch, *Palestine Diary*, p. 169. See also: Genihovsky, *Jerusalem Stories*, p. 79.

54. Newton, *Fifty Years in Palestine*, p. 193.

55. Ch. N. Bialik on the Hebrew University, Organization of Friends of the Hebrew University in Palestine, 1935, p. 9.

Kisch diary, 2 Apr. 1925, CZA S 25/3272.

56. "Lord Balfour's Tour," London *Times*, 6 Apr. 1925, p. 13.

Kisch, *Palestine Diary*, p. 166.

"Balfour in Palestine" (in Hebrew), *Ha-Olam*, 3 Apr. 1925, p. 278ff.

"Lord Balfour at Damascus," London *Times*, 11 Apr. 1925, p. 10.

183 H.C. Debs 5.s. col. 564, 4 May 1925.

57. Herbert Samuel to Mugras, 1 May 1915; correspondence regarding Samuel's request to remain in Palestine, ISA P/649/12.

58. Shlonsky to Levine, undated, Levine Papers, with the kind permission of the Munin family.

59. "Insurance in Palestine," *Monthly Pioneer*, Sept. 1928, p. 14.

60. The Palace to Levine, 19 Dec. 1928, Levine Papers. With the kind permission of the Munin family.

61. Gad Frumkin, *The Way of a Judge in Jerusalem* (in Hebrew) (Tel Aviv: Dvir, 1954), p. 221.

62. Neil Caplan, *Palestine Jewry and the Arab Question, 1917–1925* (London: Frank Cass, 1978), p. 141ff.

63. Uri Keisari, "The Fate of Alter Levine" (in Hebrew), *Do'ar HaYom*, 3 Nov. 1933, p. 2; Uri Keisari, "Asaf Halevy and Alter Levine" (in Hebrew), *Ha'aretz*, 28 Sept. 1947, p. 3.

Dov Kimche, *Book of Small Essays* (in Hebrew) (Reuven Mas, 1938), p. 80ff.

64. Kroyanker, *Jerusalem Architecture*, p. 388ff.

65. David Ben-Gurion, *Memoirs* (in Hebrew) (Tel Aviv: Am Oved, 1971), vol. I, p. 207.

66. Keisari, "The Fate of Alter Levine," p. 2; Keisari, "Asaf Halevy and Alter Levine," p. 3.

67. Agnon to Levine, 26 Feb. 1928, Levine Papers. With the kind permission of the Munin family.

10: YEFIM GORDIN COMES TO PALESTINE

1. Gordin to his parents, 28 May 1928. Letters of Yefim Gordin, later Chaim Shalom Halevi. Quoted with the kind permission of his son.

2. Moshe Lissak, "Immigration, Absorption, and the Building of Society in Palestine: Israel in the 1920s, 1918–1930," in *The History of the Jewish Yishuv in Palestine from the Time of the First Aliya (The British Mandate)* (in Hebrew), ed. Moshe Lissak and Gabriel Cohen (Jerusalem: Israel Academy of Sciences, Bialik Institute, 1994), part II, pp. 199, 214.

U. Schmeltz, "Migration," *Encyclopedia Judaica*, vol. XVI, p. 1518ff.

3. Gideon Biger, *Crown Colony or National Home: The Influence of British Rule on Palestine, 1917–1930: A Geographical-Historical Examination* (in Hebrew) (Jerusalem: Yad Ben-Zvi, 1983), p. 174.

4. The Zionist Organization in London to all Zionist Federations, 18 Apr. 1919, CZA L3/31 I.

Minutes of the eighth session of the Temporary Council of the Jews of Palestine, 22–23 Oct. 1919, p. 11.

Ben Baruch, "Closing the Gates" (in Hebrew), *Ha'aretz*, 23 Dec. 1920, p. 2.

5. David Ben-Gurion, *Memoirs* (in Hebrew) (Tel Aviv: Am Oved, 1971), vol. I, p. 198.

6. Baruch Ben-Avram and Henry Nir, *Studies in the Third Aliya: Image and Reality* (in Hebrew) (Jerusalem: Yad Ben-Zvi, 1995), p. 21.

Biger, *Crown Colony or National Home*, p. 174.

Immigration survey (1925), CZA S6/5208.

7. Weizmann and others with Samuel, 3 July 1920, CZA Z4/3766.

8. Lissak, "Immigration, Absorption, and the Building of Society in Palestine," part II, p. 218.
9. Weizmann and others to Samuel, 3 July 1920, CZA Z4/3766.
10. Directive on immigration no. 2, 17 Dec. 1920, CZA Z4/1287.
11. Weizmann to Samuel, 22 Nov. 1919, *The Letters and Papers of Chaim Weizmann*, ed. Jehuda Reinharz (New Brunswick, NJ, and Jerusalem: Transaction Books, Rutgers University, and Israel Universities Press, 1977), vol. IX, p. 270.
12. Samuel to Weizmann, 20 Jan. 1920, CZA Z4/16146.
13. Eder, Ruppin, and others to Herbert Samuel, 2 July 1920, ISA M/1/33.
Lissak, "Immigration, Absorption, and the Building of Society in Palestine," part II, p. 216ff.
National Council Executive to the Colonial Secretary, 21 Apr. 1925, Knesset Yisrael, National Council, *Book of Documents* (Jerusalem: 1949), p. 84. See also: CZA S25 /2591.
M. Mossek, *Palestine Immigration Policy Under Sir Herbert Samuel* (London: Frank Cass, 1978), p. 127.
Shuckburgh to the Colonial Office, 25 Mar. 1925, PRO CO 733/110.
14. Edwin Samuel, *A Lifetime in Jerusalem* (Jerusalem: Israel Universities Press, 1970), p. 79.
15. Mossek, *Palestine Immigration Policy Under Sir Herbert Samuel*, p. 43.
16. Digest of letters, 14 Mar. 1923, CZA S6/267.
Lissak, "Immigration, Absorption, and the Building of Society in Palestine," part II, p. 219ff.
Ben-Gurion, *Memoirs*, vol. I, p. 279.
17. Samuel to the Advisory Committee, 19 May 1919, CZA Z4/16009.
Ruppin to the High Commissioner, 1 Aug. 1920, ISA M/1/33.
Eder and others to the High Commission, 2 July 1920, CZA M/1/33.
Weizmann to Graham, 11 July 1919, in *The Letters and Papers of Chaim Weizmann*, vol. IX, p. 170ff. See also: E. Samuel, *A Lifetime in Jerusalem*, p. 81.
Kisch diary, 10 June 1930, CZA S25/838.
18. The Zionist Executive in Palestine to the Palestinian Office, 15 Nov. 1922 and 8 May 1922, CZA S6/267.
Immigration directive no. 2, 17 Dec. 1920, CZA Z4/1287.
Ben-Avram and Nir, *Studies in the Third Aliya*, p. 113.
19. "Self-Defense," *Kontrass,* vol. IV, no. 78 (11 May 1921), p. 31.
20. Ettinger to the Zionist Commission, 10 June 1919, CZA L3/31 I.
Yehuda Erez, ed., *Book of the Third Aliya* (Tel Aviv: Am Oved, 1964), vol. I, pp. 219, 411.
Ben-Avram and Nir, *Studies in the Third Aliya*, p. 144.
21. Lissak, "Immigration, Absorption, and the Building of Society in Palestine," part II, p. 237ff.
22. The Palestinian Office Eliash, 6 Mar. 1919, CZA L4/568. See also: Zionist Commission, 22 May 1919, CZA L3/31 I.
Zionist Commission to the Zionist Organization, 13 Aug. 1920, CZA L3/289.
Immigration Department to the Palestinian Offices, 14 Mar. 1923, CZA S6/267.
23. Assistance Center to de Sola Pool, 20 Aug. 1920, and de Sola Pool to Rabbi Kook, 11 Oct. 1920, CZA L3/202.
24. Immigration directive no. 2, 17 Dec. 1920, CZA Z4/1287. See also: Immigration Department to Palestinian Office, 23 Jan. 1923, CZA S6/267 I.
25. Theodor Herzl, *The Jewish State* (in Hebrew) (Tel Aviv: Yediot Aharonot, 1978), p. 54.
Berl Katznelson, *The Writings of Berl Katznelson* (in Hebrew) (Tel Aviv: Mapai, n.d.), vol. I, p. 113.
Ben-Avram and Nir, *Studies in the Third Aliya*, pp. 32, 35.
26. Douglas V. Duff, *Bailing with a Teaspoon* (London: John Long, 1953), pp. 75–77. See also: Y. G. to the Zionist Commission, 9 Oct. 1921, CZA L3/474.
27. Yosi Ben-Artzi, "The Judaization of Haifa and Its Development in the Mandatory

Period" (in Hebrew), in *Haifa in Its Development, 1918–1948* (in Hebrew), ed. Mordecai Naor and Yosi Ben-Artzi (Jerusalem: Yad Ben-Zvi, 1989), p. 31. See also: May Seikaly, *Haifa: Transformation of an Arab Society, 1918–1939* (London: Tauris, 1995), p. 49.

28. Shimon Stern, "Hadar Ha-Karmel: The Center of Jewish Life in Haifa" (in Hebrew), in Naor Ben-Artzi, *Haifa in Its Development*, p. 38ff.

29. Gordin to his parents, 8 and 16 June 1926.

30. Gordin to his parents, 6 June 1926.

31. L. and Hannah Majero, *Lod: Memoirs* (in Hebrew); mimeographed edition, self-published, 1965.

32. Gordin to his parents, 6 July 1926.

33. Gordin to his parents, 28 Aug. 1926.

34. Gordin to his parents, 10 Aug. 1926.

35. Ilan Shchori, *A Dream That Became a City* (in Hebrew) (Tel Aviv: Avivim, 1990), p. 368.

36. Natan Herpo, "From Dream Houses to Box Houses" (in Hebrew), in *Tel Aviv at Its Beginnings, 1909–1934* (in Hebrew), ed. Mordecai Naor (Jerusalem: Yad Ben-Zvi, 1984), p. 91ff.
    Alter Levine, *Scroll of the East* (in Hebrew) (Dekel, 1915).

37. Lissak, "Immigration, Absorption, and the Building of Society in Palestine," part II, p. 235ff.

38. Lissak, "Immigration, Absorption, and the Building of Society in Palestine," part II, pp. 287ff., 214.

39. Gideon Biger, "Geddes's Plan to Design the Physical Image of Tel Aviv in 1925," in *Proceedings of the Tenth World Congress of Jewish Studies* (Jerusalem: World Union of Jewish Studies, 1990), division B, vol. I, p. 384ff.
    Geddes to Eder, 2 May 1925, CZA L12/39. See also: Hellen Meller, *Patrick Geddes, Social Evolutionist and City Planner* (London: Routledge, 1990).

40. Memoirs of Moshe Levy in *Dreaming in the Sands* (in Hebrew), ed. Shimon Halfi; to be published. With the kind permission of Rachel Halfi.
    Mordechai Ben-Hillel Hacohen, *My World* (in Hebrew) (Mitzpeh, 1928), book IV, p. 147ff.

41. Ben-Avram and Nir, *Studies in the Third Aliya*, p. 69.
    Weizmann to his wife, 18 Apr. 1918, in *The Letters and Papers of Chaim Weizmann*, ed. Dvora Barzilay and Barnett Litvinoff (New Brunswick, NJ, and Jerusalem: Transaction Books, Rutgers University, and Israel Universities Press, 1977), vol. VIII, p. 131ff.

42. Edmond Fleg, *My Israel* (in Hebrew) (Am HaSefer, 1957), p. 83ff.
    Nahum Gutman, *A Small City of Few People* (in Hebrew) (Tel Aviv: Am Oved and Dvir, 1959), p. 261.

43. Memoirs of Gabriel Tzifroni, in S. Halfi, *Dreaming in the Sands*. With the kind permission of Rachel Halfi.

44. Gordin to his parents, 14 July 1926.

45. Immigration Department of the Palestine Office in Warsaw, 23 Jan., 8 May, and 4 Sept. 1923, CZA S6/267 I. See also: Lissak, *The History of the Jewish Yishuv*, part II, pp. 227, 192, 235ff.

46. Gordin to his parents, 14 Nov. 1926.

47. Gordin to his parents, 12 Apr. 1927.

48. Gordin to his parents, 2 May 1929.

49. Ilan Shchori, *Dream*, p. 371.

50. Gordin to his parents, 7 June 1927.

51. Gordin to his parents, 28 Dec. 1926; 3 Jan., 1 Feb., and 12 Aug. 1927.

52. Gordin to his parents, 1 Feb. and 17 May 1927.

53. Gordin to his parents, 28 Dec. 1926.

54. Gordin to his parents, 3 Jan. 1927.

55. Gordin to his parents, 9 Jan., 22 Sept. 1927.

56. Gordin to his parents, 19 July 1927.

57. Gordin to his parents, 6 June 1929.

58. Gordin to his parents, 27 Jan. 1928.

59. Gordin to his parents, 19 July 1927.

60. Gordin to his parents, 12 Apr., 17 May, 17 July 1927.

61. Rashid Khalidi, *Palestinian Identity: The Construction of a Modern National Conscious-ness* (New York: Columbia University Press, 1977), p. 109.
    Bramley report, 30 Nov. 1924, RCS—Bramley Papers.
    Bernard A. Rosenblatt, "Afulah Day," *New Palestine*, 19 Dec. 1924, p. 426.
    Moshe Glickson, "The Afula Matter" (in Hebrew), *Ha'aretz*, 30 Nov. 1924, p. 2ff.
    F. H. Kisch, *Palestine Diary* (London: Victor Gollancz, 1938), p. 154.
    Horace Samuel, *Unholy Memories of the Holy Land* (London: Hogarth Press, 1930), p. 229ff.

62. Dan Giladi, "Afula: 'City of the Valley' or City Against the Valley?" in *Jezreel Valley, 1900–1967* (in Hebrew), ed. Mordecai Naor (Jerusalem: Yad Ben-Zvi, 1993), p. 95ff. See also: Iris Glazer, "The Valley of Jezreel: Social Ideologies and Settlement Landscape, 1920–1929," *Studies in Zionism*, vol. XI, no. 1 (1990), pp. 11ff.

63. Gordin to his parents, 8 Sept. 1926.

64. Gordin to his parents, 28 Sept. 1926.

65. Gordin to his parents, 9 Aug.; 7, 14, 10 Nov.; 1 Dec. 1926.

66. Gordin to his parents, 16 Jan. 1927.

67. Gordin to his parents, 7 Feb. 1927.

68. Gordin to his parents, 19 Aug. 1927.

69. Gordin to his parents, 28 June 1928.

70. Gordin to his parents, 3 Apr. 1928.

71. Gordin to his parents, 14 Sept. 1927.

72. Gordin to his parents, 24 Oct. 1926.

73. Joseph Klausner, *Jesus of Nazareth* (in Hebrew) (Tel Aviv: Masada, 1945), p. 448.
    David N. Myers, *Re-inventing the Jewish Past* (New York: Oxford University Press, 1995), p. 94ff.

74. Gordin to his parents, 8 Mar. 1927.

75. Gordin to his parents, 15 Mar. 1928.

76. Gordin to his parents, 15 Apr. 1928.

77. Gordin to his parents, 1 Feb. 1927.

78. Gordin to his parents, 3 Jan., 5 Apr., 6 June 1927.

79. Gordin to his parents, 11 Dec. 1927.

80. Gordin to his parents, 28 Dec. 1926.

81. Gordin to his parents, 27 Jan., 11 Dec. 1928.

82. Gordin to his parents, 6 June 1929.

83. Gordin to his parents, 11 July, 9 Nov., and 28 Dec. 1926.

11: A NEW MAN

1. Moshe Lissak, "Immigration, Absorption, and the Building of Society in Palestine: Israel in the 1920s, 1918–1930" (in Hebrew), in *The History of the Jewish Yishuv in Palestine from the Time of the First Aliya (The British Mandate)*, ed. Moshe Lissak and Gabriel Cohen (Jerusalem: Israel Academy of Sciences, Bialik Institute, 1994), part II, p. 191.

2. Henry Near, *The Kibbutz Movement* (Oxford: Oxford University Press, 1992), p. 138.
    David Canaani, ed., *Encyclopedia of the Social Sciences* (in Hebrew) (Tel Aviv: Sifriat Poalim, 1920), vol. V, p. 343.

3. Near, *The Kibbutz Movement*, p. 7ff.
    Yona Oren (Shifmiller), "Kibbutz Upper Bitaniya" (in Hebrew), in *Book of the Third Aliya* (in Hebrew), ed. Yehuda Erez (Tel Aviv: Am Oved, 1964), p. 417.

Yehuda Erez, *Book of the Third Aliya* (in Hebrew) (Tel Aviv: Am Oved, 1964), vol. II, p. 725ff.

Sylvie Fogiel-Bijaoui, "From Revolution to Motherhood: The Case of Women in the Kibbutz, 1910–1948," in *Jewish Women in Pre-State Israel*, ed. Deborah Bernstein (New York: State University of New York, 1992), p. 211ff.

4. Shlomo Bar-Yosef (Schlomo Horowitz), "Shomriya" (in Hebrew), in *Book of the Third Aliya*, vol. II, p. 419.

5. Erez, *Book of the Third Aliya*, vol. I, p. 472.

6. Dan Giladi, *The Yishuv During the Period of the Fourth Aliya (1924–1929)* (in Hebrew) (Tel Aviv: Am Oved, 1973), p. 71ff.

7. Baruch Ben-Avram and Henry Nir, *Studies in the Third Aliya: Image and Reality* (in Hebrew) (Jerusalem: Yad Ben-Zvi, 1995), p. 100.

8. Takhi, "From the Diary of a Member of Kibbutz B" (in Hebrew), in *Book of the Third Aliya*, vol. I, p. 429ff.

9. Numbers 32:20–21, 31–32; Joshua 6:1–13.
David Ben-Gurion, *Memoirs* (in Hebrew), (Tel Aviv: Am Oved, 1971), vol. I, p. 336.

10. Ben-Gurion, *Memoirs*, vol. I, p. 263; see also pp. 300, 323, 329, 336, 337.

11. II Chronicles 36:23 *Ch. N. Bialik on the Hebrew University* (in Hebrew) (Jerusalem: Friends of the Hebrew University in Palestine, 1925), p. 9.

12. Henry Nir, "Who Is a Pioneer?" (in Hebrew), in *Tora B* (Tel Aviv: HaKibbutz HaMe'uhad, 1992), p. 228ff. See also: Erez, *Book of the Third Aliya*, vol. I, p. 7ff.

13. Hagit Levsky, *The Jewish National Fund in Theory and Practice in the Period of the British Mandate* (in Hebrew) (Institute for the Study of the History of the Jewish National Fund and the Settlement of the Country, 1993), p. 10.
Ben-Avram and Nir, *Studies in the Third Aliya*, pp. 47, 114.
Shmuel Almog, "Redemption in Zionist Rhetoric" (in Hebrew), *Redemption of the Land in Palestine: Idea and Practice* (in Hebrew), ed. Ruth Kark (Jerusalem: Yad Ben-Zvi, 1990), p. 13ff.

14. Gordin to his parents, 8 June 1926. See also: S. Z. Abramov, *On a Party That Disappeared and on Liberalism* (in Hebrew) (Tel Aviv: Dvir, 1995), p. 97ff.

15. Ben-Avram and Nir, *Studies in the Third Aliya*, pp. 36, 54, 80.

16. Mordechai Ben-Hillel Hacohen, "Settlement in the Cities" (in Hebrew), *Hadashot min Ha-Aretz Ha-Kedosha*, 24 Sept. 1919, p. 4. See also: Mordechai Ben-Hillel Hacohen, "Places to Sit" (in Hebrew), *Ha'aretz*, 22 Feb. 1920, p. 1ff.
Joseph Klausner, "In Praise of Tel Aviv" (in Hebrew), *Ha'aretz*, 15 Apr. 1921, p. 2.
M. Kleinman, "The Renewal of Zionist Life" (Hebrew), *Ha'aretz*, 3 Nov. 1921, p. 3.
Dizengoff in the Zionist Executive, May 1927, CZA Z4/273/1.
Undated memorandum praising urban settlement, CZA L3/70.
Yigal Drori, *Between Right and Left: The "Civil Circles" in the Twenties* (in Hebrew) (Tel Aviv: Mifalim Universitaim, 1990), p. 107ff.
Dan Giladi, "The Return to 'The Land of Our Fathers'" (in Hebrew), in *An Entrepreneurial Alternative to Zionist Policy* (in Hebrew), ed. Z. D. Levontin (Israel Center for Economic and Social Advancement, 1994).
Weizmann to Bella Berligne, 8 Nov. 1919, in *The Letters and Papers of Chaim Weizmann*, ed. Jehuda Reinharz (New Brunswick, NJ, and Jerusalem: Transaction Books, Rutgers University, and Israel Universities Press, 1977), vol. IX, p. 251ff. See also: Yigal Drori, "The Positions of Jabotinsky, Glickson, and Levontin on the Question of Land for Settlement at the Beginning of the 1920s" (in Hebrew), in *Redemption of the Land in Palestine*, p. 199ff.

17. Ben-Gurion, *Memoirs*, vol. I, p. 425.
Drori, *Between Right and Left*.

18. Moshe Glickson, "On the Economic Situation" (in Hebrew), *Ha'aretz*, 15 Jan. 1925, p. 2.
Ben-Avram and Nir, *Studies in the Third Aliya*, p. 39.

19. Ilan Troen, "Tel Aviv in the 1920's and 1930's: Competing Ideologies in the Shaping of the Zionist Metropolis," *Proceedings of the Tenth World Congress of Jewish Studies* (Jerusalem: World Union of Jewish Studies, 1990), division B, vol. 1, p. 391ff.

20. *Kathedra* 83 (Apr. 1997) (cover picture). See also: Batia Dunar, ed., *Living with a Dream* (in Hebrew) (Tel Aviv: Dvir, 1989).
Anita Shapira, *New Jews, Old Jews* (in Hebrew) (Tel Aviv: Am Oved, 1997), p. 155ff.
Oz Almog, *The Sabra: A Portrait* (in Hebrew) (Tel Aviv: Am Oved, 1997).
Arthur Ruppin, *Chapters of My Life in the Building of the Land and the Nation, 1920–1942* (in Hebrew) (Tel Aviv: Am Oved, 1968), p. 28.

21. Rafaela Bilsky Ben-Hur, *Every Individual a King: Ze'ev Jabotinsky's Social and Political Thought* (in Hebrew) (Tel Aviv: Dvir, 1988), p. 182ff.
Ben-Gurion, *Memoirs* (in Hebrew) (Tel Aviv: Am Oved, 1971), vol. I, p. 470.
Rachel Arbel, *Blue and White in Color: Visual Representations of Zionism, 1897–1947* (Tel Aviv: Diaspora Museum and Am Oved), p. 124.

22. Halevi to his parents, 20 Sept. 1928. With the kind permission of his son.

23. Ben-Avram and Nir, *Studies in the Third Aliya*, pp. 31, 80.
Y. Luria, "School and Revival" (in Hebrew), *Ha'aretz*, 22 Aug. 1921, p. 3.
M. Zogorodsky, "Graduates" (in Hebrew), *Ha'aretz*, 7 Sept. 1921, p. 2.
Weizmann to his wife, 18 Apr. 1918, in *The Letters and Papers of Chaim Weizmann*, ed. Dvora Barzilay and Barnett Litvinoff (New Brunswick, NJ, and Jerusalem: Transaction Books, Rutgers University, and Israel Universities Press, 1977), vol. VIII, p. 132.

24. Nurit Reichel, "'Roots' or 'Horizons': A Portrait of the Desired Israeli Pupil in the Years 1889–1933" (in Hebrew), *Kathedra* 83 (Apr. 1997), p. 55ff.

25. Ben-Avram and Nir, *Studies in the Third Aliya*, p. 96.

26. Yehuda Erez, ed., *Book of the Third Aliya* (in Hebrew) (Tel Aviv: Am Oved, 1964), vol. II. See also: Ben-Avram and Nir, *Studies in the Third Aliya*, p. 84ff.

27. Tsiona Rabau, *In Tel Aviv on the Sands* (in Hebrew) (Tel Aviv: Masada, 1973), p. 103ff.

28. Giladi, *The Yishuv During the Period of the Fourth Aliya*, p. 169.

29. Ben-Avram and Nir, *Studies in the Third Aliya*, pp. 36ff., 39.
A.T., "People of the Land" (in Hebrew), *Ha'aretz*, 26 Jan. 1920, p. 1.
Weizmann to Samuel, 22 Nov. 1919, in Reinharz,*The Letters and Papers of Chaim Weizmann*, vol. IX, p. 270.

30. Ben-Avram and Nir, *Studies in the Third Aliya*, p. 27ff.

31. Anita Shapira, "The Dream and Its Shattering: The Political Development of the Trumpeldor Labor Battalion, 1920–1927" (in Hebrew) (diss., Tel Aviv University, 1967), p. 94.

32. Halevi to his parents, 2 June 1926. With the kind permission of his son.

33. Giladi, *The Yishuv During the Period of the Fourth Aliya*, p. 180.
Nadav Halevy, *The Economic Development of the Jewish Yishuv in Palestine, 1917–1947* (in Hebrew) (Falk Institute, 1979), p. 27.

34. Halevi to his parents, 14 Nov. 1926. With the kind permission of his son.

35. N. Halevy, *The Economic Development of the Jewish Yishuv in Palestine*, p. 21.

36. Moshe Lissak, "Immigration, Absorption, and the Building of Society in Palestine," part II, p. 215.
Giladi, *The Yishuv During the Period of the Fourth Aliya*, p. 229ff.

37. Ben-Gurion, *Memoirs*, vol. I, pp. 334, 546.

38. Moshe Lissak, "Immigration, Absorption, and the Building of Society in Palestine," part II, p. 282. See also: Nachum Gross, "The Economic Policy of the British Mandatory Administration in Palestine" (in Hebrew), *Kathedra* 24 (July 1982), p. 169.

39. Evyatar Friesel, *Zionist Policy After the Balfour Declaration 1917–1922* (in Hebrew) (Tel Aviv: Tel Aviv University, 1977), p. 176.
Reports of the Experts Submitted to the Joint Palestine Survey Commission (Boston, 1928).
Ussishkin's response to the reorganization report, CZA L3/655.

40. Halevi to his parents, 19 July 1927. With the kind permission of his son.
41. Halevi to his parents, 28 May 1929. With the kind permission of his son.
42. Halevi to his parents, 14 Nov. 1926. With the kind permission of his son.
43. Ben-Avram and Nir, *Studies in the Third Aliya*, pp. 131, 134.
44. Halevi to his parents, 24 June 1927. With the kind permission of his son.
45. Tsiona Rabau, *In Tel Aviv on the Sands*, p. 108ff. See also: Ilan Shchori, *Dream*, p. 364ff.
46. Halevi to his parents, 19 July 1927. With the kind permission of his son.
47. Halevi to his parents, 27 July 1927, 11 Dec. 1928. With the kind permission of his son.
48. Halevi to his parents, 23 Nov. 1927. With the kind permission of his son.
49. A. D. Gordon, "A Bit of Observation" (in Hebrew), in *The Writings of A. D. Gordon* (in Hebrew), ed. Sh. H. Bergman and A. L. Shochat (Tel Aviv: HaSifriya HaTzionit, 1952), vol. I, p. 124.
50. CZA S25/6733. See also CZA J1/68.
51. Stein to Kisch, 4 Mar. 1927, CZA S25/6733.
52. Tsiona Rabau, *In Tel Aviv on the Sands*, p. 108ff.; Natan Donewitz, *Tel Aviv: Sands That Became a City* (in Hebrew) (Tel Aviv: Schocken, 1959), p. 71.
    Chancellor to his son, 17 Oct. 1930, RHL, Chancellor Papers, 16:3, f. 113.
53. Kisch diary, 5 Dec. 1923, CZA S25/564.
54. Halevi-Arlosoroff correspondence, 1932, CZA S25/6733.
55. Halevi to his parents, 23 Nov. 1927. With the kind permission of his son.
56. Sarah Thon to Meir Wilkansky, 9 Oct. 1919. Rafi Thon, *The Struggle for Equal Rights for Women: The Story of Sarah Thon* (in Hebrew) (published by the author, 1995), p. 216. See also: Natan Efrati, "The Revival of the Hebrew Language and the Zionist Movement" (in Hebrew), *Leshonenu Le-Am*, vol. 48, no. 3 (Apr.-June 1997), p. 93ff.
57. Arieh L. Pilovsky, "Language, Culture, and Nationalism in the New Yishuv: The Public Debate over the Plan to Establish a Chair in Yiddish in Jerusalem at the End of 1927" (in Hebrew), *Katedra* 21 (Oct. 1982), p. 103ff.
58. Halevi to his parents, 2 Jan. 1928. With the kind permission of his son.
59. Halevi to his parents, 20 Apr. 1928. With the kind permission of his son.
60. Pilovsky, "Language, Culture, and Nationalism in the New Yishuv," p. 122.
    Menachem Brinker, *To the Tiberian Alley* (in Hebrew) (Tel Aviv: Am Oved, 1990), p. 209.
    Mordecai Neuman to the Committee on English Affairs (undated), CZA S25/7470.
    Reichel, " 'Roots' or 'Horizons,' " p. 55ff., CZA S25/6731.
    Reichel, " 'Roots' or 'Horizons,' " Apr. 1997, p. 55ff., CZA S25/6731.
61. Halevi to his parents, 9 May 1927. With the kind permission of his son.
62. Pilovsky, "Language, Culture, and Nationalism in the New Yishuv," p. 107.
63. Halevi to his parents, 25 Dec. 1927. With the kind permission of his son. See also: David N. Myers, *Re-inventing the Jewish Past* (New York: Oxford University Press, 1995), p. 76ff.
64. National Council to the high commissioner, 28 Jan. 1923; Deedes to the National Council, 16 Feb. 1923, Knesset Yisrael, National Council, *Book of Documents*, 1949, p. 64ff.
65. CZA S25/6743 and CZA S25/6742. See also: CZA J36.
66. Yisrael Amikam, *Twenty-two Letters Fighting for their Rights* (in Hebrew) (n.p.,), 1947. David Tidhar, *Encyclopedia of the Pioneers and Builders of the Yishuv* (in Hebrew) (Sifriat Rishonim, 1961), vol. XI, p. 3,799.
67. Halevi to his parents, 2 Jan. 1928. With the kind permission of his son.

12: NEGOTIATIONS WITH FRIENDS

1. Ylana Miller, *Government and Society in Rural Palestine, 1920–1948* (Austin: University of Texas Press, 1985).
   Baruch Kimmerling and Joel S. Migdal, *Palestinians: The Making of a People* (New York: Free Press, 1993).

Mohammed Yazbek, "Arab Migration to Haifa, 1933–1948: Quantitative Analysis According to Arab Sources" (in Hebrew), *Katedra* 45 (Sept. 1987), p. 131ff.

Yosef Washitz, "Migration of Villagers to Haifa in the Mandatory Period: A Process of Urbanization?" (in Hebrew), *Katedra* 45 (Sept. 1987), p. 113ff.

Gad Gelbar, "Trends in the Demographic Development of the Arabs of Palestine, 1870–1948" (in Hebrew), *Katedra* 45 (Sept. 1987), p. 42ff.

Rachelle Taqqu, "Peasants into Workmen: Internal Labor Migration and the Arab Village Community Under the Mandate," in *Palestinian Society and Politics*, ed. Joel S. Migdal (Princeton: Princeton University Press, 1980), p. 261ff.

2. Gideon Shilo, "The Life and Diaries of a Palestinian Educator of Jerusalem" (in Hebrew) in Khalil al-Sakakini, *Such Am I, O World* (in Hebrew) (Jerusalem: Keter, 1990), pp. 14, 146.

3. Intelligence Report no. 107, 3 July, and Intelligence Report no. 146, 13 Aug. 1920, CZA L4/793.

Yehoshua Porat, *The Growth of the Palestinian Arab National Movement, 1918–1929* (in Hebrew) (Tel Aviv: Am Oved, 1976), vol. I, p. 30ff.

Survey of the Arab press, CZA Z4/1250; S25/517. See also: Rashid Khalidi, *Palestinian Identity: The Construction of a Modern National Consciousness* (New York: Columbia University Press, 1977), p. 145ff.

4. Porat, *The Growth of the Palestinian National Movement*, vol. I, p. 102.

5. Shmuel Almog, "Redemption in Zionist Rhetoric," in *Redemption of the Land in Palestine: Idea and Practice*, ed. Ruth Kark (in Hebrew) (Jerusalem: Yad Ben-Zvi, 1990), p. 13ff.

6. Irit Amit and Ruth Kark, *Joshua Chankin: Two Loves* (in Hebrew) (Tel Aviv: Milo, 1996). Kenneth W. Stein, *The Land Question in Palestine, 1917–1939* (Chapel Hill: University of North Carolina Press, 1984), pp. 227, 39, 4, 210.

7. Pazner to Ruppin, 1 June 1939, CZA S25/7448.

Yosef Weitz, *The Question of the Dispossession of the Arabs*, 20 Mar. 1946, CZA S25/10685. *Our Relations with the Arabs* (no author or date, apparently 1920), CZA L/353.

8. Hagi Levsky, *The Jewish National Fund in Theory and Practice in the Period of the British Mandate* (in Hebrew) (Institute for the Study of the History of the Jewish National Fund and the Settlement of the Country, 1993), p. 9ff.

Iris Gracier, "The Valley of Jezreel: Social Ideologies and Settlement Landscape, 1920–1929," *Studies in Zionism*, vol. XI, no. 1 (1990), p. 1ff. See also: F. H. Kisch, *Palestine Diary* (London: Victor Gollancz, 1938), p. 118.

9. Khalidi, *Palestinian Identity*, p. 81.

Mohammed Izzat Darwazza, *Ninety-five Years of Life: Memories and Meditations* (in Arabic) (Jerusalem: Arab Thought Forum, 1993), p. 201.

Adnan abu-Gazaleh, "Arab Cultural Nationalism in Palestine During the British Mandate," *Journal of Palestine Studies*, vol. I, no. 3 (1972), p. 37ff.

10. The Royal Institute of International Affairs, *Great Britain and Palestine, 1915–1936* (London: Royal Institute of International Affairs, 1937), p. 50ff.

11. Stein, *The Land Question in Palestine*.

Walter Lehn with Uri Davis, *The Jewish National Fund* (London: Kegan Paul International, 1988).

12. Arieh L. Avineri, *Jewish Settlement and the Charge of Dispossession, 1878–1948* (in Hebrew) (Tel Aviv: Ha-Kibbutz Ha-Me'uhad, 1980), p. 112ff. See also: Yitzhak Ulshan, *Din U-Devarim* (Memoirs) (in Hebrew) (Tel Aviv: Schocken, 1978), p. 141.

13. Sakakini, *Such Am I, O World*, pp. 158, 163.

14. Sellers of Land to the Jews, 5 Jan. 1937, CZA S25/9783. See also: Eliahu Eilat, "Conversations with Musa Alami" (in Hebrew), *Yahadut Zemananu*, vol. II (1985), p. 27.

15. Stein, *The Land Question in Palestine*, p. 228ff. See also: Rashid Khalidi, "The Land Question in Palestine, 1917–1939," *Journal of Palestine Studies*, vol. XVII, no. 1 (Autumn 1987), p. 146ff.

Letter by Kenneth Stein, *Journal of Palestine Studies*, vol. XVII, no. 4 (Summer 1988), p. 252ff.

16. Weizmann to Samuel, 22 Nov. 1919, in *The Letters and Papers of Chaim Weizmann*, ed. Jehuda Reinharz (New Brunswick, NJ, and Jerusalem: Transaction Books, Rutgers University, and Israel Universities Press, 1977), vol. IX, p. 257.
Weizmann to Sokolow, 21 Aug. 1920, in *The Letters and Papers of Chaim Weizmann*, ed. Bernard Wasserstein (New Brunswick, NJ, and Jerusalem: Transaction Books, Rutgers University, and Israel Universities Press, 1977), vol. X, p. 22.
Weizmann to Cowan, 24 Sept. 1921, in Wasserstein, *The Letters and Papers of Chaim Weizmann*, vol. X, p. 256.

17. Yoav Gelber, *The Roots of the Lily* (in Hebrew) (Tel Aviv: Ministry of Defense, 1992).

18. Thon to the Zionist Executive, 29 Dec. 1925, CZA S25/517.
Kisch to Bodtzky, 6 Oct. 1932, CZA S25/3029.

19. Kalvarisky to the Zionist Executive, 18 July 1923, CZA S25/4380.
Kalvarisky to the Zionist Executive in London, 2 July 1925, CZA S25/4793.

20. Kisch to the political secretary, 28 Mar. 1923, CZA S25/10320.
Stein to Kisch, 10 Apr. 1923, CZA S25/10320.

21. Activities of the Arab Secretariat of the National Council (1922), CZA S25/4384.
Kisch diary, 27 Oct. and 26 Apr. 1923, CZA S25/564.

22. Kisch memorandum, 19 May 1925, CZA S25/517.
Ze'ev Sternhall, *Building a Nation or Rectifying Society?* (in Hebrew) (Tel Aviv: Am Oved, 1995).
Gad Frumkin, *The Way of a Judge in Jerusalem* (in Hebrew) (Tel Aviv: Dvir, 1954), p. 288.

23. Baruch Katinka, *From Then to Now* (in Hebrew) (Kiryat Sefer, 1965), p. 257ff.
Tayasir Jabara, *Palestinian Leader: Hajj Amin Al-Hussayni, Mufti of Jerusalem* (Princeton: Kingston Press, 1985), p. 64ff.
Nasser Eddin Nashashibi, *Jerusalem's Other Voice* (London: Ithaca Press, 1990), p. 79ff.
Yehoshua Porat, *From Disturbances to Rebellion* (in Hebrew) (Tel Aviv: Am Oved, 1978), p. 79.
David Kroyanker, *The Palace Hotel* (in Hebrew) (Jerusalem: Jerusalem Municipality, 1981).

24. David Hacohen, *Time to Tell* (in Hebrew) (Tel Aviv: Am Oved, 1974), p. 45.
Frumkin, *The Way of a Judge*, p. 288ff.
Chaim Arlosoroff, *Jerusalem Diary* (in Hebrew) (Tel Aviv: Mifleget Poalei Eretz Yisrael, 1949), pp. 205, 120ff.

25. Abadin to the Jewish Agency, 22 Sept. 1922, CZA J1/289.
Kisch diary, 1 Aug. 1924, CZA S25/565.
Weizmann to Wormser, Feb. 1923, in *The Letters and Papers of Chaim Weizmann*, ed. Bernard Wasserstein (New Brunswick, NJ, and Jerusalem: Transaction Books, Rutgers University, and Israel Universities Press, 1977), vol. XI, p. 232ff.
CZA S25/4384; J1/311 II.
Club budget and collaborator receipts, CZA S25/10302 and CZA S25/10287.

26. Kisch diary, 24 Jan. 1923, CZA S25/564.
Kisch memorandum, 13 Dec. 1922, CZA S25/518 I.
Gilikin to the National Council, 4 Dec. 1922.
Principal of the Arabic-Hebrew School in Tiberias to the secretary of the National Council, 4 Jan. 1923, CZA J1/289.

27. Kisch diary, 13 June 1923, CZA S25/564.

28. Kisch diary, 24 Jan. 1923 and Annex C, CZA S25/564.

29. Kisch diary, 30 Jan. 1923, CZA S25/564.

30. Kisch diary, 8 July 1924, CZA S25/565.

31. Kisch diary, 9 July 1923, CZA S25/564.

32. Kisch diary, 1 Feb., 5 Feb., 15 Apr., 15 June 1923, CZA S25/564.

33. Survey of the Arab newspapers published in Palestine, 19 Aug. 1921, CZA Z4/1250.
Kisch diary, 1 Aug. 1924, CZA S25/565.
Editor of Arab newspaper to the Jewish Agency, 10 July 1927, CZA S25/517.
Movement coordinator to Kisch, 5 Apr. 1923, CZA S25/4384. See also: CZA S25/10287.

34. Kisch diary, 2 Jan. 1924, CZA S25/565. See also: CZA S25/4380.

35. Kisch to the political secretary, 15 Nov. 1923, CZA S25/665.
Kisch to Weizmann, 20 June 1923, CZA S25/745.

36. Kisch diary, 17 Nov. 1924, CZA S25/565.
CZA L4/977.
Kisch to Deedes, 30 Jan. 1923 and attached documents. ISA secretariat, section 2, M/5/151.

37. David Ben-Gurion, *Memoirs* (in Hebrew) (Tel Aviv: Am Oved, 1971), vol. II, p. 145ff.
Neil Caplan, *Palestine Jewry and the Arab Question, 1917–1925* (London: Frank Cass, 1978), p. 101ff.
Kastel proposal, 1923, CZA J1/289.
Ben-Zvi in the National Council, 9 May 1923, CZA J1/7226.
Sloan to the Secretary of State and Simon Report, 1 Mar. 1935, "Records of the U.S. Consulate in Jerusalem, Palestine," Confidential Correspondence 1920–1935 (Record group 84).

38. Kisch diary, 2 Jan. 1924, CZA S25/565.
Humphrey Bowman, *Middle-East Window* (London: Longrams, Green and Co., 1942), p. 265.
Stein memorandum, 28 Feb. 1924, CZA S25/10595.
Eliezer Domke, "The Birth Pangs of the Kadoorie School" (in Hebrew) *Katedra* 35 (Apr. 1985), p. 91ff.
Rafaela Bilsky Ben-Hur, *Every Individual a King: Ze'ev Jabotinsky's Social and Political Thought* (in Hebrew) (Tel Aviv: Dvir, 1988), p. 287.

39. Ahad Ha'am to E. L. Simon, 24 May 1923, *The Letters of Ahad Ha'am* (Tel Aviv: Dvir, 1960), vol. VI, p. 253.
Kisch diary, 20 Nov. 1923, CZA S25/564.
Ben-Gurion, *Memoirs*, vol. I, p. 340.
P. A. Elsberg, "The Fight for the Mayorship of Jerusalem in the Mandatory Period" (in Hebrew), in *Topics in the History of Jerusalem in Modern Times,* ed. Eli Shaltiel (in Hebrew) (Jerusalem: Yad Ben-Zvi, 1981), p. 310.

40. Anita Shapira, *The Disillusioning Struggle: Hebrew Labor, 1929–1939* (in Hebrew) (Tel Aviv: Ha-Kibbutz Ha-Me'uhad, 1977), p. 106.
Yigal Drori, *Between Right and Left: The "Civil Circles" in the Twenties* (in Hebrew) (Tel Aviv: Mifalim Universitaim, 1990), p. 165. See also: Zachary Lockman, *Comrades and Enemies* (Berkeley: University of California Press, 1996).

41. *Berl Katznelson on the Hebrew University* (in Hebrew) (Jerusalem: n.p., 1944), p. 36.
Arlosoroff, *Jerusalem Diary*, p. 43.

42. Moshe Glickson and Moshe Smilansky (1922), in Drori, *Between Right and Left*, p. 38.
See also: Drori, *Between Right and Left*, p. 106.

43. Ze'ev Sternhall, *Building a Nation or Rectifying Society?* (in Hebrew) (Tel Aviv: Am Oved, 1986), p. 187ff.
Shabtai Teveth, *Ben-Gurion and the Arabs of Palestine* (in Hebrew) (Tel Aviv: Schocken, 1985), p. 69.

44. Anita Shapira, "A Political History of the Yishuv, 1918–1939" (in Hebrew), in *The History of the Jewish Yishuv in Palestine from the Time of the First Aliya,* ed. Moshe Lissak and Gabriel Cohen (in Hebrew) (Jerusalem: Israel Academy of Sciences, Bialik Institute, 1944), part II, pp. 79, 97.

45. The secretary for Arab affairs to Sasson Efendi, 1 Dec. 1922, CZA J1/289.
Kisch, *Palestine Diary*, p. 139.

Yehuda Nini, *Were You There or Did I Dream It: The Yemenites of Kinneret—the Story of Their Settlement and Displacement, 1912–1930* (in Hebrew) (Tel Aviv: Am Oved, 1996), p. 102.

46. Norman and Helen Bentwich, *Mandate Memoirs, 1918–1948* (London: Hogarth Press, 1965), p. 53.
47. Ben-Gurion to Eichenberg, 10 Dec. 1935, CZA S25/7188.
48. Rotenstreich to the Jewish Agency Executive, 30 Dec. 1936, CZA S25/9783.
49. Cohen diary, 9 Dec. 1935, National Library, Manuscript Division, B/514.
Internal dangers, undated (1941), CZA S25/7188.
The War for Hebrew Labor in Kfar Saba, CZA S25/7188.
CZA S25/10108.
50. List of citrus groves and workplaces in which pickets were set, 1926–1934 (in Hebrew), CZA S25/7188.
51. Halevi to his parents, 13 July 1927. With the kind permission of his son. See also: Arthur Ruppin, *Chapters of My Life in the Building of the Land and the Nation, 1920–1942* (in Hebrew) (Tel Aviv: Am Oved, 1969), p. 133.
52. Kisch diary, 12 May 1925, CZA S25/3272.
53. CZA S25/765.
54. Norman and Helen Bentwich, *Mandate Memoirs*, p. 106.
Edward Keith-Roach, *Pasha of Jerusalem* (London: Radcliffe Press, 1994), p. 99.
Douglas V. Duff, *Bailing with a Teaspoon* (London: John Long, 1953), p. 105.
55. Zvi El-Peleg, *The Grand Mufti* (in Hebrew) (Tel Aviv: Ministry of Defense, 1989), p. 29.
56. Deedes to the director of public security, apparently 1922, ISA M/S/158 I.
Francis Emily Newton, *Fifty Years in Palestine* (Wrotham: Coldharbour Press, 1948), p. 178.
57. Plumer to Amery, 28 Aug. 1925, PRO Colonial Office 733/96/40791.
Pinhas Ofer, "The Crystallization of the Mandate Regime and the Laying of the Foundations for the Jewish National Home, 1921–1931" (in Hebrew), in *The History of the Jewish Yishuv in Palestine from the Time of the First Aliya (The British Mandate)* (in Hebrew), ed. Moshe Lissak (Jerusalem: Israel Academy of Sciences, Bialik Institute, 1993), part I, p. 258ff.
58. Kisch diary, 21 Oct. 1925, CZA S25/3272.
59. N. and H. Bentwich, *Mandate Memoirs*, p. 106ff.
Keith-Roach, *Pasha of Jerusalem*, pp. 99, 115.
Frumkin, *The Way of a Judge*, p. 273.
Kisch diary, 1 Oct. 1925, CZA S25/3272.
60. Eder to Plumer, 26 July 1927, CZA S25/6832.
Kisch, *Palestine Diary*, p. 212.
N. and H. Bentwich, *Mandate Memoirs*, p. 113ff.
61. Halevi to his parents, 19 July 1927. With the kind permission of his son.
62. Yemima Rosenthal, ed., *Chronology of the History of the Jewish Yishuv in Palestine, 1917–1935* (in Hebrew) (Jerusalem: Yad Ben-Zvi, 1979), p. 144.
63. Kisch diary, 12–13 Feb. 1923, CZA S25/564.
64. Rosenthal, *Chronology of the History of the Jewish Yishuv in Palestine*, p. 144.
65. Halevi to his parents, 19 July 1927. With the kind permission of his son.
66. Horace Samuel, *Unholy Memories of the Holy Land* (London: Hogarth Press, 1930), p. 174.

13: THE NERVES OF JERUSALEM

1. *Palestine Commission on the Disturbances of August 1929*, vol. I, Colonial No. 48 (London: HMSO, 1930), p. 228ff.
F. H. Kisch, *Palestine Diary* (London: Victor Gollancz, 1938), p. 224ff.
Bernard Wasserstein, *The British in Palestine* (Oxford: Basil Blackwell, 1991), p. 154.

2. Norman and Helen Bentwich, *Mandate Memoirs, 1918–1948* (London: Hogarth Press, 1965), p. 131.

3. Douglas V. Duff, *Bailing with a Teaspoon* (London: John Long, 1953), p. 168ff.
Edward Keith-Roach, *Pasha of Jerusalem* (London: Radcliffe Press, 1994), p. 119.

4. Landau to Kisch, 21 Dec. 1928, CZA S25/2987.

5. Ronald Storrs, *Orientations* (London: Ivor Nicholson and Watson, 1939), pp. 342ff., 413. See also: Zionist Commission to the Political Committee in London, 20 May 1920, L3/240.

6. Bowman to Hall, 23 Sept. 1935, ISA secretariat section 125/32, microfilm G91-134 (1621). See also: Ben-Zvi to the chief secretary, 31 Dec. 1931, CZA S25/6731.

7. Kisch to David Yellin, 10 Apr. 1927, CZA J1/78.

8. Hacohen diary, 8 Tevet 5696, 3 Jan. 1936, National Library, Manuscript Division, 514/C. CZA 6910; S25/6286.
Chaim Arlosoroff, *Jerusalem Diary* (in Hebrew) (Tel Aviv: Mifleget Poalei Eretz Yisrael, 1949), p. 145.

9. Norman and Helen Bentwich, *Mandate Memoirs*, p. 48.
K. Y. Silman, "The Hannah Landau Affair" (in Hebrew), *Ha'aretz*, 11 June 1922, p. 3. See also: CZA S25/6910.
Storrs, *Orientations*, p. 435.

10. CZA S25/2099, S25/1364. See also: A. Caspi to Kisch, 3 June 1925, CZA S25/4274.
Ha-Olam, 12 June 1925, p. 453.
Kisch to the Zionist Organization, 6 Nov. 1928, CZA S25/420.

11. Report on Newton's activity, 19 June 1936, CZA S25/3234. See also: Cohen to Shertok, 4 July 1940, CZA S25/4803.
Francis Emily Newton, *Fifty Years in Palestine* (Wrotham: Coldharbour Press, 1948), p. 143. See also: *The Encyclopaedia Britannica*, 13th ed. (London: 1926), vol. II, p. 39.
Zionist Organization to Macmillan Publishers, 22 Oct. 1935, CZA S25/10535.

12. Moshe Sharett, *Political Diary* (in Hebrew) (Tel Aviv: Am Oved, 1971), vol I, p. 236 (24 July 1936).
David N. Myers, *Re-Inventing the Jewish Past* (New York: Oxford University Press, 1995), p. 144ff. See also: Uri Ram, "Zionist Historiography and the Invention of Modern Jewish Nationhood: The Case of Ben-Zion Dinur," *History and Memory*, vol. VII, no. 1 (Spring-Summer 1995), p. 91ff.

13. CZA S25/10063; S25/42. See also: Ashbal to Shertok, 28 Feb. 1946; U. H. (Uriel Heit-Hed) to Sherf, 4 Mar. 1946.
CZA S25/8085.

14. Tarif Khalidi, "Palestinian Historiography, 1900–1948," *Journal of Palestine Studies*, vol. X, no. 3 (Spring 1981), Issue 39, p. 59ff. See also: Adnan abu-Ghazaleh, "Arab Cultural Nationalism in Palestine During the British Mandate," *Journal of Palestine Studies*, vol. I, no. 3 (1972), p. 37ff.

15. ISA P/241 No. 1235.
Intelligence Report 98, 24 June 1920, and Intelligence Report 107, 3 July 1920, CZA L4/739. ISA P/329 No. 813.

16. Kisch to the high commissioner, 9 Jan. 1931, CZA S25/14.
Knabenshue to the State Department, "Records of the United States Consulate in Jerusalem, Palestine," Confidential Correspondence, 1920–1935 (Record group 84), CZA 10720, S25/1335.
JNF meeting, 17 Apr. 1934, CZA S25/1946.

17. CZA A199/25.

18. Bernard Wasserstein, *The British in Palestine* (Oxford: Basil Blackwell, 1991), p. 227.

19. Harry Luke, *Cities and Men* (London: Geoffrey Bles, 1953), pp. 204, 217.

20. Luke, *Cities and Men*, p. 213.

21. Horace Samuel, *Unholy Memories of the Holy Land* (London: Hogarth Press, 1930), p. 145ff. See also: Kisch, *Palestine Diary*, pp. 144, 146.

National Council to the High Commissioner, 22 Sept. 1922, ISA M/4/145.
CZA S25/2990.

22. Ronald Storrs, *Orientations* (London: Ivor Nicholson and Watson, 1939), p. 441.
Kisch, *Palestine Diary*, p. 131.
P. Dagan, "Jewish Scandal" (in Hebrew), *Do'ar HaYom*, 29 June 1924, p. 2.
"Culture" (in Hebrew), *Do'ar HaYom*, 7 Aug. 1924, p. 4.
"Culture," (in Hebrew), *Ha'aretz*, 15 July 1924, p. 4.

23. Storrs, *Orientations*, pp. 342ff., 413ff.
Zionist Commission to the Political Committee in London, 20 May 1920, CZA L3/240.

24. "The British Administration and Its Attitude to the Building of the National Home, 1942–1947," CZA S25/36.

25. Storrs, *Orientations*, p. 458.
Mayir Verete, Sir Ronald Storrs, 20 Jan. 1946, CZA S25/8033.

26. List of land sellers, 5 Jan. 1937, S25/9783.
Wasserstein, *The British in Palestine*, p. 224.

27. Knabenshue report, 2 Dec. 1929.
"Records of the United States Consulate in Jerusalem, Palestine," Confidential Correspondence, 1920–1935 (Record group 84). See also: ISA M/5/146.
Rachel Arbel, *Blue and White in Color: Visual Representations of Zionism, 1897–1947* (Tel Aviv: Diaspora Museum and Am Oved, 1997).

28. Halevi to his parents, 12 Apr. 1928. With the kind permission of his son.

29. Avraham Sela, "The Western Wall Events (1929): A Turning Point Between Jews and Arabs?" (in Hebrew), in *Jerusalem in Zionist Consciousness and Action* (in Hebrew), ed. Hagit Levsky (Merkhaz Zalman Shazar, 1989), p. 261ff.
Yehoshua Porat, *The Growth of the Palestinian Arab National Movement, 1918–1929* (in Hebrew) (Tel Aviv: Am Oved, 1976), vol. I, p. 210ff.

30. Anita Shapira, "A Political History of the Yishuv, 1918–1939" (in Hebrew), in *The History of the Jewish Yishuv in Palestine from the Time of the First Aliya* (in Hebrew), ed. Moshe Lissak (Jerusalem: Israel Academy of Sciences, Bialik Institute, 1994), part II, p. 60ff.

31. Shmuel Katz, *Jabo* (in Hebrew) (Tel Aviv: Dvir, 1993), vol. II, p. 705.

32. Ben-Gurion to the National Council, 16 Oct. 1928, CZA J1/7232.

33. National Council declaration, 26 Sept. 1928, Knesset Yisrael, National Council, "Book of Documents," 1949, p. 119ff.

34. Keith-Roach, *Pasha of Jerusalem*, p. 121.

35. Conversation with Chancellor, 15 Oct. 1928, CZA S25/29.
Chancellor's farewell speech, 26 Aug. 1921, RHL, Chancellor papers, 15:5,ff. 17–18.
The mufti to Nathan Straus, 3 Jan. 1929, CZA S25/3477.

36. Chancellor to his son, 8 Oct. 1929, 5 Oct. 1930, RHL, Chancellor Papers, 16:3 f.18, 100–02
Chancellor to the mufti, 8 Oct. 1929, RHL, Chancellor Papers, 14:1 ff.106–16.

37. Yemima Rosenthal, ed., *Chronology of the History of the Jewish Yishuv in Palestine, 1917–1935* (in Hebrew) (Jerusalem: Yad Ben-Zvi, 1979), p. 164ff.
Edwin Samuel, *A Lifetime in Jerusalem* (Jerusalem: Israel Universities Press, 1970), p. 104.

38. Halevi to his parents, 27 Sept. 1928. With the kind permission of his son.

39. Halevi to his parents, 18 Oct. 1928. With the kind permission of his son.

40. Halevi to his parents, 1 Oct. 1928. With the kind permission of his son.

41. Kisch to Rothschild, 28 Aug. 1929, CZA S25/1.

42. Halevi to his parents, 1 Oct., 18 Oct. 1928. With the kind permission of his son.

43. Yitzhak Olshan, *Memoirs* (in Hebrew) (Tel Aviv: Schocken, 1978), p. 124.

44. Halevi to his parents, 12 Aug. 1929. With the kind permission of his son.

45. Halevi to his parents, 21 Aug. 1929. With the kind permission of his son.

46. Wasserstein, *The British in Palestine*, p. 233.

47. Halevi to his parents, 21 Aug. 1929. With the kind permission of his son.

48. Archdale diary, p. 2, "Records of the United States Consulate in Jerusalem, Palestine,"

Confidential Correspondence, 1920–1935 (Record group 84). See also: Announcement of the Zionist Executive and National Council, 28 Aug. 1929, Knesset Yisrael, National Council, *Book of Documents*, 1949, p. 134ff.

49. Kingsley-Heath Report, ISA P/1052/1.
    Halevi to his parents, 21 Aug. 1929. With the kind permission of his son. See also: Duff, *Bailing with a Teaspoon*, p. 194ff.

50. Kisch, *Palestine Diary*, p. 248ff.
    Samuel, *A Lifetime in Jerusalem*, p. 109.

51. Keith-Roach, *Pasha of Jerusalem*, p. 117.
    David Ben-Gurion, *Memoirs* (in Hebrew) (Tel Aviv: Am Oved, 1971), vol I, p. 366.

52. Harry Luke, *Cities and Men*, vol. III, p. 24ff.

53. Harry Luke, *Cities and Men*, vol. III, p. 15ff. See also: [Yitzhak Ben Zvi] memorandum, 21 Aug. 1929, CZA A215/45.
    Zemora to Ben-Zvi, 27 Sept. 1929, CZA S25/9110.
    Palestine Commission on the Disturbances of August 1929, vol. I, Colonial No. 48 (HMSO: London, 1930).
    Evidence of Khadra, 27th sitting, 30 Nov. 1929, vol. I, p. 481ff.
    Evidence of Braude, 33rd sitting, 9 Dec. 1929, vol. II, p. 584ff.

54. Halevi to his parents, 1 Aug. 1929. With the kind permission of his son.

14: HEBRON, 1929

1. Harry Luke, *Cities and Men* (London: Geoffrey Bles, 1956), vol. III, p. 18.
   Report on events, "Records of the United States Consulate in Jerusalem, Palestine," Confidential Correspondence, 1920–1935 (Record group 84).
   Edward Keith-Roach, *Pasha of Jerusalem* (London: Radcliffe Press, 1994), p. 107.
   Palestine Commission on the Disturbances of August 1929, Colonial No. 48 (London: HMSO, 1930), Evidence of the Mufti, 28th–30th sittings, 2–4 Dec. 1929, vol. I, p. 492; vol. II, p. 543.

2. Report on events, "Records of the United States Consulate in Jerusalem, Palestine," Confidential Correspondence, 1920–1935 (Record group 84).
   Edwin Samuel, *A Lifetime in Jerusalem* (Jerusalem: Israel Universities Press, 1970), p. 106ff.

3. Luke, *Cities and Men*, vol. III, p. 18.
   Palestine Commission on the Disturbances of August 1929, Colonial No. 48 (London: HMSO, 1930), Evidence of the Mufti, 28th–30th sittings, 2–4 Dec. 1929, vol. I, p. 492; vol. II, p. 543.

4. Archdale diary, p. 3.
   "Records of the United States Consulate in Jerusalem, Palestine," Confidential Correspondence, 1920–1935 (Record group 84).
   Yitzhak Ben-Zvi (?), The Beginning of the Attack in Jerusalem (undated), CZA A215/45. See also: Diary of O.C. British Section DDSP, J. Nunro.

5. Report of Events, "Records of the United States Consulate in Jerusalem, Palestine," Confidential Correspondence, 1920–1935 (Record group 84). See also: Report of Mr. Kingsley Heath.
   Palestine Commission on the Disturbances of August 1929, Colonial No. 48 (London: HMSO 1930), evidence of Shammas, 21st sitting, 23 Nov. 1929, vol. I, p. 386ff.

6. S. Y. Agnon, *From Myself to Myself* (in Hebrew) (Tel Aviv: Schocken, 1976), p. 404.

7. Keith-Roach, *Pasha of Jerusalem*, p. 123.
   Martin Kolinsky, *Law, Order and Riots in Mandatory Palestine, 1928–1935* (London: St. Martin's Press, 1993), p. 79.

8. Samuel, *A Lifetime in Jerusalem*, p. 108.

9. Archdale diary, p. 1ff.

"Records of the United States Consulate in Jerusalem, Palestine," Confidential Correspondence, 1920–1935 (Record group 84).

10. Uri Brenner, *Ha-Kibbutz Ha-Me'uhad in the Haganah, 1923–1939* (in Hebrew) (Tel Aviv:
Ha-Kibbutz Ha-Me'uhad, 1980), p. 8.
Margery Bentwich to her family, 26 July 1929. With the kind permission of Ari Shavit.
Yitzhak Ben-Zvi (?), The Beginning of the Attack in Jerusalem (undated), CZA A215/45.
See also: Archdale diary, pp. 7, 10.
"Records of the United States Consulate in Jerusalem, Palestine," Confidential Corre-
spondence, 1920–1935 (Record group 84).

11. Cafferata, unpublished draft memoirs; Clayton to Cafferata, 18 July 1921; Cafferata to
his mother, 4 Aug. 1929. With the kind permission of his daughter.

12. Cafferata, unpublished draft memoirs; Clayton to Cafferata, 18 July 1921; Cafferata to
his mother, 4 Aug. 1929. With the kind permission of his daughter.

13. Eliash report, CZA S25/4601.
The City Committee of the Jews of Hebron, 20 May 1921, CZA J1/78.

14. *Palestine Commission on the Disturbances of August 1929*, Colonial No. 48 (London:
HMSO 1930), Report by Mr. Cafferata, vol. II, p. 983ff.
ISA, government publications, 01/3/381.

15. *Palestine Commission on the Disturbances of August 1929*, Colonial No. 48 (London:
HMSO 1930), Report by Mr. Cafferata, vol. II, p. 984.
Oded Avishar, "When Disturbances Occur" ("*Bifpro'a Pra'ot*") (in Hebrew), in *The
Hebron Massacre of 1929* (in Hebrew), ed. Rehavam Ze'evi (Havatzelet, 1994), p. 31ff.

16. Agnon, *From Myself to Myself*, p. 402. See also: Dan Laor, *S. Y. Agnon: A Biography* (in
Hebrew) (Tel Aviv: Schocken, 1998), p. 207ff.

17. Margery Bentwich to her family, 26 July 1929. With the kind permission of Ari Shavit.
Cafferata testimony at the Markha trial, *Report of the Commission of Inquiry* (in
Hebrew), 2nd ed. (Tel Aviv: [1930?]), p. 46.

18. Schneurson testimony and Markha testimony, Markha trial, *Report of the Commission
of Inquiry*, pp. 46, 65.

19. Report of Mr. Cafferata, *Palestine Commission on the Disturbances of August 1929*, Colonial No. 48 (London: HMSO 1930), vol. II, p. 984.
Y. L. Grodzinsky, "From the Scroll of Hebron" (in Hebrew), in Ze'evi, *The Hebron Massacre of 1929*, p. 52.

20. Testimony summaries, CZA S25/4601.
Rehavam Ze'evi, ed., *The Hebron Massacre of 1929* (in Hebrew), pp. 26ff., 69ff.
Report on events, "Records of the United States Consulate in Jerusalem, Palestine,"
Confidential Correspondence, 1920–1935 (Record group 84).

21. Halevi to his parents, 16 Sept. 1929. With the kind permission of his son.

22. David Ben-Gurion, *Memoirs* (in Hebrew) (Tel Aviv: Am Oved, 1971), vol. I, p. 349.
Ze'evi, *The Hebron Massacre of 1929*, p. 7.

23. Norman and Helen Bentwich, *Mandate Memoirs, 1918–1948* (London: Hogarth Press,
1965), p. 135.
Cafferata to his mother, 29 Nov. 1929. With the kind permission of his daughter.

24. Report on events, "Records of the United States Consulate in Jerusalem, Palestine,"
Confidential Correspondence, 1920–1935 (Record group 84).

25. Ze'evi, *The Hebron Massacre of 1929*, p. 41.
Jews Saved by Arabs, CZA S25/4472 and CZA S25/3409. See also: Oded Avishar, ed., *The
Hebron Book* (in Hebrew) (Jerusalem: Keter, 1978), p. 80ff.

26. Horowitz to Kisch, 10 Nov. 1929, CZA S25/3409.

27. Agnon, *From Myself to Myself*, p. 404ff.
Halevi to his parents, 30 Oct. 1929. With the kind permission of his son.

28. Levine to Abramson, 23 Oct. 1929. With the kind permission of the Munin family.

29. Kolinsky, *Law, Order and Riots in Mandatory Palestine*, p. 49.

F. H. Kisch, *Palestine Diary* (London: Victor Gollancz, 1938), p. 255. See also: Mohammed al-Tawil, "How the Events in Safed Began," CZA S25/9105.

30. Reply of the Palestinian Arab Executive to the High Commissioner's Proclamation, CZA S25/4184.

Arthur Ruppin, *Chapters of My Life in the Building of the Land and the Nation, 1920–1942* (in Hebrew) (Tel Aviv: Am Oved, 1968), p. 177.

CZA S25/4519. See also: The National Council on the Announcement of the Arab Executive, 6 Sept. 1929, Knesset Yisrael, National Council, *Book of Documents* (Jerusalem: n.p., 1949), p. 139ff.

Report of the Commission on Palestine Disturbances of August 1929, Cmd. 3530 (London: HMSO, 1930), p. 65.

31. Agnon, *From Myself to Myself*, p. 406.

32. Archdale diary, p. 15ff.

33. Chancellor to Passfield, 7 Sept. 1929, RHL, Chancellor papers, 12:5, f.1.

Kolinsky, *Law, Order and Riots in Mandatory Palestine*, p. 56.

Pinhas Ofer, "The Crystallization of the Mandatory Regime and the Laying of the Foundations for the Jewish National Home, 1922–1931" (in Hebrew), in *The History of the Jewish Yishuv in Palestine from the Time of the First Aliya (The British Mandate)* (in Hebrew), ed. Moshe Lissak (Jerusalem: Israel Academy of Sciences, Bialik Institute, 1993), part I, p. 287.

34. Chancellor to his son, 8 Oct. 1929, RHL, Chancellor papers, 16:3, f.18.

35. Chancellor to his son, 23 Oct. 1929, RHL, Chancellor papers, 16:3, f.35. See also: Kisch diary, 28 Jan. 1931, CZA L9/158.

15: BREAKFAST AT CHEQUERS

1. Chancellor to Passfield, 10 Nov. 1929, RHL, Chancellor Papers, 12:5, f.95. See also: Martin Kolinsky, *Law, Order and Riots in Mandatory Palestine, 1928–1935* (London: St. Martin's Press, 1993), p. 91ff.

2. Chaim Weizmann, *Trial and Error* (London: Hamish Hamilton, 1949), p. 412.

3. Chancellor to his son, 20 Oct. 1929, RHL, Chancellor Papers, 16:3, f. 26–31.

4. McDonnel to Chancellor, 18 Oct. 1921, RHL, Chancellor Papers, 17:3, f. 125.

Chaim Arlosoroff, *Jerusalem Diary* (in Hebrew) (Tel Aviv: Mifleget Poalei Eretz Yisrael, 1949), p. 205.

5. Norman and Helen Bentwich, *Mandate Memoirs, 1918–1948* (London: Hogarth Press, 1965), p. 139.

Chancellor to Passfield, 10 Sept. 1929, RHL, Chancellor Papers, 12:5 f. 29.

The Arabs of Nablus to the chief justice, 12 Sept. 1929, RHL, Chancellor Papers, 12:5, f.32.

Bentwich to Chancellor, 1 Oct. 1929, RHL, Chancellor Papers, 12:5, f. 45.

Memorandum of the Arab Executive, 2 Oct. 1929, RHL, Chancellor Papers, 14:1, f. 85.

N. and H. Bentwich, *Mandate Memoirs*, p. 137ff.

6. Kolinsky, *Law, Order and Riots in Mandatory Palestine*, p. 87ff.

7. Chancellor to his son, 13 Jan., 1 June 1930, RHL, Chancellor Papers, 16:3, ff. 80–84; f. 94.

F. H. Kisch, *Palestine Diary* (London: Victor Gollancz, 1938), p. 310.

8. Kisch diary, 17 June 1930, CZA S25/838.

Chancellor to his son, 14 Feb. 1931, RHL, Chancellor Papers, 16:3, ff. 100–02.

9. Kisch, *Palestine Diary*, p. 260. See also: Kisch with Chancellor, 10 Sept. 1929, RHL, Chancellor Papers, 14:1, ff. 36–37.

10. Kisch, *Palestine Diary*, pp. 267, 279ff. CZA S25/4472.

Rehavam Ze'evi, ed., *The Hebron Massacre of 1929* (in Hebrew) (Havatzelet, 1994), p. 86ff.

Bernard Wasserstein, *The British in Palestine* (Oxford: Basil Blackwell, 1991), p. 237.

N. and H. Bentwich, *Mandate Memoirs*, p. 134.

11. Kisch diary, 16 Sept. 1929, CZA S25/838.

12. Kisch diary, 11 Sept. 1929, CZA S25/838. See also: CZA S25/10008.

13. S. Y. Agnon, *From Myself to Myself* (in Hebrew) (Tel Aviv: Schocken, 1976), p. 406.
    N. and H. Bentwich, *Mandate Memoirs*, p. 133.
    Chancellor to his son, 5 Oct., 14 Nov. 1930, RHL, Chancellor Papers, 16:3, ff. 26–31; 128–36.

14. Kisch, *Palestine Diary*, pp. 287ff., 261.

15. "Liverpool Man's Heroism in Palestine," *Liverpool Echo*, 31 Aug. 1929.
    Official Gazette, 25 Sept. 1929, p. 998.

16. Instructions to the press, 10 Sept. 1929, CZA S25/3336.

17. Chancellor to his son, 11 Sept. 1929, RHL, Chancellor Papers, 16:3, f. 15.
    Kisch, *Palestine Diary*, p. 270.
    Kisch diary, 11–12 Sept. 1929, CZA S25/838.

18. Speech at the Zionist Congress, 1931, in David Ben-Gurion, *Memoirs* (in Hebrew) (Tel Aviv: Am Oved, 1971), vol. I, p. 466. See also: Shabtai Teveth, *Ben-Gurion and the Arabs of Palestine* (in Hebrew) (Tel Aviv: Schocken, 1985), p. 136.

19. Shmuel Katz, *Jabo* (in Hebrew) (Tel Aviv: Dvir, 1993), vol. I, p. 741ff.
    David Ben-Gurion, *Memoirs* (in Hebrew) (Tel Aviv: Am Oved, 1971), vol. I, p. 164.
    Arthur Ruppin, *Chapters of My Life in the Building of the Land and the Nation, 1920–1942* (in Hebrew) (Tel Aviv: Am Oved, 1968), p. 175.

20. Halevi to his parents, 4 and 16 Aug. 1929. With the kind permission of his son.

21. Kisch to Rothschild, 28 Aug. 1929, CZA S25/1. See also: CZA S25/3833.

22. Alan Saunders to Cafferata, Oct. 1929; Cafferata to Christopher Sykes, 30 Apr. 1964. With the kind permission of his daughter.

23. Pinhas Ofer, "The Crystallization of the Mandatory Regime and the Laying of the Foundations for the Jewish National Home, 1922–1931," in *The History of the Jewish Yishuv in Palestine from the Time of the First Aliya (The British Mandate)* (in Hebrew), ed. Moshe Lissak (Jerusalem: Israel Academy of Sciences, Bialik Institute, 1993), part I, pp. 286ff., 303ff.

24. Gabriel Sheffer, "Shapers of Mandatory Policy: Stereotypes or Flesh and Blood" (in Hebrew), *Keshet*, no. 48 (1970), p. 174.

25. Chancellor to his son, 3 Nov. 1929, RHL, Chancellor Papers, 16:3, ff. 26–31.

26. The mufti to the Commission of Inquiry, *Report of the Commission of Inquiry* (in Hebrew), 2nd ed. (Tel Aviv: [1930?]), part IV, p. 98.
    Palestine Commission on the Disturbances of August 1929, Colonial No. 48 (London: HMSO 1930), Evidence of the Mufti, 29th sitting, 3 Dec. 1929, vol. I, p. 509.
    Chancellor to his son, 12 Oct. 1929, RHL, Chancellor Papers, 16:3, ff. 26–31.

27. Ben-Gurion, *Memoirs*, vol. I, p. 344.
    Yehoshua Porat, *The Growth of the Palestinian Arab National Movement, 1918–1929* (in Hebrew) (Tel Aviv: Am Oved, 1976), vol. I, p. 210.
    Zvi El-Peleg, *The Grand Mufti* (in Hebrew) (Tel Aviv: Ministry of Defense, 1989), p. 22ff.
    Philip Mattar, "The Role of the Mufti of Jerusalem in the Political Struggle over the Western Wall, 1928–1929," *Middle Eastern Studies*, vol. XIX, no. 1 (Jan. 1983), p. 104ff.

28. The mufti to the commission of inquiry, *Report of the Commission of Inquiry* (in Hebrew), 2nd ed. (Tel Aviv: [1930?]), part IV, p. 92.

29. Chancellor to his son, 11 Nov. 1929, RHL, Chancellor Papers, 16:3, f. 53.
    Chancellor with Arab representatives, 9 Sept. 1929, RHL, Chancellor Papers, 14:1, f. 2.
    Chancellor to his son, 12 Oct. 1929, RHL, Chancellor Papers, 16:3, ff. 26–31.

30. Chancellor to his son, 12 Oct. 1929, RHL, Chancellor Papers, 16:3, ff. 26.

31. Chancellor to his son, 13 Jan. 1930, 18 Oct. 1930, RHL, Chancellor Papers, 11:1, ff. 27–28.

32. Chancellor to his son, 12 Oct. 1930; 12 Oct. 1929, RHL, Chancellor Papers, 16:3, ff. 26–31.

33. Gabriel Sheffer, "Shapers of Mandatory Policy," p. 174.

34. Chancellor to his son, 6 Oct. 1929, RHL, Chancellor Papers, 16:3, f. 18.

G. Sheffer, "Intentions and Results of British Policy in Palestine: Passfield's White Paper," *Middle Eastern Studies*, vol. IX, no. 1 (Jan. 1973), p. 45.

35. Chancellor to Plumer, 3 Oct. 1928, RHL, Chancellor Papers, 11:1, ff. 27–28.
Chancellor to the colonial secretary, 17 Jan. 1930, PRO CO733/182 77050 pt. I. See also: Pinhas Ofer, "The Crystallization of the Mandatory Regime," part I, p. 290ff.

36. Chancellor to his son, 18 Oct. 1930, RHL, Chancellor Papers, 16:3, ff. 114–18.

37. A J. P. Taylor, *English History, 1914–1945* (Oxford: Clarendon Press, 1965), p. 276.

38. Sheffer, "Intentions and Results of British Policy in Palestine," p. 45.

39. "Anti-Zionist MPs," July 1922, Weizmann Archive.

40. N. and H. Bentwich, *Mandate Memoirs*, p. 142.
Chancellor to his son, 16 Nov. 1930, RHL, Chancellor Papers, 16:3, f. 128.
Alan Bullock, *Ernest Bevin: Trade Union Leader* (New York: W.W. Norton, 1960), p. 457.

41. Chaim Weizmann, *Trial and Error* (London: Hamish Hamilton, 1949), p. 410ff.
Gabriel Sheffer, "The Image of the Palestinians and the Yishuv as a Factor in Shaping Mandatory Policy in the 1930s" (in Hebrew), *Ha-Tzionut* III (1973), p. 287.

42. Chancellor to his son, 26 Oct. 1930, RHL, Chancellor Papers, 16:3, f. 123.

43. Wedgwood to Chancellor and others, 26 July 1928, RHL, Chancellor Papers, 11:1, 17–18.
Ben-Gurion, *Memoirs*, vol. V, pp. 93, 125.
Ben-Gurion, *Memoirs*, vol. I, pp. 305, 307. See also: Josiah Wedgwood, *The Seventh Dominion* (London: Labour Publishing Co., 1928).

44. Chancellor to his son, 18 Oct. 1930, RHL, Chancellor Papers, 16:3, ff. 114–18.
Chancellor to Davidson, 7 Mar. 1937, RHL, Chancellor Papers, 15:7, ff. 69–72.
George Rendel, *The Sword and the Olive* (London: John Murray, 1957), p. 120.
Chancellor to his son, 12 Oct. 1929, RHL, Chancellor Papers, 16:3, ff. 26–31.

45. Weizmann, *Trial and Error*, pp. 410, 406, 416.
Ofer, "The Crystallization of the Mandatory Regime," part I, p. 290ff.
The Royal Institute of International Affairs, *Great Britain and Palestine, 1915–1936* (New York: Oxford University Press, 1937), p. 54ff. See also: Reaction of the National Council, Knesset Yisrael, National Council, *Book of Documents* (Jerusalem: n.p., 1949), p. 143ff.

46. Katz, *Jabo*, vol. II, p. 816.
Norman Rose, *Chaim Weizmann* (New York: Viking, 1986), p. 290ff.

47. Ben-Gurion, *Memoirs*, vol. I, pp. 420, 428.
Shabtai Teveth, *The Burning Ground* (Tel Aviv: Schocken, 1980), vol. II, p. 180ff.

48. Ben-Gurion, *Memoirs*, vol. I, p. 483.

49. Ben-Gurion, *Memoirs*, vol. III, p. 140. See also: Ben-Gurion, *Memoirs*, vol. V, p. 367.

50. Knabenshue to the secretary of state, 20 Oct. 1931, "Records of the United States Consulate in Jerusalem, Palestine," Confidential Correspondence, 1920–1935 (Record group 84).

51. Chancellor to his son, 14 and 15 Nov. 1930, 13 Mar. 1931, RHL, Chancellor Papers, 16:3, ff. 128–36; ff. 157–61.

52. Draft of article, RHL, Chancellor Papers, 11:7, ff. 67–78.
Chancellor to his son, 12 Oct. 1929, 23 Oct. 1930, RHL, Chancellor Papers, 16:3, ff. 26–31; 119–22.

53. Chancellor to his son, 13 Jan., 21 Feb. 1930; Chancellor to Birchenough (undated), RHL, Chancellor Papers, 16:3, ff. 80–87; 12:7, f.8.
Chancellor's farewell speech, 26 Aug. 1931, RHL, Chancellor Papers, 15:5, f. 17.

54. Procedure for Civil Marriage of Mr. Cafferata and Miss Ford-Dunn, Apr. 5, 1930. With the kind permission of his daughter.
"Palestine Hero and His Bride," *Liverpool Echo*, 22 Apr. 1930.

16: HAMLET IN BIR ZEIT

1. David Kroyanker, *Jerusalem Architecture: Building in the British Mandate Period* (in Hebrew) (Jerusalem: Keter, 1991), p. 81ff.

2. The American consulate to the State Department, 4 July 1935, "Records of the United States Consulate in Jerusalem, Palestine," Confidential Correspondence, 1920–1935 (Record group 84).
   Battershill diary, 14 Aug. 1937, 1 Jan. 1939, RHL, Battershill Papers, 12:6, ff. 5–11; 48–56.
3. Horace Samuel, *Unholy Memories of the Holy Land* (London: Hogarth Press, 1930), p. 189.
4. Beatrice Magnes, *Episodes* (Berkeley: Judah L. Magnes Memorial Museum, 1977), p. 79.
5. Amos Oz, *Panther in the Basement* (in Hebrew) (Jerusalem: Keter, 1995), p. 37.
6. Antonius to his daughter, 16 July 1930, ISA P/1051/5.
7. Edward Keith-Roach, *Pasha of Jerusalem* (London: Radcliffe Press, 1994), p. 212ff.
   Wauchope to Battershill, 20 Sept. 1937, RHL, Battershill Papers, 1:4, f. 7.
   Battershill diary, 29 Nov. 1938, RHL, Battershill Papers, 12:6, ff. 24–27.
   Battershill diary, 15 Dec. 1938, RHL, Battershill Papers, 12:6, ff. 24–27.
8. Chaim Arlosoroff, *Jerusalem Diary* (in Hebrew) (Tel Aviv: Mifleget Poalei Eretz Yisrael, 1949), pp. 195, 164, 181, 237.
9. Arlosoroff, *Jerusalem Diary*, p. 168.
10. Correspondence between Arlosoroff and Wauchope, May 1932, CZA S25/30.
11. Plan for Establishing Good Relations with British Officials, 1931, CZA S25/7753.
12. Joseph F. Broadhurst, *From Vine Street to Jerusalem* (London: Stanley Paul, 1936), p. 223.
13. Mikhail Golinkin, *From the Sanctuaries of Yefet to the Tents of Shem* (in Hebrew) (Committee for the Publication of the Golinkin Memoirs, 1950).
    "Culture," *Ha'aretz*, 9 Mar. 1923, p. 4.
14. Ronald Storrs, *Orientations* (London: Ivor Nicholson and Watson, 1939), p. 440.
    Tel Aviv Municipality to Moshe Shertok, 28 May 1934, CZA S25/9725.
15. Magnes, *Episodes*, pp. 108, 116, 151.
16. Arlosoroff, *Jerusalem Diary*, p. 224.
    Magnus Hirschfeld, *Men and Women: The World Journey of a Sexologist* (New York: G. P. Putnam's Sons, 1935), p. 291.
17. Hacohen diary, 14 Heshvan 5695 (2 Nov. 1934), 1 Menachem-Av (31 July 1934), National Library, Manuscript Division, 514/B.
18. Wauchope file, CZA S25/30.
19. Keith-Roach, *Pasha of Jerusalem*, p. 132ff.
    Battershill diary, 14 Aug. 1937, 1 Jan. 1939, RHL, Battershill Papers, 12:6, ff. 1–4. See also: American Consulate to the State Department, 4 July 1935, "Records of the United States Consulate in Jerusalem, Palestine," Confidential Correspondence, 1920–1935 (Record group 84).
    David Hacohen, *Time to Tell* (in Hebrew) (Tel Aviv: Am Oved, 1974), p. 63.
20. CZA S25/31/2.
    Norman and Helen Bentwich, *Mandate Memoirs, 1918–1948* (London: Hogarth Press, 1965), p. 153.
    Wauchope to Ormsby-Gore, 24 June 1936, PRO CO 733/297 75156.
21. Chief Secretary to the Jewish Agency, 17 July 1930, CZA S25/4472.
22. Haim Hanegbi, "My Hebron: A Story of a Different Love" (in Hebrew), *Koteret Rashit*, 20 July 1983, p. 20ff. See also: Arlosoroff, *Jerusalem Diary*, p. 250.
23. David Ben-Gurion, *Memoirs* (in Hebrew) (Tel Aviv: Am Oved, 1971), vol I, p. 364.
24. Martin Kolinsky, *Law, Order and Riots in Mandatory Palestine, 1928–1935* (London: St. Martin's Press, 1993), p. 181.
25. Edwin Samuel, *A Lifetime in Jerusalem* (Jerusalem: Israel Universities Press, 1970), p. 111.
    Edwin Samuel to his father, 17 Sept. 1929, ISA P/653/85.
26. Baruch Katinka, *From Then to Now* (in Hebrew) (Kiryat Sefer, 1965), p. 260.
27. Edward Keith-Roach, *Pasha of Jerusalem*, p. 130.
28. Humphrey Bowman, *Middle-East Window* (London: Longrams, Green and Co., 1942), p. 305.
29. Knabenshue to the State Department, 2 Dec. 1929, "Records of the United States Con-

sulate in Jerusalem, Palestine," Confidential Correspondence, 1920–1935 (Record group 84).

Arthur Ruppin, *Chapters of My Life in the Building of the Land and the Nation, 1920–1942* (in Hebrew) (Tel Aviv: Am Oved, 1968), p. 178.

30. Levine to Hoofien, 27 Oct. 1929; Hoofien to Levine, 31 Oct. 1929. With the kind permission of the Munin family.

31. Levine papers. With the kind permission of the Munin family.

32. Alter Levine, "Go and We Will Go" (Lecha Ve-Nelecha), National Library, Manuscript Division.

33. Asaf Halevy Ish Yerushalayim, *Scroll of the East (Megilat Kedem)* (in Hebrew) (Dekel, 1915), pp. 308ff.

34. Khalil al-Sakakini, *Such Am I, O World* (in Hebrew) (Jerusalem: Keter, 1990), p. 167.
Sakakini diary, 1940, n.d. With the kind permission of his daughters.

35. Yemima Rosenthal ed., *Chronology of the History of the Jewish Yishuv in Palestine, 1917–1935* (in Hebrew) (Jerusalem: Yad Ben-Zvi, 1979), p. 196ff.

36. Arab congresses, 30 Nov. 1930, "Records of the United States Consulate in Jerusalem, Palestine," Confidential Correspondence, 1920–1935 (Record group 84).
Arlosoroff to Kisch [1929?], CZA S25/4164.

37. Yuval Arnon-Ohana, "The Al-Istiqlal Party: The Beginning of Palestinian Radicalism, 1930–1937" (in Hebrew), *Katedra* 12 (July 1979), p. 91ff. See also: Yehoshua Porat, *From Riots to Rebellion: The Arab National Movement, 1929–1939* (in Hebrew) (Tel Aviv: Am Oved, 1978), p. 147ff.

38. ISA P/326 no. 621.
Kolinsky, *Law, Order and Riots in Mandatory Palestine*, p. 172ff.

39. Sakakini, *Such Am I, O World*, p. 169.

40. Report of the Commission of Inquiry, *Palestine Gazette*, no. 420 (7 Feb. 1934), p. 95ff., ISA P/326/621.

41. Sakakini, *Such Am I, O World*, p. 171.

42. Sakakini, *Such Am I, O World*, p. 170.

43. CZA S25/4949.

44. Shabtai Teveth, *The Arlosoroff Murder* (in Hebrew) (Tel Aviv: Schocken, 1982); State of Israel, Commission of Inquiry into the Murder of Dr. Chaim Arlosoroff, "Report," 1985.

45. Yosef Heller, *Leh'i, 1940–1949* (in Hebrew) (Jerusalem: Merkaz Zalman Shazar and Keter, 1989), vol. I, p. 19ff.; vol. II, p. 531ff.
Battershill diary, 21 Nov. 1937, RHL, Battershill Papers, 10:3, ff. 5–24.

46. Morrison diary, pp. 19, 5, 16, IWM, Morrison Papers.

47. Morrison diary, pp. 11, 8, 20, IWM, Morrison Papers.

48. Moshe Lissak, "Immigration, Absorption, and the Building of Society in Palestine—Israel in the 1920s, 1918–1930" (in Hebrew), in *The History of the Jewish Yishuv in Palestine from the Time of the First Aliya (The British Mandate)* (in Hebrew), ed. Moshe Lissak and Gabriel Cohen (Jerusalem: Israel Academy of Sciences, Bialik Institute, 1994), part II, p. 287ff.
Hacohen diary, 3 Heshvan 5695 (12 Oct. 1934), National Library, Manuscript Division, B/514.

49. May Seikaly, *Haifa: Transformation of an Arab Society, 1918–1939* (London: I. B. Tauris, 1995), p. 49.

50. Tom Segev, *The Seventh Million* (New York: Hill and Wang, 1993), p. 15ff.

51. *A Survey of Palestine Prepared for the Anglo-American Committee of Inquiry* (Jerusalem: Government Printer, 1946), vol. II, p. 703. See also: Alfred Boneh on the economic situation of the Arabs, 22 Sept. 1936, CZA S25/30002.
Smilansky report, 22 June 1932, S25/7599.

52. Pevsner to Ruppin, 1 June 1930, CZA S25/7448.

53. Bowman, *Middle-East Window*, p. 261.

54. Antonius memorandum (1942), ISA P/1052/4. See also: M. F. Abcarius, *Palestine*

Through the Fog of Propaganda (London: Hutchinson and Co., 1946), p. 100.

Yehoshua Ben-Hanania, "The History of Arab Education in Palestine" (in Hebrew), *Har Ha-Mizrah*, 26 Nov. 1943, p. 5ff.; 10 Dec. 1943, p. 10ff.; 24 Dec. 1943, p. 5ff.; 14 Jan. 1944, p. 5ff.; 28 Jan. 1944, p. 6ff.; 11 Feb. 1944, p. 4ff.; 7 Apr. 1944, p. 4ff.

A Survey of Palestine Prepared for the Anglo-American Committee of Inquiry (Jerusalem: Government Printer, 1946), vol. III, p. 1147.

55. A. L. Tibawi, *Arab Education in Mandatory Palestine* (London: Luzac and Co., 1956), p. 78. See also: Roderic D. Matthews and Matta Arkawi, *Education in Arab Countries of the Near East* (Washington: American Council on Education, 1949), p. 217ff.

Ya'akov Reuveni, *The Mandatory Administration in Palestine, 1920–1948: A Historical Political Analysis* (in Hebrew) (Ramat Gan: Bar-Ilan University, 1993), p. 164.

56. The Distribution of Educational Benefits in Palestine, MEC, Farrell Papers. Wauchope to the colonial secretary, 31 Dec. 1932, PRO CO 733/230 17240.

57. Reuveni, *The Mandatory Administration in Palestine*, pp. 164, 170ff.

Tibawi, *Arab Education in Mandatory Palestine*, p. 273.

McNair Report, p. 43ff, ISA M/4388/01/3/267.

58. *Palestine and Transjordan: Report of the Financial Commission*, Middle East No. 43 (London: HMSO, July 1931), p. 84ff., ISA M/01/3/313.

59. Bowman, *Middle-East Window*, p. 279.

Tibawi, *Arab Education in Mandatory Palestine*, p. 79.

60. Farrell to the chief secretary, 7 Oct. 1935, ISA M/125/E/61/35.

Tibawi, *Arab Education in Mandatory Palestine*, p. 80ff.

61. Sakakini, *Such Am I, O World*, p. 153.

62. Tibawi, *Arab Education in Mandatory Palestine*, p. 80ff.

Farrell to the chief secretary, 12 Apr. 1932, ISA M/124/5 (microfilm G 91-134-1064).

Bowman, *Middle-East Window*, p. 258. See also: Ylana Miller, *Government and Society in Rural Palestine, 1920–1948* (Austin: University of Texas Press, 1985), p. 102ff.

63. Abdul Majid Hurshid file, ISA, education department, M/1019.

64. Musa Kazim al-Husseini to the high commissioner, 29 Sept. 1932, PRO CO 733/230 17240.

A-Dif'a, 30 Sept. 1946.

Tibawi, *Arab Education in Mandatory Palestine*, p. 165. See also: *Palestine Royal Commission Report*, Cmd. 5479 (London: HMSO, 1937), p. 337.

65. "School Year in Palestine," pp. 5ff., 58. MEC, Wilson Papers.

66. Bernard De Bunsen, "Memoirs," manuscript with unnumbered pages. With the kind permission of his widow.

Wauchope to the colonial secretary, 31 Dec. 1932, PRO CO 733/230 17240.

Palestine Royal Commission Report, Cmd. 5479 (London: HMSO, 1937), p. 337.

Tibawi, *Arab Education in Mandatory Palestine*, p. 165.

67. *Palestine and Transjordan: Report of the Financial Commission*, Middle East No. 43, p. 89.

68. Wauchope to Lawrence, 25 May 1935, PRO CO 733/273 75077.

Farrell memorandum, 23 Oct. 1939, PRO CO 733/431 76031.

69. Farrell diary, p. 10, MEC, Farrell Papers.

70. Mahmoud Yazbek, "Arab Migration to Haifa, 1933–1948: A Quantitative Analysis according to Arab Sources" (in Hebrew), *Katedra* 45 (Sept. 1987), p. 131ff.

Yosef Vashitz, "Village Migration to Haifa in the Mandatory Period: Process or Urbanization?" (in Hebrew), *Katedra* 45 (Sept. 1987), p. 113ff.

Gad Gilbar, "Trends in the Demographic Development of Palestinian Arabs, 1870–1948" (in Hebrew), *Katedra* 45 (Sept. 1987), p. 42ff.

Rachelle Taqqu, "Peasants into Workmen: Internal Labor Migration and the Arab Village Community Under the Mandate," in *Palestinian Society and Politics*, ed. Joel S. Migdal (Princeton: Princeton University Press, 1980), p. 261ff.

71. Kisch and others to the high commissioner, 7 May 1929; Chancellor to Amery, 15 May 1929, PRO CO 733/165 67049.

72. Miller, *Government and Society in Rural Palestine 1920–1948*.
    Baruch Kimmerling and Joel S. Migdal, *Palestinians: The Making of a People* (New York: Free Press, 1993).

17: KHALIL AL-SAKAKINI BUILDS A HOME

1. Organization and Activity of Arab Bands in Palestine (in Hebrew), 12 Oct. 1936, CZA S25/3441.
2. Khalil al-Sakakini, *Such Am I, O World* (in Hebrew) (Jerusalem: Keter, 1990), pp. 165, 174.
3. Report of the American Consulate in Jerusalem, 23 Oct. 1935, Ely Palmer to the secretary of state, "Records of the United States Consulate in Jerusalem, Palestine," Confidential Correspondence, 1920–1935 (Record group 84).
4. CZA S25/4224.
   Shai Lachman, "Arab Rebellion and Terrorism in Palestine, 1929–1939: The Case of Sheikh Izz al-Din al-Qassam and His Movement," in *Zionism and Arabism in Palestine and Israel*, ed. Elie Kedourie and Sylvia G. Haim (London: Frank Cass, 1982), p. 52ff.
   A. Shleifer, "The Life and Thought of Izz-al-Din al-Qassam," *Islamic Quarterly*, vol. XXIII, no. 2 (2nd quarter), 1979.
5. Ben-Gurion at the Mapai Central Committee, 29 Sept. 1936, LPA, 23/36, section 2.
6. Lachman, "Arab Rebellion and Terrorism in Palestine," p. 71.
   Yehoshua Porat, *From Riots to Rebellion: The Arab National Movement, 1929–1939* (in Hebrew) (Tel Aviv: Am Oved, 1978), p. 218.
7. Berl Katznelson at the Political Committee, 4 May 1936, in David Ben-Gurion, *Memoirs* (in Hebrew) (Tel Aviv: Am Oved, 1971), vol. III, p. 157.
8. Leila Khaled, *My People Shall Live* (London: Hodder and Stoughton, 1973), p. 23.
9. Sakakini diary, 28 June, 30 June 1936. With the kind permission of his daughters.
   Ezra Danin, ed., *Documents and Images from the Archives of the Arab Gangs in the Events of 1936–1939* (in Hebrew) (Jerusalem: Magnes, 1981).
10. "School Year in Palestine," p. 24, MEC, Wilson Papers.
11. Baruch Kimmerling and Joel S. Migdal, *Palestinians: The Making of a People* (New York: Free Press, 1993), p. 96ff.
    Joseph Nevo, "Palestinian-Arab Violent Activity During the 1930s," in *Britain and the Middle East in the 1930s*, ed. Michael J. Cohen and Martin Kolinsky (London: Macmillan, 1992), p. 169ff,
    Porat, *From Riots to Rebellion*, pp. 195ff., 228.
    Ylana Miller, *Government and Society in Rural Palestine, 1920–1948* (Austin: University of Texas Press, 1985), p. 121ff.
12. Pealy to Chancellor, 23 June 1936, RHL, Chancellor Papers, 22: MF40, pp. 2–4.
13. Morrison diary, p. 13ff., IWM, Morrison Papers.
14. "School Year in Palestine," pp. 47, 24, MEC, Wilson Papers.
15. Habas, *The Book of the Events*, 5696, p. 644.
    Wauchope to Ben-Gurion, 17 May 1936, CZA S25/31.
    Sakakini to his son, 19 May 1936. With the kind permission of his daughters.
16. Sakakini, *Such Am I, O World*, p. 188.
    Sakakini to his son, 13 June 1936. With the kind permission of his daughters.
17. Hala Sakakini, *Jerusalem and I* (Amman: n.p. 1987), p. 78.
18. Sakakini, *Such Am I, O World*, p. 180.
19. Morrison diary, p. 30, IWM, Morrison Papers.
20. Elihau Stern, ed., *Chronology of the New Jewish Yishuv in Palestine, 1936–1947* (in Hebrew) (Jerusalem: Yad Ben-Zvi, 1974), p. 14.
    Beginning of Disturbances, Summary of Events and Facts, CZA S25/4180. See also: CZA S25/4244.
    Chaim Shalmoni, ed., *Yizkor* (Moses Press, undated).

Bracha Habas, ed., *The Book of the Events of 5696* (in Hebrew) (Tel Aviv: Davar, 1937), p. 635.

21. *Survey of Palestine Prepared for the Anglo-American Committee of Inquiry* (Jerusalem: Government Printer, 1946), vol. I, pp. 38, 46, 49. See also: Stern, *Chronology of the New Jewish Yishuv in Palestine*, pp. 15, 20, 55, 60, 74, 80, 103, 108.
Habas, *The Book of the Events of 5696*, p. 691.

22. Moshe Sharett, *Political Diary* (in Hebrew) (Tel Aviv: Am Oved, 1969), vol. I, p. 121.

23. Battershill to Shuckburgh, 21 Nov. 1937, RHL, Battershill Papers, 10:3, ff. 5–24.

24. Sakakini, *Such Am I, O World*, p. 187.

25. Sakakini diary, 10 June, 13 June, 16 June 1936; 30 Apr., 5 May, 7 May, 23 May 1936. With the kind permission of his daughters.

26. Memorandum, 18 Mar. 1937 (apparently), CZA S25/9783.
Zvi El-Peleg, *The Grand Mufti* (in Hebrew) (Tel Aviv: Ministry of Defense, 1989), p. 44ff.
Tayasir Jbara, *Palestinian Leader: Hajj Amin Al-Hussayni, Mufti of Jerusalem* (Princeton: Kingston Press, 1985), p. 141ff.
Philip Mattar, *The Mufti of Jerusalem* (New York: Columbia University Press, 1988), p. 65ff.

27. Sakakini, *Such Am I, O World*, p. 13ff.

28. Sakakini diary, 4 Nov. 1933. With the kind permission of his daughters.

29. Porat, *From Riots to Rebellion*, p. 204.

30. Ya'akov Solomon to the Royal Commission, 4 Nov. 1936, CZA S25/4675. See also: ISA M/222.

31. Sakakini, *Such Am I, O World*, pp. 185, 161.

32. CZA S25/8233.

33. Ted Swedenburg, *Memoirs of Revolt* (Minneapolis: University of Minnesota Press, 1995), p. 167ff.

34. Anwar Nusseibeh, "Pattern of Disaster: Personal Note on the Fall of Palestine," pp. 48, 52. With the kind permission of his son.

35. Sakakini diary, 30 Apr. 1936. With the kind permission of his daughters.
Porat, *From Riots to Rebellion*, p. 318.
"School Year in Palestine," pp. 11, 13, MEC, Wilson Papers.

36. Swedenburg, *Memoirs of Revolt*, p. 36.

37. Rotenstreich to the members of the Jewish Agency Executive, 30 Dec. 1936, CZA S25/9783.
Porat, *From Riots to Rebellion*, p. 208ff.

38. Netanel Katzburg, "The Second Decade of the Mandate Regime in Palestine, 1931–1939" (in Hebrew), in *The History of the Jewish Yishuv in Palestine from the Time of the First Aliya (The British Mandate)* (in Hebrew) (Jerusalem: Israel Academy of Sciences, Bialik Institute, 1993), part I, p. 376ff.
Sonia Fathi El Nimr, "The Arab Revolt of 1936–1939 in Palestine" (Ph.D. thesis, University of Exeter, 1990), p. 226.

39. Porat, *From Riots to Rebellion*, p. 253. See also: R. Zaslani to A. Kaplan, Jan. 1937, CZA S25/3441.
Moshe Sharett, *Political Diary* (in Hebrew) (Tel Aviv: Am Oved, 1968), vol. I, p. 182.

40. Ben-Gurion to the Mapai Central Committee, 29 Sept. 1936, LPA, 23/36 section 2; Ben-Gurion to the members of the Zionist Executive in London, 2 Nov. 1933, CZA S25/4224.
Shabtai Teveth, *Ben-Gurion and the Arabs of Palestine* (in Hebrew) (Tel Aviv: Schocken, 1985), p. 271.
Ben-Gurion to the Mapai Committee, 6 July 1938, LPA 23/38 section 2.

41. Sakakini, *Such Am I, O World*, p. 172ff.

42. Sakakini, *Such Am I, O World*, p. 183ff.

43. Sakakini, *Such Am I, O World*, p. 148ff.

44. Sakakini, *Such Am I, O World*, pp. 173, 177, 167, 148.

45. Sakakini to his son, 12 Dec. 1932, 7 Jan. 1933, 12 Jan. 1933, ISA P/378/2646.

46. Sakakini, *Such Am I, O World*, pp. 192, 194, p. 156ff, 175.
47. Sakakini, *Such Am I, O World*, p. 191.
48. Sakakini, *Such Am I, O World*, pp. 191, 193.

18: MADE IN PALESTINE

1. Ben-Gurion's notes of his talks with Arabs, 1934–36, CZA S25/10188.
2. Eliahu Eilat, "Conversations with Musa Alami" (in Hebrew), *Yahadut Zemananu*, vol. II, 1958, p. 22.
3. Ben-Gurion's notes of his talks with Arabs, 1934–36, CZA S25/10188.
   Moshe Sharett, *Political Diary* (in Hebrew) (Tel Aviv: Am Oved, 1971), vol. I, pp. 136, 142ff., 165ff.
   Ben-Gurion with Wauchope, 29 to 30 July, 1934, CZA S25/171/1.
   Attempts to talk with Arabs 1932–45, CZA S25/8085.
   Frumkin and others to Shertok, 28 July 1936, CZA A 199/26.
   Gad Frumkin, *The Way of a Judge in Jerusalem* (in Hebrew) (Tel Aviv: Dvir, 1954), p. 321ff.
4. David Ben-Gurion, Causes of the Riots (in Hebrew), 8 Nov. 1936, CZA S25/4180.
5. David Ben-Gurion, *Memoirs* (in Hebrew) (Tel Aviv: Am Oved, 1973), vol. III, p. 200.
6. Moshe Lissak, "Immigration, Absorption, and the Building of Society in Palestine: Israel in the 1920s, 1918–1930" (in Hebrew), in *The History of the Jewish Yishuv in Palestine from the Time of the First Aliya (The British Mandate)* (in Hebrew), ed. Moshe Lissak and Gabriel Cohen (Jerusalem: Israel Academy of Sciences, Bialik Institute, 1994), part II, p. 215.
7. Knesset Yisrael to the high commissioner, 4 Sept. 1936, CZA S25/9783.
   British administration in Palestine, 1938–40, CZA S25/7746.
   Arlosoroff to Wauchope, 16 Apr. 1933, CZA S25/30.
   Sharett, *Political Diary*, vol. I, p. 32.
   Ben-Gurion, *Memoirs*, vol. I, p. 686ff.
   Netanel Katzburg, "The Second Decade of the Mandate Regime in Palestine, 1931–1939" (in Hebrew) in *The History of the Jewish Yishuv in Palestine from the Time of the First Aliya (The British Mandate)* (in Hebrew), ed. Moshe Lissak (Jerusalem: Israel Academy of Sciences, Bialik Institute, 1933), part I, p. 337ff.
8. The Anglo-Polish Bank to Antonius, 28 Nov. 1932, ISA 65 P/330/866.
   Arab protest leaflets, ISA 65 P/325/570.
   Arab mayors to the high commissioner, 13 Nov. 1932, ISA section 65 Antonius, P/316/132.
9. Hacohen diary, 22 Elul 5694 (2 Sept. 1934), 1 Menachem-Av (31 July 1934), National Library, Manuscript Division, 514/B.
   Barlas to Arlosoroff, 17 Feb. 1932, CZA S25/2589. See also: Sharett, *Political Diary*, vol. II, p. 97.
10. Kisch to the high commissioner, 25 Aug. 1933, CZA S25/16.
    Ben-Gurion and Sharett to the high commissioner, 20 Oct. 1933, CZA S25/2596.
    Sharett with the chief secretary, 9 Nov. 1934, CZA S25/2441. See also: CZA S25/2651.
    Dalia Ofer, *Way Through the Sea* (Jerusalem: Yitzhak Ben-Zvi, 1988), p. 474.
11. Ben-Gurion, *Memoirs*, vol. II, pp. 166, 23.
12. Gabriel Sheffer, "The Image of the Palestinians and the Yishuv as a Factor in Shaping Mandatory Policy in the 1930s" (in Hebrew), *Ha-Tzionut* III (1973), p. 289.
    Wauchope to Melchett, 31 Jan. 1933, CZA S25/31/2.
    Wauchope to Arlosoroff, 6 Apr. 1933, CZA S25/30.
    Wauchope with Henrietta Szold, 27 July 1933, CZA S25/15B2. See also: Ben-Gurion, *Memoirs*, vol. III, pp. 107, 109.
    A Survey of Palestine Prepared for the Anglo-American Committee of Inquiry (Jerusalem: Government Printer, 1946), vol. I, p. 141.
13. Kenneth W. Stein, *The Land Question in Palestine, 1917–1939* (Chapel Hill: University of

North Carolina Press, 1984), p. 226. See also: JNF Executive, 6 Dec. 1937, 6 July and 8 Aug. 1938, 20 Sept., 26 Nov. 1934, CZA JNF 5 Box 695.
Chaim Arlosoroff, *Jerusalem Diary* (in Hebrew) (Tel Aviv: Mifleget Poalei Eretz Yisrael, 1949), p. 133.

14. Arieh L. Avineri, *Jewish Settlement and the Charge of Dispossession, 1878–1948* (in Hebrew) (Tel Aviv: Ha-Kibbutz Ha-Me'uhad, 1980), p. 112ff.
Pewsner to Ruppin, 1 June 1930, CZA S25/7448.
Golan to Shlossberg, 13 Sept. 1938, CZA S25/6553.

15. *A Survey of Palestine Prepared for the Anglo-American Committee of Inquiry*, vol. I, p. 296.
Arlosoroff to the French Commission, 12 July 1932, CZA A 202/119.
CZA S25/7596.

16. Alex Bein, *Immigration and Settlement in the State of Israel* (in Hebrew) (Tel Aviv: Am Oved, 1982), p. 265ff.

17. Ben-Zion Dinur, ed., *The Haganah History Book* (in Hebrew) (Tel Aviv: HaSifriya HaTzionit, Ma'archot, 1964), vol. II, part 2, p. 851ff. See also: Nachum Shadmi, *A Straight Line in the Circle of Life* (in Hebrew) (Tel Aviv: Ministry of Defense, 1995), p. 114ff.
Mordecai Naor, ed., *The Days of Huma U-Migdal, 1936–1939* (in Hebrew) (Jerusalem: Yad Ben-Zvi, 1987).

18. Sharett, *Political Diary*, vol. III, p. 80ff. See also: Jewish Agency memorandum, Apr. 1939, CZA S25/10.

19. Wauchope to Shertok, 29 Dec. 1937; Wauchope to Ben-Gurion, 30 Dec. 1937, CZA S25/31.1

20. Ze'ev Vilnai, *Tel Aviv–Jaffa: The Largest of Israel's Cities* (in Hebrew) (Ahiever, 1965), p. 33.

21. Hacohen diary, 15 Tammuz 5694 (28 June 1934); 13 Elul (24 Aug. 1934); 27 Tashrei 5695 (6 Oct. 1934), National Library, Manuscript Division, ARC 4 1068/514.
Joseph F. Broadhurst, *From Vine Street to Jerusalem* (London: Stanley Paul, 1936), p. 225ff. See also: E. C. Hodgkin, ed., *Thomas Hodgkin: Letters from Palestine, 1932–1936* (London: Quartet Books, 1986), p. 36ff.

22. W. F. Stirling, *Safety Last* (London: Hollis and Carter, 1953), p. 113.

23. Hacohen diary, 21 Heshvan 5695 (30 Oct. 1934); 27 Tishrei 5795 (6 Oct. 1934), National Library, Manuscript Division, ARC 4 1068/514.

24. Central Committee of the Union of Farmers, "Report for the Years 1936–1937" (in Hebrew), p. 9, CZA S25/4833.

25. Jewish Agency treasurer to the Anglo-Palestine Bank, 2 Feb. 1932, CZA S25/6161.

26. Sharett, *Political Diary*, vol. I, p. 336ff. See also: Sharett, *Political Diary*, vol. II, p. 423ff.

27. Wauchope to Ormsby-Gore, 24 June 1936, PRO CO 733/297 75156.
Kisch report, 14 Oct. 1931, CZA S25/30. See also: Ben-Gurion, *Memoirs*, vol. I, p. 521.
Ben-Gurion, *Memoirs*, vol. III, p. 64.
Ben-Gurion with the high commissioner, 19 to 30 July 1934, CZA S25/17/1.

28. Ben-Gurion, *Memoirs*, vol. III, p. 3.
Ben-Gurion, *Memoirs*, vol. II, pp. 330, 354.

29. Index of conversations, 1933–35, CZA S25/17/1.
Ben-Gurion, *Memoirs*, vol. II, p. 151.
Sharett, *Political Diary*, vol. I, pp. 191, 183, 186.

30. Statement by the National Council, 26 Apr. 1936, in *The Book of the Events of 5696* (in Hebrew), ed., Bracha Habas (Tel Aviv: Davar, 1937), p. 49.

31. Bracha Habas, ed., *The Book of the Events of 5696*, pp. 51, 14.

32. Ben-Gurion, *Memoirs*, vol. III, p. 122.
Shabtai Teveth, *Ben-Gurion and the Arabs of Palestine* (in Hebrew) (Tel Aviv: Schocken, 1985), pp. 272, 285.
David Ben-Gurion, The Causes of the Riots, 8 Nov. 1936, CZA S25/4180.

33. Ben-Gurion diary, 11 July 1936, Ben-Gurion Heritage Archives.

34. Yigal Ilam, *The Haganah: The Zionist Way to Power* (in Hebrew) (Tel Aviv: Zemora Bei-tan Modan), p. 68ff.
Meir Pa'il, *The Development of the Hebrew Defense Force, 1907–1948* (in Hebrew) (Tel Aviv: Ministry of Defense, 1987), p. 48ff.

35. Rabbi Benjamin and Ya'akov Patrazil, eds., *Against the Terror* (in Hebrew) (n.p., Aug. 1939).

36. Bracha Habas, "Forty Days" (in Hebrew), *Davar Le-Yeladim*, 28 May 1936, p. 3.

37. G. Karsal, *The History of the Hebrew Press in Palestine* (in Hebrew) (Tel Aviv: HaSifriya HaTzionit , 1964), p. 118ff.

38. Etzel leaflet, Aug. 1938, Jabotinksy Institute, *The Etzel in Palestine* (in Hebrew), ed. Eli Y. Tabin (Tel Aviv: Jabotinsky Institute, 1990), vol. I, p. 270ff.

39. Etzel broadside, Aug. 1938, Jabotinsky Institute, in Tabin, *The Etzel in Palestine*, vol. I, p. 272.

40. Testimony of Chaim Shalom Halevi, Jabotinsky Institute, PA 62.

41. David Niv, *The Campaigns of the Etzel* (in Hebrew) (Jerusalem: Klausner Institute, 1965). See also: Saul Zadka, *Blood in Zion* (London: Brassey's, 1995).

42. Ya'akov Amarmi and Menachem Meltzsky, *The Chronicle of the War of Independence* (in Hebrew) (Tel Aviv: Ministry of Defense, 1981).

43. Sharett, *Political Diary*, vol. III, p. 152.

44. Ya'akov Shavit, ed., *Restraint or Response* (in Hebrew) (Ramat Gan: Bar Ilan University, 1983), p. 127.

45. Ben-Gurion, *Memoirs*, vol. V, p. 220ff.; vol. II, p. 19ff.

46. Sharett, *Political Diary*, vol. III, p. 208; Ben-Gurion, *Memoirs*, vol. III, p. 129.

47. Battershill to Shuckburgh, 21 Nov. 1937, RHL, Battershill papers, 10:3, ff. 5–24.

48. Elihau Stern, ed., *Chronology of the New Jewish Yishuv in Palestine, 1936–1947* (in Hebrew) (Jerusalem: Yad Ben-Zvi, 1974), pp. 53, 56, 71. See also: Knesset Yisrael, National Council, *Book of Documents* (Jerusalem: n.p., 1949), pp. 202, 208, 219, 241.

49. Dinur, *The Haganah History Book*, vol. II, p. 840ff.

50. Dinur, *The Haganah History Book*, vol. II, part II, p. 580.
Shadmi, *A Straight Line in the Circle of Life*, p. 122.

51. Moshe Sharett, *Political Diary*, vol. II, pp. 139, 142.

52. Shadmi, *A Straight Line in the Circle of Life*, p. 123ff.
Sharett, *Political Diary*, vol. II, pp. 137, 296, 416.

53. Ben-Gurion, *Memoirs*, vol. III, pp. 444ff., 343.

54. Sharett, *Political Diary*, vol. I, pp. 189, 191, 195ff., 201ff., 205ff., 218ff., 233, 321.
Ben-Gurion, *Memoirs*, vol. III, p. 143.

55. Smilansky to Shertok, 4 Sept. 1936; Rotenstreich to the members of the Jewish Agency Executive, 30 Dec. 1930, CZA S25/9783.
Ben-Gurion, *Memoirs*, vol. III, p. 478.

56. Ben-Gurion, *Memoirs*, vol. III, pp. 343, 334, 478.
Ben-Gurion diary, 11 July 1936, Ben-Gurion Heritage Archives.

57. Sakakini diary, 30 Apr. 1936. With the kind permission of his daughters. Khalil al-Sakakini, *Such Am I, O World* (in Hebrew) (Jerusalem: Keter, 1990), p. 188.

58. CZA S25/4468.
Chaim Arlosoroff, *Jerusalem Diary*, p. 98. See also: Jerusalem Committee, 24 Dec. 1937, CZA S25/42.
Sharett, *Political Diary*, vol. III, p. 108.
Haim Hanegbi, "My Hebron: A Story of a Different Love (in Hebrew), *Koteret Rashit*, 20 July 1983, p. 20ff.

59. Internal Dangers [1941?], CZA S25/7188. See also: Moshe Shertok to the Nes Tziona Committee, 10 Aug. 1939, CZA S25/7188, CZA S25/4180.
Haifa Workers' Council to Kisch, 15 Apr. 1931; the Jewish Agency to the Histadrut, 26 June 1931, CZA S25/7156.
Negotiations with a private contractor (1932), CZA S25/7165; negotiations with the

director of the train (1942), CZA S25/10078.

Kopplewitz to the Jewish Agency Executive, 14 Oct. 1935, CZA S25/7164.

Details of the visit of Dr. Werner Senator and Yosef Rabinowitz to Hadera, 4 Nov. 1931, CZA S25/7188.

Minutes of a meeting with the Agriculture Committee, Petach Tikva, 14 Dec. 1935, CZA S25/10146.

60. Meir Livni, *The Forgotten Struggle: The Association for Palestinian Products—the Agricultural Department, 1936–1949* (in Hebrew) (published by the author, 1990), pp. 121, 2, 160, 8.

61. "We Will Eat the Products of Our Economy" (in Hebrew) (unsigned), *Davar LeYeladim*, 4 June 1936, p. 16; Leah Goldberg, "Thirty Days for Palestinian Products" (in Hebrew), *Davar Le-Yeladim*, 16 June 1936, p. 16.

Ian Black, *Zionism and the Arabs, 1936–1939* (New York: Garland Publishing, 1986), p. 39ff.

62. Ben-Gurion, *Memoirs*, vol. I, p. 476.

Ha'aretz, 3 July 1919, p. 1.

63. Instilling Hebrew, 26 May 1941, CZA S25/6734.

5704, The Year of Naturalization and the Hebrew Name, Jewish Agency, 1944.

64. Yoram Bar-Gil, *Homeland and Geography in One Hundred Years of Zionist Education* (in Hebrew) (Tel Aviv: Am Oved, 1993), p. 76. See also: Services in the field of instruction, CZA S53/556.

The System of Education of the Jewish Community in Palestine, Colonial No. 201 (London: HMSO, 1946), p. 5.

ISA M/4388/01/267.

The Distribution of Educational Benefits in Palestine (1945), p. 10ff., MEC, Farrell Papers.

65. Bernard De Bunsen, "Memoirs," manuscript with unnumbered pages. With the kind permission of his widow.

66. Guggenheimer Fund, 13 Mar. 1940, Podhurzer to Guggenheimer, 13 Mar. 1940, CZA S25/3979.

Shertok to Ben-Zvi, 14 Apr. 1940, CZA S25/3055.

67. The Distribution of Educational Benefits in Palestine (1945), p. 10ff., MEC, Farrell Papers.

68. Plumer to Eder, 26 July 1927, CZA S25/6832.

69. *Palestine and Transjordan: Report of the Financial Commission*, Middle East No. 43 (London: HMSO, 1931), p. 89.

Ben-Gurion, *Memoirs*, vol. II, p. 14.

70. Ben-Gurion, *Memoirs*, vol. II, p. 419; vol. III, p. 327; vol. IV, p. 250.

Sharett, *Political Diary*, vol. I, p. 363.

71. Sharett, *Political Diary*, vol. I, pp. 328, 347; vol. III, p. 39.

Weizmann to Shertok, 2 Oct. 1936, in *The Letters and Papers of Chaim Weizmann*, ed. Yemima Rosenthal (New Brunswick, NJ: Transaction Books, 1979), Vol. XVII, p. 352.

72. Ben-Gurion, *Memoirs*, vol. I, p. 521.

73. Ben-Gurion, *Memoirs*, vol. V, p. 208. See also: Ben-Gurion, *Memoirs*, vol. I, pp. 412, 473.

74. Ben-Gurion, *Memoirs*, vol. II, p. 145; vol. III, p. 203.

75. Ben-Gurion, *Memoirs*, vol. I, p. 675.

Ben-Gurion, *Memoirs*, vol. II, p. 5.

76. Ben-Gurion, *Memoirs*, vol. IV, p. 266.

77. Shmuel Katz, *Jabo* (in Hebrew) (Tel Aviv: Dvir, 1993), vol. II, p. 971.

78. Ben-Gurion, *Memoirs*, vol. III, pp. 24, 28, 41, 64, 85.

79. Ben-Gurion, *Memoirs*, vol. III, pp. 143, 105. See also: Moshe Sharett, *Political Diary*, vol. II, p. 273.

80. Ben-Gurion, *Memoirs*, vol. II, pp. 87, 571.

81. Ben-Gurion, *Memoirs*, vol. V, pp. 220, 402.

82. Ben-Gurion, *Memoirs*, vol. V, p. 398.

83. Ben-Gurion, *Memoirs*, vol. V, p. 402ff.
Ben Gurion, *Memoirs*, vol. VI, pp. 209, 233, 228.

84. Ben-Gurion, *Memoirs*, vol. I, pp. 672, 132.

85. Report of the Immigration Department of the Jewish Agency 1937–39, CZA S6/923.
Immigration of Unfit People, CZA S7/563.
Instructions on Choosing Children, 26 Oct. 1939, CZA S6/3340.

86. CZA S25/5900; CZA S6/47009.

87. "Repatriation of Chronic and Incurable Cases," National Council of the Jewish Community of Palestine, *Bulletin on Social Welfare in Palestine*, vol. II, no. 3–4 (Dec-Jan. 1937), p. 54.

88. Sharett, *Political Diary*, vol. I, pp. 247, 345, 255.

89. Ruppin, *Chapters of My Life in the Building of the Land and the Nation*, p. 292.

90. Ben-Gurion, *Memoirs*, vol. VI, p. 511ff; vol. V, p. 220.

91. Ben-Gurion, *Memoirs*, vol. II, p. 304; vol. I, pp. 180, 366.

92. Ben-Gurion, *Memoirs*, vol. III, pp. 298, 415; vol. V, p. 416.
Kisch to Brodetsky, 3 Dec. 1928, CZA S25/1.
Ben-Gurion to Ussishkin, 11 Nov. 1936, Ben-Gurion Heritage Archives.
Sharett, *Political Diary*, vol. III, pp. 103, 279ff., 294.

19: THE STORY OF A DONKEY

1. Foreign Office to Colonial Office, 6 Nov. 1939, PRO FO 371/23251.

2. David Ben-Gurion, *Memoirs* (in Hebrew) (Tel Aviv: Am Oved, 1974), vol. IV, pp. 220, 222.
Norman Rose, ed., *Baffy: The Diaries of Blanche Dugdale, 1936–1947* (London: Vallentine, Mitchell, 1973), p. 50ff.

3. Rose, *Baffy*, p. 68.

4. Rose, *Baffy*, p. 47ff.

5. Moshe Sharett, *Political Diary* (in Hebrew) (Tel Aviv: Am Oved, 1971), vol. II, p. 46.

6. David Ben-Gurion, *Memoirs* (in Hebrew) (Tel Aviv: Am Oved, 1973), vol. III, p. 416.

7. Minute by Sir George Rendell, 4 June 1936, PRO FO 371/20035.
Martin Kolinsky, "The Collapse and Restoration of Public Security," in *Britain and the Middle East in the 1930s*, ed. Michael J. Cohen and Martin Kolinsky (London: Macmillan, 1992), p. 150.
Edward Keith-Roach, *Pasha of Jerusalem* (London: Radcliffe Press, 1994), p. 131.

8. CZA S25/9793. See also: Francis Emily Newton, *Fifty Years in Palestine* (Wrotham: Coldharbour Press, 1948), p. 287.
"Demolitions at Jaffa," *Times*, 4 July 1936, p. 14.

9. "Demolitions at Jaffa," *Times*, 4 July 1936, p. 14.

10. ISA (Antonius archive), P/324/534; P 329/814.
Sharett, *Political Diary*, vol. I, pp. 183, 186.
Keith-Roach, *Pasha of Jerusalem*, p. 185.
Gad Frumkin, *The Way of a Judge in Jerusalem* (in Hebrew) (Tel Aviv: Dvir, 1954), p. 345.
Yehoshua Porat, *From Riots to Rebellion: The Arab National Movement, 1929–1939* (in Hebrew) (Tel Aviv: Am Oved, 1978), p. 236.

11. Asaf Lahovsky, "Colonial Images and English Law in the Supreme Court of Mandatory Palestine" (in Hebrew), *Zemanim* 56 (Summer 1996), p. 87ff.
Ronen Shamir, *The Colonies of Law: Colonialism, Zionism and Law in Early Mandate Palestine* (Cambridge: Cambridge University Press, 2000), p. 12.

12. Michael J. Cohen, "Sir Arthur Wauchope, the Army, and the Rebellion in Palestine, 1936," *Middle East Studies*, vol. 9, no. 1 (Jan. 1973), p. 27.

Pealy to Chancellor, 23 June 1936, RHL, Chancellor Papers, 22: MF40, pp. 2–4.
PRO CO 733/314 75528/44, part III.

13. Netanel Katzburg, "The Second Decade of the Mandate Regime in Palestine, 1931–1939" (in Hebrew), in *The History of the Jewish Yishuv in Palestine from the Time of the First Aliya (The British Mandate)* (in Hebrew), ed. Moshe Lissak (Jerusalem: Israel Academy of Sciences, Bialik Institute, 1993), part I, pp. 332, 343ff.

14. Katzburg, "The Second Decade of the Mandate Regime in Palestine," part I, p. 339ff.

15. Wauchope to Ormsby-Gore, 24 June 1936, PRO CO 733/297 75156.
Ormsby-Gore in Parliament, 19 June 1936, 313 H.C. Deb. 5s, cols. 1313–95.
Vansittart notes, 9 June 1936, PRO FO 371/20035.

16. Katzburg, "The Second Decade of the Mandate Regime in Palestine," p. 383.

17. Secretary of State for the Colonies to Rathbone, 26 June 1936, and oral parliamentary question, 30 June 1936, ULL, Eleanor Rathbone Papers, RP XIV 2.5 (51).

18. Ben-Gurion, *Memoirs*, vol. IV, p. 3.
Husseini to the Peel Commission, 12 Jan. 1937, CZA S25/4590.

19. Ben-Gurion, *Memoirs*, vol. IV (1937), p. 18.

20. Peel to Ormsby-Gore, 20 Dec. 1936, PRO CAB 24/267.
Palestine Royal Commission Report, Cmd. 5479 (London: HMSO, 1937), p. 394.

21. *Palestine: Statement of Policy*, Cmd. 5513 (London: HMSO, 1937).

22. Rose, *Baffy*, pp. 25, 47.

23. *Palestine: Statement of Policy*, Cmd. 5513 (London: HMSO, 1937).

24. B. H. Liddell Hart, *Europe in Arms* (London: Faber and Faber, 1937), pp. 57, 59.
Sharett, *Political Diary*, vol. II, p. 90.
Herbert Sidebotham, "Some General Considerations on British Imperial Interests in Palestine," CZA S25/407.
Sharett, *Political Diary*, vol. III, p. 16.

25. Sharett, *Political Diary*, vol. II, p. 24; vol. III, p. 28. See also: Committee of Imperial Defence, Strategical aspects of the partition of Palestine, 16 Feb. 1938, PRO FO 371/21870 E876/G.

26. Keith-Roach, *Pasha of Jerusalem*, p. 190.

27. Porat, *From Riots to Rebellion*, p. 271ff.

28. *Palestine Royal Commission Report*, Cmd. 5479 (London: HMSO, 1937), p. 390ff.
Mendelsohn memorandum (undated), CZA S25/10060.

29. Newton to Chancellor, 12 July 1937, RHL, Chancellor Papers, 15:7, ff. 58–60.

30. Shmuel Dotan, *The Polemic over Partition in Mandatory Period* (in Hebrew) (Jerusalem: Yad Ben-Zvi, 1979). See also: Meir Avizohar and Yeshayahu Friedman, *Studies in the Partition Plan, 1938–1947* (in Hebrew) (Be'ersheba: Ben-Gurion University, 1984).

31. Ben-Gurion, *Memoirs*, vol. IV, pp. 267, 290ff.
Ben-Gurion to his son, 5 Oct. 1937, Ben-Gurion Heritage Archives.
Ben-Gurion diary, 12 July 1937, Ben-Gurion Heritage Archives.

32. Ben-Gurion diary, 12 July 1937, Ben-Gurion Heritage Archives.
Ben-Gurion, *Memoirs*, vol. IV, p. 296.

33. Raphael Patai, ed., *The Complete Diaries of Theodor Herzl* (New York: Herzl Press, 1960), vol. I, p. 88.

34. Minutes of the fifth session of the Temporary Committee of the Jews of Palestine, 9–11 June 1919, CZA J1/8777.

35. Israel Zangwill, *The Voice of Jerusalem* (London: William Heinemann, 1920), p. 93.

36. Jehuda Reinharz, *Chaim Weizmann: The Making of a Statesman* (New York: Oxford University Press, 1993), p. 280.
Max Nordau, *Zionist Writings* (in Hebrew) (Tel Aviv: HaSifriya HaTzionit, 1954), vol. IV, p. 107.
Knesset Yisrael, National Council, *Book of Documents* (Jerusalem: n.p., 1949), p. 11.

37. Granovsky in the JNF Executive, 6 July 1938, CZA.
Ben-Gurion, *Memoirs*, vol. IV, p. 366.

38. Thon to Kisch, 2 June 1931, CZA S25/9836.
39. Ruppin and Ussishkin in the Jewish Agency Executive, 12 June 1938, CZA.
40. Ussishkin, Zochowitzky, and Ben-Gurion in the Jewish Agency Executive, 12 June 1938, CZA.
41. Ben-Gurion, *Memoirs*, vol. IV, pp. 440, 298.
42. Ben-Gurion to his son, 27 June 1937, Ben-Gurion Heritage Archives.
43. Mendelsohn memorandum (undated), CZA S25/10060.
44. Committee on Population Transfer (1937), CZA S25/3737 (see also CZA S25/10060).
    Boneh Report, July 1937, CZA S25/8128. See also: Yossi Katz: "Discussions of the Jewish Agency Committee on Population Transfer 1937–1938," *Tzion* 12 (1988), p. 167ff.
45. Ben-Gurion, *Memoirs*, vol. III, p. 324; vol. V, p. 208ff.
    Oppenheimer Memorandum, July 1937, CZA S25/8127.
    A. Berlin at the Jewish Agency Executive, 12 June 1938, CZA.
46. Ben-Gurion, *Memoirs*, vol. V, p. 404. See also: Survey of the situation in Iraq, Apr. 1938, CZA S25/5167.
47. Sharett, *Political Diary*, vol. IV, p. 376.
48. Mendelsohn memorandum (undated), CZA S25/10060.
    Yosef Gorny, *Policy and Imagination* (in Hebrew) (Jerusalem: Yad Ben-Zvi, 1993), p. 162.
49. Bachi report, Dec. 1944, CZA S25/8223.
50. Shabtai Teveth, "The Incarnations of Transfer in Zionist Thinking" (Hebrew), *Ha'aretz*, 23 Sept. 1988, p. B5; *Ha'aretz*, 25 Sept. 1988, p. 14ff.
    Benny Morris, "'And Books and Parchments Are Accustomed to Age': A New Look at Central Zionist Documents" (in Hebrew), *Alpayim* 12 (1996), p. 73ff.; *Alpayim* 13 (1996), p. 201ff.; *Alpayim* 15 (1997), p. 174ff.
    Nur Masalha, *Expulsion of the Palestinians: The Concept of "Transfer" in Zionist Political Thought, 1882–1948* (Washington, DC: Institute for Palestine Studies, 1992).
    Efraim Karsh, *Fabricating Israeli History: The "New Historians"* (in Hebrew) (Tel Aviv: Hakibbutz Hamenchad, 1999).
51. Ben-Gurion, *Memoirs*, vol. IV (1937), p. 424.
    Minorities Committee, minutes, 23 June 1923, CZA S25/8929.
52. Minutes, 7 Dec. 1937, CZA S25/42. See also: Katznelson and Ben-Gurion at the Jewish Agency Executive, 12 June 1938, CZA.
53. Husseini at the London talks, 16 Feb. 1939, ISA P/319 no. 65 (Antonius); Husseini at the London talks, 6 Mar. 1939, ISA P/320 no. 388 (Antonius).
54. Yosef Gorny, *The Arab Question and the Jewish Problem* (in Hebrew) (Tel Aviv: Am Oved, 1985), p. 51.
    Aharon Kedar, "On the History of Brit Shalom in the Years 1925–1928" (in Hebrew), in *Studies in the History of Zionism* (in Hebrew), ed. Yehuda Bauer et al. (Jerusalem: Hebrew University, 1976), p. 224ff. See also: Susan Lee Hattis, *The Bi-National Idea in Palestine During the Mandatory Times* (Haifa: Shikmona, 1970).
    Robert Weltsch, "Zum XIV. Zionistenkongress," *Juedische Rundschau*, 14 Aug. 1925, p. 1.
55. Shalom Ratzbi, "Central Europeans in Brit Shalom and the Question of the Use of Force" (in Hebrew), *Zemanim* 58 (Spring 1997), p. 78ff.
56. Edwin Samuel to his father, 22 Sept. 1929, ISA P/653/85. See also: Edwin Samuel, *A Lifetime in Jerusalem* (Jerusalem: Israel Universities Press, 1970), p. 94ff.
57. Political Proposals by the Brit Shalom Society for Cooperation Between Jews and Arabs in Palestine, Aug. 1930, CZA Z4/3948.
    Arthur Ruppin, *Chapters of My Life in the Building of the Land and the Nation, 1920–1942* (in Hebrew) (Tel Aviv: Am Oved, 1968), p. 196.
58. Arthur A. Goren, ed., *Dissenter in Zion* (Cambridge: Harvard University Press, 1928), p. 272ff.
59. Brit Shalom to Weizmann, 7 Mar. 1930, CZA S24/3122.
    Members of Ihud to the presidium of the Zionist Executive Committee, 2 Sept. 1942, CZA S25/2962.

60. Magnes memorandum to the Anglo-American Commission of Inquiry, 2 Sept. 1942, CZA S25/2962.

61. Kisch to Brit Shalom, 13 July 1931, CZA S25/3122.

62. Chaim Margalit-Kalvarisky, Platform for a Jewish-Arab Agreement, 4 Aug. 1930, CZA S25/8085.
Sasson to Shertok, 27 Aug. and 10 Oct. 1941, CZA S25/3140 I.
Ben-Gurion, *Memoirs*, vol. I, pp. 405, 413.
Ben-Gurion, *Memoirs*, vol. V, pp. 29ff., 71ff.

63. Ben-Gurion, *Memoirs*, vol. I, pp. 298ff., 337ff., 562.
Jewish Agency survey of public figures on the future of relations with the Arabs (Oct. 1928), CZA S25/4164.
Ben-Gurion, *Memoirs*, vol. II, p. 53.
Ben-Gurion with the Kidma Mizraha Association, 1936, CZA S25/9785.
Jewish Agency Executive with the Ihud Association, 23 Sept. 1942. See also: Shabtai Teveth, *Ben-Gurion and the Arabs of Palestine* (in Hebrew) (Tel Aviv: Schocken, 1985), p. 158ff.

64. Kastel to Weizmann, 23 Aug. 1921, CZA Z4/1250.
Avishar to the National Council, 30 May 1923, CZA J1/23.
Yitzhak Epstein to the National Council, 10 Sept. 1924, CZA J1/78.
Gorny, *The Arab Question and the Jewish Problem*, pp. 51, 53.
Report of the Arab Secretariat of the National Council, 1922, CZA S25/4384.
Memorandum of the Arab Department of the National Council, 20 Dec. 1922, CZA J1/289.

65. Khalil al-Sakakini, *Such Am I, O World* (in Hebrew) (Jerusalem: Keter, 1990), p. 212ff.

66. Hala Sakakini, *Jerusalem and I* (Amman: n.p., 1987), p. 54ff.

67. Sakakini, *Such Am I, O World*, p. 187.

68. Sakakini diary, 24 Oct., 15 Jan. 1935; 20 June 1936. With the kind permission of his daughters.

69. German Propaganda in Palestine 1939–1940, PRO WO 106/1594.
CZA S25/. See also: PRO FO 371/23233 E2568.
Memorandum, A. H. Cohen, "November Events in Northern Palestine" (in Hebrew), 20 Jan. 1936, CZA S25/4224.
Zaslani to Kaplan, Jan. 1937, CZA S25/3441.

70. Sakakini diary, 7 June 1936. With the kind permission of his daughters. See also: Porat, *From Riots to Rebellion*, pp. 62, 100ff., 148.
Moshe Shemesh, "The Position of the Jaffa Newspaper *Falastin* Towards the Axis and Democratic Countries" (in Hebrew), *Iyunim Bitkumat Israel: Studies in Zionism* (in Hebrew), vol. II (1992), p. 245ff.
Baruch Kimmerling and Joel S. Migdal, *Palestinians: The Making of a People* (New York: Free Press, 1993), p. 133ff.

71. Max Domarus, ed., *Hitler-Reden* (Wiesbaden: R. Loweit, 1973), p. 956.

72. "School Year in Palestine," p. 65, MEC, Wilson Papers.

73. "Memoirs of Shraga Goren and Yisrael Melishkevitz" (in Hebrew), Lavon Institute for the Study of the Labor Movement.
Knabenshue to the secretary of state, 7 Nov. 1931, "Records of the United States Consulate in Jerusalem, Palestine," Confidential Correspondence, 1920–1935 (Record group 84).
Lev Louis Greenberg, "Strike of the Jewish-Arab Drivers Organization" (in Hebrew), in *Arabs and Jews in the Mandatory Period* (in Hebrew), ed. Ilan Pappe (Institute for the Study of Peace, 1995), p. 175ff

74. Tevet, *Ben-Gurion and the Arabs of Palestine*, p. 106.

75. Ben-Gurion, *Memoirs*, vol. IV, p. 172. See also: A.A. to M.Sh., 26 June 1936, CZA S25/9783.
Ben-Zvi to Shertok, 11 June 1939, CZA S25/3029. See also: CZA S25/7967; S 25/3032.
Sharett, *Political Diary*, vol. III, p. 219.

76. Sharett, *Political Diary*, vol. II, p. 387.
    Ben-Gurion, *Memoirs*, vol. IV, p. 174.
77. Hacohen diary, 3 Av 5695 (2 Aug. 1935), National Library, Manuscript Division, 514/B.
78. Aharon Amir, ed., *Land of Contention: The Contention for Palestine as Reflected in Hebrew Literature* (in Hebrew) (Tel Aviv: Ministry of Defense, 1992).
    Ehud Ben-Ezer, ed., *In the Homeland of Opposing Yearnings: The Arab in Hebrew Literature* (in Hebrew) (Tel Aviv: Zemora Bitan, 1992).
79. CZA S25/42, CZA S25/8929.
80. Minutes by L. Baggallay, 16 Apr. 1938, PRO FO 371/21870 E2547/G.
81. *Palestine Partition Commission Report*, Cmd. 5854 (London: HMSO, 1938).
82. Ben-Gurion to Ben-Tzion Katz, 1 Sept. 1957, Ben-Gurion Heritage Archives. See also: Aaron Kleiman, *Divide or Rule: British Policy and the Partition of Palestine—a Lost Opportunity? 1936–1939* (Jerusalem: Yad Ben-Zvi, 1983).
83. Battershill diary, 29 Apr. 1937, pp. 1–4, RHL, Battershill Papers, 12:6, ff. 1–4.
84. Battershill diary, 10 Oct. 1938, pp. 24–32, RHL, Battershill Papers, 12:6ff. 24–32. See also: R. Zaslani to E. Kaplan, Jan. 1937, CZA S25/3441.
85. Morrison diary, p. 30, IWM, Morrison papers.

20: IRELAND IN PALESTINE

1. *Great Britain and Palestine, 1915–1945* (London: Royal Institute of International Affairs, 1946), p. 116.
   Moshe Sharett, *Political Diary* (in Hebrew) (Tel Aviv: Am Oved, 1968), vol. I, p. 323.
   Randall to Shuckburgh, 2 Nov. 1937, PRO 371/20318.
2. Michael J. Cohen, "Sir Arthur Wauchope, the Army, and the Rebellion in Palestine, 1936," *Middle East Studies*, vol. 9, no. 1 (Jan. 1973), p. 31.
   Wauchope to Battershill, 26 Oct. 1937, RHL, Battershill Papers, 10:4, ff. 32–35.
   Sharett, *Political Diary*, vol. III, p. 47.
   Sharett to Wauchope, 28 Apr. 1938, CZA S25/31.1
3. David Ben-Gurion, *Memoirs* (in Hebrew) (Tel Aviv: Am Oved, 1982), vol. V, pp. 95, 118, 114, 176.
   Collie Knox, *It Might Have Been You* (London: Chapman and Hall, 1933), p. 189ff.
4. Sharett, *Political Diary*, vol. III, pp. 109, 212.
5. MacMichael to Tegart, 4 June 1939, MEC Charles Tegart Papers, 4:4.
6. Edward Keith-Roach, *Pasha of Jerusalem* (London: Radcliffe Press, 1994), p. 191.
7. Douglas V. Duff, *Bailing with a Teaspoon* (London: John Long, 1953), p. 168. PRO CO 733/413 75900/6.
   Alleged Ill-Treatment of Prisoners in Palestine, MEC, JEM LXV/5.
8. Bruce Hoffman, *The Failure of British Strategy Within Palestine, 1939–1947* (Ramat Gan: Bar Ilan University Press, 1983), p. 80.
   Martin Kolinsky, "The Collapse and Restoration of Public Security," in *Britain and the Middle East in the 1930s*, ed. Michael J. Cohen and Martin Kolinsky (London: Macmillan, 1992), p. 155.
9. Eliahu Sasson and Ezra Danin, 17 Dec. 1939, CZA S25/3140.
10. The Arab Internees in the Palestine Prisons, MEC, JEM LXV/4.
    Nigel Hamilton, *Monty: The Making of a General* (London: Hamish Hamilton, 1981), p. 288ff.
11. *Report of the Anglo-American Committee of Enquiry Regarding the Problems of European Jewry and Palestine*, Cmd. 6808 (London: HMSO, 1946), p. 68.
    Statistical Abstracts of Palestine 1939 (Jerusalem: Office of Statistics, 1939), Section XVI, line 30.
    Statistical Abstracts of Palestine 1940 (Jerusalem: Office of Statistics, 1940), Section XVII, line 84.
12. Keith-Roach, *Pasha of Jerusalem*, p. 198.

13. Alec Seath Kirkbride, *A Crackle of Thorns* (London: John Murray, 1956), p. 100ff.

14. Keith-Roach, *Pasha of Jerusalem*, p. 1980.

15. Kirkbride, *A Crackle of Thorns*, p. 100.

16. Young Offenders Ordinance (in Hebrew), *Ha'aretz*, 15 Aug. 1918, p. 1.
    ISA section 2 Secretariat M/252/34 (microfilm 1662 692-116). See also: Tegart to O'Connor, 18 Feb. 1939, KCL, O'Connor Papers, 3/4/26.

17. Gad Frumkin, *The Way of a Judge in Jerusalem* (in Hebrew) (Tel Aviv: Dvir, 1954), p. 252.

18. "School Year in Palestine," pp. 59, 25, 40, MEC, Wilson Papers.

19. Morrison diary, p. 21, IWM, Morrison Papers.

20. Frances E. Newton, *Searchlight on Palestine: Punitive Measures in Palestine*, MEC, JEM LXV/4.
    "School Year in Palestine," p. 17, MEC, Wilson Papers.

21. Haining to O'Connor, 13 Dec. 1938, KCL, O'Connor Papers, 3/2/8. See also: "School Year in Palestine," p. 40, MEC, Wilson Papers.
    Sonia Fathi El Nimr, "The Arab Revolt of 1936–1939 in Palestine" (Ph.D. thesis, University of Exeter, 1990), p. 110.
    The Bishop in Jerusalem to Ormsby-Gore, 6 Apr. 1938, MEC, JEM LXV/5.

22. E. D. Forster diary, 8–13 May 1939, MEC, Forster Papers.
    MacMichael to MacDonald, 13 Nov. 1939, PRO 371/23241.

23. Conduct of British Troops and Police, PRO CO 733/413 75900/3.
    The Bishop in Jerusalem to the Archbishop of Canterbury, MEC, JEM LXV/3.
    Newton to the Bishop in Jerusalem, 27 June 1938, MEC, JEM LXV/3.

24. ISA M/552.
    Haining to Tegart, 25 June 1938, MEC, Tegart Papers, 4:4.
    MacMichael to MacDonald, 13 Nov. 1939, PRO 371/23241.
    Martin Kolinsky, "The Collapse and Restoration of Public Security," in Cohen and Kolinsky, *Britain and the Middle East in the 1930s*.

25. The village of Raji, 12 July 1943; the village of Siris, 5 Oct. 1944, ISA M/500–53.
    Sharett, Political Diary, vol. I, p. 168.

26. "School Year in Palestine," pp. 26ff., 54, 37, MEC, Wilson Papers.

27. Kolinsky, "The Collapse and Restoration of Public Security," in Cohen and Kolinsky, *Britain and the Middle East in the 1930s*, p. 156.
    Acting chief secretary to Pollock, 5 Aug. 1938, PRONI D/1581/4/6.

28. Bruce Hoffman, *The Failure of British Strategy Within Palestine*, p. 81. See also: MacMichael to MacDonald, 13 Nov. 1939, PRO 371/23241.
    India Office to Foreign Office, 11 Nov. 1939, PRO 371-23241 E7439.

29. Anwar Nusseibeh, "Pattern of Disaster: Personal Note on the Fall of Palestine," p. 24. With the kind permission of his son.

30. "School Year in Palestine," p. 13ff., MEC, Wilson Papers.
    Khalil Zaki to the high commissioner, 5 July 1938, ISA M/551.

31. "School Year in Palestine," p. 69ff., MEC, Wilson Papers. See also: Story of a citrus grove guard, CZA S25/4180.

32. Assistant district commissioner Samaria to the district commissioner Haifa and Samaria district, PRONI D/1581/4/6.
    Kolinsky, "The Collapse and Restoration of Public Security," in Cohen and Kolinsky, *Britain and the Middle East in the 1930s*, p. 158.

33. Geoffrey Morton, *Just the Job* (London: Hodder and Stoughton, 1957), p. 98.

34. Battershill diary, 15 Jan. 1939, RHL, Battershill Papers, 12:6, ff. 49–50.
    Moshe Sharett, *Political Diary*, vol. III, p. 282.

35. Knesset Yisrael to the National Council Executive, 28 June 1936, CZA S25/4394.
    CZA S25/6286 (1940), S 25/6910 (1939), S 25/6286 (1938).

36. Sharett, *Political Diary*, vol. II, p. 419.
    O'Connor to Haining, 15 Dec. 1938, KCL, O'Connor Papers, 3/2/1.

37. Stewart to the chief secretary, 3 June 1936; office of the chief secretary to Stuart, 3 June 1936, MEC, JEM LXV/5.
   Battershill diary, 15 May 1939, RHL, Battershill Papers, 12:6, f. 49.
38. Haining to O'Connor, 13 Dec. 1938, KCL, O'Connor Papers, 3/2/8.
   MacMichael to MacDonald, 13 Nov. 1939, PRO 371/23241. See also: Atrocities in the Holy Land, CZA S25/3156.
39. Battershill to Shuckburgh, 21 Nov. 1937, RHL, Battershill Papers, 10:3, ff. 5–24.
40. Haining to Tegart, 8 Aug. 1938, MEC, Charles Tegart Papers, 4:4.
41. Sharett, *Political Diary*, vol. III, p. 190.
42. Fathi El Nimr, "The Arab Revolt of 1936–1939 in Palestine," p. 207.
   Perrott to O'Connor, 18 Oct. 1938, KCL, O'Connor Papers, 3/2/1. See also: A. J. Sherman, *Mandate Days* (London: Thames and Hudson, 1997), p. 109ff.
43. The consul general in Alexandria to the ambassador in Cairo, 20 Mar. 1939, PRO FO 371/23233.
   Ben-Gurion, *Memoirs*, vol. III, p. 373.
   Sharett, *Political Diary*, vol. II, p. 445.
44. Yehoshua Porat, *From Riots to Rebellion: The Arab National Movement, 1929–1939* (in Hebrew) (Tel Aviv: Am Oved, 1978), p. 280ff.
45. Nusseibeh, "Pattern of Disaster," p. 14. With the kind permission of his son.
46. Sharett, *Political Diary*, vol. II, p. 18.
   The Arab Policeman in the Mandatory Period (Tel Aviv: Ministry of Defense, n.d.).
47. Sharett, *Political Diary*, vol. III, p. 329ff.
48. Sharett, *Political Diary*, vol. II, pp. 379, 405ff., 382, 374.
49. Sharett diary, 7 July 1938, CZA A 245/6.
50. Sharett, *Political Diary*, vol. I, pp. 174, 268; vol. II, p. 452; vol. III, pp. 204, 166, 321.
51. *Great Britain and Palestine, 1915–1945*, p. 116.
52. Police inspector general to Gan Shlomo company, 28 May 1936, and additional correspondence, CZA S25/4180.
53. CZA S25/3156.
   Keith-Roach, *Pasha of Jerusalem*, p. 142.
54. Keith-Roach, *Pasha of Jerusalem*, p. 191.
55. David Hacohen, *Time to Tell* (in Hebrew) (Tel Aviv: Am Oved, 1974), pp. 69, 96.
56. *Great Britain and Palestine, 1915–1945*, p. 116.
57. Trevor Royle, *Orde Wingate: Irregular Soldier* (London: Weidenfeld and Nicolson, 1995), p. 98.
   John Bierman, Celin Smith, *Fire in the Night: Wingate of Burma, Ethiopia, and Zion* (New York: Random House, 2000).
   Sharett, *Political Diary*, vol. II, p. 201.
   David Frumkin, *A Peace to End All Peace: Creating the Modern Middle East, 1914–1922* (New York: Henry Holt, 1989), p. 317.
58. Hacohen, *Time to Tell*, p. 127ff.
59. Liddell Hart to Churchill, 11 Nov. 1938, Haganah Archive, 80/69/5.
   Sharett, *Political Diary*, vol. II, p. 201.
60. CZA S24/8768 and S25/10685.
   Ben-Gurion, *Memoirs*, vol. V, p. 242.
   Mordecai Naor, *Lexicon of the Haganah Defense Force* (in Hebrew) (Tel Aviv: Ministry of Defense, 1992), p. 140.
   CZA S25/10685.
61. Sharett, *Political Diary*, vol. III, p. 201ff.
   Yigal Ilam, *The Haganah: The Zionist Way to Power* (in Hebrew) (Tel Aviv: Zemora Beitan Modan), p. 98.
62. Tzion Cohen, *To Tehran and Back* (in Hebrew) (Tel Aviv: Ministry of Defense, 1995), p. 52ff.
   Testimony of Shlomo, CZA S24/8768 and S25/10685.

63. Yigal Peicovitch to the temporary additional constables, 26 Oct. 1938, CZA S25/8768.
Cohen, *To Tehran and Back*, p. 52.
64. Haining to O'Connor, 13 Dec. 1938, KCL, O'Connor Papers, 3/2/8.
65. Lieberman to Tzimbal, 9 Sept. 1938, CZA S25/8768.
66. Testimonies of Shlomo, Arieh, and Yonatan, CZA S24/8768.
Testimony of Chaim Levakow, CZA S24/8768.
Wingate report, 9 Sept. 1938, CZA S25/10685.
67. Cohen, *To Tehran and Back*, p. 54ff.
Testimony of Efraim Krasner, CZA S24/10685.
68. The Development of the Special Night Squads, 25 July 1939, CZA S25/254.
69. Sharett, *Political Diary*, vol. III, p. 202.
The Development of the Special Night Squads, 25 July 1939, CZA S25/254.
70. Battershill diary, 13 Nov. 1938, RHL, Battershill Papers, 12:6, ff. 24–47.
71. Haining to Tegart, 25 June 1938, MEC, Tegart Papers, 4:4. See also: MacDonald to Haining, 15 Oct. 1938, MEC, Haining Papers.
Haining to War Office, 2 Dec. 1938, PRO WO 106/1594C.
72. Montgomery to O'Connor, 26 Nov. 1938, KCL O'Connor Papers, 3/4/4.
73. General Service Medal (Army and Royal Air Force), "Palestine" Bar.
Dorling and Granville, ed., *Ribbons and Medals* (London: Spink and Son, 1960), p. 92.
74. Hamilton, *Monty*, p. 228ff.
75. Sharett, *Political Diary*, vol. I (1936), p. 153.
76. Tom Bowden, *The Breakdown of Public Security: The Case of Ireland, 1916–1921, and Palestine, 1936–1939* (London: Sage Publications, 1977), p. 1.
77. Ben-Gurion, *Memoirs*, vol. II, p. 531.
78. Peake to Chancellor, 26 Apr. 1938, RHL, Chancellor Papers, 22: MF40, ff. 6–10.
79. Ormsby-Gore to Chamberlain, 9 Jan. 1938, PRO FO371/21863. See also: Norman Rose, ed., *Baffy: The Diaries of Blanche Dugdale, 1936–1947* (London: Vallentine, Mitchell, 1973), p. 47ff.
Bateman to Oliphant, 30 Aug. 1938, and comments of the Egyptian Department, PRO FO 371/21881 E5726/G.
80. Glubb to Chancellor, 30 Aug. 1938, RHL, Chancellor Papers, 22: MF40, ff. 6–10.
81. Khalil al-Sakakini, *Such Am I, O World* (in Hebrew) (Jerusalem: Keter, 1990), p. 186.
82. Hacohen, *Time to Tell*, p. 19.
83. Hacohen, *Time to Tell*, p. 104.
84. Sharett, *Political Diary*, vol. III, p. 296; vol. I, p. 283.
Ben-Gurion, *Memoirs*, vol. II, p. 165.
85. Sharett, *Political Diary*, vol. II, p. 307.
86. Tegart to MacMichael (undated), MEC, Tegart Papers, 4:4.
Sharett with the high commissioner, 8 Feb. 1934, CZA S25/17/1.
Haining to Tegart, 7 May 1939, MEC, Tegart Papers, 4:4.
87. Sharett, *Political Diary*, vol. II, p. 58ff.
Gandhi's statement in *The Bond* (Jerusalem: Rubin Mass, 1939), p. 39
Ben-Gurion, *Memoirs*, vol. I, p. 429ff.; vol. IV, p. 234.
88. Peake to Chancellor, 20 Dec. 1937, RHL, Chancellor Papers, 22:MF40, ff. 6–10.
Minutes by R. J. Campbell, PRO FO 371/20035 E3483.
Policy in Palestine on the Outbreak of War, 26 Sept. 1938, PRO FO 371/21865 E5603/G.
89. Ormsby-Gore to Chamberlain, 9 Jan. 1938, PRO FO 371/21862 E559/G.
Policy in Palestine on the Outbreak of War, 26 Sept. 1938, PRO FO 371/21865 E5603/G.
Rose, *Baffy*, p. 123.
123rd Cabinet Conclusions, 27 Jan. 1939, PRO FO 371/23242 E8134. See also: Meir Avizohar, "Militant Zionism" (in Hebrew), in Ben-Gurion, *Memoirs*, vol. VI, p. 55.
Ronald Zweig, *Britain and Palestine During the Second World War* (Woodbridge: Boydell Press, 1986), p. 153ff.
Sharett, *Political Diary*, vol. IV, p. 278.

90. Bateman to Oliphant, 30 Aug. 1938, PRO FO 371/21881 E5726/G. See also: Ormsby-Gore to Chamberlain, 9 Jan. 1938, PRO FO371/21862 E559/G.

91. Chamberlain to the Cabinet Committee on Palestine, 20 Apr. 1939, PRO CAB 24/285 C.P. 89[39].

92. Policy in Palestine on the Outbreak of War, 26 Sept. 1938, PRO FO 371/21865 E5603/G. Ronald W. Zweig, "The Palestine Problem in the Context of Colonial Policy on the Eve of the Second World War," in Cohen and Kolinsky, *Britain and the Middle East in the 1930s*, p. 206ff.

93. Netanel Katzburg, "The Second Decade of the Mandate Regime in Palestine, 1931–1939" (in Hebrew), in *The History of the Jewish Yishuv in Palestine from the Time of the First Aliya (The British Mandate)* (in Hebrew), ed. Moshe Lissak (Jerusalem: Israel Academy of Sciences, Bialik Institute, 1993), part I, p. 417ff.

94. Sharett, *Political Diary*, vol. IV, p. 24ff.

95. Ben-Gurion to the Jewish Agency Executive, 11 Dec. 1938, CZA.

96. Arab Women's Committee to Mrs. Antonius, 30 Jan. 1939, ISA M/1053/11. See also: Zulika Shihabi and others to the high commissioner, 2 Mar. 1939, ISA P/403/3554.

97. Ben-Gurion, *Memoirs*, vol. VI, pp. 122, 127.
Sharett, *Political Diary*, vol. IV, p. 26.
First session, 7 Feb. 1939, ISA P/319/299 file 65.

98. Second session, 4 Mar. 1939, ISA P/319 file 65.

99. Sharett, *Political Diary*, vol. IV, p. 36.
Rose, *Baffy*, p. 123.
Second session, 4 Mar. 1939, ISA P/319 file 65.

100. Bernard Wasserstein, *Britain and the Jews of Europe, 1939–1945* (Oxford: Oxford University Press, 1988), p. 7.
British Guiana as a Second Jewish National Home, PRO FO 371/24568 1063.
Ben-Gurion, *Memoirs*, vol. VI, p. 525. CZA S25/9892; S25/9811; S25/9819; S25/9892; S25/5180. See also: Meir Michaelis, *Mussolini and the Jews* (in Hebrew) (Jerusalem: Yad Vashem, 1978), p. 243ff.
Zweig, *Britain and Palestine During the Second World War*, p. 45.

101. MacDonald to Alami, 21 Nov. 1938, ISA P/325 File 65.

102. Ben-Gurion, *Memoirs*, vol. VI, pp. 130, 240, 158.
Informal Discussions with Arab and Jewish Delegates, 24 Feb. 1939, ISA P/325/570.
Ben-Gurion, *Memoirs*, vol. VI, p. 158.

103. Avizohar, "Militant Zionism," in Ben-Gurion, *Memoirs*, vol. VI, p. 52.

104. Ben-Gurion, *Memoirs*, vol. VI, p. 147.
Rose, *Baffy*, p. 139.

105. Rose, *Baffy*, p. 137.
Sharett, *Political Diary*, vol. IV, p. 277.

106. J. C. Hurewitz, *Diplomacy in the Near and Middle East: A Documentary Record, 1914–1956* (Princeton: D. Vansittart Norstant Company, 1956), p. 218ff. See also: Bernard Joseph [Dov Yosef], *The British Regime in Palestine* (in Hebrew) (Jerusalem: Bialik Institute, 1948), p. 289ff.

107. Ben-Gurion, *Memoirs*, vol. VI, p. 200ff.

108. Ben-Gurion, *Memoirs*, vol. VI, p. 507.

109. Ben-Gurion, *Memoirs*, vol. VI, p. 189.

110. CZA S25/7747; S 25/6287; S 25/6286.
War Office to Colonial Office, 6 Mar. 1940, PRO FO 371/24563 E1023.
Sharett, *Political Diary*, vol. IV, p. 296.

111. Ya'akov Amrami and Menachem Meltzsky, *The Chronicle of the War of Independence* (in Hebrew) (Tel Aviv: Ministry of Defense, 1981), p. 24ff.
Benyamin Zaroni, *Proud and Generous and Cruel* (in Hebrew) (Tel Aviv: Milo, 1992).
The Etzel in the Land of Israel: Collected Sources and Documents (in Hebrew) (Tel Aviv: Jabotinsky Institute, 1990), vol. I, p. 326ff.

112. Ben-Gurion, *Memoirs*, vol. VI, pp. 222, 235, 540.
     W. H. Auden, *Collected Shorter Poems, 1927–1957* (London: Faber and Faber, 1966), p. 157.
113. MacMichael to Tegart, 4 June 1939, MEC, Tegart Papers, 4:4.
114. Montgomery to Brooke, 21 July 1939, PRO WO 216/49.
115. Morrison diary, p. 38, IWM, Morrison Papers.
116. Montgomery to Brooke, 21 July 1939, PRO WO 216/49.
117. Ormsby-Gore to Chamberlain, 9 Jan. 1938, PRO FO 371/21862 E 559/1/31.
     Sharett, *Political Diary*, vol. III, p. 209.
118. Peake to Chancellor, 26 Apr. 1938, RHL, Chancellor Papers, 22: MF 40, ff. 6–10.
     Shuckburgh memorandum, 27 Mar. 1938, PRO CO 733/426 75872/16.
119. Chaim Weizmann, *Trial and Error* (London: Hamish Hamilton, 1949), p. 468.
120. Battershill diary, 14 Aug., 20 May 1937; 10 Oct. 1935ff., RHL, Battershill Papers, 12:6, ff. 1–4.
121. MacMichael to Tegart, 4 June 1939, MEC, Tegart Papers, 4:4. See also: Keith-Roach, *Pasha of Jerusalem*, pp. 195, 222.
     Battershill diary, 6 Nov. 1938, RHL, Battershill Papers, 12:6, ff. 24–47.
     Pollock to his father, 2 Sept. 1939, PRONI 581/2/8.

PART III: RESOLUTION (1939–48)

1. Jane Lancaster to Golda Meyerson, 3 Feb. 1947, and additional documents CZA S25/5552.

21: HUNTING SEASON

1. Khalil al-Sakakini, *Such Am I, O World* (in Hebrew) (Jerusalem: Keter, 1990), p. 199ff.
2. Hala Sakakini, *Jerusalem and I* (Amman: n.p., 1987), pp. 76ff., 130ff.
3. Cohen diary, 24 July 1939 to 9 Feb. 1940, Haganah Archive, P. 80.276.
4. Cohen diary, 26 Mar. 1946, 25 Mar. 1947, Haganah Archive, P. 80.276.
5. Arthur Ruppin, *Chapters of My Life in the Building of the Land and the Nation, 1920–1942* (in Hebrew) (Tel Aviv: Am Oved, 1968), p. 344.
6. Cohen diary, 7 July 1940, Haganah Archive, P. 80.276.
7. David Ben-Gurion, *Memoirs* (in Hebrew) (Tel Aviv: Am Oved, 1987), vol. VI, pp. 205, 220.
   Ben-Gurion to MacMichael, 2 Apr. 1994, CZA S25/147.
8. Ben-Gurion at the Mapai Central Committee, 12 Sept. 1939, Labor Party Archive, 23/39.
9. Memorandum by Eyres, 11 Oct. 1939, PRO FO 371/23240 E6852, f. 141.
   Ben-Gurion at the Mapai Central Committee, 12 Sept. 1939, Labor Party Archive, 23/39.
10. Ben-Gurion, *Memoirs*, vol. VI, pp. 292, 327.
    Ronald Zweig, *Britain and Palestine During the Second World War* (Woodbridge: Boydell Press, 1986), p. 5.
    Martin Kolinsky, *Britain's War in the Middle East: Strategy and Diplomacy, 1930–42* (London: Macmillan, 1999), p. 203ff.
11. PRO FO 371/23251 E7479; PRO FO 371/23251 E7635, E 7675, E8148.
    Weizmann to MacDonald, 2 Oct. 1939, PRO FO 371/23242 E8142.
    Norman Rose, ed., *Baffy: The Diaries of Blanche Dugdale, 1936–1947* (London: Vallentine, Mitchell, 1973), p. 153.
    PRO FO 371/24563 E1926 f. 180.
12. High commissioner's report, 29 Dec. 1939, PRO FO 371/24563 E 1066.
    Mordecai Naor, *Lexicon of the Haganah Defense Force* (in Hebrew) (Tel Aviv: Ministry of Defense, 1992), p. 138.
13. Minutes by Coverly-Price and additional responses, 5 June 1940, PRO FO 371/24566 E2044. See also: Policy in Palestine on the Outbreak of War, 26 Sept. 1938, PRO FO

371/21865 E5603/G.

Yoav Gelber, *The Chronicle of Volunteerism* (in Hebrew) (Jerusalem: Yad Yitzhak Ben-Zvi, 1983), vol. III.

14. Rose, *Baffy*, p. 165ff.

Weizmann to the Jewish Agency Executive, 22 Oct. 1942, in *The Letters and Papers of Chaim Weizmann*, ed. Michael J. Cohen (New Brunswick, NJ, and Jerusalem: Transaction Books, Rutgers University, and Israel Universities Press, 1979), vol. XX, p. 361. See also: Ben-Gurion, *Memoirs*, vol. VI, p. 163.

David Ben-Gurion, *Chimes of Independence* (in Hebrew) (Tel Aviv: Am Oved, 1993), p. 359.

15. Shmuel Katz, *Jabo* (in Hebrew) (Tel Aviv: Dvir, 1993), vol. II, pp. 1, 127.

16. Yosef Heller, *Leh'i, 1940–1949* (in Hebrew) (Jerusalem: Merkaz Zalman Shazar and Ketev, 1989).

17. Sh. Gorlik, "*The Good Soldier Schweik* and the Enlistment Notice" (in Hebrew), *Ha'aretz*, 13 Sept. 1939, p. 2.

Cohen diary, 29 Nov. 1940, Haganah Archive, P. 30.276.

18. Cohen diary, 15–23 June, 31 July 1941, Haganah Archive, P. 80.276.

19. CZA S25/359.

Ya'akov Markovsky, *The Special Ground Forces of the Palmach* (in Hebrew) (Tel Aviv: Ministry of Defense, 1989).

20. Ezra Danin, *Zionist Under All Conditions* (in Hebrew) (Kidum, 1987), p. 157.

Becher to Shertok, 16 July 1942, CZA S6/3840.

Tom Segev, *The Seventh Million* (New York: Hill and Wang, 1993), p. 67ff. See also: CZA S25/4752.

21. Cohen diary, 20 Jan. 1941, Haganah Archive, P. 80.276.

Naor, *Lexicon of the Haganah Defense Force*, p. 344ff.

22. Tzvika Dror, *Warrior with No Rank (Biography of Yitzhak Sadeh)* (in Hebrew) (Tel Aviv: Ha-Kibbutz Ha-Me'uhad, 1996), p. 122.

23. Alex Bein, *Immigration and Settlement in the State of Israel* (in Hebrew) (Tel Aviv: Am Oved, 1982), p. 271ff.

24. Cohen diary, 15 June 1942 to 8 Feb. 1943, Haganah Archive, P. 80.276.

25. Oz Almog, *The Sabra: A Portrait* (in Hebrew) (Tel Aviv: Am Oved, 1997).

26. Menachem Begin, *The Revolt* (in Hebrew) (Ahiasaf, 1981), p. 54.

27. Yehudah Slotzky, *Haganah History Book* (in Hebrew) (Tel Aviv: Am Oved, 1973), vol. III, part I, p. 628ff.

28. Slotzky, *Haganah History Book*, vol. III, part I, p. 182ff. See also: Bruce Hoffman, *The Failure of British Strategy Within Palestine, 1939–1947* (Tel Aviv: Bar Ilan University Press, 1983), pp. 13, 48ff.

29. The Siege of Givat Haim, 29 Nov. 1945, CZA S25/7034; 7528; 7699.

30. CZA S25/134.

31. Geoffrey Morton, *Just the Job* (London: Hodder and Stoughton, 1957), p. 141ff.

Moshe Savorai, *The Libel Trial in the Circumstances of the Murder of Yair* (in Hebrew) (published by the author, 1997).

32. *The Etzel in the Land of Israel: Collected Sources and Documents* (in Hebrew) (Jabotinsky Institute, 1990), vol. III, p. 172ff.

Saul Zadka, *Blood in Zion* (London: Brassey's, 1995), p. 42.

33. Zadka, *Blood in Zion*, p. 28.

34. Report on the attempt to assassinate the high commissioner, Aug. 1944, PRO WO 201/89.

Heller, *Leh'i*, vol. I, pp. 185, 208.

Norman Rose, "Churchill and Zionism," in *Churchill*, ed. Robert Blake and Wm. Roger Louis (Oxford: Oxford University Press, 1993), p. 164.

35. Cohen diary, 16 Nov. 1944, Haganah Archive, P. 80.276.

36. *The Etzel in the Land of Israel*, vol. I, p. 340ff.; vol. III, p. 139.

37. Yehuda Lapidot, *The Season* (in Hebrew) (Tel Aviv: Jabotinsky Institute, 1994). See also: Etzel organization, 12 Aug. 1941, CZA S25/4352.
CZA S25/5678 (Yerushalmi affair); CZA S25/10672 (Yedidiya Segal et al.)
Altman to the CID, 21 Aug. 1941, Haganah Archive 47/61.
Kollek to the police inspector general, 18 June 1945, CZA S25/6202.
Sharett to Gort, 23 Nov. 1944, CZA S25/6830.
38. Henry Gurney, "Palestine Postscript," p. 14, MEC, Gurney Papers, GUR 1/2.
39. Henry Gurney, "Palestine Postscript," p. 3, MEC, Gurney Papers, GUR 1/2.
Barker to Weizmann, 18 June 1946, CZA S25/6908.
40. Sneh with Begin, 9 Oct. 1944, CZA S25/206.
41. Norman Rose, *Baffy*, p. 142.
42. Report of the Immigration Department of the Jewish Agency, 1939–1946, p. 3, CZA S6/924. See also: *a Survey of Palestine Prepared for the Anglo-American Committee of Inquiry* (Jerusalem: Government Printer, 1946), vol. I, p. 183.
43. Zweig, *Britain and Palestine During the Second World War*, p. 146.
A Survey of Palestine Prepared for the Anglo-American Committee of Inquiry, vol. I, p. 183.
Report of the Immigration Department of the Jewish Agency, 1939–1946, p. 10, CZA S6/924.
44. Martin to Lloyd, 21 Nov. 1940, PRO PREM 4/51/1.
45. Lloyd to Churchill, 21 Nov. 1940, PRO PREM 4/51/1.
Weizmann to the high commissioner, 24 Jan. 1941, and associated correspondence, CZA S25/6287.
Dror, *Warrior with No Rank*, p. 180ff.
46. Zweig, *Britain and Palestine During the Second World War*, p. 118ff.
PRO CAB 65/26[29] (42) 5 Mar., 1942; CAB 65/26[64] (42) 18 May 1942.
CAB 65/28[168] (42) 14 Dec. 1942.
47. Martin to Lloyd, 21 Nov. 1940, PRO PREM 4/51/1.
Zweig, *Britain and Palestine During the Second World War*, p. 112.
48. Zweig, *Britain and Palestine During the Second World War*, pp. 27, 86ff., 174, 171, 108ff.
49. *Annual Abstract of Statistics No. 84* (London: HMSO, 1947), p. 33.
50. Bernard Wasserstein, *Britain and the Jews of Europe, 1939–1945* (Oxford: Oxford University Press, 1988).
51. Ben-Gurion to Kastner, 2 Feb. 1958, ISA, Prime Minister's Office, 5432/16.
52. Sakakini, *Such Am I, O World*, p. 205.
53. Sakakini diary, 1 Mar. 1942. With the kind permission of his daughters.
Sakakini, *Such Am I, O World*, p. 215ff.
54. Khalil al-Sakakini, "The Jewish People Are Insane," 9 Dec. 1936, ISA P/354/1899.
55. Sakakini, *Such Am I, O World*, p. 217.
56. G.E. To A.Sh., 19 Aug. 1940, CZA S25/3140.
Kalvarisky with students, 7 Dec. 1941, CZA Z4/15185.
57. War Office to Colonial Office, 19 Sept. 1939, PRO FO 371/23245 E 6543 f.78.
Colonial Office to War Office, 26 Sept. 1939, PRO FO 371/23245 E 6659 f.83. See also: Moshe Shemesh, "The Position of the Jaffa Newspaper *Falastin* Towards the Axis and Democratic Countries" (in Hebrew), *Studies in Zionism*, vol. II (1992), p. 245ff.
Report of the High Commissioner, 1 Dec. 1939–29 Feb. 1940, PRO FO 371/24563 E 1066 f.116.
Report of the High Commissioner, 25 June 1940, PRO FO 371/24563 E2414 f.198.
Colonial Office to Foreign Office, 22 Nov. 1940, PRO FO 371/24565 E 2792 f.153.
Colonial Office to Foreign Office, 8 Mar. 1940, PRO FO 371/24563 E1066 f.68.
58. German penetration (no date), ISA P/403 3537.
59. The mufti's activities in Beirut, CZA S25/3641.
Report from Beirut, 15 Oct. 1939, PRO FO 371/23240 E70361 f.220. See also: Whereabouts and activities of the Mufti, PRO FO 371/27124 E351-E2276; E5639; E6731; E6494; E6504.
60. Husseini with Hitler, 30 Nov. 1941, *Akten zur Deutschen Auswaertigen Politik, 1918–1945*

(Goettingen: Vandehork & Ruprecht, 1970), *Serie D: 1937–1941*, vol. XIII. 2, *Die Kriegs-jahre*, Sechster Band, Zweiter Halbband, p. 718.

61. Leonard Mosley, *The Cat and the Mice* (London: Arthur Barker, 1958), p. 29.
62. German penetration (no date), ISA P/403/3537.
63. Heller, *Leh'i*, vol. II, p. 530.
64. Draft letter by Dr. T. Canaan [1938?], ISA P/1051/9.
65. George Antonius, *The Arab Awakening: The Story of the Arab National Movement* (London: Hamish Hamilton, 1938), p. 411. See also: Azmi Bishara, "The Arabs and the Holocaust" (in Hebrew), *Zemanim* 53 (Summer 1995), p. 54ff.; Dan Machman, "Arabs, Zionists, Bishara, and the Holocaust" (in Hebrew), *Zemanim* 54 (Fall 1995); Azmi Bishara, "On Nationalism and Universalism" (in Hebrew), *Zemanim* 55 (Winter 1996), p. 102ff.
66. Anwar Nusseibeh, "Pattern of Disaster: Personal Note on the Fall of Palestine," p. 14. With the kind permission of his son.
67. Ben-Gurion with MacMichael, 2 Apr. 1944, CZA S25/197.
   Zweig, *Britain and Palestine During the Second World War*, pp. 149, 163.
68. Ben-Gurion with MacMichael, 2 Apr. 1944, CZA S25/197.
   Golda Meyerson with the chief secretary, 29 Jan. 1947, and with the high commissioner, 31 July 1947; Herzog with the high commissioner, 1 Feb. 1947, CZA S25/5601.
   Meyerson with the high commissioner, 17 Dec. 1947, CZA S25/22.
69. Sari Sakakini to his sisters, 3 Jan. 1945, ISA P 375/2561.
70. "My Best Friend" (June 1945), ISA P/393/3155.
71. ISA P/403/3554.
72. Sakakini to his son, 7 Jan. 1933, ISA P/378/2646.
   Sari Sakakini, personal form (1946), ISA P/337/1060.
73. Cohen diary, 20 Mar. to 26 June 1944, Haganah Archive, P. 80.276.
74. Cohen diary, 8 May 1945, Haganah Archive, P. 80.276.
   Ben-Gurion diary, 8 May 1945, Ben-Gurion Heritage Archives.
   Sakakini, *Such Am I, O World*, p. 219.

22: "GIVE ME A COUNTRY WITHOUT WARS"

1. Barker to Antonius, undated, ISA P/867.
2. George Antonius, *The Arab Awakening: The Story of the Arab National Movement* (London: Hamish Hamilton, 1938). See also: Fouad Ajami, *The Dream Palace of the Arabs* (New York: Pantheon Books, 1998), p. 16ff.
3. Khalil al-Sakakini, *Such Am I, O World* (in Hebrew) (Jerusalem: Keter, 1990), p. 211.
4. Antonius's letters to his wife, ISA P/1051/2.
5. Anwar Nusseibeh, "Pattern of Disaster: Personal Note on the Fall of Palestine," pp. 170, 176. With the kind permission of his son.
   Tom Segev, "Katy and the General" (in Hebrew), *Ha'aretz Supplement*, 15 June 1979, p. 16ff.
6. Richard Crossman, *Palestine Mission* (London: Hamish Hamilton, n.d.), p. 132. See also: Hadara Lazar, *The Mandatories* (in Hebrew) (Jerusalem: Keter, 1990), p. 114.
   Edward Keith-Roach, *Pasha of Jerusalem* (London: Radcliffe Press, 1994), p. 149ff.
7. Barker to Antonius, 24 Oct. 1946, ISA P/867.
8. Barker to Antonius, 26 Oct. 1946, ISA P/867.
9. Cohen diary, 12–22 May 1945, 2 and 19 Mar. 1946, Haganah Archive, P. 80.276.
10. Yehudah Slotzky, *Haganah History Book* (in Hebrew) (Tel Aviv: Am Oved, 1973), vol. III, part II, p. 874.
11. Cohen diary, 26 Mar. 1946, Haganah Archive, P. 80.276.
12. Cohen diary, 28 Mar. 1946, Haganah Archive, P. 80.276.
13. CZA S25/6090.
14. Ben-Gurion to the National Council, 1 Apr. 1947, CZA S25/5645.

15. David Ben-Gurion, *Chimes of Independence* (in Hebrew) (Tel Aviv: Am Oved, 1993), pp. 65, 67, 318, 328.
16. Cohen diary, 28 July and 4 Aug. 1947, Haganah Archive, P. 80.276.
17. Shlomo Lev-Ami, *In Struggle and in Rebellion* (in Hebrew) (Tel Aviv: Ministry of Defense, n.d.), p. 259ff.
    Saul Zadka, *Blood in Zion* (London: Brassey's, 1995), p. 56.
18. Wedgwood in the House of Lords, 15 Dec. 1942, 125 H.L. Deb. 5.s., col. 543.
19. Cafferata to Wedgewood, 26 Mar. 1943. With the kind permission of his daughter.
20. Raymond Cafferata, "Tiger Hill." With the kind permission of his daughter.
21. Memoirs of Noam Zisman, Alfred Barad, and Ya'akov Salomon. Haganah Archive principal symbol 195-65, secondary 195-25, 195-57, 195-64, Jabotinsky Institute.
22. Board of Enquiry: Mr. Cafferata's Wound, 16 July 1931. With the kind permission of his daughter.
23. Cafferata papers. With the kind permission of his daughter.
24. Nechemia Ben-Tor [Erziah], *Today I Will Write with a Pen* (in Hebrew) (Ya'ir, 1991), p. 254ff.
25. Cafferata to Martin, 17 July 1946. With the kind permission of his daughter.
26. Segev, "Katy and the General," p. 19.
27. Nicholas Bethell, *The Palestine Triangle* (London: André Deutsch, 1979), p. 267ff.
    R. D. Wilson, *Cordon and Search* (Aldershot: Gale and Polden, 1949), p. 56ff.
28. Barker to Antonius, 10 Oct. 1946, ISA P/867.
29. Thurston Clarke, *By Blood and Fire* (New York: G. P. Putnam's Sons, 1981).
30. Bernard Montgomery, *Memoirs* (London: Collins, 1958), p. 426ff. See also: Michael J. Cohen, *Palestine and the Great Powers, 1945–1948* (Princeton: Princeton University Press, 1982), p. 231ff.
31. David Ben-Gurion, *Memoirs* (in Hebrew) (Tel Aviv: Am Oved, 1987), vol. VI, p. 223.
    Bernard Montgomery, *Memoirs* (London: Collins, 1958), p. 387ff.
32. Oliver Lindsay, *Once a Grenadier* (London: Leo Cooper, 1996), p. 22.
33. PRO WO 208/1706.
34. *Ha-Praklit*, Feb. 1946, p. 58ff.
35. Bruce Hoffman, *The Failure of British Strategy Within Palestine, 1939–1947* (Tel Aviv: Bar Ilan University Press, 1983), p. 76ff.
36. Churchill in Parliament, 31 Jan. 1947, 432 H.C. Deb. 5.s, col. 1343.
37. Hugh Thomas, *John Strachey* (London: Eyre Methuen, 1973), p. 229.
38. David Ben-Gurion, *Towards the End of the Mandate* (in Hebrew) (Tel Aviv: Am Oved, 1993), p. 192.
39. Ge'ula Cohen, *Historic Encounter* (in Hebrew) (Ya'ir, 1986), pp. 41ff., 98ff., 144.
    Ben-Gurion, *Chimes of Independence*, pp. 66, 317ff.
40. David Niv, *The Campaigns of the Etzel* (in Hebrew) (Jerusalem: Klausner Institute, 1976), vol. V, pp. 103ff., 135ff., 161ff.
41. Ben-Gurion, *Chimes of Independence*, p. 317.
42. Montgomery, *Memoirs*, p. 387ff.
43. Cohen, *Palestine and the Great Powers*, p. 94.
    Segev, "Katy and the General," p. 19.
    Nicholas Bethell, *The Palestine Triangle* (Jerusalem and Tel Aviv: Steimatzky's Agency, 1979), p. 253.
44. Barker to Antonius, 14, 17, 21, and 27 Apr. 1947, ISA P/867.
45. Barker to Antonius, 8 June 1947, ISA P/867/9.
    Weizman testimony, Jabotinsky Institute, 8/29/18.
46. Prime Minister's Personal Minute, 1 Mar. 1941. PRO FO 371/27126 E739/G, f. 147.
    Hoffman, *The Failure of British Strategy Within Palestine*, p. 30.
    CZA S25/6287; 6910; 7034; 7699. See also: RHL, Dudley-Nigg Papers.
47. Lecture by Martin Charteris, Sept. 1946, CZA S25/7697.
48. R. D. Wilson, *Cordon and Search* (Aldershot: Gale and Polden, 1949), pp. 15, 87.

49. Wilson, *Cordon and Search*, p. 45ff.
50. Cohen, *Palestine and the Great Powers*, p. 74.
51. Telma Eligon and Rafi Pesachson, eds., *1,001 Songs* (in Hebrew) (Tel Aviv: Kinneret, 1983), p. 265ff.
52. Wilson, *Cordon and Search*, p. 60.
53. Oliver Lindsay, *Once a Grenadier* (London: Leo Cooper, 1996), p. 21.
54. Wilson, *Cordon and Search*, pp. 203, 45ff., 90, 11ff.
    Lindsay, *Once a Grenadier*, p. 23.
55. Nathan Alterman, *The Seventh Column* (in Hebrew) (Tel Aviv: HaKibbutz Ha-Me'uhad, 1977), vol. I, p. 80.
    Wilson, *Cordon and Search*, p. 205.
56. Kollek to Sherf, 2 Sept. 1946, CZA S25/498.
    Report by Eban, 10 and 17 Mar. 1947, CZA S25/8942.
    Sherf to Kollek, 1 Oct. 1946, CZA S25/498.
57. *Labour Party Annual Conference Report* (London: 1944), p. 9.
58. Cohen diary, 14 Nov., 10 June 1945, Haganah Archive, P. 80.276.
59. Cohen diary, 26 Nov., 25 June 1945, Haganah Archive, P. 80.276.
60. Lecture by Aharon Cohen, 15 July 1947, CZA S25/5435.
    Cohen diary, 20 June 1945, Haganah Archive, P. 80.276.
61. Alan Bullock, *Ernest Bevin: Foreign Secretary, 1945–1951* (New York: W. W. Norton, 1983), p. 164.
    Golda Meir, *My Life* (London: Futura, 1975), p. 164.
    CZA S25/7034; 7548; 7689; 7690; 7691; 7693.
62. "Nazi Britain," broadsides, CZA S25/2069.
63. Y.S. [Sahar?] with Grey, 27 Jan. 1947, CZA S25/6202.
    ISA M/119/31, microfilm chief secretariat, G 91-130 (1008; 1383).
64. Call to the Yishuv to Turn in Terrorists to the Police (in Hebrew), Apr. 1947, CZA S25/5645.
65. Meyerson to Locker, 9 Feb. 1947, CZA S25/2647.
66. A. Braverman to the district commissioner, 16 Dec. 1945, ISA M/365.
    Ben-Eliezer to the deputy district commissioner of the Netanya district, 6 Mar. 1945, ISA M/111/14.
    Microfilm, chief secretariat: G 91/125 (132).
    The Ethiopian consul to the chief secretary, 1 Aug. 1946, ISA M/57/117.
    Microfilm chief secretariat G 91-129 (1467).
    ISA M/4341/27 Microfilm chief secretariat: G 91 130 (279).
    ISA M/120/28 Microfilm chief secretariat: G 91 130 (2007).
67. Beit Yisrael neighborhood council to the high commissioner, 1 Aug. 1946, ISA M/117/57.
    Microfilm chief secretariat: G 91-129 (1470).
    R. Schreibman to the high commissioner, 29 Nov. 1945, ISA M/365.
    Kibbutz Shefayim to the high commissioner, 18 Nov. 1946, ISA M/119/14.
    Microfilm chief secretariat, G 91-130 (1599).
68. Beer to the high commissioner, 13 Feb. 1947, and additional correspondence. ISA M/119/39.
    Microfilm chief secretariat, G 91-130 (730).
69. Friends of the Palestine Folk Opera to the chief secretary, 26 Dec. 1946, ISA M/129/51.
    Microfilm chief secretariat, G 91-136 (311).
    Edwin Samuel to the chief secretary, 17 Dec. 1946, ISA M/129/44.
    Microfilm chief secretariat, G 91-136 (135).
    Press release, 4 July 1948, De Bunsen Papers. With the kind permission of his widow.
70. Wilson, *Cordon and Search*, p. 13.
71. Ben-Gurion, *Memoirs*, vol. III, p. 364.
72. A Parade in Honour of the Birthday of H. M. King George VI, 12 June 1947, PRONI D/1581/4/3.

73. Jardine to De Bunsen, 20 Aug. 1948, De Bunsen Papers, quoted with the kind permission of his widow.
74. Alan Cunningham, "Palestine: The Last Days of the Mandate," *International Affairs*, vol. XXIV (1948), p. 490.
75. Lindsay, *Once a Grenadier*, p. 27.

23: THE LAST SALUTE

1. Kalinov to Kupferberg, 12 Feb. 1946, CZA S25/5900.
   R. Ipka Mistabra, "Liberated Darling" (in Hebrew), *Yediot Aharonot*, 22 June 1945, p. 2.
2. Elihau Stern, ed., *Chronology of the New Jewish Yishuv in Palestine, 1936–1947* (in Hebrew) (Jerusalem: Yad Ben-Zvi, 1974), p. 172.
   Yehuda Koren, "The English Officer's Woman" (in Hebrew), *Davar Ha-Shavu'a*, 28 Nov. 1986, p. 12.
3. Yitzhak Abadai, *Between Us and the English* (in Hebrew) (Jerusalem: Kiriyat Sefer, 1977).
4. A. J. Sherman, *Mandate Days* (London: Thames and Hudson, 1997), p. 186.
5. Hadara Lazar, *The Mandatories* (in Hebrew) (Jerusalem: Keter, 1990), p. 109ff.
   Bryant to Geiger, 31 July 1948. Quoted with her kind permission.
6. Henry Gurney, *Palestine Postscript*, p. 11, MEC, Gurney Papers, GUR 1/2.
7. Minutes of a meeting held in the Department of Public Works, 8 Oct. 1947. In the possession of Lotte Geiger. Quoted with her kind permission.
   Chief Secretary's Office, *Withdrawal*, 2 Dec. 1947.
   De Bunsen Papers. With the kind permission of his widow.
8. Hope-Simpson to Chancellor, 30 Aug., 15 Oct. 1945, RHL, Chancellor Papers, 16:6, ff. 73–76.
9. Gurney diary, pp. 53, 28. MEC, Gurney Papers, GUR 1/1.
10. The Arrangements for the New Immigrants in Palestine, 1944–1945 (in Hebrew), CZA S25/556.
    Tom Segev, *1949: The First Israelis* (New York: Henry Holt and Co., 1998).
11. The Arrangements for the New Immigrants in Palestine, 1944–1945 (in Hebrew), CZA S25/556.
12. Samuel in the House of Lords, 10 Nov. 1945, 138 H.L. Deb. 5.s. col. 495.
13. PRO PREM 8/256.
    Alan Bullock, *Ernest Bevin: Trade Union Leader* (New York: W. W. Norton, 1960), p. 167.
    Dean Acheson, *Present at the Creation* (New York: New American Library, 1970), p. 234.
14. Khalil al-Sakakini, *Such Am I, O World* (in Hebrew) (Jerusalem: Keter, 1990), p. 221.
15. Acheson, *Present at the Creation*, p. 246.
    Wm. Roger Louis, "British Imperialism and the End of the Palestine Mandate," in *The End of the Palestine Mandate*, ed. Wm. Roger Louis and Robert W. Stookey (Austin: The University of Texas Press, 1986), p. 15ff.
16. Meir Avizohar, "The Hourglass" (in Hebrew), in David Ben-Gurion, *Chimes of Independence* (Tel Aviv: Am Oved, 1993), p. 5.
    David Ben-Gurion, *Chimes of Independence*, p. 253.
17. David Ben-Gurion, *Towards the End of the Mandate* (in Hebrew) (Tel Aviv: Am Oved, 1993), p. 379.
18. Michael J. Cohen, *Palestine and the Great Powers, 1945–1948* (Princeton: Princeton University Press, 1982), p. 217ff.
19. Ben-Gurion with Bevin, 3 Feb. 1947, CZA S25/7568.
20. Ben-Gurion, *Towards the End of the Mandate*, p. 355.
    Ben-Gurion with Bevin, 29 Jan., 3, 6 Feb. 1947, CZA S25/7568.
21. "*Sunday Express* and *Daily Mail*," in Saul Zadka, *Blood in Zion* (London: Brassey's, 1995), p. 181ff.
    Beely to the prime minister, 31 Dec. 1946, PRO FO 371/61761.

22. Brigadier Peto in Parliament, 25 Feb. 1947, 433 H.C. Deb. 5.s., col. 1934.
23. Churchill to Parliament, 31 Jan. 1947, 432 H.C. Deb. 5.s., col. 1348. See also: Churchill to Parliament, 3 Mar. 1947, 434 H.C. Deb. 5.s., col. 35.
Churchill to Parliament, 12 Nov. 1946, 430 H.C. Deb. 5.s., col. 26.
Prime minister in Cabinet, 20 Sept. 1947, PRO CAB 128/10.
24. Churchill in Parliament, 31 Jan. 1947, 432 H.C. Deb. 5.s., col. 1348.
The Palestine Problem (1945), PRO WO 210/192.
Memorandum by Joint Planning Staff, 26 September 1947, PRO AIR 20/2461. J.P. (47) 130 Final.
The Chief to the Air Staff in Cabinet, 14 Feb. 1947, PRO CAB 128/9.
Dalton in Cabinet, 20 Sept. 1947, PRO CAB 128/10.
Gurney diary, p. 38, MEC, Gurney Papers, GUR 1/1.
25. Correlli Barnett, *The Lost Victory: British Dreams, British Realities, 1945–1950* (London: Macmillan, 1995), p. 53ff.
Louis, "British Imperialism and the End of the Palestine Mandate," p. 53ff.
26. Michael J. Cohen, *Palestine and the Great Powers, 1945–1948* (Princeton: Princeton University Press, 1982), p. 268.
27. Ben-Gurion in the Jewish Agency Executive, 12 Oct. 1947, CZA S25/22.
28. Ben-Gurion, *Chimes of Independence*, p. 55.
29. Unsigned letter, 5 May 1941, CZA S25/7967.
Weizmann with Roosevelt, 11 June 1943, Weizmann Papers.
Yaron Ran, *The Roots of the Jordanian Option* (in Hebrew) (Zitrin, 1991). See also: Meyerson with Abdallah, 17 Nov. 1947, CZA S25/4004.
30. Anwar Nusseibeh, "Pattern of Disaster: Personal Note on the Fall of Palestine," p. 12. With the kind permission of his son.
31. Cohen, *Palestine and the Great Powers*, p. 260ff.
32. Henry Gurney, "Palestine Postscript," p. 14, MEC, Gurney Papers, GUR 1/2.
Gurney diary, p. 22, MEC, Gurney Papers, GUR 1/1.
33. Ben-Gurion, *Chimes of Independence*, p. 217ff.
Menachem Friedman, "And These Are the Generations of the Status Quo: Religion and State in Israel" (in Hebrew), in *The Transition from Yishuv to State, 1947–1948* (in Hebrew), ed. Varda Pilovsky (Haifa: Haifa University, 1990), p. 47ff.
34. Louis, "British Imperialism and the End of the Palestine Mandate," p. 23ff.
35. Michaeli to the Jewish Agency, 18 Dec. 1947, CZA S25/10039.
Cohen, *Palestine and the Great Powers*, p. 139.
36. Cohen diary, 27–30 Nov. 1947, Haganah Archive, P. 80.276.
37. Sakakini diary, 20 June 1946. With the kind permission of his daughters.
38. Barker to Antonius, 14 and 27 May, 21 June, 6 July 1947, ISA P/867.
39. Barker to Antonius, 27 May 1947, ISA P/867.
40. Barker to Antonius, 27 Oct., 6 and 16 Dec. 1947, ISA P/867.
41. Barker to Antonius, 1 Dec. 1947, ISA P/867.
42. Barker to Antonius, 19 Sept. and 1 Oct. 1947, ISA P/867.
43. Barker to Antonius, 6 July 1947, ISA P/867.
44. Barker to Antonius, 3 July 1947, ISA P/867.
45. Eliahu Eilat, "Conversations with Musa Alami," *Yahadut Zemananu*, vol. II (1985), p. 35.
46. Proposed Arab Department (n.d.), ISA P/375/2562.
Sakakini to Pinkerton, 18 May 1945, 16 Mar. 1947, ISA P/337/1060.
47. Sakakini to Alami, 13 Apr. and 4 May 1945, ISA P/375/2561.
Sakakini to Alami, 21 Apr. 1946, ISA P/335/969.
Sakakini to Alami, 5 Apr. 1947, ISA P/337/1060.
48. Isa Khalaf, *Politics in Palestine* (Albany: State University of New York Press, 1991), p. 138ff.
49. Eilat, "Conversations with Musa Alami," pp. 1, 43.
50. Stern, *Chronology of the New Jewish Yishuv in Palestine*, p. 280.

51. Haim Levenberg, *Military Preparations of the Arab Community in Palestine, 1945–1948* (London: Frank Cass, 1993), p. 179ff.
52. Ben-Gurion diary, 20 Apr. 1948, Ben-Gurion Heritage Archives.
53. Cohen diary, 7 Dec. 1947, Haganah Archive, P. 80.276/3.
54. Cohen diary, 25 Dec. 1947, Haganah Archive, P. 80.276/3.
55. Sakakini, *Such Am I, O World*, pp. 230, 227, 228.
56. Sakakini, *Such Am I, O World*, p. 229.
57. Letters to Adnan al-Yehiya, ISA 65 P/392 (03149).
58. Sakakini, *Such Am I, O World*, p. 232.
    Danny Rubinstein, "Why Did Abdel-Kader Speak English?" (in Hebrew), *Ha'aretz*, 6 Nov. 1998, p. B7.
59. Pollock to his wife, 10 Apr. 1948, PRONI D/1 581/2/9.
60. Fawzi to Adnan, 12 Apr. 1948, ISA 65 P/392 (03149).
61. Nusseibeh, "Pattern of Disaster," p. 152ff. With the kind permission of his son.
62. Uri Milstein, *The History of the War of Independence* (in Hebrew) (Tel Aviv: Zemora Bitan, 1991), vol. IV, p. 201ff.
63. Sakakini, *Such Am I, O World*, p. 232.
64. Hala Sakakini, *Jerusalem and I* (Amman: n.p., 1987), p. 121ff.
    ISA, minutes of cabinet meeting, 9 June 1948 (classified portion); see: Tom Segev, "The First Secrets" (in Hebrew), *Ha'aretz*, 3 Feb. 1995, p. 5.
65. H. Sakakini, *Jerusalem and I*, p. 118.
66. Yitzhak Levi, *Nine Measures* (in Hebrew) (Tel Aviv: Ma'archot, 1986), p. 342ff.
    Milstein, *The History of the War of Independence*, vol. IV, p. 251ff.
    De Bunsen diary, 11 Apr. 1948. With the kind permission of his widow.
    Gurney diary, p. 59. MEC, Gurney Papers, GUR 1/1.
67. Sakakini, *Such Am I, O World*, p. 243.
    H. Sakakini, *Jerusalem and I*, p. 140.
68. Netanel Lorch, *The Events of the War of Independence* (in Hebrew) (Masada, 1989), p. 195.
69. C. S. Halevi and A. Bezhezhinsky, *In a Double Siege* (in Hebrew) (Hadar, 1982).
70. Nusseibeh, "Pattern of Disaster," p. 178ff. With the kind permission of his son.
71. CZA S25/9679; 10046.
72. Benny Morris, *The Birth of the Palestine Refugee Problem, 1947–1949* (Cambridge: Cambridge University Press, 1988).
73. Sakakini, *Such Am I, O World*, p. 243.
74. Nusseibeh, "Pattern of Disaster," p. 194. With the kind permission of his son.
75. Ben-Gurion diary, 1 May 1948, Ben-Gurion Heritage Archives.
76. "Political and Diplomatic Documents, Dec. 1947–May 1948," ISA, 1980, p. 703ff.
77. Khalaf, *Politics in Palestine*, p. 132.
78. Nusseibeh, "Pattern of Disaster," pp. 32, 80. With the kind permission of his son.
79. Nusseibeh, "Pattern of Disaster," p. 56ff. With the kind permission of his son.
80. Khalaf, *Politics in Palestine*, p. 155.
81. Nusseibeh, "Pattern of Disaster," pp. 13, 15, 39, 43, 56, 60, 80ff., 98ff., 102ff., 161, 208. With the kind permission of his son.
82. Nusseibeh, "Pattern of Disaster," pp. 78ff., 209ff. With the kind permission of his son.
83. Tom Segev, "The First Secrets" (in Hebrew), *Ha'aretz*, 3 Feb. 1995, p. 5.
84. Levenberg, *Military Preparations of the Arab Community in Palestine*, p. 186.
85. PRO AIR 23/8342-5; 23/8350.
    Evacuation of Palestine, Progress Reports, Feb.–Apr. 1948, PRO WO 216/249.
86. Framework plan for receiving control of the country, 17 Oct. 1947, CZA S25/3735.
87. Ben-Gurion with Gurney, 13 Oct. 1947, CZA S25/22.
88. Reuven Zalani to Golda Meyerson, 16 Nov. 1947, CZA S25/4065.
89. Henry Gurney, "Palestine Postscript," p. 11, MEC, Gurney Papers, GUR 1/2.

90. Gurney diary, p. 83, MEC, Gurney Papers, GUR 1/1.
    Keith-Roach to Parkinson, 30 Sept. 1936, PRO CO 733/316 75528/71.
91. Pollock memorandum, 20 Mar. 1948, PRONI D/1581/4/2.
    "Political and Diplomatic Documents, Dec. 1947–May 1948," ISA, 1980, p. 703ff.
92. Khalaf, *Politics in Palestine*, p. 199ff.
93. Chief Secretary's Office, Central Problems Common to All Departments, 2 Dec. 1947,
    De Bunsen papers. With the kind permission of his widow.
    G. H. A. MacMillan, The Planning of the Evacuation of Palestine, IWM, MacMillan
    Papers.
94. Gurney diary, pp. 5, 104, MEC, Gurney Papers, GUR 1/1.
    Henry Gurney, "Palestine Postscript," p. 25, MEC, Gurney Papers, GUR 1/2
95. De Bunsen, 24 Mar. 1948. With the kind permission of his widow.
96. Memorandum (village school in Tarshiha), 6 Nov. 1946, ISA M/125/19.
    A Survey of Palestine Prepared for the Anglo-American Committee of Inquiry (Jeru-
    salem: Government Printer, 1946), vol. II, p. 638.
97. Khalaf, *Politics in Palestine*, pp. 162, 203ff.
98. Gurney diary, pp. 5, 37, 53, MEC, Gurney Papers, GUR 1/1.
    Henry Gurney, "Palestine Postscript," p. 3ff., MEC, Gurney Papers, GUR 1/2.
99. Colonel Gomme-Duncan in Parliament, 14 May 1948, 450 H.C. Deb. 5.s., col. 2426.
    Alan Cunningham, "Palestine: The Last Days of the Mandate," *International Affairs*,
    vol. XXIV (1948), p. 481.
    Gurney diary, pp. 5, 37, 53, MEC, Gurney Papers, GUR 1/1.
    Henry Gurney, "Palestine Postscript," pp. 3ff., 15, MEC, Gurney Papers, Gur 1/2.
    Naomi Shepherd, *Ploughing Sand: British Rule in Palestine, 1917–1948* (London: John
    Murray, 1999).
100. Pollock to his wife, 9, 12, 13, and 30 Nov. 1947, PRONI D/1581/2/9.
101. Pollock to his wife, 11 Jan., 22 Feb. 1948, PRONI D/1581/2/9. See also: CZA S25/10391;
     4145.
     Testimony of Ya'akov Solomon, Haganah Archive, 178.62 (47).
102. Nusseibeh, "Pattern of Disaster," p. 128. With the kind permission of his son.
103. Drakeford to the Jewish Agency, 3 Jan. 1948; Sakharov to Drakeford, 20 Jan. 1948, CZA
     S25/6195; letter to Meyerson, 15 Nov. 1947, CZA S25/8178.
104. Bryant diary. With the kind permission of Lotte Geiger. See also: Tom Segev, "The
     Absolution of Michael Bryant" (in Hebrew), *Ha'aretz*, 18 Sept. 1992.
     Dov Yosef, *Faithful City* (in Hebrew) (Tel Aviv: Schocken, 1964).
105. British consul in Haifa to Foreign Office, 13 Aug. 1948, PRO FO 371/68656.
106. Evacuation of Security Areas, 17 May 1948, CZA S25/10526.
107. Gurney diary, p. 106ff. MEC, Gurney Papers, GUR 1/1.
108. De Bunsen diary. With the kind permission of his widow.
109. Pollock diary, 14 May 1948, PRONI D/1581/3/20.
110. Pollock report, 23 July 1948; speech by MacMillan. PRONI D/1 581/4/2.
111. PRONI D/1581/4/3.
112. Pollock diary, 29–30 June 1948, PRONI D/1581/3/20.
113. Arthur Koestler, *Promise and Fulfillment* (London: Macmillan, 1949), p. 226.
     Uri Yafeh, "Orde Wingate's Bible" (in Hebrew), in *First to Battle* (in Hebrew), ed. Galia
     Yardeni (Tel Aviv: Ha-Kibbutz Ha-Me'uhad, 1967), p. 56ff.; Tom Segev, "Two Holding
     the Bible" (in Hebrew), *Ha'aretz*, 27 Feb. 1998, p. B7.

ACKNOWLEDGMENTS

The period of the British Mandate has interested many writers; my first thanks go to all my predecessors. I found most of the books and articles they wrote in the National and University Library in Jerusalem. I would like to express my gratitude to the staff of the lending department, the reading rooms, and the periodical department.

This study is based on thousands of files containing uncounted documents. Most of these are preserved in historical archives in Israel, Great Britain, and the United States. The Israeli archives are the Central Zionist Archive, the Israel State Archives, the Weizmann Archives, the Ben-Gurion Heritage Archives, the archive of the Institute for the Study of the Labor Movement, the Labor Party Archive, the Haganah Archive, the Jabotinsky Institute Archive, and the Yair House.

The British archives are the Public Records Office, the Imperial War Museum, the British Library, and the Liddell-Hart Centre, King's College, all in London; the Middle East Centre, St. Antony's College, Oxford; the Rhodes House Library, Oxford; the Bodleian Library, Oxford; the Cambridge University Library; and the Sidney Jones Library, University of Liverpool.

I owe special thanks also to the Public Records Office of Northern Ireland, which gracefully opened for my inspection the diaries and letters of James H. H. Pollock, one of the first Britons to enter Palestine and one of the last to leave.

Some of the material that served me is kept in the National Archives, Washington; in the Jewish Theological Seminary, New York; and in the Institute for Contemporary History, Munich, Germany.

There are not enough words to thank all these institutions and their staff for their effective and generous help and wise advice. Special thanks must go to Clare Brown of St. Antony's College.

A great deal of the material that lies at the foundation of this book belongs to private individuals and is made public here for the first time; I owe great thanks to all of them. Donna Maria Isabel de la Cierva, condesa de Montefuerte, Madrid, opened before me that personal diary of her father, Antonio de la Cierva Lewita, Conde de Ballobar, who served during World War I as the Spanish consul in Jerusalem. We located the condesa thanks to the wonders of the Internet; by the time her father's fascinating diary reached me I had also gained the generous assistance of the Spanish historian Eduardo Manzano Moreno; of the Israeli historian Shlomo Ben-Ami; and of Dr. Dan Simon, director of the Sourasky Library at Tel Aviv University. Julio Adin helped me translate the diary.

The Munin family of Jerusalem provided me with a real treasure, the personal and literary papers of their grandfather, Alter Levine, a.k.a. Asaf Halevy the Jerusalemite. In this context I also owe thanks to poet and novelist Anton Shammas.

Hala and Dumia Sakakini of Ramallah permitted me to study the original diary written by their father, the noted educator and writer Khalil al-Sakakini. This document is of unparalleled importance and has thus far been published only in part, in Arabic and in Hebrew. This is the place to express my heartfelt gratitude also to Hussein Hamza, scholar of Arabic literature, who aided me in translating the diary and who invested much time and understanding in his work on the rest of the Arab material that served as a foundation of this book.

Veronica Robertson of Liverpool was kind enough to make available to me chapters of an autobiography, letters, and other material from the papers of her father, Raymond Cafferata, commander of the Hebron police in 1929. Lady de Bunsen made available to me the diary and other material from the papers of her husband, Sir Bernard de Bunsen, director of the education department in Palestine. Major Peter Lewis made available to me the relevant volume of the Official History of the Grenadier Guards prior to its publication.

Ari Shavit permitted me to quote from the writings of Margery Bentwich of Jerusalem. Rachel Halfi graciously showed me, before their publication, chapters from memoirs collected by her father, Avraham Halfi, from Tel Aviv's founders and early residents.

Shlomo Halevy of Jerusalem made available to me several dozen letters sent by his father from Palestine to his parents in Vilna. In this context I owe special thanks to Yoram Mayorek, director of the Central Zionist Archives, who drew the existence of these letters to my attention.

Lotte Geiger of Jerusalem showed me the diary entries of her friend Michael Bryant and also permitted me to quote several personal letters.

I would like to thank Dr. Sari Nusseibeh, president of Al-Kuds University, for having allowed me to examine the personal memoirs written by his father, one of the leaders of the Arab public in Jerusalem. In this context I also owe thanks to Italian journalist Lorenzo Cremonesi.

Many other people also assisted me with advice and personal information: Col. Avner Paz, director of the History and Information Branch of the Israeli Air Force; Gidon Hermel; and Avraham Kushnir. I owe special thanks also to Anthony French, senior counsel of the UNTSO command in Jerusalem, for hosting me at Government House.

The research that preceded the writing of this book took three years, and during that time I was assisted by two young, brilliant, and original scholars, Ofer Nur and Jonathan Cummings. Each of them, in his own way, not only helped me locate material but also benefited me with his analysis and understanding. They invested great thought and diligence in their work, and provided me with friendship as well. For that I am especially grateful.

Avi Katzman edited my Hebrew manuscript with great talent and wisdom. He always found the golden mean between an iron and a friendly hand, and saved me from no few gaffes. Haim Watzman, who translated the book into English, also helped improve the manuscript. It is a pleasant duty to thank my agent and friend, Deborah Harris.

INDEX

Aal, Dr. Abdal, 326
Abadin, Ibrahim, 280
Abdallah, Emir of Transjordan, 158–59, 412, 496n
Abujzhdid, Yitzhak, 324
Achdut HaAvoda (Jewish labor party), 176
Adamson, Richard, 131, 135
Agnon, Shmuel Yosef, 174, 182, 223, 315, 320, 326, 327, 331, 384
agriculture, 225, 229, 249–59, 279–81, 285–88
Alami, Musa, 81, 109, 275, 366, 375–76, 437, 439, 469n, 499–500, 509
Al-Fula (village, *later* Afula), 242–43
aliyas, 225, 261
Allenby, Gen. Sir Edmund, 22–23, 25, 26, 46, 49, 54–57, 72–76, 85–86, 89, 96, 99, 118n, 131, 140, 142, 147, 156, 179, 180, 219, 222, 348
Allenby, Lady, 55–56, 85n
Allenby, Michael, 55–56
Allon, Yigal, 386–87, 431, 470
Alterman, Nathan, 481, 482
Altneuland (Herzl), 345
Amery, Leopold, 336
Amikam, Yisrael, 264, 268–69
AMZIC (American Zionist Commonwealth), 242–43
Andrews, Lewis, 6, 367n, 414, 415, 417, 426
Ansari, Sami al-, 366
anthem issue, 98, 299
anti-British terrorism, by Jews, 457–58, 472–86
antisemitism, of British, 33, 35n, 40–41, 93, 95, 479–80
Antonius, George, 2, 8, 45, 300, 343–44, 376, 377n, 398n, 437, 464–65, 469
Antonius, Katy, 8, 398n, 437, 448, 468, 469–70, 476, 479, 480, 498–99
Arab Awakening, The (Antonius), 469n
Arab Club, 106–7, 128
Arab federation idea, 375–76

Arab Higher Committee, 368, 426, 503, 509–10, 517
Arabic Language Academy, 300
Arab-Jewish conference, St. James's, 437–40
Arab-Jewish conflicts, 109, 122, 221, 276, 348: and binational proposal, 408–14; and Brenner, 174–76; British caught between, 167, 197–201, 332, 334; commissions on, 9–10: hatred as source of, 307–9; and Paris Peace Conferences, 129–39; and rise of Nazi Germany, 411–13; and Samuel, 172, 189–94; and Western Wall controversy, 72–73, 295–98, 303–17, 334; and Zionists, 113–16
Arab-Jewish self-government, 375–76, 400
Arab Language Academy in Cairo, 502
Arab League, 499–500, 510
Arab Legion, 103, 501
Arab national movement, 81, 102–9, 180–81, 216n, 271–83, 350, 359–63, 375–77, 401–2, 462–65; and land sales to Jews, 275, 276. *See also* Istiqlal Party
Arab rebellion: against Turks, 46, 81, 110; of 1936, 366–74, 376–77, 379, 382–92, 388, 398–401, 414, 432–33, 441–43; of 1939, 6, 490. *See also* Arab terrorism; and specific incidents
Arab riots of 1929, 314–17, 325, 328–41. *See also* Hebron massacre
Arab(s): and Balfour Declaration, 46, 49; bribery of, 195, 276–83, 412, 417n, 496n; and British, 5, 6, 46, 47n, 55, 91–95, 145, 154, 167–69, 289–90, 333n, 334–35, 398n, 400n, 436–38, 450, 462–63; and casualties of terrorism, 367n; and Churchill, 158–59; culture of, 151–54, 300, 410; and discussions leading to mandate, 120–22; dispossessed of land, 114, 115, 242–43, 274–75, 354, 358–59, 379, 405; and early Mandate, 270–71; and education, 145–46, 171, 284, 354–58, 391, 514; expulsion of, 493n, 511n, 512; farmers, 104,